THE

ALMANAC

OF

HIGHER

EDUCATION

1991

THE
ALMANAC
OF
HIGHER
EDUCATION
1991

The Editors of
The Chronicle of Higher Education

The University of Chicago Press
Chicago and London

The University of Chicago Press, Chicago 60637
The University of Chicago Press, Ltd., London

International Standard Serial Number 1044-3096
International Standard Book Number 0-226-18456-0

∞ The paper used in this publication meets the minimum requirements of the American National Standard for Information Sciences–Permanence of Paper for Printed Library Materials, ANSI Z39.48-1984.

The Nation

FACULTY AND STAFF

RESOURCES

INSTITUTIONS

The States

Enrollment by Race

Higher Education in the 80's

The Nation

SEVERAL YEARS OF PUBLIC CRITICISM about high costs and questionable quality have stung many of the nation's 3,500 colleges and universities. Now increasingly tight budgets and predictions of a national economic downturn may exacerbate an already tense situation.

Like the rest of the decade, 1991 is bound to be a year of tough choices, choices that can no longer be deferred.

Signs that some colleges and universities are making those choices are already visible. Several prominent private universities, such as Stanford and Columbia, have made it clear that they will streamline administrative procedures, and close down programs, to meet the new financial realities.

Many public institutions, walking a tightrope between their own goals and the wishes of legislators, will have to balance pressures to educate more students with less money.

The message: Higher education can no longer do everything. And it will have to perform some of its basic missions better than in the past.

Despite the mood of uncertainty and the bleak financial forecast, academe hasn't given up on some of its grandest plans. Several universities are conducting path-breaking "mega-fund-raising" campaigns. Researchers are moving ahead on gene-therapy experiments that could lead to cures to diseases once thought mysterious. A growing number of colleges and universities are planning student or faculty exchanges with newly democratized higher-education institutions in Eastern Europe.

At home, however, soaring tuition costs have prompted outside scrutiny about what students are getting for their money. Legislators and several authors have questioned whether the typical college professor spends too much time on research and too little time in the classroom.

At the same time, complaints continue that college graduates just don't know enough. And universities with big-time athletic programs remain under fire, accused of producing professional stars, not student-athletes.

Few of these are new matters. But the perennial problem of too few dollars from both the federal government and many states is likely to usher in an especially tense year.

Scarce resources have also generated questions about federally financed "big science" projects that some scientists believe are taking money away from young researchers. Glitches in the $1.5-billion Hubble Space Telescope project and the escalating costs of the Superconducting Supercollider have led some in

Congress to ask whether projects of such scope make sense, especially in tight economic times.

Generally, the budget outlook for higher education is downbeat. The rising federal deficit, now estimated at $169-billion, applies a brake to significant growth in most areas. What may increase even more is Congressional dissatisfaction with student-aid programs. Worries over the financial problems of the Higher Education Assistance Foundation, one of the largest guarantors of federally insured student loans, have raised questions about the soundness of the entire student-loan system.

Financial aid will be one of many topics on the table during hearings over re-authorizing the federal Higher Education Act. Many of the lawmakers most involved in policies affecting higher education were re-elected in November 1990 but the House Education and Labor Committee, which oversees the reauthorization, will have a new chairman. There, William D. Ford, Democrat of Michigan, is replacing the retiring Augustus F. Hawkins, Democrat of California. Mr. Ford has also decided to assume the chairmanship of the House panel's Subcommittee on Postsecondary Education.

In most states, the budget outlook can be summed up in one word: tight.

As a result, pressure to keep down tuition will be felt at public universities as well as private ones. In many states where education is a priority, elementary and secondary schools generally will continue to get first crack at the available funds.

After several flush years, states such as Connecticut, New Jersey, and Virginia face the sobering reality of cutting programs to make up major deficits.

An excess of students will make life difficult in such states as Arizona, California, and Florida. There educators are being asked to serve larger student populations—populations that include growing numbers of blacks, Hispanics, and Asians—on budgets that are likely to hold steady.

C AMPUS LIFE is likely to be marked by continuing debates over efforts to diversify the student population and to broaden the perspectives included in the undergraduate curriculum.

The interest in multiculturalism will take different forms. At some institutions, like the College of Wooster, all freshmen will participate in a course that focuses on racism and sexism. Other institutions offer seminars on diversity during freshman week and in the residence halls.

Such programs are part of an all-out effort to recruit and retain minority undergraduates, as well as to ease campus tensions. Those plans have caused resentment, however, with the backlash seen in new questions about preferential treatment policies. A smattering of white-student unions have sprung up in response.

Student activism may be swelling. Much of it is consumer-oriented: Undergraduates are protesting large classes and mushrooming service fees. But campuses are also seeing increased interest in public service, a resurgent black militancy, and students mobilized around the environment, reproductive rights, and gay and lesbian issues.

Who will teach the students of this decade and next has become an increasingly pressing problem. A wave of faculty retirements is predicted in the coming years. Already the academic job market in long-stagnant humanities disciplines is opening up. But in other fields, such as business and computer science, academe goes begging for qualified professors.

A similar recruiting derby may occur within higher education as well. Bidding wars between top-flight universities over "star" faculty members have become the norm.

Perhaps most worrisome to educators is the erosion of public confidence in higher education. Members of Congress and a prominent national commission are promising to take action if the National Collegiate Athletic Association doesn't put some teeth in efforts to reform college sports. Science watchdogs continue to complain that university researchers are profiting from their discoveries. Animal-rights activists contend that animals are being maimed and killed for no purpose.

How American higher education answers those and other challenges may offer clues to how it will fare as the 21st century approaches.

DEMOGRAPHICS

Population: 248,239,000

Age distribution:
Up to 17 .... 25.8%
18 to 24 .... 10.6%
25 to 34 .... 17.7%
35 and older 45.9%

Racial and ethnic distribution:
American Indian 0.7%
Asian 1.6%
Black 11.7%
White 83.4%
Other and unknown 2.5%
Hispanic (may be any race) .. 6.4%

Educational attainment of adults:
At least 4 years of high school 66.5%
At least 1 to 3 years of college 31.9%
At least 4 years of college ... 16.2%

Per-capita personal income: $17,596

New high-school graduates in:
1990-91 (estimate) 2,474,032
2000-01 (estimate) 2,790,373

New GED diploma recipients: 364,287

High-school dropout rate: 28.9%

POLITICAL LEADERSHIP

President:
George Bush (R), term ends 1993

Vice-President:
Dan Quayle (R), term ends 1993

Secretary of Education:
Lauro F. Cavazos

COLLEGES AND UNIVERSITIES

Higher education:
Public 4-year institutions 595
Public 2-year institutions 968
Private 4-year institutions 1,532
Private 2-year institutions 440
Total 3,535

Vocational institutions: 7,071

FACULTY MEMBERS

Full-time faculty members:
At public institutions 255,731
At private institutions 100,553

Proportion who are women:
At public institutions 29.3%
At private institutions 28.5%

Proportion with tenure:
At public institutions 67.5%
At private institutions 58.3%

Average pay of full-time professors:
At public 4-year institutions $37,840
At public 2-year institutions $32,209
At private 4-year institutions $35,355
At private 2-year institutions $21,824

STUDENTS

Enrollment:
At public 4-year
   institutions 5,543,987
At public 2-year
   institutions 4,612,388
At private 4-year
   institutions 2,631,021
At private 2-year institutions 255,722
Undergraduate 11,304,160
   First-time freshmen ... 2,376,296
Graduate 1,471,862
Professional 267,096
American Indian 92,534
Asian 496,688
Black 1,129,580
Hispanic 679,962
White 10,283,176
Foreign 361,178
Total 13,043,118

Enrollment highlights:
Women 54.0%
Full-time 57.0%
Minority 18.9%
Foreign 2.8%
10-year change in total
   enrollment .... Up 15.8%

Proportion of enrollment made up of minority students:
At public 4-year institutions . 16.9%
At public 2-year institutions . 23.0%

At private 4-year institutions   15.3%
At private 2-year institutions   23.7%

Degrees awarded:
Associate 435,537
Bachelor's 993,362
Master's 298,733
Doctorate 34,839
Professional 70,415

Residence of new students: 81% of all freshmen attended colleges in their home states.

Test scores: Students averaged 18.6 on the A.C.T. and 900 on the S.A.T.

MONEY

Average tuition and fees:
At public 4-year institutions . $1,781
At public 2-year institutions .. $758
At private 4-year institutions $8,446
At private 2-year institutions $5,324

Expenditures:
Public institutions . $63,193,853,000
Private institutions $34,341,889,000

State funds for higher-education operating expenses: $40,887,722,000
Two-year change: Up 12%

State spending on student aid:
Need-based: $1,639,121,000;
   1,398,512 awards
Non–need-based: $217,162,000;
   252,859 awards
Other: $235,964,000

Total spending on research and development by doctorate-granting universities: $14,743,186,000
Sources:
Federal government 59.9%
State and local governments .. 8.2%
Industry 6.5%

The institution itself 18.2%
Other 7.2%

**Federal spending on education
and student aid (selected programs):**
Vocational and
    adult education $824,083,000
GI Bill $599,796,000
Pell Grants $4,909,927,000

Total federal spending on college-

**and university-based research
and development:** $7,717,052,000
Selected programs:
Department of Health and
    Human Services . $4,127,351,000
National Science
    Foundation $998,296,000
Department
    of Defense $1,194,161,000
Department
    of Agriculture $321,444,000
Department of Energy $408,042,000

	1989 population	Rank	Educational attainment of adults in 1980			1990-91 high-school graduates	High-school dropout rate in 1988
			4 years of high school	1-3 years of college	4 years of college		
Alabama	4,118,000	22	56.5%	24.7%	12.2%	40,690	25.1%
Alaska	527,000	50	82.5%	43.7%	21.1%	6,040	34.5%
Arizona	3,556,000	24	72.4%	38.0%	17.4%	31,543	38.9%
Arkansas	2,406,000	33	55.5%	22.3%	10.8%	26,715	22.8%
California	29,063,000	1	73.5%	42.0%	19.6%	245,259	34.1%
Colorado	3,317,000	26	78.6%	44.1%	23.0%	33,255	25.3%
Connecticut	3,239,000	27	70.3%	35.9%	20.7%	30,330	15.1%
Delaware	673,000	46	68.6%	32.4%	17.5%	7,056	28.3%
D.C.	604,000	48	67.1%	41.5%	27.5%	4,153	41.8%
Florida	12,671,000	4	66.7%	31.6%	14.9%	96,266	42.0%
Georgia	6,436,000	11	56.4%	27.9%	14.6%	65,017	39.0%
Hawaii	1,112,000	39	73.8%	38.8%	20.3%	11,781	30.9%
Idaho	1,014,000	42	73.7%	37.2%	15.8%	11,707	24.6%
Illinois	11,658,000	6	66.5%	31.4%	16.2%	116,539	24.4%
Indiana	5,593,000	14	66.4%	24.6%	12.5%	63,746	23.7%
Iowa	2,840,000	29	71.5%	28.6%	13.9%	31,316	14.2%
Kansas	2,513,000	32	73.3%	34.2%	17.0%	25,793	19.8%
Kentucky	3,727,000	23	53.1%	21.8%	11.1%	38,730	31.0%
Louisiana	4,382,000	20	57.7%	26.7%	13.9%	42,122	38.6%
Maine	1,222,000	38	68.7%	29.4%	14.4%	13,923	25.6%
Maryland	4,694,000	19	67.4%	34.9%	20.4%	44,257	25.9%
Massachusetts ..	5,913,000	13	72.2%	35.8%	20.0%	57,767	30.0%
Michigan	9,273,000	8	68.0%	30.0%	14.3%	105,516	26.4%
Minnesota	4,353,000	21	73.1%	34.5%	17.4%	49,774	9.1%
Mississippi	2,621,000	31	54.8%	25.6%	12.3%	26,544	33.1%
Missouri	5,159,000	15	63.5%	27.2%	13.9%	52,675	26.0%
Montana	806,000	44	74.4%	36.5%	17.5%	9,179	12.7%
Nebraska	1,611,000	36	73.4%	32.8%	15.5%	18,016	14.6%
Nevada	1,111,000	40	75.5%	35.1%	14.4%	9,679	24.2%
New Hampshire .	1,107,000	41	72.3%	35.1%	18.2%	11,255	25.9%
New Jersey	7,736,000	9	67.4%	31.5%	18.3%	79,005	22.6%
New Mexico	1,528,000	37	68.9%	34.7%	17.6%	16,692	28.1%
New York	17,950,000	2	66.3%	32.2%	17.9%	163,588	37.7%
North Carolina ..	6,571,000	10	54.8%	27.0%	13.2%	65,243	33.3%
North Dakota ...	660,000	47	66.4%	35.1%	14.8%	7,915	11.7%
Ohio	10,907,000	7	67.0%	26.5%	13.7%	124,293	20.4%
Oklahoma	3,224,000	28	66.0%	31.2%	15.1%	33,955	28.3%
Oregon	2,820,000	30	75.6%	38.5%	17.9%	25,125	27.0%
Pennsylvania	12,040,000	5	64.7%	24.3%	13.6%	123,070	21.6%
Rhode Island	998,000	43	61.1%	28.3%	15.4%	9,083	30.2%
South Carolina ..	3,512,000	25	53.7%	26.7%	13.4%	36,433	35.4%
South Dakota ...	715,000	45	67.9%	31.7%	14.0%	7,696	20.4%
Tennessee	4,940,000	16	56.2%	24.5%	12.6%	47,273	30.7%
Texas	16,991,000	3	62.6%	33.8%	16.9%	183,090	34.7%
Utah	1,707,000	35	80.0%	44.1%	19.9%	24,473	20.6%
Vermont	567,000	49	71.0%	34.7%	19.0%	6,206	21.3%
Virginia	6,098,000	12	62.4%	34.0%	19.1%	66,015	28.4%
Washington	4,761,000	18	77.6%	40.2%	19.0%	45,691	22.9%
West Virginia	1,857,000	34	56.0%	20.4%	10.4%	21,629	22.7%
Wisconsin	4,867,000	17	69.6%	29.2%	14.8%	55,021	15.1%
Wyoming	475,000	51	77.9%	37.9%	17.2%	5,896	11.7%
U.S.	**248,239,000**		**66.5%**	**31.9%**	**16.2%**	**2,474,032**	**28.9%**

Note: Totals may include data for service schools and outlying areas. Sources and additional notes begin on Page 266.

	Number of institutions, fall 1989					Faculty members, 1987-88	
	Public 4-year	Public 2-year	Private 4-year	Private 2-year	Vocational	Public institutions	Private institutions
Alabama	18	37	18	14	72	4,500	923
Alaska	3	0	4	1	40	577	45
Arizona	3	17	14	3	176	4,206	243
Arkansas	10	10	10	7	109	2,210	378
California	31	107	140	32	916	31,296	6,056
Colorado	13	15	17	9	119	4,347	610
Connecticut	7	17	21	3	122	3,025	2,537
Delaware	2	3	5	0	21	1,056	154
D.C..............	2	0	15	0	31	553	2,616
Florida	10	28	43	14	320	7,223	2,363
Georgia	19	28	32	16	137	5,136	1,772
Hawaii	3	6	5	0	35	1,494	95
Idaho	4	2	3	2	39	1,195	117
Illinois	12	47	91	16	359	11,788	5,938
Indiana	14	14	41	9	135	5,901	2,581
Iowa	3	15	34	6	77	3,123	1,697
Kansas	8	21	22	3	76	3,793	682
Kentucky	8	14	24	13	131	3,749	1,058
Louisiana	14	6	10	4	196	4,774	980
Maine	8	5	13	5	22	1,304	557
Maryland	14	19	21	3	180	4,561	1,259
Massachusetts ..	14	16	71	16	177	5,805	9,195
Michigan	15	29	48	5	314	10,597	1,984
Minnesota	10	26	34	11	122	4,786	2,058
Mississippi	9	20	12	6	48	3,287	321
Missouri	13	14	52	10	203	4,703	2,225
Montana	6	7	3	3	45	1,158	145
Nebraska	7	13	14	2	48	1,995	605
Nevada	2	4	1	1	55	877	n/a
New Hampshire .	5	7	12	5	28	1,023	900
New Jersey	14	19	25	4	192	5,873	2,521
New Mexico	6	16	4	0	39	2,045	88
New York	42	48	186	50	356	17,926	15,351
North Carolina ..	16	58	37	15	72	6,186	2,856
North Dakota ...	6	9	4	1	21	1,196	116
Ohio	25	36	65	26	310	10,389	4,047
Oklahoma	14	14	13	6	90	3,443	843
Oregon	8	13	24	1	113	3,735	842
Pennsylvania	43	18	103	53	366	10,403	9,002
Rhode Island	2	1	8	0	28	1,143	1,430
South Carolina ..	12	21	20	11	62	3,747	1,234
South Dakota ...	7	0	10	2	21	862	283
Tennessee	10	14	42	20	127	4,701	2,026
Texas	40	67	56	11	397	16,463	3,955
Utah	4	5	2	3	40	2,096	n/a
Vermont	4	2	13	3	11	660	673
Virginia	15	24	33	6	165	7,421	2,069
Washington	6	27	20	2	143	5,236	1,214
West Virginia	12	4	9	3	52	2,031	381
Wisconsin	13	17	28	3	99	7,960	1,476
Wyoming	1	7	0	1	14	933	n/a
U.S.	595	968	1,532	440	7,071	255,731	100,553

	Average pay of full-time faculty, 1987-88				Enrollment, fall 1988	
	Public 4-year	Public 2-year	Private 4-year	Private 2-year	Public 4-year	Public 2-year
Alabama	$32,953	$28,248	$29,234	$23,355	115,700	60,643
Alaska	$40,617	$43,608	$33,311	n/a	22,115	5,030
Arizona	$41,074	$33,975	$28,259	$18,035	93,146	148,382
Arkansas	$30,572	$23,165	$25,411	$14,600	55,352	16,601
California	$47,696	$37,266	$42,760	$24,375	484,181	1,057,124
Colorado	$36,397	$26,174	$33,813	n/a	105,270	57,632
Connecticut	$44,374	$35,428	$40,836	$23,855	64,501	41,918
Delaware	$37,624	$29,661	$29,951	n/a	22,328	9,317
D.C.	$36,743	n/a	$39,490	n/a	12,108	0
Florida	$37,552	$31,066	$31,544	$21,980	157,549	262,829
Georgia	$35,342	$28,176	$30,538	$21,346	129,692	48,159
Hawaii	$38,449	$31,526	$22,900	n/a	22,550	19,979
Idaho	$31,846	$27,348	$25,966	n/a	29,779	5,340
Illinois	$35,258	$34,067	$37,154	$21,983	193,388	328,236
Indiana	$35,748	$22,753	$33,343	$22,964	173,499	35,734
Iowa	$37,162	$25,698	$28,428	$22,440	68,872	44,391
Kansas	$32,885	$27,594	$22,135	$17,151	87,368	51,332
Kentucky	$32,950	$25,083	$25,925	$17,855	97,895	31,330
Louisiana	$29,963	$25,636	$34,227	n/a	133,830	15,519
Maine	$32,900	$24,710	$32,637	$24,664	30,198	5,716
Maryland	$37,886	$34,109	$38,114	$22,421	109,281	103,041
Massachusetts	$41,949	$30,327	$41,870	$24,007	112,800	75,971
Michigan	$39,294	$36,211	$28,990	$23,914	249,457	214,818
Minnesota	$36,911	$34,129	$31,469	$25,370	133,905	57,281
Mississippi	$29,828	$23,566	$22,841	$16,670	53,344	46,653
Missouri	$33,260	$30,400	$30,730	$22,312	116,420	62,379
Montana	$29,648	$26,793	$23,782	$22,076	27,403	3,884
Nebraska	$31,641	$24,106	$27,820	$20,975	57,107	30,676
Nevada	$37,654	$31,157	$31,381	n/a	25,179	23,467
New Hampshire .:.	$35,124	$25,874	$35,764	$13,618	23,686	6,677
New Jersey	$42,197	$34,768	$40,307	n/a	133,123	110,644
New Mexico	$33,100	$25,360	$26,496	n/a	47,396	29,998
New York	$42,719	$36,759	$38,916	$20,786	352,554	231,288
North Carolina	$36,514	$22,802	$29,136	$22,512	140,025	127,045
North Dakota	$29,959	$26,591	$23,272	$19,547	27,932	7,691
Ohio	$40,061	$29,817	$31,241	$19,676	278,424	123,080
Oklahoma	$31,763	$27,143	$29,947	$20,449	94,687	56,722
Oregon	$33,981	$29,289	$30,165	n/a	68,432	68,175
Pennsylvania	$37,233	$32,137	$36,330	$21,669	229,235	94,290
Rhode Island	$38,127	$31,108	$37,306	n/a	24,274	14,715
South Carolina	$34,051	$22,484	$28,056	$23,090	79,252	40,674
South Dakota	$28,958	n/a	$22,753	$19,330	23,898	0
Tennessee	$35,396	$26,660	$31,373	$19,106	103,791	51,818
Texas	$35,963	$29,972	$34,221	$21,241	392,103	361,091
Utah	$34,060	$26,460	$25,557	n/a	52,631	21,801
Vermont	$35,520	$27,525	$30,670	$22,235	15,762	4,205
Virginia	$40,038	$30,747	$29,758	$20,173	154,165	116,207
Washington	$37,295	$29,267	$30,417	n/a	78,070	141,033
West Virginia	$29,825	$23,644	$23,520	$19,248	60,733	9,648
Wisconsin	$37,780	$32,285	$31,090	n/a	151,146	90,712
Wyoming	$37,053	$27,889	n/a	n/a	10,773	15,138
U.S.	**$37,840**	**$32,209**	**$35,355**	**$21,824**	**5,543,987**	**4,612,388**

	Enrollment, fall 1988						
	Private 4-year	Private 2-year	All under-graduate	First-time freshmen	Graduate	Pro-fessional	Total
Alabama	18,777	4,693	178,954	43,496	17,699	3,160	199,813
Alaska	1,216	0	27,346	1,618	1,015	0	28,361
Arizona	14,269	1,989	230,262	64,668	26,048	1,476	257,786
Arkansas	9,812	2,785	77,275	18,579	5,864	1,411	84,550
California	201,539	10,720	1,560,106	280,052	163,350	30,108	1,753,564
Colorado	18,347	5,039	164,747	30,634	18,553	2,988	186,288
Connecticut	57,467	1,791	130,931	29,551	31,480	3,266	165,677
Delaware	6,615	0	34,065	7,905	3,015	1,180	38,260
D.C.	66,981	0	48,469	9,750	22,183	8,437	79,089
Florida	90,055	5,157	460,804	77,570	47,589	7,197	515,590
Georgia	42,560	10,351	196,276	50,668	27,041	7,445	230,762
Hawaii	9,768	0	46,080	8,405	5,785	432	52,297
Idaho	2,460	8,138	40,161	10,282	5,123	433	45,717
Illinois	157,965	9,385	590,929	125,551	80,767	17,278	688,974
Indiana	55,431	3,238	231,918	54,847	30,724	5,260	267,902
Iowa	45,017	2,894	137,768	37,725	17,484	5,922	161,174
Kansas	12,833	1,314	131,581	27,068	19,148	2,118	152,847
Kentucky	23,170	7,473	137,798	30,115	17,548	4,522	159,868
Louisiana	24,170	2,512	150,771	30,953	19,544	5,716	176,031
Maine	10,919	1,070	43,756	9,758	3,572	575	47,903
Maryland	35,882	875	212,645	31,699	32,494	3,940	249,079
Massachusetts	223,640	14,209	343,625	75,667	70,062	12,933	426,620
Michigan	73,399	4,906	477,704	95,821	55,088	9,788	542,580
Minnesota	48,621	4,899	214,285	48,262	24,868	5,553	244,706
Mississippi	10,258	2,617	101,515	30,291	9,628	1,729	112,872
Missouri	80,085	2,783	220,565	39,586	32,792	8,310	261,667
Montana	3,305	1,180	32,250	5,992	3,312	210	35,772
Nebraska	16,370	464	91,629	17,319	10,357	2,631	104,617
Nevada	161	25	44,517	8,182	4,132	183	48,832
New Hampshire ...	24,167	804	47,598	11,453	7,099	637	55,334
New Jersey	55,937	2,936	256,695	44,381	39,832	6,113	302,640
New Mexico	2,056	0	68,603	11,194	10,220	627	79,450
New York	393,310	30,259	819,446	170,682	160,900	27,065	1,007,411
North Carolina	59,265	6,186	298,635	65,610	27,938	5,948	332,521
North Dakota	2,659	11	35,444	8,906	2,424	425	38,293
Ohio	106,639	33,594	471,644	110,836	58,165	11,928	541,737
Oklahoma	18,434	6,464	151,995	30,525	20,810	3,502	176,307
Oregon	19,220	332	137,363	27,343	15,457	3,339	156,159
Pennsylvania	212,873	37,529	489,422	122,154	70,903	13,602	573,927
Rhode Island	35,850	0	65,954	13,419	8,594	291	74,839
South Carolina	22,963	4,868	127,488	33,985	17,888	2,381	147,757
South Dakota	7,180	382	28,308	6,085	2,729	423	31,460
Tennessee	45,087	5,710	180,156	37,475	20,821	5,429	206,406
Texas	90,024	3,974	739,128	150,518	92,638	15,426	847,192
Utah	32,080	1,026	96,586	18,900	9,740	1,212	107,538
Vermont	12,383	2,117	30,590	6,918	3,522	355	34,467
Virginia	47,766	3,078	276,339	50,768	38,829	6,048	321,216
Washington	32,337	1,648	231,422	72,493	18,663	3,003	253,088
West Virginia	7,488	2,510	70,143	16,569	8,948	1,288	80,379
Wisconsin	42,211	1,158	256,235	54,094	25,345	3,647	285,227
Wyoming	0	629	24,694	6,019	1,640	206	26,540
U.S.	2,631,021	255,722	11,304,160	2,376,296	1,471,862	267,096	13,043,118

The Nation: SUMMARY STATISTICS

	Degrees awarded, 1987-88					Test scores	
	Associate	Bachelor's	Master's	Doctorate	Pro-fessional	Test taken	Score
Alabama	5,974	16,270	4,559	289	817	A.C.T.	17.9
Alaska	661	927	318	15	0	A.C.T.	17.9
Arizona	5,466	12,348	4,970	495	404	A.C.T.	19.0
Arkansas	2,412	7,017	1,746	101	369	A.C.T.	17.6
California	47,503	88,518	31,506	4,116	7,893	S.A.T.	903
Colorado	5,825	15,144	4,397	667	872	A.C.T.	19.6
Connecticut	4,781	13,680	5,892	496	918	S.A.T.	901
Delaware	1,134	3,485	649	107	284	S.A.T.	903
D.C.	391	6,933	5,126	542	2,437	S.A.T.	850
Florida	30,661	32,345	9,828	1,200	2,046	S.A.T.	884
Georgia	6,653	19,481	5,883	737	1,875	S.A.T.	844
Hawaii	2,309	3,724	969	116	126	S.A.T.	885
Idaho	2,600	3,043	703	63	71	A.C.T.	19.1
Illinois	24,720	47,958	17,783	2,152	4,353	A.C.T.	18.8
Indiana	8,949	26,408	7,079	941	1,422	S.A.T.	867
Iowa	7,013	16,747	3,001	658	1,518	A.C.T.	20.1
Kansas	4,759	11,890	2,983	376	628	A.C.T.	19.1
Kentucky	4,915	12,074	3,333	313	1,161	A.C.T.	17.8
Louisiana	2,532	16,367	3,941	346	1,400	A.C.T.	17.1
Maine	2,069	5,168	548	25	157	S.A.T.	886
Maryland	7,061	17,334	5,414	717	1,081	S.A.T.	908
Massachusetts	13,047	41,801	15,692	1,937	3,721	S.A.T.	900
Michigan	19,298	38,939	11,904	1,238	2,341	A.C.T.	18.6
Minnesota	7,591	21,167	3,839	549	1,560	A.C.T.	19.7
Mississippi	4,504	8,486	2,082	241	473	A.C.T.	15.9
Missouri	6,711	23,029	7,920	537	2,264	A.C.T.	19.0
Montana	714	4,170	724	65	78	A.C.T.	19.8
Nebraska	2,546	8,288	1,722	248	706	A.C.T.	19.6
Nevada	857	1,943	434	28	46	A.C.T.	19.0
New Hampshire	2,369	6,778	1,596	69	172	S.A.T.	928
New Jersey	9,379	22,327	6,397	824	1,723	S.A.T.	891
New Mexico	1,760	4,778	1,798	222	164	A.C.T.	17.8
New York	46,897	87,071	33,873	3,436	6,274	S.A.T.	882
North Carolina	10,333	25,688	5,938	796	1,594	S.A.T.	841
North Dakota	1,886	4,110	584	66	114	A.C.T.	18.7
Ohio	17,651	43,521	12,238	1,459	3,207	A.C.T.	19.1
Oklahoma	5,341	13,173	4,118	349	1,031	A.C.T.	17.7
Oregon	4,823	11,251	2,869	409	845	S.A.T.	923
Pennsylvania	18,281	58,348	13,791	1,882	3,637	S.A.T.	883
Rhode Island	3,659	7,934	1,625	237	84	S.A.T.	883
South Carolina	4,776	12,136	3,535	302	683	S.A.T.	834
South Dakota	831	3,627	756	51	121	A.C.T.	19.4
Tennessee	5,908	17,159	4,435	540	1,308	A.C.T.	17.9
Texas	22,346	55,575	17,559	2,067	3,999	S.A.T.	874
Utah	3,552	10,820	2,574	418	378	A.C.T.	18.9
Vermont	1,149	4,273	830	45	98	S.A.T.	897
Virginia	8,192	25,149	6,056	746	1,699	S.A.T.	895
Washington	11,664	17,552	4,262	576	898	S.A.T.	923
West Virginia	2,419	7,260	1,824	131	308	A.C.T.	17.4
Wisconsin	8,570	25,057	5,479	812	988	A.C.T.	20.1
Wyoming	1,386	1,631	343	73	69	A.C.T.	19.4
U.S.	435,537	993,362	298,733	34,839	70,415	A.C.T./S.A.T.	18.6/900

	Minority enrollment, fall 1988				Average tuition and fees, 1989-90			
	Public 4-year	Public 2-year	Private 4-year	Private 2-year	Public 4-year	Public 2-year	Private 4-year	Private 2-year
Alabama	18.3%	19.8%	41.8%	42.2%	$1,522	$662	$5,484	$3,703
Alaska	16.2%	14.1%	25.8%	n/a	$1,280	n/a	$5,078	n/a
Arizona	13.0%	22.0%	18.9%	28.1%	$1,362	$519	$4,127	$11,007
Arkansas	15.3%	13.9%	12.9%	34.8%	$1,376	$644	$3,715	$6,102
California	33.0%	34.7%	22.8%	37.2%	$1,123	$112	$9,489	$7,664
Colorado	11.4%	15.6%	13.6%	24.1%	$1,830	$792	$9,188	$8,036
Connecticut	8.2%	15.7%	10.3%	16.0%	$2,017	$915	$11,268	$7,906
Delaware	13.0%	17.8%	12.3%	n/a	$2,768	$882	$5,388	n/a
D.C.	94.6%	n/a	30.8%	n/a	$664	n/a	$9,489	n/a
Florida	20.2%	23.3%	24.6%	40.1%	n/a	$729	$7,153	$5,519
Georgia	17.2%	20.7%	33.5%	36.6%	$1,631	$852	$7,076	$3,194
Hawaii	70.9%	74.3%	42.7%	n/a	$1,293	$410	$4,008	n/a
Idaho	4.7%	3.5%	3.6%	2.7%	$1,119	$779	$6,669	$1,400
Illinois	17.9%	27.0%	17.6%	53.4%	$2,370	$871	$8,281	$5,505
Indiana	8.1%	10.4%	7.9%	21.2%	$1,975	$1,374	$8,267	$7,412
Iowa	5.0%	4.6%	4.6%	5.4%	$1,823	$1,225	$7,945	$6,423
Kansas	7.4%	10.1%	11.6%	31.9%	$1,467	$711	$5,460	$3,962
Kentucky	7.5%	8.0%	4.0%	11.4%	$1,316	$693	$4,689	$4,669
Louisiana	27.0%	31.7%	29.1%	38.4%	$1,768	$837	$9,257	$5,648
Maine	1.5%	1.2%	3.5%	1.1%	$1,980	$1,134	$10,425	$3,787
Maryland	25.1%	22.8%	13.0%	12.9%	$2,120	$1,172	$9,914	$8,393
Massachusetts ..	7.3%	13.4%	11.6%	14.5%	$2,052	$1,332	$11,450	$7,186
Michigan	11.4%	14.3%	16.4%	28.5%	$2,484	$1,047	$6,520	$6,400
Minnesota	4.3%	4.1%	4.4%	8.7%	$2,063	$1,499	$8,776	$5,181
Mississippi	31.1%	25.1%	27.0%	42.4%	$1,858	$680	$4,828	$3,602
Missouri	8.9%	13.4%	10.9%	20.7%	$1,532	$815	$7,170	$5,554
Montana	4.3%	9.8%	5.7%	77.0%	$1,535	$877	$5,034	$1,144
Nebraska	4.1%	6.1%	7.1%	4.6%	$1,519	$919	$6,442	$3,410
Nevada	12.1%	16.5%	n/a	8.0%	$1,100	$522	$5,400	n/a
New Hampshire .	1.6%	1.6%	6.4%	3.1%	$2,196	$1,608	$10,299	$4,050
New Jersey	20.6%	21.8%	16.0%	23.4%	$2,511	$1,130	$9,398	$6,748
New Mexico	30.7%	41.9%	33.4%	n/a	$1,326	$496	$7,335	n/a
New York	29.2%	24.3%	17.0%	37.1%	$1,460	$1,412	$9,517	$5,544
North Carolina ..	21.1%	20.1%	19.3%	31.0%	$1,015	$288	$7,373	$4,880
North Dakota ...	3.0%	14.0%	6.2%	n/a	$1,604	$1,286	$5,149	$2,100
Ohio	8.5%	11.9%	10.5%	5.6%	$2,432	$1,636	$8,019	$5,690
Oklahoma	14.5%	14.1%	13.2%	27.9%	$1,309	$840	$5,133	$5,382
Oregon	8.9%	7.3%	8.2%	7.0%	$1,738	$753	$8,656	$5,250
Pennsylvania ...	9.7%	13.0%	7.4%	18.4%	$3,210	$1,419	$9,430	$5,497
Rhode Island	5.1%	9.3%	6.9%	n/a	$2,281	$1,004	$10,143	n/a
South Carolina ..	16.7%	24.5%	30.1%	39.5%	$2,162	$807	$5,914	$4,898
South Dakota ...	5.7%	n/a	11.8%	33.8%	$1,718	n/a	$6,224	$2,447
Tennessee	14.6%	15.6%	17.5%	22.9%	$1,406	$803	$6,530	$3,395
Texas	25.1%	32.0%	19.8%	33.5%	$959	$455	$6,047	$5,112
Utah	5.5%	7.7%	2.0%	15.1%	$1,429	$1,136	$1,975	$2,768
Vermont	3.2%	1.3%	3.6%	1.6%	$3,641	$2,210	$10,928	$5,979
Virginia	18.1%	16.9%	21.0%	36.4%	$2,532	$813	$7,238	$4,409
Washington	12.6%	11.3%	9.3%	9.2%	$1,710	$802	$8,096	$7,045
West Virginia	5.2%	2.5%	5.9%	6.3%	$1,591	$803	$7,197	$2,554
Wisconsin	5.4%	7.7%	8.2%	18.6%	$1,861	$1,160	$7,615	$4,001
Wyoming	4.8%	5.5%	n/a	6.8%	$1,003	$613	n/a	$6,900
U.S.	**16.9%**	**23.0%**	**15.3%**	**23.7%**	**$1,781**	**$758**	**$8,446**	**$5,324**

The Nation: SUMMARY STATISTICS

	Expenditures, 1985-86		State appropriations 1990-91
	Public institutions	Private institutions	
Alabama	$1,324,774,000	$186,596,000	$866,989,000
Alaska	$224,042,000	$10,171,000	$181,834,000
Arizona	$1,017,203,000	$52,887,000	$613,806,000
Arkansas	$528,831,000	$72,321,000	$319,014,000
California	$8,515,440,000	$3,641,630,000	$6,100,728,000
Colorado	$1,057,558,000	$160,193,000	$516,793,000
Connecticut	$562,696,000	$836,949,000	$485,846,000
Delaware	$229,377,000	$15,855,000	$122,391,000
D.C.	$88,462,000	$1,307,377,000	n/a
Florida	$1,782,180,000	$723,270,000	$1,632,302,000
Georgia	$1,255,964,000	$696,734,000	$961,283,000
Hawaii	$312,248,000	$20,964,000	$297,625,000
Idaho	$238,438,000	$49,768,000	$183,997,000
Illinois	$2,571,409,000	$2,722,294,000	$1,722,530,000
Indiana	$1,602,203,000	$530,163,000	$876,162,000
Iowa	$1,092,542,000	$353,753,000	$576,924,000
Kansas	$848,602,000	$105,193,000	$458,895,000
Kentucky	$898,718,000	$194,873,000	$607,445,000
Louisiana	$1,039,177,000	$353,433,000	$585,729,000
Maine	$216,737,000	$133,778,000	$195,912,000
Maryland	$1,064,430,000	$901,948,000	$885,085,000
Massachusetts	$980,585,000	$3,544,867,000	$697,248,000
Michigan	$2,946,336,000	$447,436,000	$1,486,694,000
Minnesota	$1,324,691,000	$521,441,000	$1,028,528,000
Mississippi	$706,380,000	$64,054,000	$443,597,000
Missouri	$999,869,000	$911,951,000	$637,378,000
Montana	$182,102,000	$22,349,000	$116,648,000
Nebraska	$537,858,000	$161,066,000	$329,121,000
Nevada	$180,107,000	$2,448,000	$163,324,000
New Hampshire	$183,959,000	$264,440,000	$72,959,000
New Jersey	$1,406,490,000	$714,733,000	$1,055,893,000
New Mexico	$456,600,000	$16,500,000	$335,466,000
New York	$3,802,602,000	$5,594,159,000	$3,142,943,000
North Carolina	$1,799,173,000	$837,291,000	$1,484,279,000
North Dakota	$288,214,000	$18,853,000	$129,756,000
Ohio	$2,718,408,000	$980,801,000	$1,520,055,000
Oklahoma	$844,829,000	$178,905,000	$509,471,000
Oregon	$880,696,000	$171,604,000	$420,047,000
Pennsylvania	$2,392,145,000	$3,169,219,000	$1,421,710,000
Rhode Island	$213,253,000	$315,651,000	$141,139,000
South Carolina	$951,848,000	$196,271,000	$644,726,000
South Dakota	$149,092,000	$51,675,000	$91,415,000
Tennessee	$1,081,052,000	$684,948,000	$743,821,000
Texas	$4,375,082,000	$993,824,000	$2,579,342,000
Utah	$669,714,000	$194,649,000	$295,884,000
Vermont	$188,112,000	$150,689,000	$59,830,000
Virginia	$1,825,156,000	$387,455,000	$1,077,934,000
Washington	$1,399,780,000	$227,211,000	$840,231,000
West Virginia	$376,293,000	$73,716,000	$262,731,000
Wisconsin	$1,754,395,000	$373,533,000	$843,543,000
Wyoming	$203,307,000	n/a	$120,719,000
U.S.	**$63,193,853,000**	**$34,341,889,000**	**$40,887,722,000**

	State spending on student aid, 1989-90	Research spending by universities fiscal 1989	Federal funds for college-and-university-based research, fiscal 1988
Alabama	$11,907,000	$207,200,000	$106,502,000
Alaska	$2,212,000	$56,701,000	$15,928,000
Arizona	$3,400,000	$223,531,000	$83,490,000
Arkansas	$4,827,000	$43,676,000	$15,599,000
California	$162,003,000	$1,845,555,000	$1,109,954,000
Colorado	$20,442,000	$226,428,000	$145,900,000
Connecticut	$32,806,000	$284,410,000	$175,972,000
Delaware	$1,582,000	$37,194,000	$15,261,000
D.C.	$1,069,000	$114,297,000	$72,668,000
Florida	$56,313,000	$385,556,000	$185,626,000
Georgia	$22,273,000	$417,287,000	$165,293,000
Hawaii	$5,953,000	$70,733,000	$39,651,000
Idaho	$638,000	$33,191,000	$8,647,000
Illinois	$204,310,000	$604,466,000	$301,297,000
Indiana	$59,315,000	$227,266,000	$111,776,000
Iowa	$58,932,000	$209,327,000	$89,074,000
Kansas	$7,550,000	$107,856,000	$37,228,000
Kentucky	$13,858,000	$83,998,000	$31,965,000
Louisiana	$9,729,000	$179,332,000	$61,456,000
Maine	$2,008,000	$19,974,000	$6,618,000
Maryland	$21,422,000	$921,848,000	$522,341,000
Massachusetts	$88,314,000	$867,521,000	$545,068,000
Michigan	$77,311,000	$486,270,000	$233,121,000
Minnesota	$69,589,000	$258,614,000	$123,621,000
Mississippi	$1,991,000	$75,175,000	$37,891,000
Missouri	$17,617,000	$255,009,000	$137,276,000
Montana	$417,000	$32,450,000	$8,554,000
Nebraska	$2,037,000	$93,916,000	$25,763,000
Nevada	$400,000	$34,146,000	$13,856,000
New Hampshire	$1,735,000	$62,172,000	$36,766,000
New Jersey	$91,689,000	$283,087,000	$104,853,000
New Mexico	$8,259,000	$136,189,000	$56,163,000
New York	$423,092,000	$1,332,139,000	$794,873,000
North Carolina	$52,123,000	$425,298,000	$246,688,000
North Dakota	$1,622,000	$27,634,000	$11,044,000
Ohio	$76,683,000	$417,275,000	$210,593,000
Oklahoma	$32,545,000	$113,279,000	$25,495,000
Oregon	$10,770,000	$161,127,000	$91,133,000
Pennsylvania	$134,014,000	$761,130,000	$452,313,000
Rhode Island	$11,254,000	$79,810,000	$47,349,000
South Carolina	$19,772,000	$120,137,000	$35,595,000
South Dakota	$594,000	$12,449,000	$4,851,000
Tennessee	$20,027,000	$214,764,000	$114,221,000
Texas	$112,047,000	$1,008,969,000	$414,370,000
Utah	$10,527,000	$164,828,000	$86,648,000
Vermont	$11,384,000	$42,743,000	$28,244,000
Virginia	$26,373,000	$258,919,000	$126,596,000
Washington	$14,136,000	$276,885,000	$200,888,000
West Virginia	$11,877,000	$39,368,000	$14,204,000
Wisconsin	$41,060,000	$336,815,000	$162,145,000
Wyoming	$241,000	$23,310,000	$9,076,000
U.S.	**$2,092,247,000**	**$14,743,186,000**	**$7,717,052,000**

The Nation: SUMMARY STATISTICS

	Federal spending on selected programs, fiscal 1989		
	Vocational education	GI Bill	Pell Grants
Alabama	$16,379,000	$18,913,000	$97,118,000
Alaska	$3,878,000	$1,908,000	$5,853,000
Arizona	$10,996,000	$14,480,000	$81,047,000
Arkansas	$9,482,000	$6,706,000	$57,616,000
California	$70,847,000	$72,280,000	$413,206,000
Colorado	$17,159,000	$15,596,000	$75,890,000
Connecticut	$1,541,000	$3,810,000	$29,773,000
Delaware	$4,065,000	$1,126,000	$28,218,000
D.C.	$4,112,000	$807,000	$13,008,000
Florida	$34,453,000	$34,227,000	$214,107,000
Georgia	$22,892,000	$19,786,000	$72,304,000
Hawaii	$4,148,000	$4,212,000	$7,454,000
Idaho	$4,147,000	$3,397,000	$27,660,000
Illinois	$34,971,000	$18,168,000	$193,859,000
Indiana	$19,936,000	$9,899,000	$106,653,000
Iowa	$9,668,000	$6,056,000	$78,590,000
Kansas	$7,605,000	$7,674,000	$72,520,000
Kentucky	$15,160,000	$8,830,000	$87,228,000
Louisiana	$17,625,000	$11,767,000	$136,558,000
Maine	$4,506,000	$2,811,000	$15,497,000
Maryland	$13,251,000	$9,193,000	$51,527,000
Massachusetts	$17,280,000	$8,139,000	$70,414,000
Michigan	$30,917,000	$15,608,000	$187,031,000
Minnesota	$13,248,000	$11,245,000	$108,850,000
Mississippi	$10,961,000	$6,234,000	$68,225,000
Missouri	$17,062,000	$13,013,000	$106,891,000
Montana	$4,095,000	$2,722,000	$21,612,000
Nebraska	$5,391,000	$6,430,000	$39,626,000
Nevada	$4,101,000	$2,933,000	$13,910,000
New Hampshire	$4,162,000	$2,283,000	$7,787,000
New Jersey	$20,337,000	$5,590,000	$73,686,000
New Mexico	$5,872,000	$6,665,000	$34,928,000
New York	$52,000,000	$16,613,000	$469,873,000
North Carolina	$24,820,000	$19,447,000	$85,566,000
North Dakota	$4,086,000	$3,042,000	$26,031,000
Ohio	$36,448,000	$21,332,000	$215,209,000
Oklahoma	$11,916,000	$12,151,000	$89,407,000
Oregon	$8,873,000	$8,455,000	$55,035,000
Pennsylvania	$38,673,000	$15,889,000	$216,502,000
Rhode Island	$4,288,000	$2,173,000	$13,507,000
South Carolina	$14,056,000	$13,280,000	$58,986,000
South Dakota	$4,099,000	$2,819,000	$26,910,000
Tennessee	$18,831,000	$11,833,000	$83,403,000
Texas	$57,359,000	$50,301,000	$327,601,000
Utah	$6,356,000	$5,047,000	$56,137,000
Vermont	$4,373,000	$725,000	$8,446,000
Virginia	$18,810,000	$23,293,000	$76,924,000
Washington	$13,595,000	$22,771,000	$83,894,000
West Virginia	$7,744,000	$2,948,000	$36,770,000
Wisconsin	$16,153,000	$9,827,000	$116,259,000
Wyoming	$3,932,000	$1,655,000	$11,500,000
U.S.	**$824,083,000**	**$599,796,000**	**$4,909,927,000**

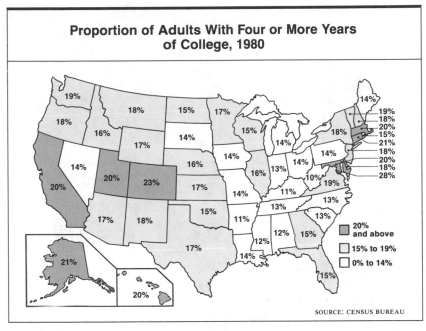

Proportion of Adults With Four or More Years of College, 1980

SOURCE: CENSUS BUREAU

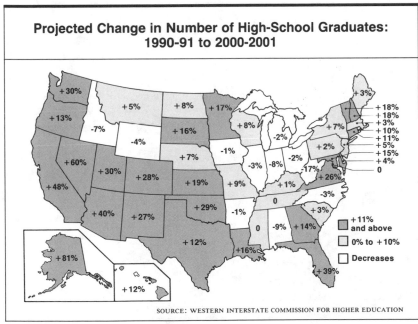

Projected Change in Number of High-School Graduates: 1990-91 to 2000-2001

SOURCE: WESTERN INTERSTATE COMMISSION FOR HIGHER EDUCATION

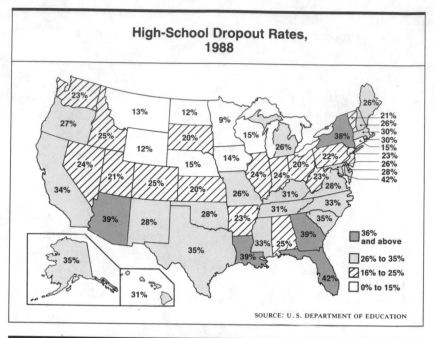

High-School Dropout Rates, 1988

23%
13% 12% 9%
26%
27% 25% 20% 15% 38% 21%
12% 26% 26%
24% 15% 14% 22% 30%
21% 25% 20% 20% 23% 30%
34% 24% 24% 23% 15%
25% 26% 31% 28% 23%
39% 28% 28% 23% 31% 33% 26%
23% 31% 35% 28%
35% 39% 42%

35%

35% 33% 25% 39%
39% 42%

31%

■ 36% and above
▨ 26% to 35%
▨ 16% to 25%
□ 0% to 15%

SOURCE: U.S. DEPARTMENT OF EDUCATION

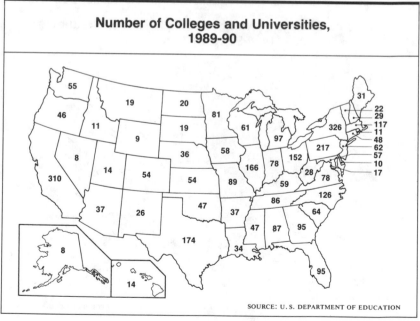

Number of Colleges and Universities, 1989-90

55
19 20 31
46 81
11 19 61 326 22
9 97 29 117
8 36 58 152 217 11
14 54 166 78 28 48
310 54 89 59 78 62
37 26 47 86 126 57
37 47 87 95 64 10
174 17
8 34 95
14

SOURCE: U.S. DEPARTMENT OF EDUCATION

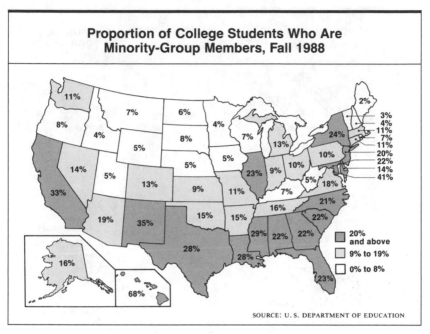

Proportion of College Students Who Are Minority-Group Members, Fall 1988

SOURCE: U. S. DEPARTMENT OF EDUCATION

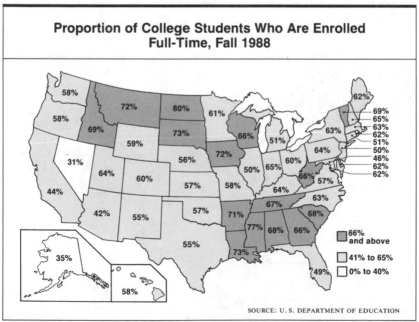

Proportion of College Students Who Are Enrolled Full-Time, Fall 1988

SOURCE: U. S. DEPARTMENT OF EDUCATION

Proportion of First-Time College Freshmen Enrolled on Campuses in Their Home States, Fall 1988

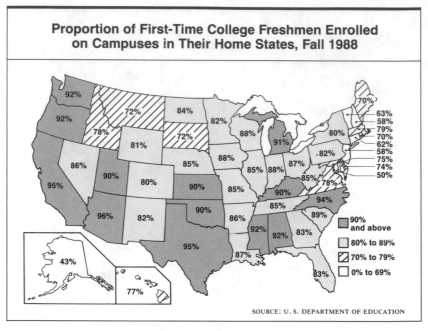

SOURCE: U. S. DEPARTMENT OF EDUCATION

States' Share of Total U.S. College Enrollment, Fall 1988

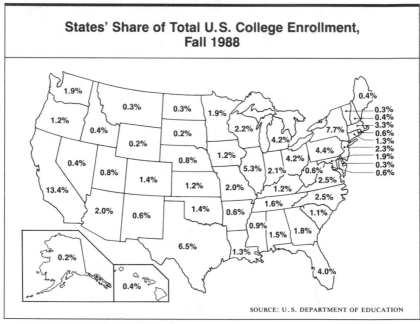

SOURCE: U. S. DEPARTMENT OF EDUCATION

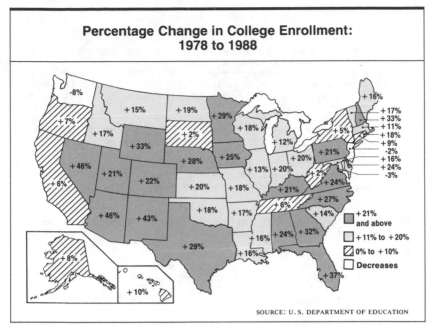

Percentage Change in College Enrollment: 1978 to 1988

SOURCE: U. S. DEPARTMENT OF EDUCATION

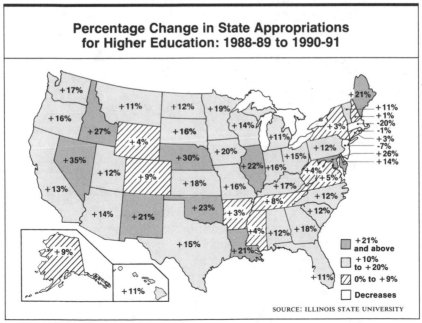

Percentage Change in State Appropriations for Higher Education: 1988-89 to 1990-91

SOURCE: ILLINOIS STATE UNIVERSITY

9 Issues Affecting Colleges: Roll Call of the States

Issue 1. Reports of Incidence of Campus Crime. These states require colleges and universities to issue reports on the incidence of crime on their campuss.

Issue 2. Tax-Exempt Bonds for College Savings. These states have programs to allow families to purchase tax-exempt bonds for college savings.

Issue 3. Prepaid Tuition Plans. These states offer pre-paid-tuition plans, which allow parents to pay a set sum of money, years in advance, for their children's education.

Issue 4. Tests of Competence in English Language for Teaching Assistants. These states require public colleges and universities to test teaching assistants for competence in English.

Issue 5. Restrictions or Taxes on Business Activities of Colleges. These states impose restrictions or taxes on the business activities of colleges and universities (or, in some instances, all non-profit groups).

Issue 6. Vandalism of Animal-Research Facilities. These states treat vandalism of animal-research facilities as a specific crime.

Issue 7. Alternative Certification for Schoolteachers. These states allow college graduates who have not completed an education major to become public-school teachers through an alternative-certification program.

Issue 8. Non-Education Majors for High-School Teachers. These states require prospective secondary-school teachers to major in a subject other than education.

Issue 9. Requirements to Assess What Students Learn. These states require public colleges and universities to set up programs to assess what students learn in college.

	Issue 1	Issue 2	Issue 3	Issue 4	Issue 5	Issue 6	Issue 7	Issue 8	Issue 9
Alabama			★		★				★
Alaska			★				★		
Arizona				★	★	★	★		
Arkansas		★					★	★	★
California	★	★					★	★	
Colorado		★			★			★	★
Connecticut	★	★					★	★	
Delaware	★	★					★	★	
Florida	★		★	★			★	★	★
Georgia	★					★	★		★
Hawaii							★	★	
Idaho				★	★	★	★		★
Illinois		★		★	★	★			

	Issue 1	Issue 2	Issue 3	Issue 4	Issue 5	Issue 6	Issue 7	Issue 8	Issue 9
Indiana		★				★			
Iowa		★	★						
Kansas		★		★		★			
Kentucky		★				★		★	
Louisiana	★	★		★	★	★	★	★	
Maine			★						
Maryland						★			
Massachusetts		★	★			★	★	★	
Michigan			★				★	★	
Minnesota						★	★	★	
Mississippi							★		★
Missouri		★	★	★	★				
Montana									
Nebraska									
Nevada								★	★
New Hampshire		★					★	★	
New Jersey	★						★	★	★
New Mexico							★		
New York							★	★	
North Carolina	★	★					★	★	
North Dakota		★		★				★	
Ohio		★	★	★					
Oklahoma			★	★			★	★	
Oregon		★							
Pennsylvania	★	★		★			★	★	
Rhode Island		★						★	
South Carolina							★		★
South Dakota		★			★				★
Tennessee	★	★		★				★	★
Texas		★		★			★	★	★
Utah					★	★	★	★	
Vermont									
Virginia	★	★					★	★	★
Washington		★						★	★
West Virginia		★	★				★		★
Wisconsin		★						★	
Wyoming			★						

A STAR INDICATES AN ACTION EITHER BY A STATE LEGISLATURE OR BY A STATEWIDE COORDINATING BOARD OR GOVERNING BOARD, AS OF NOVEMBER 1, 1990. SOURCE: CHRONICLE REPORTING

Average ACT Scores by Sex and Racial and Ethnic Group, 1990

	Score	1-year change
Men	21.0	n/a
Women	20.3	n/a
American Indian	18.0	+0.5
Asian	21.7	−0.2
Black	17.0	+0.4
Mexican-American	18.3	+0.2
Other Hispanic	19.3	0.0
White	21.2	−0.1
All	20.6	0.0

Note: The ACT Assessment is scored on a scale from 1 to 36. The figures show the performance of high-school seniors who graduated in 1990 and who took the examination as juniors or seniors. The examination was revised in October 1989; the seniors may have taken either the old or the new version of the assessment. Comparisons are based on estimates derived from research conducted to link scores earned on the two versions of the examination.

SOURCE: AMERICAN COLLEGE TESTING PROGRAM

Average SAT Scores by Sex and Racial and Ethnic Group, 1990

	Verbal section		Mathematical section	
	Score	1-year change	Score	1-year change
Men	429	− 5	499	− 1
Women	419	− 2	455	+ 1
American Indian	388	+ 4	437	+ 9
Asian	410	+ 1	528	+ 3
Black	352	+ 1	385	− 1
Mexican-American	380	− 1	429	− 1
Puerto Rican	359	− 1	405	− 1
Other Hispanic	383	− 6	434	− 2
White	442	− 4	491	0
Other	410	− 4	467	0
All	424	− 3	476	0

Note: Each section of the Scholastic Aptitude Test is scored on a scale from 200 to 800.

SOURCE: THE COLLEGE BOARD

Financial Aid to Undergraduates, Fall 1986

By type of institution	Proportion of students receiving financial assistance, by source			Type of assistance		
	Total	Federal	Other	Grants	Loans	Work-study
Public						
Doctoral	46.8%	35.5%	28.5%	36.4%	27.6%	5.8%
Other 4-year	47.3	38.4	30.0	38.1	24.9	8.1
2-year	28.5	19.9	18.1	25.4	7.8	2.4
Less-than-2-year	51.8	41.9	22.9	46.1	19.6	3.4
All	38.0	28.5	23.7	31.5	17.3	4.6
Private, not-for-profit						
Doctoral	61.8	45.7	50.8	52.2	39.5	13.0
Other 4-year	67.9	50.1	57.7	60.1	42.1	16.4
2-year	63.9	47.9	44.7	53.6	35.7	5.7
Less-than-2-year	66.2	59.4	35.5	55.5	40.4	5.0
All	65.3	48.4	54.1	56.7	40.7	14.3
Private, for-profit						
2-year and above	82.7	79.2	24.2	54.9	69.3	1.2
Less-than-2-year	84.8	81.4	13.0	63.5	71.5	0.5
All	84.0	80.6	17.2	60.3	70.7	0.8
By student characteristics						
Sex						
Men	44.5%	34.1%	27.8%	36.5%	23.9%	5.6%
Women	46.3	35.6	29.7	38.6	24.9	6.6
Racial and ethnic group						
American Indian	48.9	40.3	28.7	41.2	19.7	6.8
Asian	40.5	33.3	28.5	36.2	18.4	7.6
Black, non-Hispanic . . .	63.8	55.7	33.2	56.6	35.0	9.8
Hispanic	47.8	40.9	27.2	41.1	24.0	5.8
White, non-Hispanic . . .	43.3	32.0	28.4	35.1	23.6	5.6
Age						
23 or younger	50.0	39.0	33.5	41.2	28.7	8.4
24 to 29	42.8	34.2	21.9	34.4	22.5	3.6
30 and older	35.4	24.8	21.7	30.6	14.4	2.0
Attendance status						
Full-time	58.3	47.4	37.3	48.2	34.2	9.2
Part-time	24.4	14.4	15.0	20.3	8.4	1.1
All	45.5%	34.9%	28.8%	37.6%	24.4%	6.1%

Note: Figures are based on a survey of 59,886 students enrolled at 1,074 colleges, universities, and proprietary institutions in the fall of 1986. Details may add up to more than the total because some students received multiple types and sources of aid.
The total includes students who reported that they received aid but did not specify its source.

SOURCE: U. S. DEPARTMENT OF EDUCATION

College Enrollment by Racial and Ethnic Group, Selected Years

American Indian	1978	1980	1982	1984	1986	1988
All	78,000	84,000	88,000	84,000	90,000	93,000
Men	37,000	38,000	40,000	38,000	39,000	39,000
Women	41,000	46,000	48,000	46,000	51,000	53,000
Public	68,000	74,000	77,000	72,000	79,000	81,000
Private	9,000	10,000	10,000	11,000	11,000	11,000
4-year	35,000	37,000	39,000	38,000	40,000	42,000
2-year	43,000	47,000	49,000	46,000	51,000	50,000
Undergraduate	72,000	79,000	82,000	78,000	83,000	86,000
Graduate	4,000	4,000	5,000	5,000	5,000	6,000
Professional	1,000	1,000	1,000	1,000	1,000	1,000
Asian						
All	235,000	286,000	351,000	390,000	448,000	497,000
Men	126,000	151,000	189,000	210,000	239,000	259,000
Women	109,000	135,000	162,000	180,000	209,000	237,000
Public	195,000	240,000	296,000	323,000	371,000	406,000
Private	40,000	47,000	55,000	67,000	77,000	91,000
4-year	138,000	162,000	193,000	223,000	262,000	297,000
2-year	97,000	124,000	158,000	167,000	186,000	199,000
Undergraduate	206,000	253,000	313,000	343,000	393,000	437,000
Graduate	24,000	28,000	30,000	37,000	43,000	46,000
Professional	5,000	6,000	8,000	9,000	11,000	14,000
Black						
All	1,054,000	1,107,000	1,101,000	1,076,000	1,082,000	1,130,000
Men	453,000	464,000	458,000	437,000	436,000	443,000
Women	601,000	643,000	644,000	639,000	646,000	687,000
Public	840,000	876,000	873,000	844,000	854,000	881,000
Private	215,000	231,000	228,000	232,000	228,000	248,000
4-year	612,000	634,000	612,000	617,000	615,000	656,000
2-year	443,000	472,000	489,000	459,000	467,000	473,000
Undergraduate	975,000	1,028,000	1,028,000	995,000	996,000	1,039,000
Graduate	68,000	66,000	61,000	67,000	72,000	76,000
Professional	11,000	13,000	13,000	13,000	14,000	14,000
Hispanic						
All	417,000	472,000	519,000	535,000	618,000	680,000
Men	213,000	232,000	252,000	254,000	290,000	310,000
Women	205,000	240,000	267,000	281,000	328,000	370,000
Public	363,000	406,000	446,000	456,000	532,000	587,000
Private	55,000	66,000	74,000	79,000	86,000	93,000
4-year	190,000	217,000	229,000	246,000	278,000	296,000
2-year	227,000	255,000	291,000	289,000	340,000	384,000
Undergraduate	388,000	438,000	485,000	495,000	563,000	631,000
Graduate	24,000	27,000	27,000	32,000	46,000	39,000
Professional	5,000	7,000	7,000	8,000	9,000	9,000

Note: Because of rounding, details may not add to totals.

White	1978	1980	1982	1984	1986	1988
All	9,194,000	9,833,000	9,997,000	9,815,000	9,921,000	10,283,000
Men	4,613,000	4,773,000	4,830,000	4,690,000	4,647,000	4,712,000
Women	4,581,000	5,060,000	5,167,000	5,125,000	5,273,000	5,572,000
Public	7,136,000	7,656,000	7,785,000	7,543,000	7,654,000	7,964,000
Private	2,058,000	2,177,000	2,212,000	2,272,000	2,267,000	2,319,000
4-year	6,027,000	6,275,000	6,306,000	6,301,000	6,337,000	6,582,000
2-year	3,167,000	3,558,000	3,692,000	3,514,000	3,584,000	3,702,000
Undergraduate	7,946,000	8,556,000	8,749,000	8,484,000	8,558,000	8,907,000
Graduate	1,019,000	1,030,000	1,002,000	1,087,000	1,133,000	1,153,000
Professional	229,000	248,000	246,000	243,000	231,000	223,000
Foreign						
All	253,000	305,000	331,000	335,000	345,000	361,000
Men	180,000	211,000	230,000	231,000	233,000	235,000
Women	73,000	94,000	101,000	104,000	112,000	126,000
Public	167,000	204,000	219,000	219,000	224,000	238,000
Private	85,000	101,000	113,000	116,000	120,000	123,000
4-year	201,000	241,000	270,000	282,000	292,000	302,000
2-year	52,000	64,000	61,000	53,000	53,000	60,000
Undergraduate	169,000	208,000	220,000	216,000	205,000	205,000
Graduate	80,000	94,000	108,000	115,000	136,000	151,000
Professional	3,000	3,000	3,000	3,000	4,000	5,000
All						
Total	11,231,000	12,087,000	12,388,000	12,235,000	12,504,000	13,043,000
Men	5,621,000	5,868,000	5,999,000	5,859,000	5,885,000	5,998,000
Women	5,609,000	6,219,000	6,389,000	6,376,000	6,619,000	7,045,000
Public	8,770,000	9,456,000	9,695,000	9,458,000	9,714,000	10,156,000
Private	2,461,000	2,630,000	2,693,000	2,777,000	2,790,000	2,887,000
4-year	7,203,000	7,565,000	7,648,000	7,708,000	7,824,000	8,175,000
2-year	4,028,000	4,521,000	4,740,000	4,527,000	4,680,000	4,868,000
Undergraduate	9,757,000	10,560,000	10,875,000	10,610,000	10,798,000	11,304,000
Graduate	1,219,000	1,250,000	1,235,000	1,344,000	1,435,000	1,472,000
Professional	255,000	277,000	278,000	278,000	270,000	267,000

SOURCE: U. S. DEPARTMENT OF EDUCATION

College and University Enrollment by Level and Age of Student, Fall 1987

	Undergraduate			First-professional		
	Men	Women	Total	Men	Women	Total
Full-time students						
Under 18	1.5%	2.0%	1.8%	0.0%	0.0%	0.0%
18 to 19	34.4	37.6	36.1	0.1	0.1	0.1
20 to 21	29.8	29.2	29.5	2.6	3.6	3.0
22 to 24	18.7	13.5	16.0	40.0	40.2	40.1
25 to 29	7.8	6.5	7.2	37.6	32.4	35.7
30 to 34	3.4	4.3	3.8	10.9	11.5	11.1
35 to 39	1.7	2.9	2.3	4.5	5.9	5.0
40 to 49	1.3	2.4	1.8	2.1	3.9	2.8
50 to 64	0.3	0.5	0.4	0.4	0.7	0.5
65 and over	0.1	0.1	0.1	0.1	0.1	0.1
Age unknown	1.0	1.0	1.0	1.6	1.7	1.7
Number of full-time students ...	3,163,754	3,299,312	6,463,066	153,661	88,143	241,804
Part-time students						
Under 18	2.0%	2.0%	2.0%	0.0%	0.0%	0.0%
18 to 19	8.7	7.5	8.0	0.0	0.0	0.0
20 to 21	11.5	9.3	10.2	0.4	0.3	0.4
22 to 24	17.1	13.6	15.1	10.5	10.0	10.3
25 to 29	20.6	17.6	18.9	35.8	30.4	33.7
30 to 34	14.6	14.7	14.7	24.3	22.3	23.6
35 to 39	9.3	12.0	10.9	14.6	16.0	15.1
40 to 49	8.8	13.7	11.7	10.1	14.7	11.9
50 to 64	3.7	5.3	4.6	2.6	3.8	3.1
65 and over	1.6	2.1	1.9	0.3	0.3	0.3
Age unknown	2.1	2.1	2.1	1.4	2.1	1.7
Number of part-time students...	1,904,930	2,679,906	4,584,836	16,472	10,191	26,663
All students						
Under 18	1.7%	2.0%	1.9%	0.0%	0.0%	0.0%
18 to 19	24.7	24.1	24.4	0.1	0.1	0.1
20 to 21	22.9	20.3	21.5	2.4	3.2	2.7
22 to 24	18.1	13.5	15.6	37.1	37.1	37.1
25 to 29	12.6	11.5	12.0	37.4	32.2	35.5
30 to 34	7.6	8.9	8.3	12.2	12.6	12.3
35 to 39	4.6	7.0	5.9	5.5	6.9	6.0
40 to 49	4.1	7.4	5.9	2.9	5.0	3.7
50 to 64	1.6	2.6	2.2	0.7	1.0	0.8
65 and over	0.7	1.0	0.9	0.1	0.1	0.1
Age unknown	1.4	1.5	1.5	1.6	1.8	1.7
Total number of students	5,068,684	5,979,218	11,047,902	170,133	98,334	268,467

Note: The federal government compiles data on the age of students every two years; the latest report covers 1987.

Graduate			All levels		
Men	Women	Total	Men	Women	Total
0.0%	0.0%	0.0%	1.3%	1.8%	1.6%
0.1	0.1	0.1	30.2	34.3	32.2
1.1	1.3	1.2	26.3	26.8	26.5
22.0	24.0	22.9	19.8	14.8	17.3
36.8	30.3	33.9	11.4	8.7	10.1
19.7	16.5	18.3	5.0	5.2	5.1
10.3	11.7	10.9	2.5	3.5	3.0
6.0	11.3	8.3	1.7	3.0	2.4
1.3	2.6	1.9	0.4	0.7	0.5
0.7	0.2	0.5	0.2	0.1	0.1
2.1	1.9	2.0	1.1	1.1	1.1
293,503	233,133	526,636	3,610,918	3,620,588	7,231,506
0.1%	0.1%	0.1%	1.7%	1.7%	1.7%
0.0	0.0	0.0	7.1	6.2	6.6
0.3	0.3	0.3	9.5	7.8	8.5
8.9	8.6	8.7	15.6	12.8	14.0
28.9	23.3	25.7	22.2	18.6	20.1
23.4	18.7	20.7	16.2	15.4	15.7
16.7	18.0	17.5	10.6	13.0	12.0
14.2	20.5	17.8	9.7	14.8	12.7
3.3	5.4	4.5	3.6	5.3	4.6
0.6	0.5	0.5	1.4	1.9	1.7
3.6	4.5	4.1	2.4	2.5	2.4
399,811	525,491	925,302	2,321,213	3,215,588	5,536,801
0.1%	0.0%	0.1%	1.5%	1.8%	1.6%
0.0	0.0	0.0	21.1	21.1	21.1
0.6	0.7	0.6	19.7	17.9	18.7
14.4	13.4	13.9	18.2	13.9	15.9
32.2	25.5	28.7	15.6	13.4	14.4
21.8	18.0	19.8	9.4	10.0	9.7
14.0	16.1	15.1	5.7	8.0	6.9
10.7	17.7	14.3	4.9	8.5	6.8
2.5	4.6	3.6	1.7	2.8	2.3
0.6	0.4	0.5	0.6	0.9	0.8
3.0	3.7	3.3	1.6	1.7	1.7
693,314	758,624	1,451,938	5,932,131	6,836,176	12,768,307

SOURCE: U. S. DEPARTMENT OF EDUCATION

Projections of College Enrollment and Degrees to be Awarded, 1990-2000

	1990	1991	1992	1993	1994
Enrollment	13,213,000	13,233,000	13,126,000	13,026,000	12,955,000
Men	6,010,000	6,002,000	5,952,000	5,920,000	5,901,000
Women	7,203,000	7,231,000	7,174,000	7,106,000	7,054,000
Public institutions	10,291,000	10,308,000	10,228,000	10,154,000	10,102,000
Private institutions ...	2,922,000	2,925,000	2,898,000	2,872,000	2,853,000
Full-time students	7,428,000	7,378,000	7,274,000	7,179,000	7,117,000
Part-time students ...	5,785,000	5,855,000	5,852,000	5,847,000	5,838,000
Four-year institutions					
Total	8,289,000	8,298,000	8,224,000	8,147,000	8,086,000
Public	5,623,000	5,628,000	5,578,000	5,525,000	5,483,000
Private	2,666,000	2,670,000	2,646,000	2,622,000	2,603,000
Two-year institutions					
Total	4,924,000	4,935,000	4,902,000	4,879,000	4,869,000
Public	4,668,000	4,680,000	4,650,000	4,629,000	4,619,000
Private	256,000	255,000	252,000	250,000	250,000
Undergraduate	11,387,000	11,390,000	11,284,000	11,179,000	11,116,000
Graduate	1,545,000	1,561,000	1,560,000	1,564,000	1,559,000
First-professional	281,000	282,000	282,000	283,000	280,000
Degrees					
Associate	448,000	456,000	457,000	452,000	446,000
Bachelor's	1,005,000	995,000	1,011,000	1,016,000	1,006,000
Master's	301,000	300,000	302,000	301,000	299,000
Doctorate	34,400	34,500	34,600	34,700	34,800
First-professional	72,400	72,300	72,100	72,700	72,200

1995	1996	1997	1998	1999	2000
12,935,000	12,973,000	13,048,000	13,162,000	13,282,000	13,378,000
5,893,000	5,924,000	5,959,000	6,014,000	6,075,000	6,124,000
7,042,000	7,049,000	7,089,000	7,148,000	7,207,000	7,254,000
10,090,000	10,121,000	10,178,000	10,264,000	10,356,000	10,427,000
2,845,000	2,852,000	2,870,000	2,898,000	2,926,000	2,951,000
7,104,000	7,157,000	7,237,000	7,356,000	7,481,000	7,585,000
5,831,000	5,816,000	5,811,000	5,806,000	5,801,000	5,793,000
8,066,000	8,086,000	8,137,000	8,214,000	8,299,000	8,371,000
5,471,000	5,486,000	5,521,000	5,574,000	5,634,000	5,683,000
2,595,000	2,600,000	2,616,000	2,640,000	2,665,000	2,688,000
4,869,000	4,887,000	4,911,000	4,948,000	4,983,000	5,007,000
4,619,000	4,635,000	4,657,000	4,690,000	4,722,000	4,744,000
250,000	252,000	254,000	258,000	261,000	263,000
11,108,000	11,156,000	11,237,000	11,360,000	11,485,000	11,589,000
1,551,000	1,543,000	1,539,000	1,531,000	1,526,000	1,520,000
276,000	274,000	272,000	271,000	271,000	269,000
443,000	443,000	445,000	448,000	454,000	461,000
990,000	973,000	962,000	961,000	968,000	976,000
295,000	292,000	290,000	289,000	287,000	286,000
34,900	34,900	35,000	35,000	35,000	35,100
70,600	69,200	68,300	67,800	67,600	67,100

SOURCE: U.S. DEPARTMENT OF EDUCATION

Earned Degrees Conferred, 1987-88

	Bachelor's degrees		
	Men	Women	Total
Agriculture and natural resources	9,744	4,478	14,222
Allied health and health sciences	8,787	51,308	60,095
Architecture and environmental design	5,277	3,329	8,606
Area and ethnic studies	1,393	2,070	3,463
Business and management	129,764	113,580	243,344
Communications and communications technologies	18,588	28,117	46,705
Computer and information sciences	23,347	11,201	34,548
Education	21,005	70,008	91,013
Engineering and engineering technologies	76,607	12,184	88,791
Foreign languages	2,727	7,301	10,028
Home economics and vocational home economics	1,225	13,600	14,825
Law	413	890	1,303
Letters	13,152	26,351	39,503
Liberal / general studies	9,498	12,298	21,796
Library and archival sciences	17	106	123
Life sciences	18,261	18,500	36,761
Mathematics	8,513	7,375	15,888
Military sciences and military technologies	331	18	349
Multi / interdisciplinary studies	8,193	9,173	17,366
Parks and recreation	1,680	2,401	4,081
Philosophy and religion	3,858	2,101	5,959
Physical sciences and science technologies	12,375	5,401	17,776
Protective services	8,349	5,020	13,369
Psychology	13,484	31,477	44,961
Public affairs and social work	4,533	9,699	14,232
Social sciences	56,297	43,973	100,270
Theology	4,187	1,397	5,584
Visual and performing arts	14,106	22,494	36,600
Not classified by field of study	1,131	670	1,801
All fields	476,842	516,520	993,362

Professional Degrees Conferred, 1987-88

	Men	Women	Total
Chiropractic	1,963	669	2,632
Dentistry	3,216	1,135	4,351
Law	21,124	14,345	35,469
Medicine	10,107	4,984	15,091
Optometry	672	351	1,023
Osteopathic medicine	1,123	421	1,544
Pharmacy	383	568	951
Podiatry and podiatric medicine	495	150	645
Theological professions	5,088	1,386	6,474
Veterinary medicine	1,117	1,118	2,235
All fields	45,288	25,127	70,415

SOURCE: U.S. DEPARTMENT OF EDUCATION

Master's degrees			Doctor's degrees		
Men	Women	Total	Men	Women	Total
2,427	1,052	3,479	926	216	1,142
4,028	14,495	18,523	540	707	1,247
2,042	1,117	3,159	66	32	98
495	410	905	71	71	142
46,282	23,348	69,630	853	256	1,109
1,574	2,358	3,932	128	108	236
6,702	2,464	9,166	380	48	428
19,383	58,321	77,704	2,944	3,600	6,544
20,503	2,923	23,426	3,898	293	4,191
589	1,258	1,847	180	231	411
246	1,813	2,059	82	227	309
1,386	494	1,880	66	23	89
2,110	4,061	6,171	532	648	1,180
511	831	1,342	16	15	31
790	2,923	3,713	22	24	46
2,417	2,352	4,769	2,330	1,268	3,598
2,052	1,371	3,423	626	126	752
48	1	49	0	0	0
1,799	1,298	3,097	167	94	261
205	256	461	19	10	29
675	423	1,098	306	99	405
4,315	1,412	5,727	3,119	685	3,805
727	297	1,024	23	9	32
2,589	5,273	7,862	1,366	1,622	2,988
6,324	10,826	17,150	238	232	470
6,235	4,058	10,293	1,851	932	2,783
3,159	1,616	4,775	1,080	127	1,207
3,437	4,488	7,925	427	301	728
1,873	2,271	4,144	336	243	579
144,923	153,810	298,733	22,592	12,247	34,839

SOURCE: U. S. DEPARTMENT OF EDUCATION

Degrees Conferred by Racial and Ethnic Group, 1986-87

	American Indian	Asian	Black	Hispanic	White	Foreign
Associate						
Men	1,263	6,172	13,956	8,764	158,126	2,560
Women	1,933	5,622	21,510	10,581	203,693	2,128
Total	3,196	11,794	35,466	19,345	361,819	4,688
Bachelor's						
Men	1,819	17,249	22,499	12,864	406,751	19,598
Women	2,152	15,369	34,056	14,126	435,069	9,708
Total	3,971	32,618	56,555	26,990	841,820	29,306
Master's						
Men	517	5,238	5,151	3,330	105,573	21,455
Women	587	3,320	8,716	3,714	123,297	8,443
Total	1,104	8,558	13,867	7,044	228,870	29,898
Doctorate						
Men	58	795	488	439	14,813	5,466
Women	46	302	572	311	9,622	1,121
Total	104	1,097	1,060	750	24,435	6,587
Professional						
Men	183	1,420	1,835	1,303	41,149	632
Women	121	850	1,585	748	21,539	252
Total	304	2,270	3,420	2,051	62,688	884

SOURCE: U. S. DEPARTMENT OF EDUCATION

Proportion of High-School Graduates Who Are Enrolled in College, by Racial and Ethnic Group and Age

	White		Black		Hispanic	
	18-24	25-34	18-24	25-34	18-24	25-34
1978	31.3%	8.8%	29.7%	10.8%	27.2%	10.2%
1979	31.2	8.9	29.5	9.3	30.2	11.6
1980	32.1	8.7	27.7	9.6	29.9	9.2
1981	32.7	8.4	28.0	10.2	29.9	10.8
1982	33.3	8.7	27.9	9.5	29.2	9.7
1983	33.0	8.7	27.0	8.9	31.4	9.7
1984	33.9	8.4	27.2	8.1	29.9	9.9
1985	34.9	8.6	26.1	7.4	26.9	9.7
1986	34.5	8.0	28.6	7.8	29.4	10.4
1987	37.4	7.9	30.1	8.2	28.5	8.9
1988	38.7	7.8	28.0	7.4	30.9	8.3

Note: The figures are based on annual Census Bureau surveys of 60,000 households.

SOURCE: CENSUS BUREAU

Educational Attainment of 1980 High-School Seniors by 1986

	No high-school diploma	High-school diploma	License	Associate degree	Bachelor's degree	Professional/ graduate degree
Sex						
Men	1.0%	64.0%	10.5%	5.9%	17.6%	0.9%
Women	0.8	59.6	13.3	7.0	18.8	0.6
Racial and ethnic group						
American Indian	—	61.3	18.6	9.3	10.8	—
Asian	—	49.6	12.6	8.7	27.3	1.7
Black, non-Hispanic	1.2	69.4	13.9	5.3	9.9	0.2
Hispanic	1.7	70.2	13.8	7.3	6.8	0.1
White, non-Hispanic	0.8	60.0	11.5	6.6	20.2	0.9
Socioeconomic status						
Low	1.2	74.1	12.3	5.5	6.6	0.2
Low-middle	0.5	66.7	13.6	8.0	11.1	0.2
High-middle	0.1	58.4	12.9	7.7	20.4	0.6
High	—	45.7	8.7	6.3	37.1	2.2
High-school program						
General	0.8	69.7	12.6	6.5	10.2	0.2
Academic	0.1	45.6	8.8	7.2	36.6	1.8
Vocational	0.6	72.8	16.2	6.9	3.6	0.0
Type of high school						
Public	1.0	63.2	12.1	6.6	16.4	0.7
Catholic	—	47.4	11.9	6.4	32.8	1.6
Other private	—	52.3	7.0	3.9	36.7	0.1
Postsecondary education plans						
No plans	1.4	83.5	12.7	2.1	0.2	—
Attend voc/tech school ..	0.3	72.5	17.7	8.4	1.1	—
Attend college less than 4 years	0.2	65.5	14.4	13.1	6.8	—
Earn bachelor's degree ..	—	48.3	8.2	6.9	35.8	0.7
Earn advanced degree ..	0.1	43.5	7.9	4.9	40.6	3.0
1980 enrollment status						
Part-time 2-year public college	0.7	66.4	17.7	8.8	6.5	—
Part-time 4-year public college	2.7	57.1	15.4	1.6	22.6	0.6
Full-time 2-year public college	—	49.5	11.7	20.7	17.6	0.5
Full-time 4-year public college	—	41.7	7.6	4.5	44.9	1.3
Full-time 4-year private college	—	31.1	8.8	5.1	51.9	3.0
Not a student	1.8	78.2	12.8	3.6	3.5	0.2
Total	0.9%	61.8%	11.9%	6.5%	18.2%	0.7%

Note: Figures are based on data from "High School and Beyond," a longitudinal study of more than 10,500 students who were high-school seniors in 1980. They show students' highest level of education achieved by the spring of 1986.
Because of rounding, figures may not add to 100 per cent. A dash indicates less than 0.5 per cent.
Socioeconomic status was determined by parental education, family income, father's occupation, and household characteristics in 1980.

SOURCE: U.S. DEPARTMENT OF EDUCATION

Characteristics of Recipients of Doctorates, 1988

	Arts and humanities	Business and management	Education
Doctoral degrees conferred	3,553	1,039	6,349
Median age at conferral	35.4	34.8	40.5
Median number of years from bachelor's degree to doctorate	12.2	11.6	16.9
Median number of years registered as a graduate student	8.5	6.9	8.1
Proportion with bachelor's degree in same field as doctorate	56.7%	36.9%	36.9%
Sex			
Male	55.7%	76.2%	44.8%
Female	44.3	23.8	55.2
Citizenship			
United States	78.4	58.5	83.1
Non-U.S., permanent visa	4.7	7.9	2.7
Non-U.S., temporary visa	9.7	24.5	7.5
Unknown	7.1	9.0	6.7
Planned postdoctoral study			
Fellowship	4.0%	0.5%	2.0%
Research associateship	1.5	0.7	1.3
Traineeship	0.3	0.5	0.6
Other	1.4	0.5	0.9
Planned postdoctoral employment			
Educational institution	66.1	75.6	63.1
Industry or business	5.5	7.8	6.3
Government	2.3	1.9	7.4
Non-profit organization	4.8	0.5	4.9
Other or unknown	4.0	0.9	3.5
Postdoctoral status unknown	10.2	11.3	10.0
Primary postdoctoral employment activity			
Research and development	6.6%	32.0%	5.5%
Teaching	70.2	57.7	35.5
Administration	5.6	3.7	37.4
Professional services	5.9	1.7	11.8
Other	5.2	1.4	2.5
Unknown	6.5	3.5	7.2

[1] Excludes business and management, which is listed separately.
[2] Includes degree categories not listed separately.

Engineering	Life sciences	Physical sciences	Social sciences	Other professional fields[1]	All fields[2]
4,190	6,143	5,309	5,769	1,053	33,456
31.0	31.9	30.3	34.1	37.9	33.8
8.1	8.9	7.4	10.5	14.6	10.5
5.9	6.5	6.1	7.4	7.9	6.9
76.4%	55.4%	67.3%	54.5%	23.6%	54.7%
93.2%	63.2%	83.4%	55.0%	59.6%	64.8%
6.8	36.8	16.6	45.0	40.4	35.2
42.4	71.3	60.8	74.8	73.3	69.3
8.7	4.9	4.7	3.8	4.2	4.8
41.1	17.3	27.8	12.3	11.3	18.5
7.7	6.4	6.7	9.1	11.2	7.5
5.2%	30.8%	17.6%	8.4%	1.3%	11.4%
12.6	17.4	24.3	3.7	1.0	9.7
1.3	1.6	0.7	1.5	0.7	1.0
0.4	3.5	0.7	1.0	0.8	1.3
24.0	19.9	20.3	36.8	50.1	39.2
34.5	7.3	20.3	12.1	7.2	13.2
7.2	6.3	4.4	8.9	7.0	6.2
0.7	2.0	0.8	10.4	14.9	4.3
2.6	2.4	1.4	5.4	2.5	3.1
11.4	9.0	9.6	11.9	14.4	10.5
64.0%	44.6%	61.9%	22.7%	11.9%	28.3%
20.6	28.7	24.7	29.7	46.6	36.3
2.1	5.9	1.7	6.3	13.1	13.2
5.1	9.8	3.9	33.5	16.6	13.0
2.2	3.5	2.0	3.4	5.2	3.1
6.0	7.5	5.7	4.4	6.6	6.1

SOURCE: NATIONAL RESEARCH COUNCIL

Student Financial Aid, 1989-90

Total spending, by source

Federally supported programs
Generally available aid

Pell Grants	$4,476,000,000
Supplemental Educational Opportunity Grants	442,000,000
State Student Incentive Grants	72,000,000
College Work-Study	780,000,000
Perkins Loans	844,000,000
Income Contingent Loans	6,000,000
Stafford Student Loans	9,660,000,000
Supplemental Loans for Students	1,839,000,000
Parent Loans for Undergraduate Students	801,000,000
Subtotal	18,920,000,000
Specially directed aid	
Veterans	601,000,000
Military	366,000,000
Other grants	112,000,000
Other loans	350,000,000
Subtotal	1,428,000,000
Total federal aid	20,355,000,000
State grant programs	1,785,000,000
Institutionally awarded aid	5,728,000,000
Total federal, state, and institutional aid	$27,860,000,000

Number of recipients and average award per recipient, selected programs

Program	Recipients	Amount
Pell Grants	3,200,000	$1,399
Supplemental Educational Opportunity Grants	633,000	699
College Work-Study	835,000	934
Perkins Loans	826,000	1,022
Stafford Student Loans	3,696,000	2,614
Supplemental Loans for Students	688,000	2,673
Parent Loans for Undergraduate Students	256,000	3,128
State Grants and State Student Incentive Grants	1,651,000	1,124

Note: Figures are estimates and include assistance to undergraduate and graduate students.
Several of the federal programs include small amounts of money from sources other than the federal government. For example, College Work-Study includes some contributions by institutions, although most of the funds in the program are federal.
Federal spending for State Student Incentive Grants is reported under federal programs; state spending for those grants is reported in the "state grants" category.
Funds for Stafford Student Loans, Supplemental Loans for Students, and Parent Loans for Undergraduate Students come mostly from private sources. The federal government subsidizes interest payments and repays defaults. Amounts reported represent loan commitments rather than amounts loaned, but the difference between the two is insignificant.
Veterans' benefits are payments for postsecondary education and training to veterans and their dependents.
Military aid covers the Armed Forces Health Professions Scholarship program; Reserve Officers Training Corps programs for the Air Force, Army, and Navy; and tuition assistance for military personnel on active duty.
Because of rounding, details may not add to totals.

SOURCE: THE COLLEGE BOARD

Attitudes and Characteristics of Freshmen, Fall 1989

	Men	Women	Total
Racial/ethnic background:			
American Indian	0.8%	1.0%	0.9%
Asian-American	3.3	2.6	2.9
Black	7.8	10.3	9.2
Mexican-American	1.2	1.5	1.4
Puerto Rican-American	0.8	0.9	0.8
White	85.6	83.3	84.3
Other	2.1	2.0	2.1
Number of other colleges applied to for admission this year:			
None	30.2	32.3	31.3
One	14.2	16.2	15.3
Two	16.8	16.6	16.7
Three	15.6	14.8	15.2
Four	9.7	8.4	9.0
Five	6.1	5.4	5.7
Six or more	7.5	6.3	6.9
Number of other college acceptances (of those with multiple applications):			
None	16.3	15.4	15.8
One	25.9	28.1	27.1
Two	23.8	23.7	23.7
Three	17.1	16.9	17.0
Four	8.9	8.4	8.6
Five	4.0	3.9	3.9
Six or more	4.1	3.6	3.8
College attended is student's:			
First choice	69.0	68.7	68.9
Second choice	22.2	23.4	22.9
Third choice	5.5	5.3	5.4
Other	3.3	2.5	2.9
Highest degree planned:			
None	1.2	0.9	1.1
Vocational certificate	1.3	0.6	0.9
Associate (or equivalent)	3.9	5.0	4.5
Bachelor's	33.1	31.6	32.3
Master's	36.3	37.6	37.0
Ph.D. or Ed.D.	12.0	11.5	11.7
M.D., D.O., D.D.S., or D.V.M.	5.4	6.0	5.7
LL.B. or J.D.	4.9	4.9	4.9
B.D. or M.Div.	0.4	0.2	0.3
Other	1.5	1.7	1.6
Concern about financing college:			
None	39.9	32.2	35.7
Some	49.3	52.7	51.2
Major	10.8	15.1	13.1

Note: The statistics are based on a survey of 216,362 freshmen entering 403 two-year and four-year institutions in the fall of 1989. The figures were statistically adjusted to represent the total population of 1.6 million first-time, full-time freshmen. Because of rounding or multiple responses, figures may add to more than 100 per cent.

Continued on Following Page

Attitudes and Characteristics of Freshmen, Fall 1989, continued

	Men	Women	Total
Reasons noted as very important in deciding to go to college:			
Could not find job	6.3%	7.5%	7.0%
To get away from home	14.5	15.5	15.0
To be able to get a better job	75.4	76.3	75.9
To gain a general education and appreciation of ideas	55.0	68.9	62.5
To improve reading and study skills	35.8	44.4	40.5
Parent wanted me to go	32.4	36.2	34.3
Nothing better to do	3.0	1.9	2.4
To become a more cultured person	29.5	40.8	35.6
To be able to make more money	75.6	69.3	72.2
To learn more about things that interest me	67.9	76.2	72.4
To prepare for graduate or professional school	47.3	55.1	51.5
Students estimate chances are very good that they will:			
Change major field	12.2	14.2	13.3
Change career choice	10.4	13.7	12.2
Fail one or more courses	1.5	1.2	1.4
Graduate with honors	13.6	11.8	12.6
Be elected to student office	3.5	3.3	3.4
Get a job to pay college expenses	31.0	37.9	34.7
Work full-time while attending college	3.4	3.7	3.6
Join a social fraternity or sorority	15.5	19.9	17.9
Play varsity athletics	19.5	10.4	14.6
Be elected to an honor society	7.3	7.7	7.5
Make at least a B average	41.4	40.7	41.0
Get tutoring in some courses	10.5	14.3	12.6
Work at outside job	16.9	22.9	20.1
Seek vocational counseling	3.9	4.8	4.4
Seek individual counseling	3.0	3.8	3.4
Participate in student protests	5.5	7.1	6.3
Need extra time to complete degree	7.2	7.5	7.4
Transfer to another college	10.9	12.6	11.8
Drop out permanently	1.0	0.7	0.8
Drop out temporarily	1.3	1.0	1.1
Get bachelor's degree	66.7	70.1	68.5
Be satisfied with college	44.8	53.8	49.7
Find job in preferred field	66.4	72.1	69.5
Marry while in college	3.5	6.0	4.8
Political views:			
Far left	2.4	1.5	1.9
Liberal	19.3	23.7	21.7
Middle of the road	49.5	57.1	53.6
Conservative	26.6	16.7	21.3
Far right	2.3	0.9	1.5
Objectives considered essential or very important:			
Becoming accomplished in a performing art	10.7	11.5	11.1
Becoming an authority in own field	67.8	64.1	65.8

	Men	Women	Total
Objectives considered essential or very important:			
Obtaining recognition from colleagues for contributions to field	56.1%	54.0%	55.0%
Influencing the political structure	22.4	17.7	19.9
Influencing social values	35.2	46.1	41.1
Raising a family	68.5	69.0	68.8
Having administrative responsibility for the work of others	44.9	42.6	43.6
Being very well-off financially	79.5	71.9	75.4
Helping others who are in difficulty	49.0	68.7	59.7
Making a theoretical contribution to science	20.7	14.1	17.1
Writing original works	12.2	12.7	12.5
Creating artistic work	12.4	12.6	12.5
Becoming successful in own business	50.1	40.8	45.1
Becoming involved in programs to clean up environment	28.3	24.3	26.1
Developing a meaningful philosophy of life	40.0	41.6	40.8
Participating in a community-action program	20.2	25.9	23.3
Helping to promote racial understanding	32.5	37.6	35.3
Keeping up to date with political affairs	43.4	36.0	39.4
Agree strongly or somewhat that:			
Government is not doing enough to protect the consumer	64.7	71.5	68.4
Government is not doing enough to promote disarmament	58.8	76.2	68.1
Government is not doing enough to control pollution ...	84.8	87.6	86.3
Taxes should be raised to reduce the federal deficit	32.6	25.5	28.8
Abortion should be legal	63.6	65.5	64.7
The death penalty should be abolished	18.4	23.8	21.3
It is all right for two people who like each other to have sex even if they've known each other for a very short time	65.1	36.4	49.7
Married women's activities are best confined to home and family	32.3	20.4	25.9
A couple should live together before marriage	57.3	45.0	50.7
Marijuana should be legalized	20.1	13.7	16.7
Busing to achieve racial balance in schools is all right ..	56.1	56.0	56.0
It is important to have laws prohibiting homosexual relationships	57.3	35.1	45.4
Colleges should not invest in companies that do business in South Africa	54.1	44.2	48.8
The chief benefit of college is that it increases one's earning power	75.6	66.8	70.9
Employers should be allowed to require employees or job applicants to take drug tests	76.5	78.9	77.8
The best way to control AIDS is through widespread, mandatory testing	66.9	67.5	67.2
Just because a man thinks that a woman has "led him on" does not entitle him to have sex with her	79.0	92.8	86.4
The government should do more to control the sale of handguns	67.2	87.6	78.2
A national health-care plan is needed to cover everybody's medical costs	72.1	79.0	75.8

SOURCE: "THE AMERICAN FRESHMAN: NATIONAL NORMS FOR FALL 1989," BY ALEXANDER W. ASTIN, PUBLISHED BY AMERICAN COUNCIL ON EDUCATION AND UNIVERSITY OF CALIFORNIA AT LOS ANGELES

Foreign Students' Countries of Origin, 1989-90

Country or territory	Students	Country or territory	Students
China	33,390	Kuwait	2,280
Taiwan	30,960	Panama	2,260
Japan	29,840	Sri Lanka	2,210
India	26,240	Kenya	2,200
Republic of Korea	21,710	Norway	2,160
Canada	17,870	Trinidad & Tobago	2,160
Malaysia	14,110	South Africa	2,050
Hong Kong	11,230	Ethiopia	2,020
Indonesia	9,390	Vietnam	1,850
Iran	7,440	Netherlands	1,840
United Kingdom	7,100	Argentina	1,810
Pakistan	7,070	Cyprus	1,750
West Germany	6,750	Australia	1,740
Thailand	6,630	Sweden	1,740
Mexico	6,540	Egypt	1,700
France	5,340	Bahamas	1,640
Jordan	5,250	Syria	1,500
Philippines	4,540	Haiti	1,490
Nigeria	4,480	Honduras	1,470
Lebanon	4,450	United Arab Emirates	1,450
Singapore	4,440	Ireland	1,380
Greece	4,430	El Salvador	1,370
Saudi Arabia	4,110	Cameroon	1,240
Brazil	3,730	Switzerland	1,240
Spain	3,640	Ecuador	1,170
Turkey	3,400	Morocco	1,140
Colombia	3,320	Chile	1,100
Israel	2,910	Yugoslavia	1,070
Jamaica	2,850	Bolivia	1,060
Peru	2,750	Costa Rica	1,060
Venezuela	2,740	Ghana	1,030
Bangladesh	2,470	Guatemala	1,030
Nicaragua	2,450	Poland	1,010
Italy	2,370		

Note: Includes only countries with over 1,000 students in U.S. institutions.

SOURCE: INSTITUTE OF INTERNATIONAL EDUCATION

Educational Attainment of the U.S. Population

Highest level reached	Men	Women	Total
Doctorate	0.9%	0.2%	0.6%
Professional	1.6	0.4	1.0
Master's	4.1	3.0	3.5
Bachelor's	13.0	11.0	11.9
Associate	4.0	4.4	4.2
Vocational	1.5	2.7	2.1
Some college, no degree	18.0	17.2	17.6
High-school diploma	33.9	39.2	36.6
No high-school diploma	23.0	22.0	22.5

Note: The figures are based on a 1987 survey of 11,100 households. They cover the civilian, resident population of adults age 18 and older.

SOURCE: CENSUS BUREAU

Institutions Enrolling the Most Foreign Students, 1989-90

Miami-Dade Community College	5,518
University of Southern California	3,705
University of Texas at Austin	3,588
University of Wisconsin at Madison	3,295
Boston University	3,248
University of California at Los Angeles	3,126
Ohio State University main campus	2,887
Columbia University	2,849
University of Illinois at Urbana-Champaign	2,794
University of Pennsylvania	2,778
Southern Illinois University at Carbondale	2,615
University of Minnesota–Twin Cities	2,555
University of Michigan at Ann Arbor	2,465
University of Maryland at College Park	2,397
University of Houston at University Park	2,332
Northeastern University	2,288
Purdue University main campus	2,277
Michigan State University	2,270
University of Arizona	2,253
Harvard University	2,246
George Washington University	2,207
State University of New York at Buffalo	2,192
Iowa State University	2,160
Texas A&M University main campus	2,156
University of California at Berkeley	2,143
Cornell University	2,138
Arizona State University	2,132
New York University	2,102
Stanford University	2,081
Indiana University at Bloomington	2,066
Pennsylvania State University main campus	2,059
Massachusetts Institute of Technology	2,049
California State University at Los Angeles	2,028
Rutgers University	1,988
University of Iowa	1,888
University of Florida	1,880
New Jersey Institute of Technology	1,864
University of Hawaii at Manoa	1,850
University of Kansas	1,837
Oregon State University	1,817

SOURCE: INSTITUTE OF INTERNATIONAL EDUCATION

Campuses With the Largest Enrollments, Fall 1988

University of Minnesota–Twin Cities	61,556
Ohio State University main campus	53,661
University of Texas at Austin	50,106
Michigan State University	44,480
Miami-Dade Community College	43,880
Arizona State University	43,426
University of Wisconsin at Madison	43,364
Texas A&M University	39,163
University of Illinois at Urbana-Champaign	38,337
Pennsylvania State University main campus	37,269
University of Maryland at College Park	36,681
Purdue University main campus	36,517
University of Michigan at Ann Arbor	36,001
University of Arizona	34,725
University of California at Los Angeles	34,371
San Diego State University	34,155
Indiana University at Bloomington	33,776
University of Washington	33,460
University of Florida	33,282
California State University at Long Beach	33,179
Rutgers University at New Brunswick	32,901
Northeastern University	32,385
Temple University	32,139
Northern Virginia Community College	31,896
Macomb Community College	31,462
University of Cincinnati main campus	31,432
University of Southern California	30,831
Wayne State University	30,751
New York University	30,750
University of Houston–University Park	30,372
St. Louis Community College	30,291
Houston Community College	30,236
Brigham Young University main campus	30,226
University of California at Berkeley	30,102
University of Iowa	30,001
University of South Florida	29,912
California State University at Northridge	29,401
Boston University	28,555
University of Pittsburgh main campus	28,524
State University of New York at Buffalo	28,005
University of Massachusetts at Amherst	27,918
University of Akron main campus	27,818
Louisiana State University	27,348
University of Georgia	27,176
Oakland Community College	26,854
Pima Community College	26,810
College of Du Page	26,489
Iowa State University	26,475
San Jose State University	26,456
University of South Carolina at Columbia	26,435

Community College of the Air Force	26,354
University of Kansas main campus	26,020
Tarrant County Junior College District	25,946
Florida State University	25,907
El Camino College	25,789
North Carolina State University at Raleigh	25,725
University of Connecticut	25,374
University of Wisconsin at Milwaukee	25,212
University of Tennessee at Knoxville	24,985
Western Michigan University	24,861
Indiana University–Purdue University at Indianapolis	24,808
Texas Tech University	24,605
University of North Texas	24,498
University of New Mexico main campus	24,433
City College of San Francisco	24,408
Virginia Polytechnic Institute and State University	24,280
Northern Illinois University	24,255
Southern Illinois University at Carbondale	24,217
Harvard University	24,194
San Francisco State University	24,138
University of Colorado at Boulder	24,065
University of Illinois at Chicago	23,986
University of Nebraska at Lincoln	23,985
University of Utah	23,756
University of North Carolina at Chapel Hill	23,626
University of Missouri at Columbia	23,568
California State University at Sacramento	23,478
San Diego Mesa College	23,410
University of Texas at Arlington	23,383
California State University at Fullerton	23,376
Cleveland Institute of Electronics	23,373
Eastern Michigan University	23,060
University of Toledo	22,806
Kent State University main campus	22,753
Orange Coast College	22,365
Illinois State University	22,322
University of Kentucky	22,230
University of Oklahoma at Norman	22,224
Georgia State University	22,176
University of Pennsylvania	22,169
Syracuse University main campus	22,086
Cuyahoga Community College District	22,010
De Anza College	21,948
Broward Community College	21,682
San Antonio College	21,593
Lansing Community College	21,470
Austin Community College	21,418
University of Louisville	21,313
Oklahoma State University main campus	21,258
Portland Community College	20,904

SOURCE: U. S. DEPARTMENT OF EDUCATION

Number of Colleges by Enrollment, Fall 1988

	Universities	Other 4-year institutions	2-year institutions	All institutions
Public institutions				
Under 200	0	2	7	9
200 to 499	0	10	31	41
500 to 999	0	28	100	128
1,000 to 2,499	0	110	299	409
2,500 to 4,999	0	98	217	315
5,000 to 9,999	8	138	184	330
10,000 to 19,999	29	93	94	216
20,000 to 29,999	33	18	21	72
30,000 or more	24	2	5	31
All	94	499	958	1,551
Private institutions				
Under 200	0	283	121	404
200 to 499	0	232	162	394
500 to 999	0	295	103	398
1,000 to 2,499	0	454	41	495
2,500 to 4,999	6	144	3	153
5,000 to 9,999	24	43	1	68
10,000 to 19,999	24	7	1	32
20,000 to 29,999	4	0	1	5
30,000 or more	4	0	0	4
All	62	1,458	433	1,953
All institutions				
Under 200	0	285	128	413
200 to 499	0	242	193	435
500 to 999	0	323	203	526
1,000 to 2,499	0	564	340	904
2,500 to 4,999	6	242	220	468
5,000 to 9,999	32	181	185	398
10,000 to 19,999	53	100	95	248
20,000 to 29,999	37	18	22	77
30,000 or more	28	2	5	35
All	156	1,957	1,391	3,504

Note: Figures exclude approximately 60 institutions that did not report enrollment.

SOURCE: U. S. DEPARTMENT OF EDUCATION

Colleges With the Most Freshman National Merit Scholars, 1989

	Number of scholars	Number sponsored by institution
Harvard and Radcliffe Colleges	314	0
University of Texas at Austin	217	163
Stanford University	203	0
Rice University	198	130
Yale University	169	0
Princeton University	141	0
Carleton College	123	102
Massachusetts Institute of Technology	113	0
University of Chicago	111	83
Georgia Institute of Technology	109	78
Texas A&M University	109	84
University of Florida	96	85
Northwestern University	94	55
University of Michigan	87	0
Duke University	83	9
Brigham Young University	82	60
Michigan State University	80	67
Virginia Polytechnic Institute and State University	75	58
University of California at Los Angeles	74	60
University of Houston	69	58
University of New Orleans	69	62
Brown University	61	0
Cornell University	60	0
Bowling Green State University	58	44
University of California at Berkeley	55	4
Washington University (Mo.)	54	31
Williams College	53	0
University of California at San Diego	51	39
University of Oklahoma	50	40
University of Kansas	49	40
Harvey Mudd College	48	43
Trinity University	47	36
University of Minnesota–Twin Cities	47	37
Florida State University	46	40
Baylor University	44	35
University of Arizona	43	30
Macalester College	42	34
Iowa State University	40	39
Vanderbilt University	40	24
Oberlin College	39	27
University of Illinois at Urbana–Champaign	39	0
University of Iowa	39	25

Note: The table shows the total number of National Merit Scholarship winners and the number whose scholarships were paid for by the institution, not by the National Merit Scholarship Corporation or other corporate sponsors. The rankings were determined by The Chronicle from an alphabetical listing in the corporation's annual report.

SOURCE: NATIONAL MERIT SCHOLARSHIP CORPORATION

Average Faculty Salaries, 1989-90

	Public		Private, independent	
Doctoral institutions	Salary	1-year increase	Salary	1-year increase
Professor	$57,520	5.9%	$68,360	6.8%
Associate professor	42,010	6.0	46,440	7.1
Assistant professor	35,380	5.8	39,110	7.5
Instructor	24,570	4.7	30,610	8.2
Lecturer	27,420	—	34,510	—
All ranks	45,490	5.9	53,690	7.0
Comprehensive institutions				
Professor	49,610	6.4	51,000	7.0
Associate professor	39,690	6.5	39,740	6.7
Assistant professor	32,730	6.8	32,780	7.1
Instructor	25,110	7.3	26,470	7.2
Lecturer	25,630	—	29,510	—
All ranks	40,140	6.4	40,370	6.9
Baccalaureate institutions				
Professor	43,270	5.4	46,830	6.1
Associate professor	35,850	4.8	35,940	6.2
Assistant professor	29,650	4.7	29,520	6.5
Instructor	24,220	4.3	24,100	5.6
Lecturer	25,400	—	29,170	—
All ranks	34,420	4.9	36,320	6.2
2-year institutions with academic ranks				
Professor	43,000	5.7	31,560	6.9
Associate professor	35,990	6.3	27,830	9.1
Assistant professor	30,560	5.8	24,620	9.6
Instructor	25,850	5.7	18,840	4.5
Lecturer	22,040	—	—	—
All ranks	34,560	5.9	25,210	8.1
Institutions without academic ranks				
All	34,510	5.6	27,320	5.6
All institutions except institutions without academic ranks				
Professor	53,210	6.0	59,600	6.7
Associate professor	40,250	6.1	41,210	6.8
Assistant professor	33,530	6.1	34,030	7.1
Instructor	25,040	5.1	26,030	7.0
Lecturer	26,500	—	33,050	—
All ranks	41,920	6.0	45,080	6.8

Note: Salary figures are based on 2,127 institutions; percentage increases are based on 1,717 institutions.
— No data reported.

Church-related		All	
Salary	1-year increase	Salary	1-year increase
$61,210	7.0%	$59,920	6.2%
43,810	6.4	42,830	6.2
36,330	7.6	36,110	6.2
31,190	4.8	25,710	5.4
27,400	—	29,110	—
46,380	6.9	47,080	6.2
48,020	7.7	49,710	6.5
38,090	6.9	39,250	6.5
31,900	5.9	32,640	6.7
25,160	7.3	25,250	5.6
33,960	—	26,290	—
38,510	6.9	40,010	6.5
37,620	6.6	42,180	6.1
31,410	6.1	34,030	5.8
26,390	5.9	28,210	5.8
22,030	5.6	23,210	5.1
21,240	—	25,860	—
30,480	6.2	33,400	5.8
26,040	4.2	42,430	5.7
25,130	5.5	35,540	6.4
22,490	5.3	30,080	5.9
18,570	4.3	25,240	5.7
—	—	22,040	—
23,000	6.1	33,950	6.0
22,400	3.8	34,390	5.6
44,320	7.0	53,540	6.3
35,320	6.4	39,590	6.3
29,080	6.2	32,970	6.3
23,110	5.9	24,890	5.4
27,110	—	27,780	—
34,910	6.6	41,650	6.1

SOURCE: AMERICAN ASSOCIATION OF UNIVERSITY PROFESSORS

Median Salaries of Chief Executive and Academic Officers, 1989-90

Type of institution by size of budget	Chief executive officer	Chief academic officer
Doctoral		
Up to $104-million	$112,000	$91,200
$104-million to $202-million	127,745	95,000
$202-million to $318-million	124,420	111,300
$318-million or more	140,000	122,375
All	126,027	101,000
Comprehensive		
Up to $25-million	$90,200	$69,000
$25-million to $37-million	95,000	78,123
$37-million to $59-million	96,000	82,412
$59-million or more	114,088	92,881
All	97,268	79,144
Baccalaureate		
Up to $7.7-million	$69,360	$49,236
$7.7-million to $13-million	80,000	57,500
$13-million to $19-million	90,000	64,574
$19-million or more	104,545	75,000
All	85,675	60,674
2-year		
Up to $6-million	$66,092	$49,800
$6-million to $9.7-million	71,100	54,641
$9.7-million to $18-million	79,380	59,153
$18-million or more	85,005	68,332
All	73,708	56,844

Note: The figures are based on reports of 1,390 colleges and universities.

SOURCE: COLLEGE AND UNIVERSITY PERSONNEL ASSOCIATION

Median Salaries of Administrators, 1989-90

	All institutions
Executive	
Chief executive of a system	$91,400
Assistant to chief executive of a system	57,553
Chief executive of a single institution	87,000
Assistant to chief executive of single institution	45,600
Executive vice-president	73,978
Academic	
Chief academic officer	$67,000
Chief health-professions officer	83,208
Director, library services	43,903
Circulation librarian	26,623
Acquisitions librarian	30,603
Technical-services librarian	31,308
Public-services librarian	32,818
Reference librarian	28,900
Director, institutional research	46,066
Associate director, institutional research	37,692
Director, educational-media services	34,001
Director, learning-resources center	37,500
Director, international studies	46,188
Director, academic computer center	46,013
Associate director, academic computer center	39,520
Administrator, grants and contracts	44,612
Dean, agriculture	81,750
Dean, architecture	81,622
Dean, arts and letters	58,000
Dean, arts and sciences	66,000
Dean, business	66,000
Dean, communications	53,318
Dean, continuing education	50,000
Dean, dentistry	110,000
Dean, education	64,000
Dean, engineering	81,200
Dean, extension	59,014
Dean, fine arts	57,928
Dean, graduate programs	65,199
Dean, health-related professions	60,000
Dean, home economics	72,200
Dean, humanities	50,400
Dean, instruction	55,533
Dean, law	109,472
Dean, library and information sciences	62,000
Dean, mathematics	48,270
Dean, medicine	151,410
Dean, music	55,456
Dean, nursing	56,200
Dean, pharmacy	86,964
Dean, public health	94,000
Dean, sciences	53,577
Dean, social sciences	49,789
Dean, social work	75,042
Dean, special programs	45,030
Dean, undergraduate programs	58,027
Dean, veterinary medicine	100,428
Dean, vocational education	52,146
Administrative	
Chief business officer	$63,307
Chief administrative officer	64,403

Continued on Following Page

Median Salaries of Administrators, continued

Administrative, continued	All institutions
Chief financial officer	$58,463
Director, health and safety	42,000
Director, telecommunications	41,000
Chief planning officer	57,780
Chief budget officer	50,900
Associate budget director	40,000
Chief planning and budget officer	64,316
General counsel	66,700
Staff attorney	50,117
Chief personnel and human-resources officer	46,875
Associate director, personnel	37,450
Manager, benefits	30,577
Manager, training and development	35,692
Manager, employee relations	39,000
Manager, labor relations	50,562
Manager, employment	31,000
Manager, wage and salary	34,297
Manager, personnel information systems	34,152
Director, affirmative action and equal employment	46,482
Associate director, affirmative action	35,000
Director, personnel and affirmative action	37,979
Director, computer center	49,896
Associate director, computer center	42,000
Data-base administrator	40,200
Systems analyst, highest level	37,449
Systems analyst, lowest level	30,160
Programmer analyst, highest level	30,770
Programmer analyst, lowest level	24,638
Director, administrative computer center	45,360
Associate director, administrative computer center	38,135
Director, information systems	52,860
Director, physical plant	45,000
Associate director, physical plant	37,596
Manager, landscape and grounds	29,000
Manager, building maintenance trades	32,498
Manager, technical trades	34,225
Manager, custodial services	28,090
Manager, power plant	35,877
Comptroller	46,783
Manager, payroll	28,991
Director, accounting	38,798
Staff accountant, highest level	28,434
Staff accountant, lowest level	23,000
Bursar	34,400
Associate bursar	28,896
Director, purchasing	36,968
Associate director, purchasing	32,566
Director, bookstore	27,500
Associate director, bookstore	24,268
Director, internal audit	44,647
Director, auxiliary services	45,601
Manager, mail services	21,446
Director, campus security	33,722
Director, risk management and insurance	46,900
Administrator, hospital medical center	122,715

External affairs	
Director, medical-center public relations	$51,230
Director, medical-center personnel	50,280

	All institutions
Chief development officer	$58,000
Director, annual giving	34,200
Director, corporate and foundation relations	40,000
Coordinator, resource development	27,910
Director, estate planning	42,390
Chief public-relations officer	40,700
Director, governmental relations	62,000
Chief development and public-relations officer	64,700
Director, alumni affairs	33,600
Director, development and alumni affairs	43,741
Director, special and deferred gifts	41,077
Director, community services	40,598
Director, publications	33,809
Associate director, publications	26,363
Manager, printing services	29,640
Director, information office	33,638
Director, news bureau	30,030

Student services

	All institutions
Chief student-affairs officer	$54,463
Director, admissions	41,974
Associate director, admissions	30,000
Admissions counselor	20,911
Academic adviser	24,278
Director, admissions and registrar	47,393
Registrar	37,899
Associate registrar	31,409
Assistant registrar	25,493
Director, admissions and financial aid	47,079
Director, student financial aid	36,897
Associate director, student financial aid	27,294
Director, food services	37,240
Associate director, food services	32,020
Director, student housing	33,900
Associate director, student housing	28,080
Housing officer, administrative operations	29,800
Housing officer, residential life	24,913
Director, foreign students	31,333
Director, student union	37,792
Associate director, student union	30,800
Student-union business manager	30,579
Director, student activities	30,000
Director, student placement	33,845
Director, student counseling	39,908
Associate director, student counseling	34,725
Director, student health services, physician	70,008
Director, student health services, nurse	26,466
Director, campus ministries	30,269
Director, athletics	47,175
Men's	49,700
Women's	36,228
Director, sports information	26,204
Director, campus recreation	30,626
Director, enrollment management	47,580
Director, minority affairs	35,000
Director, conferences	35,508

Note: The figures are based on reports of 1,390 colleges and universities and are meant to provide a broad overview of salaries in higher education.

SOURCE: COLLEGE AND UNIVERSITY PERSONNEL ASSOCIATION

Faculty Attitudes and Activities, 1988-89

POLITICAL CHARACTERIZATION
Liberal ....
Moderately liberal ....
Middle of the road ....
Moderately conservative ....
Conservative ....

SCHOLARLY ACTIVITIES
Major interests:
Primarily research ....
Primarily teaching ....
In both, but leaning toward research ....
In both, but leaning toward teaching ....

WORKING CONDITIONS
Rate as excellent or good at own Institution:
Own salary ....
Own teaching load ....
Academic reputation of department outside the institution ....
Intellectual environment ....
Administration ....
Quality of life ....
Sense of community ....

VIEWS ON TENURE
Agree strongly or with reservations that:
In my department tenure is now more difficult to achieve than it was five years ago ....
Many young faculty members at this institution will leave because it is "tenured in" ....
The abolition of faculty tenure would, on the whole, improve the quality of American
    higher education ....
In my department it is difficult for a person to achieve tenure if he or she does not publish ...
At my institution publications used for tenure and promotion are just "counted," not
    qualitatively measured ....
At my institution we need better ways, besides publications, to evaluate the scholarly
    performance of the faculty ....
The pressure to publish reduces the quality of teaching at my university ....
Teaching effectiveness should be the primary criterion for promotion of faculty ....
At my campus academic freedom would be protected whether faculty members could get tenure
    or not ....

VIEWS ON UNDERGRADUATE EDUCATION
Rate own institution excellent or somewhat better than adequate in:
Providing undergraduates with a general education ....
Preparing undergraduates for a vocation or career ....
Strengthening the values of undergraduates ....
Creating opportunities for undergraduates to engage in public service ....

All institutions, by sex			By type of institution				
Men	Women	All	Research	Doctoral	Compre-hensive	Liberal arts	Two-year
23%	29%	25%	34%	24%	26%	24%	19%
31	33	32	33	33	33	35	29
17	14	16	16	15	14	14	18
21	20	21	14	21	20	21	26
7	4	6	3	7	7	6	9
7%	4%	6%	18%	8%	3%	2%	1%
41	50	44	10	21	39	49	77
26	18	23	48	37	20	14	6
26	28	27	25	34	38	35	16
48%	45%	48%	46%	30%	40%	29%	62%
49	45	47	58	49	37	39	50
64	70	66	67	53	55	62	79
45	43	45	52	39	31	52	49
36	38	36	28	30	32	47	45
53	46	51	48	45	43	56	57
35	38	37	25	30	32	56	45
54%	54%	54%	61%	70%	65%	51%	37%
19	21	20	21	22	23	26	14
27	32	29	25	27	28	32	32
57	45	54	94	89	65	39	6
38	38	38	42	52	54	33	19
68	68	68	69	77	79	69	55
36	34	35	52	53	41	22	14
58	73	62	22	41	68	76	92
43	45	44	35	37	38	52	55
74%	77%	75%	62%	69%	73%	84%	85%
73	79	75	62	69	71	71	89
36	41	37	24	32	34	70	43
29	31	30	23	28	29	53	31

Continued on Following Page

Faculty Attitudes and Activities, continued

VIEWS ON UNDERGRADUATE EDUCATION, continued
Agree strongly or with reservations that:

Undergraduates at my institution are not getting as good an education today as they did five years ago ....

State-mandated assessment requirements threaten the quality of undergraduate education and intrude on institutional autonomy ....

The number of general-education courses required of all undergraduates should be increased

I enjoy interacting informally with undergraduates outside the classroom ....

Undergraduates should seek out faculty only during posted office hours ....

Grade inflation is a problem at my institution ....

I find myself not grading as "hard" as I should ....

The undergraduates with whom I have close contact are seriously underprepared in basic skills such as those required for written and oral communication ....

VIEWS ON ADMINISTRATIVE AND EDUCATIONAL ISSUES
Agree strongly or with reservations that at own institution:

The administration supports academic freedom ....

The institution is managed effectively ....

Faculty members who become administrators soon lose sight of what it means to be a teacher or to do research ....

The institution spends too much time and money teaching students what they should have learned in high school ....

The institution has serious financial problems ....

There are more part-time and adjunct faculty members who work at the institution than there were five years ago ....

The institution is as interested now in increasing the numbers of women and minority members on the faculty as it was five years ago ....

I am satisfied with the results of affirmative action ....

Issues raised by affirmative action are causing serious strains among the faculty in the department ....

The normal academic requirements should be relaxed in appointing members of minority groups to the faculty at this institution ....

Agree strongly or with reservations that:

Performing sponsored research for a private company is not a proper university activity .....

Too many students ill-suited to academic life are now enrolling in colleges and universities ..

There has been a widespread lowering of standards in American higher education ....

My job is the source of considerable personal strain ....

I tend to subordinate all aspects of my life to my work ....

This is a poor time for any young person to begin an academic career ....

If I had it to do over again, I would not become a college teacher ....

I may leave this profession within the next five years ....

I often wish I had entered another profession ....

I feel trapped in a profession with limited opportunities for advancement ....

Note: The figures are based on a national survey conducted in February 1989 of 9,996 faculty members at 306 colleges and universities. The response rate was 54.5 per cent. The figures cover the 1988-89 academic year, and are weighted by type of institution. The responses to the attitude and activity questions cover full-time faculty members only, while the responses to the question on characteristics cover both full- and part-time faculty members. Figures may not add to 100 per cent because of rounding, multiple responses, or the omission of "neutral" or other response categories.

All institutions, by sex			By type of institution				
Men	Women	All	Research	Doctoral	Compre-hensive	Liberal arts	Two-year
18%	19%	18%	17%	18%	19%	14%	20%
45	43	44	45	42	43	51	44
37	38	37	40	33	34	33	41
84	81	83	77	83	85	92	84
13	19	15	15	15	13	12	16
63	62	62	64	64	62	65	60
49	49	49	48	49	50	54	48
74	77	75	68	70	73	64	85
68%	65%	67%	63%	61%	62%	75%	74%
49	53	50	37	44	46	61	61
52	53	52	47	50	55	39	58
69	66	68	60	64	73	56	73
42	39	41	51	47	48	38	28
56	63	58	38	50	57	55	75
72	61	69	69	69	65	66	72
50	48	49	44	47	48	46	55
15	16	16	14	16	13	8	20
9	6	8	11	8	9	9	5
25	27	25	24	21	25	28	27
64	63	64	54	59	66	61	70
65	72	67	60	63	67	68	73
40	51	44	48	46	45	48	38
39	43	40	46	42	44	47	32
20	19	20	22	22	20	17	18
15	14	15	14	16	17	14	13
31	32	31	26	32	33	33	34
17	19	17	14	19	20	15	19
19	21	20	14	20	22	18	22

SOURCE: CARNEGIE FOUNDATION FOR THE ADVANCEMENT OF TEACHING

College Experiences in Faculty Recruiting, 1989

	2-year	Bacca-laureate	Compre-hensive	Doctoral	Total
The quality of applicants has declined					
Yes, generally	11%	2%	4%	3%	6%
Yes, in a few fields	29	40	24	16	31
No	60	57	72	80	63
It has taken longer to find qualified people					
Yes, generally	20	26	14	13	20
Yes, in a few fields	44	36	61	55	45
No	36	39	24	32	34
Institution has had greater difficulty in getting top applicants to accept positions					
Yes, generally	22	24	20	15	22
Yes, in a few fields	44	28	51	57	41
No	34	48	28	28	37
A lower percentage of offers is being accepted					
Yes, generally	11	19	10	10	13
Yes, in a few fields	24	18	32	38	25
No	64	63	58	52	62
Institution has hired some faculty members in advance of an expected vacancy					
Yes, generally	1	7	6	6	4
Yes, in a few fields	4	10	17	34	10
No	95	83	77	60	86
Institution has hired some faculty members at salaries above the salary scale					
Yes, generally	8	10	16	12	10
Yes, in a few fields	24	47	65	75	41
No	67	43	19	13	48
Institution has hired new junior faculty members at a salary above that of some senior faculty members in the same department					
Yes, generally	2	5	7	5	4
Yes, in a few fields	13	27	40	56	25
No	85	68	53	39	71
Institution has moved part-time faculty members into full-time positions					
Yes, generally	14	4	2	2	8
Yes, in a few fields	51	58	44	31	50
No	36	38	53	67	42
Institution has had situations in which recruitment involved dual-career couples					
Yes, generally	4	13	8	9	8
Yes, in a few fields	22	37	63	78	38
No	75	50	28	14	55
Institution has assisted the spouse's job search for a dual-career couple					
Yes, generally	4	14	14	18	10
Yes, in a few fields	19	26	48	61	29
No	76	60	39	21	61

Note: The figures are based on responses to a survey sent to senior administrators at 444 colleges in the spring of 1990 and describe experiences in recruiting full-time professors in 1989-90. The response rate was 82 per cent. Because of rounding, figures may not add to 100 per cent.

SOURCE: AMERICAN COUNCIL ON EDUCATION

Employees in Colleges and Universities, Fall 1987

| | Full-Time | | | Part-Time | | | |
	Men	Women	All	Men	Women	All	Total
Professional							
Executive, administrative, managerial.....	80,524	48,285	128,809	2,358	2,552	4,910	133,719
Faculty	373,546	149,874	523,420	155,867	113,783	269,650	793,070
Part-time research assistants	0	0	0	98,608	62,856	161,464	161,464
Non-faculty professionals...	121,958	173,546	295,504	17,590	36,628	54,218	349,722
Non-professional							
Technical, para-professional....	57,152	78,882	136,034	11,238	20,105	31,343	167,377
Clerical, secretarial	28,597	321,532	350,129	15,673	69,632	85,305	435,434
Skilled crafts	55,363	2,521	57,884	1,841	786	2,627	60,511
Service, maintenance ...	123,097	74,192	197,289	20,655	18,293	38,948	236,237
Total.............	840,237	848,832	1,689,069	323,830	324,635	648,465	2,337,534

SOURCE: U.S. DEPARTMENT OF EDUCATION

Employment of Faculty Members, 1987

	Public 4-year	Private 4-year	Public 2-year	Other	All
Number of faculty members ...	319,000	218,000	218,000	70,000	825,000
Regular full-time	72%	58%	41%	63%	60%
Regular part-time	14	21	35	20	22
Temporary full-time	4	3	1	1	3
Temporary part-time	9	19	23	16	16

Note: The figures are based on a 1988 survey of administrators at 480 colleges and universities. The response rate was 88 per cent. The figures are adjusted to represent the distribution of all professors whose regular assignment includes instruction. The category of "Other" institutions includes private two-year colleges and specialized institutions. "Temporary" faculty members include visiting, acting, and adjunct professors. Because of rounding, figures may not add to 100 per cent.

SOURCE: U.S. DEPARTMENT OF EDUCATION

Distribution of Full-Time Faculty Members by Rank, 1987

	Public 4-year	Private 4-year	Public 2-year	Other	All
Full professor	38%	31%	12%	23%	30%
Associate professor	27	27	11	22	24
Assistant professor	24	29	11	31	24
Instructor	5	7	33	13	11
Other	5	6	34	10	11

Note: The figures are based on a 1988 survey of administrators at 480 colleges and universities. The response rate was 88 per cent. The category of "Other" institutions includes private two-year colleges and specialized institutions. Because of rounding, figures may not add to 100 per cent.

SOURCE: U.S. DEPARTMENT OF EDUCATION

Distribution of Full-Time Faculty Members by Age and Discipline at Four-Year Institutions, 1987

	Under 30	30 to 44	45 to 54	55 to 64	65 and over	Average age
Agriculture and home economics	2%	47%	32%	19%	1%	45
Business	2	50	28	17	2	45
Education	2	30	35	30	3	49
Engineering	1	35	31	31	3	48
Fine arts	4	40	35	17	4	46
Health sciences..............	1	46	28	20	5	46
Humanities	1	32	35	27	5	49
Natural sciences	1	41	39	17	2	47
Social sciences	1	43	34	17	5	47
Other	2	38	31	23	5	48
All	1	40	33	21	4	47

Note: The figures are based on a 1988 survey of 11,013 faculty members at 480 colleges and universities. The response rate was 76 per cent. Figures may not add to 100 per cent because of rounding.

SOURCE: U.S. DEPARTMENT OF EDUCATION

Total Return on College Endowments

	Periods ending June 30, 1989			
	1 year	3 years	5 years	10 years
All investment pools...........................	+14.1%	+9.4%	+15.7%	+13.7%
By size				
$25-million and under........................	+13.1%	+8.4%	+14.4%	+12.7%
$25-million to $100-million	+14.0	+9.6	+15.7	+13.3
$100-million to $400-million	+15.3	+9.8	+16.6	+14.4
$400-million or more...........................	+14.3	+10.1	+16.6	+15.0
By type of institution				
Public	+14.2%	+9.3%	+15.6%	+13.2%
Private.......................................	+14.1	+9.4	+15.8	+13.9
Comparative measurements				
Standard & Poor's 500 Index	+20.6%	+11.9%	+20.0%	+16.9%
Shearson Lehman Hutton				
Government / Corporate Bond Index	+12.3	+8.1	+14.4	+11.3
Shearson Lehman Hutton				
Government Bond Index	+12.1	+7.8	+13.8	+11.5
Consumer Price Index	+5.3	+4.2	+3.6	+5.4

Note: Total-return rates represent change in market value, plus dividends and interest, for periods ending June 30, 1989, based on data for investment pools at 330 colleges and universities.

SOURCE: NATIONAL ASSOCIATION OF COLLEGE AND UNIVERSITY BUSINESS OFFICERS

Top 10 Institutions in Voluntary Support, 1988-89

Stanford University	$188,635,513
Harvard University	185,353,003
Cornell University	157,072,064
Yale University	122,755,800
University of Pennsylvania	121,945,814
Columbia University	110,422,711
University of Southern California	102,628,589
University of Wisconsin at Madison	102,232,856
Duke University	102,016,708
University of Minnesota	100,170,258

SOURCE: COUNCIL FOR AID TO EDUCATION

College and University Endowments Over $115-Million, 1989

	Market value June 30, 1989
Harvard University	$4,478,976,000
University of Texas System	3,021,474,000
Princeton University	2,483,829,000
Yale University	2,336,495,000
Stanford University	1,775,000,000
Columbia University	1,460,356,000
Texas A&M University System	1,304,536,000
Washington University	1,294,209,000
Massachusetts Institute of Technology	1,256,165,000
University of Chicago	973,697,000
Rice University	970,817,000
Emory University	923,612,000
Northwestern University	893,680,000
Cornell University	823,000,000
University of Pennsylvania	761,408,000
Dartmouth College	632,027,000
Vanderbilt University	556,567,000
University of Notre Dame	542,501,000
New York University	540,315,000
University of Rochester	538,078,000
Johns Hopkins University	527,209,000
Rockefeller University	522,663,000
California Institute of Technology	477,879,000
University of Southern California	459,828,000
University of Virginia	446,476,000
Duke University	426,183,000
University of Michigan	422,809,000
Brown University	398,100,000
Case Western Reserve University	381,075,000
Wellesley College	341,746,000
Southern Methodist University	334,643,000
University of Delaware	329,280,000
Smith College	325,759,000
Swarthmore College	304,911,000
Grinnell College	294,328,000
Carnegie Mellon University	291,271,000
Williams College	290,637,000
Ohio State University	287,298,000
Wake Forest University	284,670,000
Wesleyan University	275,138,000
University of Cincinnati	273,133,000
University of Tulsa [1]	272,720,000
Pomona College	271,053,000
Trinity University [1]	266,670,000
Amherst College	266,506,000
George Washington University	265,772,000
University of Richmond	265,310,000
University of Pittsburgh	259,144,000
Berea College	252,052,000
Boston College [1]	250,005,000
University of Minnesota	247,438,000

	Market value June 30, 1989
Loyola University of Chicago	$246,236,000
Georgetown University	240,674,000
Baylor University [1]	235,316,000
Vassar College	226,953,000
Lehigh University	225,628,000
Tulane University	221,424,000
Oberlin College	220,870,000
Middlebury College	216,920,000
Rensselaer Polytechnic Institute	209,406,000
Kansas University Endowment Association	203,595,000
University of Florida Foundation	198,207,000
Lafayette College	187,117,000
Thomas Jefferson University	185,229,000
Pennsylvania State University	166,850,000
Mount Holyoke College	163,664,000
Saint Louis University	160,779,000
Georgia Institute of Technology	158,174,000
Carleton College	157,632,000
Rochester Institute of Technology	155,630,000
University of Nebraska	155,284,000
University of North Carolina at Chapel Hill	151,562,000
Boston University	150,547,000
University of Washington	147,978,000
Occidental College	145,211,000
Washington State University	144,697,000
Brandeis University	144,618,000
Bowdoin College	144,156,000
Syracuse University	144,015,000
University of Minnesota Foundation	142,453,000
University of Miami [1]	142,363,000
Academy of the New Church	140,016,000
Rush-Presbyterian St. Luke's Medical Center	135,353,000
University of Alabama System [2]	135,000,000
Bryn Mawr College	133,917,000
Purdue University	133,431,000
University of Missouri	131,968,000
Tufts University	130,666,000
Colgate University	123,309,000
Colorado College	123,047,000
Earlham College	122,247,000
State University of New York at Buffalo	119,044,000
American University of Beirut	117,544,000
University of Illinois Foundation	117,478,000

Note: Table includes institutions participating in the comparative-performance study by the National Association of College and University Business Officers.
[1] As of May 31
[2] As of September 30

SOURCE: NATIONAL ASSOCIATION OF COLLEGE AND UNIVERSITY BUSINESS OFFICERS

Trends in College Revenues and Expenditures, 1980-81 to 1986-87

	Revenues		Expenditures	
	Public institutions	Private institutions	Public institutions	Private institutions
1980-81	$43,195,617,000	$22,389,172,000	$42,279,806,000	$21,773,132,000
1981-82	47,270,822,000	24,920,034,000	46,219,134,000	24,120,314,000
1982-83	50,412,086,000	27,183,640,000	49,572,918,000	26,362,831,000
1983-84	54,545,275,000	29,872,012,000	53,086,644,000	28,906,716,000
1984-85	59,794,159,000	32,678,536,000	58,314,550,000	31,636,713,000
1985-86	65,004,632,000	35,432,985,000	63,193,853,000	34,341,889,000
1986-87	69,613,289,000	39,196,539,000	67,653,838,000	38,109,719,000

SOURCE: U. S. DEPARTMENT OF EDUCATION

Largest Endowments per Student, 1989

Private institutions	Students	Amount
Academy of the New Church	315	$444,495
Princeton University	6,235	398,369
California Institute of Technology	1,741	274,485
Harvard University	16,961	264,075
Rice University	4,002	242,583
Agnes Scott College	488	235,293
Swarthmore College	1,332	228,912
Grinnell College	1,294	227,456
Yale University	10,538	221,721
Pomona College	1,384	195,848

Public institutions		
Virginia Military Institute Foundation	1,318	65,785
Oregon Health Sciences University Foundation ...	1,281	34,411
Texas A&M University System	50,000	26,091
University of Virginia	17,546	25,446
University of Texas System	123,482	24,469
University of Delaware	16,844	19,549
Georgia Institute of Technology	12,053	13,123
University of Cincinnati	22,570	12,102
College of William and Mary	7,023	10,487
University of Michigan	44,169	9,573

Note: Based on market value of endowments on June 30, 1989, and full-time-equivalent enrollment for fall 1988.

SOURCE: NATIONAL ASSOCIATION OF COLLEGE AND UNIVERSITY BUSINESS OFFICERS

Revenues and Expenditures of Colleges and Universities, 1986-87

	Public institutions		Private institutions	
	1986-87	Per cent of total	1986-87	Per cent of total
Revenues				
Tuition and fees	$10,198,633,000	14.7%	$15,507,194,000	39.6%
Appropriations				
Federal	1,434,295,000	2.1	221,950,000	0.6
State	28,974,665,000	41.6	362,454,000	0.9
Local	2,289,420,000	3.3	4,713,000	—
Government grants and contracts				
Federal	5,793,699,000	8.3	6,454,104,000	16.5
State	1,465,213,000	2.1	506,970,000	1.3
Local	245,594,000	0.4	259,594,000	0.7
Private gifts, grants, and contracts...	2,292,985,000	3.3	3,659,697,000	9.3
Endowment income	349,779,000	0.5	2,028,179,000	5.2
Sales and services				
Educational activities	1,771,760,000	2.5	870,145,000	2.2
Auxiliary enterprises	7,092,985,000	10.2	4,271,203,000	10.9
Hospitals	5,910,785,000	8.5	3,367,048,000	8.6
Other	1,793,474,000	2.6	1,683,287,000	4.3
Total current-fund revenues	69,613,289,000	100.0	39,196,539,000	100.0
Expenditures				
Instruction	$23,359,057,000	34.5%	$10,352,089,000	27.2%
Research	6,258,625,000	9.3	3,093,684,000	8.1
Public service	2,727,593,000	4.0	720,860,000	1.9
Academic support	5,048,232,000	7.5	2,527,219,000	6.6
Student services...................	3,158,991,000	4.7	1,816,922,000	4.8
Institutional support	6,042,593,000	8.9	4,042,069,000	10.6
Plant operation and maintenance....	5,308,631,000	7.8	2,510,400,000	6.6
Scholarships and fellowships........	1,751,671,000	2.6	3,024,430,000	7.9
Mandatory transfers	704,040,000	1.0	508,448,000	1.3
Auxiliary enterprises	7,135,393,000	10.5	3,901,940,000	10.2
Hospitals	5,904,212,000	8.7	3,268,802,000	8.6
Other	254,799,000	0.4	2,342,856,000	6.1
Total current-fund expenditures	67,653,838,000	100.0	38,109,719,000	100.0

Note: A dash indicates less than 0.5 per cent. Because of rounding, details may not add up to totals.

SOURCE: U.S. DEPARTMENT OF EDUCATION

Range of 1990-91 Tuition at Four-Year Institutions

	Number of colleges	Average tuition and fees	Proportion of total enrollment
Private institutions			
$15,000 or more	37	$15,518	6.2%
14,000 — 14,999	37	14,503	7.0
13,000 — 13,999	26	13,482	3.3
12,000 — 12,999	28	12,516	3.8
11,000 — 11,999	45	11,471	4.1
10,000 — 10,999	82	10,421	8.0
9,000 — 9,999	105	9,444	10.9
8,000 — 8,999	121	8,497	13.2
7,000 — 7,999	145	7,515	10.4
6,000 — 6,999	145	6,485	9.8
5,000 — 5,999	99	5,537	7.1
4,000 — 4,999	123	4,507	7.4
3,000 — 3,999	83	3,418	3.0
2,000 — 2,999	59	2,531	3.7
1,000 — 1,999	12	1,699	1.7
Less than $1,000	9	425	0.3
Total	1,156	—	100.0%
Public institutions			
$3,000 or more	24	$3,578	4.9%
2,000 — 2,999	105	2,359	26.3
1,500 — 1,999	147	1,730	31.3
1,000 — 1,499	138	1,315	24.7
500 — 999	37	903	11.3
Less than $500	9	466	1.5
Total	460	—	100.0%

Note: Includes only those institutions that provided final or estimated 1990-91 tuition and fees by August 15, 1990.

SOURCE: THE COLLEGE BOARD

Average College Costs, 1990-91

	Public colleges		Private colleges	
	Resident	Commuter	Resident	Commuter
4-year colleges				
Tuition and fees	$1,809	$1,809	$9,391	$9,391
Books and supplies	464	464	479	479
Room and board*	3,161	1,459	4,153	1,610
Transportation	456	776	432	757
Other	1,101	1,086	863	938
Total	$6,991	$5,594	$15,318	$13,175
2-year colleges				
Tuition and fees	$884	$884	$5,003	$5,003
Books and supplies	452	452	436	436
Room and board*	—	1,520	3,481	1,280
Transportation	—	857	472	691
Other	—	941	864	804
Total	—	$4,654	$10,256	$8,214

Note: The figures are weighted by enrollment to reflect the charges incurred by the average undergraduate enrolled at each type of institution.

* Room not included for commuter students.
— Insufficient data.

SOURCE: THE COLLEGE BOARD

Voluntary Support for Higher Education, 1988-89

			Percentage change	
Sources	Amount	Per cent	1-year	5-year
Alumni	$2,292,000,000	25.7%	+12.2%	+75.6%
Other individuals	2,077,000,000	23.3	+7.8	+57.8
Corporations	1,947,000,000	21.8	+5.1	+53.2
Foundations	1,742,000,000	19.5	+8.4	+61.1
Religious organizations	237,000,000	2.7	+20.0	+44.5
Other	632,000,000	7.1	+10.0	+44.5
Total	$8,925,000,000	100%	+8.8%	+59.4%

SOURCE: COUNCIL FOR AID TO EDUCATION

Major Gifts to Higher Education Since 1967

Emory University: Robert W. Woodruff, $105-million, 1979.
Stanford University: David Packard, $70-million, 1986.
University of Miami: James L. Knight, $56-million, 1986.
California Institute of Technology: Arnold and Mabel Beckman Foundation, $50-million, 1986.
Cornell University Medical Center: anonymous, $50-million, 1983.

Stanford University: William R. Hewlett, $50-million, 1986.
United Negro College Fund: Walter Annenberg, $50-million, 1990.
University of Richmond: E. Claiborne Robins, $50-million, 1969.
Yale University: Paul Mellon, $47-million, 1967.
University of Texas Southwestern Medical Center: Harold C. Simmons, $41-million, 1988.

Vanderbilt University: Harold Sterling Vanderbilt, $41-million, 1970.
California Institute of Technology: Liliore Green Rains, $40-million, 1986.
Loyola Marymount University: Liliore Green Rains, $40-million, 1986.
Pomona College: Liliore Green Rains, $40-million, 1986.
Stanford University: Liliore Green Rains, $40-million, 1986.

University of Illinois: Arnold and Mabel Beckman Foundation, $40-million, 1985.
Asbury Theological Seminary: Ralph Waldo Beeson, $39-million, 1990.
Samford University: Ralph Waldo Beeson, $39-million, 1990.
Georgia Institute of Technology: George Woodruff, $37.5-million, 1987.
Carnegie Mellon University: anonymous, $35-million, 1976.

National College of Education: Michael W. Louis, $33-million, 1989.
University of Notre Dame: Edward J. DeBartolo, $33-million, 1989.
University of Miami: Harcourt M. & Virginia W. Sylvester Foundation, $32.5-million, 1986.
New York University: Leonard N. Stern, $30-million, 1988.
New York University: Lawrence A. and Robert P. Tisch, $30-million, 1989.

University of Houston: Cullen Foundation, $30-million, 1990.
University of Oklahoma: Bill D. Saxon, $30-million, 1981.
Trinity University: Norine Randle Murchison, $27.1-million, 1986.
Baylor College of Medicine: Albert B. Alkek, $25-million, 1988.
Columbia University: John M. Kluge, $25-million, 1987.

Columbia University: John M. Kluge, $25-million, 1990.
Ohio State University: Leslie H. Wexner, $25-million, 1987.
Southern Methodist University: Robert H. and Nancy Dedman, $25-million, 1981.
University of Minnesota: Curtis L. Carlson, $25-million, 1985.
University of Pennsylvania: Saul P. Steinberg, $25-million, 1989.

University of Rochester: Charles F. Hutchison, $25-million, 1976.
University of Texas M. D. Anderson Cancer Center: Col. C. P. Simpson and Anna Crouchet
    Simpson, $24-million, 1989.
Princeton University: Laurance S. Rockefeller, $21-million, 1990.
Cornell College (Iowa): Richard and Norma Small, $20-million, 1990.

Cornell University: Samuel C. Johnson, $20-million, 1984.
New York University: Paulette Goddard, $20-million, 1990.
Northwestern University: Walter Annenberg, $20-million, 1989.
Spelman College: Bill Cosby, $20-million, 1988.
University of Richmond: Mr. and Mrs. Robert Jepson, Jr., $20-million, 1987.

University of Texas Southwestern Medical Center: H. Ross Perot, $20-million, 1987.
Yale University: the Bass Family, $20-million, May 1990.
Yale University: the Bass Family, $20-million, October 1990.

Note: Includes gifts by individual donors to colleges and universities from 1967 to November 1990.

SOURCE: CHRONICLE REPORTING

Top Institutions in Research-and-Development Spending, Fiscal Year 1989

	Total funds for research & development
Johns Hopkins University	$648,395,000
Massachusetts Institute of Technology	287,157,000
Cornell University	286,733,000
Stanford University	285,994,000
University of Wisconsin at Madison	285,982,000
University of Michigan	280,905,000
University of Minnesota	258,614,000
Texas A&M University	250,706,000
University of California at Los Angeles	227,828,000
University of Washington	221,712,000
Pennsylvania State University	219,930,000
University of California at San Francisco	219,446,000
University of California at San Diego	216,991,000
University of Illinois at Urbana-Champaign	210,590,000
University of California at Berkeley	209,967,000
Harvard University	209,519,000
University of Texas at Austin	193,337,000
University of California at Davis	180,297,000
Georgia Institute of Technology	174,664,000
University of Arizona	174,119,000
University of Pennsylvania	173,744,000
Columbia University	172,145,000
Yale University	171,139,000
Ohio State University	162,690,000
University of Southern California	162,013,000
University of Maryland at College Park	149,510,000
University of Georgia	145,953,000
University of Colorado	143,694,000
Baylor College of Medicine	134,681,000
Duke University	131,090,000
North Carolina State University	128,891,000
Washington University	128,419,000
University of Florida	125,770,000
University of Tennessee System	124,820,000
Rutgers University	124,574,000
Purdue University	124,323,000
University of Rochester	123,997,000
Louisiana State University	122,357,000
University of North Carolina at Chapel Hill	122,097,000
Michigan State University	121,456,000
Northwestern University	118,991,000
University of Pittsburgh	111,265,000
University of Masachusetts	110,644,000
University of Chicago	109,429,000
University of Connecticut	109,328,000

Note: Figures cover only research-and-development expenditures in science and engineering, and exclude spending in such disciplines as the arts, education, the humanities, law, and physical education.

SOURCE: NATIONAL SCIENCE FOUNDATION

Non-Profit Institutions Receiving the Largest Contracts From the Defense Department, Fiscal Year 1989

	Amount
Massachusetts Institute of Technology	$410,578,000
Aerospace Corporation	301,430,000
Mitre Corporation	384,216,000
Johns Hopkins University	327,647,000
IIT Research Institute	78,151,000
University of California	56,507,000
Charles S. Draper Laboratory	54,986,000
Pennsylvania State University	53,950,000
Rand Corporation	50,953,000
Carnegie Mellon University	49,023,000
SRI International	45,624,000
Institute for Defense Analyses	42,811,000
University of Texas	33,362,000
Stanford University	32,192,000
Analytic Services Inc.	32,078,000
Georgia Tech Research Corporation	31,945,000
Utah State University	31,705,000
University of Minnesota	30,255,000
University of Southern California	29,363,000
Battelle Memorial Institute	29,003,000
University of Washington	22,921,000
University of Dayton	20,918,000
New Mexico State University	17,811,000
University of Illinois	16,958,000
Logistics Management Institute	16,321,000
South Carolina Research Authority	14,225,000
Woods Hole Oceanographic Institution	14,071,000
Cornell University	12,095,000
Environmental Research Institute of Michigan	11,045,000
Southern Research Institute	10,015,000

Note: The table includes colleges, universities, and other non-profit organizations that received more than $10-million in Department of Defense contracts. The contracts were for research, development, testing, and evaluation for military projects and for civilian water-resource projects. Other types of funding are not included in this table.

SOURCE: U.S. DEPARTMENT OF DEFENSE

Administrators' Views on Institutional Status, 1990

	2-year	Bacca-laureate	Compre-hensive	Doctoral	All
Percentage rating own institution as "excellent" or "very good":					
Ability to attract and hold good faculty members .	62%	54%	56%	63%	59%
Adequacy of faculty compensation	38	19	35	41	32
Overall financial condition of the institution	43	49	50	46	47
Level of trust in senior administrators	46	46	45	35	45
Extent of collegiality among faculty members	50	49	45	37	48
Ability to attract good students	30	35	39	53	34
Ability to attract black students	20	18	16	25	19
Ability to attract Hispanic students	21	8	13	24	15
Ability to attract and retain adult students	70	60	46	23	60
Percentage rating own institution as "fair" or "poor":					
Ability to attract and hold good faculty members .	5%	12%	6%	3%	7%
Adequacy of faculty compensation	28	44	21	29	32
Overall financial condition of the institution	18	29	17	21	22
Level of trust in senior administrators	14	20	14	9	16
Extent of collegiality among faculty members	8	14	11	6	10
Ability to attract good students	24	18	15	6	19
Ability to attract black students	52	66	42	46	54
Ability to attract Hispanic students	62	75	51	55	64
Ability to attract and retain adult students	6	24	19	27	15

Note: The figures are based on responses to a survey sent to senior administrators at 444 colleges and universities in the spring of 1990. The response rate was 82 per cent. Percentages reporting "good" are omitted.

SOURCE: AMERICAN COUNCIL ON EDUCATION

Administrators' Views of Challenges Facing Institutions in the Next Five Years

Percentage of administrators citing each challenge:	2-year	Bacca-laureate	Compre-hensive	Doctoral	All
Adequate finances	62%	40%	47%	64%	52%
Fund raising	7	22	10	15	13
Maintain enrollment	19	31	34	34	27
Enrollment growth	11	15	8	12	12
Assessment	14	7	9	4	10
Maintain quality	19	21	25	18	21
Strengthen curriculum	15	16	21	15	16
Serve new needs and populations ..	7	11	9	6	9
Effective faculty	12	17	13	14	14
Recruitment and retention of faculty members	16	13	31	27	18
Other faculty issues	31	29	23	12	27
Diversity	21	24	32	30	24
Facilities and technology	45	30	28	28	36

Note: The figures are based on responses to a survey sent to senior administrators at 444 colleges and universities in the spring of 1990. The response rate was 82 per cent.

SOURCE: AMERICAN COUNCIL ON EDUCATION

Administrators' Views of Enrollment Changes in the Next Five Years

Percentage expecting these enrollment changes at own institution:	2-year	Bacca-laureate	Compre-hensive	Doctoral	All
Increase of 30% or more	4%	7%	2%	4%	5%
Increase of 21% to 29%	6	10	7	0	7
Increase of 11% to 20%	22	19	15	0	19
Increase of 1% to 10%...................	61	42	52	41	52
No change	3	17	18	34	12
Decrease of 1% to 10%.................	4	4	6	21	5

Note: The figures are based on responses to a survey sent to senior administrators at 444 colleges and universities in the spring of 1990. The response rate was 82 per cent.

SOURCE: AMERICAN COUNCIL ON EDUCATION

Holdings of Top Research Libraries, 1988-89

	Rank[1]	Volumes in library	Volumes added	Current serials	Total staff	Total expenditures[2]
Harvard University	1	11,781,270	336,649	102,000	1,065	$40,905,537
University of California at Berkeley.............	2	7,366,672	195,076	103,944	773	29,480,699
University of California at Los Angeles	3	5,976,588	188,733	93,549	728	29,349,137
Stanford University[3]	4	5,753,147	320,601	56,343	610	28,674,297
Yale University[3]	5	8,718,619	188,616	52,496	680	26,896,746
University of Illinois at Urbana-Champaign	6	7,561,615	188,468	92,445	540	17,194,948
Columbia University	7	5,894,135	166,476	63,841	656	22,852,784
University of Texas	8	6,066,136	181,571	78,446	589	17,925,133
University of Toronto	9	5,821,745	181,590	34,053	716	24,574,320
University of Michigan	10	6,237,521	119,296	68,299	592	21,111,158
Cornell University[3]	11	5,144,830	126,812	61,369	527	19,487,745
University of Washington..	12	4,815,209	152,461	49,282	493	18,936,832
University of Wisconsin ...	13	4,908,985	108,834	48,085	508	19,091,165
University of Minnesota ...	14	4,537,087	97,527	47,010	465	19.213,314
University of Chicago	15	5,063,051	96,350	50,663	367	14,852,685
Rutgers University[3]	16	3,129,861	113,110	28,433	525	21,860,812
University of North Carolina	17	3,635,509	127,838	41,758	413	15,245,467
Princeton University	18	4,175,904	110.908	31,414	383	15,966,013
Ohio State University	19	4,338,474	99,622	32,005	462	16,127,336
Pennsylvania State University	20	3,043,837	85,650	30,345	449	16,668,127
Indiana University	21	4,045,828	87,861	25,699	465	15,425,406
Arizona State University[3]	22	2,466,274	133,883	34,001	381	13,877,587
University of Georgia[3]	23	2,788,311	100,079	57,950	352	11,668,634
University of Pennsylvania	24	3,576,227	86,296	30,419	369	15,434,175
University of California at Davis................	25	2,306,831	89,236	51,486	332	15,038,004
Duke University	26	3,757,814	96,563	30.018	319	13,758,604
University of British Columbia	27	2,817,779	109,572	21,499	415	14,144,640
University of Virginia	27	3,091,445	102,040	25,693	366	15,257,838
University of Arizona......	27	3,424,698	99,861	28,808	386	13,232,559
New York University	30	3,031,621	74,628	29,499	382	16,424,012
University of Florida	30	2,782,279	100,629	29,542	389	14,385,607
Michigan State University	32	3,373,215	114,521	28,754	325	12,306,366
University of Alberta[3]	33	2,844,697	83,889	19,426	402	13,371,072
University of Southern California[3]	34	2,580,183	55,566	37,297	371	14,338,464
University of Pittsburgh ...	35	2,789,211	91,980	22,259	355	11,901,697
Johns Hopkins University .	36	2,784,642	65,648	20,327	324	14,217,404
McGill University	36	2,477,288	98,201	17,447	318	12,759,722
University of Iowa	38	3,018,599	93,259	24,119	266	10,553,903
University of Kansas	38	2,793,134	71,272	27,857	316	11,446,035
University of California at San Diego	40	1,888,207	65,414	30,225	339	13,457,087
University of Maryland	41	1,993,077	68,531	22,526	342	12,115,457
Wayne State University....	42	2,309,698	80,239	24,588	238	11,320,503

Continued on Following Page

Holdings of Top Research Libraries, continued

	Rank[1]	Volumes in library	Volumes added	Current serials	Total staff	Total expenditures[2]
Howard University	43	1,729,875	60,884	27,931	224	$11,427,835
University of Western Ontario	44	1,912,689	71,644	18,860	291	10,183,315
University of Hawaii	45	2,312,229	70,287	32,257	236	8,712,084
University of California at Santa Barbara	46	1,927,290	67,973	21,497	250	11,036,818
University of Connecticut[3]	47	2,210,528	70,032	19,499	233	12,122,828
Georgetown University....	47	1,737,381	71,282	21,241	296	10,765,556
University of Laval	49	1,723,632	72,012	15,184	271	10,574,873
Massachusetts Institute of Technology	50	2,141,174	52,288	21,019	258	9,916,248
Louisiana State University	51	2,408,565	83,661	19,917	276	8,002,404
Boston University.........	52	1,711,215	53,264	29,155	277	9,406,578
Vanderbilt University......	52	1,810,919	60,993	19,348	303	9,827,362
University of Illinois at Chicago	54	1,610,165	55,925	17,660	295	10,367,454
Washington University (Mo.)	54	2,221,176	53,549	18,841	235	10,069,892
University of South Carolina	56	2,367,144	74,903	19,009	194	8,531,967
University of Cincinnati ...	56	1,693,173	58,255	19,027	285	10,996,517
University of Delaware	56	1,898,511	61,888	23,490	234	8,964,237
Emory University	56	1,820,956	58,526	16,733	257	10,741,274
University of Massachusetts	60	2,345,974	72,624	16,655	204	9,192,395
Purdue University	61	1,867,691	60,029	21,042	271	8,696,953
Syracuse University.......	61	2,285,707	43,468	20,614	269	8,929,768
University of New Mexico .	63	1,667,749	52,525	16,177	348	10,645,139
Texas A&M University.....	63	1,840,334	55,598	17,088	304	9,811,822
York University (Ontario)..	65	1,746,261	58,687	19,582	245	9,286,452
Brigham Young University	66	1,997,272	73,741	18,715	330	9,213,729
Brown University	67	2,172,889	50,664	13,464	265	9,406,004
University of Rochester[3] ..	68	2,639,518	53,898	13,959	258	8,112,657
University of Colorado	68	2,227,963	53,930	15,084	221	9,558,177
University of Kentucky	70	2,118,822	43,917	19,123	278	7,892,099
University of Tennessee ...	70	1,833,491	42,320	20,761	255	8,093,394
University of Notre Dame..	72	1,929,116	76,728	16,602	190	6,772,138
University of Miami	72	1,656,659	52,333	15,478	255	9,095,200
University of California at Irvine................	74	1,395,955	54,085	16,467	228	10,481,056
University of Missouri.....	75	2,446,491	38,961	17,073	238	7,520,902
Southern Illinois University	76	2,039,345	46,037	21,275	250	7,851,734
Dartmouth College	77	1,774,175	53,544	20,533	173	7,982,175
University of Utah	78	1,757,847	53,739	14,338	229	7,367,725
Virginia Polytechnic Institute and State University	79	1,673,005	46,367	18,412	221	8,051,309
Florida State University[3] ..	80	1,764,116	49,714	18,656	231	7,468,986
University of Nebraska	81	1,967,758	46,367	17,626	209	7,081,454
University of Waterloo	82	1,630,870	52,492	14,598	206	7,637,308
Temple University[3]	82	2,034,523	38,777	15,171	232	7,602,237

	Rank[1]	Volumes in library	Volumes added	Current serials	Total staff	Total expenditures[2]
University of Oregon	84	1,844,650	41,937	21,024	217	$7,736,764
Iowa State University	84	1,792,018	43,218	18,627	218	7,508,324
Queen's University at Kingston	84	1,748,868	36,848	15,747	218	7,999,497
State University of New York at Stony Brook	87	1,654,860	42,737	11,211	224	9,090,506
Washington State University	88	1,561,376	34,616	21,962	209	7,843,297
Tulane University[3]	89	1,759,026	44,575	16,767	180	6,950,382
University of Oklahoma ...	90	2,261,724	39,348	17,588	183	6,617,399
Kent State University[3]	91	2,010,760	35,110	10,561	251	8,893,468
University of Manitoba	91	1,491,876	35,260	12,368	232	8,197,539
Case Western Reserve University	93	1,559,365	33,112	12,345	181	6,708,322
McMaster University	94	1,338,532	44,879	11,607	200	8,506,271
University of Guelph	95	1,837,164	57,981	12,987	155	5,432,538
University of Saskatchewan	95	1,372,707	52,592	10,748	179	7,358,922
University of Alabama.....	97	1,772,934	42,959	17,441	176	6,137,694
North Carolina State University	98	1,263,969	34,343	13,349	220	8,341,223
University of Houston	99	1,598,010	38,222	16,490	205	6,355,605
Oklahoma State University[3] 100		1,524,543	47,767	11,976	186	6,806,752
University of California at Riverside 101		1,414,570	47,757	9,103	191	6,609,674
State University of New York at Albany[3] 102		1,253,476	37,432	14,756	167	6,544,051
Georgia Institute of Technology..........103		1,611,773	35,753	23,580	122	4,525,114
Colorado State University	104	1,182,764	45,006	11,284	141	6,373,166
Rice University	n/a	1,403,820	36,127	12,153	148	5,744,939
State University of New York at Buffalo	n/a	2,534,391	60,888	23,264	293	11,008,544

Note: Institutions are asked to report figures for their main campuses only, unless a branch campus is indicated. The list excludes Northwestern University; officials there would not submit survey data because of a U.S. Justice Department investigation concerning alleged collusion by some universities in the setting of tuition and student-aid levels.

[1] Based on an index developed by the Association of Research Libraries to measure the relative size of university libraries. The index takes into account the number of volumes held, number of volumes added during the previous fiscal year, number of current serials, total expenditures, and size of staff. It does not measure a library's services, the quality of its collections, or its success in meeting the needs of users. Two institutions chose not to have their index figure calculated; they appear at the end of the list.

[2] Figures for Canadian libraries are expressed in U.S. dollars.

[3] Includes branches as well as the main institution.

n/a   Data not available.

SOURCE: ASSOCIATION OF RESEARCH LIBRARIES

Leading Research Universities

Boston University
California Institute of Technology
Carnegie Mellon University
Case Western Reserve University
Colorado State University
Columbia University
Cornell University
Duke University
Georgia Institute of Technology
Harvard University
Howard University
Indiana University at Bloomington
Johns Hopkins University
Louisiana State University
Massachusetts Institute of Technology
Michigan State University
New Mexico State University
New York University
North Carolina State University
Northwestern University
Ohio State University
Oregon State University
Pennsylvania State University
Princeton University
Purdue University
Rockefeller University
Rutgers University
Stanford University
State University of New York at Stony Brook
Texas A&M University
University of Arizona
University of California at Berkeley
University of California at Davis
University of California at Irvine
University of California at Los Angeles

University of California at San Diego
University of California at San Francisco
University of Chicago
University of Cincinnati
University of Colorado at Boulder
University of Connecticut
University of Florida
University of Georgia
University of Hawaii at Manoa
University of Illinois at Chicago
University of Illinois at Urbana-Champaign
University of Iowa
University of Kentucky
University of Maryland at College Park
University of Miami
University of Michigan at Ann Arbor
University of Minnesota–Twin Cities
University of Missouri at Columbia
University of New Mexico
University of North Carolina at Chapel Hill
University of Pennsylvania
University of Pittsburgh
University of Rochester
University of Southern California
University of Tennessee at Knoxville
University of Texas at Austin
University of Utah
University of Virginia
University of Washington
University of Wisconsin at Madison
Virginia Polytechnic Inst. and State University
Vanderbilt University
Washington University
Yale University
Yeshiva University

Note: These institutions were classified as Research Universities I by the Carnegie Foundation for the Advancement of Teaching. Most offer a full range of baccalaureate programs, are committed to graduate education through the doctoral degree, and give a high priority to research. Each received at least $33.5-million in federal support in 1983, 1984, and 1985, and each awarded at least 50 Ph.D. degrees in 1983-84. The classification was published in 1987 and is based on institutional data covering 1982 through 1985. It is the latest such information available.

SOURCE: CARNEGIE FOUNDATION FOR THE ADVANCEMENT OF TEACHING

Selective Liberal-Arts Colleges

Agnes Scott College
Albion College
Albright College
Allegheny College
Alma College
Amherst College
Antioch University
Augustana College (Ill.)
Austin College
Barat College
Bard College
Barnard College
Bates College
Beloit College
Benedictine College
Bennington College
Bethany College (W.Va.)
Birmingham Southern
  College
Blackburn College
Borromeo College of Ohio
Bowdoin College
Bryn Mawr College
Bucknell University
Carleton College
Carroll College (Wis.)
Centenary College
  of Louisiana
Centre College of Kentucky
Chatham College
Chestnut Hill College
Claremont McKenna College
Coe College
Colby College
Colgate University
College of Mount
  Saint Vincent
College of the Holy Cross
College of Wooster
Colorado College
Connecticut College
Cornell College
Davidson College
De Pauw University
Denison University
Dickinson College
Drew University
Earlham College
Eckerd College
Emmanuel College
Franklin and Marshall
  College

Furman University
Gettysburg College
Goddard College
Gordon College
Goshen College
Goucher College
Grinnell College
Guilford College
Gustavus Adolphus College
Hamilton College
Hamline University
Hampden-Sydney College
Hampshire College
Hanover College
Hartwick College
Haverford College
Hendrix College
Hobart and William Smith
  Colleges
Hollins College
Hope College
Houghton College
Juniata College
Kalamazoo College
Kenyon College
King College
Knox College
Lafayette College
Lake Forest College
Lawrence University
Lebanon Valley College
Lewis and Clark College
Luther College
Macalester College
MacMurray College
Manhattanville College
Marlboro College
Marymount Manhattan
  College
Middlebury College
Mills College
Millsaps College
Mount Holyoke College
Muhlenberg College
Nebraska Wesleyan
  University
Neumann College
Oberlin College
Occidental College
Oglethorpe University
Pitzer College
Pomona College

Principia College
Radcliffe College
Randolph-Macon College
Randolph-Macon Woman's
  College
Reed College
Regis College (Mass.)
Rhodes College
Ripon College
Rockford College
St. John's College–Main
  Campus
St. John's College at Santa Fe
Saint John's University
  (Minn.)
St. Lawrence University
Saint Olaf College
Salem College
Sarah Lawrence College
Scripps College
Skidmore College
Smith College
State University of New York
  College at Purchase
Swarthmore College
Sweet Briar College
Thomas More College
Trinity College (Conn.)
Union College (N.Y.)
University of Dallas
University of the South
Ursinus College
Vassar College
Virginia Military Institute
Wabash College
Wartburg College
Washington and Jefferson
  College
Washington and Lee
  University
Washington College
Wellesley College
Wells College
Wesleyan University
Western Maryland College
Westmont College
Wheaton College (Ill.)
Wheaton College (Mass.)
Whitman College
Willamette University
Williams College

Note: These institutions were classified as Liberal Arts Colleges I by the Carnegie Foundation for the Advancement of Teaching and are highly selective, primarily undergraduate colleges that award more than half of their baccalaureate degrees in arts-and-science fields. The classification was published in 1987 and is based on institutional data covering 1982 through 1985. It is the latest such information available.

SOURCE: CARNEGIE FOUNDATION FOR THE ADVANCEMENT OF TEACHING

The States

ALABAMA

TRYING to limit pork-barrel projects at Alabama colleges is next to impossible because in Alabama politics and higher education are inextricable.

Despite perennial complaints from some state officials and public-interest groups, that tradition is expected to continue. Legislators pride themselves on how well they take care of the colleges in their districts and think nothing of paying for a new building or blocking a policy to satisfy the folks back home.

In 1990, some college presidents even appeared in campaign commercials for their favorite state legislators. Meanwhile, the Alabama Commission on Higher Education has been struggling to restrain the colleges, many of which hope to expand their academic programs and missions.

Gov. Guy Hunt has tried to curb the legislators' interference with institutions' academic missions. But even though he is popular in the state, as a Republican he has been unable to sway the overwhelmingly Democratic Legislature. Governor Hunt, who was re-elected in November 1990, also has tried to slow the proliferation of academic programs.

Alabama lawmakers face strong pressure to limit state spending. Like many other states, Alabama has seen a decline in projected revenues, and its agriculture-based economy is stagnant.

An unwelcome legacy of Alabama's past is visible in a continuing legal battle over desegregation. State leaders say they fully support the concept of racial integration in higher education. But civil-rights activists, the federal government, and Alabama officials still cannot agree—despite decades of court battles—on whether segregation still exists and, if so, what should be done about it. More court hearings are under way, and 1991 could see significant rulings in the case.

Black colleges have a long tradition in Alabama. Along with two public black universities and two black community colleges, the state is home to Tuskegee University, a private institution that also receives some state financial support.

The two universities with the most political clout are archrivals, Auburn University and the University of Alabama. Their athletic battles are major events in the state, and the rivalry extends to budgetary matters, as well.

The Alabama Commission on Higher Education serves as the coordinating board for public higher education and has the authority to approve new

ALABAMA
Continued

programs and recommend budgets. Campus governing boards, however, tend to have more clout than the commission. Community colleges are governed by the Board of Education, an elected body.

DEMOGRAPHICS

Population: 4,118,000   (Rank: 22)

Age distribution:
Up to 17 .... 26.9%
18 to 24 .... 10.9%
25 to 34 .... 17.2%
35 and older 45.0%

Racial and ethnic distribution:
American Indian 0.2%
Asian 0.3%
Black 25.6%
White 73.8%
Other and unknown 0.1%
Hispanic (may be any race) .. 0.9%

Educational attainment of adults:
At least 4 years of high school 56.5%
At least 1 to 3 years of college 24.7%
At least 4 years of college ... 12.2%

Per-capita personal income: $13,625

New high-school graduates in:
1990-91 (estimate) 40,690
2000-01 (estimate) 37,063

New GED diploma recipients: 6,907

High-school dropout rate: 25.1%

POLITICAL LEADERSHIP

Governor: Guy Hunt (R), term ends 1995

Governor's higher-education adviser: Anita Buckley, 11 South Union Street, State House, Montgomery 36130; (205) 242-7130

U.S. Senators: Howell Heflin (D), term ends 1997; Richard C. Shelby (D), term ends 1993

U.S. Representatives:
5 Democrats, 2 Republicans
Tom Bevill (D), Glen Browder (D), Sonny Callahan (R), Bud Cramer (D), William L. Dickinson (R), Ben Erdreich (D), Claude Harris (D)

Legislature: Senate, 28 Democrats, 8 Republicans; House, 82 Democrats, 23 Republicans

COLLEGES AND UNIVERSITIES

Higher education:
Public 4-year institutions 18
Public 2-year institutions 37
Private 4-year institutions 18
Private 2-year institutions 14
Total 87

Vocational institutions: 72

Statewide coordinating board:
Commission on Higher Education
One Court Square, Suite 221
Montgomery 36104
(205) 269-2700
Henry J. Hector, executive director

Private-college association:
Council for the Advancement of
   Private Colleges in Alabama
6 Office Park Circle, Suite 112
Birmingham 35223
(205) 879-1673
Wayne Anderson, president

Institutions censured by the AAUP:
Alabama State University,
Auburn University, Talladega College

Institution under NCAA sanctions:
Alabama A&M University

FACULTY MEMBERS

Full-time faculty members:
At public institutions 4,500
At private institutions 923

Proportion who are women:
At public institutions 33.8%
At private institutions 32.4%

Proportion with tenure:
At public institutions 70.0%
At private institutions 45.9%

Average pay of full-time professors:
At public 4-year institutions $32,953
At public 2-year institutions $28,248
At private 4-year institutions $29,234
At private 2-year institutions $23,355

STUDENTS

Enrollment:
At public 4-year institutions 115,700
At public 2-year institutions . 60,643
At private 4-year institutions 18,777
At private 2-year institutions . 4,693
Undergraduate 178,954
  First-time freshmen 43,496
Graduate 17,699
Professional 3,160
American Indian 438
Asian 1,596
Black 38,978
Hispanic 1,121
White 153,884
Foreign 3,796
Total 199,813

Enrollment highlights:
Women 52.8%
Full-time 67.8%
Minority 21.5%
Foreign 1.9%

10-year change in total
  enrollment .... Up 23.7%

Proportion of enrollment made up of minority students:
At public 4-year institutions . 18.3%
At public 2-year institutions . 19.8%
At private 4-year institutions 41.8%
At private 2-year institutions 42.2%

Degrees awarded:
Associate 5,974
Bachelor's 16,270
Master's 4,559
Doctorate 289
Professional 817

Residence of new students: State residents made up 79% of all freshmen enrolled in Alabama; 92% of all Alabama residents who were freshmen attended college in their home state.

Test scores: Students averaged 17.9 on the A.C.T., which was taken by 53% of Alabama's high-school seniors.

MONEY

Average tuition and fees:
At public 4-year institutions . $1,522
At public 2-year institutions .. $662
At private 4-year institutions $5,484
At private 2-year institutions $3,703

Expenditures:
Public institutions .. $1,324,774,000
Private institutions ... $186,596,000

State funds for higher-education operating expenses: $866,989,000
Two-year change: Up 12%

State spending on student aid:
Need-based: $2,245,000; 3,942 awards
Non–need-based: $4,771,000;
  7,478 awards
Other: $4,891,000

ALABAMA

Continued

**Salary of chief executive
of largest public 4-year campus:**
James E. Martin, Auburn University
main campus: $137,500

**Total spending on research and
development by doctorate-granting
universities:** $207,200,000

Sources:
Federal government 55.4%
State and local governments .. 8.9%
Industry 7.8%
The institution itself 19.9%
Other 7.9%

**Federal spending on education
and student aid (selected programs):**
Vocational and
    adult education $16,379,000
GI Bill $18,913,000
Pell Grants $97,118,000

**Total federal spending on college-
and university-based research
and development:** $106,502,000

Selected programs:
Department of Health
    and Human Services $65,518,000
National Science
    Foundation $5,412,000
Department of Defense $10,904,000
Department
    of Agriculture $7,610,000
Department of Energy .. $1,614,000

Largest endowment:
University of Alabama
    System $135,000,000

Top fund raisers:
Auburn University $17,659,000
University of Alabama
    at Birmingham $17,325,000

University of Alabama
    at Tuscaloosa $16,482,000

MISCELLANY

■ The campus of the University of
Alabama is the site of a museum devoted to Paul W. (Bear) Bryant, the
legendary football coach, and the university's football team. The museum
includes more than 1,000 films of
games.

■ Tuskegee University is a national
historic site because of its importance
in black history. The site includes the
George Washington Carver Museum,
which has exhibits on some of the uses
Carver devised for the peanut and
sweet potato. The university also pre-
serves the home of Booker T. Washington, which was built by Tuskegee
students.

■ Each January, the Senior Bowl
All-Star Football Classic is played in
Mobile.

■ Some dispute exists as to which
college in Alabama is the oldest. The
state's first constitution, in 1819, required the establishment of the University of Alabama; its doors swung
open in 1831. It had been beaten to the
punch, however, by Athens Academy
(now Athens State College), whose
first class was held in 1822.

ALASKA

THE University of Alaska System is the dominant higher-education enterprise in the 49th

state, and, like the state itself, it encompasses a lot of diverse territory.

Since 1987, when the university absorbed most of the state's community colleges in a money-saving move, it has had an expansive mission, offering everything from vocational courses for health-care technicians to doctoral programs in polar studies and geology.

While most students receive their education at one of the university's 11 main campuses, the university has also been aggressive in its use of technology to reach students in "bush" communities such as Nome, where many students commute to classrooms by snowmobile to hear lessons over speaker phones.

The university's far-reaching educational ventures now also extend to the Soviet Union. American university students and scientists have recently undertaken several exchanges with their Soviet counterparts to study ecological and climatic issues in Siberia and northern Alaska.

Looking to attract more sponsored research, the university in 1990 persuaded the Legislature to approve an exemption to the state's public-records law that will allow its researchers to keep their findings private while the studies are under way. University officials had argued that the open-records requirements could have discouraged some potential research sponsors.

The exemption is just one example of the university's good standing with the Legislature, a phenomenon that university officials trace to 1988, when voters rejected a challenge to the community-college merger. Legislators saw the vote in the university's favor as a public endorsement of the university's overall operations.

In recent years, lagging oil revenues have prevented the Legislature from showing the university favor where it really counts—in budgets. But university officials, mindful of Alaska's dependence on oil prices, say they are pleased with the level of state support the university has received relative to other state operations. With oil prices again on the rise because of the crisis in the Persian Gulf, money could flow more freely. And the new Governor, Walter J. Hickel, has pledged to make education "the highest" financing priority.

DEMOGRAPHICS

Population: 527,000   (Rank: 50)

Age distribution:
Up to 17	31.3%
18 to 24	11.8%
25 to 34	19.0%
35 and older	38.0%

Racial and ethnic distribution:
American Indian	16.0%
Asian	2.1%
Black	3.4%
White	77.6%
Other and unknown	0.9%
Hispanic (may be any race)	2.4%

Educational attainment of adults:
At least 4 years of high school 82.5%
At least 1 to 3 years of college 43.7%
At least 4 years of college ... 21.1%

Per-capita personal income: $21,656

New high-school graduates in:
1990-91 (estimate) 6,040
2000-01 (estimate) 10,944

New GED diploma recipients: 1,199

High-school dropout rate: 34.5%

ALASKA
Continued

POLITICAL LEADERSHIP

Governor: Walter J. Hickel (Ind), term ends 1995

Governor's higher-education adviser: n/a

U.S. Senators: Frank H. Murkowski (R), term ends 1993; Ted Stevens (R), term ends 1997

U.S. Representative:
0 Democrats, 1 Republican
Don Young (R)

Legislature: Senate, 10 Democrats, 10 Republicans; House, 24 Democrats, 16 Republicans

COLLEGES AND UNIVERSITIES

Higher education:
Public 4-year institutions 3
Public 2-year institutions 0
Private 4-year institutions 4
Private 2-year institutions 1
Total 8

Vocational institutions: 40

Statewide coordinating board:
Alaska Commission on
  Postsecondary Education
400 Willoughby Avenue
Box FP
Juneau 99811
(907) 465-2854
Jane Byers Maynard,
executive director

Private-college association:
None

Institutions censured by the AAUP:
None

Institutions under NCAA sanctions:
None

FACULTY MEMBERS

Full-time faculty members:
At public institutions 577
At private institutions 45

Proportion who are women:
At public institutions 29.6%
At private institutions 37.8%

Proportion with tenure:
At public institutions 44.9%
At private institutions .... n/a

Average pay of full-time professors:
At public 4-year institutions $40,617
At public 2-year institutions $43,608
At private 4-year institutions $33,311
At private 2-year institutions ... n/a

STUDENTS

Enrollment:
At public 4-year institutions . 22,115
At public 2-year institutions .. 5,030
At private 4-year institutions . 1,216
At private 2-year institutions 0
Undergraduate 27,346
  First-time freshmen 1,618
Graduate 1,015
Professional 0
American Indian 2,233
Asian 784
Black 1,048
Hispanic 522
White 23,613
Foreign 161
Total 28,361

Enrollment highlights:
Women 57.1%
Full-time 34.6%

Minority 16.3%
Foreign 0.6%
10-year change in total
   enrollment .... Up 7.6%

**Proportion of enrollment made up
of minority students:**
At public 4-year institutions . 16.2%
At public 2-year institutions . 14.1%
At private 4-year institutions   25.8%
At private 2-year institutions ... n/a

Degrees awarded:
Associate 661
Bachelor's 927
Master's 318
Doctorate 15
Professional 0

Residence of new students: State residents made up 78% of all freshmen
enrolled in Alaska; 43% of all Alaska
residents who were freshmen attended college in their home state.

Test scores: Students averaged 17.9
on the A.C.T., which was taken by
36% of Alaska's high-school seniors.

MONEY

Average tuition and fees:
At public 4-year institutions . $1,280
At public 2-year institutions .... n/a
At private 4-year institutions $5,078
At private 2-year institutions ... n/a

Expenditures:
Public institutions $224,042,000
Private institutions $10,171,000

**State funds for higher-education
operating expenses:** $181,834,000
Two-year change: Up 9%

State spending on student aid:
Need-based: $228,000; 152 awards

Non–need-based: $1,984,000;
   number of awards n/a
Other: None

**Salary of chief executive
of largest public 4-year campus:**
Donald F. Behrend, University of
   Alaska at Anchorage: $108,600

**Total spending on research and
development by doctorate-granting
universities:** $56,701,000
Sources:
Federal government 47.0%
State and local governments .. 3.7%
Industry 5.4%
The institution itself 38.6%
Other 5.3%

**Federal spending on education
and student aid (selected programs):**
Vocational and
   adult education $3,878,000
GI Bill $1,908,000
Pell Grants $5,853,000

**Total federal spending on college-
and university-based research
and development:** $15,928,000
Selected programs:
Department of Health
   and Human Services ... $674,000
National Science
   Foundation $6,999,000
Department of Defense ... $596,000
Department
   of Agriculture $1,464,000
Department of Energy $953,000

Largest endowment:
University of Alaska .. $28,500,000

Top fund raiser:
University of Alaska
   at Fairbanks $1,329,000

MISCELLANY

■ The University of Alaska's North

ALASKA

Continued

Slope Higher Education Center, located in Barrow, is the northernmost campus in the country. The westernmost is Northwest Community College, in Nome.

■ The University of Alaska at Fairbanks is one of some three dozen universities belonging to the Arctic Research Consortium of the United States, a group that provides logistical support for researchers interested in working in the Arctic and serves as a forum for sharing information about frozen regions of the globe.

■ The oldest higher-education institution in Alaska is Sheldon Jackson College, founded in 1878.

ARIZONA

HIGHER-EDUCATION officials in Arizona are caught between rising enrollments and the state's inability to finance public services for its rapidly growing population. In five of the last six years, budget increases for the universities were followed by mid-year cutbacks.

Gov. Rose Mofford, a Democrat, has struggled for three years to find a solution to the state's perennial budget problems, but without success. She decided not to seek re-election, but the race to succeed her was so close that she is expected to serve until a successor is selected in a run-off election. Neither the Democrat, Terry Goddard, nor the Republican, Fife Sy-

mington, won 50 per cent of the vote, the requirement for victory.

Mr. Goddard, who is the Mayor of Phoenix, wants to use off-campus classes and telecommunications to increase enrollment at two-year colleges. Mr. Symington, a businessman, wants to start a new state agency to coordinate all financial aid for college-bound students. He also says he would support legislation to provide free tuition and books at state universities for any student meeting certain academic and financial requirements.

Whoever replaces Ms. Mofford will play a pivotal role, as state lawmakers grapple with the politically sensitive issue of tax reform. She leaves behind a recommendation from a joint legislative committee that the state broaden its tax base.

In the past, the Legislature has opted for politically expedient taxes that could be paid by tourists. But a series of deficits and a growing need for public services are putting new pressure on legislators to act decisively. In the meantime, the state's three public-university presidents can expect to receive what are basically standstill budgets in the face of major enrollment growth.

The state's universities are at or near capacity, and higher-education officials are becoming increasingly concerned about their ability to serve students at the crowded institutions. The Arizona Board of Regents has appointed a task force of legislators and community-college and university officials to review the financing formula for higher education and to develop an enrollment-management plan.

Arizona has large Hispanic and American Indian populations that are a growing proportion of the citizenry. Consequently, the state's institutions are developing a variety of programs to recruit and retain minority students.

Two boards, both with governing and coordinating responsibilities, oversee the state's public colleges and universities: the Board of Regents for the three universities, and the State Board of Directors for community colleges.

DEMOGRAPHICS

Population: 3,556,000   (Rank: 24)

Age distribution:

Up to 17	27.6%
18 to 24	10.5%
25 to 34	17.2%
35 and older	44.7%

Racial and ethnic distribution:

American Indian	5.7%
Asian	0.9%
Black	2.8%
White	83.2%
Other and unknown	7.5%
Hispanic (may be any race)	16.2%

Educational attainment of adults:

At least 4 years of high school	72.4%
At least 1 to 3 years of college	38.0%
At least 4 years of college	17.4%

Per-capita personal income: $15,802

New high-school graduates in:

1990-91 (estimate)	31,543
2000-01 (estimate)	44,295

New GED diploma recipients: 7,292

High-school dropout rate: 38.9%

POLITICAL LEADERSHIP

Governor: Rose Mofford (D) will serve until a successor is chosen in a run-off election to be held in early 1991

Governor's higher-education adviser: n/a

U.S. Senators: Dennis DeConcini (D), term ends 1995; John S. McCain (R), term ends 1993

U.S. Representatives:
1 Democrat, 4 Republicans
Jim Kolbe (R), Jon L. Kyl (R), John J. Rhodes, III (R), Bob Stump (R), Morris K. Udall (D)

Legislature: Senate, 17 Democrats, 13 Republicans; House, 27 Democrats, 33 Republicans

---

COLLEGES AND UNIVERSITIES

Higher education:

Public 4-year institutions	3
Public 2-year institutions	17
Private 4-year institutions	14
Private 2-year institutions	3
Total	37

Vocational institutions: 176

Statewide coordinating board:
Arizona Board of Regents
3030 North Central Avenue
Suite 1400
Phoenix 85012
(602) 255-4082
Molly C. Broad, executive director

Private-college association:
None

Institutions censured by the AAUP:
None

Institutions under NCAA sanctions:
None

ARIZONA
Continued

FACULTY MEMBERS

Full-time faculty members:
At public institutions 4,206
At private institutions 243

Proportion who are women:
At public institutions 26.0%
At private institutions 32.9%

Proportion with tenure:
At public institutions 66.6%
At private institutions .... n/a

Average pay of full-time professors:
At public 4-year institutions $41,074
At public 2-year institutions $33,975
At private 4-year institutions $28,259
At private 2-year institutions $18,035

STUDENTS

Enrollment:
At public 4-year institutions . 93,146
At public 2-year institutions 148,382
At private 4-year institutions 14,269
At private 2-year institutions . 1,989
Undergraduate 230,262
First-time freshmen 64,668
Graduate 26,048
Professional 1,476
American Indian 8,301
Asian 5,340
Black 7,263
Hispanic 26,082
White 203,748
Foreign 7,052
Total 257,786

Enrollment highlights:
Women 53.0%
Full-time 42.1%
Minority 18.7%

Foreign 2.7%
10-year change in total
enrollment .... Up 46.0%

Proportion of enrollment made up of minority students:
At public 4-year institutions . 13.0%
At public 2-year institutions . 22.0%
At private 4-year institutions 18.9%
At private 2-year institutions 28.1%

Degrees awarded:
Associate 5,466
Bachelor's 12,348
Master's 4,970
Doctorate 495
Professional 404

Residence of new students: State residents made up 87% of all freshmen enrolled in Arizona; 96% of all Arizona residents who were freshmen attended college in their home state.

Test scores: Students averaged 19.0 on the A.C.T., which was taken by 36% of Arizona's high-school seniors.

MONEY

Average tuition and fees:
At public 4-year institutions . $1,362
At public 2-year institutions .. $519
At private 4-year institutions $4,127
At private 2-year institutions $11,007

Expenditures:
Public institutions .. $1,017,203,000
Private institutions $52,887,000

State funds for higher-education operating expenses: $613,806,000
Two-year change: Up 14%

State spending on student aid:
Need-based: $3,400,000; 5,000 awards
Non–need-based: None
Other: None

**Salary of chief executive
of largest public 4-year campus:**
Lattie F. Coor, Arizona State
   University: $151,002

**Total spending on research and
development by doctorate-granting
universities:** $223,531,000
Sources:
Federal government 47.1%
State and local governments .. 3.6%
Industry 5.6%
The institution itself 38.4%
Other 5.3%

**Federal spending on education
and student aid (selected programs):**
Vocational and
   adult education $10,996,000
GI Bill $14,480,000
Pell Grants $81,047,000

**Total federal spending on college-
and university-based research
and development:** $83,490,000
Selected programs:
Department of Health
   and Human Services $34,002,000
National Science
   Foundation $15,027,000
Department of Defense . $9,759,000
Department
   of Agriculture $3,512,000
Department of Energy .. $3,567,000

Largest endowment:
University of Arizona . $55,300,000

Top fund raisers:
University of Arizona . $40,332,000
Arizona State University $25,704,000
Northern Arizona
   University $3,918,000

MISCELLANY

■ Engineering students at Northern
Arizona University have helped bring
solar-generated electricity to 150
homes and a community center on a
Navajo reservation 150 miles north of
the campus. Fifty students installed
solar panels on the roofs of the houses
and of an abandoned schoolhouse that
is serving as a community center.

■ The University of Arizona has
added a brief and controversial passage to its faculty-promotion guidelines: Tenured professors who are no
longer professionally active in their
disciplines and who would not meet
their institutions' current tenure standards are not allowed to evaluate their
colleagues for promotion and tenure.

■ In the desert 20 miles north of
Tucson, scientists and architects are
assembling a 2½-acre structure that
they hope will take the first realistic
stab at answering the question: Could
settlers on another planet set up a self-
sustaining environment? Known as
Biosphere II, the building will be
stocked with 3,800 species of plants,
insects, and animals (including eight
Homo sapiens who will live there for
two years).

■ Scholars at the University of Arizona and Northern Arizona University are assembling a Hopi-English dic-
tionary, the first of any of the Pueblo
languages of the American Southwest.

■ The oldest institution of higher
education in Arizona is Arizona State
University, founded in 1886.

ARKANSAS

I N 1988 the "A + Arkansas" coalition of business and political leaders used the slogan "Because Ar-

ARKANSAS

Continued

kansas Can't Afford to Fail'' to promote a push for both higher-education reforms and new taxes to pay for them.

So far, the campaign may merit only an "Incomplete."

At first the coalition's effort did lead to several reforms in higher education, but the effort has stalled because the state has failed to find new money to sustain the push.

The lack of funds has also hindered the state's efforts to improve its overall college-going rate, which ranks among the lowest in the nation.

Political pundits blame Gov. Bill Clinton, a Democrat, for the stalemate. While Mr. Clinton has championed new laws to eliminate duplicate programs, improve graduation rates, and evaluate faculty members more stringently, his critics say his national political ambitions have alienated potential allies in the General Assembly who could have helped him win a tax increase.

Other political analysts note, however, that powerful business and agricultural interests have resisted new taxes, creating formidable obstacles.

Meanwhile, low salaries have led to sagging morale, which has prompted many faculty members to flee to better-paying states.

Mr. Clinton, who has been Governor for 10 years, easily won another term in November 1990. He also won approval for a new state-sponsored college-savings bond program that will help families save for college and raise money to build and refurbish public-college buildings.

Arkansas has one public historically black college and three private ones. Public colleges and universities are governed by their own institutional boards, but the Arkansas Board of Higher Education, the statewide coordinating agency, has recently been given greater authority to create new academic programs and supervise athletic budgets.

DEMOGRAPHICS

Population: 2,406,000   (Rank: 33)

Age distribution:
Up to 17 .... 27.0%
18 to 24 .... 10.4%
25 to 34 .... 15.6%
35 and older 46.9%

Racial and ethnic distribution:
American Indian 0.6%
Asian 0.3%
Black 16.3%
White 82.7%
Other and unknown 0.1%
Hispanic (may be any race) .. 0.8%

Educational attainment of adults:
At least 4 years of high school 55.5%
At least 1 to 3 years of college 22.3%
At least 4 years of college ... 10.8%

Per-capita personal income: $12,901

New high-school graduates in:
1990-91 (estimate) 26,715
2000-01 (estimate) 26,416

New GED diploma recipients: 6,341

High-school dropout rate: 22.8%

POLITICAL LEADERSHIP

Governor: Bill Clinton (D), term ends 1995

Governor's higher-education adviser: Kathy VanLaningham, State Capitol, Room 205, Little Rock 72201; (501) 682-2345

U.S. Senators: Dale Bumpers (D), term ends 1993; David Pryor (D), term ends 1997

U.S. Representatives:
3 Democrats, 1 Republican
Bill Alexander (D), Beryl Anthony, Jr. (D), John Paul Hammerschmidt (R), Ray Thornton (D)

General Assembly: Senate, 31 Democrats, 4 Republicans; House, 92 Democrats, 8 Republicans

COLLEGES AND UNIVERSITIES

Higher education:
Public 4-year institutions 10
Public 2-year institutions 10
Private 4-year institutions 10
Private 2-year institutions 7

Total 37

Vocational institutions: 109

Statewide coordinating board:
Board of Higher Education
1220 West Third Street
Little Rock 72201
(501) 371-1441
Diane Gilleland, director

Private-college association:
Independent Colleges of Arkansas
One Riverfront Place, Suite 610
North Little Rock 72114
(501) 378-0843
E. Kearney Dietz, president

Institutions censured by the AAUP:
Phillips County Community College, Southern Arkansas University,

University of the Ozarks (governing board)

Institutions under NCAA sanctions:
None

FACULTY MEMBERS

Full-time faculty members:
At public institutions 2,210
At private institutions 378

Proportion who are women:
At public institutions 34.0%
At private institutions 27.8%

Proportion with tenure:
At public institutions 61.2%
At private institutions 69.4%

Average pay of full-time professors:
At public 4-year institutions $30,572
At public 2-year institutions $23,165
At private 4-year institutions $25,411
At private 2-year institutions $14,600

STUDENTS

Enrollment:
At public 4-year institutions . 55,352
At public 2-year institutions . 16,601
At private 4-year institutions . 9,812
At private 2-year institutions . 2,785
Undergraduate 77,275
    First-time freshmen 18,579
Graduate 5,864
Professional 1,411
American Indian 380
Asian 668
Black 11,361
Hispanic 366
White 70,180
Foreign 1,595
Total 84,550

Enrollment highlights:
Women 56.5%
Full-time 71.1%

ARKANSAS
Continued

Minority 15.4%
Foreign 1.9%
10-year change in total
   enrollment .... Up 16.9%

Proportion of enrollment made up of minority students:
At public 4-year institutions . 15.3%
At public 2-year institutions . 13.9%
At private 4-year institutions 12.9%
At private 2-year institutions 34.8%

Degrees awarded:
Associate 2,412
Bachelor's 7,017
Master's 1,746
Doctorate 101
Professional 369

Residence of new students: State residents made up 85% of all freshmen enrolled in Arkansas; 86% of all Arkansas residents who were freshmen attended college in their home state.

Test scores: Students averaged 17.6 on the A.C.T., which was taken by 59% of Arkansas's high-school seniors.

MONEY

Average tuition and fees:
At public 4-year institutions . $1,376
At public 2-year institutions .. $644
At private 4-year institutions $3,715
At private 2-year institutions $6,102

Expenditures:
Public institutions $528,831,000
Private institutions $72,321,000

State funds for higher-education operating expenses: $319,014,000
Two-year change: Up 3%

State spending on student aid:
Need-based: $3,905,000;
  11,906 awards
Non–need-based: $749,000;
  375 awards
Other: $173,000

Salary of chief executive of largest public 4-year campus:
Daniel E. Ferritor, University
  of Arkansas main campus: $89,872

Total spending on research and development by doctorate-granting universities: $43,676,000
Sources:
Federal government 32.5%
State and local governments . 27.9%
Industry 9.4%
The institution itself 21.8%
Other 8.3%

Federal spending on education and student aid (selected programs):
Vocational and
  adult education $9,482,000
GI Bill $6,706,000
Pell Grants $57,616,000

Total federal spending on college- and university-based research and development: $15,599,000

Selected programs:
Department of Health
  and Human Services . $5,538,000
National Science
  Foundation $1,030,000
Department of Defense ... $365,000
Department
  of Agriculture $5,702,000
Department of Energy $783,000

Largest endowment:
Hendrix College $49,950,000

Top fund raisers:
Harding University $6,048,000

Ouachita Baptist
University $4,394,000
Arkansas College $3,645,000

MISCELLANY

■ Former Sen. J. William Fulbright, the creator of the program of international scholarly and student exchanges that bears his name, served as president of the University of Arkansas from 1939 to 1941.

■ The University of Arkansas has decided to leave the Southwest Athletic Conference and compete in the Southeastern Conference, a move that many college sports officials expected to set off a flurry of conference switching by big-time sports programs.

■ Henderson State University and Ouachita Baptist University—separated by only a street and a ravine in their hometown of Arkadelphia—are serious rivals. Every year the two compete in a football classic called "the Battle of the Ravine."

■ The oldest institution of higher education in Arkansas is the University of the Ozarks, founded in 1834. It is affiliated with the United Presbyterian Church, U.S.A.

CALIFORNIA

WHEN Californians voted in 1990 to raise the state's spending ceiling, they also raised the hopes of higher-education officials who had feared their institutions would be unable to accommodate a projected enrollment increase of 700,000 within 15 years.

For a decade, the restrictive state budget formula had created headaches for higher-education officials facing a series of ever-increasing projections for college enrollment. The latest projections indicate that the number of students will climb to 2.5 million by 2005.

In recent years, the state's voter-imposed spending limits forced its public colleges to make do with small increases and little or no hope of adequate ones in the future. College officials said the limits threatened the state's "master plan" for higher education, which guarantees admission to one of California's four-year institutions to every qualified resident of the state. The plan places a high priority on serving minority students.

But passage of the measure—known as Proposition 111—does not mean that the universities will be rolling in money. To reduce a $3.6-billion deficit, legislators have already done almost everything but beg or steal, and the next few years are expected to be financially tight.

Higher-education officials had hoped the passage of Proposition 111 would make state lawmakers less reluctant to support tax increases. But the resounding defeat of almost all of the bond measures on the November ballot—including a $450-million higher-education capital-improvement bond—has diminished those hopes. Nor is the state's new Republican Governor, Pete Wilson, talking about tax increases. His interest in higher education focuses on such issues as assessing student performance.

Universities now are trying to determine how they can finance the new campuses and buildings they need to accommodate enrollment growth. The University of California, for example, says it needs three new campuses. The search for the first—in California's Central Valley near Fresno—is under way.

If enrollment projections are accurate, the California Community College system, which already has 107 campuses, may need at least 23 more. In addition, the California State University System will have to expand its 20 existing campuses.

The C.S.U. expansion, however, may be threatened by controversies over the system's management. The chancellor, W. Ann Reynolds, resigned in April 1990 amid criticism from lawmakers and faculty members over a plan adopted by her Board of Trustees to increase the salaries of some administrative employees. Ms. Reynolds's salary soared from $136,000 to $195,000 under the plan. The credibility of the system may depend on whoever is chosen to succeed Ms. Reynolds.

In 1963, higher education in California was divided into three separately governed systems: the University of California, the California State University, and the community colleges.

U.C. is the only doctorate-granting system and offers admission to the top eighth of the state's high-school graduates. C.S.U. offers bachelor's- and master's-degree programs to students from the top third of their high-school classes. The community colleges have an open admissions policy.

By limiting expensive doctoral and research programs to the U.C. system, California has avoided some of the costly competition between systems that is found in other states. But some say the emphasis on research and graduate programs at U.C. has hurt the quality of undergraduate education. The community colleges, in theory, provide an inexpensive way for students to prepare for the four-year institutions, but relatively few students actually transfer.

Despite the criticisms, California is committed to the system and is trying to make it work. The California Postsecondary Education Commission— the state's coordinating board—and the Legislature have rebuffed C.S.U. officials who regularly seek authority to grant doctorates. Lawmakers also support a transfer program that would guarantee two-year college students admission to one of the public-university systems.

However, California's growing minority populations are presenting new challenges to the systems. Few black and Hispanic students qualify for enrollment in the selective institutions, and those who do enroll complain about hostile campus environments. Asian Americans claim that elite universities have imposed informal quotas to limit Asian Americans' enrollment and that the community colleges do not offer programs that recent immigrants need.

California residents are strong proponents of the state's low-tuition policies. Community-college tuition, for example, is $100 a year.

The tuition gap between the state's public and private institutions, however, has widened substantially. Private colleges have lobbied for increased state support of student-aid programs. In particular, the officials of those colleges want the maximum state grant to students attending their institutions to equal the subsidy for each student at public institutions (about $7,000). The current grant maximum is about $5,200.

While public institutions dwarf the private institutions, the private colleges and universities play an important role in the state. They include prestigious research universities, such as Stanford University, the University of Southern California, and the California Institute of Technology; liberal-arts colleges, such as Claremont McKenna, Mills, and Pomona; and such specialized institutions as the California Institute of the Arts and the Monterey Institute of International Studies.

DEMOGRAPHICS

Population: 29,063,000 (Rank: 1)

Age distribution:
Up to 17	26.5%
18 to 24	10.4%
25 to 34	18.9%
35 and older	44.2%

Racial and ethnic distribution:
American Indian	1.0%
Asian	5.5%
Black	7.7%
White	77.0%
Other and unknown	8.8%
Hispanic (may be any race)	19.2%

Educational attainment of adults:
At least 4 years of high school	73.5%
At least 1 to 3 years of college	42.0%
At least 4 years of college	19.6%

Per-capita personal income: $19,929

New high-school graduates in:
1990-91 (estimate)	245,259
2000-01 (estimate)	362,558

New GED diploma recipients: 9,468

High-school dropout rate: 34.1%

POLITICAL LEADERSHIP

Governor: Pete Wilson (R), term ends 1995

Governor's higher-education adviser: n/a

U.S. Senators: Alan Cranston (D), term ends 1993; 1 vacancy

U.S. Representatives:
26 Democrats, 19 Republicans
Glenn M. Anderson (D), Anthony C. Beilenson (D), Howard L. Berman (D), Barbara Boxer (D), George E. Brown, Jr. (D), Tom Campbell (R), Gary Condit (D), C. Christopher Cox (R), Randy Cunningham (R), William E. Dannemeyer (R), Ronald V. Dellums (D), Julian C. Dixon (D), Calvin Dooley (D), John Doolittle (R), Robert K. Dornan (R), David Dreier (R), Mervyn M. Dymally (D), Don Edwards (D), Vic Fazio (D), Elton Gallegly (R), Wally Herger (R), Duncan Hunter (R), Robert J. Lagomarsino (R), Tom Lantos (D), Richard H. Lehman (D), Mel Levine (D), Jerry Lewis (R), Bill Lowery (R), Matthew G. Martinez (D), Robert T. Matsui (D), Alfred A. (Al) McCandless (R), George Miller (D), Norman Y. Mineta (D), Carlos J. Moorhead (R), Ron Packard (R), Leon E. Panetta (D), Nancy Pelosi (D), Frank Riggs (R), Dana Rohrabacher (R), Edward R. Roybal (D), Fortney Pete Stark (D), William M. Thomas (R), Esteban Edward Torres (D), Maxine Waters (D), Henry A. Waxman (D)

Legislature: Senate, 25 Democrats, 13 Republicans, 1 Independent, 1 vacancy; House, 49 Democrats, 31 Republicans

CALIFORNIA
Continued

COLLEGES AND UNIVERSITIES

Higher education:
Public 4-year institutions 31
Public 2-year institutions 107
Private 4-year institutions 140
Private 2-year institutions 32
Total 310

Vocational institutions: 916

Statewide coordinating board:
California Postsecondary Education
   Commission
1020 12th Street, 3rd Floor
Sacramento 95814
(916) 445-1000
Kenneth B. O'Brien,
executive director

Private-college association:
Association of Independent California
   Colleges and Universities
1100 11th Street, Suite 315
Sacramento 95814
(916) 446-7626
William J. Moore, president

Institutions censured by the AAUP:
Sonoma State University,
University of Judaism

Institutions under NCAA sanctions:
None

FACULTY MEMBERS

Full-time faculty members:
At public institutions 31,296
At private institutions 6,056

Proportion who are women:
At public institutions 27.9%
At private institutions 25.5%

Proportion with tenure:
At public institutions 72.1%
At private institutions 60.7%

Average pay of full-time professors:
At public 4-year institutions $47,696
At public 2-year institutions $37,266
At private 4-year institutions $42,760
At private 2-year institutions $24,375

STUDENTS

Enrollment:
At public 4-year institutions   484,181
At public 2-year
   institutions 1,057,124
At private 4-year institutions 201,539
At private 2-year institutions   10,720
Undergraduate 1,560,106
   First-time freshmen 280,052
Graduate 163,350
Professional 30,108
American Indian 20,600
Asian 205,929
Black 114,388
Hispanic 215,397
White 1,131,731
Foreign 65,519
Total 1,753,564

Enrollment highlights:
Women 53.9%
Full-time 44.0%
Minority 33.0%
Foreign 3.7%
10-year change in total
   enrollment .... Up 6.3%

**Proportion of enrollment made up
of minority students:**
At public 4-year institutions . 33.0%
At public 2-year institutions . 34.7%
At private 4-year institutions   22.8%
At private 2-year institutions   37.2%

Degrees awarded:
Associate 47,503

Bachelor's 88,518
Master's 31,506
Doctorate 4,116
Professional 7,893

Residence of new students: State residents made up 90% of all freshmen enrolled in California; 95% of all California residents who were freshmen attended college in their home state.

Test scores: Students averaged 903 on the s.a.t., which was taken by 45% of California's high-school seniors.

MONEY

Average tuition and fees:
At public 4-year institutions . $1,123
At public 2-year institutions .. $112
At private 4-year institutions $9,489
At private 2-year institutions $7,664

Expenditures:
Public institutions .. $8,515,440,000
Private institutions . $3,641,630,000

State funds for higher-education operating expenses: $6,100,728,000

Two-year change: Up 13%

State spending on student aid:
Need-based: $162,003,000;
79,886 awards
Non–need-based: None
Other: None

Salary of chief executive of largest public 4-year campus:
Charles E. Young, University of California at Los Angeles: $165,000

Total spending on research and development by doctorate-granting universities: $1,845,555,000

Sources:
Federal government 69.4%

State and local governments .. 2.4%
Industry 4.5%
The institution itself 17.4%
Other 6.3%

Federal spending on education and student aid (selected programs):
Vocational and
    adult education $70,847,000
GI Bill $72,280,000
Pell Grants $413,206,000

Total federal spending on college- and university-based research and development: $1,109,954,000

Selected programs:
Department of Health
    and Human Services $609,383,000
National Science
    Foundation $164,689,000
Department of Defense $148,010,000
Department
    of Agriculture $15,401,000
Department of Energy . $68,081,000

Largest endowment:
Stanford University $1,775,000,000

Top fund raisers:
Stanford University .. $188,636,000
University of Southern
    California $102,629,000
University of California
    at Los Angeles $72,825,000

MISCELLANY

■ For a half hour every Wednesday, employees of Santa Monica College—including switchboard operators and the president—stop everything and read whatever they like. The experiment is aimed at encouraging more people to read.

■ A California jury in March 1990 awarded a former professor at the Claremont Graduate School more

CALIFORNIA

Continued

than $1-million in what was thought to be one of the largest awards ever in a discrimination case. The professor, who is black, had sued the college, claiming he had been denied tenure because of his race.

■ A chemical with the odor of skunk oil is being sold in the student store at the University of California at Los Angeles as a defense against sexual assault.

■ The University of California at Davis hopes to entice more law-school students into public-interest jobs after graduation by helping them repay their college loans. The Loan Repayment Assistance Program was created in response to the dwindling number of graduates who go on to work for non-profit organizations.

■ Stanford University has adopted an anti-harassment policy that penalizes students who bother or intimidate others because of their race, sex, handicap, religion, sexual orientation, or national or ethnic origin.

■ The Board of Trustees of Mills College in 1990 reversed its decision to admit male undergraduates by 1991, thus bowing to protests by students, faculty members, and alumnae.

■ Chang-Lin Tien became the first Asian American to head one of the University of California's nine campuses when he took over as chancellor at Berkeley in July 1990. An expert in the field of heat-transfer technology, Mr. Tien was executive vice-chancellor of the university's Irvine campus

at the time of his appointment to the Berkeley post.

■ The oldest institutions of higher education in California are the University of the Pacific (an independent institution) and Santa Clara University (a Roman Catholic institution), both founded in 1851.

COLORADO

I N Colorado, the strong interest that state political leaders take in overseeing higher-education policy is matched by the aggressive posture of the state's colleges and universities themselves.

The public universities are among the most active in the country in pursuing federal and private research dollars and in recruiting high-technology industries. The University of Colorado, in particular, has been rewarded for its efforts: US West Advanced Technologies selected the university's new research park in Boulder as the site for the company's sought-after research center.

The Boulder campus also has a long tradition of attracting many of its students from out of state, a circumstance that sometimes bothers residents, who want their tax dollars spent on Coloradans.

Prodded by the General Assembly and the Commission on Higher Education—the statewide coordinating board—the public institutions have also undertaken programs to measure how well students are being taught and to improve the graduation rates of minority students. The next focus of attention will probably be to reform the way teachers are certified, a campaign pledge of Gov. Roy Romer, a Democrat who was re-elected in November 1990 to a second term.

The state's 15 community colleges have seen a dramatic enrollment growth in the past three years. The colleges are highly regarded for their innovative worker-training programs, developed in cooperation with businesses.

Concern over the growing "tuition gap" between Colorado's public institutions and the state's private, non-profit colleges has also been a political issue in recent years. Private-college leaders were able to persuade lawmakers in 1988 to enact a program to provide direct payments to the institutions based on their enrollment, but so far the colleges have been unable to get legislators to follow through with money for the assistance program. The General Assembly has, however, agreed to change the formula for state financial aid to provide needy private-college students with additional money for their tuition and other college costs.

DEMOGRAPHICS

Population: 3,317,000   (Rank: 26)

Age distribution:
Up to 17 .... 26.0%
18 to 24 .... 10.7%
25 to 34 .... 19.8%
35 and older 43.5%

Racial and ethnic distribution:
American Indian 0.7%
Asian 1.2%
Black 3.5%
White 89.7%
Other and unknown 4.9%
Hispanic (may be any race) . 11.8%

Educational attainment of adults:
At least 4 years of high school 78.6%
At least 1 to 3 years of college 44.1%
At least 4 years of college ... 23.0%

Per-capita personal income: $17,553

New high-school graduates in:
1990-91 (estimate) 33,255
2000-01 (estimate) 42,699

New GED diploma recipients: 5,978

High-school dropout rate: 25.3%

POLITICAL LEADERSHIP

Governor: Roy Romer (D), term ends 1995

Governor's higher-education adviser: Joy Fitzgerald, State Capitol, Room 124, Denver 80203; (303) 866-4585

U.S. Senators: Hank Brown (R), term ends 1997; Timothy E. Wirth (D), term ends 1993

U.S. Representatives:
3 Democrats, 3 Republicans
Wayne Allard (R), Ben Nighthorse Campbell (D), Joel Hefley (R), Dan Schaefer (R), Patricia Schroeder (D), David E. Skaggs (D)

General Assembly: Senate, 12 Democrats, 23 Republicans; House, 27 Democrats, 38 Republicans

---

COLLEGES AND UNIVERSITIES

Higher education:
Public 4-year institutions 13
Public 2-year institutions 15
Private 4-year institutions 17
Private 2-year institutions 9
Total 54

COLORADO

Continued

Vocational institutions: 119

Statewide coordinating board:
Commission on Higher Education
1300 Broadway, 2nd Floor
Denver 80203
(303) 866-2723
David A. Longanecker,
executive director

Private-college association:
Independent Higher Education
of Colorado
387 Denver Club Building
518 17th Street
Denver 80202
(303) 571-5559
Toni Worcester, executive director

Institutions censured by the AAUP:
Colorado School of Mines,
University of Northern Colorado

Institutions under NCAA sanctions:
None

FACULTY MEMBERS

Full-time faculty members:
At public institutions 4,347
At private institutions 610

Proportion who are women:
At public institutions 22.8%
At private institutions 29.0%

Proportion with tenure:
At public institutions 69.8%
At private institutions 68.6%

Average pay of full-time professors:
At public 4-year institutions $36,397
At public 2-year institutions $26,174

At private 4-year institutions $33,813
At private 2-year institutions ... n/a

STUDENTS

Enrollment:
At public 4-year institutions 105,270
At public 2-year institutions . 57,632
At private 4-year institutions 18,347
At private 2-year institutions . 5,039
Undergraduate 164,747
    First-time freshmen 30,634
Graduate 18,553
Professional 2,988
American Indian 1,654
Asian 4,050
Black 5,078
Hispanic 13,452
White 157,982
Foreign 4,072
Total 186,288

Enrollment highlights:
Women 52.5%
Full-time 60.4%
Minority 13.3%
Foreign 2.2%
10-year change in total
    enrollment .... Up 22.3%

**Proportion of enrollment made up
of minority students:**
At public 4-year institutions . 11.4%
At public 2-year institutions . 15.6%
At private 4-year institutions 13.6%
At private 2-year institutions 24.1%

Degrees awarded:
Associate 5,825
Bachelor's 15,144
Master's 4,397
Doctorate 667
Professional 872

Residence of new students: State residents made up 78% of all freshmen enrolled in Colorado; 80% of all Colorado residents who were freshmen attended college in their home state.

Test scores: Students averaged 19.6 on the A.C.T., which was taken by 60% of Colorado's high-school seniors.

MONEY

Average tuition and fees:
At public 4-year institutions . $1,830
At public 2-year institutions .. $792
At private 4-year institutions $9,188
At private 2-year institutions $8,036

Expenditures:
Public institutions .. $1,057,558,000
Private institutions ... $160,193,000

State funds for higher-education operating expenses: $516,793,000

Two-year change: Up 9%

State spending on student aid:
Need-based: $10,548,000;
 15,020 awards
Non–need-based: $9,894,000;
 11,933 awards
Other: None

Salary of chief executive of largest public 4-year campus:
James N. Corbridge, Jr., University of Colorado at Boulder: $120,800

Total spending on research and development by doctorate-granting universities: $226,428,000

Sources:
Federal government 73.7%
State and local governments .. 4.7%
Industry 6.4%
The institution itself 7.8%
Other 7.3%

Federal spending on education and student aid (selected programs):
Vocational and
 adult education $17,159,000
GI Bill $15,596,000
Pell Grants $75,890,000

Total federal spending on college- and university-based research and development: $145,900,000

Selected programs:
Department of Health
 and Human Services $65,582,000
National Science
 Foundation $22,252,000
Department of Defense $12,527,000
Department
 of Agriculture $4,665,000
Department of Energy .. $5,918,000

Largest endowment:
Colorado College $123,047,000

Top fund raisers:
University of Colorado $40,150,000
University of Denver .. $11,783,000
Colorado College $7,455,000

MISCELLANY

■ The U.S. Air Force Academy is located in Colorado Springs.

■ Colorado State University is the only land-grant institution in the country to offer a baccalaureate program in equine sciences. Students in the program at the Fort Collins campus take courses ranging from anatomy to rider-instructor training at the Colorado State Equine Teaching Center, which includes a 300-foot-by-200-foot indoor arena.

■ The Colorado School of Mines campus houses a geology museum with mineral collections from around the world. The Golden campus is also

COLORADO
Continued

home to an Interior Department National Earthquake Center, which records temblors from as far away as the South China Sea.

■ The Naropa Institute in Boulder is the country's only college based on Buddhism.

■ Denver is the home of two national higher-education associations dealing with state governments. The Education Commission of the States is a group of governors, educators, and legislators, and the State Higher Education Executive Officers represents the directors of state coordinating boards.

■ The oldest institution of higher education in Colorado is the University of Denver, an independent institution founded in 1864.

CONNECTICUT

THE economic boom that Connecticut and other New England states enjoyed in the mid-1980's is over. In recent years, the state has been racked by successive budget crises.

In early 1990 the revenue shortages and the ensuing problems drove Gov. William A. O'Neill's approval ratings to the lowest level ever. Consequently, Mr. O'Neill, a Democrat, did not seek election to a third term. His successor, former Sen. Lowell P. Weicker, Jr., who ran as a third-party candidate, has called for tax reform. Connecticut has an 8-per-cent sales tax, but no levy on income. That tax structure is no longer providing adequate financing for state services, the new Governor says.

For many years, the state relied on private colleges and universities to educate its citizens. Yale University, for example—founded in 1701—is 180 years older than the University of Connecticut. Yale is not the state's only prominent higher-education institution; Connecticut College and Wesleyan University also have national reputations.

But in the 1980's, public higher education assumed a new role. Students in Connecticut are now older, more likely to want to study part time, and more likely to be members of minority groups. Many programs have been developed in the last 10 years to serve the growing population of non-traditional students. Those programs, however, are now being threatened by the state's revenue woes.

While lawmakers have paid more attention to public institutions in recent years, private colleges continue to be influential. Connecticut offers generous grants for private-college students and provides financial subsidies to cities and towns whose tax bases are reduced by the presence of colleges.

In New Haven, particularly, town-gown relations have taken center stage. Although other universities have made voluntary contributions to their cities for years, Yale refused to make such payments until 1990. Yale officials agreed to pay New Haven more than $1.16-million to cover the costs of campus fire protection in 1990-91.

Yale also agreed to place its golf course on the city's tax rolls, bringing

New Haven $304,000 a year. In exchange, the city has agreed to waive its right to try to remove the tax-exempt status of other Yale properties.

The Board of Governors for Higher Education is the statewide coordinating board, with powers to set wide-ranging policies. It has used its authority to push colleges to recruit more minority students and to assess what college students learn.

The two-year institutions are now supervised by a single governing board called the Board of Trustees of Technical and Community Colleges. The University of Connecticut and the Connecticut state-college system are governed by separate boards.

DEMOGRAPHICS

Population: 3,239,000   (Rank: 27)

Age distribution:
Up to 17	23.4%
18 to 24	10.3%
25 to 34	16.9%
35 and older	49.5%

Racial and ethnic distribution:
American Indian	0.2%
Asian	0.7%
Black	7.0%
White	90.5%
Other and unknown	1.7%
Hispanic (may be any race)	4.0%

Educational attainment of adults:
At least 4 years of high school	70.3%
At least 1 to 3 years of college	35.9%
At least 4 years of college	20.7%

Per-capita personal income: $24,683

New high-school graduates in:
1990-91 (estimate)	30,330
2000-01 (estimate)	33,576

New GED diploma recipients: 3,636

High-school dropout rate: 15.1%

POLITICAL LEADERSHIP

Governor: Lowell P. Weicker, Jr. (Ind), term ends 1995

Governor's higher-education adviser: n/a

U.S. Senators: Christopher J. Dodd (D), term ends 1993; Joe Lieberman (D), term ends 1995

U.S. Representatives:
3 Democrats, 3 Republicans
Rosa DeLauro (D), Gary Franks (R), Sam Gejdenson (D), Nancy L. Johnson (R), Barbara B. Kennelly (D), Christopher Shays (R)

General Assembly: Senate, 20 Democrats, 16 Republicans; House, 89 Democrats, 62 Republicans

---

COLLEGES AND UNIVERSITIES

Higher education:
Public 4-year institutions	7
Public 2-year institutions	17
Private 4-year institutions	21
Private 2-year institutions	3
Total	48

Vocational institutions: 122

Statewide coordinating board:
Board of Governors for
  Higher Education
61 Woodland Street
Hartford 06105
(203) 566-5766
Norma Foreman Glasgow,
commissioner of higher education

CONNECTICUT
Continued

Private-college association:
Connecticut Conference of
  Independent Colleges
36 Gillett Street
Hartford 06105
(203) 522-0271
Michael A. Gerber, president

Institutions censured by the AAUP:
None

Institutions under NCAA sanctions:
None

FACULTY MEMBERS

Full-time faculty members:
At public institutions 3,025
At private institutions 2,537

Proportion who are women:
At public institutions 27.3%
At private institutions 25.7%

Proportion with tenure:
At public institutions 71.7%
At private institutions 58.5%

Average pay of full-time professors:
At public 4-year institutions $44,374
At public 2-year institutions $35,428
At private 4-year institutions $40,836
At private 2-year institutions $23,855

STUDENTS

Enrollment:
At public 4-year institutions . 64,501
At public 2-year institutions . 41,918
At private 4-year institutions 57,467
At private 2-year institutions . 1,791
Undergraduate 130,931
  First-time freshmen 29,551

Graduate 31,480
Professional 3,266
American Indian 398
Asian 3,528
Black 8,930
Hispanic 4,824
White 143,934
Foreign 4,063
Total 165,677

Enrollment highlights:
Women 56.4%
Full-time 50.6%
Minority 10.9%
Foreign 2.5%
10-year change in total
  enrollment .... Up 8.7%

**Proportion of enrollment made up
of minority students:**
At public 4-year institutions .. 8.2%
At public 2-year institutions . 15.7%
At private 4-year institutions 10.3%
At private 2-year institutions 16.0%

Degrees awarded:
Associate 4,781
Bachelor's 13,680
Master's 5,892
Doctorate 496
Professional 918

Residence of new students: State residents made up 78% of all freshmen enrolled in Connecticut; 62% of all Connecticut residents who were freshmen attended college in their home state.

Test scores: Students averaged 901 on the S.A.T., which was taken by 74% of Connecticut's high-school seniors.

MONEY

Average tuition and fees:
At public 4-year institutions . $2,017
At public 2-year institutions .. $915

At private 4-year institutions $11,268
At private 2-year institutions $7,906

Expenditures:
Public institutions $562,696,000
Private institutions ... $836,949,000

State funds for higher-education operating expenses: $485,846,000
Two-year change: Up 3%

State spending on student aid:
Need-based: $20,929,000;
17,500 awards
Non–need-based: $200,000; 20 awards
Other: $11,677,000

Salary of chief executive of largest public 4-year campus:
Harry J. Hartley (interim), University of Connecticut: $137,000

Total spending on research and development by doctorate-granting universities: $284,410,000
Sources:
Federal government 65.8%
State and local governments .. 1.9%
Industry 4.1%
The institution itself 20.0%
Other 8.1%

Federal spending on education and student aid (selected programs):
Vocational and
   adult education $1,541,000
GI Bill $3,810,000
Pell Grants $29,773,000

Total federal spending on college- and university-based research and development: $175,972,000
Selected programs:
Department of Health
   and Human Services $135,088,000
National Science
   Foundation $13,967,000

Department of Defense $10,865,000
Department
   of Agriculture $1,563,000
Department of Energy .. $9,064,000

Largest endowment:
Yale University $2,336,495,000

Top fund raisers:
Yale University $122,756,000
Wesleyan University .. $12,330,000
University of Hartford . $10,197,000

MISCELLANY

■ Winnie the Pooh, the bear in A. A. Milne's collection of children's stories, was honored with a scholarship named for him at Yale University. The $6,000 prize will go each year to an English major with financial need. The character was a favorite of an alumnus, Barry Campbell Good. Mr. Good's wife, Stormy Good, decided a Pooh scholarship would be a fitting memorial to her husband, who died in 1988.

■ Maya Ying Lin, the architect who designed the Vietnam Veterans Memorial in Washington, is drafting plans for a new monument to honor women at Yale University. Yale, which is Ms. Lin's alma mater, first admitted women in 1970.

■ David F. Machell, a psychologist at Western Connecticut State University, has identified what he thinks is an emotional disorder unique to the professoriate—"professorial melancholia." Afflicted professors suffer from low self-esteem, resent their students, and feel misunderstood, depressed, and isolated.

■ The U.S. Coast Guard Academy is located in New London.

■ Yale University is the oldest institution of higher education in Connecticut. It was founded in 1701. In 1831, it had the distinction of running the nation's first endowment drive, which raised $107,000.

DELAWARE

SINCE the stock-market crash in October 1987, the watchword among Delaware legislators considering spending issues has been "caution." Gov. Michael N. Castle has tried to keep a lid on spending increases, but he also has been trying to increase state revenues by trying to persuade more international corporations to call Delaware home.

Delaware's political spotlight has not focused on higher education in recent years. Governor Castle, a Republican, tends instead to concentrate on education in the public schools.

If their political fate is to be ignored, the economic fate of Delaware's public colleges and universities is linked closely to the state's economy. That, in turn, is linked to the national economy, since many major companies are incorporated in Delaware.

Throughout much of the state's history the dominant corporation has been E. I. du Pont de Nemours & Company, the chemical manufacturer and a significant financial contributor to the state's higher-education system. The company's role has sometimes been a source of controversy, with critics contending that the company and members of the du Pont family have had too much influence on state policy.

Delaware has a well-articulated system of higher education, with two public four-year institutions—the University of Delaware and Delaware State College—and a three-campus community-college system.

Delaware State is a black college that historically did not receive much state money. But in recent years, under prodding from the federal government, the state has changed that. State officials have also tried to attract more black students and faculty members to the University of Delaware. But local civil-rights advocates say the university needs to do more to make black students feel welcome, and say that the state college needs additional financing. Separate governing boards control the university, the state college, and the community colleges. The statewide coordinating board, the Delaware Postsecondary Education Commission, has limited powers.

DEMOGRAPHICS

Population: 673,000   (Rank: 46)

Age distribution:
Up to 17	25.0%
18 to 24	11.0%
25 to 34	18.4%
35 and older	45.5%

Racial and ethnic distribution:
American Indian	0.2%
Asian	0.8%
Black	16.1%
White	82.1%
Other and unknown	0.8%
Hispanic (may be any race)	1.6%

Educational attainment of adults:
At least 4 years of high school 68.6%
At least 1 to 3 years of college 32.4%
At least 4 years of college ... 17.5%

Per-capita personal income: $18,483

New high-school graduates in:
1990-91 (estimate) 7,056
2000-01 (estimate) 7,364

New GED diploma recipients: 795

High-school dropout rate: 28.3%

POLITICAL LEADERSHIP

Governor: Michael N. Castle (R), term ends 1993

Governor's higher-education adviser: Helen K. Foss, 820 North French Street, Wilmington 19801; (302) 577-3210

U.S. Senators: Joseph R. Biden, Jr. (D), term ends 1997; William V. Roth, Jr. (R), term ends 1995

U.S. Representative:
1 Democrat, 0 Republicans
Thomas R. Carper (D)

General Assembly: Senate, 15 Democrats, 6 Republicans; House, 17 Democrats, 24 Republicans

---

COLLEGES AND UNIVERSITIES

Higher education:
Public 4-year institutions 2
Public 2-year institutions 3
Private 4-year institutions 5
Private 2-year institutions 0
Total 10

Vocational institutions: 21

Statewide coordinating board:
Delaware Postsecondary Education
 Commission
820 North French Street
Wilmington 19801
(302) 577-3240
John F. Corrozi, executive director

Private-college association:
None

Institutions censured by the AAUP:
None

Institutions under NCAA sanctions:
None

FACULTY MEMBERS

Full-time faculty members:
At public institutions 1,056
At private institutions 154

Proportion who are women:
At public institutions 34.0%
At private institutions 44.8%

Proportion with tenure:
At public institutions 60.2%
At private institutions 34.4%

Average pay of full-time professors:
At public 4-year institutions $37,624
At public 2-year institutions $29,661
At private 4-year institutions $29,951
At private 2-year institutions ... n/a

STUDENTS

Enrollment:
At public 4-year institutions . 22,328
At public 2-year institutions .. 9,317
At private 4-year institutions . 6,615
At private 2-year institutions 0
Undergraduate 34,065
 First-time freshmen 7,905
 Graduate 3,015
 Professional 1,180

DELAWARE
Continued

American Indian 68
Asian 545
Black 4,313
Hispanic 356
White 32,315
Foreign 663
Total 38,260

Enrollment highlights:
Women 57.3%
Full-time 61.5%
Minority 14.0%
Foreign 1.7%
10-year change in total
    enrollment . . . . Up 23.7%

Proportion of enrollment made up of minority students:
At public 4-year institutions . 13.0%
At public 2-year institutions . 17.8%
At private 4-year institutions 12.3%
At private 2-year institutions . . . n/a

Degrees awarded:
Associate 1,134
Bachelor's 3,485
Master's 649
Doctorate 107
Professional 284

Residence of new students: State residents made up 57% of all freshmen enrolled in Delaware; 74% of all Delaware residents who were freshmen attended college in their home state.

Test scores: Students averaged 903 on the s.a.t., which was taken by 58% of Delaware's high-school seniors.

MONEY

Average tuition and fees:
At public 4-year institutions . $2,768
At public 2-year institutions . . $882
At private 4-year institutions $5,388
At private 2-year institutions   . . . n/a

Expenditures:
Public institutions $229,377,000
Private institutions $15,855,000

State funds for higher-education operating expenses: $122,391,000
Two-year change: Up 14%

State spending on student aid:
Need-based: $1,196,000; 1,422 awards
Non–need-based: $203,000;
    194 awards
Other: $183,000

Salary of chief executive of largest public 4-year campus:
David P. Roselle, University
    of Delaware: salary n/a

Total spending on research and development by doctorate-granting universities: $37,194,000
Sources:
Federal government 45.9%
State and local governments . . 7.0%
Industry 11.0%
The institution itself 29.9%
Other 6.2%

Federal spending on education and student aid (selected programs):
Vocational and
    adult education $4,065,000
GI Bill $1,126,000
Pell Grants $28,218,000

Total federal spending on college- and university-based research and development: $15,261,000
Selected programs:
Department of Health
    and Human Services . $2,290,000
National Science
    Foundation $4,137,000

Department of Defense . $3,594,000
Department
of Agriculture $1,712,000
Department of Energy $660,000

Largest endowment:
University of Delaware $329,280,000

Top fund raiser:
University of Delaware $11,244,000

MISCELLANY

■ Goldey Beacom College is the result of a merger arranged by two Wilmington proprietary-school owners: H. S. Goldey and W. H. Beacom. The two men ran separate and competing secretarial schools until 1951, when they merged. The college became a four-year institution in 1974.

■ Widener University is in Chester, Pa., but the university has two campuses in Wilmington, Del.: Brandywine College of Widener University and the Widener University School of Law.

■ The oldest higher-education institution in the state is the University of Delaware, founded in 1833.

DISTRICT OF COLUMBIA

TRANSITION is the key word for higher education in the District of Columbia. Many campuses are either welcoming or searching for new presidents, and in some cases the changes have been difficult.

The American University was stunned early in 1990 by the resigna-

tion of President Richard Berendzen and then by revelations that he had made obscene phone calls from his office. Mr. Berendzen had been credited with increasing the university's visibility, and his departure prompted some to wonder whether the campus's gains would be reversed.

The controversy continued late into the year as students and faculty members protested a plan for the university to pay Mr. Berendzen $1-million to sever his ties to the institution.

At the University of the District of Columbia, the only public university in Washington, the Board of Trustees ousted President Rafael L. Cortada. Mr. Cortada had been feuding with the trustees and faculty members for several years. He continued a tradition of short tenures for presidents at the troubled university.

Students at the university became so fed up in the fall of 1990 that they shut down the campus with several days of protests. Washington's new Mayor, Sharon Pratt Dixon, says she agrees with the students and will appoint new trustees to manage the university.

Washington already has several new university presidents: I. King Jordan at Gallaudet, Stephen Joel Trachtenberg at George Washington, the Rev. Leo J. O'Donovan at Georgetown, and Franklyn G. Jenifer at Howard. Because Gallaudet and Howard depend on federal funds for a large part of their operating budgets, supporters of the two universities have been pleased by the rave reviews their new presidents have been receiving from Congress. Gallaudet educates deaf students and is a focal point for pride among deaf people. Howard historically has been one of the country's leading black institutions.

The universities in the district are as

DISTRICT OF COLUMBIA

Continued

diverse as those of many larger states. U.D.C. serves city residents, many of whom are not well prepared for college. The private colleges are much wealthier and tend to serve students from elsewhere.

The only public higher-education board is the Board of Trustees of U.D.C. The Mayor's office acts as a coordinating board. In addition, many of the college leaders have informal relationships with public and private institutions in Washington's Maryland and Virginia suburbs.

DEMOGRAPHICS

Population: 604,000 (Rank: 48)

Age distribution:
Up to 17	23.0%
18 to 24	10.3%
25 to 34	19.5%
35 and older	47.2%

Racial and ethnic distribution:
American Indian	0.2%
Asian	1.1%
Black	70.3%
White	27.4%
Other and unknown	1.1%
Hispanic (may be any race)	2.8%

Educational attainment of adults:
At least 4 years of high school 67.1%
At least 1 to 3 years of college 41.5%
At least 4 years of college ... 27.5%

Per-capita personal income: $23,491

New high-school graduates in:
1990-91 (estimate)	4,153
2000-01 (estimate)	4,164

New GED diploma recipients: 575

High-school dropout rate: 41.8%

POLITICAL LEADERSHIP

Mayor: Sharon Pratt Dixon (D)

Mayor's higher-education adviser: n/a

U.S. Senators: None

U.S. Representative:
Delegate Eleanor Holmes Norton (D); non-voting

Legislature: n/a

COLLEGES AND UNIVERSITIES

Higher education:
Public 4-year institutions	2
Public 2-year institutions	0
Private 4-year institutions	15
Private 2-year institutions	0
Total	17

Vocational institutions: 31

Statewide coordinating board:
Office of Postsecondary Education Research and Assistance
2100 Martin Luther King Avenue, S.E.
Suite 401
Washington 20020
(202) 727-3685
Eloise C. Turner, chief

Private-college association:
Consortium of Universities of the Washington Metropolitan Area
1717 Massachusetts Avenue, N.W.
Suite 101
Washington 20036
(202) 265-1313
Monte P. Shepler, president

Institution censured by the AAUP:
Catholic University of America

Institutions under NCAA sanctions:
None

FACULTY MEMBERS

Full-time faculty members:
At public institutions 553
At private institutions 2,616

Proportion who are women:
At public institutions 36.5%
At private institutions 30.7%

Proportion with tenure:
At public institutions .... n/a
At private institutions 63.1%

Average pay of full-time professors:
At public 4-year institutions $36,743
At public 2-year institutions .... n/a
At private 4-year institutions $39,490
At private 2-year institutions ... n/a

STUDENTS

Enrollment:
At public 4-year institutions . 12,108
At public 2-year institutions 0
At private 4-year institutions   66,981
At private 2-year institutions 0
Undergraduate 48,469
  First-time freshmen 9,750
Graduate 22,183
Professional 8,437
American Indian 134
Asian 2,494
Black 23,926
Hispanic 2,114
White 41,348
Foreign 9,073
Total 79,089

Enrollment highlights:
Women 52.9%
Full-time 62.1%

Minority 40.9%
Foreign 11.5%
10-year change in total
  enrollment .... Down 3.3%

**Proportion of enrollment made up
of minority students:**
At public 4-year institutions . 94.6%
At public 2-year institutions .... n/a
At private 4-year institutions   30.8%
At private 2-year institutions ... n/a

Degrees awarded:
Associate 391
Bachelor's 6,933
Master's 5,126
Doctorate 542
Professional 2,437

Residence of new students: Residents made up 18% of all freshmen enrolled in the District of Columbia; 50% of all District of Columbia residents who were freshmen attended college in the District.

Test scores: Students averaged 850 on the s.a.t., which was taken by 68% of the District of Columbia's high-school seniors.

MONEY

Average tuition and fees:
At public 4-year institutions .. $664
At public 2-year institutions .... n/a
At private 4-year institutions $9,489
At private 2-year institutions ... n/a

Expenditures:
Public institutions $88,462,000
Private institutions . $1,307,377,000

**State funds for higher-education
operating expenses:** n/a

Two-year change: n/a

DISTRICT
OF COLUMBIA

Continued

State spending on student aid:
Need-based: $1,069,000; 790 awards
Non–need-based: None
Other: None

**Salary of chief executive
of largest public 4-year campus:**
Miles Mark Fisher, IV (interim),
   University of the District of
   Columbia: $89,816

**Total spending on research and
development by doctorate-granting
universities:** $114,297,000

Sources:
Federal government 74.0%
Local government 0.4%
Industry 6.5%
The institution itself 14.2%
Other 4.9%

**Federal spending on education
and student aid (selected programs):**
Vocational and
   adult education $4,112,000
GI Bill $807,000
Pell Grants $13,008,000

**Total federal spending on college-
and university-based research
and development:** $72,668,000

Selected programs:
Department of Health
   and Human Services $43,850,000
National Science
   Foundation $4,612,000
Department of Defense $12,928,000
Department
   of Agriculture $921,000
Department of Energy .. $1,112,000

Largest endowment:
George Washington
   University $265,772,000

Top fund raisers:
Georgetown University $30,115,000
George Washington
   University $17,834,000
Howard University $8,860,000

MISCELLANY

■ Howard University houses the
Moorland-Spingarn Research Center,
widely recognized as the largest re-
pository of materials documenting the
history of people of African descent.

■ George Washington University
enrolled foreign students from more
nations than any other institution in
the country in 1989-90, with its 2,207
international students coming from
125 different countries. American
University ranked a close second,
with 1,382 foreign students from 123
nations.

■ George Washington University
plans to give $7-million in scholar-
ships to District of Columbia public-
school students whom it admits between 1990 and 2000. The institution
expects to award 50 such scholarships
in the 10-year period. It estimates that
total costs will average about $35,000
per student per year over the decade.

■ The oldest institution of higher
education in the District of Columbia
is Georgetown University, a Roman
Catholic institution founded in 1789.
First called Georgetown College, it
became a university in 1815 when it
received the first university charter
granted by the federal government.
Georgetown's colors are blue and
gray, representing the unification of
the North and South after the Civil
War.

FLORIDA

LORIDA faces some daunting challenges in the 1990's. Because of its staggering growth, the state's 28 community colleges are jammed and many of its nine public universities have raised admissions standards to control enrollment.

The growth in student population has not been matched by a growth in financial support from the state. Higher-education officials expect, however, that the pressing demands for more money will soon force the state to raise taxes.

The new Democratic Governor, Lawton Chiles, a former U.S. Senator, is considered more amenable to a tax increase than was the Republican he defeated, Bob Martinez. Mr. Martinez served one term.

If the state had more money, higher-education officials say, their institutions would fare well. The Legislature has generally supported increases for college and university operations and has created several programs through which state funds are provided to match private donations for endowed chairs or new facilities.

Private colleges, many of which are less well established than their public counterparts, have complained that such programs hurt their own fund-raising efforts. But several of the private institutions—particularly the University of Miami, with its prestigious medical school—have also benefited from contracts with the state to provide programs that public institutions do not offer.

The Legislature is known for taking a more-than-casual interest in higher-education issues, at times using its budget authority to focus on such concerns as undergraduate education. At other times, lawmakers have been known to use a budget bill to provide a university job for a departing colleague. Several legislators work for private and public colleges, prompting increased concern about the potential for conflicts of interest.

As might be expected in such a large and diverse state, ethnic and regional issues are important in politics. Although Florida has recently begun pumping more money into academic programs in the Miami and Fort Lauderdale areas, politicians and higher-education leaders in fast-growing south and central Florida complain that state financing still favors the older institutions, the University of Florida and Florida State University, in the north.

Florida's basic-skills test, a prerequisite for graduating from community college or enrolling in junior- or senior-level college classes, has also been controversial, particularly after state education officials predicted that a disproportionate number of black and Hispanic students would fail the test once the passing score was raised. In response, the state postponed raising the score on part of the test and provided institutions with more money to establish remedial classes for students unprepared to pass the examination.

The Postsecondary Education Planning Commission is the statewide coordinating board, but most of the power lies with the Legislature, the Board of Regents for the nine universities, and the elected Cabinet, which includes an Education Commissioner. There is also a Board of Community Colleges, but the boards at the individual institutions enjoy much control over the operations of their institutions.

FLORIDA
Continued

DEMOGRAPHICS

Population: 12,671,000   (Rank: 4)

Age distribution:
Up to 17 .... 22.7%
18 to 24 .... 9.4%
25 to 34 .... 15.5%
35 and older 52.4%

Racial and ethnic distribution:
American Indian 0.3%
Asian 0.6%
Black 13.8%
White 84.0%
Other and unknown 1.3%
Hispanic (may be any race) .. 8.8%

Educational attainment of adults:
At least 4 years of high school 66.7%
At least 1 to 3 years of college 31.6%
At least 4 years of college ... 14.9%

Per-capita personal income: $17,647

New high-school graduates in:
1990-91 (estimate) 96,266
2000-01 (estimate) 133,351

New GED diploma recipients: 25,279

High-school dropout rate: 42.0%

POLITICAL LEADERSHIP

Governor: Lawton Chiles (D), term ends 1995

Governor's higher-education adviser: n/a

U.S. Senators: Bob Graham (D), term ends 1993; Connie Mack (R), term ends 1995

U.S. Representatives:
9 Democrats, 10 Republicans
Jim Bacchus (D), Charles E. Bennett (D), Michael Bilirakis (R), Dante B. Fascell (D), Sam Gibbons (D), Porter J. Goss (R), Earl Hutto (D), Andy Ireland (R), Craig T. James (R), Harry Johnston (D), William Lehman (D), Tom Lewis (R), Bill McCollum (R), Pete Peterson (D), Ileana Ros-Lehtinen (R), E. Clay Shaw, Jr. (R), Lawrence J. Smith (D), Cliff Stearns (R), C.W. Bill Young (R)

Legislature: Senate, 23 Democrats, 17 Republicans; House, 74 Democrats, 46 Republicans

COLLEGES AND UNIVERSITIES

Higher education:
Public 4-year institutions 10
Public 2-year institutions 28
Private 4-year institutions 43
Private 2-year institutions 14
Total 95

Vocational institutions: 320

Statewide coordinating board:
Postsecondary Education
  Planning Commission
Florida Education Center
Tallahassee 32399
(904) 488-7894
William Proctor, executive director

Private-college association:
Independent Colleges
  and Universities of Florida
5005 Central Avenue
St. Petersburg 33710
(813) 321-2258
George P. Russell, executive director

Institution censured by the AAUP:
Saint Leo College

Institutions under NCAA sanctions:
Florida A&M University, University of Florida

FACULTY MEMBERS

Full-time faculty members:
At public institutions 7,223
At private institutions 2,363

Proportion who are women:
At public institutions 29.5%
At private institutions 25.1%

Proportion with tenure:
At public institutions 68.7%
At private institutions 53.8%

Average pay of full-time professors:
At public 4-year institutions $37,552
At public 2-year institutions $31,066
At private 4-year institutions $31,544
At private 2-year institutions $21,980

STUDENTS

Enrollment:
At public 4-year institutions 157,549
At public 2-year institutions 262,829
At private 4-year institutions 90,055
At private 2-year institutions . 5,157
Undergraduate 460,804
First-time freshmen 77,570
Graduate 47,589
Professional 7,197
American Indian 1,509
Asian 9,331
Black 48,396
Hispanic 54,513
White 386,687
Foreign 15,154
Total 515,590

Enrollment highlights:
Women 54.5%
Full-time 49.0%
Minority 22.7%

Foreign 2.9%
10-year change in total
enrollment .... Up 36.7%

Proportion of enrollment made up of minority students:
At public 4-year institutions . 20.2%
At public 2-year institutions . 23.3%
At private 4-year institutions 24.6%
At private 2-year institutions 40.1%

Degrees awarded:
Associate 30,661
Bachelor's 32,345
Master's 9,828
Doctorate 1,200
Professional 2,046

Residence of new students: State residents made up 78% of all freshmen enrolled in Florida; 83% of all Florida residents who were freshmen attended college in their home state.

Test scores: Students averaged 884 on the s.a.t., which was taken by 44% of Florida's high-school seniors.

MONEY

Average tuition and fees:
At public 4-year institutions .... n/a
At public 2-year institutions .. $729
At private 4-year institutions $7,153
At private 2-year institutions $5,519

Expenditures:
Public institutions .. $1,782,180,000
Private institutions ... $723,270,000

State funds for higher-education operating expenses: $1,632,302,000
Two-year change: Up 11%

State spending on student aid:
Need-based: $21,700,000;
21,563 awards

FLORIDA
Continued

Non–need-based: $34,613,000;
23,060 awards
Other: None

**Salary of chief executive
of largest public 4-year campus:**
John V. Lombardi, University
of Florida: $185,000

**Total spending on research and
development by doctorate-granting
universities:** $385,556,000
Sources:
Federal government 51.9%
State and local governments .. 6.7%
Industry 5.4%
The institution itself 29.3%
Other 6.8%

**Federal spending on education
and student aid (selected programs):**
Vocational and
    adult education $34,453,000
GI Bill $34,227,000
Pell Grants $214,107,000

**Total federal spending on college-
and university-based research
and development:** $185,626,000
Selected programs:
Department of Health
    and Human Services $81,003,000
National Science
    Foundation $19,671,000
Department of Defense $44,823,000
Department
    of Agriculture $8,062,000
Department of Energy . $19,236,000

Largest endowment:
University of Florida
    Foundation $198,207,000

Top fund raisers:
University of Miami ... $62,816,000
University of Florida .. $58,677,000
University of South
    Florida $14,863,000

MISCELLANY

■ Every year Rollins College declares a surprise campus holiday—
called Fox Day—on which classes are
canceled and a cement fox statue is
planted on the campus quadrangle.

■ Students at Miami-Dade Community College who enrolled in fall 1990
in programs in health sciences, graphic arts, funeral services, or police
training will get their tuition and fee
payments back if they can't find jobs
in their fields after graduation. Em-
ployers in the four fields are having
difficulty finding qualified employees
in Dade County.

■ Florida Atlantic University is
providing every black freshman with a
scholarship that amounts to free tuition for the next four years.

■ Students at Eckerd College don't
have to leave Fido at home. The college has set aside two residence halls
where students can live with their
pets.

■ Miami-Dade Community College
is believed to be the first community
college to establish endowed chairs
for its faculty members.

■ Floridians disagree about which
institution of higher education is the
oldest. Some cite Florida State University, which was founded in 1851 as
Seminary West of the Suwannee but
did not offer college-level classes until
1857. Others name the University of

Florida, founded in 1853. Rollins College, founded in 1885, says it is the first institution to be chartered as an "institution of higher learning," not as a seminary or a prep school.

GEORGIA

J OE FRANK HARRIS, a Democrat, made public-school reform the cornerstone of his eight years as Governor. Higher-education officials are counting on his successor, Zell Miller, to make improving the state's university system a top priority.

Mr. Miller, a Democrat and the former Lieutenant Governor, has a simple but ambitious goal: He wants the University System of Georgia to become the standard by which other public universities measure themselves.

Mr. Miller wants to establish a higher-education capital-and-equipment trust fund; increase the number of scholarship programs; formalize Atlanta's research quadrangle, which is anchored by Emory University and the three public universities in the Atlanta area; and raise faculty salaries.

In the meantime, higher-education officials are looking at other ways to make their salary-and-benefits packages more attractive to prospective faculty members. The University System of Georgia won legislative authorization to offer new faculty members the option of either joining a national pension plan or participating in the state teachers' retirement system, which requires an employee to serve 10 years before qualifying for benefits.

Led by the Board of Regents, the governing and coordinating body for all public colleges, many of Georgia's institutions have raised admission standards, attracted top faculty members, and started new research programs in the last few years. State financial support has been good, and reforms at the state's public schools have produced students who are better prepared for college than many of their predecessors.

Racial issues, however, continue to plague the university system. Although the U.S. Department of Education has declared that Georgia's public colleges are no longer segregated, black students still do not enroll or graduate in numbers proportionate to their share of the population as a whole. The public black colleges have complained that state policies limit their enrollments and missions.

On the other hand, Georgia is home to some of the nation's finest private black colleges, and they have been thriving in recent years. Helped by major gifts and a rising applicant pool, institutions such as Morehouse and Spelman Colleges have been gaining in national stature.

Private higher education is by no means limited to black colleges. Georgia has many small, church-related colleges. In addition, Emory University offers nationally respected research programs and attracts much notice for the programs sponsored by the Jimmy Carter Presidential Library.

DEMOGRAPHICS

Population: 6,436,000   (Rank: 11)

Age distribution:

Up to 17	27.9%
18 to 24	11.3%
25 to 34	17.6%
35 and older	43.2%

GEORGIA

Continued

Racial and ethnic distribution:
American Indian 0.2%
Asian 0.5%
Black 26.8%
White 72.3%
Other and unknown 0.2%
Hispanic (may be any race) .. 1.1%

Educational attainment of adults:
At least 4 years of high school 56.4%
At least 1 to 3 years of college 27.9%
At least 4 years of college ... 14.6%

Per-capita personal income: $16,053

New high-school graduates in:
1990-91 (estimate) 65,017
2000-01 (estimate) 74,370

New GED diploma recipients: 12,686

High-school dropout rate: 39.0%

POLITICAL LEADERSHIP

Governor: Zell Miller (D), term ends 1995

Governor's higher-education adviser: n/a

U.S. Senators: Wyche Fowler, Jr. (D), term ends 1993; Sam Nunn (D), term ends 1997

U.S. Representatives:
9 Democrats, 1 Republican
Doug Barnard, Jr. (D), George (Buddy) Darden (D), Newt Gingrich (R), Charles Hatcher (D), Ed Jenkins (D), Ben Jones (D), John Lewis (D), Richard Ray (D), J. Roy Rowland (D), Lindsay Thomas (D)

General Assembly: Senate, 45 Democrats, 11 Republicans; House, 145 Democrats, 35 Republicans

---

COLLEGES AND UNIVERSITIES

Higher education:
Public 4-year institutions 19
Public 2-year institutions 28
Private 4-year institutions 32
Private 2-year institutions 16
Total 95

Vocational institutions: 137

Statewide coordinating board:
Board of Regents
University System of Georgia
244 Washington Street, S.W.
Atlanta 30334
(404) 656-2203
H. Dean Propst, chancellor

Private-college association:
Association of Private Colleges
and Universities in Georgia
945 East Paces Ferry Road
Suite 1730
Atlanta 30326
(404) 233-5434
William W. Kelly, executive director

Institutions censured by the AAUP:
None

Institutions under NCAA sanctions:
None

FACULTY MEMBERS

Full-time faculty members:
At public institutions 5,136
At private institutions 1,772

Proportion who are women:
At public institutions 32.3%
At private institutions 32.7%

Proportion with tenure:
At public institutions 63.8%
At private institutions 49.5%

Average pay of full-time professors:
At public 4-year institutions $35,342
At public 2-year institutions $28,176
At private 4-year institutions $30,538
At private 2-year institutions $21,346

STUDENTS

Enrollment:
At public 4-year institutions 129,692
At public 2-year institutions . 48,159
At private 4-year institutions 42,560
At private 2-year institutions 10,351
Undergraduate 196,276
First-time freshmen 50,668
Graduate 27,041
Professional 7,445
American Indian 428
Asian 3,237
Black 43,029
Hispanic 2,336
White 176,235
Foreign 5,497
Total 230,762

Enrollment highlights:
Women 53.4%
Full-time 66.4%
Minority 21.8%
Foreign 2.4%
10-year change in total
enrollment .... Up 32.0%

Proportion of enrollment made up of minority students:
At public 4-year institutions . 17.2%
At public 2-year institutions . 20.7%
At private 4-year institutions 33.5%
At private 2-year institutions 36.6%

Degrees awarded:
Associate 6,653
Bachelor's 19,481

Master's 5,883
Doctorate 737
Professional 1,875

Residence of new students: State residents made up 80% of all freshmen enrolled in Georgia; 83% of all Georgia residents who were freshmen attended college in their home state.

Test scores: Students averaged 844 on the S.A.T., which was taken by 57% of Georgia's high-school seniors.

MONEY

Average tuition and fees:
At public 4-year institutions . $1,631
At public 2-year institutions .. $852
At private 4-year institutions $7,076
At private 2-year institutions $3,194

Expenditures:
Public institutions .. $1,255,964,000
Private institutions ... $696,734,000

State funds for higher-education operating expenses: $961,283,000
Two-year change: Up 18%

State spending on student aid:
Need-based: $5,005,000;
14,099 awards
Non–need-based: $15,810,000;
16,042 awards
Other: $1,458,000

Salary of chief executive of largest public 4-year campus:
Charles B. Knapp, University
of Georgia: $132,000 from state
plus $16,000 from private donations

Total spending on research and development by doctorate-granting universities: $417,287,000
Sources:
Federal government 49.0%

GEORGIA
Continued

State and local governments .. 9.6%
Industry 8.5%
The institution itself 30.0%
Other 2.9%

**Federal spending on education
and student aid (selected programs):**
Vocational and
  adult education $22,892,000
GI Bill $19,786,000
Pell Grants $72,304,000

**Total federal spending on college-
and university-based research
and development:** $165,293,000

Selected programs:
Department of Health
  and Human Services $73,544,000
National Science
  Foundation $12,922,000
Department of Defense $48,483,000
Department
  of Agriculture $9,444,000
Department of Energy . $11,184,000

Largest endowment:
Emory University $923,612,000

Top fund raisers:
Emory University $31,703,000
Georgia Institute
  of Technology $25,513,000
University of Georgia . $20,629,000

MISCELLANY

■ Merian Randall, a 31-year-old mother of three children, in 1990 became the first non-traditional student to be crowned homecoming queen at Georgia State University.

■ Both the University of Georgia and the University of North Carolina claim to be the oldest public university in the country.

■ The University of Georgia library holds nearly 60,000 pieces of material about the author of *Gone With the Wind,* Margaret Mitchell.

■ The oldest institution of higher education in the state is the University of Georgia, founded in 1785.

HAWAII

WITH a flourishing, tourism-based economy to feed them, Hawaii's colleges and universities have been adept at putting their locale to good use in their academic and research programs.

But the geography of the 1,500-mile archipelago also can be a burden: The University of Hawaii System is called upon to satisfy a wide variety of educational demands for the many students who cannot travel outside the state for higher education.

Occasionally strains develop as college leaders attempt to balance community demands for a full range of educational services at each of the three main campuses against the Legislature's calls for savings through reductions in duplicative programs. (The university system is governed by a single Board of Regents and also includes six community colleges.)

The university is known for its programs in marine biology, geology, and tropical environments. Its astronomy programs have won international acclaim, due in large part to the university's owning land at the summit on Mauna Kea, considered one of the best sites in the world for ground-based telescopes.

The university has also been a leader in Pacific Rim studies, which examine the cultures, economies, and histories of the nations that border the Pacific Ocean. The university's proximity to those nations has helped it attract students and scholars from many Asian countries, adding to the islands' already-rich ethnic mix. Gov. John Waihee, III, a Democrat who was re-elected in November 1990 to a second term, has been a strong supporter of the university's science programs and its efforts to recruit more minority and disadvantaged students.

DEMOGRAPHICS

Population: 1,112,000   (Rank: 39)

Age distribution:
Up to 17 .... 25.8%
18 to 24 .... 11.4%
25 to 34 .... 17.6%
35 and older 45.1%

Racial and ethnic distribution:
American Indian 0.3%
Asian 61.2%
Black 1.8%
White 34.4%
Other and unknown 2.3%
Hispanic (may be any race) .. 7.4%

Educational attainment of adults:
At least 4 years of high school 73.8%
At least 1 to 3 years of college 38.8%
At least 4 years of college ... 20.3%

Per-capita personal income: $18,472

New high-school graduates in:
1990-91 (estimate) 11,781
2000-01 (estimate) 13,133

New GED diploma recipients: 1,271

High-school dropout rate: 30.9%

POLITICAL LEADERSHIP

Governor: John Waihee, III (D), term ends 1995

Governor's higher-education adviser: Patricia Brandt, State Capitol, Room 410, Honolulu 96813; (808) 548-3031

U.S. Senators: Daniel K. Akaka (D), term ends 1997; Daniel K. Inouye (D), term ends 1993

U.S. Representatives:
2 Democrats, 0 Republicans
Neil Abercrombie (D), Patsy Mink (D)

Legislature: Senate, 22 Democrats, 3 Republicans; House, 45 Democrats, 6 Republicans

COLLEGES AND UNIVERSITIES

Higher education:
Public 4-year institutions 3
Public 2-year institutions 6
Private 4-year institutions 5
Private 2-year institutions 0
Total 14

Vocational institutions: 35

Statewide coordinating board:
University of Hawaii Board
   of Regents
Bachman Hall, Room 209
2444 Dole Street
Honolulu 96822
(808) 956-8213
Albert J. Simone, president

Private-college association:
None

HAWAII
Continued

Institutions censured by the AAUP:
None

Institutions under NCAA sanctions:
None

FACULTY MEMBERS

Full-time faculty members:
At public institutions 1,494
At private institutions 95

Proportion who are women:
At public institutions 29.5%
At private institutions 42.1%

Proportion with tenure:
At public institutions 66.6%
At private institutions 34.4%

Average pay of full-time professors:
At public 4-year institutions $38,449
At public 2-year institutions $31,526
At private 4-year institutions $22,900
At private 2-year institutions ... n/a

STUDENTS

Enrollment:
At public 4-year institutions . 22,550
At public 2-year institutions . 19,979
At private 4-year institutions . 9,768
At private 2-year institutions 0
Undergraduate 46,080
    First-time freshmen 8,405
Graduate 5,785
Professional 432
American Indian 194
Asian 31,008
Black 957
Hispanic 844
White 15,700
Foreign 3,594
Total 52,297

Enrollment highlights:
Women 53.1%
Full-time 57.8%
Minority 67.8%
Foreign 6.9%
10-year change in total
    enrollment .... Up 10.0%

Proportion of enrollment made up of minority students:
At public 4-year institutions . 70.9%
At public 2-year institutions . 74.3%
At private 4-year institutions 42.7%
At private 2-year institutions ... n/a

Degrees awarded:
Associate 2,309
Bachelor's 3,724
Master's 969
Doctorate 116
Professional 126

Residence of new students: State residents made up 88% of all freshmen enrolled in Hawaii; 77% of all Hawaii residents who were freshmen attended college in their home state.

Test scores: Students averaged 885 on the s.a.t., which was taken by 52% of Hawaii's high-school seniors.

MONEY

Average tuition and fees:
At public 4-year institutions . $1,293
At public 2-year institutions .. $410
At private 4-year institutions $4,008
At private 2-year institutions ... n/a

Expenditures:
Public institutions $312,248,000
Private institutions $20,964,000

State funds for higher-education operating expenses: $297,625,000
Two-year change: Up 11%

State spending on student aid:
Need-based: $755,000; 900 awards
Non–need-based: None
Other: $5,198,000

**Salary of chief executive
of largest public 4-year campus:**
Albert J. Simone, University
of Hawaii at Manoa: $95,000

**Total spending on research and
development by doctorate-granting
universities:** $70,733,000
Sources:
Federal government 57.4%
State and local governments . 35.0%
Industry 1.1%
The institution itself 5.2%
Other 1.3%

**Federal spending on education
and student aid (selected programs):**
Vocational and
    adult education $4,148,000
GI Bill $4,212,000
Pell Grants $7,454,000

**Total federal spending on college-
and university-based research
and development:** $39,651,000

Selected programs:
Department of Health
    and Human Services . $7,572,000
National Science
    Foundation $9,881,000
Department of Defense . $2,140,000
Department
    of Agriculture $3,666,000
Department of Energy .. $1,712,000

Largest endowment:
University of Hawaii .. $49,941,000

Top fund raisers:
University of Hawaii ... $8,200,000
Chaminade University
    of Honolulu $590,000

MISCELLANY

■ One of the University of Hawaii's public two-year colleges is named Leeward Community College; another is named Windward Community College.

■ The East-West Center, adjacent to the University of Hawaii's Manoa campus, was established by Congress in 1960 "to promote better relations and understanding between the United States and the nations of Asia and the Pacific through cooperative study, training, and research."

■ The oldest institution of higher education in Hawaii is the University of Hawaii at Manoa, founded in 1907.

IDAHO

MOST Idaho residents favor spending more money on education, according to a survey conducted by Boise State University. The big question is whether the legislators and Governor will be able to reach agreement on that or any other issue.

This Rocky Mountain state was in the national spotlight in 1990 because the Legislature passed what would have been the nation's most restrictive state abortion law. But half an hour after the Republican-dominated Legislature adjourned, Democratic Gov. Cecil D. Andrus vetoed the bill. As activists on both sides of the issue marshaled their forces, the controversy led to 20 contested primary races and a heated gubernatorial campaign.

IDAHO

Continued

Although Governor Andrus was re-elected last fall, some observers worry that differences over abortion will make it difficult for politicians to cooperate on other issues, such as higher education.

If Idaho's politicians and residents are ready to focus on higher-education financing after the election, the state's recent economic upswing may make it possible to put dollars behind campaign promises of more support. Higher-education officials say more money is essential.

In the 1980's the three mainstays of Idaho's economy—mining, timber, and agriculture—experienced sharp downturns. As a result, the colleges have been trying to maintain quality programs under financial conditions so uncertain that institutions have feared for their accreditation.

Both Governor Andrus and key legislators have been pushing for more funds for Idaho's colleges. Higher-education officials have welcomed the attention but have sometimes been caught in the middle of debates between Mr. Andrus and the Legislature about which branch of government was doing more for education.

Idaho has one board for coordinating and governing all levels of education. It is called the State Board of Education when it is dealing with elementary and secondary schools and the Board of Regents when dealing with colleges and universities.

DEMOGRAPHICS

Population: 1,014,000   (Rank: 42)

Age distribution:

Up to 17 .... 30.0%
18 to 24 .... 10.4%
25 to 34 .... 16.6%
35 and older 43.1%

Racial and ethnic distribution:

American Indian 1.1%
Asian 0.7%
Black 0.3%
White 95.8%
Other and unknown 2.1%
Hispanic (may be any race) .. 3.9%

Educational attainment of adults:

At least 4 years of high school 73.7%
At least 1 to 3 years of college 37.2%
At least 4 years of college ... 15.8%

Per-capita personal income: $13,707

New high-school graduates in:

1990-91 (estimate) 11,707
2000-01 (estimate) 10,885

New GED diploma recipients: 813

High-school dropout rate: 24.6%

POLITICAL LEADERSHIP

Governor: Cecil D. Andrus (D), term ends 1995

Governor's higher-education adviser: Jeff Shinn, State House, Room 122, Boise 83720; (208) 334-3138

U.S. Senators: Larry E. Craig (R), term ends 1997; Steve Symms (R), term ends 1993

U.S. Representatives:
2 Democrats, 0 Republicans
Larry LaRocco (D), Richard H. Stallings (D)

Legislature: Senate, 21 Democrats, 21 Republicans; House, 27 Democrats, 57 Republicans

COLLEGES AND UNIVERSITIES

Higher education:
Public 4-year institutions 4
Public 2-year institutions 2

Private 4-year institutions 3
Private 2-year institutions 2

Total 11

Vocational institutions: 39

Statewide coordinating board:
State Board of Education
650 West State Street, Room 307
Boise 83720
(208) 334-2270
Rayburn Barton, executive director
for higher education

Private-college association:
None

Institutions censured by the AAUP:
None

Institutions under NCAA sanctions:
None

FACULTY MEMBERS

Full-time faculty members:
At public institutions 1,195
At private institutions 117

Proportion who are women:
At public institutions 25.4%
At private institutions 21.4%

Proportion with tenure:
At public institutions 63.1%
At private institutions 51.0%

Average pay of full-time professors:
At public 4-year institutions $31,846
At public 2-year institutions $27,348
At private 4-year institutions $25,966
At private 2-year institutions ... n/a

STUDENTS

Enrollment:
At public 4-year institutions . 29,779
At public 2-year institutions .. 5,340
At private 4-year institutions . 2,460
At private 2-year institutions . 8,138
Undergraduate 40,161
   First-time freshmen 10,282
Graduate 5,123
Professional 433
American Indian 373
Asian 541
Black 280
Hispanic 653
White 42,695
Foreign 1,175
Total 45,717

Enrollment highlights:
Women 52.7%
Full-time 68.8%
Minority 4.1%
Foreign 2.6%
10-year change in total
   enrollment .... Up 16.5%

**Proportion of enrollment made up
of minority students:**
At public 4-year institutions .. 4.7%
At public 2-year institutions .. 3.5%
At private 4-year institutions . 3.6%
At private 2-year institutions . 2.7%

Degrees awarded:
Associate 2,600
Bachelor's 3,043
Master's 703
Doctorate 63
Professional 71

Residence of new students: State residents made up 59% of all freshmen enrolled in Idaho; 78% of all Idaho residents who were freshmen attended college in their home state.

IDAHO

Continued

Test scores: Students averaged 19.1 on the A.C.T., which was taken by 58% of Idaho's high-school seniors.

MONEY

Average tuition and fees:
At public 4-year institutions . $1,119
At public 2-year institutions .. $779
At private 4-year institutions $6,669
At private 2-year institutions $1,400

Expenditures:
Public institutions $238,438,000
Private institutions $49,768,000

State funds for higher-education operating expenses: $183,997,000

Two-year change: Up 27%

State spending on student aid:
Need-based: $491,000; 900 awards
Non–need-based: $147,000; 98 awards
Other: None

Salary of chief executive of largest public 4-year campus:
John H. Keiser, Boise State
    University: $96,900

Total spending on research and development by doctorate-granting universities: $33,191,000

Sources:
Federal government 37.9%
State and local governments . 24.4%
Industry 12.7%
The institution itself 24.5%
Other 0.4%

Federal spending on education and student aid (selected programs):
Vocational and
    adult education $4,147,000

GI Bill $3,397,000
Pell Grants $27,660,000

Total federal spending on college- and university-based research and development: $8,647,000

Selected programs:
Department of Health
    and Human Services ... $943,000
National Science
    Foundation $748,000
Department of Defense ... $239,000
Department
    of Agriculture $3,693,000
Department of Energy $735,000

Largest endowment:
University of Idaho ... $35,000,000

Top fund raisers:
Boise State University .. $2,489,000
Northwest Nazarene
    College $2,167,000
College of Idaho $1,498,000

MISCELLANY

■ The College of Southern Idaho is the only two-year college in the state that runs a museum—the Herrett Museum. It houses about 5,000 prehistoric artifacts from North, Central, and South America. The collection includes items from the Maya and Inca civilizations, as well as some 12,000-year-old tools from the Clovis culture.

■ Idaho State University attracts thousands of rodeo fans every spring when it holds the Dodge National Circuit Finals Rodeo in its Minidome. The event—sponsored by the Professional Rodeo Circuit Association—brings cowboys and cowgirls from across the country to compete for the championship.

■ Boise State University claims to

be the only institution in the country that uses a synthetic football field that isn't green. It's blue.

■ The oldest institution of higher education in Idaho is Ricks College, a Mormon institution founded in 1888.

ILLINOIS

HIGHER education in Illinois is rarely removed from politics, a situation that both helps and hinders colleges and universities.

These days, for example, the public institutions are tasting the fruits of their political labors: generous budget increases thanks to a special, two-year income-tax surcharge. The tax had been sought for several years, but passed only after Chicago city officials and legislators pressured legislative leaders to enact it so they too could receive some money.

Traditionally, however, higher-education policy making has been affected by regional and institutional political rivalries—the result of the decentralized nature of public-college governance. Although there is a Board of Higher Education, which serves as a coordinating board, five separate governing boards manage colleges across the state, and the systems frequently compete against each other for money and students.

Historically, the leader in that competition is the University of Illinois's flagship campus at Urbana-Champaign, one of the nation's leading public research universities. But institutions elsewhere in the state have become more aggressive in their pursuit

of financing, often recruiting their local legislators to help them.

Illinois is also home to the City Colleges of Chicago, a money-starved system of eight community colleges that serve some of the neediest students in the nation. Plagued for years by high dropout rates and low public support, the system is beginning to gain credibility with politicians by reducing its budget and increasing the number of students taking college-level courses.

The infusion of new money from the tax surcharge has tamed college rivalries of late, but the tax is due to expire in 1991. Public-college leaders have reason to hope it will be extended, since the new Governor, Jim Edgar, a Republican, campaigned on a risky pledge to continue the tax. He defeated a candidate who opposed doing so.

Another higher-education issue is how best to serve the graduate and professional needs of the Chicago suburbs, which are home to many high-technology companies and the Argonne and Fermi National Laboratories. The area has historically been served by private institutions, such as the Illinois Institute of Technology, but now regional public universities, among them Northern Illinois University and the Chicago branch of the University of Illinois, are eager to extend their presence there. The state is considering building a new facility in the area for use by public and private institutions, but private colleges have opposed it, saying it would be a needless expenditure of public funds.

Private institutions in Illinois are diverse. The state is home to national research institutions like the University of Chicago and Northwestern University as well as such small liberal-arts colleges as North Central and Rockford Colleges. Chicago is also a

ILLINOIS
Continued

center for Catholic higher education, with De Paul and Loyola Universities, the Catholic Theological Union, and Montay and Saint Xavier Colleges.

In general, the private colleges have enjoyed good relations with the state.

DEMOGRAPHICS

Population: 11,658,000   (Rank: 6)

Age distribution:
Up to 17	25.6%
18 to 24	10.5%
25 to 34	17.9%
35 and older	46.0%

Racial and ethnic distribution:
American Indian	0.2%
Asian	1.5%
Black	14.7%
White	81.1%
Other and unknown	2.6%
Hispanic (may be any race)	5.6%

Educational attainment of adults:
At least 4 years of high school	66.5%
At least 1 to 3 years of college	31.4%
At least 4 years of college	16.2%

Per-capita personal income: $18,824

New high-school graduates in:
1990-91 (estimate)	116,539
2000-01 (estimate)	113,383

New GED diploma recipients: 16,281

High-school dropout rate: 24.4%

POLITICAL LEADERSHIP

Governor: Jim Edgar (R), term ends 1995

Governor's higher-education adviser: n/a

U.S. Senators: Alan J. Dixon (D), term ends 1993; Paul Simon (D), term ends 1997

U.S. Representatives:
15 Democrats, 7 Republicans
Frank Annunzio (D), Terry L. Bruce (D), Cardiss Collins (D), Jerry F. Costello (D), John W. Cox, Jr. (D), Philip M. Crane (R), Richard J. Durbin (D), Lane Evans (D), Harris W. Fawell (R), J. Dennis Hastert (R), Charles A. Hayes (D), Henry J. Hyde (R), William O. Lipinski (D), Edward R. Madigan (R), Robert H. Michel (R), John Edward Porter (R), Glenn Poshard (D), Dan Rostenkowski (D), Marty Russo (D), George E. Sangmeister (D), Gus Savage (D), Sidney R. Yates (D)

General Assembly: Senate, 31 Democrats, 28 Republicans; House, 72 Democrats, 46 Republicans

---

COLLEGES AND UNIVERSITIES

Higher education:
Public 4-year institutions	12
Public 2-year institutions	47
Private 4-year institutions	91
Private 2-year institutions	16
Total	166

Vocational institutions: 359

Statewide coordinating board:
Board of Higher Education
500 Reisch Building
4 West Old Capitol Square
Springfield 62701
(217) 782-2551
Richard D. Wagner,
executive director

Private-college association:
Federation of Independent Illinois
  Colleges and Universities
Myers Building, Suite 506
One West Old State Capitol Plaza
Springfield 62701
(217) 789-1400
Donald E. Fouts, president

Institution censured by the AAUP:
Illinois College of Optometry

Institution under NCAA sanctions:
University of Illinois at
  Urbana-Champaign

FACULTY MEMBERS

Full-time faculty members:
At public institutions 11,788
At private institutions 5,938

Proportion who are women:
At public institutions 29.3%
At private institutions 27.3%

Proportion with tenure:
At public institutions 74.8%
At private institutions 61.8%

Average pay of full-time professors:
At public 4-year institutions $35,258
At public 2-year institutions $34,067
At private 4-year institutions $37,154
At private 2-year institutions $21,983

STUDENTS

Enrollment:
At public 4-year institutions   193,388
At public 2-year institutions   328,236
At private 4-year institutions 157,965
At private 2-year institutions . 9,385
Undergraduate 590,929
  First-time freshmen 125,551
Graduate 80,767
Professional 17,278
American Indian 1,972

Asian 27,798
Black 83,090
Hispanic 40,784
White 521,510
Foreign 13,820
Total 688,974

Enrollment highlights:
Women 54.2%
Full-time 50.3%
Minority 22.8%
Foreign 2.0%
10-year change in total
  enrollment .... Up 12.7%

**Proportion of enrollment made up
of minority students:**
At public 4-year institutions . 17.9%
At public 2-year institutions . 27.0%
At private 4-year institutions 17.6%
At private 2-year institutions 53.4%

Degrees awarded:
Associate 24,720
Bachelor's 47,958
Master's 17,783
Doctorate 2,152
Professional 4,353

Residence of new students: State residents made up 92% of all freshmen enrolled in Illinois; 85% of all Illinois residents who were freshmen attended college in their home state.

Test scores: Students averaged 18.8 on the A.C.T., which was taken by 61% of Illinois's high-school seniors.

MONEY

Average tuition and fees:
At public 4-year institutions . $2,370
At public 2-year institutions .. $871
At private 4-year institutions $8,281
At private 2-year institutions $5,505

ILLINOIS
Continued

Expenditures:
Public institutions .. $2,571,409,000
Private institutions . $2,722,294,000

State funds for higher-education operating expenses: $1,722,530,000

Two-year change: Up 22%

State spending on student aid:
Need-based: $180,800,000;
111,100 awards
Non–need-based: $19,385,000;
23,533 awards
Other: $4,125,000

Salary of chief executive of largest public 4-year campus:
Morton W. Weir, University of
Illinois at Urbana-Champaign:
$133,600

Total spending on research and development by doctorate-granting universities: $604,466,000

Sources:
Federal government 55.9%
State and local governments .. 5.9%
Industry 6.5%
The institution itself 24.9%
Other 6.8%

Federal spending on education and student aid (selected programs):
Vocational and
adult education $34,971,000
GI Bill $18,168,000
Pell Grants $193,859,000

Total federal spending on college- and university-based research and development: $301,297,000

Selected programs:
Department of Health
and Human Services $151,226,000

National Science
Foundation $68,752,000
Department of Defense $30,112,000
Department
of Agriculture $9,523,000
Department of Energy . $21,827,000

Largest endowment:
University of Chicago $973,697,000

Top fund raisers:
University of Illinois .. $73,096,000
Northwestern
University $68,523,000
University of Chicago . $66,604,000

MISCELLANY

■ A cooperative program between Bradley University and Illinois Central College allows substance abusers to complete their formal education. The program, "Learning to Live Again," identifies people who have the ability to earn either an associate or a four-year degree.

■ The University of Illinois at Urbana-Champaign is now the proud owner of the original, uncensored manuscript of James Jones's 1951 novel *From Here to Eternity,* which is considered pretty strong stuff even in its published version.

■ The School of the Art Institute of Chicago is selling for $5.4-million the former Playboy Mansion, which it received as a gift. The 72-room building, which was once the home of *Playboy* magazine's founder, Hugh Hefner, features an indoor swimming pool and a bowling alley. The institute has used it as a dormitory since 1984.

■ The oldest higher-education institution in Illinois is McKendree College, which was founded in 1828 and is affiliated with the United Methodist Church.

INDIANA

ALTHOUGH Indiana has many respected public universities, it has historically lagged behind other states in the proportion of high-school graduates who attend college.

In northern Indiana, in particular, where the economy has been dominated by automobile-related industries, residents traditionally have not needed a college degree to find well-paying jobs. But declines in the auto industry have changed that picture in recent years, and state officials have been trying to encourage more people to attend college.

Institutions are designing recruitment programs for ninth-graders and working with secondary-school systems to help students get any remedial help they may need. Democratic Gov. Evan Bayh, meanwhile, has called for greater efforts to attract minority and non-traditional students.

Like the governors of other "Rust Belt" states, Governor Bayh says Indiana's economic health is linked to higher education. He has called for increased financing for public colleges and universities.

In the 1990 legislative session, Indiana University officials worked hard to avoid getting caught up in a bitter abortion debate that was raging in the General Assembly. One bill would have prohibited abortions at public facilities, including the Indiana University teaching hospital. The bill was approved by the state's House of Representatives but was killed in the Senate.

The Commission for Higher Education, the statewide coordinating board, is responsible for planning and reviewing budgets and academic programs. The seven public systems are governed by individual boards.

Indiana is home to many private colleges, including a number of small liberal-arts institutions affiliated with religious groups. Among them are Bethel, Earlham, Franklin, Goshen, and Saint Mary-of-the-Woods Colleges.

Indiana also boasts one of the nation's premier Roman Catholic institutions, the University of Notre Dame, which is influential around the state and the nation.

The "Win One for the Gipper" legend in college athletics was born in Indiana under the great Notre Dame football coach, Knute Rockne. The state's enthusiasm for sports endures today, centering on the Indiana University basketball team coached by Bob Knight. While Mr. Knight is extremely popular in Indiana, some higher-education officials worry that his tremendous influence in the state distorts the university's academic priorities.

DEMOGRAPHICS

Population: 5,593,000   (Rank: 14)

Age distribution:

Up to 17	26.1%
18 to 24	10.9%
25 to 34	17.5%
35 and older	45.4%

Racial and ethnic distribution:

American Indian	0.2%
Asian	0.4%
Black	7.6%

INDIANA

Continued

White 91.2%
Other and unknown 0.6%
Hispanic (may be any race) .. 1.6%

Educational attainment of adults:
At least 4 years of high school 66.4%
At least 1 to 3 years of college 24.6%
At least 4 years of college ... 12.5%

Per-capita personal income: $15,779

New high-school graduates in:
1990-91 (estimate) 63,746
2000-01 (estimate) 58,855

New GED diploma recipients: 9,035

High-school dropout rate: 23.7%

POLITICAL LEADERSHIP

Governor: Evan Bayh (D), term ends 1993

Governor's higher-education adviser: Marci Reddick, State House, Room 206, Indianapolis 46204; (317) 232-6109

U.S. Senators: Dan Coats (R), term ends 1997; Richard G. Lugar (R), term ends 1995

U.S. Representatives:
8 Democrats, 2 Republicans
Dan Burton (R), Lee H. Hamilton (D), Andrew Jacobs, Jr. (D), Jim Jontz (D), Jill L. Long (D), Frank McCloskey (D), John T. Myers (R), Tim Roemer (D), Philip R. Sharp (D), Peter J. Visclosky (D)

General Assembly: Senate, 24 Democrats, 26 Republicans; House, 52 Democrats, 48 Republicans

COLLEGES AND UNIVERSITIES

Higher education:
Public 4-year institutions 14
Public 2-year institutions 14
Private 4-year institutions 41
Private 2-year institutions 9
Total 78

Vocational institutions: 135

Statewide coordinating board:
Commission for Higher Education
101 West Ohio Street, Suite 550
Indianapolis 46204
(317) 232-1900
Clyde Ingle, commissioner for higher education

Private-college association:
Independent Colleges and
   Universities of Indiana
200 South Meridian Street, Suite 220
Indianapolis 46225
(317) 635-2655
William Du Bois, Jr., president

Institution censured by the AAUP:
Concordia Theological Seminary

Institutions under NCAA sanctions:
None

FACULTY MEMBERS

Full-time faculty members:
At public institutions 5,901
At private institutions 2,581

Proportion who are women:
At public institutions 30.5%
At private institutions 25.1%

Proportion with tenure:
At public institutions 65.1%
At private institutions 64.2%

Average pay of full-time professors:
At public 4-year institutions $35,748
At public 2-year institutions $22,753
At private 4-year institutions $33,343
At private 2-year institutions $22,964

STUDENTS

Enrollment:
At public 4-year institutions   173,499
At public 2-year institutions . 35,734
At private 4-year institutions   55,431
At private 2-year institutions . 3,238
Undergraduate 231,918
  First-time freshmen 54,847
Graduate 30,724
Professional 5,260
American Indian 604
Asian 3,329
Black 14,723
Hispanic 3,686
White 239,057
Foreign 6,503
Total 267,902

Enrollment highlights:
Women 52.2%
Full-time 64.6%
Minority 8.5%
Foreign 2.4%
10-year change in total
  enrollment . . . . Up 20.2%

**Proportion of enrollment made up
of minority students:**
At public 4-year institutions . . 8.1%
At public 2-year institutions . 10.4%
At private 4-year institutions . 7.9%
At private 2-year institutions   21.2%

Degrees awarded:
Associate 8,949
Bachelor's 26,408
Master's 7,079
Doctorate 941
Professional 1,422

Residence of new students: State residents made up 75% of all freshmen enrolled in Indiana; 88% of all Indiana residents who were freshmen attended college in their home state.

Test scores: Students averaged 867 on the s.a.t., which was taken by 54% of Indiana's high-school seniors.

MONEY

Average tuition and fees:
At public 4-year institutions . $1,975
At public 2-year institutions . $1,374
At private 4-year institutions $8,267
At private 2-year institutions $7,412

Expenditures:
Public institutions . . $1,602,203,000
Private institutions . . . $530,163,000

**State funds for higher-education
operating expenses:** $876,162,000
Two-year change: Up 16%

State spending on student aid:
Need-based: $58,395,000;
  45,500 awards
Non–need-based: $920,000;
  816 awards
Other: None

**Salary of chief executive
of largest public 4-year campus:**
Steven C. Beering, Purdue University
  main campus: $160,000

**Total spending on research and
development by doctorate-granting
universities:** $227,266,000
Sources:
Federal government 59.9%
State and local governments . . 8.3%
Industry 8.1%
The institution itself 19.2%
Other 4.5%

INDIANA

Continued

Federal spending on education and student aid (selected programs):
Vocational and
  adult education $19,936,000
GI Bill $9,899,000
Pell Grants $106,653,000

Total federal spending on college- and university-based research and development: $111,776,000
Selected programs:
Department of Health
  and Human Services $52,305,000
National Science
  Foundation $24,699,000
Department of Defense $11,657,000
Department
  of Agriculture $6,749,000
Department of Energy . $10,925,000

Largest endowment:
University of
  Notre Dame $542,501,000

Top fund raisers:
University of
  Notre Dame $44,928,000
Indiana University $40,354,000
Purdue University $25,674,000

MISCELLANY

■ Despite a crackdown by university officials, the "Nude Olympics" continue at Purdue University. The annual event started 20 years ago when students dared each other to run naked across a dormitory quadrangle on one of the coldest nights of the year.

■ The University of Notre Dame earned $1-million in royalties from licensed merchandise in 1989, the largest amount received by any college or university.

■ One of Purdue University's original faculty members was Harvey Washington Wiley, who was a professor from 1874 to 1883. Founder of the institution's first chemical laboratory, a popular teacher, and the first baseball coach, he shocked the board of trustees by riding a high-wheeled bicycle around town. Later he went to work for the U.S. Department of Agriculture and was regarded as the "father" of the Pure Food and Drug Act.

■ The oldest institution of higher education in Indiana is Vincennes University, a two-year college founded in 1801 as the Jefferson Academy and renamed in 1806.

IOWA

I OWANS boast about being the nation's education leaders and Iowa's Governor, Terry E. Branstad, spearheaded the National Governors' Association study of education.

Mr. Branstad, a Republican, has increased the state's spending on faculty salaries and has expanded tuition-assistance programs at public colleges and universities. But during his re-election campaign the Governor promised to significantly increase schoolteachers' salaries. Some higher-education officials are afraid that keeping his campaign promise may limit the Governor's ability to increase state spending for higher education.

How much Mr. Branstad will be

able to do depends on the strength of Iowa's agriculture-based economy. After a major economic slump in the mid-1980's, Iowa is on the rebound, and financial support for higher education is on the rise. But as states from coast to coast experience revenue shortfalls, Iowa legislators have become increasingly cautious about their revenue predictions.

Although research on agriculture is well financed and is watched closely by state agricultural organizations, higher education in Iowa belies many of the other stereotypes of farm states.

The Iowa Writer's Workshop, for example, is a nationally known program at the University of Iowa that competes with New York City as a mecca for aspiring authors. High-technology research programs are also prominent at that university and at Iowa State University.

Public higher education in Iowa operates on two levels: The Board of Regents runs the three public universities, and the state Board of Education governs the community colleges, which in Iowa are called "area colleges."

Private higher education is important in Iowa. The state does not have public four-year liberal-arts colleges, so such programs are available only at private institutions. Coe, Cornell, and Grinnell Colleges are typical of the small private colleges throughout the state. Their students are eligible for state student-aid grants that are unusually high for the Midwest.

DEMOGRAPHICS

Population: 2,840,000   (Rank: 29)

Age distribution:
Up to 17 .... 24.9%
18 to 24 .... 10.3%
25 to 34 .... 17.4%
35 and older 47.3%

Racial and ethnic distribution:
American Indian 0.2%
Asian 0.5%
Black 1.4%
White 97.5%
Other and unknown 0.4%
Hispanic (may be any race) .. 0.9%

Educational attainment of adults:
At least 4 years of high school 71.5%
At least 1 to 3 years of college 28.6%
At least 4 years of college ... 13.9%

Per-capita personal income: $15,487

New high-school graduates in:
1990-91 (estimate) 31,316
2000-01 (estimate) 31,478

New GED diploma recipients: 4,006

High-school dropout rate: 14.2%

POLITICAL LEADERSHIP

Governor: Terry F. Branstad (R), term ends 1995

Governor's higher-education adviser: Phillip Dunshee, State House, Des Moines 50319; (515) 281-5211

U.S. Senators: Charles E. Grassley (R), term ends 1993; Tom Harkin (D), term ends 1997

U.S. Representatives:
2 Democrats, 4 Republicans
Fred Grandy (R), Jim Leach (R), Jim Lightfoot (R), David R. Nagle (D), Jim Nussle (R), Neal Smith (D)

General Assembly: Senate, 28 Democrats, 21 Republicans, 1 vacancy; House, 55 Democrats, 45 Republicans

IOWA

Continued

COLLEGES AND UNIVERSITIES

Higher education:
Public 4-year institutions 3
Public 2-year institutions 15
Private 4-year institutions 34
Private 2-year institutions 6
Total 58

Vocational institutions: 77

Statewide coordinating boards:
State Board of Regents
Old State Historical Building
Des Moines 50319
(515) 281-3934
R. Wayne Richey, executive director

Department of Education
Division of Community Colleges
Grimes State Office Building
Des Moines 50319
(515) 281-8260
Joann Horton, administrator

Private-college association:
Iowa Association of Independent
    Colleges and Universities
307 Equitable Building
604 Locust Street
Des Moines 50309
(515) 282-3175
John V. Hartung, president

Institution censured by the AAUP:
University of Osteopathic Medicine
    and Health Sciences

Institutions under NCAA sanctions:
None

FACULTY MEMBERS

Full-time faculty members:
At public institutions 3,123
At private institutions 1,697

Proportion who are women:
At public institutions 28.6%
At private institutions 28.2%

Proportion with tenure:
At public institutions 72.2%
At private institutions 58.4%

Average pay of full-time professors:
At public 4-year institutions $37,162
At public 2-year institutions $25,698
At private 4-year institutions $28,428
At private 2-year institutions $22,440

STUDENTS

Enrollment:
At public 4-year institutions . 68,872
At public 2-year institutions . 44,391
At private 4-year institutions   45,017
At private 2-year institutions . 2,894
Undergraduate 137,768
    First-time freshmen 37,725
Graduate 17,484
Professional 5,922
American Indian 457
Asian 2,056
Black 3,511
Hispanic 1,402
White 147,933
Foreign 5,815
Total 161,174

Enrollment highlights:
Women 51.8%
Full-time 72.0%
Minority 4.8%
Foreign 3.6%
10-year change in total
    enrollment .... Up 24.8%

Proportion of enrollment made up of minority students:
At public 4-year institutions .. 5.0%
At public 2-year institutions .. 4.6%
At private 4-year institutions . 4.6%
At private 2-year institutions . 5.4%

Degrees awarded:
Associate 7,013
Bachelor's 16,747
Master's 3,001
Doctorate 658
Professional 1,518

Residence of new students: State residents made up 83% of all freshmen enrolled in Iowa; 88% of all Iowa residents who were freshmen attended college in their home state.

Test scores: Students averaged 20.1 on the A.C.T., which was taken by 60% of Iowa's high-school seniors.

MONEY

Average tuition and fees:
At public 4-year institutions . $1,823
At public 2-year institutions . $1,225
At private 4-year institutions $7,945
At private 2-year institutions $6,423

Expenditures:
Public institutions .. $1,092,542,000
Private institutions ... $353,753,000

State funds for higher-education operating expenses: $576,924,000

Two-year change: Up 20%

State spending on student aid:
Need-based: $32,101,000;
  17,958 awards
Non–need-based: $1,196,000;
  2,077 awards
Other: $25,635,000

Salary of chief executive of largest public 4-year campus:
Hunter R. Rawlings, III, University of Iowa: $164,000

Total spending on research and development by doctorate-granting universities: $209,327,000
Sources:
Federal government 49.4%
State and local governments . 11.9%
Industry 7.0%
The institution itself 29.0%
Other 2.7%

Federal spending on education and student aid (selected programs):
Vocational and
  adult education $9,668,000
GI Bill $6,056,000
Pell Grants $78,590,000

Total federal spending on college- and university-based research and development: $89,074,000
Selected programs:
Department of Health
  and Human Services $60,513,000
National Science
  Foundation $6,579,000
Department of Defense . $3,460,000
Department
  of Agriculture $6,828,000
Department of Energy .. $1,202,000

Largest endowment:
Grinnell College $294,328,000

Top fund raisers:
University of Iowa $31,227,000
Iowa State University . $19,344,000
Coe College $8,488,000

MISCELLANY

■ Cornell College claims to be the only college or university in the country to have its entire campus—110

IOWA

Continued

acres—listed on the National Register of Historic Places. The college was established in 1853.

■ In 1990 Drake University installed computers in the dormitory rooms of all freshmen and some upperclassmen. Some 560 rooms were outfitted with Apple Macintosh SE computers and Imagewriter printers, with all of the computers connected to the campus's network.

■ Cornell College requires all faculty members to be versed in at least the outlines of feminist scholarship in their discipline.

■ The Herbert Hoover Library, which contains most of the late President's papers, is located in West Branch.

■ The oldest higher-education institution in Iowa is Loras College, a Roman Catholic institution founded in 1839.

KANSAS

KANSAS lawmakers have a new Governor and a new political mandate to shift financial responsibility for some local programs to the state.

Higher-education officials fear that the changes may pose financial problems for them. Former Gov. Mike Hayden, a Republican, lost his re-election bid in 1990 over a controversial tax plan he helped enact. The new Democratic Governor, Joan Finney, is expected to try to reform the state's tax system in 1991.

But unless more tax revenue is found for the final legislative package, higher-education officials say budget cuts for colleges and universities are inevitable.

Still, Governor Finney advocates continued support for "Margin of Excellence," a program to increase faculty salaries and provide money for both new and existing programs at state institutions.

Like other farm states, Kansas saw its economy hit hard in the 1980's, and spending on higher education suffered. And the state has been trying to restore those cuts through the "Margin of Excellence" program.

The state embarked on the three-year plan in 1987 and the Kansas Board of Regents received full financing for the first and second years. But a weakened farm economy and budgetary restraints prompted legislators to defer completing the plan in 1990. Higher-education officials say they will try to get additional money for the last stages of the plan in the next budget session.

While the regents have raised many Kansans' hopes for a high-quality university system, the board has failed to meet its goal of setting admissions standards for the state's public institutions. Legislators cite the state's strong populist traditions each time they reject proposals to end its policy of admitting all high-school graduates.

The Board of Regents serves as the coordinating board for all higher education in the state and as the governing board for the six state universities and a two-year technical institute. The regents have approved a plan to merge the technical institute with Kansas State University; the plan will go to the Legislature in 1991.

Community colleges are governed by local boards under the supervision of the state Board of Education.

DEMOGRAPHICS

Population: 2,513,000   (Rank: 32)

Age distribution:
Up to 17 .... 26.2%
18 to 24 .... 10.3%
25 to 34 .... 17.6%
35 and older 45.9%

Racial and ethnic distribution:
American Indian 0.8%
Asian 0.7%
Black 5.3%
White 91.8%
Other and unknown 1.4%
Hispanic (may be any race) .. 2.7%

Educational attainment of adults:
At least 4 years of high school 73.3%
At least 1 to 3 years of college 34.2%
At least 4 years of college ... 17.0%

Per-capita personal income: $16,498

New high-school graduates in:
1990-91 (estimate) 25,793
2000-01 (estimate) 30,717

New GED diploma recipients: 5,268

High-school dropout rate: 19.8%

POLITICAL LEADERSHIP

Governor: Joan Finney (D), term ends 1995

Governor's higher-education adviser: n/a

U.S. Senators: Bob Dole (R), term ends 1993; Nancy Landon Kassebaum (R), term ends 1997

U.S. Representatives:
2 Democrats, 3 Republicans
Dan Glickman (D), Jan Meyers (R), Dick Nichols (R), Pat Roberts (R), Jim Slattery (D)

Legislature: Senate, 18 Democrats, 22 Republicans; House, 63 Democrats, 62 Republicans

COLLEGES AND UNIVERSITIES

Higher education:
Public 4-year institutions 8
Public 2-year institutions 21
Private 4-year institutions 22
Private 2-year institutions 3
Total 54

Vocational institutions: 76

Statewide coordinating board:
Kansas Board of Regents
Capitol Tower
400 S.W. 8th Street, Suite 609
Topeka 66603
(913) 296-3421
Stanley Z. Koplik, executive director

Private-college association:
Kansas Independent
   College Association
Capitol Federal Building, Room 515
Topeka 66603
(913) 235-9877
Robert N. Kelly, executive director

Institutions censured by the AAUP:
None

Institution under NCAA sanctions:
University of Kansas

KANSAS

Continued

FACULTY MEMBERS

Full-time faculty members:
At public institutions 3,793
At private institutions 682

Proportion who are women:
At public institutions 26.9%
At private institutions 32.3%

Proportion with tenure:
At public institutions 70.0%
At private institutions 42.0%

Average pay of full-time professors:
At public 4-year institutions $32,885
At public 2-year institutions $27,594
At private 4-year institutions $22,135
At private 2-year institutions $17,151

STUDENTS

Enrollment:
At public 4-year institutions . 87,368
At public 2-year institutions . 51,332
At private 4-year institutions 12,833
At private 2-year institutions . 1,314
Undergraduate 131,581
First-time freshmen 27,068
Graduate 19,148
Professional 2,118
American Indian 1,826
Asian 2,089
Black 6,300
Hispanic 2,910
White 134,878
Foreign 4,844
Total 152,847

Enrollment highlights:
Women 54.2%
Full-time 57.3%
Minority 8.9%

Foreign 3.2%
10-year change in total
enrollment .... Up 20.0%

Proportion of enrollment made up of minority students:
At public 4-year institutions .. 7.4%
At public 2-year institutions . 10.1%
At private 4-year institutions 11.6%
At private 2-year institutions 31.9%

Degrees awarded:
Associate 4,759
Bachelor's 11,890
Master's 2,983
Doctorate 376
Professional 628

Residence of new students: State residents made up 82% of all freshmen enrolled in Kansas; 90% of all Kansas residents who were freshmen attended college in their home state.

Test scores: Students averaged 19.1 on the A.C.T., which was taken by 66% of Kansas' high-school seniors.

MONEY

Average tuition and fees:
At public 4-year institutions . $1,467
At public 2-year institutions .. $711
At private 4-year institutions $5,460
At private 2-year institutions $3,962

Expenditures:
Public institutions $848,602,000
Private institutions ... $105,193,000

State funds for higher-education operating expenses: $458,895,000
Two-year change: Up 18%

State spending on student aid:
Need-based: $7,129,000; 4,802 awards
Non–need-based: $35,000; 100 awards
Other: $386,000

**Salary of chief executive
of largest public 4-year campus:**
Gene A. Budig, University of Kansas:
$126,990

**Total spending on research and
development by doctorate-granting
universities:** $107,856,000
Sources:
Federal government 41.1%
State and local governments . 22.4%
Industry 4.8%
The institution itself 28.0%
Other 3.7%

**Federal spending on education
and student aid (selected programs):**
Vocational and
    adult education $7,605,000
GI Bill $7,674,000
Pell Grants $72,520,000

**Total federal spending on college-
and university-based research
and development:** $37,228,000

Selected programs:
Department of Health
    and Human Services $16,941,000
National Science
    Foundation $4,617,000
Department of Defense . $1,450,000
Department
    of Agriculture $7,385,000
Department of Energy .. $1,888,000

Largest endowment:
Kansas University Endowment
    Association $203,595,000

Top fund raisers:
University of Kansas .. $26,607,000
Kansas State University $12,656,000
Washburn University ... $6,624,000

MISCELLANY

■ Donald E. Mock, a professor of
entomology at Kansas State University, received more than 2,700 tick specimens when newspapers and maga-
zines across the state reprinted an arti-
cle on the bugs that he had written for
county extension agents. In the arti-
cle, Mr. Mock asked readers to send
him samples of ticks. Medicine vials
containing ticks soon arrived in Mr.
Mock's mail, sometimes at the rate of
30 packages a day.

■ Emporia State University and the
town of Emporia are raising money to
create a National Teachers Hall of
Fame. The facility, which would be
adjacent to a one-room rural schoolhouse on the university campus,
would include a museum of American
education and a conference and study
center.

■ The oldest higher-education institution in Kansas is Highland Community College, which was chartered in
1857. The oldest four-year university
in the state is Baker University, a
United Methodist institution, which
received its charter just three days after Highland did.

KENTUCKY

IN early 1990 the University of Kentucky took its fight for more state
financing to the public in a series of
television, radio, and newspaper ad-
vertisements centered on the theme
"U.K. is worth it."

Whether it swayed the taxpayers is
unclear. But the campaign seems to
have made little impact on one key
player, Gov. Wallace G. Wilkinson.
Mr. Wilkinson, a Democrat, continues to rail at public-college leaders for

KENTUCKY
Continued

wasting money and to tweak the institutions for giving faculty members teaching loads that are so light, he says, that "they're almost not working anymore."

For years, college leaders have complained that the state does not finance their institutions adequately, a complaint that can be attributed partly to Kentucky's conservatism and resistance to taxes.

Under a state Supreme Court order to make its public-school financing more equitable, Kentucky raised taxes in 1990 and overhauled its elementary- and secondary-school systems. The actions had no direct higher-education component, but many colleges and universities won money for new buildings when the Governor agreed to add new projects in exchange for support from individual legislators for the new taxes.

The General Assembly did, however, approve the new College Access Program sought by Governor Wilkinson. He says the plan, which promises any needy resident free tuition for the first two years of college, is designed to make 14 years of public education available to every Kentuckian.

Higher-education policy making in the Bluegrass State is often polarized by racial and regional politics. Black students at predominantly white institutions have complained that the campuses are hostile environments. Meanwhile, supporters of Kentucky State University—the historically black institution—say the state does not provide it with adequate financing.

Regional politics have come into play in debates over financing for the

University of Kentucky, the state's flagship, and the University of Louisville, which wants more resources and programs on its campus. Louisville is nearer the state's population center.

The Kentucky Council on Higher Education is the statewide coordinating board. Another board governs the University of Kentucky and all community colleges. Seven other public institutions are governed by their own boards.

Private higher education in Kentucky consists mostly of small, church-related colleges.

DEMOGRAPHICS

Population: 3,727,000   (Rank: 23)

Age distribution:
Up to 17 .... 25.9%
18 to 24 .... 11.1%
25 to 34 .... 17.5%
35 and older 45.5%

Racial and ethnic distribution:
American Indian 0.1%
Asian 0.3%
Black 7.1%
White 92.3%
Other and unknown 0.1%
Hispanic (may be any race) .. 0.7%

Educational attainment of adults:
At least 4 years of high school 53.1%
At least 1 to 3 years of college 21.8%
At least 4 years of college ... 11.1%

Per-capita personal income: $13,743

New high-school graduates in:
1990-91 (estimate) 38,730
2000-01 (estimate) 39,156

New GED diploma recipients: 10,463

High-school dropout rate: 31.0%

POLITICAL LEADERSHIP

Governor: Wallace G. Wilkinson (D), term ends 1991

Governor's higher-education adviser: Jack Foster, State Capitol Building, Room 105, Frankfort 40601; (502) 564-2611

U.S. Senators: Wendell H. Ford (D), term ends 1993; Mitch McConnell (R), term ends 1997

U.S. Representatives:
4 Democrats, 3 Republicans
Jim Bunning (R), Larry J. Hopkins (R), Carroll Hubbard, Jr. (D), Romano L. Mazzoli (D), William H. Natcher (D), Carl C. Perkins (D), Harold Rogers (R)

General Assembly: Senate, 27 Democrats, 11 Republicans; House, 68 Democrats, 32 Republicans

COLLEGES AND UNIVERSITIES

Higher education:
Public 4-year institutions 8
Public 2-year institutions 14
Private 4-year institutions 24
Private 2-year institutions 13
Total 59

Vocational institutions: 131

Statewide coordinating board:
Council on Higher Education
1050 U.S. 127 South, Suite 101
Frankfort 40601
(502) 564-3553
Gary S. Cox, executive director

Private-college association:
Council of Independent Kentucky
Colleges and Universities
P.O. Box 668
Danville 40422
(606) 236-3533
John W. Frazer, executive director

Institution censured by the AAUP:
Murray State University

Institution under NCAA sanctions:
University of Kentucky

FACULTY MEMBERS

Full-time faculty members:
At public institutions 3,749
At private institutions 1,058

Proportion who are women:
At public institutions 32.4%
At private institutions 36.2%

Proportion with tenure:
At public institutions 68.2%
At private institutions 51.7%

Average pay of full-time professors:
At public 4-year institutions $32,950
At public 2-year institutions $25,083
At private 4-year institutions $25,925
At private 2-year institutions $17,855

STUDENTS

Enrollment:
At public 4-year institutions . 97,895
At public 2-year institutions . 31,330
At private 4-year institutions   23,170
At private 2-year institutions . 7,473
Undergraduate 137,798
First-time freshmen 30,115
Graduate 17,548
Professional 4,522
American Indian 427
Asian 1,078

KENTUCKY

Black 9,296
Hispanic 683
White 146,703
Foreign 1,681
Total 159,868

Enrollment highlights:
Women 57.2%
Full-time 64.1%
Minority 7.3%
Foreign 1.1%
10-year change in total
    enrollment .... Up 20.5%

Proportion of enrollment made up of minority students:
At public 4-year institutions .. 7.5%
At public 2-year institutions .. 8.0%
At private 4-year institutions . 4.0%
At private 2-year institutions 11.4%

Degrees awarded:
Associate 4,915
Bachelor's 12,074
Master's 3,333
Doctorate 313
Professional 1,161

Residence of new students: State residents made up 88% of all freshmen enrolled in Kentucky; 90% of all Kentucky residents who were freshmen attended college in their home state.

Test scores: Students averaged 17.8 on the A.C.T., which was taken by 58% of Kentucky's high-school seniors.

MONEY

Average tuition and fees:
At public 4-year institutions . $1,316
At public 2-year institutions .. $693

At private 4-year institutions $4,689
At private 2-year institutions $4,669

Expenditures:
Public institutions $898,718,000
Private institutions ... $194,873,000

State funds for higher-education operating expenses: $607,445,000

Two-year change: Up 17%

State spending on student aid:
Need-based: $13,858,000;
    23,375 awards
Non–need-based: None
Other: None

Salary of chief executive of largest public 4-year campus:
Charles T. Wethington, Jr.,
    University of Kentucky: $130,500

Total spending on research and development by doctorate-granting universities: $83,998,000
Sources:
Federal government 39.2%
State and local governments .. 8.5%
Industry 8.9%
The institution itself 36.4%
Other 6.9%

Federal spending on education and student aid (selected programs):
Vocational and
    adult education $15,160,000
GI Bill $8,830,000
Pell Grants $87,228,000

Total federal spending on college- and university-based research and development: $31,965,000
Selected programs:
Department of Health
    and Human Services $16,717,000
National Science
    Foundation $2,871,000

Department of Defense ... $970,000
Department
    of Agriculture $8,131,000
Department of Energy .. $1,946,000

Largest endowment:
Berea College $252,052,000

Top fund raisers:
University of Kentucky $17,270,000
University of Louisville $12,006,000
Berea College $11,751,000

MISCELLANY

■ Kentucky State University officials have threatened to expel students who are caught having sex in dormitory rooms.

■ The University of Kentucky added a woman's touch to its men's basketball program, becoming the first university in the National Collegiate Athletic Association's Division I to hire a female assistant coach.

■ The University of Kentucky plans to establish an Equine Research Hall of Fame to recognize some unsung heros of the horse industry—scientists who perform basic biomedical research on the animals. Each member of the hall of fame will receive a plaque and a statuette of a horse.

■ Former Democratic Gov. Martha Layne Collins, who pushed for more money and improved educational quality at Kentucky's public colleges and universities in the early 1980's, was named in June 1990 as president of St. Catharine College, a Roman Catholic institution.

■ Berea College, established in 1855 to serve needy students from Appalachia, charges no tuition but has a compulsory work program to help offset the lack of tuition revenue.

■ The oldest higher-education institution in the state is Transylvania University, founded in 1780. Kentucky's 1857-58 legislature repealed the bill establishing Transylvania as a university, and it operated until 1865 as a high school. Since then it has been a liberal-arts college.

LOUISIANA

T HE Louisiana Legislature repeatedly made headlines in 1990 by writing a series of bills that made civil libertarians cringe. One measure would have required that records and tapes carry labels if they contained offensive lyrics. Two others would have sent physicians to prison for 10 years for performing abortions.

The measures were vetoed by the Governor, Buddy Roemer, as some lawmakers fumed and threatened to come back with even stronger bills. But in the midst of the wrangling over morality, Louisiana lawmakers adopted a budget bill that gave faculty members at state colleges their first substantial raise in years and provided $180-million for maintenance and construction on public campuses.

State officials had been grappling with budget crises for the past 10 years because the oil and gas industries were in a slump and because Louisiana voters strongly opposed tax increases. But after years of scant budget growth, the 1990 Legislature approved raising $420-million in new revenue by extending some temporary taxes, and lawmakers decided to give a big portion of the increase to higher education.

In part, the increase can be credited to intense lobbying by the state's college and university presidents. But a brain drain from the state also alarmed legislators. Faculty members, particularly those at Louisiana State University, were frustrated by shortages of money and equipment, and many were lured away by leading research institutions in other states.

Two other long-standing problems have yet to be resolved—the segregation of Louisiana's public institutions and the debate about the structure of higher education.

Civil-rights groups and the federal government have been challenging the legality of Louisiana's higher-education system since 1970. Then, in November 1990, a federal judge threw out the case.

Federal District Judge Charles Schwartz, Jr., said that an appeals-court ruling in a Mississippi desegregation case had changed the legal standards for proving the existence of illegal segregation in higher education. Under the new standards, with which he said he disagreed, Judge Schwartz said he had no choice but to reverse his earlier finding that Louisiana was operating a segregated system.

In 1989 the federal court issued an order, which mirrored a proposal supported by Governor Roemer. The order required the state to eliminate its coordinating board and its three boards for college and university systems. They would have been replaced with a single governing body.

But officials at Southern University, the nation's only public black higher-education system, were vehemently opposed to both the court order and the Governor's plan. They said the new board would ignore the interests of black students. Although the order has been withdrawn, the Governor says he will continue his fight for a single board to govern higher education.

Another major higher-education issue in Louisiana is admission standards. The state's strong populist tradition has led most public institutions to operate on an open-admission basis.

Although the vast majority of Louisiana students attend public colleges, the state also has private institutions, which exert considerable political influence. Tulane University has long been regarded as a leader, and Dillard and Xavier Universities are respected private black colleges.

DEMOGRAPHICS

Population: 4,382,000   (Rank: 20)

Age distribution:

Up to 17	29.0%
18 to 24	11.1%
25 to 34	18.3%
35 and older	41.5%

Racial and ethnic distribution:

American Indian	0.3%
Asian	0.6%
Black	29.4%
White	69.3%
Other and unknown	0.3%
Hispanic (may be any race)	2.4%

Educational attainment of adults:

At least 4 years of high school	57.7%
At least 1 to 3 years of college	26.7%
At least 4 years of college	13.9%

Per-capita personal income: $12,921

New high-school graduates in:
1990-91 (estimate) 42,122
2000-01 (estimate) 48,723

New GED diploma recipients: 6,601

High-school dropout rate: 38.6%

POLITICAL LEADERSHIP

Governor: Buddy Roemer (D), term ends 1992

Governor's higher-education adviser: John Kennedy, P.O. Box 94004, Baton Rouge 70804; (504) 342-7015

U.S. Senators: John B. Breaux (D), term ends 1993; J. Bennett Johnston (D), term ends 1997

U.S. Representatives:
4 Democrats, 4 Republicans
Richard H. Baker (R), James A. Hayes (D), Clyde C. Holloway (R), Jerry Huckaby (D), William Jefferson (D), Bob Livingston (R), Jim McCrery (R), W.J. (Billy) Tauzin (D)

Legislature: Senate, 33 Democrats, 6 Republican; House, 86 Democrats, 18 Republicans, 1 Independent

COLLEGES AND UNIVERSITIES

Higher education:
Public 4-year institutions 14
Public 2-year institutions 6
Private 4-year institutions 10
Private 2-year institutions 4

Total 34

Vocational institutions: 196

Statewide coordinating board:
State of Louisiana Board
 of Regents
150 Riverside Mall, Suite 129
Baton Rouge 70803
(504) 342-4253
Sammie W. Cosper, commissioner of higher education

Private-college association:
Louisiana Association of Independent
 Colleges and Universities
320 Riverside Mall, Suite 104
Baton Rouge 70801
(504) 389-9885
William Arceneaux, president

Institutions censured by the AAUP:
None

Institutions under NCAA sanctions:
Grambling State University,
Northwestern State University,
Southeastern Louisiana University

FACULTY MEMBERS

Full-time faculty members:
At public institutions 4,774
At private institutions 980

Proportion who are women:
At public institutions 33.6%
At private institutions 30.3%

Proportion with tenure:
At public institutions 56.0%
At private institutions 53.6%

Average pay of full-time professors:
At public 4-year institutions $29,963
At public 2-year institutions $25,636
At private 4-year institutions $34,227
At private 2-year institutions ... n/a

STUDENTS

Enrollment:
At public 4-year institutions 133,830
At public 2-year institutions . 15,519

LOUISIANA

Continued

At private 4-year institutions 24,170
At private 2-year institutions . 2,512
Undergraduate 150,771
  First-time freshmen 30,953
Graduate 19,544
Professional 5,716
American Indian 624
Asian 2,507
Black 41,213
Hispanic 3,283
White 123,362
Foreign 5,042
Total 176,031

Enrollment highlights:
Women 54.9%
Full-time 73.0%
Minority 27.9%
Foreign 2.9%
10-year change in total
  enrollment .... Up 15.7%

**Proportion of enrollment made up
of minority students:**
At public 4-year institutions . 27.0%
At public 2-year institutions . 31.7%
At private 4-year institutions 29.1%
At private 2-year institutions 38.4%

Degrees awarded:
Associate 2,532
Bachelor's 16,367
Master's 3,941
Doctorate 346
Professional 1,400

Residence of new students: State residents made up 83% of all freshmen enrolled in Louisiana; 87% of all Louisiana residents who were freshmen attended college in their home state.

Test scores: Students averaged 17.1 on the A.C.T., which was taken by 62% of Louisiana's high-school seniors.

MONEY

Average tuition and fees:
At public 4-year institutions . $1,768
At public 2-year institutions . . $837
At private 4-year institutions $9,257
At private 2-year institutions $5,648

Expenditures:
Public institutions . . $1,039,177,000
Private institutions . . . $353,433,000

**State funds for higher-education
operating expenses:** $585,729,000
Two-year change: Up 21%

State spending on student aid:
Need-based: $2,006,000; 3,343 awards
Non–need-based: $723,000;
  2,384 awards
Other: $7,000,000

**Salary of chief executive
of largest public 4-year campus:**
William E. Davis, Louisiana State
  University: $121,500

**Total spending on research and
development by doctorate-granting
universities:** $179,332,000
Sources:
Federal government 37.0%
State and local governments . 24.0%
Industry 4.5%
The institution itself 26.1%
Other 8.4%

**Federal spending on education
and student aid (selected programs):**
Vocational and
  adult education $17,625,000
GI Bill $11,767,000
Pell Grants $136,558,000

Total federal spending on college-and university-based research and development: $61,456,000

Selected programs:
Department of Health
  and Human Services $38,826,000
National Science
  Foundation $4,750,000
Department of Defense . $5,672,000
Department
  of Agriculture $5,482,000
Department of Energy .. $2,580,000

Largest endowment:
Tulane University $221,424,000

Top fund raisers:
Tulane University $24,013,000
Xavier University
  of Louisiana $5,086,000
Loyola University
  of New Orleans $4,493,000

MISCELLANY

■ Law students at Tulane University are working for the release of elderly prisoners at the Louisiana State Penitentiary at Angola. Under the university's Project for Older Prisoners, law students have volunteered to visit convicts over age 55 to determine their health needs and make recommendations for their release to the pardon and parole boards.

■ Xavier University of Louisiana is the only historically black Roman Catholic college in the country.

■ The Louisiana Ornithological Society was started by a group of biologists and ornithologists at Louisiana State University in Baton Rouge in 1945. The group's 350 members—amateurs and professionals—still flock to Cameron, La., every April and October to watch the migration of birds crossing the Gulf of Mexico.

■ The oldest higher-education institution in the state is Centenary College of Louisiana. It is affiliated with the United Methodist Church and was founded in 1825.

MAINE

HIGHER education in Maine has always attracted strong support from politicians, but lawmakers don't always have the money to back up their enthusiasm.

The state's economy is in a recession. Because of an economic slowdown and revenue shortfall, the state had to trim its 1989-91 biennial budget. The University of Maine System lost $9.6-million of its $283.6-million biennial budget, and about $6.6-million of those cuts will have to be made in the 1990-91 fiscal year.

The economic slowdown comes in the middle of a campaign to increase the number of state residents who attend college. To attract more Maine students to higher education, state officials have been pumping money into the seven-campus university system and state scholarship programs.

Gov. John R. McKernan, Jr., a Republican starting his second term, has been supportive of higher education, but it is unclear whether he will be able to provide additional funds for colleges in the current economic climate.

The cost of attending college continues to be an issue in Maine. The strength of the state's private institutions of higher education has led

MAINE

Continued

Maine to offer generous student-aid programs. State officials also continue to grapple with the competition between the University of Southern Maine, a fast-growing institution in Portland, and the university system's flagship campus in Orono. Orono faculty members fear the growth at Southern Maine will come at the expense of their own programs.

Maine is among the New England states in which private higher education is older and more prestigious than public higher education. The state is well known for its private, liberal-arts institutions. Bates, Bowdoin, and Colby Colleges all have national reputations and predate the University of Maine.

DEMOGRAPHICS

Population: 1,222,000   (Rank: 38)

Age distribution:
Up to 17 .... 25.0%
18 to 24 .... 10.8%
25 to 34 .... 17.1%
35 and older 47.1%

Racial and ethnic distribution:
American Indian 0.4%
Asian 0.3%
Black 0.3%
White 99.0%
Other and unknown 0.1%
Hispanic (may be any race) .. 0.4%

Educational attainment of adults:
At least 4 years of high school 68.7%
At least 1 to 3 years of college 29.4%
At least 4 years of college ... 14.4%

Per-capita personal income: $16,248

New high-school graduates in:
1990-91 (estimate) 13,923
2000-01 (estimate) 14,326

New GED diploma recipients: 3,307

High-school dropout rate: 25.6%

POLITICAL LEADERSHIP

Governor: John R. McKernan, Jr. (R), term ends 1995

Governor's higher-education adviser: Mark LeDuc, State House, Station No. 1, Augusta 04333; (207) 289-3531

U.S. Senators: William S. Cohen (R), term ends 1997; George J. Mitchell (D), term ends 1995

U.S. Representatives:
1 Democrat, 1 Republican
Thomas Andrews (D), Olympia J. Snowe (R)

Legislature: Senate, 22 Democrats, 13 Republicans; House, 97 Democrats, 54 Republicans

COLLEGES AND UNIVERSITIES

Higher education:
Public 4-year institutions 8
Public 2-year institutions 5
Private 4-year institutions 13
Private 2-year institutions 5
Total 31

Vocational institutions: 22

Statewide coordinating board:
University of Maine System
Board of Trustees
107 Maine Avenue
Bangor 04401
(207) 947-0336
Robert L. Woodbury, chancellor

Private-college association:
Maine Independent College
  and University Association
College of the Atlantic
105 Eden Street
Bar Harbor 04609
(207) 288-5015
Louis Rabineau, president

Institution censured by the AAUP:
Husson College

Institutions under NCAA sanctions:
None

FACULTY MEMBERS

Full-time faculty members:
At public institutions 1,304
At private institutions 557

Proportion who are women:
At public institutions 27.0%
At private institutions 33.4%

Proportion with tenure:
At public institutions 60.4%
At private institutions 51.4%

Average pay of full-time professors:
At public 4-year institutions $32,900
At public 2-year institutions $24,710
At private 4-year institutions $32,637
At private 2-year institutions $24,664

STUDENTS

Enrollment:
At public 4-year institutions . 30,198
At public 2-year institutions .. 5,716
At private 4-year institutions 10,919
At private 2-year institutions . 1,070
Undergraduate 43,756
  First-time freshmen 9,758
Graduate 3,572
Professional 575
American Indian 235
Asian 260

Black 263
Hispanic 135
White 46,748
Foreign 262
Total 47,903

Enrollment highlights:
Women 55.7%
Full-time 62.2%
Minority 1.9%
Foreign 0.5%
10-year change in total
  enrollment .... Up 15.5%

**Proportion of enrollment made up
of minority students:**
At public 4-year institutions .. 1.5%
At public 2-year institutions .. 1.2%
At private 4-year institutions . 3.5%
At private 2-year institutions . 1.1%

Degrees awarded:
Associate 2,069
Bachelor's 5,168
Master's 548
Doctorate 25
Professional 157

Residence of new students: State residents made up 71% of all freshmen enrolled in Maine; 70% of all Maine residents who were freshmen attended college in their home state.

Test scores: Students averaged 886 on the s.a.t., which was taken by 60% of Maine's high-school seniors.

MONEY

Average tuition and fees:
At public 4-year institutions . $1,980
At public 2-year institutions . $1,134
At private 4-year institutions $10,425
At private 2-year institutions $3,787

MAINE

Continued

Expenditures:
Public institutions $216,737,000
Private institutions ... $133,778,000

State funds for higher-education operating expenses: $195,912,000
Two-year change: Up 21%

State spending on student aid:
Need-based: $2,008,000; 4,400 awards
Non–need-based: None
Other: None

Salary of chief executive of largest public 4-year campus:
Dale W. Lick, University of Maine at Orono: $118,085

Total spending on research and development by doctorate-granting universities: $19,974,000
Sources:
Federal government 41.5%
State and local governments .. 2.9%
Industry 20.0%
The institution itself 32.9%
Other 2.7%

Federal spending on education and student aid (selected programs):
Vocational and
   adult education $4,506,000
GI Bill $2,811,000
Pell Grants $15,497,000

Total federal spending on college- and university-based research and development: $6,618,000
Selected programs:
Department of Health
   and Human Services ... $872,000
National Science
   Foundation $1,901,000

Department of Defense $92,000
Department
   of Agriculture $2,463,000
Department of Energy 0

Largest endowment:
Bowdoin College $144,156,000

Top fund raisers:
University of Maine ... $10,351,000
Bowdoin College $9,888,000
Colby College $3,509,000

MISCELLANY

■ Salad-bar scraps mixed with manure are used by the Waste Utilization Research Group at the University of Maine to generate electricity. The anaerobic digestion, as the process is called, produces more than $8,000 worth of electricity a year.

■ The College of the Atlantic invited high-school seniors to a Sunday-afternoon yacht party on a 90-feet sailing craft that the institution had docked at New York's South Street Seaport.

■ In 1858 Bowdoin College bestowed an honorary degree upon Mississippi Sen. Jefferson Davis. When Davis assumed the Presidency of the Confederacy, the college was pressured to rescind the award. At the end of the Civil War, Davis lost his freedom and his citizenship, but not his Bowdoin degree.

■ The College of the Atlantic, a private institution in Bar Harbor that was established in 1969, offers a single degree program—in human ecology.

■ The University of Maine's two northernmost campuses, at Fort Kent and Presque Isle, enroll many students whose native language is French. The classes, with the exception of French, are taught in English, since the students are bilingual. They come from Quebec and parts of Maine with French-speaking populations.

■ Bowdoin is the oldest higher-education institution in Maine. It was founded in 1794.

MARYLAND

HIGHER education in Maryland, like just about everything else, is dominated by Gov. William Donald Schaefer.

Mr. Schaefer, who won a second term last fall, has made higher education one of his priorities. During his administration, financial support for colleges and universities has increased by half. He has also strengthened the coordinating board, more clearly defined the role of campus presidents, and fought to bring most of the state's public institutions into the University of Maryland System.

But it may not be easy to maintain that momentum.

The once-thriving economy has cooled a little. The 1990 budget was somewhat tighter than college officials would have liked. And some members of the General Assembly have complained that they have not seen any positive results from Governor Schaefer's reorganization of higher education, or from the budget increases that the campuses have received.

Maryland's large black population watches higher education almost as closely as the legislature does. Many black lawmakers say the state does not do enough to support its public black colleges or to attract black students to other institutions.

Another contentious issue in the state involves higher education in Baltimore. Residents there continue to push for more programs, but advocates of the University of Maryland's flagship campus at College Park fear any expansion by the system's five Baltimore-area campuses.

For example, city officials and a panel of trustees of the Community College of Baltimore persuaded legislators to have the state take over the city-run institution. The Higher Education Commission, the state coordinating board, supported the move because the commissioners believed that the college could offer inner-city residents better programs if it had more money and more interaction with the rest of public higher education.

But advocates of the University of Maryland in College Park resisted the move because they said it would increase the competition for state dollars.

Community colleges and two four-year institutions remain outside the University of Maryland system.

Private colleges have long been influential in Maryland politics. The state has many liberal-arts institutions, among them Goucher and St. John's.

Maryland is also home to the Johns Hopkins University, a nationally known research university. In the last two years, Johns Hopkins, like many similar institutions around the country, has been developing new strategies to deal with tight budgets.

MARYLAND

Continued

DEMOGRAPHICS

Population: 4,694,000 (Rank: 19)

Age distribution:
Up to 17 .... 24.7%
18 to 24 .... 10.9%
25 to 34 .... 18.0%
35 and older 46.3%

Racial and ethnic distribution:
American Indian 0.2%
Asian 1.6%
Black 22.7%
White 75.1%
Other and unknown 0.4%
Hispanic (may be any race) .. 1.5%

Educational attainment of adults:
At least 4 years of high school 67.4%
At least 1 to 3 years of college 34.9%
At least 4 years of college ... 20.4%

Per-capita personal income: $21,013

New high-school graduates in:
1990-91 (estimate) 44,257
2000-01 (estimate) 51,039

New GED diploma recipients: 5,412

High-school dropout rate: 25.9%

POLITICAL LEADERSHIP

Governor: William Donald Schaefer (D), term ends 1995

Governor's higher-education adviser: Judy Sachwald, State House, Annapolis 21401; (301) 974-3004

U.S. Senators: Barbara A. Mikulski (D), term ends 1993; Paul S. Sarbanes (D), term ends 1995

U.S. Representatives:
5 Democrats, 3 Republicans
Helen Delich Bentley (R), Beverly B. Byron (D), Benjamin L. Cardin (D), Wayne Gilchrest (R), Steny H. Hoyer (D), C. Thomas McMillen (D), Kweisi Mfume (D), Constance A. Morella (R)

General Assembly: Senate, 38 Democrats, 9 Republicans; House, 116 Democrats, 25 Republicans

COLLEGES AND UNIVERSITIES

Higher education:
Public 4-year institutions 14
Public 2-year institutions 19
Private 4-year institutions 21
Private 2-year institutions 3
Total 57

Vocational institutions: 180

Statewide coordinating board:
Maryland Higher Education
    Commission
Jeffrey Building
16 Francis Street
Annapolis 21401
(301) 974-2971
Shaila R. Aery,
secretary of higher education

Private-college association:
Maryland Independent College
    and University Association
208 Duke of Gloucester Street
Annapolis 21401
(301) 269-0306
J. Elizabeth Garraway, president

Institutions censured by the AAUP:
Maryland Institute College of Art,
Morgan State University

Institution under NCAA sanctions:
University of Maryland
at College Park

FACULTY MEMBERS

Full-time faculty members:
At public institutions 4,561
At private institutions 1,259

Proportion who are women:
At public institutions 35.1%
At private institutions 28.9%

Proportion with tenure:
At public institutions 66.1%
At private institutions 48.4%

Average pay of full-time professors:
At public 4-year institutions $37,886
At public 2-year institutions $34,109
At private 4-year institutions $38,114
At private 2-year institutions $22,421

STUDENTS

Enrollment:
At public 4-year institutions 109,281
At public 2-year institutions 103,041
At private 4-year institutions 35,882
At private 2-year institutions .. 875
Undergraduate 212,645
First-time freshmen 31,699
Graduate 32,494
Professional 3,940
American Indian 688
Asian 9,962
Black 39,530
Hispanic 4,327
White 188,900
Foreign 5,672
Total 249,079

Enrollment highlights:
Women 56.1%
Full-time 46.1%
Minority 22.4%

Foreign 2.3%
10-year change in total
enrollment .... Up 16.0%

**Proportion of enrollment made up
of minority students:**
At public 4-year institutions . 25.1%
At public 2-year institutions . 22.8%
At private 4-year institutions 13.0%
At private 2-year institutions 12.9%

Degrees awarded:
Associate 7,061
Bachelor's 17,334
Master's 5,414
Doctorate 717
Professional 1,081

Residence of new students: State residents made up 83% of all freshmen enrolled in Maryland; 75% of all Maryland residents who were freshmen attended college in their home state.

Test scores: Students averaged 908 on the S.A.T., which was taken by 59% of Maryland's high-school seniors.

MONEY

Average tuition and fees:
At public 4-year institutions . $2,120
At public 2-year institutions . $1,172
At private 4-year institutions $9,914
At private 2-year institutions $8,393

Expenditures:
Public institutions .. $1,064,430,000
Private institutions ... $901,948,000

**State funds for higher-education
operating expenses:** $885,085,000
Two-year change: Up 26%

State spending on student aid:
Need-based: $15,468,000;
19,661 awards

MARYLAND

Continued

Non–need-based: $5,899,000;
3,320 awards

Other: $55,000

**Salary of chief executive
of largest public 4-year campus:**
William E. Kirwan, University
of Maryland at College Park:
$143,377

**Total spending on research and
development by doctorate-granting
universities:** $921,848,000

Sources:

Federal government 76.6%
State and local governments .. 6.9%
Industry 3.8%
The institution itself 10.0%
Other 2.7%

**Federal spending on education
and student aid (selected programs):**
Vocational and
adult education $13,251,000
GI Bill $9,193,000
Pell Grants $51,527,000

**Total federal spending on college-
and university-based research
and development:** $522,341,000

Selected programs:
Department of Health
and Human Services $184,220,000
National Science
Foundation $22,785,000
Department of Defense $278,413,000
Department
of Agriculture $4,526,000
Department of Energy .. $8,172,000

Largest endowment:
Johns Hopkins
University $527,209,000

Top fund raisers:
Johns Hopkins
University $84,062,000
University of Maryland $19,645,000
Loyola College $6,433,000

MISCELLANY

■ The University of Maryland at
College Park is home to the new National Public Broadcasting Archives,
sponsored by the university and the
Academy for Educational Development in Washington.

■ Goucher College has waived its
$35 application fee for people who are
recommended by its former students.
The action is part of an effort by
Goucher to boost its enrollment and
involve the alumni and alumnae.

■ Students at Morgan State University met in 1990 with Gov. William
Donald Schaefer to demand that the
state provide more funds for their historically black university. The meeting came in the midst of a week-long
sit-in at a campus administration
building by students who were protesting, among other things, a tuition
increase and poor dormitory conditions. State officials subsequently
promised to correct the conditions
that provoked the demonstrations.

■ The oldest institution of higher
education in Maryland is Washington
College, founded in 1782.

MASSACHUSETTS

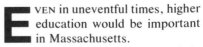

EVEN in uneventful times, higher
education would be important
in Massachusetts.
The Bay State is, after all, the birth-

place of American higher education. It is also home to elite private colleges like Amherst, Smith, Wellesley, and Williams, and to many of the world's foremost research institutions, including Harvard University and the Massachusetts Institute of Technology. Many of the high-technology companies that have developed in the state also owe their start to the scientific resources of those institutions.

Recent developments, however, have made colleges and universities particularly big news.

Most devastating have been the state's declining economy and its deepening budget problems, which in the last two years have forced painful cuts in financing for the state's 27 public institutions. The reductions have led institutions to eliminate courses, limit enrollments, and drastically raise tuition, all of which have outraged students.

The economic problems have also had a big impact on university management. Because of the budget uncertainty, the Board of Regents of Higher Education, which governs the 27 institutions, suspended its search to replace its chancellor, Franklyn G. Jenifer, who left to become president of Howard University. And when the president of the University of Massachusetts resigned, its Board of Trustees decided to give the chancellor of the Amherst campus the additional title of president of the entire three-campus system.

Public-college leaders have long complained that the state's generous financial-aid programs for private-college students deprive their institutions of needed resources. The public-college officials say the recent cuts are a further reflection of the state's traditional indifference to public higher education.

The standing of the public institutions has also been damaged, however, by a series of financial scandals in the late 1980's that involved top college administrators on a few campuses.

The public institutions' frustration is especially bitter because the state's economic woes follow a period when the state was beginning to provide generous increases to public higher education.

Private higher education has also been in the papers lately. The biggest news was the campaign of Boston University's outspoken president, John Silber, for Governor. The reputation of B.U. became a significant issue in the campaign, which Mr. Silber ultimately lost. The victor, William Weld, a Republican, succeeds Michael S. Dukakis, who did not seek re-election.

At Harvard, President Derek C. Bok has announced that he will retire in 1991. That transition could delay the start of what is expected to be a $2-billion fund-raising campaign at the university.

M.I.T., which offered its presidency to several unwilling candidates, has recently welcomed Charles M. Vest, the provost of the University of Michigan, as its new president.

Massachusetts continues to win praise in education circles for its efforts to improve public-school teaching. The state has raised teacher-training requirements and authorized an experiment that allows Boston University to operate the public schools in the city of Chelsea.

The state is also home to many of the nation's leading women's colleges—including Wellesley College, whose seemingly innocent invitation to Barbara Bush to speak at its 1990 commencement sparked a national

MASSACHUSETTS

Continued

debate over the role of women in today's society.

DEMOGRAPHICS

Population: 5,913,000   (Rank: 13)

Age distribution:
Up to 17	22.6%
18 to 24	11.1%
25 to 34	18.3%
35 and older	48.0%

Racial and ethnic distribution:
American Indian	0.2%
Asian	0.9%
Black	3.9%
White	93.7%
Other and unknown	1.3%
Hispanic (may be any race)	2.5%

Educational attainment of adults:
At least 4 years of high school	72.2%
At least 1 to 3 years of college	35.8%
At least 4 years of college	20.0%

Per-capita personal income: $22,174

New high-school graduates in:
1990-91 (estimate)	57,767
2000-01 (estimate)	59,491

New GED diploma recipients: 8,655

High-school dropout rate: 30.0%

POLITICAL LEADERSHIP

Governor: William F. Weld (R), term ends 1995

Governor's higher-education adviser: n/a

U.S. Senators: Edward M. Kennedy (D), term ends 1995; John F. Kerry (D), term ends 1997

U.S. Representatives:
10 Democrats, 1 Republican
Chester G. Atkins (D), Silvio O. Conte (R), Brian J. Donnelly (D), Joseph D. Early (D), Barney Frank (D), Joseph P. Kennedy, II (D), Edward J. Markey (D), Nicholas Mavroules (D), John Joseph Moakley (D), Richard E. Neal (D), Gerry E. Studds (D)

General Court: Senate, 24 Democrats, 16 Republicans; House, 120 Democrats, 40 Republicans

---

COLLEGES AND UNIVERSITIES

Higher education:
Public 4-year institutions	14
Public 2-year institutions	16
Private 4-year institutions	71
Private 2-year institutions	16
Total	117

Vocational institutions: 177

Statewide coordinating board:
Massachusetts Board of Regents
   of Higher Education
One Ashburton Place
Boston 02108
(617) 727-7785
Randolph Bromery, acting chancellor

Private-college association:
Association of Independent Colleges
   and Universities in Massachusetts
11 Beacon Street, Suite 1224
Boston 02108
(617) 742-5147
Clare M. Cotton, president

Institutions censured by the AAUP:
American International College,
Bridgewater State College,
Nichols College

Institutions under NCAA sanctions:
None

FACULTY MEMBERS

Full-time faculty members:
At public institutions 5,805
At private institutions 9,195

Proportion who are women:
At public institutions 32.7%
At private institutions 27.7%

Proportion with tenure:
At public institutions 72.2%
At private institutions 56.9%

Average pay of full-time professors:
At public 4-year institutions $41,949
At public 2-year institutions $30,327
At private 4-year institutions $41,870
At private 2-year institutions $24,007

STUDENTS

Enrollment:
At public 4-year institutions 112,800
At public 2-year institutions . 75,971
At private 4-year institutions 223,640
At private 2-year institutions 14,209
Undergraduate 343,625
First-time freshmen 75,667
Graduate 70,062
Professional 12,933
American Indian 1,157
Asian 13,731
Black 17,777
Hispanic 11,628
White 362,797
Foreign 19,530
Total 426,620

Enrollment highlights:
Women 55.3%
Full-time 62.9%
Minority 10.9%
Foreign 4.6%
10-year change in total
enrollment .... Up 11.0%

Proportion of enrollment made up of minority students:
At public 4-year institutions .. 7.3%
At public 2-year institutions . 13.4%
At private 4-year institutions 11.6%
At private 2-year institutions 14.5%

Degrees awarded:
Associate 13,047
Bachelor's 41,801
Master's 15,692
Doctorate 1,937
Professional 3,721

Residence of new students: State residents made up 68% of all freshmen enrolled in Massachusetts; 79% of all Massachusetts residents who were freshmen attended college in their home state.

Test scores: Students averaged 900 on the s.a.t., which was taken by 72% of Massachusetts' high-school seniors.

MONEY

Average tuition and fees:
At public 4-year institutions . $2,052
At public 2-year institutions . $1,332
At private 4-year institutions $11,450
At private 2-year institutions $7,186

Expenditures:
Public institutions $980,585,000
Private institutions . $3,544,867,000

State funds for higher-education operating expenses: $697,248,000

Two-year change: Down 20%

State spending on student aid:
Need-based: $65,494,000;
47,055 awards
Non–need-based: $1,569,000;
1,549 awards
Other: $21,251,000

MASSACHUSETTS

Continued

**Salary of chief executive
of largest public 4-year campus:**
Joseph D. Duffey, University
of Massachusetts at Amherst:
$109,000

**Total spending on research and
development by doctorate-granting
universities:** $867,521,000
Sources:
Federal government 71.7%
State and local governments .. 2.1%
Industry 9.1%
The institution itself 6.8%
Other 10.4%

**Federal spending on education
and student aid (selected programs):**
Vocational and
    adult education $17,280,000
GI Bill $8,139,000
Pell Grants $70,414,000

**Total federal spending on college-
and university-based research
and development:** $545,068,000
Selected programs:
Department of Health
    and Human Services $256,108,000
National Science
    Foundation $98,547,000
Department of Defense $86,439,000
Department
    of Agriculture $15,604,000
Department of Energy . $53,232,000

Largest endowment:
Harvard University $4,478,976,000

Top fund raisers:
Harvard University .. $185,353,000
Massachusetts Institute
    of Technology $95,719,000
Brandeis University ... $42,939,000

MISCELLANY

■ In a major policy shift, Harvard University agreed in 1989 to disregard the sexual orientation and marital status of faculty members and graduate students seeking to lease university housing.

■ Under a policy adopted in 1990 at the Massachusetts Institute of Technology, most parties, dances, and concerts must end no later than 12:30 a.m. M.I.T. officials established the policy to help reduce the number of people who try to attend campus events even though they are not affiliated with the institute.

■ Clark University is offering a money-back guarantee to students who eat in its dining halls. But those who are dissatisfied with the food are asked to raise the issue with the dining-hall manager and try to find reasonable alternatives before getting their money back.

■ A group of students at Harvard University has created the Society of Nerds and Geeks to promote the importance of learning for learning's sake.

■ Smith College is keeping its retired professors involved through a group called O.B.N.D. Members of the club, whose initials stand for "Old But Not Dead," meet each month, usually arranging for a current Smith professor to give a lecture. Twice a year, dinners or musical events are held.

■ Lasell Junior College, founded in 1851, is the oldest private junior college in the United States.

■ Harvard University, founded in 1636, is the country's oldest institution of higher education.

MICHIGAN

MICHIGAN has been in the vanguard of efforts to curb college costs and improve the campus climate for minority students—two of higher education's most pressing goals.

But it is still unclear whether the state's many efforts will prove effective.

The best known of those is the state's prepaid-tuition program, created in 1986 by former Gov. James J. Blanchard, a Democrat. The plan has been popular with citizens, but critics say the state has ignored the potential income-tax liability for participants. One of those critics is the new Governor, John M. Engler, a Republican who defeated Mr. Blanchard in November 1990. One study has questioned the financial soundness of the program in light of continually rising tuition rates. Mr. Engler said he would propose allowing contract holders to opt out of the plan and get their money back.

Governor Blanchard was critical of recent college tuition increases, and many institutions, particularly the University of Michigan, are taking the criticism to heart. The university, among the most prestigious public institutions in the country, recently announced an efficiency and cost-cutting program that could become a model for other public universities in the state and nation.

That chain of events also typifies how higher-education policy often develops in the state's unusually pluralistic governance system. There is no statewide governing or coordinating board. Public colleges and universities are run by their own independent boards, three of which—those at the University of Michigan and at Michigan State and Wayne State Universities—are selected in statewide partisan elections. The boards enjoy considerable autonomy, although their decisions are frequently influenced by the Governor and the money committees in the Legislature. Community colleges are run by local boards.

Competition among public institutions for funds is often intense, and lobbyists from the state's well-organized private-college sector also play an active role.

The private institutions and their students are eligible for state aid, and typically are treated generously by lawmakers who value the service that several of them provide to the inner-city residents of Detroit. Most of the private colleges in the state are small liberal-arts institutions.

Public colleges continue to wrestle with race-related issues in hiring and the curriculum. Recent efforts by institutions to enact anti-racism policies have raised questions of free speech. The University of Michigan is now considering a new policy, because its first proposal was declared unconstitutional by a federal judge.

DEMOGRAPHICS

Population: 9,273,000   (Rank: 8)

Age distribution:

Up to 17	26.4%
18 to 24	11.0%
25 to 34	17.7%
35 and older	44.9%

MICHIGAN

Continued

Racial and ethnic distribution:
American Indian 0.5%
Asian 0.7%
Black 12.9%
White 85.2%
Other and unknown 0.7%
Hispanic (may be any race) .. 1.8%

Educational attainment of adults:
At least 4 years of high school 68.0%
At least 1 to 3 years of college 30.0%
At least 4 years of college ... 14.3%

Per-capita personal income: $17,444

New high-school graduates in:
1990-91 (estimate) 105,516
2000-01 (estimate) 103,729

New GED diploma recipients: 11,549

High-school dropout rate: 26.4%

POLITICAL LEADERSHIP

Governor: John Engler (R), term ends 1995

Governor's higher-education adviser: n/a

U.S. Senators: Carl Levin (D), term ends 1997; Donald W. Riegle, Jr. (D), term ends 1995

U.S. Representatives:
11 Democrats, 7 Republicans
David E. Bonior (D), Wm. S. Broomfield (R), Dave Camp (R), Bob Carr (D), Barbara-Rose Collins (D), John Conyers, Jr. (D), Robert W. Davis (R), John D. Dingell (D), William D. Ford (D), Paul B. Henry (R), Dennis M. Hertel (D), Dale E. Kildee (D),
Sander M. Levin (D), Carl D. Pursell (R), Bob Traxler (D), Frederick S. Upton (R), Guy Vander Jagt (R), Howard Wolpe (D)

Legislature: Senate, 18 Democrats, 20 Republicans; House, 61 Democrats, 49 Republicans

COLLEGES AND UNIVERSITIES

Higher education:
Public 4-year institutions 15
Public 2-year institutions 29
Private 4-year institutions 48
Private 2-year institutions 5

Total 97

Vocational institutions: 314

Statewide coordinating board:
State Department of Education
P.O. Box 30008
Lansing 48909
(517) 373-3357
Gary D. Hawks, deputy
superintendent of public instruction

Private-college association:
Association of Independent Colleges
  and Universities of Michigan
650 Michigan National Tower
Lansing 48933
(517) 372-9160
Edward O. Blews, Jr., president

Institutions censured by the AAUP:
Hillsdale College, Olivet College,
University of Detroit

Institutions under NCAA sanctions:
None

FACULTY MEMBERS

Full-time faculty members:
At public institutions 10,597
At private institutions 1,984

Proportion who are women:
At public institutions 26.6%
At private institutions 30.3%

Proportion with tenure:
At public institutions 72.4%
At private institutions 58.2%

Average pay of full-time professors:
At public 4-year institutions $39,294
At public 2-year institutions $36,211
At private 4-year institutions $28,990
At private 2-year institutions $23,914

STUDENTS

Enrollment:
At public 4-year institutions 249,457
At public 2-year institutions 214,818
At private 4-year institutions 73,399
At private 2-year institutions . 4,906
Undergraduate 477,704
   First-time freshmen 95,821
Graduate 55,088
Professional 9,788
American Indian 3,122
Asian 8,607
Black 51,494
Hispanic 7,718
White 458,194
Foreign 13,445
Total 542,580

Enrollment highlights:
Women 54.7%
Full-time 51.0%
Minority 13.4%
Foreign 2.5%
10-year change in total
   enrollment .... Up 11.8%

Proportion of enrollment made up of minority students:
At public 4-year institutions . 11.4%
At public 2-year institutions . 14.3%
At private 4-year institutions 16.4%
At private 2-year institutions 28.5%

Degrees awarded:
Associate 19,298
Bachelor's 38,939
Master's 11,904
Doctorate 1,238
Professional 2,341

Residence of new students: State residents made up 85% of all freshmen enrolled in Michigan; 91% of all Michigan residents who were freshmen attended college in their home state.

Test scores: Students averaged 18.6 on the A.C.T., which was taken by 57% of Michigan's high-school seniors.

MONEY

Average tuition and fees:
At public 4-year institutions . $2,484
At public 2-year institutions . $1,047
At private 4-year institutions $6,520
At private 2-year institutions $6,400

Expenditures:
Public institutions .. $2,946,336,000
Private institutions ... $447,436,000

State funds for higher-education operating expenses: $1,486,694,000
Two-year change: Up 11%

State spending on student aid:
Need-based: $76,09o3,000;
   55,411 awards
Non–need-based: None
Other: $1,218,000

Salary of chief executive of largest public 4-year campus:
John A. DiBiaggio, Michigan State
   University: $142,000

MICHIGAN

Continued

Total spending on research and development by doctorate-granting universities: $486,270,000

Sources:
Federal government 54.2%
State and local governments .. 7.4%
Industry 7.4%
The institution itself 23.8%
Other 7.2%

Federal spending on education and student aid (selected programs):
Vocational and
adult education $30,917,000
GI Bill $15,608,000
Pell Grants $187,031,000

Total federal spending on college- and university-based research and development: $233,121,000

Selected programs:
Department of Health
and Human Services $135,827,000
National Science
Foundation $41,357,000
Department of Defense $15,272,000
Department
of Agriculture $10,723,000
Department of Energy . $11,186,000

Largest endowment:
University of Michigan $422,809,000

Top fund raisers:
University of Michigan $70,712,000
Michigan State
University $50,627,000
Wayne State University $14,370,000

MISCELLANY

■ A vote for a union in 1990 by faculty members at Mercy College of Detroit ended a three-year drought in the organization of full-time, tenure-system professors at four-year institutions.

■ A solar-powered car called Sunrunner, built in 1990 by engineering students at the University of Michigan, beat cars entered by students at 31 other universities in the 11-day Sunrayce USA, sponsored by General Motors Corporation.

■ An Ann Arbor physician is trying to help students pay for college by inviting them to play a game he has invented called "Scholarship." The game, which is similar to Trivial Pursuit, was invented by John Zettelmaier, a general practitioner who hopes to sell it in stores to generate revenue for a scholarship fund.

■ An "ugly art" auction at Concordia College helped raise $2,100 for its athletics program in 1989. The college's staff and faculty donated their tackiest pieces rummaged out of basements and attics—including portrayals of Elvis and coconut sculptures.

■ The University of Michigan boasts what may be the largest university computer room in the country. It's a 14,000-square-foot space that holds 260 Apple Macintosh computers and 70 I.B.M. PC's.

■ Local citizens joined Lake Superior State University's faculty members and students on the first day of spring 1990 to burn a papier-mâché snowman for the 20th year running.

■ The oldest institution of higher education in the state is the University of Michigan, founded in 1817.

MINNESOTA

MINNESOTA'S economy is strong, but lawmakers are well aware that budget projections in many other states have been revised downward. As a result, they have been trying to hold the line on spending.

Accordingly, the Legislature passed a state bond measure for campus expansion that requires colleges to cover about a third of the interest costs. But there's a catch—institutions cannot raise tuition to cover their debt-service costs.

What are the colleges supposed to do? The lawmakers expect them to cut spending, reallocate existing revenues—or forgo their building plans.

Meanwhile, concern about the management of the University of Minnesota, prompted by a series of financial scandals in 1988, has eased. Nils Hasselmo's first big task as president of the university was convincing then-Gov. Rudy Perpich, a Democrat, and state legislators that the institution was straightening out its problems. So far, he has succeeded.

The state's new Governor, Arne Carlson, was an active participant on a 10-member panel convened in 1989 by the University of Minnesota to review finances and operations following the scandals. University officials say Mr. Carlson, a Republican and former State Auditor, showed a deep understanding of higher-education issues and concerns, but they note that other pressing issues in the state will probably capture more of his attention as Governor.

Lawmakers, meanwhile, have shifted their attention from the management issue to improving the quality of higher education in the state's major metropolitan area. A study commissioned by the state coordinating board found that the Minneapolis–St. Paul area lacked the research facilities and high-technology training programs it needed as an up-and-coming urban center.

The report recommended changing the missions of the University of Minnesota–Twin Cities and Metropolitan State University. The University of Minnesota would focus on science and technology and develop stronger ties to industry, while Metropolitan State would expand its undergraduate program. The Legislature has asked the Minnesota Higher Education Coordinating Board to review the study and develop a plan to put its recommendations into effect.

The coordinating board conducts statewide planning for all the systems. While the board is not powerful, it has been influential because of the high quality of its studies on policy issues. The University of Minnesota, Minnesota State University, and community-college systems have separate governing boards.

Private higher education is also healthy in Minnesota. The state has some nationally known liberal-arts institutions, such as Carleton and Macalester Colleges, as well as many institutions affiliated with Lutheran groups. The private colleges have an effective lobby.

DEMOGRAPHICS

Population: 4,353,000 (Rank: 21)

Age distribution:

Up to 17	26.0%
18 to 24	10.4%
25 to 34	18.2%
35 and older	45.5%

MINNESOTA
Continued

Racial and ethnic distribution:

American Indian 0.9%
Asian 0.8%
Black 1.3%
White 96.7%
Other and unknown 0.3%
Hispanic (may be any race) .. 0.8%

Educational attainment of adults:
At least 4 years of high school 73.1%
At least 1 to 3 years of college 34.5%
At least 4 years of college ... 17.4%

Per-capita personal income: $17,657

New high-school graduates in:
1990-91 (estimate) 49,774
2000-01 (estimate) 58,248

New GED diploma recipients: 5,098

High-school dropout rate: 9.1%

POLITICAL LEADERSHIP

Governor: Arne Carlson (R), term ends 1995

Governor's higher-education adviser: n/a

U.S. Senators: Dave Durenberger (R), term ends 1995; Paul Wellstone (D), term ends 1997

U.S. Representatives:
6 Democrats, 2 Republicans
James L. Oberstar (D), Timothy J. Penny (D), Collin Peterson (D), Jim Ramstad (R), Martin Olav Sabo (D), Gerry Sikorski (D), Bruce F. Vento (D), Vin Weber (R)

Legislature: Senate, 46 Democrats, 21 Republicans; House, 80 Democrats, 54 Republicans

---

COLLEGES AND UNIVERSITIES

Higher education:

Public 4-year institutions 10
Public 2-year institutions 26
Private 4-year institutions 34
Private 2-year institutions 11

Total 81

Vocational institutions: 122

Statewide coordinating board:
Minnesota Higher Education
  Coordinating Board
400 Capitol Square Building
550 Cedar Street
St. Paul 55101
(612) 296-9665
David R. Powers, executive director

Private-college association:
Minnesota Private College Council
Park Square Court, Suite 560
400 Sibley Street
St. Paul 55101
(612) 228-9061
David B. Laird, Jr., president

Institutions censured by the AAUP:
None

Institution under NCAA sanctions:
University of Minnesota–Twin Cities

FACULTY MEMBERS

Full-time faculty members:
At public institutions 4,786
At private institutions 2,058

Proportion who are women:
At public institutions 26.8%
At private institutions 32.0%

Proportion with tenure:
At public institutions 71.4%
At private institutions 61.7%

Average pay of full-time professors:
At public 4-year institutions $36,911
At public 2-year institutions $34,129
At private 4-year institutions $31,469
At private 2-year institutions $25,370

STUDENTS

Enrollment:
At public 4-year institutions   133,905
At public 2-year institutions . 57,281
At private 4-year institutions   48,621
At private 2-year institutions . 4,899
Undergraduate 214,285
    First-time freshmen 48,262
Graduate 24,868
Professional 5,553
American Indian 1,731
Asian 3,929
Black 3,274
Hispanic 1,507
White 229,422
Foreign 4,843
Total 244,706

Enrollment highlights:
Women 54.7%
Full-time 60.5%
Minority 4.4%
Foreign 2.0%
10-year change in total
    enrollment .... Up 29.4%

Proportion of enrollment made up
of minority students:
At public 4-year institutions .. 4.3%
At public 2-year institutions .. 4.1%
At private 4-year institutions . 4.4%
At private 2-year institutions . 8.7%

Degrees awarded:
Associate 7,591
Bachelor's 21,167
Master's 3,839
Doctorate 549
Professional 1,560

Residence of new students: State residents made up 80% of all freshmen enrolled in Minnesota; 82% of all Minnesota residents who were freshmen attended college in their home state.

Test scores: Students averaged 19.7 on the A.C.T., which was taken by 46% of Minnesota's high-school seniors.

MONEY

Average tuition and fees:
At public 4-year institutions . $2,063
At public 2-year institutions . $1,499
At private 4 year institutions $8,776
At private 2-year institutions $5,181

Expenditures:
Public institutions .. $1,324,691,000
Private institutions ... $521,441,000

State funds for higher-education
operating expenses: $1,028,528,000
Two-year change: Up 19%

State spending on student aid:
Need-based: $68,000,000;
    62,470 awards
Non–need-based: None
Other: $1,589,000

Salary of chief executive
of largest public 4-year campus:
Nils Hasselmo, University
    of Minnesota–Twin Cities: $152,300

Total spending on research and
development by doctorate-granting
universities: $258,614,000
Sources:
Federal government 51.4%
State and local governments . 16.4%

MINNESOTA

Continued

Industry 4.8%
The institution itself 16.9%
Other 10.5%

**Federal spending on education
and student aid (selected programs):**
Vocational and
  adult education $13,248,000
GI Bill $11,245,000
Pell Grants $108,850,000

**Total federal spending on college-
and university-based research
and development:** $123,621,000

Selected programs:
Department of Health
  and Human Services $84,295,000
National Science
  Foundation $16,831,000
Department of Defense . $5,416,000
Department
  of Agriculture $7,378,000
Department of Energy .. $4,990,000

Largest endowment:
University
  of Minnesota $247,438,000

Top fund raisers:
University
  of Minnesota $100,170,000
Mayo Medical School . $31,925,000
St. Olaf College $7,332,000

MISCELLANY

■ In 1989 Minnesota became the first state to enact specific legislation aimed at those who create and distribute computer "viruses" or other destructive computer programs. Violators of the law could face up to $50,000 in fines and 10 years in jail.

■ At Christmas 1989, a sprig of mistletoe that hung in an academic office at Moorhead State University became the subject of news reports across the country and even overseas. After a few professors complained that the sprig could encourage sexual harassment, it was removed at the suggestion of the university president.

■ Minnesotans battle over which institution of higher education is the oldest in the state. The University of Minnesota–Twin Cities was chartered in 1851 but did not admit a freshman class until 1869. Hamline University slipped in with its charter in 1854, and commenced classes that same year.

MISSISSIPPI

Mississippi's drive to improve education has encountered a major hurdle that could have a serious impact on the state's recent successes with its public colleges and universities: The 1990 Legislature approved a series of reforms to improve public schools, but provided no money to pay for them.

That has created a "chicken-egg" situation, in the words of one state higher-education leader. By 1995, state leaders want to raise admissions standards at public institutions by requiring freshmen to have taken a foreign language and basic laboratory sciences. But because many school districts still do not have the resources to offer those college-preparatory courses, some legislators and civil-rights activists worry that disadvantaged students will be excluded from college.

Mississippi's legacy of segregation makes the issue especially sensitive. Many of the poorest school districts are also predominantly black, and civil-rights activists say that raising admissions standards could effectively deny black citizens access to higher education.

Nonetheless, Gov. Ray Mabus, a Democrat, and his Commissioner of Higher Education, W. Ray Cleere, are committed to the plan. They intend to ask the Board of Trustees of State Institutions of Higher Learning—the coordinating and governing board for all eight public four-year colleges—and the State Board for Community and Junior Colleges to approve the higher standards, and then work to win financial backing for the school reforms.

Finding that money could prove difficult. Despite declines in its oil- and agriculture-based economy, the state has provided substantial salary increases to teachers and college faculty members in recent years, and has financed much-needed renovations on many campus buildings. But the economy is not growing enough to support further increases without a tax hike.

The state has yet to satisfy civil-rights leaders who say its public-college system still discriminates against black students. They say the predominantly white institutions do not do enough to recruit minority students or create a comfortable climate for them once they reach the campuses. The state is home to three predominantly black public institutions—Alcorn State, Jackson State, and Mississippi Valley State Universities—as well as several private black colleges and two-year institutions.

Mississippi has other private colleges, most of which are small and affiliated with religious groups.

DEMOGRAPHICS

Population: 2,621,000 (Rank: 31)

Age distribution:
Up to 17 .... 29.3%
18 to 24 .... 11.4%
25 to 34 .... 16.6%
35 and older 42.7%

Racial and ethnic distribution:
American Indian 0.3%
Asian 0.3%
Black 35.2%
White 64.1%
Other and unknown 0.1%
Hispanic (may be any race) .. 1.0%

Educational attainment of adults:
At least 4 years of high school 54.8%
At least 1 to 3 years of college 25.6%
At least 4 years of college ... 12.3%

Per-capita personal income: $11,724

New high-school graduates in:
1990-91 (estimate) 26,544
2000-01 (estimate) 26,490

New GED diploma recipients: 5,466

High-school dropout rate: 33.1%

POLITICAL LEADERSHIP

Governor: Ray Mabus (D), term ends 1992

Governor's higher-education adviser: Pickett Wilson, State Capitol, P.O. Box 139, Jackson 39205; (601) 359-3150

U.S. Senators: Thad Cochran (R), term ends 1997; Trent Lott (R), term ends 1995

MISSISSIPPI

Continued

U.S. Representatives:
5 Democrats, 0 Republicans
Mike Espy (D), G.V. (Sonny) Montgomery (D), Mike Parker (D), Gene
Taylor (D), Jamie L. Whitten (D)

Legislature: Senate, 43 Democrats, 9
Republicans; House, 104 Democrats,
18 Republicans

COLLEGES AND UNIVERSITIES

Higher education:
Public 4-year institutions 9
Public 2-year institutions 20
Private 4-year institutions 12
Private 2-year institutions 6
Total 47

Vocational institutions: 48

Statewide coordinating boards:
Board of Trustees of State Institutions
    of Higher Learning
3825 Ridgewood Road
Jackson 39211
(601) 982-6611
W. Ray Cleere, commissioner

State Board for Community
    and Junior Colleges
3825 Ridgewood Road
Jackson 39211
(601) 982-6518
Olon E. Ray, executive director

Private-college association:
Mississippi Association
    of Independent Colleges
P.O. Drawer 1198
Clinton 39060
(601) 925-3400
Johnnie Ruth Hudson,
executive director

Institutions censured by the AAUP:
None

Institutions under NCAA sanctions:
None

FACULTY MEMBERS

Full-time faculty members:
At public institutions 3,287
At private institutions 321

Proportion who are women:
At public institutions 41.9%
At private institutions 37.1%

Proportion with tenure:
At public institutions 53.4%
At private institutions 38.0%

Average pay of full-time professors:
At public 4-year institutions $29,828
At public 2-year institutions $23,566
At private 4-year institutions $22,841
At private 2-year institutions $16,670

STUDENTS

Enrollment:
At public 4-year institutions . 53,344
At public 2-year institutions . 46,653
At private 4-year institutions   10,258
At private 2-year institutions . 2,617
Undergraduate 101,515
    First-time freshmen 30,291
Graduate 9,628
Professional 1,729
American Indian 337
Asian 604
Black 30,367
Hispanic 316
White 79,451
Foreign 1,797
Total 112,872

Enrollment highlights:
Women 56.7%
Full-time 77.0%

Minority 28.5%
Foreign 1.6%
10-year change in total
   enrollment .... Up 15.7%

**Proportion of enrollment made up
of minority students:**
At public 4-year institutions . 31.1%
At public 2-year institutions . 25.1%
At private 4-year institutions 27.0%
At private 2-year institutions 42.4%

Degrees awarded:
Associate 4,504
Bachelor's 8,486
Master's 2,082
Doctorate 241
Professional 473

Residence of new students: State residents made up 87% of all freshmen enrolled in Mississippi; 92% of all Mississippi residents who were freshmen attended college in their home state.

Test scores: Students averaged 15.9 on the A.C.T., which was taken by 64% of Mississippi's high-school seniors.

MONEY

Average tuition and fees:
At public 4-year institutions . $1,858
At public 2-year institutions .. $680
At private 4-year institutions $4,828
At private 2-year institutions $3,602

Expenditures:
Public institutions $706,380,000
Private institutions $64,054,000

State funds for higher-education operating expenses: $443,597,000

Two-year change: Up 4%

State spending on student aid:
Need-based: $1,243,000; 2,200 awards
Non–need-based: $748,000;
   142 awards
Other: None

**Salary of chief executive
of largest public 4-year campus:**
Donald W. Zacharias, Mississippi
   State University: $95,000

**Total spending on research and
development by doctorate-granting
universities:** $75,175,000
Sources:
Federal government 42.7%
State and local governments . 27.3%
Industry 7.1%
The institution itself 12.8%
Other 10.1%

**Federal spending on education
and student aid (selected programs):**
Vocational and
   adult education $10,961,000
GI Bill $6,234,000
Pell Grants $68,225,000

**Total federal spending on college-
and university-based research
and development:** $37,891,000
Selected programs:
Department of Health
   and Human Services . $6,977,000
National Science
   Foundation $1,203,000
Department of Defense $12,109,000
Department
   of Agriculture $9,545,000
Department of Energy .. $4,239,000

Largest endowment:
University of Mississippi $37,707,000

Top fund raisers:
University of Mississippi $12,410,000
Mississippi State
   University $11,336,000
Mississippi College $3,757,000

MISSISSIPPI
Continued

MISCELLANY

■ Children's books by more than 1,000 authors and illustrators are part of a research collection at the University of Southern Mississippi's McCain Library.

■ The lead plaintiff in the *Adams* case, the landmark desegregation lawsuit that ultimately involved 18 Southern and border states, was Kenneth Adams, a resident of Brandon. He was 16 years old when the suit was filed in 1970. A federal appeals court dismissed the case in June 1990.

■ The University of Mississippi is home of the Center for the Study of Southern Culture, a leading institute in the growing field of regional studies.

■ The oldest institution of higher education in the state is Mississippi College, a Southern Baptist institution founded in 1826.

MISSOURI

I N 1990 two of Missouri's most influential citizen's groups examined the state's public colleges and universities and declared them "chronically underfunded."

The diagnosis, from organizations of business and community leaders from Kansas City and St. Louis, came as no surprise to higher-education leaders and some legislators. They had been arguing for more money for several years, but without success.

However, the new appeal—for an immediate infusion of $300-million for operating expenses and an additional $311-million for computers and building renovations—went unheeded by the General Assembly and Republican Gov. John Ashcroft.

For some politicians, Missouri voters' strong support for low taxes was reason enough to reject the pleas.

Others say Missouri must re-evaluate whether it needs so many colleges in sparsely populated areas before the state commits new funds to higher education.

That reassessment, they say, should cover not only the nine independently governed regional institutions but also the way the University of Missouri allocates its resources, which must be shared among the flagship campus in rural Columbia and the newer branches that serve such major metropolitan regions as Kansas City and St. Louis.

Community leaders in those cities say their branches do not receive an adequate portion of the university's resources.

A Board of Curators governs the University of Missouri System, and each of the 10 community colleges is governed by its own board.

The analysis by the citizen's groups also highlighted other issues facing the public colleges.

It said colleges should recruit more minority faculty members and students, increase their inventory of basic and advanced scientific and engineering equipment, and extend community-college districts to areas currently not served by them.

Although private colleges in Missouri do not now have as much clout as public institutions, their influence is gradually increasing as the number of students who attend the state's many church-related institutions continues to grow. Two other private institutions, Washington University and Saint Louis University, are particularly respected. Washington's research programs have given it a national reputation, and the institution is known for its ability to attract big donations.

Missouri has a Coordinating Board for Higher Education, which is gaining respect in policy-making matters.

The biggest splash in Missouri higher education in the last year may have come from the state Attorney General's office. In an effort to crack down on unscrupulous trade schools, the attorneys created a fake trade school to show how easy it is to win accreditation from some organizations.

DEMOGRAPHICS

Population: 5,159,000   (Rank: 15)

Age distribution:
Up to 17 .... 25.3%
18 to 24 .... 10.2%
25 to 34 .... 17.2%
35 and older 47.3%

Racial and ethnic distribution:
American Indian 0.3%
Asian 0.5%
Black 10.5%
White 88.4%
Other and unknown 0.3%
Hispanic (may be any race) .. 1.1%

Educational attainment of adults:
At least 4 years of high school 63.5%
At least 1 to 3 years of college 27.2%
At least 4 years of college ... 13.9%

Per-capita personal income: $16,292

New high-school graduates in:
1990-91 (estimate) 52,675
2000-01 (estimate) 57,473

New GED diploma recipients: 7,698

High-school dropout rate: 26.0%

POLITICAL LEADERSHIP

Governor: John Ashcroft (R), term ends 1993

Governor's higher-education adviser: Karen Gallagher, State Capitol, P.O. Box 720, Jefferson City 65102; (314) 751-3222

U.S. Senators: Christopher S. Bond (R), term ends 1993; John C. Danforth (R), term ends 1995

U.S. Representatives:
6 Democrats, 3 Republicans
William (Bill) Clay (D), E. Thomas Coleman (R), Bill Emerson (R), Richard A. Gephardt (D), Mel Hancock (R), Joan Kelly Horn (D), Ike Skelton (D), Harold L. Volkmer (D), Alan Wheat (D)

General Assembly: Senate, 22 Democrats, 11 Republicans, 1 vacancy; House, 98 Democrats, 65 Republicans

---

COLLEGES AND UNIVERSITIES

Higher education:
Public 4-year institutions 13
Public 2-year institutions 14
Private 4-year institutions 52
Private 2-year institutions 10
Total 89

Vocational institutions: 203

MISSOURI

Continued

Statewide coordinating board:
Coordinating Board for
  Higher Education
101 Adams Street
Jefferson City 65101
(314) 751-2361
Charles J. McClain, commissioner
of higher education

Private-college association:
Independent Colleges and
  Universities of Missouri
514 Earth City Expressway, Suite 244
Earth City 63045
(314) 739-4770
Charles V. Gallagher, president

Institutions censured by the AAUP:
Concordia Seminary,
Metropolitan Community Colleges

Institution under NCAA sanctions:
University of Missouri at Columbia

FACULTY MEMBERS

Full-time faculty members:
At public institutions 4,703
At private institutions 2,225

Proportion who are women:
At public institutions 27.2%
At private institutions 32.3%

Proportion with tenure:
At public institutions 65.9%
At private institutions 58.6%

Average pay of full-time professors:
At public 4-year institutions $33,260
At public 2-year institutions $30,400
At private 4-year institutions $30,730
At private 2-year institutions $22,312

STUDENTS

Enrollment:
At public 4-year institutions 116,420
At public 2-year institutions . 62,379
At private 4-year institutions 80,085
At private 2-year institutions . 2,783
Undergraduate 220,565
  First-time freshmen 39,586
Graduate 32,792
Professional 8,310
American Indian 840
Asian 3,922
Black 20,110
Hispanic 2,610
White 228,721
Foreign 5,464
Total 261,667

Enrollment highlights:
Women 53.8%
Full-time 57.6%
Minority 10.7%
Foreign 2.1%
10-year change in total
  enrollment .... Up 18.3%

**Proportion of enrollment made up
of minority students:**
At public 4-year institutions .. 8.9%
At public 2-year institutions . 13.4%
At private 4-year institutions 10.9%
At private 2-year institutions 20.7%

Degrees awarded:
Associate 6,711
Bachelor's 23,029
Master's 7,920
Doctorate 537
Professional 2,264

Residence of new students: State residents made up 79% of all freshmen enrolled in Missouri; 85% of all Missouri residents who were freshmen attended college in their home state.

Test scores: Students averaged 19.0 on the A.C.T., which was taken by 60% of Missouri's high-school seniors.

MONEY

Average tuition and fees:
At public 4-year institutions . $1,532
At public 2-year institutions .. $815
At private 4-year institutions $7,170
At private 2-year institutions $5,554

Expenditures:
Public institutions $999,869,000
Private institutions ... $911,951,000

State funds for higher-education operating expenses: $637,378,000

Two-year change: Up 16%

State spending on student aid:
Need-based: $10,814,000;
　8,600 awards
Non–need-based: $6,543,000;
　3,309 awards
Other: $260,000

Salary of chief executive of largest public 4-year campus:
Haskell M. Monroe, University of Missouri at Columbia: $110,500 from state plus $10,000 from private sources

Total spending on research and development by doctorate-granting universities: $255,009,000

Sources:
Federal government 54.8%
State and local governments .. 5.7%
Industry 9.9%
The institution itself 23.4%
Other 6.3%

Federal spending on education and student aid (selected programs):
Vocational and
　adult education $17,062,000
GI Bill $13,013,000
Pell Grants $106,891,000

Total federal spending on college- and university-based research and development: $137,276,000

Selected programs:
Department of Health
　and Human Services $108,317,000
National Science
　Foundation $9,822,000
Department of Defense . $2,278,000
Department
　of Agriculture $7,902,000
Department of Energy .. $2,332,000

Largest endowment:
Washington
　University $1,294,209,000

Top fund raisers:
Washington University $49,339,000
University of Missouri . $38,412,000
Saint Louis University . $16,071,000

MISCELLANY

■ Hammonds House, a state-of-the-art residence hall at Southwest Missouri State University, offers sun-tanning beds and delivers food to students' rooms.

■ Harris-Stowe State College was founded in 1857 as the first teacher-education college west of the Mississippi River.

■ Lincoln University, a land-grant institution, has a predominantly black enrollment of resident students and a predominantly white enrollment of commuter students, most of them Jef-

MISSOURI

Continued

ferson City residents taking evening courses.

■ The National Association of Intercollegiate Athletics, the governing body for about 500 small-college sports programs, has its headquarters in Missouri.

■ The oldest higher-education institution in Missouri is Saint Louis University, a Roman Catholic institution founded in 1818.

MONTANA

MONTANA is one of the biggest yet most sparsely populated states in the nation, and many people there believe it has too many colleges.

That view has attracted attention in the past decade because lagging revenues from the state's stagnant agricultural and mining economy have forced Montana to slash higher-education budgets repeatedly. But thus far, advocates of the current higher-education structure have been able to convince lawmakers that closing institutions would hurt students' chances to go to college.

A citizens' committee appointed by the Governor is studying the state's long-term higher-education needs, and college officials hope a result will be a push for tax reform. For their part, the colleges say the problem is not with the quality of their programs but rather with the level of financial support they receive from the state.

The committee and higher-education officials, however, may have a difficult time convincing lawmakers and voters that additional revenue is needed. Montana is one of five states with no sales tax, and politicians aggressively avoid any appearance of supporting one.

The Board of Regents of Higher Education is the governing board for all public institutions in the state.

Montana has several small, private colleges. In addition, the state is home to tribally controlled colleges that serve Montana's American Indian population. Among them are Fort Belknap, Little Big Horn, and Stone Child Colleges.

DEMOGRAPHICS

Population: 806,000 (Rank: 44)

Age distribution:

Up to 17	27.0%
18 to 24	9.8%
25 to 34	17.4%
35 and older	45.9%

Racial and ethnic distribution:

American Indian	4.8%
Asian	0.4%
Black	0.2%
White	94.2%
Other and unknown	0.4%
Hispanic (may be any race)	1.3%

Educational attainment of adults:

At least 4 years of high school	74.4%
At least 1 to 3 years of college	36.5%
At least 4 years of college	17.5%

Per-capita personal income: $14,078

New high-school graduates in:

1990-91 (estimate)	9,179
2000-01 (estimate)	9,600

New GED diploma recipients: 1,471

High-school dropout rate: 12.7%

POLITICAL LEADERSHIP

Governor: Stan Stephens (R), term ends 1993

Governor's higher-education adviser: Marilyn Miller, State Capitol, Helena 59620; (406) 444-3111

U.S. Senators: Max Baucus (D), term ends 1997; Conrad R. Burns (R), term ends 1995

U.S. Representatives:
1 Democrat, 1 Republican
Ron Marlenee (R), Pat Williams (D)

Legislature: Senate, 29 Democrats, 21 Republicans; House, 60 Democrats, 39 Republicans, 1 undecided race

---

COLLEGES AND UNIVERSITIES

Higher education:
Public 4-year institutions 6
Public 2-year institutions 7
Private 4-year institutions 3
Private 2-year institutions 3
Total 19

Vocational institutions: 45

Statewide coordinating board:
Montana University System
33 South Last Chance Gulch
Helena 59620
(406) 444-6570
John M. Hutchinson,
commissioner of higher education

Private-college association:
None

Institutions censured by the AAUP:
None

Institutions under NCAA sanctions:
None

FACULTY MEMBERS

Full-time faculty members:
At public institutions 1,158
At private institutions 145

Proportion who are women:
At public institutions 22.6%
At private institutions 33.1%

Proportion with tenure:
At public institutions 62.0%
At private institutions 56.2%

Average pay of full-time professors:
At public 4-year institutions $29,648
At public 2-year institutions $26,793
At private 4-year institutions $23,782
At private 2-year institutions $22,076

STUDENTS

Enrollment:
At public 4-year institutions . 27,403
At public 2-year institutions .. 3,884
At private 4-year institutions . 3,305
At private 2-year institutions . 1,180
Undergraduate 32,250
    First-time freshmen 5,992
Graduate 3,312
Professional 210
American Indian 2,068
Asian 135
Black 141
Hispanic 269
White 32,472
Foreign 687
Total 35,772

Enrollment highlights:
Women 52.4%
Full-time 72.2%

MONTANA

Continued

Minority 7.4%
Foreign 1.9%
10-year change in total
   enrollment .... Up 15.0%

Proportion of enrollment made up of minority students:
At public 4-year institutions .. 4.3%
At public 2-year institutions .. 9.8%
At private 4-year institutions . 5.7%
At private 2-year institutions 77.0%

Degrees awarded:
Associate 714
Bachelor's 4,170
Master's 724
Doctorate 65
Professional 78

Residence of new students: State residents made up 86% of all freshmen enrolled in Montana; 72% of all Montana residents who were freshmen attended college in their home state.

Test scores: Students averaged 19.8 on the A.C.T., which was taken by 54% of Montana's high-school seniors.

MONEY

Average tuition and fees:
At public 4-year institutions . $1,535
At public 2-year institutions .. $877
At private 4-year institutions $5,034
At private 2-year institutions $1,144

Expenditures:
Public institutions $182,102,000
Private institutions $22,349,000

State funds for higher-education operating expenses: $116,648,000
Two-year change: Up 11%

State spending on student aid:
Need-based: $417,000; 1,300 awards
Non–need-based: None
Other: None

Salary of chief executive of largest public 4-year campus:
William J. Tietz, Montana State
   University: $89,000

Total spending on research and development by doctorate-granting universities: $32,450,000
Sources:
Federal government 35.6%
State and local governments . 24.4%
Industry 10.0%
The institution itself 29.4%
Other 0.6%

Federal spending on education and student aid (selected programs):
Vocational and
   adult education $4,095,000
GI Bill $2,722,000
Pell Grants $21,612,000

Total federal spending on college- and university-based research and development: $8,554,000
Selected programs:
Department of Health
   and Human Services . $1,844,000
National Science
   Foundation $1,962,000
Department of Defense ... $249,000
Department
   of Agriculture $2,645,000
Department of Energy $238,000

Largest endowment:
University of Montana
   Foundation $16,600,000

Top fund raisers:
Carroll College $1,297,000
Montana College of Mineral
   Science and Technology $872,000
Eastern Montana College . $692,000

MISCELLANY

■ Little Big Horn College, a two-year college run by the Crow Indians, enrolled one of its largest classes ever during the fall 1989 semester—the equivalent of 200 full-time students, compared with 32 in 1982. In addition to para-professional and academic-transfer programs, the college offers courses in Crow history and language.

■ The oldest institution of higher education in Montana is Rocky Mountain College, an interdenominational institution founded in 1878.

NEBRASKA

HISTORICALLY, the University of Nebraska at Lincoln has dominated higher education in this Great Plains state. But in 1990 the chairmen of the legislature's appropriations and education committees set in motion a plan to end the university's monopoly.

The legislature, called the Unicameral, is trying to give more power to the relatively weak Nebraska Coordinating Commission for Postsecondary Education. Specifically, the Unicameral wants to develop a comprehensive higher-education system that will offer quality programs throughout the state.

Lawmakers hope an invigorated coordinating commission will see the economic and educational value of improving some of the state's regional institutions. The institutions are important because Nebraska is so large that many people cannot travel to Lincoln. The legislature's plan required an amendment to the state constitution, which was approved in the November 1990 election.

Voters elected a new Governor, Ben Nelson, a Democrat who wants to increase minority enrollment at state universities by improving financial aid, recruitment, and counseling.

At least one controversial higher-education issue has been resolved: The much-debated fate of Kearney State College was settled in May 1990 when the Nebraska Supreme Court approved a law that moves Kearney from the state-college system to the university system. Some supporters of the University of Nebraska at Lincoln fought the plan, saying it would hurt the main campus. During the gubernatorial campaign, Mr. Nelson criticized his Republican opponent, Gov. Kay A. Orr, for failing to show leadership in the debate over Kearney State.

Tensions persist, however, between private colleges and state institutions over the spending of public money on financial aid for students at private colleges. And public institutions have tried to remove a seat for a private-college representative from the state coordinating commission.

DEMOGRAPHICS

Population: 1,611,000   (Rank: 36)

Age distribution:

Up to 17	26.3%
18 to 24	10.4%
25 to 34	17.4%
35 and older	45.9%

Racial and ethnic distribution:

American Indian	0.6%
Asian	0.5%
Black	3.1%
White	95.1%

NEBRASKA
Continued

Other and unknown 0.8%
Hispanic (may be any race) .. 1.8%

Educational attainment of adults:
At least 4 years of high school 73.4%
At least 1 to 3 years of college 32.8%
At least 4 years of college ... 15.5%

Per-capita personal income: $15,446

New high-school graduates in:
1990-91 (estimate) 18,016
2000-01 (estimate) 19,257

New GED diploma recipients: 2,350

High-school dropout rate: 14.6%

POLITICAL LEADERSHIP

Governor: Ben Nelson (D), term ends 1995

Governor's higher-education adviser: n/a

U.S. Senators: J. James Exon (D), term ends 1997; Bob Kerrey (D), term ends 1995

U.S. Representatives:
1 Democrat, 2 Republicans
Bill Barrett (R), Doug Bereuter (R), Peter Hoagland (D)

Unicameral: Nonpartisan legislature

COLLEGES AND UNIVERSITIES

Higher education:
Public 4-year institutions 7
Public 2-year institutions 13

Private 4-year institutions 14
Private 2-year institutions 2
Total 36

Vocational institutions: 48

Statewide coordinating board:
Nebraska Coordinating Commission
  for Postsecondary Education
State Capitol, 6th Floor
P.O. Box 95005
Lincoln 68509
(402) 471-2847
Bruce G. Stahl, executive director

Private-college association:
Association of Independent Colleges
  and Universities of Nebraska
521 South 14th Street, Suite 302
Lincoln 68508
(402) 434-2818
Thomas J. O'Neill, Jr., president

Institutions censured by the AAUP:
None

Institutions under NCAA sanctions:
None

FACULTY MEMBERS

Full-time faculty members:
At public institutions 1,995
At private institutions 605

Proportion who are women:
At public institutions 24.9%
At private institutions 29.3%

Proportion with tenure:
At public institutions 65.9%
At private institutions 60.3%

Average pay of full-time professors:
At public 4-year institutions $31,641
At public 2-year institutions $24,106
At private 4-year institutions $27,820
At private 2-year institutions $20,975

STUDENTS

Enrollment:

At public 4-year institutions . 57,107
At public 2-year institutions . 30,676
At private 4-year institutions 16,370
At private 2-year institutions .. 464
Undergraduate 91,629
  First-time freshmen 17,319
Graduate 10,357
Professional 2,631
American Indian 625
Asian 948
Black 2,520
Hispanic 1,220
White 97,630
Foreign 1,674
Total 104,617

Enrollment highlights:

Women 53.8%
Full-time 55.6%
Minority 5.2%
Foreign 1.6%
10-year change in total
  enrollment .... Up 28.1%

**Proportion of enrollment made up
of minority students:**

At public 4-year institutions .. 4.1%
At public 2-year institutions .. 6.1%
At private 4-year institutions . 7.1%
At private 2-year institutions . 4.6%

Degrees awarded:

Associate 2,546
Bachelor's 8,288
Master's 1,722
Doctorate 248
Professional 706

Residence of new students: State residents made up 86% of all freshmen enrolled in Nebraska; 85% of all Nebraska residents who were freshmen attended college in their home state.

Test scores: Students averaged 19.6 on the A.C.T., which was taken by 69% of Nebraska's high-school seniors.

MONEY

Average tuition and fees:

At public 4-year institutions . $1,519
At public 2-year institutions .. $919
At private 4-year institutions $6,442
At private 2-year institutions $3,410

Expenditures:

Public institutions $537,858,000
Private institutions ... $161,066,000

State funds for higher-education operating expenses: $329,121,000

Two-year change: Up 30%

State spending on student aid:

Need-based: $2,037,000; 2,500 awards
Non–need-based: None
Other: None

**Salary of chief executive
of largest public 4-year campus:**

Martin A. Massengale, University
  of Nebraska at Lincoln: $124,800

**Total spending on research and
development by doctorate-granting
universities:** $93,916,000

Sources:

Federal government 39.2%
State and local governments . 24.5%
Industry 9.7%
The institution itself 22.3%
Other 4.4%

**Federal spending on education
and student aid (selected programs):**

Vocational and
  adult education $5,391,000
GI Bill $6,430,000
Pell Grants $39,626,000

NEBRASKA

Continued

Total federal spending on college- and university-based research and development: $25,763,000

Selected programs:
Department of Health
and Human Services $11,990,000
National Science
Foundation $3,966,000
Department of Defense ... $655,000
Department
of Agriculture $4,971,000
Department of Energy $578,000

Largest endowment:
University of Nebraska $155,284,000

Top fund raisers:
University of Nebraska $34,553,000
Creighton University .. $26,519,000
Nebraska Wesleyan
University $2,785,000

MISCELLANY

■ Tractors from China, France, Italy, Germany, Japan, the Soviet Union, and the United States are sent to the University of Nebraska's Lincoln campus to be tested at the Tractor Testing Lab.

■ The Natural Science Museum at the University of Nebraska features one of the most extensive collections of prehistoric fossils in the world.

■ The University of Nebraska at Omaha is the home of the only academic center in the Western Hemisphere devoted exclusively to the study of Afghanistan.

■ The oldest institution of higher education in Nebraska is Peru State College, founded in 1867.

NEVADA

IT IS probably no coincidence that Nevada, a state with some of the lowest taxes in the country, also saw one of the nation's biggest population surges in the past decade.

The two factors are combining to create serious enrollment pressures at the state's two public universities and four community colleges. As a result, higher-education and civic leaders are starting to suggest that it's time for the state to look beyond its traditional sources of income—tourism and gambling —in order to increase financing for higher education and other public services.

The University of Nevada, an aggressive system with four-year campuses in Reno and Las Vegas, has made a concerted push in recent years to enhance its scientific and research facilities.

At times the system's ambitions have put it at odds with state officials in Carson City—most notably in late 1989, when the system agreed to conduct research for the Department of Energy on developing a nuclear-waste dump in the state, a project that state lawmakers vehemently oppose.

But the university's efforts to upgrade its stature have generally enjoyed backing from the Legislature and Gov. Bob Miller, a Democrat who won re-election in November 1990.

The system has also recognized the need to find money from other sources. In 1990 the University of Nevada at Reno began a six-year, $105-

million fund-raising drive. The Las Vegas campus has shown an aptitude for attracting federal funds, including $10-million for a National Supercomputing Center for Energy and the Environment.

The Board of Regents of the University of Nevada system, an elected body, governs all public higher education in the state. The regents also oversee the state's Desert Research Institute, which is devoted to scientific and social studies on topics related to water, air, energy, and geology.

DEMOGRAPHICS

Population: 1,111,000 (Rank: 40)

Age distribution:
Up to 17 .... 25.0%
18 to 24 .... 10.0%
25 to 34 .... 20.2%
35 and older 44.8%

Racial and ethnic distribution:
American Indian 1.8%
Asian 1.9%
Black 6.4%
White 87.8%
Other and unknown 2.1%
Hispanic (may be any race) .. 6.7%

Educational attainment of adults:
At least 4 years of high school 75.5%
At least 1 to 3 years of college 35.1%
At least 4 years of college ... 14.4%

Per-capita personal income: $19,269

New high-school graduates in:
1990-91 (estimate) 9,679
2000-01 (estimate) 15,515

New GED diploma recipients: 2,760

High-school dropout rate: 24.2%

POLITICAL LEADERSHIP

Governor: Bob Miller (D), term ends 1995

Governor's higher-education adviser: Scott Craigie, Capitol Complex, Carson City 89710; (702) 687-5670

U.S. Senators: Richard H. Bryan (D), term ends 1995; Harry Reid (D), term ends 1993

U.S. Representatives:
1 Democrat, 1 Republican
James H. Bilbray (D), Barbara F. Vucanovich (R)

Legislature: Senate, 11 Democrats, 10 Republicans; House, 22 Democrats, 20 Republicans

COLLEGES AND UNIVERSITIES

Higher education:
Public 4-year institutions 2
Public 2-year institutions 4
Private 4-year institutions 1
Private 2-year institutions 1
Total 8

Vocational institutions: 55

Statewide coordinating board:
University of Nevada System
2601 Enterprise Road
Reno 89512
(702) 784-4901
Mark H. Dawson, chancellor

Private-college association:
None

Institutions censured by the AAUP:
None

Institution under NCAA sanctions:
University of Nevada at Las Vegas

NEVADA
Continued

FACULTY MEMBERS

Full-time faculty members:
At public institutions 877
At private institutions .... n/a

Proportion who are women:
At public institutions 27.3%
At private institutions .... n/a

Proportion with tenure:
At public institutions 59.7%
At private institutions .... n/a

Average pay of full-time professors:
At public 4-year institutions $37,654
At public 2-year institutions $31,157
At private 4-year institutions $31,381
At private 2-year institutions ... n/a

STUDENTS

Enrollment:
At public 4-year institutions . 25,179
At public 2-year institutions . 23,467
At private 4-year institutions .. 161
At private 2-year institutions ... 25
Undergraduate 44,517
  First-time freshmen 8,182
Graduate 4,132
Professional 183
American Indian 667
Asian 1,603
Black 2,242
Hispanic 2,324
White 41,304
Foreign 692
Total 48,832

Enrollment highlights:
Women 54.7%
Full-time 31.4%
Minority 14.2%

Foreign 1.4%
10-year change in total
  enrollment .... Up 45.6%

Proportion of enrollment made up of minority students:
At public 4-year institutions . 12.1%
At public 2-year institutions . 16.5%
At private 4-year institutions ... n/a
At private 2-year institutions . 8.0%

Degrees awarded:
Associate 857
Bachelor's 1,943
Master's 434
Doctorate 28
Professional 46

Residence of new students: State residents made up 89% of all freshmen enrolled in Nevada; 86% of all Nevada residents who were freshmen attended college in their home state.

Test scores: Students averaged 19.0 on the A.C.T., which was taken by 42% of Nevada's high-school seniors.

MONEY

Average tuition and fees:
At public 4-year institutions . $1,100
At public 2-year institutions .. $522
At private 4-year institutions $5,400
At private 2-year institutions ... n/a

Expenditures:
Public institutions $180,107,000
Private institutions $2,448,000

State funds for higher-education operating expenses: $163,324,000
Two-year change: Up 35%

State spending on student aid:
Need-based: $400,000; 400 awards
Non–need-based: None
Other: None

**Salary of chief executive
of largest public 4-year campus:**
Robert C. Maxson, University
    of Nevada at Las Vegas: $141,400

**Total spending on research and
development by doctorate-granting
universities:** $34,146,000
Sources:
Federal government 51.6%
State and local governments .. 5.3%
Industry 12.0%
The institution itself 27.3%
Other 3.9%

**Federal spending on education
and student aid (selected programs):**
Vocational and
    adult education $4,101,000
GI Bill $2,933,000
Pell Grants $13,910,000

**Total federal spending on college-
and university-based research
and development:** $13,856,000
Selected programs:
Department of Health
    and Human Services . $2,682,000
National Science
    Foundation $2,272,000
Department of Defense $90,000
Department
    of Agriculture $1,211,000
Department of Energy $593,000

Largest endowment:
University of Nevada
System $56,056,000

Top fund raisers: n/a

MISCELLANY

■ The University of Nevada at
Reno is using $3.5-million it will re-
ceive as a result of an unusual court
decision to give local students scholarships for college. In 1990 a district
judge ordered a construction company to pay the university the $3.5-mil-
lion because of damages from con-
struction-related dust.

■ The only Basque-studies program
in the Western Hemisphere is at the
University of Nevada at Reno. It is
primarily a research institute, with
four full-time research faculty members and four to six visiting researchers from around the world at any given
time during the academic year. There
are 20,000 Basque-related volumes in
the library.

■ The oldest institution of higher
education in the state is the University
of Nevada at Reno, founded in 1874.

NEW HAMPSHIRE

B Y tradition, politicians survive
in New Hampshire only if
they "take the pledge"
against taxes.

The practice is a good indicator of
the state's conservative character but
a source of continuing financial trou-
ble for its public colleges and universities, which already feel overshadowed
by the state's many private colleges.

The state has no sales tax or person-
al-income tax, so even if Gov. Judd
Gregg and the legislature were of a
mind to give the public institutions
more money, they would have few
sources to draw from. Mr. Gregg, a
Republican, was re-elected in November 1990 to a second two-year term.

The state has two public higher-education systems: the University of
New Hampshire and the vocational-
technical system.

NEW HAMPSHIRE
Continued

The financial squeeze was especially tight last year because of a slowdown in the agricultural and manufacturing economy. Some students were so angry over a mid-semester tuition hike—a result of cuts in college budgets—that they refused to pay and sued the University of New Hampshire, claiming the increase violated their contract with the institution.

Nearly half of all students in New Hampshire attend private colleges, although many of the more prestigious of those institutions, particularly Dartmouth College, draw their students from throughout the country.

Dartmouth has been a pioneer in encouraging students to use computers in their academic work. It is also home to the *Dartmouth Review*, a newspaper privately financed by conservative benefactors. The *Review* is known for its criticism of affirmative action and divestment, and has spawned a series of imitators on other campuses.

DEMOGRAPHICS

Population: 1,107,000 (Rank: 41)

Age distribution:
Up to 17 .... 25.3%
18 to 24 .... 11.1%
25 to 34 .... 18.2%
35 and older 45.3%

Racial and ethnic distribution:
American Indian 0.2%
Asian 0.4%
Black 0.4%
White 98.9%

Other and unknown 0.1%
Hispanic (may be any race) .. 0.6%

Educational attainment of adults:
At least 4 years of high school 72.3%
At least 1 to 3 years of college 35.1%
At least 4 years of college ... 18.2%

Per-capita personal income: $20,267

New high-school graduates in:
1990-91 (estimate) 11,255
2000-01 (estimate) 13,223

New GED diploma recipients: 1,677

High-school dropout rate: 25.9%

POLITICAL LEADERSHIP

Governor: Judd Gregg (R), term ends 1993

Governor's higher-education adviser: Nancy Baybutt, State House, Concord 03301; (603) 271-2121

U.S. Senators: Warren Rudman (R), term ends 1993; Robert Smith (R), term ends 1997

U.S. Representatives:
1 Democrat, 1 Republican
Dick Swett (D), Bill Zeliff (R)

General Court: Senate, 11 Democrats, 13 Republicans; House, 135 Democrats, 265 Republicans

---

COLLEGES AND UNIVERSITIES

Higher education:
Public 4-year institutions 5
Public 2-year institutions 7
Private 4-year institutions 12
Private 2-year institutions 5
Total 29

Vocational institutions: 28

Statewide coordinating board:
New Hampshire Postsecondary
  Education Commission
Two Industrial Park Drive
Concord 03301
(603) 271-2555
James A. Busselle, executive director

Private-college association:
None

Institutions censured by the AAUP:
None

Institutions under NCAA sanctions:
None

FACULTY MEMBERS

Full-time faculty members:
At public institutions 1,023
At private institutions 900

Proportion who are women:
At public institutions 27.3%
At private institutions 30.0%

Proportion with tenure:
At public institutions 71.2%
At private institutions 47.3%

Average pay of full-time professors:
At public 4-year institutions $35,124
At public 2-year institutions $25,874
At private 4-year institutions $35,764
At private 2-year institutions $13,618

STUDENTS

Enrollment:
At public 4-year institutions . 23,686
At public 2-year institutions .. 6,677
At private 4-year institutions 24,167
At private 2-year institutions .. 804
Undergraduate 47,598
  First-time freshmen 11,453

Graduate 7,099
Professional 637
American Indian 190
Asian 541
Black 611
Hispanic 647
White 52,433
Foreign 912
Total 55,334

Enrollment highlights:
Women 53.8%
Full-time 65.0%
Minority 3.7%
Foreign 1.6%
10-year change in total
  enrollment .... Up 33.2%

**Proportion of enrollment made up
of minority students:**
At public 4-year institutions .. 1.6%
At public 2-year institutions .. 1.6%
At private 4-year institutions . 6.4%
At private 2-year institutions . 3.1%

Degrees awarded:
Associate 2,369
Bachelor's 6,778
Master's 1,596
Doctorate 69
Professional 172

Residence of new students: State residents made up 49% of all freshmen enrolled in New Hampshire; 58% of all New Hampshire residents who were freshmen attended college in their home state.

Test scores: Students averaged 928 on the S.A.T., which was taken by 67% of New Hampshire's high-school seniors.

MONEY

Average tuition and fees:
At public 4-year institutions . $2,196
At public 2-year institutions . $1,608

NEW HAMPSHIRE
Continued

At private 4-year institutions $10,299
At private 2-year institutions $4,050

Expenditures:
Public institutions $183,959,000
Private institutions ... $264,440,000

State funds for higher-education operating expenses: $72,959,000

Two-year change: Up 1%

State spending on student aid:
Need-based: $925,000; 1,760 awards
Non–need-based: $10,000; 10 awards
Other: $800,000

Salary of chief executive of largest public 4-year campus:
Dale F. Nitzschke, University of New Hampshire: $120,000

Total spending on research and development by doctorate-granting universities: $62,172,000

Sources:
Federal government 67.3%
State and local governments .. 4.3%
Industry 4.7%
The institution itself 15.0%
Other 8.7%

Federal spending on education and student aid (selected programs):
Vocational and
   adult education $4,162,000
GI Bill $2,283,000
Pell Grants $7,787,000

Total federal spending on college- and university-based research and development: $36,766,000

Selected programs:
Department of Health
   and Human Services $19,232,000

National Science
   Foundation $4,271,000
Department of Defense . $2,400,000
Department
   of Agriculture $1,661,000
Department of Energy .. $1,041,000

Largest endowment:
Dartmouth College ... $632,027,000

Top fund raisers:
Dartmouth College $47,455,000
Colby-Sawyer College .. $1,953,000
St. Anselm College $1,757,000

MISCELLANY

■ Since 1977, St. Anselm College has required all freshmen and sophomores to take a two-year, interdisciplinary humanities program called "Portraits of Human Greatness." The students examine the ideas and values of Western civilization by devoting several weeks at a time to historical figures such as Lorenzo de Medici, Calvin, and Darwin.

■ Dartmouth College has computerized 600 years' worth of analyses of Dante's the *Divine Comedy*.

■ Dartmouth College, founded in 1769, is the oldest higher-education institution in New Hampshire.

NEW JERSEY

I N the 1980's New Jersey's economy was strong, and Thomas H. Kean, a Republican, was the quintessential "education governor."

The state created a series of new programs to improve the quality of public higher education, emphasizing teacher education, high technology, and educating minority students.

Now Mr. Kean is president of Drew University; New Jersey's economy has gone flat; and the new Governor, James J. Florio, a Democrat, has had the unpleasant task of slashing programs and raising taxes to make up a $3-billion deficit.

Already many higher-education programs have been subjected to budget cuts—including some of the programs created with so much enthusiasm just a few years earlier. The cuts have also led to double-digit tuition increases on campuses across the state.

The cuts may hamper efforts by New Jersey's colleges to improve their services to the state's large black, Hispanic, and working-class-immigrant populations. Members of those groups have not attended college in large numbers in the past, and many higher-education officials fear that the loss of special programs for such students would discourage them from enrolling.

At the same time, the state faces a leadership vacuum in higher education. Edward J. Bloustein, the president of Rutgers University, died in 1989. He was succeeded by Francis L. Lawrence, provost of Tulane University. The presidents of many of the state's other public and private institutions have retired or resigned in recent years. T. Edward Hollander, chancellor of the Department of Higher Education, quit in June 1990 to become a faculty member at Rutgers.

Governor Florio pushed through a major change in the way New Jersey supports its public schools. Under the new plan, impoverished districts would get much more money than in the past, and the hope is that more

students from those districts would be able to get quality educations and continue in college. Continuing protests from taxpayers, college students, and others over the Governor's tax hikes and budget cuts, however, have prompted him to reconsider his tax-reform package, including parts of his public-school financing plan.

New Jersey has had a strong tradition of private higher education since Princeton University was founded in 1746. Under Mr. Kean's leadership, Drew is expected to become more prominent than it has been in the past. Other important private institutions in New Jersey include Rider College and Fairleigh Dickinson and Seton Hall Universities.

The state also has a long political tradition of strong local governments, which has led state leaders to eschew a statewide community-college system in favor of one that is largely controlled and financed by localities.

The Board of Higher Education coordinates postsecondary education. Its staff is the Department of Higher Education, headed by a chancellor who is a member of the Governor's cabinet. There are 31 governing boards for public institutions.

DEMOGRAPHICS

Population: 7,736,000   (Rank: 9)

Age distribution:

Up to 17	23.7%
18 to 24	10.2%
25 to 34	16.7%
35 and older	49.4%

Racial and ethnic distribution:

American Indian	0.1%
Asian	1.5%
Black	12.6%
White	83.6%

NEW JERSEY
Continued

Other and unknown 2.2%
Hispanic (may be any race) .. 6.7%

Educational attainment of adults:
At least 4 years of high school 67.4%
At least 1 to 3 years of college 31.5%
At least 4 years of college ... 18.3%

Per-capita personal income: $23,778

New high-school graduates in:
1990-91 (estimate) 79,005
2000-01 (estimate) 82,886

New GED diploma recipients: 5,636

High-school dropout rate: 22.6%

POLITICAL LEADERSHIP

Governor: James J. Florio (D), term
ends 1994

**Governor's higher-education advis-
er:** Tom Corcoran, State House, CN-
001, Trenton 08625; (609) 777-1243

U.S. Senators: Bill Bradley (D), term
ends 1997; Frank R. Lautenberg (D),
term ends 1995

U.S. Representatives:
8 Democrats, 6 Republicans
Robert Andrews (D), Bernard J.
Dwyer (D), Dean A. Gallo (R), Frank
J. Guarini (D), William J. Hughes (D),
Frank Pallone, Jr. (D), Donald M.
Payne (D), Matthew J. Rinaldo (R),
Robert A. Roe (D), Marge Roukema
(R), Jim Saxton (R), Christopher H.
Smith (R), Robert G. Torricelli (D),
Richard A. Zimmer (R)

Legislature: Senate, 23 Democrats, 17

Republicans; House, 43 Democrats,
37 Republicans

COLLEGES AND UNIVERSITIES

Higher education:
Public 4-year institutions 14
Public 2-year institutions 19
Private 4-year institutions 25
Private 2-year institutions 4
Total 62

Vocational institutions: 192

Statewide coordinating board:
Board of Higher Education
20 West State Street, CN542
Trenton 08625
(609) 292-4310
Edward D. Goldberg,
acting chancellor

Private-college association:
Association of Independent Colleges
 and Universities in New Jersey
P.O. Box 206
Summit 07901
(201) 277-3738
John B. Wilson, president

Institutions censured by the AAUP:
Camden County College,
Rider College

Institution under NCAA sanctions:
Upsala College

FACULTY MEMBERS

Full-time faculty members:
At public institutions 5,873
At private institutions 2,521

Proportion who are women:
At public institutions 33.7%
At private institutions 25.2%

Proportion with tenure:
At public institutions 75.5%
At private institutions 63.8%

Average pay of full-time professors:
At public 4-year institutions $42,197
At public 2-year institutions $34,768
At private 4-year institutions $40,307
At private 2-year institutions ... n/a

STUDENTS

Enrollment:
At public 4-year institutions 133,123
At public 2-year institutions 110,644
At private 4-year institutions 55,937
At private 2-year institutions . 2,936
Undergraduate 256,695
First-time freshmen 44,381
Graduate 39,832
Professional 6,113
American Indian 847
Asian 11,196
Black 28,831
Hispanic 17,894
White 232,047
Foreign 11,825
Total 302,640

Enrollment highlights:
Women 55.0%
Full-time 49.9%
Minority 20.2%
Foreign 3.9%
10-year change in total
enrollment .... Down 1.8%

Proportion of enrollment made up of minority students:
At public 4-year institutions . 20.6%
At public 2-year institutions . 21.8%
At private 4-year institutions 16.0%
At private 2-year institutions 23.4%

Degrees awarded:
Associate 9,379
Bachelor's 22,327

Master's 6,397
Doctorate 824
Professional 1,723

Residence of new students: State residents made up 86% of all freshmen enrolled in New Jersey; 58% of all New Jersey residents who were freshmen attended college in their home state.

Test scores: Students averaged 891 on the S.A.T., which was taken by 69% of New Jersey's high-school seniors.

MONEY

Average tuition and fees:
At public 4-year institutions . $2,511
At public 2-year institutions . $1,130
At private 4-year institutions $9,398
At private 2-year institutions $6,748

Expenditures:
Public institutions .. $1,406,490,000
Private institutions ... $714,733,000

State funds for higher-education operating expenses: $1,055,893,000
Two-year change: Down 7%

State spending on student aid:
Need-based: $85,372,000;
55,860 awards
Non–need-based: $6,317,000;
5,071 awards
Other: None

Salary of chief executive of largest public 4-year campus:
Francis L. Lawrence, Rutgers
University at New Brunswick:
$170,000

Total spending on research and development by doctorate-granting universities: $283,087,000
Sources:
Federal government 41.8%

NEW JERSEY
Continued

State and local governments . 15.9%
Industry 5.9%
The institution itself 29.2%
Other 7.2%

**Federal spending on education
and student aid (selected programs):**
Vocational and
  adult education $20,337,000
GI Bill $5,590,000
Pell Grants $73,686,000

**Total federal spending on college-
and university-based research
and development:** $104,853,000
Selected programs:
Department of Health
  and Human Services $47,115,000
National Science
  Foundation $24,902,000
Department of Defense $12,728,000
Department
  of Agriculture $3,726,000
Department of Energy .. $5,418,000

Largest endowment:
Princeton University $2,483,829,000

Top fund raisers:
Princeton University .. $80,316,000
Rutgers University ... $24,615,000
Seton Hall University .. $6,606,000

MISCELLANY

■ Women studying science and
math at Rutgers University's Doug-
lass College have a dormitory designed especially for them. The building, named after two former deans of
the women's college, provides housing for 110 students, a resource library, and a microcomputer facility.

■ In 1990 Princeton University received a $21-million gift from Laur-
ance S. Rockefeller to establish a center for the study and teaching of human values.

■ Upsala College daily changes the
international flags flying on its campus
to represent the cultural and ethnic diversity of the student population.

■ Princeton University is the oldest
institution of higher education in New
Jersey. It was founded in 1746.

NEW MEXICO

ICHARD E. PECK, the new president of the University of New
Mexico, had to hit the ground
running. Before he moved into his office on the Albuquerque campus, a
lawsuit was filed to open the records
of the presidential search, and Hispanic groups complained because a
Hispanic was not a finalist.

The complaints were not meant to
be critical of Mr. Peck. Rather, they
were an outgrowth of the pressure that
political and demographic changes in
this Southwestern state have placed
on higher education.

The University of New Mexico has
been feeling the political impact of the
Democrat-controlled Legislature
more than any other state institution.
Since the Democratic majority elected
Hispanic lawmakers to lead the House
of Representatives and the Senate, the
university and its affirmative-action
policies have been under scrutiny as
never before.

Former Gov. Garrey E. Carruthers,
a Republican and a former professor

of agricultural economics at New Mexico State University, has also taken a strong interest in higher education. He was limited to one term.

The new Governor, Bruce King, has served in the post twice before, in 1971-74 and 1979-82, and was generous to higher education.

But since then, state revenues from oil and gas have dwindled. Although the state's economy is becoming more diverse, New Mexico lawmakers are not awash in dollars.

The state's Commission on Higher Education has been urging lawmakers to change the financing formula for higher education. The commission says it would be more efficient and less expensive to have the two-year institutions do the majority of the lower-division and remedial instruction. A new formula would offer the research institutions incentives to pursue more graduate and upper-division work and, at the same time, give the smaller institutions incentives to undertake more lower-division and remedial work.

The Commission on Higher Education, whose members are appointed by the Governor, is the statewide coordinating agency for postsecondary education. There are 11 governing boards for public institutions.

Only three private, non-profit colleges operate in the state. One is St. John's College in Santa Fe, which is affiliated with St. John's College in Maryland.

DEMOGRAPHICS

Population: 1,528,000   (Rank: 37)

Age distribution:
Up to 17 .... 29.7%
18 to 24 .... 10.5%
25 to 34 .... 17.3%
35 and older 42.5%

Racial and ethnic distribution:
American Indian 8.2%
Asian 0.6%
Black 1.8%
White 76.0%
Other and unknown 13.3%
Hispanic (may be any race) . 36.6%

Educational attainment of adults:
At least 4 years of high school 68.9%
At least 1 to 3 years of college 34.7%
At least 4 years of college ... 17.6%

Per-capita personal income: $13,140

New high-school graduates in:
1990-91 (estimate) 16,692
2000-01 (estimate) 21,195

New GED diploma recipients: 3,487

High-school dropout rate: 28.1%

POLITICAL LEADERSHIP

Governor: Bruce King (D), term ends 1995

Governor's higher-education adviser: n/a

U.S. Senators: Jeff Bingaman (D), term ends 1995; Pete V. Domenici (R), term ends 1997

U.S. Representatives:
1 Democrat, 2 Republicans
Bill Richardson (D), Steven Schiff (R), Joe Skeen (R)

Legislature: Senate, 26 Democrats, 16 Republicans; House, 49 Democrats, 21 Republicans

NEW MEXICO

Continued

COLLEGES AND UNIVERSITIES

Higher education:
Public 4-year institutions 6
Public 2-year institutions 16
Private 4-year institutions 4
Private 2-year institutions 0

Total 26

Vocational institutions: 39

Statewide coordinating board:
Commission on Higher Education
1068 Cerrillos Road
Santa Fe 87501
(505) 827-8300
Kathleen M. Kies, executive director

Private-college association:
New Mexico Association
of Independent Colleges
P.O. Box 3593
Albuquerque 87190
(505) 473-6271
Robert E. Rhodes, executive director

Institutions censured by the AAUP:
None

Institutions under NCAA sanctions:
None

FACULTY MEMBERS

Full-time faculty members:
At public institutions 2,045
At private institutions 88

Proportion who are women:
At public institutions 27.7%
At private institutions 23.9%

Proportion with tenure:
At public institutions 59.7%
At private institutions 58.1%

Average pay of full-time professors:
At public 4-year institutions $33,100
At public 2-year institutions $25,360
At private 4-year institutions $26,496
At private 2-year institutions ... n/a

STUDENTS

Enrollment:
At public 4-year institutions . 47,396
At public 2-year institutions . 29,998
At private 4-year institutions . 2,056
At private 2-year institutions 0
Undergraduate 68,603
    First-time freshmen 11,194
Graduate 10,220
Professional 627
American Indian 4,546
Asian 929
Black 1,667
Hispanic 20,221
White 50,647
Foreign 1,440
Total 79,450

Enrollment highlights:
Women 54.5%
Full-time 54.8%
Minority 35.1%
Foreign 1.8%
10-year change in total
    enrollment .... Up 42.6%

**Proportion of enrollment made up
of minority students:**
At public 4-year institutions . 30.7%
At public 2-year institutions . 41.9%
At private 4-year institutions 33.4%
At private 2-year institutions ... n/a

Degrees awarded:
Associate 1,760
Bachelor's 4,778

Master's 1,798
Doctorate 222
Professional 164

Residence of new students: State residents made up 84% of all freshmen enrolled in New Mexico; 82% of all New Mexico residents who were freshmen attended college in their home state.

Test scores: Students averaged 17.8 on the A.C.T., which was taken by 55% of New Mexico's high-school seniors.

MONEY

Average tuition and fees:
At public 4-year institutions . $1,326
At public 2-year institutions .. $496
At private 4-year institutions $7,335
At private 2-year institutions ... n/a

Expenditures:
Public institutions $456,600,000
Private institutions $16,500,000

State funds for higher-education operating expenses: $335,466,000

Two-year change: Up 21%

State spending on student aid:
Need-based: $5,309,000; 7,072 awards
Non–need-based: $2,950,000;
  1,969 awards
Other: None

**Salary of chief executive
of largest public 4-year campus:**
Richard E. Peck, University
  of New Mexico: $135,000

Total spending on research and development by doctorate-granting universities: $136,189,000

Sources:
Federal government 56.4%

State and local governments . 10.7%
Industry 12.1%
The institution itself 13.1%
Other 7.7%

**Federal spending on education
and student aid (selected programs):**
Vocational and
  adult education $5,872,000
GI Bill $6,665,000
Pell Grants $34,928,000

**Total federal spending on college-
and university-based research
and development:** $56,163,000

Selected programs:
Department of Health
  and Human Services . $9,584,000
National Science
  Foundation $5,416,000
Department of Defense $15,658,000
Department
  of Agriculture $2,530,000
Department of Energy .. $1,894,000

Largest endowment:
University of
  New Mexico $38,080,000

Top fund raisers:
University of
  New Mexico $12,012,000
New Mexico Military
  Institute $1,312,000
College of Santa Fe $782,000

MISCELLANY

■ The Lea County Cowboy Hall of Fame and Western Heritage Center pays tribute to ranching and rodeo with historical exhibits. The center is located at the New Mexico Junior College campus.

■ The Los Alamos National Laboratory, one of three national laboratories that the University of California

NEW MEXICO

Continued

system operates for the Energy Department, grew out of federal nuclear research done in the 1940's, including the Manhattan Project.

■ The oldest institution of higher education in the state is the New Mexico State University main campus, founded in 1888.

NEW YORK

HIGHER education in New York is diverse and sophisticated. Its constellation of private institutions includes nationally renowned research institutions like Columbia, Cornell, and Rockefeller Universities; small liberal-arts colleges like Colgate University and Vassar College; specialized institutions like the Juilliard School and Cooper Union; and a host of other influential colleges and universities, including Fordham and Syracuse Universities.

The state is also home to two mammoth public-university systems: the State University of New York and the City University of New York. Both include community colleges, professional schools, and research universities.

The SUNY campus in Buffalo, which has been upgrading its research facilities, was admitted to the select ranks of the Association of American Universities in 1989, joining five private institutions in the state that already were members.

Private higher education wields considerable political clout in the Empire State. Not only is New York one of only six states to provide funds directly to private institutions, but it also devotes a considerable portion of its generous student-aid budget to students who attend private colleges.

In fact, New York is the leading state provider of student financial aid. About 20 per cent of all the money spent by states for financial aid in 1989-90 was spent by New York, which also provided 35 per cent of all the state assistance to graduate students.

With its Liberty Partnership and Liberty Scholarship programs, the state has also been a pioneer in the growing "mentoring" movement, which promises financial assistance and counseling to school children interested in college.

Gov. Mario M. Cuomo, a Democrat re-elected to a third term in 1990, cites those programs as examples of his commitment to improving access to higher education. Mr. Cuomo also says he would like to restore free tuition to the state's public institutions, but he has never offered a budget that would allow that to happen.

Indeed, both public- and private-college leaders in New York complain that the Governor's actions rarely match his rhetoric. Those leaders have come to rely heavily on the Legislature for support. As a result, the annual budget-making process typically draws the state's well-organized student associations and faculty unions to Albany for lobbying campaigns.

Budgets have been especially tight in recent years, and fears that they would result in higher tuition have prompted sit-ins and protests on several campuses.

The issue has become especially political at CUNY, where minority students are in the majority on many campuses. Some student activists and faculty members say the tight budgets are a sign that the state is uninterested in supporting a university system that has come to be dominated by needy Caribbean, Hispanic, and black students.

The question of tuition will probably preoccupy CUNY's new chancellor, W. Ann Reynolds. Ms. Reynolds resigned under fire as chancellor of the California State University system and was quickly named by the CUNY Board of Trustees to replace Joseph S. Murphy, who had decided to return to teaching. SUNY has its own board.

Cornell, a private university that operates four SUNY units, is the state's land-grant institution.

New York City is also a center for American philanthropy and for literary and artistic life, both of which have an impact on higher education.

Grant seekers regularly travel to New York to meet with leaders of such organizations as the Ford, Rockefeller, and Andrew W. Mellon Foundations and the Carnegie Corporation. The city is also home to the New York Public Library and many major publishing houses and journals.

DEMOGRAPHICS

Population: 17,950,000   (Rank: 2)

Age distribution:
Up to 17 .... 24.2%
18 to 24 .... 10.6%
25 to 34 .... 16.9%
35 and older 48.3%

Racial and ethnic distribution:
American Indian 0.3%
Asian 1.9%
Black 13.7%
White 79.9%
Other and unknown 4.3%
Hispanic (may be any race) .. 9.5%

Educational attainment of adults:
At least 4 years of high school 66.3%
At least 1 to 3 years of college 32.2%
At least 4 years of college ... 17.9%

Per-capita personal income: $21,073

New high-school graduates in:
1990-91 (estimate) 163,588
2000-01 (estimate) 174,425

New GED diploma recipients: 31,569

High-school dropout rate: 37.7%

POLITICAL LEADERSHIP

Governor: Mario M. Cuomo (D), term ends 1995

Governor's higher-education adviser: Daniel Kinley, State Capitol, Executive Chamber, Albany 12224; (518) 474-8390

U.S. Senators: Alfonse M. D'Amato (R), term ends 1993; Daniel Patrick Moynihan (D), term ends 1995

U.S. Representatives:
21 Democrats, 13 Republicans
Gary L. Ackerman (D), Sherwood L. Boehlert (R), Thomas J. Downey (D), Eliot L. Engel (D), Hamilton Fish, Jr. (R), Floyd H. Flake (D), Benjamin A. Gilman (R), Bill Green (R), George J. Hochbrueckner (D), Frank Horton (R), Amo Houghton (R), John J. LaFalce (D), Norman F. Lent (R), Nita M. Lowey (D), Thomas J. Manton (D), David O'B. Martin (R), Raymond J. McGrath (R), Matthew F. McHugh (D), Michael R. McNulty (D), Susan Molinari (R), Robert J. Mrazek (D),

NEW YORK

Henry J. Nowak (D), Major R. Owens (D), Bill Paxon (R), Charles B. Rangel (D), James H. Scheuer (D), Charles E. Schumer (D), José E. Serrano (D), Louise McIntosh Slaughter (D), Stephen J. Solarz (D), Gerald B. H. Solomon (R), Edolphus Towns (D), James T. Walsh (R), Ted Weiss (D)

Legislature: Senate, 26 Democrats, 35 Republicans; House, 95 Democrats, 55 Republicans

---

COLLEGES AND UNIVERSITIES

Higher education:

Public 4-year institutions 42
Public 2-year institutions 48

Private 4-year institutions 186
Private 2-year institutions 50

Total 326

Vocational institutions: 356

Statewide coordinating board:
New York State Education
   Department
Cultural Education Center
Room 5B28
Albany 12230
(518) 474-5851
Donald J. Nolan, deputy
commissioner for higher and
continuing education

Private-college association:
Commission on Independent Colleges
   and Universities in New York
17 Elk Street
P.O. Box 7289
Albany 12224
(518) 436-4781
C. Mark Lawton, president

Institutions censured by the AAUP:
New York University School of
Medicine, Onondaga Community
College, State University of New
York, Yeshiva University

Institutions under NCAA sanctions:
Adelphi University, State University
of New York College at Plattsburgh

FACULTY MEMBERS

Full-time faculty members:
At public institutions 17,926
At private institutions 15,351

Proportion who are women:
At public institutions 30.6%
At private institutions 28.9%

Proportion with tenure:
At public institutions 70.7%
At private institutions 59.1%

Average pay of full-time professors:
At public 4-year institutions $42,719
At public 2-year institutions $36,759
At private 4-year institutions $38,916
At private 2-year institutions $20,786

STUDENTS

Enrollment:
At public 4-year institutions 352,554
At public 2-year institutions 231,288
At private 4-year institutions 393,310
At private 2-year institutions 30,259
Undergraduate 819,446
   First-time freshmen 170,682
Graduate 160,900
Professional 27,065
American Indian 3,619
Asian 44,043
Black 111,000
Hispanic 70,739
White 742,572
Foreign 35,438
Total 1,007,411

Enrollment highlights:

Women 55.5%
Full-time 62.7%
Minority 23.6%
Foreign 3.5%
10-year change in total
   enrollment .... Up 5.4%

Proportion of enrollment made up of minority students:

At public 4-year institutions . 29.2%
At public 2-year institutions . 24.3%
At private 4-year institutions 17.0%
At private 2-year institutions 37.1%

Degrees awarded:

Associate 46,897
Bachelor's 87,071
Master's 33,873
Doctorate 3,436
Professional 6,274

Residence of new students: State residents made up 64% of all freshmen enrolled in New York; 80% of all New York residents who were freshmen attended college in their home state.

Test scores: Students averaged 882 on the S.A.T., which was taken by 70% of New York's high-school seniors.

MONEY

Average tuition and fees:

At public 4-year institutions . $1,460
At public 2-year institutions . $1,412
At private 4-year institutions $9,517
At private 2-year institutions $5,544

Expenditures:

Public institutions .. $3,802,602,000
Private institutions . $5,594,159,000

State funds for higher-education operating expenses: $3,142,943,000

Two-year change: Up 3%

State spending on student aid:

Need-based: $392,000,000;
  315,166 awards
Non–need-based: $30,707,000;
  65,950 awards
Other: $385,000

Salary of chief executive of largest public 4-year campus:

Steven B. Sample, State University
  of New York at Buffalo: $133,775

Total spending on research and development by doctorate-granting universities: $1,332,139,000

Sources:
Federal government 65.1%
State and local governments .. 5.2%
Industry 5.3%
The institution itself 12.9%
Other 11.5%

Federal spending on education and student aid (selected programs):

Vocational and
  adult education $52,000,000
GI Bill $16,613,000
Pell Grants $469,873,000

Total federal spending on college- and university-based research and development: $794,873,000

Selected programs:
Department of Health
  and Human Services $517,965,000
National Science
  Foundation $114,133,000
Department of Defense $67,909,000
Department
  of Agriculture $9,576,000
Department of Energy . $41,594,000

Largest endowment:

Columbia University $1,460,356,000

Top fund raisers:

Cornell University ... $157,072,000
Columbia University . $110,423,000
New York University .. $61,850,000

NEW YORK
Continued

MISCELLANY

■ After Candace Mills, a black student at Union College, married a white man, she found that little had been written about interracial relationships. She has started publishing a magazine called *Interrace,* which addresses issues of interracial and transcultural adoption, and interracial dating and marriage.

■ The State University of New York College at New Paltz has started a program aimed at helping students cope with homesickness. As part of the new program, the residence-life office matches homesick students with student counselors.

■ Wayne Palmer, a Utica College mathematics professor, has raised approximately $8,000 in scholarship money by collecting 150,000 cans for recycling. Since 1983 he has walked from classroom to classroom at the end of each day, collecting aluminum cans left behind by students. The 5 cents per can that he receives from the recycler is added to the scholarship fund.

■ Cornell University's Mann Library is assisting a project to put the core literature of world agriculture on compact disks. The library is preparing a list of the most significant books, journals, working papers, and other materials in eight agricultural disciplines from the past 200 years. Commercial companies will then put the full texts of these materials on 40 five-inch compact disks that will hold the equivalent of 10 million pages.

■ One of the coldest places on the earth is an Ithaca physics laboratory, where Cornell University researchers are studying the behavior of matter as it is cooled to 10-millionths of a degree above absolute zero.

■ A group of students at Syracuse University started an organization to persuade universities to focus less on research and more on undergraduate teaching. The organization, Undergraduates for a Better Education, held its second national conference in 1989.

■ All students at Cooper Union, an engineering, architecture, and art institution in Manhattan, receive a full scholarship covering tuition, room, and board. Peter Cooper, the inventor and entrepreneur who founded the institution in 1859, required the full scholarships as a condition of his donating the school's original endowment.

■ *The Elements of Style,* the classic writing guide by William Strunk, Jr., and E. B. White, is based on a privately printed book with the same title used in a Cornell University English class in 1919. At the time, Strunk was the professor and White was one of his students.

■ The oldest higher-education institution in New York is Columbia University, founded in 1754.

NORTH CAROLINA

THE North Carolina model of university-business interaction is one that many states wish to emulate.

"The Triangle," a relatively recent addition to North Carolina's geography, is a prime example of how higher education and industry can work together. In North Carolina's case, cooperation revitalized an economy that once depended on agriculture and textiles.

At the corners of the triangle are three research universities: Duke and North Carolina State Universities and the University of North Carolina at Chapel Hill. In the region between those campuses, high-technology businesses have thrived, using—and adding to—the resources of the three universities.

The state's community colleges, however, have had a difficult time keeping up as the state's economy shifted to high-technology and service industries. The community colleges and vocational institutes were geared to produce workers for the state's factories and farms.

Now business leaders say the two-year institutions should be graduating students with critical-thinking skills. As a result, two-year-college officials have begun a major push to improve academic programs, raise faculty salaries, recruit more minority students, and enhance job-training programs.

North Carolina's General Assembly provided some money for improvements, but the state's economy has had only modest growth in recent years. In addition, a top budget priority has been repairing the extensive damage caused by Hurricane Hugo when it whirled through Charlotte.

The University of North Carolina system is governed by a single board, with a less-powerful board providing advice for each campus. The relationships between individual campuses and the university's central administration have been a constant source of friction, especially for Chapel Hill.

The community-college system is governed locally, with coordination by a state board.

Duke is the most famous of North Carolina's private institutions, attracting students from around the country and the world. Many other private colleges in the state, most of them affiliated with religious groups, are also gaining popularity and prestige. In the last few years, however, Southern Baptist institutions have been fighting bitterly over control of faculty appointments and curricula.

Historically black colleges in North Carolina play an important role in both public and private higher education. The state has five traditionally black public colleges and seven private ones.

Racial issues continue to be among the most difficult problems facing college officials in North Carolina. Black enrollment at most institutions is not proportionate to the number of blacks in the state's population. Some North Carolina institutions, however, have ambitious plans to attract minority students and faculty members. Duke, for example, is trying to hire at least one black faculty member for each of its academic departments.

DEMOGRAPHICS

Population: 6,571,000   (Rank: 10)

Age distribution:

Up to 17	25.0%
18 to 24	11.3%
25 to 34	17.6%
35 and older	46.1%

Racial and ethnic distribution:

American Indian	1.1%
Asian	0.4%

NORTH CAROLINA
Continued

Black 22.4%
White 75.8%
Other and unknown 0.2%
Hispanic (may be any race) .. 1.0%

Educational attainment of adults:
At least 4 years of high school 54.8%
At least 1 to 3 years of college 27.0%
At least 4 years of college ... 13.2%

Per-capita personal income: $15,198

New high-school graduates in:
1990-91 (estimate) 65,243
2000-01 (estimate) 63,230

New GED diploma recipients: 13,552

High-school dropout rate: 33.3%

POLITICAL LEADERSHIP

Governor: James G. Martin (R), term ends 1993

Governor's higher-education adviser: George A. Kahdy, 116 West Jones Street, Raleigh 27603; (919) 733-5811

U.S. Senators: Jesse Helms (R), term ends 1997; Terry Sanford (D), term ends 1993

U.S. Representatives:
7 Democrats, 4 Republicans
Cass Ballenger (R), Howard Coble (R), W.G. (Bill) Hefner (D), Walter B. Jones (D), H. Martin Lancaster (D), J. Alex McMillan (R), Stephen L. Neal (D), David E. Price (D), Charles Rose (D), Charles Taylor (R), Tim Valentine (D)

General Assembly: Senate, 36 Demo-crats, 14 Republicans; House, 82 Democrats, 37 Republicans, 1 Independent

---

COLLEGES AND UNIVERSITIES

Higher education:
Public 4-year institutions 16
Public 2-year institutions 58

Private 4-year institutions 37
Private 2-year institutions 15

Total 126

Vocational institutions: 72

Statewide coordinating boards:
University of North Carolina
General Administration
P.O. Box 2688
Chapel Hill 27515
(919) 962-6981
C. D. Spangler, president

State Department of Community
  Colleges
200 West Jones Street
Raleigh 27603
(919) 733-7051
Robert W. Scott, president

Private-college association:
North Carolina Association
  of Independent Colleges
  and Universities
879A Washington Street
Raleigh 27605
(919) 832-5817
John T. Henley, president

Institutions censured by the AAUP:
Southeastern Baptist Theological Seminary, Wingate College

Institution under NCAA sanctions:
North Carolina State University

FACULTY MEMBERS

Full-time faculty members:
At public institutions 6,186
At private institutions 2,856

Proportion who are women:
At public institutions 33.2%
At private institutions 30.4%

Proportion with tenure:
At public institutions 59.0%
At private institutions 52.5%

Average pay of full-time professors:
At public 4-year institutions $36,514
At public 2-year institutions $22,802
At private 4-year institutions $29,136
At private 2-year institutions $22,512

STUDENTS

Enrollment:
At public 4-year institutions   140,025
At public 2-year institutions   127,045
At private 4-year institutions   59,265
At private 2-year institutions . 6,186
Undergraduate 298,635
 First-time freshmen 65,610
Graduate 27,938
Professional 5,948
American Indian 2,620
Asian 4,353
Black 58,267
Hispanic 2,249
White 260,563
Foreign 4,469
Total 332,521

Enrollment highlights:
Women 56.0%
Full-time 62.7%
Minority 20.6%
Foreign 1.3%
10-year change in total
 enrollment .... Up 26.6%

Proportion of enrollment made up of minority students:
At public 4-year institutions . 21.1%
At public 2-year institutions . 20.1%
At private 4-year institutions   19.3%
At private 2-year institutions   31.0%

Degrees awarded:
Associate 10,333
Bachelor's 25,688
Master's 5,938
Doctorate 796
Professional 1,594

Residence of new students: State residents made up 81% of all freshmen enrolled in North Carolina; 94% of all North Carolina residents who were freshmen attended college in their home state.

Test scores: Students averaged 841 on the S.A.T., which was taken by 55% of North Carolina's high-school seniors.

MONEY

Average tuition and fees:
At public 4-year institutions . $1,015
At public 2-year institutions .. $288
At private 4-year institutions $7,373
At private 2-year institutions $4,880

Expenditures:
Public institutions .. $1,799,173,000
Private institutions ... $837,291,000

State funds for higher-education operating expenses: $1,484,279,000
Two-year change: Up 12%

State spending on student aid:
Need-based: $5,989,000; 7,849 awards
Non–need-based: $23,297,000;
 24,330 awards
Other: $22,837,000

NORTH CAROLINA

Continued

**Salary of chief executive
of largest public 4-year campus:**
Larry K. Monteith, North Carolina
State University: $117,130

**Total spending on research and
development by doctorate-granting
universities:** $425,298,000
Sources:
Federal government 61.6%
State and local governments . 14.4%
Industry 9.7%
The institution itself 11.0%
Other 3.3%

**Federal spending on education
and student aid (selected programs):**
Vocational and
   adult education $24,820,000
GI Bill $19,447,000
Pell Grants $85,566,000

**Total federal spending on college-
and university-based research
and development:** $246,688,000
Selected programs:
Department of Health
   and Human Services $182,570,000
National Science
   Foundation $17,818,000
Department of Defense $14,277,000
Department
   of Agriculture $12,421,000
Department of Energy .. $5,878,000

Largest endowment:
Duke University $426,183,000

Top fund raisers:
Duke University $102,017,000
University of North Carolina
   at Chapel Hill $49,215,000
University of North Carolina
   at Raleigh $25,938,000

MISCELLANY

■ Photographs that line the walls of Duke University's Center for Documentary Studies tell a story. Indeed, that's what the center is all about. It was established to bring together specialists from a variety of fields—history, photography, medicine, and law—to record through oral histories and other kinds of narrative, still photographs, and film the lives of people who don't make it into official documents.

■ Warren Wilson College has a 15-hours-a-week work requirement for all on-campus students, and a dean of work to administer the program.

■ Pembroke State University was founded to teach American Indians, and its student body is still about one-third Indian.

■ The University of North Carolina and the University of Georgia both claim to be the oldest public university in the country.

■ The oldest institution of higher education in North Carolina is Salem College, a Moravian institution founded in 1772.

NORTH DAKOTA

IN 1989 North Dakota lawmakers approved a series of tax increases and then appropriated new money for faculty pay raises and academic programs.
But midway through the academic

year voters were given a chance to ratify the tax increases. Their answer was a resounding No. Two tax increases were repealed and a third, which had not yet taken effect, was rejected. Suddenly the state budget was $98-million in the red.

Gov. George A. Sinner, a Democrat who was once president of the state's Board of Higher Education, is favorably disposed toward giving higher education more money. But the state's economy has been weakened in recent years by declines in agriculture and the energy industry. After the voters turned down the tax increases, Mr. Sinner told higher-education officials they would have to make major budget cuts.

The short-term solutions included increasing tuition and putting the faculty pay raises on hold. But the North Dakota Board of Higher Education, the state's governing board for public colleges, decided that long-term solutions would require more-centralized control of the state's public institutions.

The board moved quickly to make the Commissioner of Higher Education the chancellor of the North Dakota University System, giving him more power in leading public higher education in the state. In making the changes, the board also adopted a plan under which mission statements for all four-year and research institutions would be more sharply focused, some duplicate programs would be eliminated, and enrollments at the state's four largest institutions would be capped or reduced.

No campuses were closed, however. The 11 state colleges and universities, which are widely scattered, have become vital to the economies of their communities, and it is unlikely that political leaders would risk the out-rage involved in shutting down a campus.

DEMOGRAPHICS

Population: 660,000   (Rank: 47)

Age distribution:
Up to 17	27.1%
18 to 24	10.6%
25 to 34	18.2%
35 and older	44.1%

Racial and ethnic distribution:
American Indian	3.1%
Asian	0.4%
Black	0.4%
White	96.0%
Other and unknown	0.2%
Hispanic (may be any race) ..	0.6%

Educational attainment of adults:
At least 4 years of high school	66.4%
At least 1 to 3 years of college	35.1%
At least 4 years of college ...	14.8%

Per-capita personal income: $13,563

New high-school graduates in:
1990-91 (estimate)	7,915
2000-01 (estimate)	8,559

New GED diploma recipients: 778

High-school dropout rate: 11.7%

POLITICAL LEADERSHIP

Governor: George A. Sinner (D), term ends 1992

Governor's higher-education adviser: Carol M. Siegert, State Capitol, Bismarck 58505; (701) 224-2200

U.S. Senators: Quentin N. Burdick (D), term ends 1995; Kent Conrad (D), term ends 1993

NORTH DAKOTA
Continued

U.S. Representative:
1 Democrat, 0 Republicans
Byron L. Dorgan (D)

Legislative Assembly: Senate, 26 Democrats, 26 Republicans, 1 vacancy; House, 48 Democrats, 58 Republicans

---

COLLEGES AND UNIVERSITIES

Higher education:
Public 4-year institutions 6
Public 2-year institutions 9
Private 4-year institutions 4
Private 2-year institutions 1
Total 20

Vocational institutions: 21

Statewide coordinating board:
Board of Higher Education
State Capitol Building, 10th Floor
Bismarck 58505
(701) 224-2960
Thomas J. Clifford, interim chancellor

Private-college association:
North Dakota Independent College
   Fund
University of Mary
7500 University Drive
Bismarck 58504
(701) 255-7500
Ernest B. Borr, executive director

Institutions censured by the AAUP:
None

Institutions under NCAA sanctions:
None

FACULTY MEMBERS

Full-time faculty members:
At public institutions 1,196
At private institutions 116

Proportion who are women:
At public institutions 25.7%
At private institutions 44.8%

Proportion with tenure:
At public institutions 61.9%
At private institutions .... n/a

Average pay of full-time professors:
At public 2-year institutions $29,959
At public 2-year institutions $26,591
At private 4-year institutions $23,272
At private 2-year institutions $19,547

STUDENTS

Enrollment:
At public 4-year institutions . 27,932
At public 2-year institutions .. 7,691
At private 4-year institutions . 2,659
At private 2-year institutions ... 11
Undergraduate 35,444
   First-time freshmen 8,906
Graduate 2,424
Professional 425
American Indian 1,486
Asian 212
Black 215
Hispanic 137
White 35,231
Foreign 1,012
Total 38,293

Enrollment highlights:
Women 47.9%
Full-time 80.0%
Minority 5.5%
Foreign 2.6%
10-year change in total
   enrollment .... Up 18.5%

**Proportion of enrollment made up
of minority students:**
At public 4-year institutions .. 3.0%
At public 2-year institutions . 14.0%
At private 4-year institutions . 6.2%
At private 2-year institutions ... n/a

Degrees awarded:
Associate 1,886
Bachelor's 4,110
Master's 584
Doctorate 66
Professional 114

Residence of new students: State residents made up 71% of all freshmen enrolled in North Dakota; 84% of all North Dakota residents who were freshmen attended college in their home state.

Test scores: Students averaged 18.7 on the A.C.T., which was taken by 66% of North Dakota's high-school seniors.

MONEY

Average tuition and fees:
At public 4-year institutions . $1,604
At public 2-year institutions . $1,286
At private 4-year institutions $5,149
At private 2-year institutions $2,100

Expenditures:
Public institutions $288,214,000
Private institutions $18,853,000

**State funds for higher-education
operating expenses:** $129,756,000

Two-year change: Up 12%

State spending on student aid:
Need-based: $1,540,000; 2,540 awards
Non–need-based: $82,000; awards n/a
Other: None

**Salary of chief executive
of largest public 4-year campus:**
Thomas J. Clifford, University
   of North Dakota: $92,880

**Total spending on research and
development by doctorate-granting
universities:** $27,634,000
Sources:
Federal government 70.2%
State and local governments .. 3.3%
Industry 9.1%
The institution itself 13.7%
Other 3.6%

**Federal spending on education
and student aid (selected programs):**
Vocational and
   adult education $4,086,000
GI Bill $3,042,000
Pell Grants $26,031,000

**Total federal spending on college-
and university-based research
and development:** $11,044,000

Selected programs:
Department of Health
   and Human Services . $1,701,000
National Science
   Foundation $659,000
Department of Defense ... $350,000
Department
   of Agriculture $5,894,000
Department of Energy .. $1,196,000

Largest endowment:
University of North Dakota
   Foundation $31,177,000

Top fund raisers:
University of
   North Dakota $3,539,000
Jamestown College $1,628,000
University of Mary $832,000

MISCELLANY

■ Smoking is prohibited on all 11

NORTH DAKOTA
Continued

public campuses in North Dakota. The ban, which was approved by the state Board of Higher Education, applies in all university facilities except outdoor stadiums and dormitories.

■ Four of North Dakota's two-year colleges are controlled by Indian tribes—Fort Berthold Community College, Little Hoop Community College, Standing Rock College, and Turtle Mountain Community College.

■ The oldest institution of higher education in North Dakota is the University of North Dakota in Grand Forks, founded in 1883.

OHIO

L IKE many states in the "Rust Belt," Ohio underwent a dramatic economic transition in the last decade, and higher education played an important role in the change.

After the recession of the late 1970's and early 1980's hit many of the state's traditional manufacturing industries, state officials made a strong push to diversify Ohio's economic base.

Former Gov. Richard F. Celeste and state legislators have come to view higher education as a partner in their economic strategy—moving from an industrial to a service-based economy. Ohio's program to support joint university-and-business research, named for Thomas Alva Edison, is one of the most highly regarded in the nation.

Through most of his two terms, Governor Celeste, a Democrat, pushed for major increases in operating funds for public higher education. Lately, however, those increases have been smaller as economic growth has stagnated.

Under state law, Governor Celeste could not seek re-election. In November 1990 voters elected the former Mayor of Cleveland, George Voinovich, to succeed him.

Mr. Voinovich, a Republican, says he won't allow tuition rates to exceed the rate of inflation. He advocates forgivable loans for students majoring in mathematics or science as long as they live and work in Ohio for four years after graduation.

He also has proposed the creation of "AccessOhio," an interest-free student-loan program exclusively for middle-income families.

In addition to a new Governor, Ohio college officials will be working with a new chancellor of the state Board of Regents. Elaine H. Hairston is the first woman to head the system. She was the board's vice-chancellor for academic and special programs.

The governance of higher education in Ohio is highly decentralized. The Board of Regents serves as the statewide coordinating agency, and each institution has its own board. Some operate branch campuses as well.

Ohio is known for its many huge campuses. The Ohio State University enrolls more than 50,000 students and the University of Cincinnati more than 30,000.

The state is also home to many small, private, liberal-arts colleges, like the College of Wooster, Denison University, Kenyon College, and

Oberlin College, which has one of the country's outstanding music schools.

Ohio also has many proprietary schools. Following scandals about the management and academic quality of some trade schools, state regulations were toughened.

DEMOGRAPHICS

Population: 10,907,000   (Rank: 7)

Age distribution:
Up to 17 .... 25.8%
18 to 24 .... 10.5%
25 to 34 .... 17.1%
35 and older 46.5%

Racial and ethnic distribution:
American Indian 0.1%
Asian 0.5%
Black 10.0%
White 89.0%
Other and unknown 0.4%
Hispanic (may be any race) .. 1.1%

Educational attainment of adults:
At least 4 years of high school 67.0%
At least 1 to 3 years of college 26.5%
At least 4 years of college ... 13.7%

Per-capita personal income: $16,373

New high-school graduates in:
1990-91 (estimate) 124,293
2000-01 (estimate) 121,753

New GED diploma recipients: 11,007

High-school dropout rate: 20.4%

POLITICAL LEADERSHIP

Governor: George Voinovich (R), term ends 1995

Governor's higher-education adviser: n/a

U.S. Senators: John Glenn (D), term ends 1993; Howard M. Metzenbaum (D), term ends 1995

U.S. Representatives:
11 Democrats, 10 Republicans
Douglas Applegate (D), John Boehner (R), Dennis E. Eckart (D), Edward F. Feighan (D), Paul E. Gillmor (R), Willis D. Gradison, Jr. (R), Tony P. Hall (D), David Hobson (R), Marcy Kaptur (D), John R. Kasich (R), Charles Luken (D), Bob McEwen (R), Clarence E. Miller (R), Mary Rose Oakar (D), Michael G. Oxley (R), Donald J. Pease (D), Ralph Regula (R), Thomas C. Sawyer (D), Louis Stokes (D), James A. Traficant, Jr. (D), Chalmers P. Wylie (R)

General Assembly: Senate, 12 Democrats, 21 Republicans; House, 61 Democrats, 38 Republicans

COLLEGES AND UNIVERSITIES

Higher education:
Public 4-year institutions 25
Public 2-year institutions 36
Private 4-year institutions 65
Private 2-year institutions 26
Total 152

Vocational institutions: 310

Statewide coordinating board:
Ohio Board of Regents
30 East Broad Street
3600 State Office Tower
Columbus 43266
(614) 466-6000
Elaine H. Hairston, chancellor

Private-college association:
Association of Independent Colleges
   and Universities of Ohio
17 South High Street, Suite 1020
Columbus 43215
(614) 228-2196
Larry H. Christman, president

OHIO
Continued

Institutions censured by the AAUP:
None

Institutions under NCAA sanctions:
Cleveland State University,
University of Cincinnati

FACULTY MEMBERS

Full-time faculty members:
At public institutions 10,389
At private institutions 4,047

Proportion who are women:
At public institutions 27.7%
At private institutions 27.1%

Proportion with tenure:
At public institutions 70.9%
At private institutions 61.0%

Average pay of full-time professors:
At public 4-year institutions $40,061
At public 2-year institutions $29,817
At private 4-year institutions $31,241
At private 2-year institutions $19,676

STUDENTS

Enrollment:
At public 4-year institutions 278,424
At public 2-year institutions 123,080
At private 4-year institutions 106,639
At private 2-year institutions 33,594
Undergraduate 471,644
　First-time freshmen 110,836
Graduate 58,165
Professional 11,928
American Indian .... , 1,272
Asian 6,140
Black 38,130
Hispanic 4,552

White 478,222
Foreign 13,421
Total 541,737

Enrollment highlights:
Women 51.3%
Full-time 60.3%
Minority 9.5%
Foreign 2.5%
10-year change in total
　enrollment .... Up 20.2%

**Proportion of enrollment made up
of minority students:**
At public 4-year institutions .. 8.5%
At public 2-year institutions . 11.9%
At private 4-year institutions 10.5%
At private 2-year institutions . 5.6%

Degrees awarded:
Associate 17,651
Bachelor's 43,521
Master's 12,238
Doctorate 1,459
Professional 3,207

Residence of new students: State residents made up 86% of all freshmen enrolled in Ohio; 87% of all Ohio residents who were freshmen attended college in their home state.

Test scores: Students averaged 19.1 on the A.C.T., which was taken by 52% of Ohio's high-school seniors.

MONEY

Average tuition and fees:
At public 4-year institutions . $2,432
At public 2-year institutions . $1,636
At private 4-year institutions $8,019
At private 2-year institutions $5,690

Expenditures:
Public institutions .. $2,718,408,000
Private institutions ... $980,801,000

State funds for higher-education operating expenses: $1,520,055,000

Two-year change: Up 15%

State spending on student aid:
Need-based: $50,700,000;
  69,000 awards
Non–need-based: $25,983,000;
  41,219 awards
Other: None

Salary of chief executive of largest public 4-year campus:
E. Gordon Gee, Ohio State University
  main campus: $155,000

Total spending on research and development by doctorate-granting universities: $417,275,000

Sources:
Federal government 58.1%
State and local governments . 11.8%
Industry 6.3%
The institution itself 14.9%
Other 9.0%

Federal spending on education and student aid (selected programs):
Vocational and
  adult education $36,448,000
GI Bill $21,332,000
Pell Grants $215,209,000

Total federal spending on college- and university-based research and development: $210,593,000

Selected programs:
Department of Health
  and Human Services $117,041,000
National Science
  Foundation $19,219,000
Department of Defense $32,075,000
Department
  of Agriculture $7,056,000
Department of Energy .. $5,182,000

Largest endowment:
Case Western Reserve
  University $381,075,000

Top fund raisers:
Ohio State University . $68,577,000
Case Western Reserve
  University $35,148,000
University of Cincinnati $23,980,000

MISCELLANY

■ The College of Wooster's freshman seminars focus on how American society is shaped by race, gender, class, and cultural differences. The college requires all freshmen to take the seminars.

■ An alcohol-free night club called the SAC at Baldwin-Wallace College attracts students with plush sofas, a pulsating sound-and-light system, a snack bar, and an atmosphere free of drunk, rowdy customers.

■ King Juan Carlos of Spain has agreed to help establish a Spanish-studies chair at the Ohio State University by 1992. The university expects the Spanish government to donate $625,000 for the chair's $1.25-million endowment. The university will finance the remaining portion.

■ About two-thirds of the problems reported on the Ohio State University's "classroom hot line" in fall 1989 were resolved within an hour. The hot line, which had 528 calls, is a number that professors can call if they have technical problems or if something is amiss in their classrooms (no chalk, no heat, etc.).

■ Wittenberg University sophomores are required to sign up for community-service programs that deal

OHIO
Continued

with literacy, health, physically disabled people, the elderly, and the environment. The university also allows undergraduates to propose their own volunteer programs. Students must complete 30 hours of service to graduate.

■ In 1863 Daniel Alexander Payne, a bishop in the African Methodist Episcopal Church, was named president of Wilberforce University, making him the first black university president.

■ The oldest higher-education institution in the state is Ohio University, founded in 1804.

OKLAHOMA

OKLAHOMA has taken several important steps in recent years to improve the quality and financial management of its public colleges and universities.

But the state still faces many challenges, particularly as its higher-education leaders struggle to raise academic quality. That effort has been difficult because of populist political forces that have resisted stricter admissions standards and shown a readiness to become involved in college affairs.

Still, a new public-school reform and financing package enacted in the 1990 legislative session is expected to contribute to the drive for quality by providing prospective college students with better academic preparation.

The Legislature has also supported efforts to attract the brightest high-school graduates to state institutions by increasing financing for a special scholarship program.

Another program, which matches private donations with state contributions, has created 65 new endowed chairs at the public institutions since 1988.

Even so, in a state still hobbled by declines in its oil-dependent economy, money is a perennial concern.

Much of the impetus for the changes comes from the Board of Regents, a coordinating body whose authority is frequently checked by the governing boards of the 17 public colleges and universities. The regents have, however, restored some credibility to the public colleges, several of which were tarnished by financial scandals in the late 1980's. The regents, under Chancellor Hans Brisch, have also imposed new policies that prevent university foundations from spending their money on political campaigns.

Mr. Brisch and the regents are also proposing tougher academic requirements for students in extracurricular activities, including athletes—a move that is likely to irk some people in this football-crazy state.

The regents will probably find an ally in the new Governor, David Walters, a businessman and former administrator at the University of Oklahoma. Mr. Walters, a Democrat, favors more money for faculty salaries, university research, and scholarships.

Oklahoma has also been struggling to attract more minority students to higher education, and black legislators frequently complain that the state's only predominantly black public institution, Langston University, needs more money.

Most private colleges in Oklahoma are church-related. The best known of those is Oral Roberts University, which gained notoriety in 1987 when its founder and namesake said the institution needed to raise $8-million or he would be "called home" to heaven. In 1990, Mr. Roberts closed down the institution's nine-year-old medical school. He cited financial reasons, but several faculty members said the minister's interference had driven away many doctors who could have helped it succeed.

DEMOGRAPHICS

Population: 3,224,000   (Rank: 28)

Age distribution:
Up to 17 .... 26.5%
18 to 24 .... 10.6%
25 to 34 .... 17.5%
35 and older 45.4%

Racial and ethnic distribution:
American Indian 5.7%
Asian 0.7%
Black 6.8%
White 86.0%
Other and unknown 0.9%
Hispanic (may be any race) .. 1.9%

Educational attainment of adults:
At least 4 years of high school 66.0%
At least 1 to 3 years of college 31.2%
At least 4 years of college ... 15.1%

Per-capita personal income: $14,154

New high-school graduates in:
1990-91 (estimate) 33,955
2000-01 (estimate) 43,780

New GED diploma recipients: 4,485

High-school dropout rate: 28.3%

POLITICAL LEADERSHIP

Governor: David Walters (D), term ends 1995

Governor's higher-education adviser: n/a

U.S. Senators: David L. Boren (D), term ends 1997; Don Nickles (R), term ends 1993

U.S. Representatives:
4 Democrats, 2 Republicans
Bill Brewster (D), Mickey Edwards (R), Glenn English (D), James M. Inhofe (R), Dave McCurdy (D), Mike Synar (D)

Legislature: Senate, 37 Democrats, 11 Republicans; House, 68 Democrats, 32 Republicans, 1 vacancy

---

COLLEGES AND UNIVERSITIES

Higher education:
Public 4-year institutions 14
Public 2-year institutions 14
Private 4-year institutions 13
Private 2-year institutions 6
Total 47

Vocational institutions: 90

Statewide coordinating board:
Oklahoma State Regents
   for Higher Education
500 Education Building
State Capitol Complex
Oklahoma City 73105
(405) 524-9100
Hans Brisch, chancellor

OKLAHOMA
Continued

Private-college association:
Oklahoma Association of
Independent Colleges and
Universities
114 East Sheridan, Suite 101
Oklahoma City 73104
(405) 235-0587
James A. Reid, president

Institutions censured by the AAUP:
Central State University,
Southern Nazarene University

Institutions under NCAA sanctions:
Oklahoma State University,
University of Oklahoma

FACULTY MEMBERS

Full-time faculty members:
At public institutions 3,443
At private institutions 843

Proportion who are women:
At public institutions 29.8%
At private institutions 31.2%

Proportion with tenure:
At public institutions 59.2%
At private institutions 51.0%

Average pay of full-time professors:
At public 4-year institutions $31,763
At public 2-year institutions $27,143
At private 4-year institutions $29,947
At private 2-year institutions $20,449

STUDENTS

Enrollment:
At public 4-year institutions . 94,687
At public 2-year institutions . 56,722
At private 4-year institutions 18,434
At private 2-year institutions . 6,464

Undergraduate 151,995
  First-time freshmen 30,525
Graduate 20,810
Professional 3,502
American Indian 8,014
Asian 2,787
Black 11,777
Hispanic 2,534
White 145,486
Foreign 5,709
Total 176,307

Enrollment highlights:
Women 53.7%
Full-time 57.3%
Minority 14.7%
Foreign 3.2%
10-year change in total
  enrollment .... Up 18.0%

**Proportion of enrollment made up
of minority students:**
At public 4-year institutions . 14.5%
At public 2-year institutions . 14.1%
At private 4-year institutions 13.2%
At private 2-year institutions 27.9%

Degrees awarded:
Associate 5,341
Bachelor's 13,173
Master's 4,118
Doctorate 349
Professional 1,031

Residence of new students: State residents made up 91% of all freshmen enrolled in Oklahoma; 90% of all Oklahoma residents who were freshmen attended college in their home state.

Test scores: Students averaged 17.7 on the A.C.T., which was taken by 57% of Oklahoma's high-school seniors.

MONEY

Average tuition and fees:
At public 4-year institutions . $1,309
At public 2-year institutions .. $840
At private 4-year institutions $5,133
At private 2-year institutions $5,382

Expenditures:
Public institutions $844,829,000
Private institutions ... $178,905,000

State funds for higher-education operating expenses: $509,471,000

Two-year change: Up 23%

State spending on student aid:
Need-based: $13,105,000;
 17,225 awards
Non need-based: $2,370,000;
 706 awards
Other: $17,070,000

Salary of chief executive of largest public 4-year campus:
Richard L. Van Horn, University of
 Oklahoma at Norman: $137,000
 from state plus $10,000 from
 private sources

Total spending on research and development by doctorate-granting universities: $113,279,000

Sources:
Federal government 29.2%
State and local governments .. 4.5%
Industry 5.0%
The institution itself 53.0%
Other 8.3%

Federal spending on education and student aid (selected programs):
Vocational and
 adult education $11,916,000
GI Bill $12,151,000
Pell Grants $89,407,000

Total federal spending on college- and university-based research and development: $25,495,000

Selected programs:
Department of Health
 and Human Services . $9,962,000
National Science
 Foundation $3,966,000
Department of Defense . $1,485,000
Department
 of Agriculture $6,139,000
Department of Energy .. $1,398,000

Largest endowment:
University of Tulsa ... $272,720,000

Top fund raisers:
University of Oklahoma $21,374,000
Oklahoma State
 University $15,245,000
University of Tulsa $5,517,000

MISCELLANY

■ An anti-hazing law passed in 1990 prohibits any act that "recklessly or intentionally" endangers the health or safety of a high-school or college student. The law applies to students at both public and private institutions. Individual violators are subject to a maximum fine of $500, 90 days in jail, or both. An organization found guilty could be fined up to $1,500 and lose all privileges accorded to it by a school or college.

■ Historically black Langston University and the city in which it is located are both named for John Mercer Langston, a 19th-century black leader who served as vice-president of Howard University, as president of Virginia State College for Negroes (now Virginia State University), and as President Rutherford B. Hayes's resident minister in Haiti.

OKLAHOMA

Continued

■ The oldest institution of higher education in Oklahoma is Bacone College, founded in 1880.

OREGON

IF Oregon officials have not yet resolved how best to raise academic standards at public universities, increase faculty pay, and improve educational opportunities in Portland, the state's major metropolitan region, it has not been for lack of trying.

The state's ambitious and inventive proposals, however, usually have fallen victim to financial or political concerns.

In 1989, for example, the state announced a new program to limit enrollment and raise academic standards at its two research universities, the University of Oregon and Oregon State University, only to suspend the policy less than a year later for financial reasons. Thomas A. Bartlett, the chancellor of the State System of Higher Education, said the plan would help universities by allowing them to concentrate their resources. But faced with mounting deficits in college athletics programs, Mr. Bartlett and the Board of Higher Education (which governs all eight public colleges and universities) later suspended the limits because they needed the tuition income.

Voters previously rejected a proposal for a statewide tax on beer to support college sports. Then the Legislative Assembly's strategy for providing raises to public-college faculty members with the income from a network of video-poker machines faltered when local officials moved to ban the games.

And a new limit on local property taxes—approved by voters in November 1990—will create even more financial burdens on public colleges. An even greater share of the financing for public schools will shift to the state, leaving far less money available for higher education.

The newly elected Governor, Democrat Barbara Roberts, is a strong supporter of higher education, however, and said during her campaign that she would be willing to raise taxes to support it.

Oregon has a well-organized group of private colleges, including Reed, Lewis and Clark, and Marylhurst.

Many of those institutions are in the Portland area, where a Governor's Commission examining the region's higher-education resources hopes to involve private colleges in cooperative ventures with public institutions. Governor Roberts has also promoted that idea.

The proposals were developed to deal with a shortage of graduate programs in the Portland area, particularly in the high-technology fields important to businesses that the state hopes to attract to diversify its lumber-based economy.

Several of the state's 13 community colleges are clustered around Portland, and they too are expected to be made part of a regional consortium. Oregon is also developing a telecommunications network to extend higher education to rural regions.

DEMOGRAPHICS

Population: 2,820,000 (Rank: 30)

Age distribution:
Up to 17 .... 24.7%
18 to 24 .... 9.9%
25 to 34 .... 18.3%
35 and older 47.1%

Racial and ethnic distribution:
American Indian 1.2%
Asian 1.6%
Black 1.4%
White 94.8%
Other and unknown 1.1%
Hispanic (may be any race) .. 2.5%

Educational attainment of adults:
At least 4 years of high school 75.6%
At least 1 to 3 years of college 38.5%
At least 4 years of college ... 17.9%

Per-capita personal income: $15,919

New high-school graduates in:
1990-91 (estimate) 25,125
2000-01 (estimate) 28,365

New GED diploma recipients: 5,990

High-school dropout rate: 27.0%

POLITICAL LEADERSHIP

Governor: Barbara Roberts (D), term ends 1995

Governor's higher-education adviser: n/a

U.S. Senators: Mark O. Hatfield (R), term ends 1997; Bob Packwood (R), term ends 1993

U.S. Representatives:
4 Democrats, 1 Republican
Les AuCoin (D), Peter A. DeFazio (D), Mike Kopetski (D), Robert F. (Bob) Smith (R), Ron Wyden (D)

Legislative Assembly: Senate, 20 Democrats, 10 Republicans; House, 29 Democrats, 31 Republicans

---

COLLEGES AND UNIVERSITIES

Higher education:
Public 4-year institutions 8
Public 2-year institutions 13
Private 4-year institutions 24
Private 2-year institutions 1
Total 46

Vocational institutions: 113

Statewide coordinating board:
Oregon Office of Educational
    Policy and Planning
225 Winter Street, N.E.
Salem 97310
(503) 378-3921
Paul E. Bragdon, director

Private-college association:
Oregon Independent
    Colleges Association
7100 Southwest Hampton Street
Suite 222
Portland 97223
(503) 639-4541
Gary K. Andeen, executive director

Institutions censured by the AAUP:
None

Institutions under NCAA sanctions:
None

FACULTY MEMBERS

Full-time faculty members:
At public institutions 3,735
At private institutions 842

Proportion who are women:
At public institutions 31.1%
At private institutions 26.6%

OREGON

Continued

Proportion with tenure:
At public institutions 70.4%
At private institutions 56.9%

Average pay of full-time professors:
At public 4-year institutions $33,981
At public 2-year institutions $29,289
At private 4-year institutions $30,165
At private 2-year institutions ... n/a

STUDENTS

Enrollment:
At public 4-year institutions . 68,432
At public 2-year institutions . 68,175
At private 4-year institutions 19,220
At private 2-year institutions .. 332
Undergraduate 137,363
  First-time freshmen 27,343
Graduate 15,457
Professional 3,339
American Indian 1,540
Asian 6,055
Black 2,013
Hispanic 2,572
White 138,077
Foreign 5,902
Total 156,159

Enrollment highlights:
Women 52.7%
Full-time 58.3%
Minority 8.1%
Foreign 3.8%
10-year change in total
  enrollment .... Up 6.7%

Proportion of enrollment made up of minority students:
At public 4-year institutions .. 8.9%
At public 2-year institutions .. 7.3%
At private 4-year institutions . 8.2%
At private 2-year institutions . 7.0%

Degrees awarded:
Associate 4,823
Bachelor's 11,251
Master's 2,869
Doctorate 409
Professional 845

Residence of new students: State residents made up 82% of all freshmen enrolled in Oregon; 92% of all Oregon residents who were freshmen attended college in their home state.

Test scores: Students averaged 923 on the s.a.t., which was taken by 49% of Oregon's high-school seniors.

MONEY

Average tuition and fees:
At public 4-year institutions . $1,738
At public 2-year institutions .. $753
At private 4-year institutions $8,656
At private 2-year institutions $5,250

Expenditures:
Public institutions $880,696,000
Private institutions ... $171,604,000

State funds for higher-education operating expenses: $420,047,000
Two-year change: Up 16%

State spending on student aid:
Need-based: $10,770,000;
  16,235 awards
Non–need-based: None
Other: None

Salary of chief executive of largest public 4-year campus:
Myles Brand, University of Oregon: $105,000

Total spending on research and development by doctorate-granting universities: $161,127,000
Sources:
Federal government 61.5%

State and local governments . 12.9%
Industry 3.0%
The institution itself 10.3%
Other 12.2%

Federal spending on education
and student aid (selected programs):
Vocational and
   adult education $8,873,000
GI Bill $8,455,000
Pell Grants $55,035,000

Total federal spending on college-
and university-based research
and development: $91,133,000

Selected programs:
Department of Health
   and Human Services $36,071,000
National Science
   Foundation $15,379,000
Department of Defense $15,446,000
Department
   of Agriculture $7,754,000
Department of Energy .. $4,074,000

Largest endowment:
Reed College $74,528,000

Top fund raisers:
Oregon State University $15,215,000
Oregon Health Sciences
   University $13,701,000
University of Oregon .. $13,484,000

MISCELLANY

■ To achieve its goal of providing a liberal-arts curriculum with courses on America, the year-old Tokyo International University of America called on nearby Willamette—its long-time "sister university." Willamette professors taught courses on U. S. history, culture, society, and economy. The Japanese students' nine-month stay ended with a course on the history and politics of Oregon.

■ Ken Kesey, a University of Oregon professor, and 13 of his graduate creative-writing students are believed to be the first university class to have collectively written and published a novel. *Caverns*—described as a hybrid of *The Grapes of Wrath*, *The Canterbury Tales*, and the best of the Indiana Jones movie adventures—traces the exploits of 14 characters as they follow a convicted murderer on a cross-country journey.

■ Raymond P. Gleason, an assistant professor of business and economics at George Fox College, requires his students to stand when answering questions. The technique prevents students from getting by without reading and studying, thus enabling the class to cover more material in a shorter time. Although many students were initially distressed and surprised at the method, they seem to have accepted it.

■ The oldest higher-education institution in Oregon is Willamette University, founded by Christian missionaries in 1842.

PENNSYLVANIA

PENNSYLVANIA'S Gov. Robert P. Casey, a Democrat starting his second term, says that making sure higher education is affordable is the key to increasing the number of Pennsylvania high-school graduates who go to college.

But the Governor's approach—an incentive program that provides a financial bonus to institutions that keep their tuition increases below a pre-

PENNSYLVANIA
Continued

scribed cap—has frustrated administrators at research institutions, who contend that the program leaves them without the money they need.

Their lobbyists have managed to persuade the General Assembly to raise the cap above what the Democratic Governor has proposed. But for now, the idea of tuition limitations seems to be firmly in place.

Pennsylvania has a strong and unusual financial relationship with many of its public and private colleges. In addition to the 14 regional, "state-owned" colleges and universities that make up the State System of Higher Education, Pennsylvania has four "state-related" institutions. Those—Lincoln, Pennsylvania State, and Temple Universities and the University of Pittsburgh—receive substantial portions of their financing from the state. In return, the state is accorded some control over their operations.

A third set of colleges are considered "state-assisted." They are private, but they receive state money for certain academic programs. Pennsylvania also has a relatively small community-college system for a state its size.

The state is also home to prestigious private research institutions like the University of Pennsylvania and Carnegie Mellon University. Pennsylvania also has many private liberal-arts colleges. As the center of the Quaker religious belief in America, Pennsylvania is the site of three colleges founded by the Society of Friends that are considered to be among the country's elite institutions: Bryn Mawr, Haverford, and Swarthmore Colleges. The state also has two predominant-

ly black public colleges, Lincoln and Cheyney Universities. Higher-education officials have been striving to attract more minority students to colleges, particularly in light of the declines in the state's overall population and reports that the racial climate on some campuses is inhospitable to blacks.

For all the diversity of higher education in Pennsylvania, the state is known as a leader in cooperation among different types of institution. The Pennsylvania Association of Colleges and Universities is widely credited with limiting competition and promoting harmony among the various colleges.

Higher-education policies in Pennsylvania are designed to take advantage of the wealth of institutions. For example, the state's economic-development program—the Ben Franklin Partnership—awards special grants to groups of different kinds of colleges and universities that collaborate on research projects.

DEMOGRAPHICS

Population: 12,040,000   (Rank: 5)

Age distribution:

Up to 17	23.6%
18 to 24	10.2%
25 to 34	16.7%
35 and older	49.4%

Racial and ethnic distribution:

American Indian	0.1%
Asian	0.6%
Black	8.8%
White	89.9%
Other and unknown	0.6%
Hispanic (may be any race)	1.3%

Educational attainment of adults:
At least 4 years of high school 64.7%
At least 1 to 3 years of college 24.3%
At least 4 years of college ... 13.6%

Per-capita personal income: $17,269

New high-school graduates in:
1990-91 (estimate) 123,070
2000-01 (estimate) 125,917

New GED diploma recipients: 13,852

High-school dropout rate: 21.6%

POLITICAL LEADERSHIP

Governor: Robert P. Casey (D), term ends 1995

Governor's higher-education adviser: Dan Wofford, State Capitol, Room 225, Harrisburg 17120; (717) 783-9180

U.S. Senators: John Heinz (R), term ends 1995; Arlen Specter (R), term ends 1993

U.S. Representatives:
11 Democrats, 12 Republicans
Robert A. Borski (D), William F. Clinger, Jr. (R), Lawrence Coughlin (R), William J. Coyne (D), Thomas M. Foglietta (D), Joseph M. Gaydos (D), George W. Gekas (R), William F. Goodling (R), William H. Gray, III (D), Paul E. Kanjorksi (D), Joe Kolter (D), Peter H. Kostmayer (D), Joseph M. McDade (R), Austin J. Murphy (D), John P. Murtha (D), Thomas J. Ridge (R), Don Ritter (R), Rick Santorum (R), Richard T. Schulze (R), Bud Shuster (R), Robert S. Walker (R), Curt Weldon (R), Gus Yatron (D)

General Assembly: Senate, 24 Democrats, 26 Republicans; House, 108 Democrats, 95 Republicans

COLLEGES AND UNIVERSITIES

Higher education:
Public 4-year institutions 43
Public 2-year institutions 18
Private 4-year institutions 103
Private 2-year institutions 53
Total 217

Vocational institutions: 366

Statewide coordinating board:
State Department of Education
333 Market Street
Harrisburg 17126
(717) 787-5041
Charles R. Fuget, commissioner
for higher education

Private-college association:
Commission for Independent Colleges
    and Universities of Pennsylvania
800 North Third Street
Harrisburg 17102
(717) 232-8649
Francis J. Michelini, president

Institutions censured by the AAUP:
Alvernia College, Grove City College, Temple University

Institution under NCAA sanctions:
Robert Morris College

FACULTY MEMBERS

Full-time faculty members:
At public institutions 10,403
At private institutions 9,002

Proportion who are women:
At public institutions 27.3%
At private institutions 26.8%

Proportion with tenure:
At public institutions 68.9%
At private institutions 61.3%

PENNSYLVANIA

Continued

Average pay of full-time professors:
At public 4-year institutions $37,233
At public 2-year institutions $32,137
At private 4-year institutions $36,330
At private 2-year institutions $21,669

STUDENTS

Enrollment:
At public 4-year institutions   229,235
At public 2-year institutions . 94,290

At private 4-year institutions 212,873
At private 2-year institutions   37,529

Undergraduate 489,422
  First-time freshmen 122,154
Graduate 70,903
Professional 13,602
American Indian 918
Asian 10,583
Black 38,415
Hispanic 6,139
White 504,972
Foreign 12,900
Total 573,927

Enrollment highlights:
Women 53.9%
Full-time 64.3%
Minority 10.0%
Foreign 2.2%
10-year change in total
   enrollment .... Up 21.4%

**Proportion of enrollment made up
of minority students:**
At public 4-year institutions .. 9.7%
At public 2-year institutions . 13.0%
At private 4-year institutions . 7.4%
At private 2-year institutions   18.4%

Degrees awarded:
Associate 18,281
Bachelor's ....'.. 58,348

Master's 13,791
Doctorate 1,882
Professional 3,637

Residence of new students: State residents made up 77% of all freshmen enrolled in Pennsylvania; 82% of all Pennsylvania residents who were freshmen attended college in their home state.

Test scores: Students averaged 883 on the S.A.T., which was taken by 64% of Pennsylvania's high-school seniors.

MONEY

Average tuition and fees:
At public 4-year institutions . $3,210
At public 2-year institutions . $1,419
At private 4-year institutions $9,430
At private 2-year institutions $5,497

Expenditures:
Public institutions .. $2,392,145,000
Private institutions . $3,169,219,000

**State funds for higher-education
operating expenses:** $1,421,710,000

Two-year change: Up 12%

State spending on student aid:
Need-based: $133,429,000;
   120,009 awards
Non–need-based: $585,000;
   226 awards
Other: None

**Salary of chief executive
of largest public 4-year campus:**
Joab L. Thomas, Pennsylvania State
   University main campus: salary n/a

**Total spending on research and
development by doctorate-granting
universities:** $761,130,000

Sources:
Federal government 61.6%

State and local governments .. 4.2%
Industry 12.0%
The institution itself 14.4%
Other 7.7%

**Federal spending on education
and student aid (selected programs):**
Vocational and
    adult education $38,673,000
GI Bill $15,889,000
Pell Grants $216,502,000

**Total federal spending on college-
and university-based research
and development:** $452,313,000

Selected programs:
Department of Health
    and Human Services $238,290,000
National Science
    Foundation $51,686,000
Department of Defense $115,134,000
Department
    of Agriculture $9,801,000
Department of Energy . $16,097,000

Largest endowment:
University of
    Pennsylvania $761,408,000

Top fund raisers:
University of
    Pennsylvania $121,946,000
Pennsylvania State
    University $55,181,000
Carnegie Mellon
    University $31,224,000

MISCELLANY

■ The University of Pennsylvania
has the oldest medical school in the
country, founded in 1765.

■ In a landmark decision, the Supreme Court unanimously ruled in
1990 that the University of Pennsylvania could not withhold confidential
peer-review documents from a federal

agency investigating a discrimination
complaint.

■ Bucknell University students can
board the Bison Express, a chartered
bus that takes them to explore New
York, Washington, or Philadelphia.
The trips give students at the small
liberal-arts college, which one university official jokes is "centrally isolated," the chance to explore urban at-
tractions.

■ Established in 1834, the Dickinson School of Law is the nation's oldest independent law school.

■ Learning-disabled students may
get a college degree through an innovative program at College Misericor-
dia that uses tutoring, note-taking
services, and talking computers and
calculators.

■ The University of Pennsylvania,
founded in 1740, is the nation's oldest
full-fledged university. (Harvard,
which dates to 1636, was founded as a
college.)

RHODE ISLAND

I N the mid-1980's Rhode Island was
booming. State revenues were up
and the business community was
flourishing. But now—like the rest of
New England—Rhode Island is in the
grip of a recession.

Higher education, particularly the
University of Rhode Island, has been
hit hard by budget cuts. Last year,
then-Gov. Edward D. DiPrete, a Republican, reversed his no-new-taxes
stance and proposed a one-cent in-

RHODE ISLAND

Continued

crease in the sales tax to help restore money to the university and other state agencies. The heated budget fight strained the relationship between the university and Mr. DiPrete and made higher education an issue in the 1990 Governor's race. Ultimately, the tax increases led to Mr. DiPrete's defeat in November 1990.

His Democratic successor, Bruce Sundlun, has expressed strong support for education. He has promised not to cut financial support for higher education in the middle of the fiscal year.

The state's reverence for higher education predates the national public-college movement by a century. Hence, private colleges have great status in Rhode Island. The state offers an array of generous scholarship programs designed to help residents attend its private colleges, including nationally regarded Brown University and the Rhode Island School of Design.

The state has adopted a "quality, not quantity" approach to public higher education, a tactic that has proved financially beneficial to its three public institutions: the University of Rhode Island, Rhode Island College, and the Community College of Rhode Island.

Despite budget problems, Governor DiPrete did find money to start a "Children's Crusade." The program established an endowment, financed with public and private funds, to help pay the cost of a college education for needy students who agree in grade school to avoid drugs and meet certain academic requirements.

The Board of Governors for Higher Education is the governing board and coordinating board for all public higher education.

DEMOGRAPHICS

Population: 998,000   (Rank: 43)

Age distribution:
Up to 17 .... 23.1%
18 to 24 .... 10.9%
25 to 34 .... 17.6%
35 and older 48.3%

Racial and ethnic distribution:
American Indian 0.3%
Asian 0.7%
Black 2.9%
White 95.1%
Other and unknown 1.0%
Hispanic (may be any race) .. 2.1%

Educational attainment of adults:
At least 4 years of high school 61.1%
At least 1 to 3 years of college 28.3%
At least 4 years of college ... 15.4%

Per-capita personal income: $17,950

New high-school graduates in:
1990-91 (estimate) 9,083
2000-01 (estimate) 9,949

New GED diploma recipients: 1,844

High-school dropout rate: 30.2%

POLITICAL LEADERSHIP

Governor: Bruce G. Sundlun (D), term ends 1993

Governor's higher-education adviser: n/a

U.S. Senators: John H. Chafee (R), term ends 1995; Claiborne Pell (D), term ends 1997

U.S. Representatives:
1 Democrat, 1 Republican
Ronald K. Machtley (R), Jack Reed (D)

General Assembly: Senate, 45 Democrats, 5 Republicans; House, 88 Democrats, 12 Republicans

COLLEGES AND UNIVERSITIES

Higher education:
Public 4-year institutions 2
Public 2-year institutions 1

Private 4-year institutions 8
Private 2-year institutions 0

Total 11

Vocational institutions: 28

Statewide coordinating board:
Office of Higher Education
301 Promenade Street
Providence 02908
(401) 277-6560
Americo W. Petrocelli, commissioner of higher education

Private-college association:
Rhode Island Independent
  Higher Education Association
Charles-Orms Building, Suite 120
10 Orms Street
Providence 02904
(401) 272-8270
Robert J. McKenna, president

Institutions censured by the AAUP:
None

Institutions under NCAA sanctions:
None

FACULTY MEMBERS

Full-time faculty members:
At public institutions 1,143
At private institutions 1,430

Proportion who are women:
At public institutions 32.5%
At private institutions 23.9%

Proportion with tenure:
At public institutions 78.1%
At private institutions 62.9%

Average pay of full-time professors:
At public 4-year institutions $38,127
At public 2-year institutions $31,108
At private 4-year institutions $37,306
At private 2-year institutions ... n/a

STUDENTS

Enrollment:
At public 4-year institutions . 24,274
At public 2-year institutions . 14,715

At private 4-year institutions 35,850
At private 2-year institutions 0

Undergraduate 65,954
  First-time freshmen 13,419
Graduate 8,594
Professional 291
American Indian 218
Asian 1,402
Black 2,185
Hispanic 1,197
White 68,139
Foreign 1,698
Total 74,839

Enrollment highlights:
Women 54.7%
Full-time 62.4%
Minority 6.8%
Foreign 2.3%
10-year change in total
  enrollment .... Up 17.8%

Proportion of enrollment made up of minority students:
At public 4-year institutions .. 5.1%
At public 2-year institutions .. 9.3%
At private 4-year institutions . 6.9%
At private 2-year institutions ... n/a

RHODE ISLAND
Continued

Degrees awarded:
Associate 3,659
Bachelor's 7,934
Master's 1,625
Doctorate 237
Professional 84

Residence of new students: State residents made up 44% of all freshmen enrolled in Rhode Island; 70% of all Rhode Island residents who were freshmen attended college in their home state.

Test scores: Students averaged 883 on the S.A.T., which was taken by 62% of Rhode Island's high-school seniors.

MONEY

Average tuition and fees:
At public 4-year institutions . $2,281
At public 2-year institutions . $1,004
At private 4-year institutions $10,143
At private 2-year institutions ... n/a

Expenditures:
Public institutions $213,253,000
Private institutions ... $315,651,000

State funds for higher-education operating expenses: $141,139,000

Two-year change: Down 1%

State spending on student aid:
Need-based: $10,134,000;
  9,500 awards
Non–need-based: $120,000; 48 awards
Other: $1,000,000

Salary of chief executive of largest public 4-year campus:
Edward D. Eddy, University of
  Rhode Island: $103,502

Total spending on research and development by doctorate-granting universities: $79,801,000

Sources:
Federal government 70.7%
State and local governments .. 4.1%
Industry 7.9%
The institution itself 14.6%
Other 2.7%

Federal spending on education and student aid (selected programs):
Vocational and
  adult education $4,288,000
GI Bill $2,173,000
Pell Grants $13,507,000

Total federal spending on college- and university-based research and development: $47,349,000

Selected programs:
Department of Health
  and Human Services $14,568,000
National Science
  Foundation $13,141,000
Department of Defense . $9,888,000
Department
  of Agriculture $1,385,000
Department of Energy .. $2,669,000

Largest endowment:
Brown University $398,100,000

Top fund raisers:
Brown University $38,237,000
University of
  Rhode Island $6,673,000
Providence College $3,034,000

MISCELLANY

■ Former private homes, a church, and a restored bank building house the studios, workshops, classrooms, dormitories, and other facilities for the Rhode Island School of Design, located on Providence's historic East Side.

- Many of the campus buildings at Salve Regina–the Newport College were once part of 19th-century estates on Newport's Cliff Walk, overlooking the Atlantic.

- Johnson & Wales University has established a program called Fast Action Study Team, which encourages employees to come up with new ideas for saving money or improving university operations. A recycling program that participants designed resulted in more than $100,000 in savings for the university in the 1988-89 fiscal year.

- The oldest institution of higher education in Rhode Island is Brown University, founded in 1764.

SOUTH CAROLINA

SOUTH CAROLINA politicians spent a lot of time on higher education in 1990, but few public-college leaders welcomed the attention.

The General Assembly was angry over the free-spending practices of University of South Carolina President James B. Holderman, who has since resigned. In the wake of revelations about his $879-a-night hotel rooms and annual chauffeur bills of $7,000, lawmakers provided only a token increase for college and university budgets. They also imposed several restrictions on all university financial practices, including limits on tuition increases.

Legislators have threatened to pass other laws that would restrict how universities spend their income from bookstores, athletics, and concession stands, and force them to open the financial records of their affiliated foundations if they refuse to do so voluntarily.

The laws apply not only to the University of South Carolina, but to other public institutions such as Clemson University, where there have been no allegations of misspending.

The actions were severe, but hardly out of character for the General Assembly, which is known for taking an active interest in the management of the state's colleges. That interest has continued despite efforts in recent years to shift more authority to the state Commission on Higher Education, the coordinating board.

South Carolina colleges have a history of appealing directly to their legislators for support, and of resisting efforts by the commission to assert more control over higher-education policy. The commission's recent decision to allow technical colleges to award associate degrees, for example, was nearly scuttled when community-college leaders threatened to have the General Assembly overturn the move as an intrusion on their mission. Most institutions are governed by their own boards.

In 1988 the state started an ambitious program to improve higher education. The program, called the "Cutting Edge," included money for new endowed professorships and improved research programs.

State higher-education policy also takes private higher education into account. The private institutions are eligible for some grants under the Cutting Edge program, and needy students at private colleges are eligible for state grants that offset the higher costs of private-college tuition.

Besides the perennial lack of mon-

SOUTH CAROLINA
Continued

ey, higher-education leaders in South Carolina are also concerned about improving the college-going rates of black citizens, who make up one-third of the state's population but only about one-fifth of the college population. Minority enrollment is even lower at the state's major institutions, the University of South Carolina and Clemson.

DEMOGRAPHICS

Population: 3,512,000 (Rank: 25)

Age distribution:
Up to 17	27.2%
18 to 24	11.5%
25 to 34	17.9%
35 and older	43.4%

Racial and ethnic distribution:
American Indian	0.2%
Asian	0.4%
Black	30.4%
White	68.8%
Other and unknown	0.2%
Hispanic (may be any race)	1.1%

Educational attainment of adults:
At least 4 years of high school 53.7%
At least 1 to 3 years of college 26.7%
At least 4 years of college ... 13.4%

Per-capita personal income: $13,634

New high-school graduates in:
1990-91 (estimate) 36,433
2000-01 (estimate) 37,610

New GED diploma recipients: 4,702

High-school dropout rate: 35.4%

POLITICAL LEADERSHIP

Governor: Carroll A. Campbell, Jr. (R), term ends 1995

Governor's higher-education adviser: Mary Willis, P.O. Box 11369, State House, Columbia 29211; (803) 734-9818

U.S. Senators: Ernest F. Hollings (D), term ends 1993; Strom Thurmond (R), term ends 1997

U.S. Representatives:
4 Democrats, 2 Republicans
Butler Derrick (D), Elizabeth J. Patterson (D), Arthur Ravenel, Jr. (R), Floyd Spence (R), John M. Spratt, Jr. (D), Robin Tallon (D)

General Assembly: Senate, 34 Democrats, 11 Republicans, 1 vacancy; House, 78 Democrats, 42 Republicans, 1 Independent, 3 vacancies

COLLEGES AND UNIVERSITIES

Higher education:
Public 4-year institutions	12
Public 2-year institutions	21
Private 4-year institutions	20
Private 2-year institutions	11
Total	64

Vocational institutions: 62

Statewide coordinating board:
Commission on Higher Education
1333 Main Street, Suite 300
Columbia 29201
(803) 253-6260
Fred R. Sheheen, commissioner

Private-college association:
South Carolina College Council
P.O. Box 12007
Columbia 29211
(803) 799-7122
Sterling L. Smith, vice-president

Institutions censured by the AAUP:
None

Institutions under NCAA sanctions:
Clemson University,
University of South Carolina

FACULTY MEMBERS

Full-time faculty members:
At public institutions 3,747
At private institutions 1,234

Proportion who are women:
At public institutions 32.0%
At private institutions 29.1%

Proportion with tenure:
At public institutions 57.8%
At private institutions 56.3%

Average pay of full-time professors:
At public 4-year institutions $34,051
At public 2-year institutions $22,484
At private 4-year institutions $28,056
At private 2-year institutions $23,090

STUDENTS

Enrollment:
At public 4-year institutions . 79,252
At public 2-year institutions . 40,674
At private 4-year institutions 22,963
At private 2-year institutions . 4,868
Undergraduate 127,488
  First-time freshmen 33,985
Graduate 17,888
Professional 2,381
American Indian 236
Asian 1,288
Black 29,247
Hispanic 863
White 113,939
Foreign 2,184
Total 147,757

Enrollment highlights:
Women 56.1%

Full-time 67.7%
Minority 21.7%
Foreign 1.5%
10-year change in total
  enrollment .... Up 13.6%

Proportion of enrollment made up of minority students:
At public 4-year institutions . 16.7%
At public 2-year institutions . 24.5%
At private 4-year institutions 30.1%
At private 2-year institutions 39.5%

Degrees awarded:
Associate 4,776
Bachelor's 12,136
Master's 3,535
Doctorate 302
Professional 683

Residence of new students: State residents made up 80% of all freshmen enrolled in South Carolina; 89% of all South Carolina residents who were freshmen attended college in their home state.

Test scores: Students averaged 834 on the S.A.T., which was taken by 54% of South Carolina's high-school seniors.

MONEY

Average tuition and fees:
At public 4-year institutions . $2,162
At public 2-year institutions .. $807
At private 4-year institutions $5,914
At private 2-year institutions $4,898

Expenditures:
Public institutions $951,848,000
Private institutions ... $196,271,000

State funds for higher-education operating expenses: $644,726,000
Two-year change: Up 12%

SOUTH CAROLINA
Continued

State spending on student aid:
Need-based: $18,191,000;
7,476 awards
Non–need-based: None
Other: $1,581,000

**Salary of chief executive
of largest public 4-year campus:**
Arthur K. Smith (interim),
University of South Carolina
at Columbia: $112,000

**Total spending on research and
development by doctorate-granting
universities:** $120,137,000

Sources:
Federal government 34.6%
State and local governments . 14.5%
Industry 6.6%
The institution itself 37.8%
Other 6.5%

**Federal spending on education
and student aid (selected programs):**
Vocational and
adult education $14,056,000
GI Bill $13,280,000
Pell Grants $58,986,000

**Total federal spending on college-
and university-based research
and development:** $35,595,000

Selected programs:
Department of Health
and Human Services $17,931,000
National Science
Foundation $4,874,000
Department of Defense . $4,041,000
Department
of Agriculture $5,798,000
Department of Energy .. $1,625,000

Largest endowment:
Furman University $73,160,000

Top fund raisers:
University of South Carolina
at Columbia $22,567,000
Clemson University ... $17,720,000
Furman University $7,517,000

MISCELLANY

■ Winthrop College has been selected as the site of South Carolina's Center for the Advancement of Teaching and School Leadership, a consortium of eight public and private higher-education institutions. The center will provide training for faculty members, as well as for schoolteachers and administrators who will work in the public schools to make fundamental organizational changes.

■ Segments of news film shot all over the world from 1919 to 1963 can be viewed in the Movietonews Film Library at the University of South Carolina's McKissick Museum.

■ Since 1982 the University of South Carolina at Columbia has been leading a nationwide effort to improve students' first year in college. The university is the site of the National Conference on the Freshman Year Experience, one of the most popular annual conferences for student-personnel administrators.

■ The oldest higher-education institution in South Carolina is the College of Charleston, founded in 1770.

SOUTH DAKOTA

SOUTH DAKOTA'S lawmakers are very supportive of higher education, but they are also very reluctant to increase taxes to pay for it. As a result, state officials are encouraged to be creative and stretch every dollar as far as it can go.

For example, the state enacted an Education Savings Bond program early in 1990. Although the program was established to help families save for college, money collected from the bond sales may be used by the state for other purposes. Revenue from the first bonds will be lent to a public-school district to finance remodeling projects and to build a new high school and elementary school.

Like other states in the Great Plains region, South Dakota has an economy based on agriculture and mining. Although that economy has been relatively strong, the state does not have the revenue to support dramatic increases in financial support for higher education. At the urging of University of South Dakota officials, the state has provided more money for faculty salaries, but professors are still among the lowest-paid in the nation.

Gov. George S. Mickelson, a Republican, pointed to his support of higher education during his successful re-election campaign. He says he will continue that support.

Some higher-education officials complain, however, that influential farming interests direct too much money to agriculture-related research at the expense of life-science, engineering, and physical-science programs—all of which could contribute to the diversification of the state's economy.

South Dakota's population of American Indians is served by the state institutions as well as by tribally controlled colleges, which receive support from the federal government.

The South Dakota Board of Regents serves as the governing and coordinating board for all public higher education.

DEMOGRAPHICS

Population: 715,000 (Rank: 45)

Age distribution:
Up to 17 .... 27.4%
18 to 24 .... 10.2%
25 to 34 .... 16.9%
35 and older 45.6%

Racial and ethnic distribution:
American Indian 6.6%
Asian 0.3%
Black 0.3%
White 92.6%
Other and unknown 0.2%
Hispanic (may be any race) .. 0.6%

Educational attainment of adults:
At least 4 years of high school 67.9%
At least 1 to 3 years of college 31.7%
At least 4 years of college ... 14.0%

Per-capita personal income: $13,685

New high-school graduates in:
1990-91 (estimate) 7,696
2000-01 (estimate) 8,913

New GED diploma recipients: 892

High-school dropout rate: 20.4%

POLITICAL LEADERSHIP

Governor: George S. Mickelson (R), term ends 1995

Governor's higher-education adviser: Howell Todd, 207 East Capitol Avenue, Pierre 57501; (605) 773-3455

U.S. Senators: Thomas A. Daschle (D), term ends 1993; Larry Pressler (R), term ends 1997

SOUTH DAKOTA
Continued

U.S. Representative:
1 Democrat, 0 Republicans
Tim Johnson (D)

Legislature: Senate, 17 Democrats, 18 Republicans; House, 24 Democrats, 46 Republicans

COLLEGES AND UNIVERSITIES

Higher education:
Public 4-year institutions 7
Public 2-year institutions 0
Private 4-year institutions 10
Private 2-year institutions 2
Total 19

Vocational institutions: 21

Statewide coordinating board:
Board of Regents
207 East Capitol Avenue
Pierre 57501
(605) 773-3455
Howell Todd, executive director

Private-college association:
South Dakota Association
  of Independent Colleges
P.O. Box 645
Sioux Falls 57101
(605) 338-6621
Jeffrey W. Hayzlett,
executive director

Institutions censured by the AAUP:
South Dakota State Colleges
  and Universities (governing board)

Institutions under NCAA sanctions:
None

FACULTY MEMBERS

Full-time faculty members:
At public institutions 862
At private institutions 283

Proportion who are women:
At public institutions 26.9%
At private institutions 39.6%

Proportion with tenure:
At public institutions 58.6%
At private institutions 56.6%

Average pay of full-time professors:
At public 4-year institutions $28,958
At public 2-year institutions .... n/a
At private 4-year institutions $22,753
At private 2-year institutions $19,330

STUDENTS

Enrollment:
At public 4-year institutions . 23,898
At public 2-year institutions 0
At private 4-year institutions . 7,180
At private 2-year institutions .. 382
Undergraduate 28,308
  First-time freshmen 6,085
Graduate 2,729
Professional 423
American Indian 1,888
Asian 122
Black 226
Hispanic 69
White 28,526
Foreign 629
Total 31,460

Enrollment highlights:
Women 54.6%
Full-time 72.9%
Minority 7.5%
Foreign 2.0%
10-year change in total
  enrollment .... Up 1.7%

Proportion of enrollment made up of minority students:
At public 4-year institutions .. 5.7%
At public 2-year institutions .... n/a
At private 4-year institutions   11.8%
At private 2-year institutions   33.8%

Degrees awarded:
Associate 831
Bachelor's 3,627
Master's 756
Doctorate 51
Professional 121

Residence of new students: State residents made up 72% of all freshmen enrolled in South Dakota; 72% of all South Dakota residents who were freshmen attended college in their home state.

Test scores: Students averaged 19.4 on the A.C.T., which was taken by 66% of South Dakota's high-school seniors.

MONEY

Average tuition and fees:
At public 4-year institutions . $1,718
At public 2-year institutions .... n/a
At private 4-year institutions $6,224
At private 2-year institutions $2,447

Expenditures:
Public institutions $149,092,000
Private institutions $51,675,000

State funds for higher-education operating expenses: $91,415,000

Two-year change: Up 16%

State spending on student aid:
Need-based: $504,000; 1,500 awards
Non–need-based: $90,000; 60 awards
Other: None

Salary of chief executive of largest public 4-year campus:
Robert T. Wagner, South Dakota
   State University: $84,000

Total spending on research and development by doctorate-granting universities: $12,449,000
Sources:
Federal government 49.5%
State and local governments . 39.4%
Industry 2.5%
The institution itself 6.7%
Other 1.8%

Federal spending on education and student aid (selected programs):
Vocational and
   adult education $4,099,000
GI Bill $2,819,000
Pell Grants $26,910,000

Total federal spending on college- and university-based research and development: $4,851,000
Selected programs:
Department of Health
   and Human Services ... $670,000
National Science
   Foundation $772,000
Department of Defense 0
Department
   of Agriculture $2,402,000
Department of Energy $265,000

Largest endowment:
University of
   South Dakota $13,695,000

Top fund raisers:
Augustana College $3,855,000
University of
   South Dakota $2,213,000
South Dakota State
   University $2,201,000

SOUTH DAKOTA
Continued

MISCELLANY

■ In its Shrine to Music Museum, the University of South Dakota houses more than 4,000 musical instruments from around the world—including one of the two Stradivari guitars still in existence.

■ South Dakota has two four-year colleges that are controlled by Indian tribal councils, as well as two tribal community colleges.

■ The oldest institution of higher education in South Dakota is the North American Baptist Seminary, founded in 1858.

TENNESSEE

GOV. NED RAY McWHERTER of Tennessee is the new chairman of the Southern Regional Education Board, and he wants to make his state's efforts to improve education a national model.

The Tennessee Higher Education Commission is developing a plan to improve the quality of instructional programs dramatically, increase higher education's ties to economic development, and enlarge its share of federal research dollars. The public-schools commissioner has prepared a plan to improve the state's elementary and secondary schools.

Mr. McWherter, a Democrat, won a second term in November. He says he will devote the next four years to improving the quality of Tennessee schools and colleges—and to increasing financial support for them.

Although the University of Tennessee has historically dominated higher education in the state, the regional and community-college system is gaining importance. The regional system is governed by the Tennessee Board of Regents.

The board's new chancellor is Otis L. Floyd, once the president of Tennessee State University, a historically black university. One of his top priorities will be to hire new presidents for three of the state's largest institutions: Tennessee, Middle Tennessee, and Memphis State Universities.

Meanwhile, Lamar Alexander, president of the University of Tennessee, is pushing ahead with his plans to make the university into a top-flight research institution. He says he wants it to be on a par with the University of Michigan and the University of North Carolina at Chapel Hill.

Mr. Alexander, Mr. McWherter's predecessor, has been the subject of much debate in Tennessee. His selection for the presidency angered many Democrats, who did not want to see the former Republican Governor head the four-campus system.

Both the regional and the university systems are coordinated by the Tennessee Higher Education Commission. In the last few years, the commission has stepped up its monitoring of yet another segment of higher education: for-profit trade schools. Many politicians believe the proprietary schools are misusing student-aid money and must be watched more closely.

The commission has also been working to make sure that the public colleges and universities attract more black students and faculty members.

Unlike most Southern states, which were covered by a single federal desegregation suit, Tennessee has its own court order, with goals for increasing black enrollment. And the state is still trying to meet several of those goals.

Many of the state's black students enroll at historically black colleges like Tennessee State, a public institution, or Fisk University, a private institution.

Several private institutions are influential in Tennessee, including the University of the South and Vanderbilt University.

DEMOGRAPHICS

Population: 4,940,000 (Rank: 16)

Age distribution:
Up to 17 .... 25.4%
18 to 24 .... 10.7%
25 to 34 .... 17.3%
35 and older 46.6%

Racial and ethnic distribution:
American Indian 0.2%
Asian 0.3%
Black 15.8%
White 83.6%
Other and unknown 0.1%
Hispanic (may be any race) .. 0.7%

Educational attainment of adults:
At least 4 years of high school 56.2%
At least 1 to 3 years of college 24.5%
At least 4 years of college ... 12.6%

Per-capita personal income: $14,694

New high-school graduates in:
1990-91 (estimate) 47,273
2000-01 (estimate) 47,131

New GED diploma recipients: 9,093

High-school dropout rate: 30.7%

POLITICAL LEADERSHIP

Governor: Ned Ray McWherter (D), term ends 1995

Governor's higher-education adviser: Billy Stair, G12 State Capitol, Nashville 37219; (615) 741-5098

U.S. Senators: Albert Gore, Jr. (D), term ends 1997; Jim Sasser (D), term ends 1995

U.S. Representatives:
6 Democrats, 3 Republicans
Bob Clement (D), Jim Cooper (D), John J. Duncan, Jr. (R), Harold E. Ford (D), Bart Gordon (D), Marilyn Lloyd (D), James H. (Jimmy) Quillen (R), Don Sundquist (R), John S. Tanner (D)

General Assembly: Senate, 19 Democrats, 14 Republicans; House, 57 Democrats, 42 Republicans

COLLEGES AND UNIVERSITIES

Higher education:
Public 4-year institutions 10
Public 2-year institutions 14
Private 4-year institutions 42
Private 2-year institutions 20
Total 86

Vocational institutions: 127

Statewide coordinating board:
Tennessee Higher
    Education Commission
Parkway Towers, Suite 1900
404 James Robertson Parkway
Nashville 37219
(615) 741-7562
Arliss L. Roaden, executive director

TENNESSEE

Private-college association:
Tennessee Council of
  Private Colleges
611 Commerce Street, Suite 2912
Nashville 37203
(615) 242-6400
Hans Giesecke, president

Institutions censured by the AAUP:
None

Institution under NCAA sanctions:
Memphis State University

FACULTY MEMBERS

Full-time faculty members:
At public institutions 4,701
At private institutions 2,026

Proportion who are women:
At public institutions 30.7%
At private institutions 25.8%

Proportion with tenure:
At public institutions 65.0%
At private institutions 54.1%

Average pay of full-time professors:
At public 4-year institutions $35,396
At public 2-year institutions $26,660
At private 4-year institutions $31,373
At private 2-year institutions $19,106

STUDENTS

Enrollment:
At public 4-year institutions 103,791
At public 2-year institutions . 51,818
At private 4-year institutions 45,087
At private 2-year institutions . 5,710
Undergraduate 180,156
  First-time freshmen 37,475

Graduate 20,821
Professional 5,429
American Indian 404
Asian 1,728
Black 28,494
Hispanic 1,166
White 170,510
Foreign 4,104
Total 206,406

Enrollment highlights:
Women 53.9%
Full-time 66.6%
Minority 15.7%
Foreign 2.0%
10-year change in total
  enrollment .... Up 6.0%

Proportion of enrollment made up of minority students:
At public 4-year institutions . 14.6%
At public 2-year institutions . 15.6%
At private 4-year institutions 17.5%
At private 2-year institutions 22.9%

Degrees awarded:
Associate 5,908
Bachelor's 17,159
Master's 4,435
Doctorate 540
Professional 1,308

Residence of new students: State residents made up 79% of all freshmen enrolled in Tennessee; 85% of all Tennessee residents who were freshmen attended college in their home state.

Test scores: Students averaged 17.9 on the A.C.T., which was taken by 61% of Tennessee's high-school seniors.

MONEY

Average tuition and fees:
At public 4-year institutions . $1,406
At public 2-year institutions .. $803

At private 4-year institutions $6,530
At private 2-year institutions $3,395

Expenditures:
Public institutions .. $1,081,052,000
Private institutions ... $684,948,000

State funds for higher-education operating expenses: $743,821,000

Two-year change: Up 8%

State spending on student aid:
Need-based: $17,295,000;
    24,599 awards
Non–need-based: $205,000; 51 awards
Other: $2,527,000

Salary of chief executive of largest public 4-year campus:
John J. Quinn, University of
    Tennessee at Knoxville: $138,375

Total spending on research and development by doctorate-granting universities: $214,764,000

Sources:
Federal government 57.8%
State and local governments . 15.1%
Industry 4.9%
The institution itself 17.2%
Other 5.1%

Federal spending on education and student aid (selected programs):
Vocational and
    adult education $18,831,000
GI Bill $11,833,000
Pell Grants $83,403,000

Total federal spending on college- and university-based research and development: $114,221,000

Selected programs:
Department of Health
    and Human Services $73,025,000
National Science
    Foundation $7,180,000
Department of Defense . $8,264,000

Department
    of Agriculture $7,254,000
Department of Energy . $11,824,000

Largest endowment:
Vanderbilt University $556,567,000

Top fund raisers:
Vanderbilt University . $36,359,000
University of Tennessee $32,159,000
University of the South . $6,212,000

MISCELLANY

■ Meharry Medical College, founded in 1876 as the Medical Department of Central Tennessee College, separated in 1915 to become the first independent medical school for blacks. Meharry claims to have trained nearly a third of the black doctors and dentists in the country. In 1987, the college was designated by the federal government as a Center for Excellence in Minority Health Education and Care.

■ David Lipscomb College, which is affiliated with the Church of Christ, in 1989 banned the cable-television channel MTV from campus sets because of its "sexually explicit and violent content."

■ The oldest institutions of higher education in the state are Tusculum College and the University of Tennessee at Knoxville, both founded in 1794.

TEXAS

TEXAS prides itself on its Old West populism, its rich ethnic history, and its reputation as

TEXAS

the home of some of the nation's most sophisticated medical and scientific research centers. The Lone Star State's giant higher-education enterprise clearly reflects those political and cultural factors.

Public colleges in Texas are large, charge low tuition, and spread across the state. But critics say that quality is too often related to their locale, the demographics of the regions they serve, or the political clout of their alumni and local legislators.

College leaders in the poor, predominantly Hispanic area of South Texas, for example, have long complained that their institutions don't receive a fair share of state funds, although in recent years the Legislature has sought to redress that by merging some institutions into larger, better-financed systems.

The two most powerful and prestigious systems are the University of Texas and Texas A&M University Systems, which enjoy special status because they receive income from a state trust fund based on oil revenue. They have invested it wisely: Their endowments are the largest of any public systems in the country.

Their wealth and traditional legislative clout have often been a source of irritation to the state's other ambitious, research-oriented institutions, including the University of Houston and Texas Tech University.

Altogether, public colleges and universities are governed by 12 different boards. Although the institutions retain much control over their day-to-day operations, the Texas Higher Education Coordinating Board is increasingly expanding its role in policy-making issues. The coordinating board is also now studying whether Texas colleges could be run more efficiently with fewer governing boards.

The board also recently took steps to encourage more black and Hispanic students to pursue doctoral degrees by offering them forgivable student loans.

The board has also become a central player in the state's effort to improve the success rates for college students taking the basic-skills test, which they must pass to move into junior- or senior-level courses. A disproportionate number of those who fail are black or Hispanic students, a fact that many attribute to the poor preparation such students receive in public schools. The Legislature spent much of 1990 fighting former Gov. William P. Clements, a Republican, over ways to overhaul public-school financing.

Mr. Clements, who has feuded with higher-education officials for many years, did not seek re-election. His successor is Ann Richards, a Democrat and former State Treasurer. Governor Richards has pledged to increase financial aid and to guarantee the future of the state's historically black colleges and universities.

Meanwhile, higher education lost one of its staunchest supporters with the retirement of Lieut. Gov. William P. Hobby.

Mr. Hobby has been one of the strongest advocates of the state's efforts to expand the universities' research capabilities and to use their faculty members' expertise to promote economic development. The state's competitive grant program for research, financed by special appropriations from the Legislature, is the largest of its kind in the nation.

Because it is moving to diversify its energy-based economy, Texas takes its research seriously. The state's pledge of $1-billion was cited as an important factor in its being selected by the U.S. Department of Energy as the site for the Superconducting Supercollider. And faculty members at several public and private medical schools, including the Baylor College of Medicine and the U.T. Health Science Center at San Antonio, have been in the forefront of state and national campaigns to block restrictions on the use of animals in scientific and medical research.

Private colleges and universities also are a force in Texas, particularly research institutions such as Rice University and those with religious ties, such as Southern Methodist and Texas Christian Universities.

DEMOGRAPHICS

Population: 16,991,000   (Rank: 3)

Age distribution:
Up to 17	29.1%
18 to 24	10.9%
25 to 34	18.5%
35 and older	41.5%

Racial and ethnic distribution:
American Indian	0.4%
Asian	0.9%
Black	12.0%
White	79.4%
Other and unknown	7.2%
Hispanic (may be any race)	21.0%

Educational attainment of adults:
At least 4 years of high school	62.6%
At least 1 to 3 years of college	33.8%
At least 4 years of college	16.9%

Per-capita personal income: $15,702

New high-school graduates in:
1990-91 (estimate)	183,090
2000-01 (estimate)	204,725

New GED diploma recipients: 33,187

High-school dropout rate: 34.7%

POLITICAL LEADERSHIP

Governor: Ann Richards (D), term ends 1995

Governor's higher-education adviser: n/a

U.S. Senators: Lloyd Bentsen (D), term ends 1995; Phil Gramm (R), term ends 1997

U.S. Representatives:
19 Democrats, 8 Republicans
Michael A. Andrews (D), Bill Archer (R), Richard K. Armey (R), Steve Bartlett (R), Joe Barton (R), Jack Brooks (D), John Bryant (D), Albert G. Bustamante (D), Jim Chapman (D), Ronald D. Coleman (D), Larry Combest (R), E de la Garza (D), Tom DeLay (R), Chet Edwards (D), Jack Fields (R), Martin Frost (D), Pete Geren (D), Henry B. Gonzalez (D), Ralph M. Hall (D), Greg Laughlin (D), Solomon P. Ortiz (D), J.J. Pickle (D), Bill Sarpalius (D), Lamar S. Smith (R), Charles W. Stenholm (D), Craig A. Washington (D), Charles Wilson (D)

Legislature: Senate, 23 Democrats, 8 Republicans; House, 94 Democrats, 56 Republicans

---

COLLEGES AND UNIVERSITIES

Higher education:
Public 4-year institutions	40
Public 2-year institutions	67
Private 4-year institutions	56
Private 2-year institutions	11
Total	174

TEXAS
Continued

Vocational institutions: 397

Statewide coordinating board:
Texas Higher Education
  Coordinating Board
P.O. Box 12788
Austin 78711
(512) 483-6100
Kenneth H. Ashworth, commissioner

Private-college association:
Independent Colleges and
  Universities of Texas
P.O. Box 13105
Austin 78711
(512) 472-9522
Carol L. McDonald, president

Institutions censured by the AAUP:
Amarillo College, Blinn College,
Frank Phillips College, Houston
Baptist University, Southwestern
Adventist College, University
of Texas of the Permian Basin

Institutions under NCAA sanctions:
Houston Baptist University,
University of Houston, University
of Texas–Pan American, West Texas
State University

FACULTY MEMBERS

Full-time faculty members:
At public institutions 16,463
At private institutions 3,955

Proportion who are women:
At public institutions 31.4%
At private institutions 27.8%

Proportion with tenure:
At public institutions 61.8%
At private institutions 55.1%

Average pay of full-time professors:
At public 4-year institutions $35,963
At public 2-year institutions $29,972
At private 4-year institutions $34,221
At private 2-year institutions $21,241

STUDENTS

Enrollment:
At public 4-year institutions   392,103
At public 2-year institutions   361,091
At private 4-year institutions   90,024
At private 2-year institutions . 3,974
Undergraduate 739,128
  First-time freshmen 150,518
Graduate 92,638
Professional 15,426
American Indian 2,756
Asian 23,642
Black 75,478
Hispanic 125,778
White 597,400
Foreign 22,138
Total 847,192

Enrollment highlights:
Women 52.8%
Full-time 54.6%
Minority 27.6%
Foreign 2.6%
10-year change in total
  enrollment .... Up 29.1%

**Proportion of enrollment made up
of minority students:**
At public 4-year institutions . 25.1%
At public 2-year institutions . 32.0%
At private 4-year institutions 19.8%
At private 2-year institutions 33.5%

Degrees awarded:
Associate 22,346
Bachelor's 55,575
Master's 17,559
Doctorate 2,067
Professional 3,999

Residence of new students: State residents made up 92% of all freshmen enrolled in Texas; 95% of all Texas residents who were freshmen attended college in their home state.

Test scores: Students averaged 874 on the s.a.t., which was taken by 42% of Texas' high-school seniors.

MONEY

Average tuition and fees:
At public 4-year institutions .. $959
At public 2-year institutions .. $455
At private 4-year institutions $6,047
At private 2-year institutions $5,112

Expenditures:
Public institutions .. $4,375,082,000
Private institutions ... $993,824,000

State funds for higher-education operating expenses: $2,579,342,000

Two-year change: Up 15%

State spending on student aid:
Need-based: $27,380,000;
  20,857 awards
Non–need-based: None
Other: $84,667,000

Salary of chief executive of largest public 4-year campus:
William H. Cunningham, University of Texas at Austin: $62,160 from state plus $111,840 from private donations

Total spending on research and development by doctorate-granting universities: $1,008,969,000
Sources:
Federal government 48.4%
State and local governments . 12.3%
Industry 6.2%
The institution itself 20.3%
Other 12.8%

Federal spending on education and student aid (selected programs):
Vocational and
  adult education $57,359,000
GI Bill $50,301,000
Pell Grants $327,601,000

Total federal spending on college- and university-based research and development: $414,370,000
Selected programs:
Department of Health
  and Human Services $239,919,000
National Science
  Foundation $39,346,000
Department of Defense $64,547,000
Department
  of Agriculture $18,466,000
Department of Energy . $21,057,000

Largest endowment:
University of Texas
  System $3,021,474,000

Top fund raisers:
Texas A&M University $50,240,000
University of Texas
  at Austin $35,464,000
University of Texas Medical
  Branch at Galveston . $26,800,000

MISCELLANY

■ Students at the University of Texas gave the institution an overall C average when they graded it in a campuswide referendum in the fall of 1989. Students gave the institution the lowest grades in learning atmosphere, class size, and ability to provide the classes that students are required to take.

■ Texas Woman's University has a residence hall for 30 single mothers and their children.

■ Texas high-school juniors and seniors can get a head start on college in a program for gifted mathematics and science students. The Texas Academy of Mathematics and Science, at the University of North Texas, allows students simultaneously to finish their last two years of high school and first two years of college.

■ President Bush has reportedly decided to set up his Presidential library at a campus in his adopted home state of Texas, and universities are already vying to provide a site for it.

■ A long-standing dispute between Texas Methodists and Baptists obscures any higher-education institution's clear claim to being the oldest in the state. Southwestern University, a private liberal-arts college affiliated with the United Methodist Church, says it was founded in 1840 as Rutersville College. Baylor University, a private institution affiliated with the Southern Baptist Church, considers that a highly questionable claim and maintains that its 1845 charter from the Republic of Texas Congress makes it the state's oldest college or university.

UTAH

FUSION confusion continues to have ramifications for Utah higher education more than a year after the University of Utah became the center of a national scientific controversy. The debate involved a claim by two professors who said they had produced fusion at room temperature.

State officials, who authorized $4.5-million in public funds to establish a National Cold Fusion Institute, are now demanding more detailed information to determine if future financing for the institute is warranted. The Legislature created the institute in a burst of enthusiasm shortly after the scientists made their announcement in March 1989. But the excitement has since subsided as scientists around the world have continued to challenge the experiment's validity.

More fallout came in June 1990, when the university's president, Chase N. Peterson, announced he would retire after a storm of protest over his use of $500,000 from the university foundation as an "anonymous" gift to the fusion institute. In late 1990, the future of the fusion institute seemed even more shaky, when one of the scientists abruptly left the university saying he wanted a one-year sabbatical and the other was reportedly in England seeking treatment for an undisclosed medical condition.

Many in the university and state now fear that the controversy will damage the university's hard-earned reputation in such fields as medicine, physics, and space-related research.

The concern is especially high because Utah's public colleges sometimes have a difficult time winning budget increases from the fiscally conservative Legislature, and the state's soaring population is placing additional strains on the public institutions.

The public colleges also regularly contend with the state's strong anti-tax movement. Higher-education officials monitor and lobby against legislation and referenda to eliminate or cut state taxes.

The Board of Regents is the governing and coordinating board for all of public higher education, which now includes two new universities formerly known as state colleges: Southern Utah State and Weber State. The Legislature approved the name changes in 1990.

For a Western state, Utah also has unusually influential private colleges. That is largely due to the enormous influence of the Mormon Church and its premier institution, Brigham Young University. Brigham Young alumni dominate many spheres of state business and government.

DEMOGRAPHICS

Population: 1,707,000   (Rank: 35)

Age distribution:
Up to 17	37.0%
18 to 24	11.8%
25 to 34	17.5%
35 and older	33.8%

Racial and ethnic distribution:
American Indian	1.4%
Asian	1.4%
Black	0.6%
White	94.7%
Other and unknown	1.9%
Hispanic (may be any race)	4.1%

Educational attainment of adults:
At least 4 years of high school	80.0%
At least 1 to 3 years of college	44.1%
At least 4 years of college	19.9%

Per-capita personal income: $13,079

New high-school graduates in:
1990-91 (estimate)	24,473
2000-01 (estimate)	31,829

New GED diploma recipients: 1,007

High-school dropout rate: 20.6%

POLITICAL LEADERSHIP

Governor: Norman H. Bangerter (R), term ends 1993

Governor's higher-education adviser: Colleen Colton, 210 State Capitol, Salt Lake City 84114; (801) 538-1000

U.S. Senators: Jake Garn (R), term ends 1993; Orrin G. Hatch (R), term ends 1995

U.S. Representatives:
2 Democrats, 1 Republican
James V. Hansen (R), William Orton (D), Wayne Owens (D)

Legislature: Senate, 10 Democrats, 19 Republicans; House, 31 Democrats, 44 Republicans

COLLEGES AND UNIVERSITIES

Higher education:
Public 4-year institutions	4
Public 2-year institutions	5
Private 4-year institutions	2
Private 2-year institutions	3
Total	14

Vocational institutions: 40

Statewide coordinating board:
Utah System of Higher Education
355 West North Temple
3 Triad Center, Suite 550
Salt Lake City 84180
(801) 538-5247
Wm. Rolfe Kerr, commissioner of higher education

Private-college association:
None

Institution censured by the AAUP:
Westminster College of Salt Lake City

UTAH
Continued

Institutions under NCAA sanctions:
None

FACULTY MEMBERS

Full-time faculty members:
At public institutions 2,096
At private institutions .... n/a

Proportion who are women:
At public institutions 22.5%
At private institutions .... n/a

Proportion with tenure:
At public institutions 61.1%
At private institutions .... n/a

Average pay of full-time professors:
At public 4-year institutions $34,060
At public 2-year institutions $26,460
At private 4-year institutions $25,557
At private 2-year institutions ... n/a

STUDENTS

Enrollment:
At public 4-year institutions . 52,631
At public 2-year institutions . 21,801
At private 4-year institutions 32,080
At private 2-year institutions . 1,026
Undergraduate 96,586
  First-time freshmen 18,900
Graduate 9,740
Professional 1,212
American Indian 1,088
Asian 1,736
Black 619
Hispanic 1,743
White 97,575
Foreign 4,777
Total 107,538

Enrollment highlights:
Women 47.1%
Full-time 63.8%
Minority 5.0%
Foreign 4.4%
10-year change in total
  enrollment .... Up 20.8%

Proportion of enrollment made up of minority students:
At public 4-year institutions .. 5.5%
At public 2-year institutions .. 7.7%
At private 4-year institutions . 2.0%
At private 2-year institutions 15.1%

Degrees awarded:
Associate 3,552
Bachelor's 10,820
Master's 2,574
Doctorate 418
Professional 378

Residence of new students: State residents made up 64% of all freshmen enrolled in Utah; 90% of all Utah residents who were freshmen attended college in their home state.

Test scores: Students averaged 18.9 on the A.C.T., which was taken by 67% of Utah's high-school seniors.

MONEY

Average tuition and fees:
At public 4-year institutions . $1,429
At public 2-year institutions . $1,136
At private 4-year institutions $1,975
At private 2-year institutions $2,768

Expenditures:
Public institutions $669,714,000
Private institutions ... $194,649,000

State funds for higher-education operating expenses: $295,884,000

Two-year change: Up 12%

State spending on student aid:
Need-based: $1,068,000; 1,690 awards
Non–need-based: $968,000; 66 awards
Other: $8,491,000

**Salary of chief executive
of largest public 4-year campus:**
Chase N. Peterson, University
  of Utah: $113,000

**Total spending on research and
development by doctorate-granting
universities:** $164,828,000

Sources:
Federal government 66.2%
State and local governments . 10.4%
Industry 3.3%
The institution itself 16.9%
Other 3.2%

**Federal spending on education
and student aid (selected programs):**
Vocational and
  adult education $6,356,000
GI Bill $5,047,000
Pell Grants $56,137,000

**Total federal spending on college-
and university-based research
and development:** $86,648,000

Selected programs:
Department of Health
  and Human Services $39,107,000
National Science
  Foundation $11,168,000
Department of Defense $24,126,000
Department
  of Agriculture $2,649,000
Department of Energy .. $4,742,000

Largest endowment:
University of Utah $55,752,000

Top fund raisers:
University of Utah $34,830,000
Utah State University . $10,540,000
Dixie College $1,527,000

MISCELLANY

■ The Repertory Dance Theatre at
the University of Utah performs more
than 200 historical and modern dance
works by choreographers from
around the country. The theater was
founded by the university and the
Rockefeller Foundation in 1966.

■ Brigham Young University has a
large population of multilingual students. They learned the languages, especially Asian ones, when they served
abroad as Mormon missionaries before attending college.

■ Following clashes between the
administration and the faculty that led
to the resignation of 17 professors in
1915, the University of Utah became
the subject of the first institutional investigation ever conducted by the
American Association of University
Professors. John Dewey, the philoso-
pher, was a member of the A.A.U.P.
investigating team.

■ The oldest institution of higher
education in the state is the University
of Utah, founded in 1850.

VERMONT

V ERMONT'S long private-college
tradition continues to have a
great impact on higher education in the Green Mountain State.
Lately, though, the weakening economy has been a more powerful influence.

Hit by a recession that is battering
all of New England, Vermont has
found itself unable to provide its pub-

lic colleges and universities with the kind of generous budgets they enjoyed during the regional boom of the mid-1980's.

The belt tightening comes at a time when legislators are making greater demands on public institutions to use new technologies, like the state's educational television network, to serve students in rural regions.

Four-year institutions and community colleges operated by the Vermont State Colleges Board of Trustees are especially hard hit by the tight budgets. They rely more heavily on state support than does the University of Vermont, which receives less than 15 per cent of its funds from the state.

The university, Vermont's premier educational institution and its land-grant college, has an unusual relationship with the state. It was founded as a private institution and began receiving state funds only in 1955. It is governed by its own Board of Trustees. The university is often regarded as elitist because of its high tuition and popularity among wealthy non-Vermonters. Its legal maneuvering to thwart a unionization effort by faculty members has inflamed some lawmakers.

The hostility in the capital, Montpelier, and in the university's hometown of Burlington dissipated significantly in 1990 when university leaders tried to be more responsive to legislative and local concerns.

Private colleges enroll about a third of Vermont's college students and rely heavily on the state's student-aid programs. They also are attuned to political trends and have not shied away from lobbying for more state financial aid.

Bennington, Middlebury, and St. Michael's Colleges are among the state's leading liberal-arts institutions. Middlebury's foreign-language programs and Bennington's innovative curriculum emphasizing independent study are nationally known.

The institutions may also have an ally in the new Governor, Richard Snelling, a Republican who in November 1990 re-captured the post he held from 1977 to 1985. Mr. Snelling says that he is a supporter of higher education, but that the state's severe economic condition will require him to give a higher priority to financing elementary and secondary schools.

DEMOGRAPHICS

Population: 567,000   (Rank: 49)

Age distribution:
Up to 17 .... 25.0%
18 to 24 .... 11.6%
25 to 34 .... 18.5%
35 and older 45.0%

Racial and ethnic distribution:
American Indian 0.2%
Asian 0.3%
Black 0.2%
White 99.1%
Other and unknown 0.1%
Hispanic (may be any race) .. 0.6%

Educational attainment of adults:
At least 4 years of high school 71.0%
At least 1 to 3 years of college 34.7%
At least 4 years of college ... 19.0%

Per-capita personal income: $16,371

New high-school graduates in:
1990-91 (estimate) 6,206
2000-01 (estimate) 7,301

New GED diploma recipients: 1,060

High-school dropout rate: 21.3%

POLITICAL LEADERSHIP

Governor: Richard A. Snelling (R), term ends 1993

Governor's higher-education adviser: n/a

U.S. Senators: James M. Jeffords (R), term ends 1995; Patrick J. Leahy (D), term ends 1993

U.S. Representative:
0 Democrats, 0 Republicans,
1 Socialist
Bernie Sanders (Socialist)

General Assembly: Senate, 15 Democrats, 15 Republicans; House, 73 Democrats, 75 Republicans, 2 Independents

COLLEGES AND UNIVERSITIES

Higher education:
Public 4-year institutions 4
Public 2-year institutions 2
Private 4-year institutions 13
Private 2-year institutions 3
Total 22

Vocational institutions: 11

Statewide coordinating board:
Vermont Higher Education
   Planning Commission
Department of Finance
   and Management
109 State Street
Montpelier 05602
(802) 828-2376
Suzanne A. Villanti,
executive director

Private-college association:
Association of Vermont
   Independent Colleges
9170 Shaw Mansion Road
Waterbury Center 05677
(802) 244-5586
Judy P. Rosenstreich,
executive director

Institutions censured by the AAUP:
None

Institutions under NCAA sanctions:
None

FACULTY MEMBERS

Full-time faculty members:
At public institutions 660
At private institutions 673

Proportion who are women:
At public institutions 25.8%
At private institutions 30.8%

Proportion with tenure:
At public institutions 63.1%
At private institutions 57.3%

Average pay of full-time professors:
At public 4-year institutions $35,520
At public 2-year institutions $27,525
At private 4-year institutions $30,670
At private 2-year institutions $22,235

STUDENTS

Enrollment:
At public 4-year institutions . 15,762
At public 2-year institutions .. 4,205
At private 4-year institutions   12,383
At private 2-year institutions . 2,117
Undergraduate 30,590
   First-time freshmen 6,918
Graduate 3,522
Professional 355
American Indian 98
Asian 407

VERMONT
Continued

Black 277
Hispanic 234
White 32,953
Foreign 498
Total 34,467

Enrollment highlights:
Women 57.2%
Full-time 68.7%
Minority 3.0%
Foreign 1.4%
10-year change in total
    enrollment .... Up 16.5%

Proportion of enrollment made up of minority students:
At public 4-year institutions .. 3.2%
At public 2-year institutions .. 1.3%
At private 4-year institutions . 3.6%
At private 2-year institutions . 1.6%

Degrees awarded:
Associate 1,149
Bachelor's 4,273
Master's 830
Doctorate 45
Professional 98

Residence of new students: State residents made up 43% of all freshmen enrolled in Vermont; 63% of all Vermont residents who were freshmen attended college in their home state.

Test scores: Students averaged 897 on the s.a.t., which was taken by 62% of Vermont's high-school seniors.

MONEY

Average tuition and fees:
At public 4-year institutions . $3,641
At public 2-year institutions . $2,210
At private 4-year institutions $10,928
At private 2-year institutions $5,979

Expenditures:
Public institutions $188,112,000
Private institutions ... $150,689,000

State funds for higher-education operating expenses: $59,830,000
Two-year change: Up 11%

State spending on student aid:
Need-based: $11,172,000;
   10,806 awards
Non–need-based: None
Other: $212,000

Salary of chief executive of largest public 4-year campus:
George H. Davis, University
   of Vermont: $125,000

Total spending on research and development by doctorate-granting universities: $42,743,000
Sources:
Federal government 66.8%
State and local governments .. 5.8%
Industry 8.2%
The institution itself 12.8%
Other 6.4%

Federal spending on education and student aid (selected programs):
Vocational and
   adult education $4,373,000
GI Bill $725,000
Pell Grants $8,446,000

Total federal spending on college- and university-based research and development: $28,244,000
Selected programs:
Department of Health
   and Human Services $21,465,000
National Science
   Foundation $1,649,000

Department of Defense ... $355,000
Department
of Agriculture $2,831,000
Department of Energy $242,000

Largest endowment:
Middlebury College .. $216,920,000

Top fund raisers:
University of Vermont . $11,829,000
Middlebury College ... $10,537,000
Norwich University $2,619,000

MISCELLANY

■ The University of Vermont is home to the Pringle Herbarium, housing more than 300,000 specimens of dried plants from all over the country. The herbarium—started at the university by Cyrus Guernsey Pringle in 1902—includes plant specimens dating back to 1820.

■ Trustees at Middlebury College in the spring of 1990 ordered the college's six fraternities to admit women or face loss of their charters. All six fraternities, which are now called houses, agreed to admit women. The trustees took the action after a special committee recommended the abolition of the fraternity system.

■ In 1819 Alden Partridge founded the American Literary, Scientific, and Military Academy in Norwich. The first private technical and military school in the world, it is now Norwich University.

■ The oldest institution of higher education in the state is the University of Vermont, founded in 1791.

VIRGINIA

VIRGINIA, home of several of the nation's oldest universities, is the center of some of the most innovative thinking and policy making in American higher education.

Governors have been doing much of that thinking. In the early 1980's, Charles S. Robb pushed for higher faculty salaries. As the decade came to a close, Gerald L. Baliles promoted general education and college courses in foreign languages and foreign cultures.

Those efforts may pale beside the actions taken by Gov. L. Douglas Wilder, a Democrat who took office in January 1990. Already Mr. Wilder has put a lid on tuition increases, ordered colleges to use existing funds if they want to start new academic programs, and pressured colleges to divest their portfolios of stocks in companies with ties to South Africa. He has demanded that colleges prepare policies to fight racism and sexism on campus. The demand is a reflection of the state's uneven progress in recruiting minority students, particularly at its predominantly white campuses.

Unlike his predecessors, Mr. Wilder has shown little reverence for Virginia's strong tradition of campus autonomy. Late in 1990, he even decided to take on the Virginia Military Institute, saying that he disagreed with its policy of admitting only men. The Governor had tried to stay out of the dispute, but spoke out after a federal judge made him a defendant in a case against v.m.i. brought by the U.S. Justice Department.

The institute's loyal alumni are among the most politically influential in the state. They are also generous:

VIRGINIA

Continued

The v.m.i. Foundation has the largest endowment per student of any public institution in the nation. Two of the state's other prestigious institutions, the University of Virginia and the College of William and Mary, are among the top 10 institutions in that ranking.

Virginia has also been a leader in the movement to assess what college students learn and has won praise for a new, imaginative strategy for overall long-range planning. Both efforts were guided by the State Council of Higher Education for Virginia, whose studies are respected across the country.

The planning strategy, prepared by the so-called Commission on the University of the 21st Century, requires institutions to justify increases in their budgets. They must also show the General Assembly how they intend to respond to technological changes and the new educational demands of the emerging global economy. The strategy is also supposed to guide the state in planning to meet an expected surge in college enrollments in the next 10 years.

The council has some influence with the legislature, but the individual Boards of Visitors of the four-year institutions retain considerable power. The State Board for Community Colleges governs two-year institutions, many of which have seen remarkable enrollment increases in recent years.

Historically black institutions in the state include Virginia State and Norfolk State Universities, which are public, and Hampton University, which is private. Other private institutions include the University of Richmond and Liberty University, which is best known for its ties to the televangelist Jerry Falwell.

DEMOGRAPHICS

Population: 6,098,000   (Rank: 12)

Age distribution:
Up to 17	24.3%
18 to 24	11.5%
25 to 34	18.4%
35 and older	45.8%

Racial and ethnic distribution:
American Indian	0.2%
Asian	1.3%
Black	18.9%
White	79.2%
Other and unknown	0.4%
Hispanic (may be any race)	1.5%

Educational attainment of adults:
At least 4 years of high school	62.4%
At least 1 to 3 years of college	34.0%
At least 4 years of college	19.1%

Per-capita personal income: $18,927

New high-school graduates in:
1990-91 (estimate)	66,015
2000-01 (estimate)	82,897

New GED diploma recipients: 8,446

High-school dropout rate: 28.4%

POLITICAL LEADERSHIP

Governor: L. Douglas Wilder (D), term ends 1994

Governor's higher-education adviser: Karen J. Petersen, P.O. Box 1475, Richmond 23212; (804) 786-3586

U.S. Senators: Charles S. Robb (D), term ends 1995; John W. Warner (R), term ends 1997

U.S. Representatives:
6 Democrats, 4 Republicans
Herbert H. Bateman (R), Thomas J. Bliley, Jr. (R), Rick Boucher (D), James Moran (D), Jim Olin (D), Lewis F. Payne, Jr. (D), Owen B. Pickett (D), Norman Sisisky (D), D. French Slaughter, Jr. (R), Frank R. Wolf (R)

General Assembly: Senate, 30 Democrats, 10 Republicans; House, 59 Democrats, 39 Republicans, 2 Independents

---

COLLEGES AND UNIVERSITIES

Higher education:
Public 4-year institutions 15
Public 2-year institutions 24
Private 4-year institutions 33
Private 2-year institutions 6
Total 78

Vocational institutions: 165

Statewide coordinating board:
State Council of Higher Education
James Monroe Building
101 North 14th Street
Richmond 23219
(804) 225-2600
Gordon K. Davies, director

Private-college association:
Council of Independent Colleges
  in Virginia
P.O. Box 1005
118 East Main Street
Bedford 24523
(703) 586-0606
Robert B. Lambeth, Jr., president

Institutions censured by the AAUP:
Virginia Community College System

Institutions under NCAA sanctions:
None

FACULTY MEMBERS

Full-time faculty members:
At public institutions 7,421
At private institutions 2,069

Proportion who are women:
At public institutions 29.0%
At private institutions 33.6%

Proportion with tenure:
At public institutions 53.7%
At private institutions 52.7%

Average pay of full-time professors:
At public 4-year institutions $40,038
At public 2-year institutions $30,747
At private 4-year institutions $29,758
At private 2-year institutions $20,173

STUDENTS

Enrollment:
At public 4-year institutions   154,165
At public 2-year institutions   116,207
At private 4-year institutions   47,766
At private 2-year institutions . 3,078
Undergraduate 276,339
    First-time freshmen 50,768
Graduate 38,829
Professional 6,048
American Indian 738
Asian 9,032
Black 44,164
Hispanic 3,783
White 257,686
Foreign 5,813
Total 321,216

Enrollment highlights:
Women 56.0%
Full-time 56.9%
Minority 18.3%
Foreign 1.8%
10-year change in total
    enrollment .... Up 24.3%

VIRGINIA

Continued

Proportion of enrollment made up of minority students:

At public 4-year institutions . 18.1%
At public 2-year institutions . 16.9%
At private 4-year institutions 21.0%
At private 2-year institutions 36.4%

Degrees awarded:

Associate 8,192
Bachelor's 25,149
Master's 6,056
Doctorate 746
Professional 1,699

Residence of new students: State residents made up 68% of all freshmen enrolled in Virginia; 78% of all Virginia residents who were freshmen attended college in their home state.

Test scores: Students averaged 895 on the S.A.T., which was taken by 58% of Virginia's high-school seniors.

MONEY

Average tuition and fees:

At public 4-year institutions . $2,532
At public 2-year institutions .. $813
At private 4-year institutions $7,238
At private 2-year institutions $4,409

Expenditures:

Public institutions .. $1,825,156,000
Private institutions ... $387,455,000

State funds for higher-education operating expenses: $1,077,934,000

Two-year change: Up 5%

State spending on student aid:

Need-based: $8,284,000; 9,700 awards
Non–need-based: $18,089,000;
    16,723 awards
Other: None

Salary of chief executive of largest public 4-year campus:

James D. McComas, Virginia
    Polytechnic Institute and State
    University: $104,621 from state
    plus $43,058 from private donations

Total spending on research and development by doctorate-granting universities: $258,919,000

Sources:
Federal government 53.9%
State and local governments . 19.0%
Industry 8.4%
The institution itself 13.3%
Other 5.5%

Federal spending on education and student aid (selected programs):

Vocational and
    adult education $18,810,000
GI Bill $23,293,000
Pell Grants $76,924,000

Total federal spending on college- and university-based research and development: $126,596,000

Selected programs:
Department of Health
    and Human Services $62,956,000
National Science
    Foundation $13,327,000
Department of Defense $10,061,000
Department
    of Agriculture $7,426,000
Department of Energy .. $6,221,000

Largest endowment:

University of Virginia $446,476,000

Top fund raisers:

University of Virginia . $47,575,000
Virginia Polytechnic Institute
    and State University $27,779,000
College of William
    and Mary $13,362,000

MISCELLANY

- The University of Virginia has contributed $15,000 to a rape-crisis center near its campus because about 20 per cent of the center's clients are students.

- Christopher Newport College has a touch of Japan on its campus: a replica of a 17th-century teahouse. The building was a gift from a Japanese newspaper and a securities company.

- Thomas Jefferson, who considered the creation of the University of Virginia one of his greatest achievements, opposed the awarding of degrees as "artificial embellishments." However, in 1831, six years after the university opened and five years after Jefferson's death, the university abandoned his no-degree policy.

- Officials of Liberty University began mandatory drug testing of students in the 1989 academic year—the first such effort at an American college or university.

- The oldest institution of higher education in Virginia is the College of William and Mary, founded in 1693.

WASHINGTON

WASHINGTON STATE would probably have enough room in its six public four-year colleges to handle its predicted increase in enrollments—if the institutions were in the right places.

But only the University of Washing-ton, the state's premier research institution, and Evergreen State College are located near populous areas: Seattle and Olympia are seeing tremendous population growth.

Those regions, along with Vancouver, the Puget Sound area, and Spokane, are also places where the state's prospective minority, part-time, and other non-traditional students are concentrated.

The state has addressed the problem with a plan to develop six new branch campuses in the next 20 years. But lawmakers did not provide as much start-up money as was sought by the three sponsoring institutions, the University of Washington and Washington State and Central Washington Universities. And with the Legislature's history of fiscal conservatism, some college leaders worry that lawmakers are not yet willing to provide budgets that adequately support the new institutions and maintain quality on existing campuses.

The economy has been buoyed, however, by a resurgence in the aerospace industry and the state's growing role as a center for international trade.

Education has been a priority for Gov. Booth Gardner, a soft-spoken Democrat who is in his second term. The Governor has made elementary and secondary education the focus of his legislative programs, which in 1990 included a dramatic change in the state's teacher-preparation requirements.

The new law, which is being phased in, eliminates education as an undergraduate major and requires teachers to obtain a master's degree within seven years of completing college or lose their teaching certification.

This year Mr. Gardner is chairman of two national organizations with education concerns: the National Gov-

WASHINGTON
Continued

ernors' Association and the Education Commission of the States.

Washington's relatively new Higher Education Coordinating Board has also begun to assume more authority in policy making. One of its biggest projects is to oversee the state's new requirement that colleges develop programs to assess how well their students are being taught. However, institutional boards and the State Board for Community Colleges, which oversees a network of 27 two-year institutions, retain considerable autonomy.

DEMOGRAPHICS

Population: 4,761,000   (Rank: 18)

Age distribution:
Up to 17	25.5%
18 to 24	10.2%
25 to 34	18.9%
35 and older	45.3%

Racial and ethnic distribution:
American Indian	1.5%
Asian	2.7%
Black	2.6%
White	91.7%
Other and unknown	1.5%
Hispanic (may be any race)	2.9%

Educational attainment of adults:
At least 4 years of high school 77.6%
At least 1 to 3 years of college 40.2%
At least 4 years of college ... 19.0%

Per-capita personal income: $17,647

New high-school graduates in:
1990-91 (estimate)	45,691
2000-01 (estimate)	59,201

New GED diploma recipients: 10,363

High-school dropout rate: 22.9%

POLITICAL LEADERSHIP

Governor: Booth Gardner (D), term ends 1993

Governor's higher-education adviser: Mike Bigelow, 300 Insurance Building, Mail Stop AQ44, Olympia 98504; (206) 586-0820

U.S. Senators: Brock Adams (D), term ends 1993; Slade Gorton (R), term ends 1995

U.S. Representatives:
5 Democrats, 3 Republicans
Rod Chandler (R), Norman D. Dicks (D), Thomas S. Foley (D), Jim McDermott (D), John Miller (R), Sid Morrison (R), Al Swift (D), Jolene Unsoeld (D)

Legislature: Senate, 24 Democrats, 25 Republicans; House, 60 Democrats, 38 Republicans

COLLEGES AND UNIVERSITIES

Higher education:
Public 4-year institutions	6
Public 2-year institutions	27
Private 4-year institutions	20
Private 2-year institutions	2
Total	55

Vocational institutions: 143

Statewide coordinating board:
Higher Education Coordinating Board
917 Lakeridge Way, GV-11
Olympia 98504
(206) 753-3241
Ann Daley, executive director

Private-college association:
Washington Friends of
  Higher Education
Westland Building, Suite 265
100 South King Street
Seattle 98104
(206) 624-9093
David M. Irwin, president

Institutions censured by the AAUP:
None

Institutions under NCAA sanctions:
None

FACULTY MEMBERS

Full-time faculty members:
At public institutions 5,236
At private institutions 1,214

Proportion who are women:
At public institutions 26.0%
At private institutions 28.4%

Proportion with tenure:
At public institutions 74.6%
At private institutions 58.8%

Average pay of full-time professors:
At public 4-year institutions $37,295
At public 2-year institutions $29,267
At private 4-year institutions $30,417
At private 2-year institutions ... n/a

STUDENTS

Enrollment:
At public 4-year institutions . 78,070
At public 2-year institutions   141,033
At private 4-year institutions 32,337
At private 2-year institutions . 1,648
Undergraduate 231,422
  First-time freshmen 72,493
Graduate 18,663
Professional 3,003
American Indian 3,444
Asian 13,492

Black 6,504
Hispanic 4,830
White 219,643
Foreign 5,175
Total 253,088

Enrollment highlights:
Women 55.2%
Full-time 57.8%
Minority 11.4%
Foreign 2.0%
10-year change in total
  enrollment .... Down 8.1%

Proportion of enrollment made up of minority students:
At public 4-year institutions . 12.6%
At public 2-year institutions . 11.3%
At private 4-year institutions . 9.3%
At private 2-year institutions . 9.2%

Degrees awarded:
Associate 11,664
Bachelor's 17,552
Master's 4,262
Doctorate 576
Professional 898

Residence of new students: State residents made up 89% of all freshmen enrolled in Washington; 92% of all Washington residents who were freshmen attended college in their home state.

Test scores: Students averaged 923 on the s.a.t., which was taken by 44% of Washington's high-school seniors.

MONEY

Average tuition and fees:
At public 4-year institutions . $1,710
At public 2-year institutions .. $802
At private 4-year institutions $8,096
At private 2-year institutions $7,045

WASHINGTON
Continued

Expenditures:
Public institutions .. $1,399,780,000
Private institutions ... $227,211,000

**State funds for higher-education
operating expenses:** $840,231,000

Two-year change: Up 17%

State spending on student aid:
Need-based: $13,625,000;
19,407 awards
Non–need-based: None
Other: $511,000

**Salary of chief executive
of largest public 4-year campus:**
William P. Gerberding, University
of Washington: $105,370 from state
plus $48,350 from private donations

**Total spending on research and
development by doctorate-granting
universities:** $276,885,000
Sources:
Federal government 74.1%
State and local governments .. 2.2%
Industry 7.7%
The institution itself 13.0%
Other 2.9%

**Federal spending on education
and student aid (selected programs):**
Vocational and
adult education $13,595,000
GI Bill $22,771,000
Pell Grants $83,894,000

**Total federal spending on college-
and university-based research
and development:** $200,888,000
Selected programs:
Department of Health
and Human Services $119,739,000

National Science
Foundation $27,134,000
Department of Defense $23,937,000
Department
of Agriculture $8,524,000
Department of Energy .. $7,782,000

Largest endowment:
University
of Washington $147,978,000

Top fund raisers:
University
of Washington $76,411,000
Seattle University $5,013,000
Gonzaga University $4,960,000

MISCELLANY

■ Seventeen veteran and retired
faculty members at Whitworth College have been the beneficiaries of an
anonymous alumnus who has invited
them to take trips, with their spouses,
anywhere in the world—on his tab.
The donor, known only as the "Mys-
tery Man," covers all travel expenses
and hotel costs and sometimes adds
$1,000 in spending money.

■ Washington State University's
partner-accommodation fund helps
spouses and homosexual partners of
faculty members find research or
teaching jobs at the institution.

■ Western Washington University
has one of the country's most highly
regarded collections of outdoor sculp-
ture. In the collection, which includes
20 large sculptures and several smaller
pieces, are works by some of the most
important—and controversial—contemporary sculptors.

■ Governor Gardner has served as
an administrator at two business

of the Harvard Business School and director of the School of Business and Economics at the University of Puget Sound.

■ The oldest institution of higher education in Washington is Whitman College, founded in 1859.

WEST VIRGINIA

T HANKS to a sweeping reorganization, higher education in West Virginia today looks different from the way it appeared in the 1980's, but many of its critical problems remain.

The new structure, engineered by Gov. Gaston Caperton, a Democrat, was designed to help the state use its scarce resources more efficiently. The reform eliminated a statewide Board of Regents that had been considered ineffective and replaced it with two new boards: One governs the research universities and professional schools that make up the new University of West Virginia System; the other oversees operations of the state's two-year and four-year colleges. Paul Marion, formerly chancellor of higher education in Arkansas, has assumed the same position at the State College System. Charles W. Manning, previously executive vice-chancellor for the Oklahoma State Regents for Higher Education, is the new university chancellor.

Still to be overcome are the deep-rooted economic and cultural traditions that hamper educational progress. West Virginia is poor, and its coal-mining economy will be further hurt in the future because federal laws to reduce air pollution will require power plants to use low-sulfur coal found in other regions.

Moreover, West Virginia ranks among the lowest in the nation in the number of high-school graduates who go on to college. So there is little grassroots political support in the state for higher education, although West Virginia University is popular in many quarters because of its football team.

West Virginia colleges have also repeatedly been criticized for trying to add to their own turf rather than coordinating their programs with other institutions.

The university also holds the dubious honor of inspiring a new federal law that affects how universities lobby Congress for funds. After it won a federal grant with the much-publicized help of a Washington lobbying firm, West Virginia's powerful Senator, Robert C. Byrd, pushed through a law that requires universities to report their relationships with private lobbyists and bars institutions from using federal grant money to pay lobbying fees.

Most private higher education in West Virginia comprises religiously affiliated institutions, including Bethany College, which has taken the lead in the state's effort to improve college-going rates. The college pledged in March 1990 to increase the number of West Virginians attending the institution by 25 per cent within the next decade and challenged other institutions to match that effort.

DEMOGRAPHICS

Population: 1,857,000   (Rank: 34)

WEST VIRGINIA
Continued

Age distribution:

Up to 17	24.9%
18 to 24	10.7%
25 to 34	16.4%
35 and older	47.9%

Racial and ethnic distribution:

American Indian	0.1%
Asian	0.3%
Black	3.3%
White	96.2%
Other and unknown	0.1%
Hispanic (may be any race)	0.7%

Educational attainment of adults:
At least 4 years of high school 56.0%
At least 1 to 3 years of college 20.4%
At least 4 years of college ... 10.4%

Per-capita personal income: $12,345

New high-school graduates in:
1990-91 (estimate) 21,629
2000-01 (estimate) 17,894

New GED diploma recipients: 3,004

High-school dropout rate: 22.7%

POLITICAL LEADERSHIP

Governor: Gaston Caperton (D), term ends 1993

Governor's higher-education adviser: Stephen E. Haid, 1018 Kanawha Boulevard East, Suite 700, Charleston 25301; (304) 348-2440

U.S. Senators: Robert C. Byrd (D), term ends 1995; John D. Rockefeller, IV (D), term ends 1997

U.S. Representatives:
4 Democrats, 0 Republicans
Alan B. Mollohan (D), Nick Joe Rahall, II (D), Harley O. Staggers, Jr. (D), Robert E. Wise, Jr. (D)

Legislature: Senate, 33 Democrats, 1 Republican; House, 74 Democrats, 26 Republicans

---

COLLEGES AND UNIVERSITIES

Higher education:

Public 4-year institutions	12
Public 2-year institutions	4
Private 4-year institutions	9
Private 2-year institutions	3
Total	28

Vocational institutions: 52

Statewide coordinating boards:
University of West Virginia System
1018 Kanawha Boulevard East
Suite 700
Charleston 25301
(304) 348-4016
Charles W. Manning, chancellor

West Virginia State College System
1018 Kanawha Boulevard East
Suite 700
Charleston 25301
(304) 348-4016
Paul Marion, chancellor

Private-college association:
West Virginia Association
   of Independent Colleges
1106 Security Building
102 Capitol Street
Charleston 25301
(304) 345-5525
Robert F. Prather, president

Institutions censured by the AAUP:
None

Institution under NCAA sanctions:
Marshall University

FACULTY MEMBERS

Full-time faculty members:
At public institutions 2,031
At private institutions 381

Proportion who are women:
At public institutions 31.4%
At private institutions 39.4%

Proportion with tenure:
At public institutions 65.1%
At private institutions 54.4%

Average pay of full-time professors:
At public 4-year institutions $29,825
At public 2-year institutions $23,644
At private 4-year institutions $23,520
At private 2-year institutions $19,248

STUDENTS

Enrollment:
At public 4-year institutions . 60,733
At public 2-year institutions .. 9,648
At private 4-year institutions . 7,488
At private 2-year institutions . 2,510
Undergraduate 70,143
  First-time freshmen 16,569
Graduate 8,948
Professional 1,288
American Indian 119
Asian 577
Black 2,876
Hispanic 335
White 75,128
Foreign 1,344
Total 80,379

Enrollment highlights:
Women 55.5%
Full-time 65.7%
Minority 4.9%
Foreign 1.7%
10-year change in total
  enrollment .... Up 1.7%

Proportion of enrollment made up of minority students:
At public 4-year institutions .. 5.2%
At public 2-year institutions .. 2.5%
At private 4-year institutions . 5.9%
At private 2-year institutions . 6.3%

Degrees awarded:
Associate 2,419
Bachelor's 7,260
Master's 1,824
Doctorate 131
Professional 308

Residence of new students: State residents made up 71% of all freshmen enrolled in West Virginia; 85% of all West Virginia residents who were freshmen attended college in their home state.

Test scores: Students averaged 17.4 on the A.C.T., which was taken by 52% of West Virginia's high-school seniors.

MONEY

Average tuition and fees:
At public 4-year institutions . $1,591
At public 2-year institutions .. $803
At private 4-year institutions $7,197
At private 2-year institutions $2,554

Expenditures:
Public institutions $376,293,000
Private institutions $73,716,000

State funds for higher-education operating expenses: $262,731,000

Two-year change: Up 4%

State spending on student aid:
Need-based: $5,272,000; 5,500 awards
Non–need-based: None
Other: $6,605,000

WEST VIRGINIA

Continued

**Salary of chief executive
of largest public 4-year campus:**
Neil S. Bucklew, West Virginia
    University: $104,572

**Total spending on research and
development by doctorate-granting
universities:** $39,368,000

Sources:
Federal government 44.0%
State and local governments .. 3.2%
Industry 10.1%
The institution itself 38.3%
Other 4.4%

**Federal spending on education
and student aid (selected programs):**
Vocational and
    adult education $7,744,000
GI Bill $2,948,000
Pell Grants $36,770,000

**Total federal spending on college-
and university-based research
and development:** $14,204,000

Selected programs:
Department of Health
    and Human Services . $4,631,000
National Science
    Foundation $1,168,000
Department of Defense . $1,028,000
Department
    of Agriculture $3,037,000
Department of Energy .. $1,136,000

Largest endowment:
Bethany College $24,134,000

Top fund raisers:
West Virginia University $10,447,000
Marshall University $7,126,000
Bethany College $4,808,000

MISCELLANY

■ A consortium of universities operates the collection of radio telescopes in Green Bank. The National Science Foundation, which finances the operation of the instruments by the National Radio Astronomy Observatory, is building a state-of-the-art, 100-meter radio telescope there that is estimated to cost $75-million.

■ West Virginia's colleges and universities have received many major federal grants, frequently with the assistance of Sen. Robert C. Byrd, a Democrat who has served as Senate Majority Leader and is chairman of the Appropriations Committee.

■ Some dispute exists over the oldest college in West Virginia. Marshall University and West Liberty State College were both founded in 1837. But Bethany College says those two institutions did not become baccalaureate-degree granting institutions until years later. Bethany believes its 1840 charter makes it the oldest institution of higher education in the state.

WISCONSIN

WISCONSIN has a long history of supporting higher education. The flagship Madison campus of the University of Wisconsin System is among the nation's most respected public institutions.

But the state's populist traditions and a more recent push for tax relief are creating worrisome financial dilemmas for the giant 26-campus system.

The Legislature is under pressure to increase spending on local schools and services, so that property taxes can be reduced. Many higher-education leaders fear that a restructuring of the tax system will drain state resources previously available to public colleges.

Other strategies to ease the financial crunch, such as enrollment limits or higher tuitions, have been resisted by lawmakers. Gov. Tommy Thompson, a Republican re-elected in November 1990 to a second term, has supported some increases to raise faculty salaries, but his major higher-education program has been a college savings-bond program.

The Legislature has not been shy about using its power to influence higher-education policy when its members feel the university leadership has not been responsive enough. That inclination recently led to a law that requires public colleges to provide students with statistics about sexual assault and rape on campuses, and to a recommendation that they require students to take ethnic-sensitivity courses.

The system has undertaken a campaign to increase its number of minority faculty members and has enacted an anti-harassment policy in response to several racial incidents. The policy, which was instituted by the Board of Regents, is being challenged by a group of students and an instructor, who say it violates their rights to free speech.

The regents govern most of public higher education, including two-year colleges. A separate Board of Vocational, Technical, and Adult Education governs other postsecondary institutions.

Private institutions include liberal-arts colleges, such as Lawrence and research institutions, such as Marquette University. Recently they have become more active in campaigns to increase state financial aid and to be included in other state programs.

DEMOGRAPHICS

Population: 4,867,000 (Rank: 17)

Age distribution:
Up to 17 .... 25.8%
18 to 24 .... 10.6%
25 to 34 .... 17.7%
35 and older 45.9%

Racial and ethnic distribution:
American Indian 0.7%
Asian 0.5%
Black 3.9%
White 94.5%
Other and unknown 0.5%
Hispanic (may be any race) .. 1.3%

Educational attainment of adults:
At least 4 years of high school 69.6%
At least 1 to 3 years of college 29.2%
At least 4 years of college ... 14.8%

Per-capita personal income: $16,449

New high-school graduates in:
1990-91 (estimate) 55,021
2000-01 (estimate) 59,529

New GED diploma recipients: 2,660

High-school dropout rate: 15.1%

POLITICAL LEADERSHIP

Governor: Tommy G. Thompson (R), term ends 1995

Governor's higher-education adviser: Tom Fonfara, State Capitol, P.O. Box 7863, Madison 53707; (608) 266-1212

WISCONSIN

Continued

U.S. Senators: Robert W. Kasten, Jr. (R), term ends 1993; Herbert Kohl (D), term ends 1995

U.S. Representatives:
4 Democrats, 5 Republicans
Les Aspin (D), Steve Gunderson (R), Gerald D. Kleczka (D), Scott Klug (R), Jim Moody (D), David R. Obey (D), Thomas E. Petri (R), Toby Roth (R), F. James Sensenbrenner, Jr. (R)

Legislature: Senate, 19 Democrats, 14 Republicans; House, 58 Democrats, 41 Republicans

---

COLLEGES AND UNIVERSITIES

Higher education:
Public 4-year institutions 13
Public 2-year institutions 17
Private 4-year institutions 28
Private 2-year institutions 3
Total 61

Vocational institutions: 99

Statewide coordinating board:
University of Wisconsin System
1720 Van Hise Hall
1220 Linden Drive
Madison 53706
(608) 262-2321
Kenneth A. Shaw, president

Private-college association:
Wisconsin Association of
  Independent Colleges and
  Universities
25 West Main Street, Suite 583
Madison 53703
(608) 256-7761
Robert E. McCarthy, president

Institution censured by the AAUP:
Marquette University

Institutions under NCAA sanctions:
None

FACULTY MEMBERS

Full-time faculty members:
At public institutions 7,960
At private institutions 1,476

Proportion who are women:
At public institutions 26.9%
At private institutions 30.1%

Proportion with tenure:
At public institutions 74.8%
At private institutions 62.9%

Average pay of full-time professors:
At public 4-year institutions $37,780
At public 2-year institutions $32,285
At private 4-year institutions $31,090
At private 2-year institutions   ... n/a

STUDENTS

Enrollment:
At public 4-year institutions   151,146
At public 2-year institutions   . 90,712
At private 4-year institutions   42,211
At private 2-year institutions   . 1,158
Undergraduate 256,235
  First-time freshmen 54,094
Graduate 25,345
Professional 3,647
American Indian 1,897
Asian 4,033
Black 9,060
Hispanic 3,497
White 261,147
Foreign 5,593
Total 285,227

Enrollment highlights:
Women 53.9%
Full-time 65.8%

Minority 6.6%
Foreign 2.0%
10-year change in total
　　enrollment .... Up 18.2%

**Proportion of enrollment made up
of minority students:**
At public 4-year institutions .. 5.4%
At public 2-year institutions .. 7.7%
At private 4-year institutions . 8.2%
At private 2-year institutions 18.6%

Degrees awarded:
Associate 8,570
Bachelor's 25,057
Master's 5,479
Doctorate 812
Professional 988

Residence of new students: State residents made up 84% of all freshmen enrolled in Wisconsin; 88% of all Wisconsin residents who were freshmen attended college in their home state.

Test scores: Students averaged 20.1 on the A.C.T., which was taken by 54% of Wisconsin's high-school seniors.

MONEY

Average tuition and fees:
At public 4-year institutions . $1,861
At public 2-year institutions . $1,160
At private 4-year institutions $7,615
At private 2-year institutions $4,001

Expenditures:
Public institutions .. $1,754,395,000
Private institutions ... $373,533,000

**State funds for higher-education
operating expenses:** $843,543,000

Two-year change: Up 14%

State spending on student aid:
Need-based: $39,181,000;
　　50,575 awards
Non–need-based: None
Other: $1,879,000

**Salary of chief executive
of largest public 4-year campus:**
Donna E. Shalala, University
　　of Wisconsin at Madison: $112,630

**Total spending on research and
development by doctorate-granting
universities:** $336,815,000
Sources:
Federal government 58.7%
State and local governments . 16.4%
Industry 4.8%
The institution itself 12.9%
Other 7.1%

**Federal spending on education
and student aid (selected programs):**
Vocational and
　　adult education $16,153,000
GI Bill $9,827,000
Pell Grants $116,259,000

**Total federal spending on college-
and university-based research
and development:** $162,145,000
Selected programs:
Department of Health
　　and Human Services $93,376,000
National Science
　　Foundation $21,417,000
Department of Defense . $9,333,000
Department
　　of Agriculture $8,062,000
Department of Energy . $14,919,000

Largest endowment:
University of Wisconsin
　　Foundation $97,849,000

Top fund raisers:
University of Wisconsin
　　at Madison $102,233,000
Marquette University .. $16,100,000
Lawrence University ... $8,494,000

WISCONSIN
Continued

MISCELLANY

■ The Board of Regents of the University of Wisconsin has voted to allow the Reserve Officers Training Corps to remain on the campus despite objections of faculty members and students that it discriminates against homosexuals.

■ Alverno College is a pioneer in the effort to assess student learning and institutional effectiveness. To graduate, students at the Roman Catholic women's college must prove they are competent in eight "abilities": communication, analysis, problem solving, valuing, social interaction, taking responsibility for the global environment, effective citizenship, and aesthetic response.

■ Grilling hamburgers and french-frying potatoes are among the tasks for undergraduates at the Burger King Fast Food Laboratory, a training facility for students in the hotel- and restaurant-management program at the University of Wisconsin–Stout.

■ The oldest institution of higher education in Wisconsin is Nashotah House, an Episcopal seminary founded in 1842.

WYOMING

WYOMING is the only state with no private non-profit colleges. It is also one of the largest and most sparsely populated states in the union.

The University of Wyoming and the state's seven community colleges therefore take seriously their responsibility for making a wide array of educational programs both accessible and affordable.

To fulfill that charge, a corps of university faculty members—nicknamed the Flying Professors—regularly travels rural regions of the state to teach classes. And for many in Wyoming's remotest regions, university personnel also provide family health care.

Because of Wyoming's membership in the Western Interstate Commission for Higher Education, students who want courses not available in the state may take them—at in-state tuition rates—in other Western states.

Wyoming was one of the first states to adopt a prepaid tuition program. The plan applies to both the university and community colleges and is open to parents or other tuition payers from outside the state.

A board of trustees governs the university, while the seven community colleges are run by the Wyoming Community College Commission. Gov. Mike Sullivan, a Democrat re-elected in November 1990 to a second term, has said he would support a new tax to raise money for the community colleges. There is no overall statewide coordinating board.

DEMOGRAPHICS

Population: 475,000   (Rank: 51)

Age distribution:
Up to 17	28.6%
18 to 24	10.7%
25 to 34	21.7%
35 and older	38.9%

Racial and ethnic distribution:
American Indian 1.8%
Asian 0.4%
Black 0.7%
White 95.1%
Other and unknown 2.0%
Hispanic (may be any race) .. 5.2%

Educational attainment of adults:
At least 4 years of high school 77.9%
At least 1 to 3 years of college 37.9%
At least 4 years of college ... 17.2%

Per-capita personal income: $14,508

New high-school graduates in:
1990-91 (estimate) 5,896
2000-01 (estimate) 5,658

New GED diploma recipients: 1,025

High-school dropout rate: 11.7%

POLITICAL LEADERSHIP

Governor: Michael Sullivan (D), term ends 1995

Governor's higher-education adviser: Jane Sabes, Herschler Building, 4th Floor East Wing, Cheyenne 82002; (307) 777-7574

U.S. Senators: Alan K. Simpson (R), term ends 1997; Malcolm Wallop (R), term ends 1995

U.S. Representative:
0 Democrats, 1 Republican
Craig Thomas (R)

Legislature: Senate, 10 Democrats, 20 Republicans; House, 22 Democrats, 42 Republicans

---

COLLEGES AND UNIVERSITIES

Higher education:
Public 4-year institutions 1
Public 2-year institutions 7

Private 4-year institutions 0
Private 2-year institutions 1
Total 9

Vocational institutions: 14

Statewide coordinating boards:
University of Wyoming
Box 3434, University Station
Laramie 82071
(307) 766-4121
Terry P. Roark, president

Wyoming Community College
  Commission
Herschler Building, 2nd Floor West
122 West 25th Street
Cheyenne 82002
(307) 777-7763
James Meznek, executive director

Private-college association:
None

Institutions censured by the AAUP:
None

Institutions under NCAA sanctions:
None

FACULTY MEMBERS

Full-time faculty members:
At public institutions 933
At private institutions .... n/a

Proportion who are women:
At public institutions 26.5%
At private institutions .... n/a

Proportion with tenure:
At public institutions 66.9%
At private institutions .... n/a

Average pay of full-time professors:
At public 4-year institutions $37,053
At public 2-year institutions $27,889

WYOMING

Continued

At private 4-year institutions ... n/a
At private 2-year institutions ... n/a

STUDENTS

Enrollment:
At public 4-year institutions . 10,773
At public 2-year institutions . 15,138
At private 4-year institutions 0
At private 2-year institutions .. 629
Undergraduate 24,694
  First-time freshmen 6,019
Graduate 1,640
Professional 206
American Indian 376
Asian 82
Black 267
Hispanic 646
White 24,668
Foreign 501
Total 26,540

Enrollment highlights:
Women 54.9%
Full-time 59.1%
Minority 5.3%
Foreign 1.9%
10-year change in total
  enrollment .... Up 33.1%

**Proportion of enrollment made up
of minority students:**
At public 4-year institutions .. 4.8%
At public 2-year institutions .. 5.5%
At private 4-year institutions ... n/a
At private 2-year institutions . 6.8%

Degrees awarded:
Associate 1,386
Bachelor's 1,631
Master's 343
Doctorate 73
Professional 69

Residence of new students: State residents made up 77% of all freshmen enrolled in Wyoming; 81% of all Wyoming residents who were freshmen attended college in their home state.

Test scores: Students averaged 19.4 on the A.C.T., which was taken by 60% of Wyoming's high-school seniors.

MONEY

Average tuition and fees:
At public 4-year institutions . $1,003
At public 2-year institutions .. $613
At private 4-year institutions ... n/a
At private 2-year institutions $6,900

Expenditures:
Public institutions $203,307,000
Private institutions .... n/a

**State funds for higher-education
operating expenses:** $120,719,000
Two-year change: Up 4%

State spending on student aid:
Need-based: $241,000; 531 awards
Non–need-based: None
Other: None

**Salary of chief executive
of largest public 4-year campus:**
Terry P. Roark, University
  of Wyoming: $113,614

**Total spending on research and
development by doctorate-granting
universities:** $23,310,000
Sources:
Federal government 59.2%
State and local governments .. 6.6%
Industry 6.6%
The institution itself 26.7%
Other 0.9%

**Federal spending on education
and student aid (selected programs):**
Vocational and
   adult education $3,932,000
GI Bill $1,655,000
Pell Grants $11,500,000

**Total federal spending on college-
and university-based research
and development:** $9,076,000

Selected programs:
Department of Health
   and Human Services ... $824,000
National Science
   Foundation $3,340,000
Department of Defense . $1,237,000
Department
   of Agriculture $1,752,000
Department of Energy $841,000

Largest endowment:
University of Wyoming $42,192,000

Top fund raiser:
University of Wyoming . $5,316,000

MISCELLANY

■ The University of Wyoming and the Northern Arapaho Indian Tribe have pooled funds to create a $1-million endowment to provide scholarships for about eight Arapaho students each year to attend the university's Laramie campus.

■ At an altitude of 7,200 feet above sea level, the University of Wyoming claims to be the highest university in the nation.

■ The trustees of Western Wyoming College have voted unanimously to ban the possession or consumption of alcohol on the campus, even by students who have reached the state's minimum drinking age of 21.

■ The oldest institution of higher education in the state is the University of Wyoming, founded in 1886.

SOURCES & NOTES

The statistics in this Almanac are meant to provide a broad view of higher education in the 50 states and the District of Columbia.

The figures are comparable from state to state, and, in all cases, they were the latest available at presstime.

The time covered by the statistics varies from item to item. For example, the racial and ethnic distribution of the adult population of the states is gathered from the decennial census; hence, the latest information is from 1980. The U.S. Department of Education typically releases statistics from its annual surveys of colleges and universities one to three years after collecting the data. As a consequence, the latest figures on academic degrees awarded, for example, cover 1987-88.

Many data that would be useful to educators and policy makers are not available for every state. For example, the Education Department has no state-by-state information on the number of part-time faculty members. Nor does the department collect information to show, on a comparable basis across the states, the proportion of high-school students who go on to college, or the proportion of college students who complete their degrees. Some states do collect such information, but those figures are not included in this Almanac because they would not always be comparable.

Because of rounding, figures may not add to 100 per cent. The designation "n/a" indicates that data are not available or not applicable. In some instances, U.S. totals may include data on service schools and outlying areas that are not shown separately.

DEMOGRAPHICS

Population:
SOURCE: Census Bureau
DATE: estimate of resident population as of July 1, 1989

Age distribution:
SOURCE: Census Bureau
DATE: estimate of resident population as of July 1, 1989

Racial and ethnic distribution:
SOURCE: Census Bureau
DATE: 1980

Educational attainment of adults:
SOURCE: Census Bureau
DATE: 1980
NOTE: Figures cover those 25 years and older.

Per-capita personal income:
SOURCE: U.S. Department of Commerce
DATE: 1989

New high-school graduates:
SOURCE: Western Interstate Commission for Higher Education
NOTE: Projections of the number of graduates in 1990-91 and 2000-01 were made in May 1988.

New GED diploma recipients:
SOURCE: American Council on Education
DATE: 1989
NOTE: General Education Development diplomas are high-school equivalency certificates awarded to high-school dropouts who pass the GED test.

High-school dropout rate:
SOURCE: U.S. Department of Education
DATE: 1988

NOTE: The figures cover public schools only, and are calculated by dividing the number of high-school graduates by the ninth-grade enrollment four years earlier. They are adjusted for interstate migration.

POLITICAL LEADERSHIP

Governor:
SOURCE: National Governors' Association

Governor's higher-education adviser:
SOURCES: Education Commission of the States; *Chronicle of Higher Education* reporting

U.S. Senators:
SOURCES: Secretary of the Senate; Associated Press

U.S. Representatives:
SOURCES: Clerk of the House of Representatives; Associated Press

Legislature:
SOURCE: National Conference of State Legislatures
NOTE: Figures represent the strength of state legislatures as of November 1990.

COLLEGES AND UNIVERSITIES

Higher education:
SOURCE: U.S. Department of Education
DATE: 1989-90

Vocational institutions:
SOURCE: U.S. Department of Education
DATE: 1989-90
NOTE: Figure includes public, private non-profit, and private for-profit non-collegiate institutions that offer post-secondary education.

Statewide coordinating board:
SOURCES: State Higher Education Executive Officers; *Chronicle of Higher Education* reporting
NOTE: These organizations are responsible for planning for public colleges and universities. Some boards also have governing authority. Those that do are indicated in the state narratives.

Private-college association:
SOURCES: National Association of Independent Colleges and Universities; *Chronicle of Higher Education* reporting

Institutions censured by the AAUP:
SOURCE: American Association of University Professors
DATE: Action as of 1990
NOTE: The A.A.U.P. censures institutions when it finds that they have violated its standards of academic freedom and tenure. The standards seek to protect the rights of faculty members to free speech without fear of penalty, and to due process in appointment, promotion, and tenure decisions. The standards are included in the 1940 Statement of Principles of Academic Freedom and Tenure, which was developed by the A.A.U.P. and the Association of American Colleges and endorsed by more than 100 other academic organizations. Censure was imposed on administrative officers at the institutions listed except for those noted.

Institutions under NCAA sanctions:
SOURCE: National Collegiate Athletic Association
DATE: Action as of November 1990

SOURCES & NOTES
Continued

FACULTY MEMBERS

Full-time faculty members;
Proportion who are women;
Proportion with tenure:
SOURCE: U.S. Department
of Education
DATE: 1987-88
NOTE: Figures cover full-time faculty members on nine-month contracts only. The figures are based on reports of those institutions that responded to the department's faculty-salary survey. Because not all colleges completed the survey, the totals are lower than figures appearing in other department tables. The tenure figures cover only those colleges that have a system of tenure.

Average pay of full-time professors:
SOURCE: U.S. Department
of Education
DATE: 1987-88
NOTE: Figures cover faculty members on nine-month contracts only.

STUDENTS

Enrollment:
SOURCE: U.S. Department
of Education
DATE: Fall 1988
NOTE: Undergraduate enrollment includes first-time freshman enrollment, which is also shown separately. The full definitions of the racial and ethnic categories are as follows: American Indian and Alaskan native; Asian and Pacific Islander; black, non-Hispanic; Hispanic; and white, non-Hispanic. Foreign students are non-resident aliens studying in the United States on a temporary basis.

Enrollment highlights:
SOURCE: U.S. Department
of Education
NOTE: The change in enrollment covers Fall 1978 to Fall 1988. All other figures cover Fall 1988. All proportions are based on total enrollment with one exception: The proportion of students who are minority-group members covers only U.S. citizens.

Proportion of enrollment made up
of minority students:
SOURCE: U.S. Department
of Education
DATE: Fall 1988

Degrees awarded:
SOURCE: U.S. Department
of Education
DATE: 1987-88

Residence of new students:
SOURCE: U.S. Department
of Education
DATE: Fall 1988
NOTE: The figures cover freshmen only.

Test scores:
SOURCES: U.S. Department
of Education; College Board
DATES: 1989 for A.C.T.; 1990 for S.A.T.
NOTE: The A.C.T.—American College Testing Program's A.C.T. Assessment—is scored on a scale from 1 to 36. The S.A.T.—the College Board's Scholastic Aptitude Test—is scored on a scale from 400 to 1,600. For each state, one score is given, depending on which test was taken by the larger number of students.

MONEY

Average tuition and fees:
SOURCE: U.S. Department
of Education

DATE: 1989-90
NOTE: Figures cover undergraduate charges and are weighted by Fall 1988 full-time-equivalent undergraduate enrollment. The figures for public institutions represent charges to state residents.

Expenditures:
SOURCE: U.S. Department of Education
DATE: 1985-86

State funds for higher-education operating expenses:
SOURCE: Edward R. Hines, Illinois State University
DATE: 1990-91
NOTE: Figures include state tax funds appropriated for colleges and universities, for student aid, and for governing and coordinating boards. They do not include funds for capital outlays and money from sources other than state taxes, such as student fees or appropriations from local governments.

State spending on student aid:
SOURCE: National Association of State Scholarship and Grant Programs
DATE: 1989-90
NOTE: "Need-based" aid covers scholarships awarded on the basis of a student's financial situation. "Non–need-based" aid includes scholarships given to reward meritorious students, to encourage students to major in particular disciplines, and to reduce the difference in tuition costs between public and private institutions. The category of "other" aid includes spending for work-study, loan-for-giveness, and loan programs. The statistics cover aid to both undergraduate and graduate students. The figures include most of the money that states

spend on student financial aid. However, some states may spend more on programs that are not specifically identified as student-aid programs.

Salary of chief executive of largest public 4-year campus:
SOURCE: *Chronicle of Higher Education* reporting
DATE: 1990-91
NOTE: Institutions were selected on the basis of Fall 1988 enrollment as reported by the U.S. Department of Education.

Total spending on research and development by doctorate-granting universities:
SOURCE: National Science Foundation
DATE: Fiscal year 1989
NOTE: Figures cover spending in science and engineering, and exclude spending in such disciplines as the arts, education, and the humanities.

Federal spending on education and student aid (selected programs):
SOURCE: Census Bureau
DATE: Fiscal year 1989

Total federal spending on college- and university-based research and development:
SOURCE: National Science Foundation
DATE: Fiscal year 1988
NOTE: Figures cover federal obligations, which are funds set aside for payments. Institutions do not always receive them in the year in which they were obligated. Figures include only spending for science and engineering projects, and exclude spending in such disciplines as the arts, education, and the humanities.

Largest endowment:
SOURCES: National Association of College and University Business

SOURCES & NOTES
Continued

Officers; *Chronicle of Higher
Education* reporting
DATE: As of June 30, 1989

Top fund raisers:
SOURCE: Council for Aid to Education
DATE: 1988-89
NOTE: Figures are based on a survey of 1,132 institutions, which together received about 85 per cent of all private contributions to colleges and universities. Rankings of institutions may be heavily influenced by the timing of fund drives, unusually large gifts, and other factors.

MISCELLANY

SOURCE: *Chronicle of Higher
Education* reporting

Enrollment by Race

THE TABLE that follows shows the distribution of enrollment by racial and ethnic group for fall 1988 at more than 3,100 colleges and universities.

The distribution is based on the institution's total enrollment, including full-time and part-time students and undergraduate and graduate students. The total enrollment appears in the last column.

The institutions are listed in alphabetical order by state. Institutions that are part of state systems of higher education appear under the system name.

The figures were compiled by the U.S. Department of Education, which conducts a survey of enrollment by race every two years. The table omits about 250 institutions that did not provide complete information to the Education Department.

Because of rounding, the figures may not add to 100 per cent.

The full definitions of the racial and ethnic groups are as follows: American Indian or Alaskan native; Asian or Pacific Islander; black, non-Hispanic; Hispanic; and white, non-Hispanic. Figures in those groups cover both U.S. citizens and resident aliens. Foreign students include all non-resident aliens who are enrolled in U.S. colleges and universities, regardless of their racial or ethnic backgrounds.

ALABAMA	American Indian	Asian	Black	Hispanic	White	Foreign	Total
Alabama A&M U	0.0%	0.3%	75.7%	0.4%	13.2%	10.5%	4,244
Alabama Aviation and Tech C	0.3	1.0	11.9	1.0	85.0	0.8	386
Alabama St U	0.0	0.0	97.1	0.4	1.4	1.0	4,045
Alexander City St JC	0.2	0.2	14.2	0.2	84.7	0.6	1,036
American Inst of Psychotherapy	0.0	0.0	5.3	0.0	94.7	0.0	38
Athens St C	0.5	0.4	5.9	0.4	92.4	0.3	2,115
Auburn U							
Main	0.1	0.5	3.5	0.4	92.5	3.0	20,553
Montgomery	0.1	1.2	15.7	0.2	82.5	0.4	5,580
Bessemer St Tech C	0.0	0.0	25.6	0.1	74.3	0.0	1,659
Birmingham Southern C	0.1	1.5	9.4	0.3	88.2	0.5	1,836
Brewer St JC	0.0	0.0	8.1	0.0	91.9	0.0	743
C A Fredd St Tech C	0.0	0.7	96.1	0.0	3.3	0.0	307
Carver St Tech C	0.0	0.0	95.0	0.0	5.0	0.0	525
Chattahoochee Valley CC	0.2	0.3	26.9	0.9	71.2	0.5	1,572
Chauncey Sparks St Tech C	0.3	0.0	35.1	0.3	64.1	0.3	370
CC of the Air Force	0.1	0.3	17.2	0.3	81.6	0.5	26,354

ALABAMA, cont.

	American Indian	Asian	Black	Hispanic	White	Foreign	Total
Concordia C	0.0%	0.0%	99.7%	0.0%	0.3%	0.0%	343
Douglas MacArthur St Tech C	0.7	0.0	13.3	0.0	85.9	0.0	427
Draughons JC	0.0	0.0	54.5	0.0	45.5	0.0	231
Enterprise St JC	0.2	1.3	10.0	2.1	86.4	0.0	2,020
Faulkner St JC	0.9	0.3	9.1	0.6	88.7	0.4	2,348
Faulkner U	0.1	0.1	25.1	0.2	73.0	1.7	1,967
Gadsden St CC	0.1	0.2	10.7	0.7	81.6	6.7	4,062
G C Wallace St CC Dothan	0.2	0.7	12.6	0.2	86.1	0.2	3,781
G C Wallace St CC Hanceville	0.0	0.1	1.6	0.0	98.2	0.1	3,382
G C Wallace St CC Selma	0.1	0.3	35.1	0.1	64.5	0.0	1,469
Harry M Ayers St Tech C	0.0	0.6	14.0	0.0	85.3	0.0	620
Hobson St Tech C	0.0	0.0	38.3	0.0	61.7	0.0	525
Huntingdon C	0.1	1.4	5.3	0.8	90.4	2.0	866
International Bible C	0.0	2.9	14.3	1.0	79.0	2.9	105
J F Drake St Tech C	0.4	0.3	38.5	0.3	58.6	1.9	694
Jacksonville St U	0.5	0.5	16.6	0.8	79.9	1.7	7,511
Jefferson Davis St JC	0.0	0.1	19.8	0.0	79.7	0.4	896
Jefferson St JC	0.4	0.4	10.3	0.2	87.9	0.8	6,042
John C Calhoun St CC	0.5	0.5	8.7	0.6	89.4	0.2	6,551
John M Patterson St Tech C	0.1	0.6	40.3	0.0	58.9	0.0	672
Judson C	0.0	0.2	4.5	0.2	94.3	0.7	402
Lawson St CC	0.0	0.0	98.9	0.0	1.1	0.0	1,105
Livingston U	0.2	0.3	25.1	0.1	73.4	0.9	1,633
Lurleen B Wallace St JC	0.1	0.0	12.3	0.2	86.2	1.2	1,009
Marion Military Inst	0.0	0.0	10.6	4.1	85.3	0.0	293
Miles C	0.0	0.0	99.7	0.0	0.3	0.0	616
Mobile C	0.2	0.2	14.7	0.0	83.2	1.7	1,054
Muscle Shoals St Tech C	0.0	0.0	15.1	0.0	84.9	0.0	730
N F Nunnelly St Tech C	0.0	0.2	19.8	0.0	80.0	0.0	515
National Ed Ctr							
National Inst of Tech	0.0	0.0	69.2	0.0	30.8	0.0	52
Northeast Alabama St JC	0.5	0.0	1.0	0.2	98.1	0.2	1,177
Northwest Alabama St JC	0.0	0.0	8.4	0.0	91.5	0.1	1,654
Northwest Alabama St Tech C	0.0	0.2	3.8	0.0	95.5	0.4	446
Oakwood C	0.0	0.0	90.8	0.0	0.0	9.2	1,233
Patrick Henry St JC	0.3	0.0	13.5	0.0	86.2	0.0	761
Reid St Tech C	1.2	0.0	24.2	0.0	74.5	0.0	326
S D Bishop St JC	0.0	0.0	73.1	0.0	25.5	1.4	1,824
Samford U	0.1	0.5	5.7	0.5	93.1	0.0	4,089
Shelton St CC	0.0	3.1	19.0	0.0	77.9	0.0	3,310
Snead St JC	0.1	0.0	0.9	0.1	98.8	0.0	1,399
Southeastern Bible C	0.0	0.0	5.0	0.0	92.8	2.2	139
Southern JC of Business							
Huntsville	0.0	0.6	43.6	0.0	55.8	0.0	509
Southern Union St JC	0.0	0.2	14.8	0.3	84.5	0.2	2,457
Southwest St Tech C	0.6	0.7	35.9	0.7	62.2	0.0	897
Spring Hill C	0.3	0.9	4.9	2.7	89.4	1.8	1,171
Stillman C	0.0	0.0	98.4	0.0	0.0	1.6	771
Talladega C	0.2	0.0	96.6	1.5	1.7	0.0	528
Trenholm St Tech C	0.0	0.0	75.8	4.0	20.2	0.0	703
Troy St U							
Main	0.6	0.9	18.1	2.4	77.4	0.6	8,039
Dothan	0.2	0.6	8.1	0.7	90.2	0.3	1,735
Montgomery	0.3	0.9	21.1	2.1	75.6	0.1	1,948
Tuskegee U	0.0	0.0	88.6	0.9	3.4	7.1	3,401
U S Sports Academy	0.0	0.4	2.1	0.8	93.8	2.9	240

	American Indian	Asian	Black	Hispanic	White	Foreign	Total
U of Alabama							
Tuscaloosa	0.2%	2.2%	8.5%	0.7%	86.3%	1.9%	18,510
Birmingham	0.1	1.0	15.8	0.2	79.6	3.2	13,886
Huntsville	0.2	2.5	5.1	0.8	88.3	3.1	7,448
U of Montevallo	0.1	0.1	7.9	0.3	89.6	2.0	2,719
U of North Alabama	0.2	0.2	7.8	0.4	91.1	0.3	5,291
U of South Alabama	0.6	1.3	9.8	0.8	83.4	4.1	10,443
Walker C	0.0	0.2	3.7	0.0	96.0	0.0	827
Walker St Tech C	0.2	0.0	5.6	0.1	94.1	0.0	2,243

ALASKA

	American Indian	Asian	Black	Hispanic	White	Foreign	Total
Alaska Bible C	4.8	0.0	1.2	1.2	85.5	7.2	83
Alaska Pacific U	10.6	2.7	6.4	3.1	74.3	2.8	639
U of Alaska							
Anchorage	4.8	3.5	5.2	2.2	83.7	0.7	13,435
Kenai Peninsula	2.7	0.5	0.5	1.3	94.7	0.2	1,503
Kodiak	7.6	5.4	1.0	2.7	83.3	0.0	628
Matanuska-Susitna	1.7	0.2	0.3	0.8	97.0	0.1	1,164
Fairbanks	10.0	2.8	3.5	1.5	81.8	0.4	6,731
Kuskokwim	59.8	1.7	1.0	1.7	35.9	0.0	301
Northwest	58.1	0.6	0.0	0.0	41.3	0.0	167
Juneau	8.4	2.2	1.9	1.3	85.6	0.6	1,949
Southeast Ketchikan	9.6	1.4	0.3	0.8	87.9	0.0	636
Southeast Sitka	17.0	1.4	0.3	1.1	80.2	0.0	631

ARIZONA

	American Indian	Asian	Black	Hispanic	White	Foreign	Total
American Graduate Sch of International Management .	0.1	0.0	0.3	1.2	70.9	27.5	1,083
American Indian Bible C	85.9	1.0	0.0	2.0	11.1	0.0	99
Arizona C of the Bible	2.4	1.6	3.2	4.8	87.2	0.8	125
Arizona St U	1.1	2.8	2.3	5.3	83.8	4.7	43,426
Arizona Western C	1.9	0.7	2.9	36.8	57.4	0.2	4,654
Central Arizona C	5.6	0.8	3.7	17.6	72.3	0.0	5,196
Cochise C	1.1	3.8	4.9	20.8	69.4	0.0	4,756
DeVry Inst of Tech	2.2	5.9	3.1	8.2	79.2	1.4	2,647
Eastern Arizona C	6.6	0.9	2.8	18.1	71.5	0.1	4,619
Frank Lloyd Wright Sch of Architecture	0.0	0.0	0.0	0.0	84.0	16.0	25
Grand Canyon C	2.6	1.2	3.4	6.2	85.4	1.2	1,813
ITT Tech Inst Phoenix	4.6	1.8	7.1	9.1	77.4	0.0	438
ITT Tech Inst Tucson	0.9	0.9	6.9	36.5	54.7	0.0	318
Maricopa County CC Dist							
Gateway CC	3.5	2.0	5.8	12.1	76.1	0.5	5,846
Glendale CC	1.1	2.3	2.3	9.0	84.6	0.7	19,200
Mesa CC	1.7	2.3	2.3	8.1	84.8	0.8	19,627
Phoenix C	2.7	1.9	4.6	13.0	77.5	0.3	13,639
Rio Salado CC	2.0	0.9	3.8	9.1	84.0	0.1	14,223
Scottsdale CC	2.7	1.2	1.2	3.0	91.4	0.5	9,141
South Mountain CC	2.1	1.7	17.6	28.7	49.3	0.6	3,177
Mohave CC	1.9	0.5	0.2	2.5	94.9	0.0	3,523
Northern Arizona U	5.2	0.8	1.4	6.0	83.0	3.6	14,995
Northland Pioneer C	22.8	0.4	0.8	7.4	68.6	0.0	6,481
Ottawa U	0.6	6.9	4.2	8.0	80.3	0.0	1,577
Pima CC	2.1	1.9	3.3	19.6	70.5	2.7	26,810

ARIZONA, cont.

	American Indian	Asian	Black	Hispanic	White	Foreign	Total
Pima CC Skill Center	13.4%	1.4%	8.5%	31.7%	45.1%	0.0%	142
Prescott C	5.1	0.3	1.4	2.0	90.5	0.7	294
Southwestern Conservative							
Baptist Bible C	1.8	0.0	3.0	3.0	91.0	1.2	166
U of Arizona	1.0	2.6	1.6	7.5	80.5	6.7	34,725
Western International U	0.0	8.5	4.8	6.8	57.6	22.3	2,291
Yavapai C	5.7	0.0	0.9	5.1	87.0	1.2	5,717

ARKANSAS

	American Indian	Asian	Black	Hispanic	White	Foreign	Total
American C	0.4	0.0	0.8	0.4	98.3	0.0	237
Arkansas Baptist C	0.0	0.0	99.6	0.0	0.4	0.0	268
Arkansas C	0.0	1.1	3.3	0.3	95.2	0.1	799
Arkansas St U							
Main	0.3	0.7	9.8	0.2	86.3	2.7	9,026
Beebe	0.8	0.7	6.7	1.2	90.6	0.0	1,823
Arkansas Tech U	0.7	0.3	2.5	0.6	95.3	0.7	3,588
Capital City JC of Business ..	0.0	0.2	44.2	0.2	55.5	0.0	573
Central Baptist C	0.0	0.5	4.9	0.0	92.3	2.2	183
Crowley's Ridge C	0.0	0.0	1.6	0.0	98.4	0.0	123
East Arkansas CC	0.0	0.2	28.8	0.3	70.7	0.0	1,269
Garland County CC	0.8	0.5	5.7	0.7	92.2	0.1	1,729
Harding U Main	0.1	0.1	1.8	0.8	94.6	2.6	3,155
Henderson St U	0.4	0.2	13.9	0.3	84.6	0.5	3,348
Hendrix C	0.0	0.6	10.6	0.2	84.8	3.8	1,203
John Brown U	1.1	0.6	0.5	0.3	88.0	9.5	874
Mississippi County CC	0.0	1.6	17.8	0.5	80.1	0.1	1,548
National Education Center ...	0.1	0.1	35.4	0.2	63.6	0.5	838
North Arkansas CC	0.9	0.3	0.1	0.2	98.4	0.0	2,457
Ouachita Baptist U	0.1	0.1	5.8	0.1	92.3	1.6	1,352
Philander Smith C	0.0	2.5	83.7	0.0	0.7	13.1	594
Phillips County CC	0.1	0.4	49.1	0.4	50.0	0.0	1,486
Rich Mountain CC	0.2	0.7	0.0	0.0	99.0	0.0	417
Shorter C	0.0	3.3	80.1	0.0	6.6	9.9	151
Southern Arkansas U							
Main	0.3	0.4	17.4	0.3	81.1	0.6	2,159
El Dorado	0.1	0.3	17.0	0.0	82.5	0.1	736
Tech	0.1	0.4	15.1	0.2	84.2	0.0	830
Southern Baptist C	0.5	0.0	2.0	0.0	96.4	1.0	589
Southern Tech C Little Rock .	0.0	0.6	36.6	0.0	62.8	0.0	629
U of Arkansas							
Little Rock	0.3	0.9	10.0	0.7	86.0	2.1	10,064
Medical Sciences	0.2	2.0	7.8	0.3	89.1	0.5	1,327
Pine Bluff	0.0	0.4	82.1	0.1	17.3	0.2	3,333
Fayetteville	0.7	1.4	4.4	0.6	88.9	4.0	13,835
Monticello	0.3	0.2	17.6	0.3	81.5	0.1	1,974
U of Central Arkansas	0.7	0.5	10.8	0.3	86.8	0.8	6,698
U of the Ozarks	0.6	0.3	4.2	0.0	81.3	13.7	795
Westark CC	0.9	2.2	2.9	0.7	93.3	0.2	4,306

CALIFORNIA

	American Indian	Asian	Black	Hispanic	White	Foreign	Total
Allan Hancock C	2.1	4.3	4.6	14.9	72.5	1.6	7,975
American Academy							
of Dramatic Arts West	0.7	2.2	5.1	4.3	74.6	13.0	138

	American Indian	Asian	Black	Hispanic	White	Foreign	Total
American Baptist Sem of the West	0.0%	8.9%	11.1%	4.4%	68.9%	6.7%	45
American Conservatory Theatre	0.0	3.4	9.5	3.4	81.6	2.0	147
American Film Inst Center for Advanced Film and Television Studies	0.0	3.5	5.0	5.0	70.0	16.5	200
Antelope Valley C	1.3	3.6	5.8	8.8	79.6	0.8	8,077
Antioch U Los Angeles	0.0	1.4	2.9	2.9	92.8	0.0	415
Antioch U San Francisco	0.4	1.2	5.4	1.7	85.4	5.8	240
Antioch U Santa Barbara	0.0	0.0	3.6	0.7	95.7	0.0	139
Armstrong C	0.0	0.8	3.2	0.0	4.8	91.3	252
Art Center C of Design	0.5	15.4	0.5	5.4	69.1	9.1	1,283
Art Inst of Southern California	0.9	4.3	0.0	5.2	85.3	4.3	116
Azusa Pacific U	0.8	3.3	3.4	5.2	75.0	12.4	2,833
Barstow C	3.4	3.7	10.7	15.3	65.2	1.7	2,233
Bethany Bible C	0.4	2.8	2.8	6.6	86.9	0.6	533
Biola U	0.3	11.4	2.7	4.1	76.7	4.8	2,587
Brooks C	3.7	8.0	10.3	9.1	63.7	5.2	750
Brooks Inst of Photography	0.3	1.9	0.6	4.8	80.5	11.8	626
Butte C	2.9	2.7	1.5	6.0	84.9	1.9	7,928
Cabrillo C	1.0	3.6	1.1	9.8	83.0	1.6	12,075
California Baptist C	0.5	4.8	9.3	6.6	70.6	8.3	666
California C of Arts and Crafts	0.5	9.2	2.6	3.9	74.2	9.5	1,118
California C of Podiatric Medicine	0.5	15.1	2.3	3.2	75.2	3.7	431
Cal Family Study Ctr	0.4	1.6	1.6	3.3	92.2	0.8	243
California Inst of the Arts	0.7	4.0	5.4	3.4	78.0	8.5	850
California Inst of Integral Studies	1.3	4.1	0.6	2.5	89.8	1.6	314
California Inst of Tech	0.1	14.4	0.5	1.7	59.3	24.0	1,841
California Lutheran U	0.5	3.2	2.9	6.0	82.8	4.5	2,749
California Maritime Academy	0.5	4.0	3.5	6.4	82.7	2.9	376
Cal Sch of Professional Psych Berkeley	0.0	2.8	3.0	3.4	89.0	1.7	464
Fresno	0.3	1.7	2.8	3.8	88.9	2.4	287
Los Angeles	0.0	4.1	7.5	6.8	79.1	2.6	468
California St U Cal Polytechnic St U San Luis Obispo	0.9	8.9	1.6	8.1	79.4	1.0	15,912
Cal St Poly U Pomona	0.8	23.6	3.9	14.5	53.8	3.5	17,905
Bakersfield	0.7	3.9	5.5	14.1	72.9	2.9	4,650
Chico	1.1	1.5	1.7	4.4	88.4	3.0	14,979
Dominguez Hill	0.8	10.1	32.3	11.6	41.3	3.9	7,460
Fresno	1.4	5.2	3.8	16.2	68.1	5.5	17,467
Fullerton	1.0	15.6	2.5	10.5	67.4	2.9	23,376
Hayward	1.3	17.1	9.4	7.1	62.3	2.8	11,757
Long Beach	0.9	18.2	5.4	10.2	62.1	3.2	33,179
Los Angeles	0.6	27.2	10.6	26.4	28.2	7.1	17,960
Northridge	0.7	12.7	5.4	10.1	69.2	2.0	29,401
Sacramento	1.3	9.8	4.4	7.4	74.8	2.2	23,478
San Bernardino	1.4	4.0	6.6	12.6	72.8	2.6	9,154
Stanislaus	1.5	4.7	3.2	10.8	77.1	2.7	4,822
Humboldt St U	2.6	2.2	2.2	4.1	87.9	1.0	6,135
San Diego St U	1.0	9.0	3.5	9.1	75.5	2.0	34,155
San Francisco St U	0.7	26.9	7.4	7.5	51.8	5.7	24,138
San Jose St U	1.0	22.0	4.1	8.8	59.9	4.2	26,456

CALIFORNIA, cont.

	American Indian	Asian	Black	Hispanic	White	Foreign	Total
California St U							
Sonoma St U	1.1%	2.7%	4.0%	5.3%	84.4%	2.3%	6,129
Career Com C of Business	0.0	11.4	43.8	4.6	40.2	0.0	219
Cerritos C	2.2	14.2	6.3	32.0	43.2	2.0	15,886
Chabot C	1.9	14.8	7.5	11.3	62.3	2.2	19,705
Chaffey CC	1.1	4.1	7.6	18.5	66.8	2.0	10,985
Chapman C	0.2	8.2	2.6	5.9	83.1	0.0	2,060
Charles R Drew U	0.0	8.1	52.5	27.3	12.1	0.0	99
Christian Heritage C	0.0	2.3	2.3	4.0	90.0	1.5	399
Church Divinity Sch of the Pacific	0.0	1.9	0.0	0.0	96.2	1.9	104
Citrus C	0.9	6.6	5.6	19.5	63.1	4.3	8,786
City C of San Francisco	0.8	36.9	9.0	11.0	36.5	5.7	24,408
Claremont Graduate Sch	0.4	3.5	3.2	3.7	80.4	8.8	1,664
Claremont McKenna C	0.4	11.1	4.2	6.1	75.1	3.2	856
Coast CC Dist							
Coastline CC	1.1	8.2	1.3	5.2	83.7	0.4	10,950
Golden West C	1.0	14.1	1.2	7.1	74.1	2.5	13,137
Orange Coast C	1.0	11.2	1.4	7.6	76.5	2.3	22,365
Cogswell C	0.4	19.3	1.2	11.5	63.8	3.7	243
C of Marin	1.4	4.4	3.3	3.8	85.0	2.1	9,817
C of Notre Dame	1.0	8.3	4.3	5.2	69.5	11.8	1,052
C of Osteopathic Medicine of the Pacific	0.7	11.8	1.2	5.1	75.9	5.3	432
C of the Canyons	0.7	3.5	1.6	8.5	85.0	0.7	4,815
C of the Desert	1.0	2.2	3.6	16.8	75.9	0.4	7,231
C of the Redwoods	4.8	2.0	1.1	2.2	89.3	0.6	6,147
C of the Sequoias	2.2	3.5	2.3	24.0	67.4	0.5	7,839
C of the Siskiyous	3.0	2.5	2.0	4.0	87.3	1.2	1,851
Columbia C Columbia	1.4	1.0	1.0	3.4	92.7	0.5	2,012
Columbia C Hollywood	0.5	4.7	7.0	6.6	60.1	21.1	213
Compton CC	0.7	1.9	60.1	30.8	4.2	2.4	3,972
Contra Costa CC Sys							
Contra Costa C	0.8	14.3	25.3	13.3	45.1	1.1	6,634
Diablo Valley C	0.7	8.3	2.8	5.7	81.8	0.7	20,255
Los Medanos C	1.2	6.1	6.4	11.8	74.5	0.0	6,367
Crafton Hills C	1.4	2.6	2.9	10.0	82.6	0.7	3,990
Cuesta CC	0.8	3.0	1.5	6.3	87.1	1.4	7,127
Cuyamaca C	1.9	4.9	1.9	9.5	81.0	0.7	3,614
D-Q U	80.0	1.1	0.0	8.3	9.4	1.1	180
DeVry Inst of Tech							
Los Angeles	0.6	18.7	11.6	28.7	38.4	2.0	2,251
Dominican C of San Rafael	0.2	4.5	3.8	4.1	80.2	7.4	665
Dominican Sch of Philosophy and Theology	0.0	11.0	2.2	5.5	73.6	7.7	91
Don Bosco Tech Inst	0.3	17.8	0.9	63.5	17.5	0.0	348
El Camino C	0.9	15.4	19.2	14.2	48.5	1.8	25,789
Fashion Inst of Design and Merchandising Costa Mesa	0.6	5.9	10.0	15.6	67.3	0.6	321
Fashion Inst of Design and Merchandising LA	0.9	6.0	9.8	15.9	66.7	0.7	2,054
Fashion Inst of Design and Merchandising San Diego	0.6	6.0	9.6	15.6	67.7	0.6	167
Fashion Inst of Design and Merchandising SF	0.8	5.8	9.8	16.1	67.0	0.5	634
Fielding Inst	0.3	0.8	3.3	0.8	94.4	0.5	644

	American Indian	Asian	Black	Hispanic	White	Foreign	Total
Foothill De Anza CC Dist							
De Anza C	1.1%	19.6%	3.8%	7.8%	63.6%	4.2%	21,948
Foothill C	1.8	11.1	4.1	5.6	74.0	3.3	12,811
Fresno Pacific C	0.8	1.4	2.0	6.7	86.0	3.1	1,317
Fuller Theological Sem	0.2	10.0	3.9	4.5	69.3	12.0	2,109
Glendale CC	1.1	13.8	1.7	19.2	53.5	10.6	12,072
Golden Gate Baptist Sem	0.3	9.6	4.7	5.7	71.1	8.6	686
Golden Gate U	0.3	10.0	6.4	3.5	73.6	6.2	8,831
Graduate Theological Union	0.0	1.5	0.8	1.0	82.3	14.4	395
Grossmont C	2.0	4.7	2.5	7.7	81.4	1.6	15,357
Hartnell C	2.0	9.4	4.2	28.3	53.9	2.2	6,762
Harvey Mudd C	0.5	17.8	0.7	2.0	77.1	1.8	551
Hebrew Union C California	0.0	0.0	0.0	0.0	100.0	0.0	48
Holy Names C	0.1	4.0	15.2	4.9	60.4	15.3	717
Humphreys C	0.5	6.4	6.6	12.2	74.3	0.0	409
Inst of Transpersonal Psychology	0.0	4.0	1.3	1.3	88.0	5.3	150
International Sch of Theology	0.0	0.0	0.0	1.8	91.1	7.1	56
ITT Tech Inst Buena Park	1.7	19.1	4.4	22.4	51.8	0.4	517
ITT Tech Inst La Mesa	0.9	7.9	9.7	17.9	61.9	1.6	546
ITT Tech Inst Sacramento	0.8	9.7	11.4	15.8	62.3	0.0	36
Jesuit Sch of Theology	0.6	5.6	0.6	4.3	66.7	22.2	162
Kern CC Dist							
Bakersfield C	2.2	3.5	5.0	15.7	72.5	1.2	10,776
Cerro Coso CC	2.3	3.3	4.0	3.6	85.6	1.3	3,673
Porterville C	2.2	3.8	3.1	18.2	70.6	2.1	2,334
Lake Tahoe CC	2.3	3.0	1.2	8.1	83.7	1.8	1,083
Lassen C	6.0	0.9	4.6	4.8	80.8	2.9	2,563
LIFE Bible C	0.8	7.3	4.6	9.7	75.5	2.2	372
Life Chiropractic C West	1.3	4.5	1.3	2.6	87.5	2.8	464
Lincoln U	0.0	4.4	1.8	1.8	26.6	65.3	271
Loma Linda U	0.5	18.2	8.2	9.9	54.2	9.0	4,392
Long Beach City C	1.2	13.9	11.9	10.5	59.2	3.2	18,378
Los Angeles C of Chiropractic	0.2	7.1	1.4	4.8	80.0	6.4	994
Los Angeles CC Dist							
East Los Angeles C	0.5	16.8	3.5	66.0	6.6	6.6	12,447
Los Angeles City C	0.5	21.5	17.4	29.8	20.6	10.1	14,479
Los Angeles Harbor C	0.5	12.7	14.8	23.5	45.9	2.6	8,319
Los Angeles Mission C	0.8	4.5	8.7	42.2	41.0	2.8	4,628
Los Angeles Pierce C	0.7	10.5	3.9	8.9	72.7	3.3	16,970
Los Angeles Southwest C	0.0	0.8	71.3	24.9	1.2	1.7	5,296
LA Trade Tech C	0.5	13.5	31.6	34.9	13.6	5.9	12,030
Los Angeles Valley C	0.6	10.7	6.7	18.2	60.7	3.0	16,457
West Los Angeles C	0.4	7.7	48.7	9.1	30.2	3.9	8,282
Los Rios CC Dist							
American River C	2.3	5.6	5.5	6.2	79.1	1.2	18,716
Cosumnes River C	2.3	7.7	9.8	7.7	71.4	1.1	8,235
Sacramento City C	2.0	13.8	11.9	12.3	55.4	4.5	14,474
Loyola Marymount U	0.2	8.8	3.5	10.2	73.8	3.5	6,479
Marymount C	0.5	7.6	6.7	6.7	64.0	14.4	1,012
Master's C	0.4	2.3	2.1	2.0	91.0	2.1	943
Mendocino C	4.1	1.5	1.2	4.2	87.9	1.0	3,455
Menlo C	0.0	2.7	0.5	1.4	82.1	13.3	592
Mennonite Brethren Biblical Sem	0.0	0.8	0.0	0.8	58.5	39.8	123
Merced C	1.2	2.7	6.2	14.4	66.1	9.4	6,854

	American Indian	Asian	Black	Hispanic	White	Foreign	Total
Mills C	0.3%	7.2%	6.9%	3.6%	74.2%	7.8%	1,038
Mira Costa C	1.1	4.3	4.6	9.7	79.3	1.0	7,517
Modesto JC	1.0	4.6	1.6	11.9	75.7	5.1	11,300
Monterey Inst of International Studies	0.0	4.4	2.1	4.2	63.8	25.5	525
Mount Saint Mary's C	0.1	11.6	9.0	32.3	46.3	0.8	1,203
Mount San Antonio C	1.0	11.1	7.4	24.9	52.5	3.2	20,563
Mount San Jacinto C	1.5	2.0	3.0	12.2	80.0	1.3	3,978
Napa Valley C	1.0	4.8	3.2	6.9	81.9	2.3	5,715
National U	0.6	6.4	10.7	5.6	74.2	2.4	12,449
New C of California	1.2	2.8	11.9	4.3	77.7	2.2	506
North Orange County CC Dist							
Cypress C	1.9	13.6	2.8	9.6	71.4	0.7	11,917
Fullerton C	1.6	10.0	2.2	14.2	71.7	0.3	17,548
Northrop U	0.1	52.7	5.1	4.2	19.4	18.5	1,190
Occidental C	0.1	11.5	3.1	6.6	74.4	4.3	1,702
Ohlone C	1.0	15.2	3.6	10.4	67.9	1.9	8,130
Otis Art Inst of Parsons Sch of Design	1.9	15.7	5.3	10.8	57.4	9.0	849
Pacific Christian C	0.4	3.7	2.2	3.3	87.4	3.0	539
Pacific Coast C	0.9	5.7	10.1	16.1	66.9	0.3	335
Pacific Coast JC Lemon Grove	0.0	48.1	20.2	14.4	17.3	0.0	104
Pacific Graduate Sch of Psychology	0.4	1.9	1.5	3.1	90.8	2.3	261
Pacific Lutheran Theological Sem	0.8	3.2	1.6	0.0	91.9	2.4	124
Pacific Oaks C	0.6	2.2	6.8	7.1	82.2	1.2	325
Pacific Sch of Religion	0.5	5.6	2.0	0.5	79.6	11.7	196
Pacific Union C	0.3	19.1	3.5	7.5	62.8	6.8	1,636
Palmer C of Chiropractic West	1.4	6.8	0.4	3.1	80.9	7.4	512
Palomar C	1.9	4.6	2.2	8.8	80.5	2.1	16,707
Pasadena City C	0.9	18.9	8.9	19.9	42.8	8.5	19,581
Patten C	0.9	12.2	38.0	17.2	30.8	0.9	221
Pepperdine U	0.7	5.6	4.2	4.5	79.0	6.0	7,146
Peralta CC Dist							
C of Alameda	2.3	14.1	34.9	8.8	36.0	4.0	4,690
Laney C	1.7	17.8	36.5	8.9	30.7	4.4	8,571
Merritt C	1.7	9.0	36.7	12.4	38.2	2.1	4,810
Vista C	1.3	7.6	14.4	8.0	68.0	0.7	3,489
Pitzer C	0.0	6.3	4.0	9.2	73.4	7.2	807
Point Loma Nazarene C	0.4	3.4	2.6	5.0	83.4	5.2	2,165
Pomona C	0.4	10.5	3.3	8.0	73.0	4.7	1,421
Queen of the Holy Rosary C	9.9	11.5	6.6	9.9	56.8	5.3	243
Rancho Santiago C	1.2	14.2	3.2	15.8	59.9	5.7	20,532
Rand Graduate Sch of Policy Studies	0.0	6.7	0.0	0.0	83.3	10.0	60
Rio Hondo C	1.7	7.8	3.9	48.3	34.2	4.0	12,048
Riverside CC	2.1	4.4	9.6	13.5	68.9	1.5	15,683
Saddleback CC Dist							
Irvine Valley C	1.1	10.8	2.2	6.1	76.6	3.2	4,678
Saddleback C	1.4	4.9	1.3	5.5	85.8	1.2	14,527
Saint John's Sem C	0.0	30.6	2.0	33.7	33.7	0.0	98
Saint Joseph's C	0.0	26.3	1.8	10.5	24.6	36.8	57
Saint Mary's C of California	0.2	2.4	4.3	5.0	85.0	3.2	3,420
Saint Patrick's Sem	0.0	21.8	0.0	18.4	49.4	10.3	87
Samuel Merritt C	0.0	14.8	8.1	2.0	73.8	1.3	149

	American Indian	Asian	Black	Hispanic	White	Foreign	Total
San Bernardino Valley C	1.8%	5.0%	13.4%	19.3%	59.2%	1.4%	10,157
San Diego CC Dist							
San Diego City C	1.5	8.9	19.2	15.2	49.2	5.9	13,737
San Diego Mesa C	1.3	9.5	4.2	8.6	73.2	3.2	23,410
San Diego Miramar C	1.7	12.6	4.6	7.0	72.0	2.2	5,378
San Francisco Art Inst	0.1	4.9	2.9	3.3	81.8	7.1	736
San Francisco C of							
Mortuary Science	0.0	0.0	14.8	6.6	73.8	4.9	61
San Francisco CC Skills Ctr ..	0.3	13.5	14.9	17.5	52.3	1.6	377
San Francisco Conservatory							
of Music	1.3	13.7	3.0	4.7	59.7	17.6	233
San Francisco Theol Sem	0.0	3.9	3.8	0.9	71.1	20.4	692
San Joaquin C of Law	0.0	2.8	1.4	7.6	87.5	0.7	144
San Joaquin Delta C	1.7	12.7	4.9	14.5	63.8	2.3	14,792
San Jose Bible C	0.0	12.8	3.7	5.3	71.3	6.9	188
San Jose / Evergreen CC Dist							
Evergreen Valley C	2.1	32.5	6.7	23.7	33.4	1.7	7,430
San Jose City C	2.9	18.6	6.3	22.0	48.7	1.4	8,767
San Mateo County CC Dist							
Cañada C	0.7	5.5	4.7	10.5	72.3	6.4	7,586
C of San Mateo	0.9	13.5	3.5	8.9	70.2	3.1	14,150
Skyline C	0.7	21.4	5.9	15.6	52.9	3.5	7,798
Santa Barbara City C	0.8	3.5	2.2	16.5	74.6	2.4	11,031
Santa Clara U	0.4	16.4	1.4	4.9	72.1	4.7	7,795
Santa Monica C	0.9	10.4	10.1	10.7	59.4	8.4	18,108
Saybrook Inst	0.5	2.6	2.6	0.0	90.2	4.1	194
Sch of Theology at Claremont	0.0	17.8	10.7	2.0	56.9	12.7	197
Scripps C	0.2	8.3	2.1	6.3	80.5	2.6	606
Shasta Bible C	0.0	0.0	0.0	0.0	100.0	0.0	35
Shasta C	3.9	1.5	0.7	3.0	89.8	1.2	8,454
Sierra C	1.9	1.5	0.8	4.0	89.7	2.0	11,637
Simpson C	0.6	19.7	5.6	2.2	69.1	2.8	178
Solano County CC	1.9	13.6	11.6	8.0	64.6	0.3	9,643
Southern California C	1.4	3.3	2.2	8.1	82.2	2.9	930
Southern California C of							
Optometry	0.3	35.5	0.3	2.9	60.3	0.8	380
Southwestern C	0.7	17.3	5.8	33.5	39.6	3.0	13,010
Southwestern U Sch of Law ..	0.3	6.8	3.3	6.0	82.5	1.2	1,036
Stanford U	0.7	9.9	5.3	6.3	62.6	15.3	14,386
Starr King Sch for the							
Ministry	0.0	0.0	0.0	0.0	100.0	0.0	47
State Center CC Dist							
Fresno City C	1.6	6.6	6.4	21.8	60.3	3.3	14,710
Kings River CC	2.5	3.9	2.6	34.2	54.1	2.7	3,078
Taft C	2.5	2.9	10.0	3.0	80.2	1.4	797
Thomas Aquinas C	0.0	2.7	0.7	4.0	80.0	12.7	150
U of California							
Berkeley	1.0	21.7	6.1	9.4	54.6	7.1	30,102
Davis	0.7	19.7	3.5	6.2	65.4	4.5	20,733
Hastings C of Law	0.5	11.6	3.9	6.1	77.9	0.0	1,367
Irvine	0.4	29.8	2.7	8.0	54.2	4.8	14,772
Los Angeles	0.7	19.8	6.4	11.9	54.7	6.4	34,371
Riverside	0.6	20.6	3.5	8.7	62.3	4.3	7,087
San Diego	0.6	17.6	3.0	8.4	65.9	4.4	16,410
San Francisco	0.8	20.1	4.1	6.2	66.3	2.5	3,759
Santa Barbara	1.0	9.9	2.8	8.5	74.9	3.0	17,743
Santa Cruz	0.9	9.5	2.7	7.9	76.8	2.3	8,816

CALIFORNIA, cont.

	American Indian	Asian	Black	Hispanic	White	Foreign	Total
U of Judaism	0.0%	0.7%	0.0%	0.0%	87.0%	12.3%	138
U of La Verne	0.4	4.8	12.0	12.4	66.5	3.9	5,376
U of the Pacific	0.4	13.8	2.6	5.0	73.4	4.8	5,607
U of Redlands	0.6	4.0	5.6	5.3	82.6	1.9	2,924
U of San Diego	0.2	3.0	1.1	5.1	87.8	2.7	5,858
U of San Francisco	0.5	9.0	4.7	6.1	68.2	11.4	7,087
U of West Los Angeles	0.7	5.4	18.5	7.7	57.2	10.6	710
Ventura County CC Dist							
Moorpark C	1.9	4.4	1.6	7.9	83.3	0.9	10,471
Oxnard C	1.9	13.5	6.0	32.8	45.7	0.1	5,542
Ventura C	1.9	4.3	1.9	17.2	74.2	0.4	11,200
Victor Valley C	1.5	3.0	7.1	8.6	79.4	0.5	4,858
West Coast Christian C	2.6	7.2	3.3	30.1	51.0	5.9	153
West Coast U	0.0	11.1	6.9	8.2	62.0	11.8	1,454
West Hills C	1.5	3.7	4.5	23.4	66.8	0.2	2,486
West Valley Mission CC Dist							
Mission C	0.9	32.1	4.7	11.8	48.3	2.1	10,170
West Valley C	0.7	8.5	2.1	7.4	79.5	1.8	12,595
Western St U C of Law							
Orange County	0.8	4.6	4.9	8.3	81.1	0.3	1,164
Western St U C of Law							
San Diego	0.5	3.2	5.8	5.0	85.4	0.0	378
Westminster Theol Sem	0.0	19.8	1.1	1.1	67.0	11.0	91
Westmont C	0.3	1.9	0.6	2.0	94.4	0.7	1,290
Whittier C	0.6	4.9	4.1	12.2	73.5	4.7	1,578
Woodbury U	0.0	8.8	8.8	17.3	44.6	20.6	875
World C West	0.0	0.9	2.7	0.0	84.8	11.6	112
Wright Inst	1.1	2.9	5.7	4.6	83.9	1.7	174

COLORADO

Aims CC	1.3	1.1	0.4	13.6	83.7	0.0	7,320
Arapahoe CC	1.4	1.4	1.2	4.9	88.6	2.5	7,040
Bel-Rea Inst of Animal Tech ..	1.2	0.0	1.2	1.8	95.8	0.0	165
Beth-El C of Nursing	0.0	2.7	2.7	7.0	87.6	0.0	185
Colorado Christian C	0.2	1.6	3.5	2.8	89.6	2.2	492
Colorado C	0.7	2.3	1.6	2.9	88.0	4.5	1,967
Colorado Inst of Art	1.2	3.0	15.2	8.4	71.1	1.1	1,220
Colorado Mountain C	0.7	0.4	0.6	3.4	94.5	0.3	8,957
Colorado Northwestern CC ..	0.6	0.0	1.0	12.2	86.0	0.2	1,344
Colorado Sch of Mines	0.4	2.5	0.7	3.3	79.0	14.2	2,316
Colorado St U Sys							
Colorado St U	0.6	1.8	1.3	2.8	89.8	3.7	19,201
Fort Lewis C	9.1	0.8	0.6	4.1	84.1	1.4	3,790
U of Southern Colorado ...	0.7	0.9	2.9	20.7	71.4	3.4	3,970
Colorado Tech C	1.4	1.3	10.5	24.2	62.5	0.0	1,147
CC of Aurora	1.1	3.3	12.4	5.1	77.9	0.2	3,593
CC of Denver	1.6	2.8	10.9	17.8	63.9	3.0	4,111
Denver Inst of Tech	2.0	2.1	4.0	17.0	75.0	0.0	807
Denver Tech C	1.4	1.9	19.6	8.5	68.4	0.3	731
Electronics Tech Inst	0.5	1.4	20.7	16.4	61.0	0.0	213
Front Range CC	0.9	3.0	1.4	8.7	85.3	0.8	5,966
Iliff Sch of Theology	1.2'	1.2	7.2	2.0	84.6	3.8	345
ITT Tech Inst	0.7	0.5	5.4	8.1	85.2	0.0	406
Lamar CC	1.2	0.2	1.6	8.3	88.6	0.2	508
Morgan CC	1.4	0.2	0.0	4.4	94.0	0.0	947
Naropa Inst	0.4	0.0	0.4	0.0	92.1	7.1	241

	American Indian	Asian	Black	Hispanic	White	Foreign	Total
National C Colorado Springs .	1.4%	0.3%	2.4%	46.1%	49.8%	0.0%	295
National C Denver	3.6	1.4	2.2	41.7	51.1	0.0	139
National C Pueblo	0.7	0.7	0.0	48.5	50.0	0.0	136
National Tech U	0.2	6.6	2.2	1.7	66.2	23.2	1,002
Nazarene Bible C	0.5	1.5	2.9	0.7	93.9	0.5	407
Northeastern JC	0.4	0.3	1.5	3.4	94.5	0.0	1,987
Otero JC	1.2	0.5	2.8	20.3	75.3	0.0	833
Parks JC	0.5	1.1	9.6	20.4	68.4	0.0	945
Pikes Peak CC	1.3	1.7	8.3	7.4	80.8	0.5	5,738
Pueblo CC	1.4	0.3	1.2	29.4	67.5	0.2	2,534
Red Rocks CC	1.0	1.4	1.1	5.5	89.6	1.3	5,173
Regis C	0.2	1.3	2.8	6.1	88.9	0.8	4,085
Saint Thomas Sem	0.0	1.6	0.8	7.4	90.2	0.0	122
St C's in Colorado							
Adams St C	1.2	1.0	2.0	21.4	73.9	0.5	2,499
Mesa St C	0.8	0.4	0.9	4.8	91.2	1.7	4,023
Metropolitan St C	0.4	2.9	4.1	8.7	83.5	0.3	15,733
Western St C	0.4	0.6	1.3	4.0	92.9	0.8	2,431
Trinidad St JC	0.3	0.2	1.3	41.6	53.7	2.9	1,581
U of Colorado							
Boulder	0.5	4.0	1.6	3.9	86.1	3.9	24,065
Colorado Springs	0.4	2.5	2.3	4.2	90.2	0.3	5,809
Denver	0.5	5.0	2.5	4.7	85.9	1.5	10,073
Health Sciences Center	0.4	3.3	1.5	5.0	88.5	1.3	1,547
U of Denver	0.6	1.9	3.1	3.2	83.7	7.5	6,875
U of Northern Colorado	0.4	1.2	1.3	4.9	91.2	1.0	9,813

CONNECTICUT

	American Indian	Asian	Black	Hispanic	White	Foreign	Total
Albertus Magnus C	0.0	0.9	8.7	3.9	83.5	3.0	635
Asnuntuck CC	0.2	1.2	5.8	1.4	90.3	1.3	1,993
Briarwood C	0.0	0.8	7.0	2.0	90.2	0.0	398
Bridgeport Engineering Inst ..	0.0	2.4	4.9	3.7	88.4	0.6	507
Charter Oak C	0.9	0.2	4.0	2.5	92.5	0.0	810
Connecticut C	0.2	2.1	3.1	1.9	88.3	4.4	1,969
Connecticut St U Sys							
Central Connecticut St U ..	0.0	1.4	3.2	1.6	93.3	0.3	14,198
Eastern Connecticut St U ..	0.7	0.4	4.4	2.1	91.3	1.0	4,447
Southern Connecticut St U	0.3	1.2	4.8	1.2	91.1	1.3	12,784
Western Connecticut St U ..	1.9	1.7	3.3	1.8	90.8	0.5	6,380
Fairfield U	0.0	0.9	1.5	1.4	95.5	0.6	4,878
Greater Hartford CC	0.1	2.9	31.4	13.2	50.2	2.2	2,927
Greater New Haven Tech C ...	0.4	2.1	9.4	6.6	80.9	0.6	808
Hartford C for Women	0.0	1.2	13.3	6.6	69.5	9.4	256
Hartford Graduate Center	0.2	3.5	1.2	0.9	93.9	0.3	2,457
Hartford Sem	0.0	1.3	13.4	0.7	83.9	0.7	149
Hartford St Tech C	0.0	5.8	8.6	3.0	82.1	0.5	955
Holy Apostles C and Sem	0.0	1.9	1.9	0.0	96.2	0.0	210
Housatonic CC	0.3	1.7	17.2	13.8	65.0	2.1	2,475
Manchester CC	0.3	1.3	5.2	2.5	90.3	0.4	5,989
Mattatuck CC	0.1	0.4	4.9	2.4	91.6	0.5	3,812
Middlesex CC	0.3	0.8	3.2	2.5	92.5	0.6	3,080
Mitchell C	0.0	6.4	5.3	4.7	82.5	1.1	1,137
Mohegan CC	0.4	1.1	4.2	2.1	91.9	0.2	2,819
Northwestern Conn CC	0.1	0.4	1.1	0.3	97.7	0.5	2,346
Norwalk CC	0.1	2.0	14.8	11.4	67.2	4.5	3,338
Norwalk St Tech C	0.3	5.6	15.2	6.7	71.8	0.5	1,101

	American Indian	Asian	Black	Hispanic	White	Foreign	Total
Paier C of Art	0.0%	0.6%	2.9%	0.0%	95.8%	0.6%	312
Post C	0.0	0.4	7.1	1.6	90.0	1.0	1,654
Quinebaug Valley CC	0.0	0.5	0.5	4.9	94.1	0.0	1,320
Quinnipiac C	0.0	0.2	0.6	0.6	98.3	0.3	2,925
Sacred Heart U	0.1	1.6	5.8	4.4	86.8	1.4	4,305
Saint Alphonsus C	0.0	0.0	16.1	9.7	74.2	0.0	31
Saint Basil's C	0.0	0.0	20.0	0.0	60.0	20.0	5
Saint Joseph C	0.2	0.7	5.9	2.4	90.6	0.1	1,634
South Central CC	0.2	0.8	17.6	7.1	72.6	1.7	3,158
Thames Valley St Tech C	0.3	1.0	2.3	2.9	93.1	0.4	1,021
Trinity C	0.0	4.4	4.2	2.6	86.8	2.0	2,043
Tunxis CC	0.2	0.7	1.8	2.1	94.5	0.7	3,254
U S Coast Guard Academy ...	0.8	4.1	1.6	2.4	90.0	1.1	892
U of Bridgeport	0.0	2.1	5.1	1.9	82.0	8.9	5,376
U of Connecticut	0.2	3.1	3.5	2.5	88.4	2.3	25,374
U of Conn Health Ctr	0.6	5.3	3.3	3.3	86.0	1.4	508
U of Hartford	0.1	1.7	4.2	1.8	86.6	5.6	7,703
U of New Haven	0.1	1.4	7.0	3.0	84.0	4.5	6,320
Waterbury St Tech C	0.2	1.2	2.8	2.6	93.3	0.0	1,522
Wesleyan U	0.1	4.2	6.7	2.2	84.5	2.2	3,428
Yale U	0.2	6.5	5.2	3.3	74.6	10.3	10,893

DELAWARE

Delaware St C	0.2	0.8	57.5	1.2	40.0	0.4	2,510
Delaware Tech and CC							
Southern	0.6	0.6	14.9	0.6	82.9	0.4	2,479
Stanton-Wilmington	0.3	1.8	13.8	2.0	81.2	1.1	5,127
Terry	0.6	1.4	14.8	1.7	81.2	0.2	1,711
Goldey Beacom C	0.2	2.4	11.5	1.3	84.6	0.1	1,827
U of Delaware	0.1	1.7	4.3	0.6	90.4	2.9	19,818
Wesley C	0.1	0.2	11.3	0.9	87.4	0.0	972
Widener U Sch of Law	0.0	0.8	2.5	0.5	96.3	0.0	1,180
Widener U Delaware	0.1	0.6	5.9	0.3	93.0	0.1	1,154
Wilmington C	0.0	0.5	17.8	1.1	80.4	0.1	1,482

DISTRICT OF COLUMBIA

American U	0.2	3.0	6.3	3.7	74.6	12.2	11,155
Catholic U of America	0.1	2.7	4.5	3.0	82.2	7.4	7,010
Corcoran Sch of Art	0.4	1.4	3.9	5.0	80.6	8.6	279
De Sales Sch of Theology	0.0	4.2	4.2	0.0	91.7	0.0	48
Defense Intelligence C	0.0	1.9	82.2	3.0	5.0	7.9	845
Dominican House of Studies .	0.0	0.0	0.0	0.0	95.6	4.4	45
Gallaudet U	0.2	1.6	6.5	3.7	75.0	13.0	2,165
George Washington U	0.3	4.7	5.8	2.3	73.4	13.6	19,232
Georgetown U	0.2	4.5	7.1	4.1	75.8	8.3	11,516
Howard U	0.1	0.8	82.1	0.5	1.4	15.2	11,617
Mount Vernon C	0.0	2.5	12.3	2.9	73.3	8.9	551
Oblate C	0.0	0.0	7.9	13.2	68.4	10.5	38
Southeastern U	0.0	12.2	51.7	0.0	9.1	27.0	801
Strayer C	0.6	3.2	46.8	2.7	19.6	27.1	1,050
Trinity C	0.0	1.2	28.0	1.7	67.3	1.9	1,125
U of the District of Columbia .	0.0	2.0	82.1	3.0	5.0	8.0	11,263
Wesley Theological Sem	0.0	2.6	18.9	1.1	75.1	2.3	349

FLORIDA

	American Indian	Asian	Black	Hispanic	White	Foreign	Total
Art Inst of Fort Lauderdale ...	0.3%	0.8%	6.1%	10.0%	80.0%	2.8%	1,893
Baptist Bible Inst	0.0	0.3	2.2	1.1	95.4	1.1	368
Barry U	0.1	1.4	9.2	18.8	63.6	6.9	5,238
Bethune Cookman C	0.0	0.3	94.5	0.4	1.0	3.8	1,860
Brevard CC	0.4	1.4	5.2	2.4	89.2	1.4	12,375
Broward CC	0.7	2.1	9.0	8.0	78.0	2.3	21,682
Caribbean Ctr for Advanced Studies Miami Inst	0.0	1.0	5.4	61.3	29.4	2.9	204
Central Florida CC	0.3	0.8	7.7	2.1	88.9	0.2	3,995
Chipola JC	0.5	0.6	13.2	0.8	84.9	0.0	1,922
Clearwater Christian C	0.3	0.0	1.4	1.1	91.5	5.7	353
C of Boca Raton	0.2	1.2	12.0	9.9	71.6	5.1	1,135
Daytona Beach CC	0.1	1.7	9.5	3.5	83.6	1.6	9,365
Eckerd C	0.1	0.9	3.1	2.4	84.4	9.1	1,293
Edison CC	0.2	0.7	2.9	2.9	92.6	0.8	7,249
Edward Waters C	0.0	0.0	85.3	0.0	0.0	14.7	597
Embry-Riddle Aeronautical U	0.5	2.5	5.1	4.0	85.9	2.1	10,766
Flagler Career Inst	0.2	2.5	34.5	46.9	15.9	0.0	441
Flagler C	0.1	0.5	1.4	1.6	95.2	1.2	1,201
Florida Christian C	0.0	0.0	1.6	0.0	98.4	0.0	123
Florida C	1.1	0.5	2.9	0.8	92.4	2.4	380
Florida CC Jacksonville	0.3	3.0	14.2	1.9	80.0	0.6	16,778
Florida Inst of Tech	0.2	1.2	3.1	3.7	77.7	14.0	6,254
Florida Keys CC	0.5	2.1	4.2	8.7	82.7	1.7	1,840
Florida Southern C	0.1	0.3	1.9	0.7	94.8	2.1	2,670
Gulf Coast CC	0.6	1.4	7.3	1.6	86.0	3.1	5,149
Hillsborough CC	0.2	2.0	8.1	9.5	79.4	0.8	15,573
Hobe Sound Bible C	1.0	0.0	0.5	1.0	87.1	10.4	202
Indian River CC	0.1	1.4	3.4	0.6	94.0	0.5	9,483
International Fine Arts C	0.0	3.4	8.5	30.9	33.6	23.5	446
ITT Tech Inst	0.0	1.5	9.4	6.8	79.5	2.8	531
Jacksonville U	0.3	2.3	5.7	4.7	83.3	3.7	2,344
Lake City CC	0.3	0.8	9.3	1.5	88.1	0.0	1,893
Lake-Sumter CC	0.1	1.0	7.7	1.0	89.9	0.2	2,078
Liberty Christian C	0.0	0.4	3.5	0.4	93.7	2.1	284
Manatee CC	0.2	0.7	3.2	0.9	93.4	1.6	7,874
Miami Christian C	0.0	3.6	15.7	28.9	50.0	1.8	166
Miami-Dade CC	0.1	1.6	14.5	53.0	26.3	4.3	43,880
National Education Center Tampa Tech Inst	0.4	2.8	20.1	5.9	70.3	0.5	1,566
New England Inst of Tech Palm Beach	0.9	2.4	14.8	9.8	70.2	1.9	580
North Florida JC	0.2	0.3	28.2	1.1	70.1	0.2	1,220
Nova U	0.3	1.1	13.8	7.8	73.7	3.3	8,759
Okaloosa-Walton JC	0.3	1.3	6.1	1.9	89.8	0.7	5,270
Orlando C	0.1	1.3	20.5	8.0	69.7	0.4	838
Palm Beach Atlantic C	0.3	0.8	6.1	3.2	89.0	0.6	1,139
Palm Beach JC	0.1	0.9	5.8	4.6	83.9	4.8	13,121
Pasco Hernando CC	0.3	1.1	2.4	1.7	94.4	0.1	3,973
Pensacola JC	1.8	3.1	9.6	0.9	84.2	0.3	10,866
Polk CC	0.1	0.8	7.7	1.8	88.3	1.3	5,879
Prospect Hall C	0.0	0.0	38.4	7.9	38.9	14.8	216
Ringling Sch of Art and Design	0.6	1.7	1.9	4.3	89.4	2.1	483
Rollins C	0.4	1.5	3.7	3.7	88.3	2.5	3,738
Saint John Vianney C Sem ...	0.0	0.0	1.6	64.1	29.7	4.7	64

FLORIDA, cont.

	American Indian	Asian	Black	Hispanic	White	Foreign	Total
Saint Johns River CC	0.2%	0.4%	5.6%	1.3%	92.0%	0.5%	2,453
Saint Leo C	1.2	1.5	14.8	3.3	78.6	0.5	5,772
Saint Petersburg JC	0.8	1.6	4.6	1.9	90.4	0.8	18,870
Saint Vincent De Paul							
Regional Sem	0.0	0.0	0.0	32.3	66.7	1.0	99
Santa Fe CC	0.2	1.6	8.0	4.4	82.6	3.3	9,633
Seminole CC	0.2	2.0	4.6	4.6	87.9	0.7	6,996
South Florida CC	0.2	1.0	14.2	5.6	79.0	0.1	1,308
Southeastern C of the							
Assemblies of God	0.6	1.0	2.0	3.1	91.0	2.3	1,155
Spurgeon Baptist Bible C	0.0	0.0	0.0	0.0	100.0	0.0	57
St U Sys of Florida							
Florida A&M U	0.0	0.6	85.5	1.3	10.8	1.9	6,396
Florida Atlantic U	0.0	2.7	5.0	5.3	82.9	4.1	11,325
Florida International U	0.1	2.5	8.8	40.1	42.8	5.8	18,128
Florida St U	0.2	0.9	6.3	3.6	86.2	2.9	25,907
U of Central Florida	0.2	2.9	3.8	4.5	86.6	2.0	18,342
U of Florida	0.1	2.8	5.8	5.1	81.6	4.5	33,282
U of North Florida	0.2	2.4	6.5	1.7	88.4	0.8	7,162
U of South Florida	0.1	2.2	3.9	5.2	86.3	2.2	29,912
U of West Florida	0.2	1.7	4.8	1.2	89.7	2.3	7,095
Stetson U	0.3	0.9	1.8	2.1	91.5	3.3	2,974
Tallahassee CC	0.3	0.7	14.8	2.7	79.2	2.2	7,264
Talmudic C of Florida	0.0	0.0	0.0	0.0	100.0	0.0	94
United Electronics Inst							
of Florida	0.2	1.0	22.9	23.1	49.3	3.4	493
U of Miami	0.1	2.6	5.6	17.7	62.6	11.3	13,828
U of Tampa	0.1	1.0	3.1	4.7	85.6	5.4	2,401
Valencia CC	0.4	2.6	7.1	7.4	80.8	1.6	14,840
Warner Southern C	0.3	0.3	6.9	0.3	89.0	3.3	363
Webber C	0.0	0.8	7.5	2.6	77.4	11.7	265

GEORGIA

	American Indian	Asian	Black	Hispanic	White	Foreign	Total
Abraham Baldwin							
Agricultural C	0.1	0.1	8.5	0.1	89.8	1.5	1,893
Agnes Scott C	0.4	1.5	7.0	2.1	85.7	3.3	517
Albany St C	0.2	0.1	82.7	0.2	16.8	0.0	2,104
Andrew C	0.0	0.0	14.2	1.7	66.1	18.0	345
Armstrong St C	0.3	1.5	13.6	0.6	82.9	1.1	3,257
Art Inst of Atlanta	0.3	0.6	29.3	1.2	67.4	1.1	1,464
Atlanta Christian C	0.0	4.1	10.1	0.0	81.7	4.1	169
Atlanta C of Art	0.0	4.3	15.7	2.9	76.3	0.8	375
Atlanta Metropolitan C	0.0	0.2	90.9	0.1	1.5	7.3	1,425
Atlanta U	0.0	2.6	78.1	0.8	4.0	14.5	1,023
Augusta C	0.2	1.7	15.5	0.9	81.1	0.5	4,827
Bainbridge C	0.1	0.4	17.1	0.2	82.1	0.0	800
Ben Hill-Irwin Tech Inst	0.0	0.0	44.9	0.0	55.1	0.0	492
Berry C	0.2	0.5	1.8	0.4	96.1	1.0	1,820
Brenau C	0.0	0.4	8.6	0.3	89.8	0.8	1,921
Brewton-Parker C	0.0	1.1	20.4	0.4	78.1	0.0	1,470
Brunswick C	0.2	0.9	17.0	1.3	79.9	0.7	1,338
Chattahoochee Tech Inst	0.1	0.9	8.7	0.6	89.7	0.1	1,708
Clayton St C	0.2	1.1	11.4	1.1	85.7	0.5	3,661
Columbia Theol Sem	0.0	3.9	4.6	0.6	87.4	3.5	541
Columbus C	0.1	2.0	17.5	1.9	77.0	1.4	3,786
Columbus Tech Inst	1.2	1.5	29.7	2.6	64.9	0.0	3,465

	American Indian	Asian	Black	Hispanic	White	Foreign	Total
Coosa Valley Tech Inst	0.1%	0.3%	8.7%	0.2%	90.7%	0.0%	943
Covenant C	0.2	0.2	2.3	0.4	93.8	3.2	533
Crandall JC	0.2	0.8	63.8	0.6	34.7	0.0	643
Dalton C	0.0	0.3	1.7	0.2	97.7	0.1	1,861
Darton C	0.2	0.6	19.8	0.4	78.9	0.2	1,887
Dekalb C	0.2	2.5	17.1	1.3	78.3	0.6	10,566
DeKalb Tech Inst	0.3	1.3	20.9	0.8	76.1	0.6	3,152
DeVry Inst of Tech	0.4	2.7	53.7	1.6	40.3	1.2	3,028
East Georgia C	0.0	0.3	13.9	0.2	85.6	0.0	617
Emmanuel C	0.0	0.0	8.3	0.0	91.7	0.0	336
Emmanuel C Sch of Christian							
Ministries	0.0	0.0	0.0	0.0	100.0	0.0	30
Emory U	0.1	2.9	6.9	1.4	82.8	5.9	9,285
Floyd JC	0.1	0.8	7.5	0.2	91.4	0.0	1,485
Fort Valley St C	0.1	0.2	92.1	0.2	5.7	1.8	1,915
Gainesville C	0.4	0.6	2.6	0.5	93.5	2.4	2,150
Georgia C	0.2	0.4	15.6	0.5	82.3	1.1	4,522
Georgia Inst of Tech	0.1	5.1	6.1	2.4	79.4	6.9	11,887
Georgia Military C	0.2	2.1	32.6	7.7	56.8	0.5	1,462
Georgia Southern C	0.1	0.5	12.2	0.3	86.2	0.8	9,843
Georgia Southwestern C	0.0	0.1	15.9	0.2	82.4	1.3	2,151
Georgia St U	0.2	2.0	16.4	1.6	76.2	3.6	22,176
Gordon C	0.4	0.6	17.6	0.2	80.8	0.4	1,389
Gupton Jones C of							
Funeral Services	0.0	0.8	14.8	2.5	80.2	1.6	243
Gwinnett Tech Inst	0.4	3.4	3.0	1.1	92.1	0.0	2,480
Heart of Georgia Tech Inst ...	0.0	0.0	23.2	0.0	76.8	0.0	289
Interdenominational							
Theol Center	0.0	0.0	88.8	0.4	2.3	8.5	260
Kennesaw St C	0.3	0.7	2.8	1.0	93.8	1.5	8,601
La Grange C	0.1	0.6	7.0	0.1	84.6	7.6	953
Lanier Tech Inst	0.2	4.0	7.0	0.4	87.9	0.4	445
Life C	0.7	0.7	2.3	2.8	91.2	2.4	1,369
Macon C	0.4	0.5	18.7	0.9	79.6	0.0	3,512
Macon Tech Inst	0.7	0.2	42.8	0.4	55.9	0.0	1,013
Massey Business C	0.0	0.0	69.0	1.7	29.0	0.2	465
Meadows JC	0.0	0.0	69.6	2.0	28.5	0.0	358
Medical C of Georgia.........	0.4	2.5	8.9	2.1	82.2	3.9	2,279
Mercer U							
Main	0.2	1.1	10.9	1.3	86.1	0.5	3,725
Atlanta	0.4	1.4	12.3	1.9	72.3	11.7	2,370
Middle Georgia C	0.3	0.8	14.7	0.5	83.4	0.3	1,464
Morehouse C	0.0	0.0	98.3	0.0	0.0	1.7	2,690
Morehouse Sch of Medicine .	0.7	5.1	76.6	5.1	10.9	1.5	137
Moultrie Area Tech Inst	0.0	0.5	23.4	0.2	75.9	0.0	586
North Georgia C	0.2	0.0	2.1	0.1	97.0	0.5	2,181
Oglethorpe U	0.1	2.6	5.7	1.0	85.8	4.9	1,042
Paine C	0.0	0.2	91.9	0.2	5.1	2.6	606
Phillips C Augusta	0.0	0.0	58.4	0.0	41.6	0.0	586
Phillips C Columbus	0.0	0.0	51.0	1.0	47.9	0.0	574
Pickens Tech Inst	0.0	0.0	0.2	0.0	99.8	0.0	612
Piedmont C	0.0	0.9	6.7	0.0	86.1	6.3	555
Reinhardt C	0.0	0.0	2.7	0.0	95.1	2.2	597
Savannah C of Art and Design	0.0	0.9	6.4	1.6	88.8	2.2	1,397
Savannah St C	0.1	0.2	81.4	0.1	14.2	4.0	1,904
Shorter C	0.0	1.0	5.3	0.0	92.3	1.4	832
South C	0.0	0.2	58.7	0.0	41.1	0.0	579

GEORGIA, cont.

	American Indian	Asian	Black	Hispanic	White	Foreign	Total
South Georgia C	0.6%	0.4%	19.2%	0.4%	77.7%	1.7%	1,010
Southern C of Tech	0.1	2.5	12.8	1.2	80.9	2.4	3,767
Spelman C	0.0	0.0	98.5	0.0	0.0	1.5	1,742
Thomas C	0.0	0.6	13.6	0.3	82.7	2.7	330
Toccoa Falls C	0.0	1.1	0.9	0.4	90.0	7.5	743
Truett McConnell C	0.0	0.0	13.9	0.0	86.1	0.0	1,488
U of Georgia	0.1	1.1	4.7	0.7	89.6	3.8	27,176
Upson Tech Inst	0.4	0.0	31.2	0.4	68.1	0.0	279
Valdosta St C	0.2	0.4	15.0	0.6	83.3	0.5	6,950
Valdosta Tech Inst	0.0	0.4	18.4	0.0	81.2	0.0	799
Watterson Career Centre	0.0	0.0	98.9	0.0	1.1	0.0	183
Waycross C	0.0	0.8	12.6	0.0	86.6	0.0	499
Wesleyan C	0.0	4.3	11.7	2.0	81.6	0.4	512
West Georgia C	0.1	0.4	14.5	0.6	83.9	0.6	6,705
Young Harris C	0.0	0.2	0.0	0.4	99.4	0.0	468

HAWAII

	American Indian	Asian	Black	Hispanic	White	Foreign	Total
Brigham Young U Hawaii	0.4	18.6	0.4	1.3	39.6	39.8	2,141
Chaminade U of Honolulu ...	0.3	31.6	6.0	2.6	56.1	3.5	2,537
Hawaii Loa C	2.3	24.2	4.8	4.1	43.2	21.5	484
Hawaii Pacific C	1.0	23.7	8.5	4.0	43.8	19.0	4,560
International C and Graduate Sch of Theology	0.0	32.6	4.3	0.0	41.3	21.7	46
U of Hawaii							
Hilo	0.4	60.8	0.5	1.8	33.6	2.8	3,634
Manoa	0.2	65.5	0.6	0.7	25.6	7.3	18,424
Honolulu CC	0.4	79.7	1.2	1.5	15.1	2.0	4,292
Kapiolani CC	0.3	73.5	0.8	1.4	23.7	0.4	5,467
Kauai CC	0.2	67.3	0.3	2.4	28.8	1.0	1,231
Leeward CC	0.3	69.1	2.2	2.2	25.6	0.7	5,439
Maui CC	0.4	60.0	0.4	1.7	35.2	2.4	1,995
West Oahu C	0.2	55.5	1.8	1.8	40.0	0.6	492
Windward CC	0.4	52.5	1.2	1.4	43.6	1.0	1,555

IDAHO

	American Indian	Asian	Black	Hispanic	White	Foreign	Total
Boise Bible C	1.5	0.0	1.5	3.0	94.0	0.0	67
C of Southern Idaho	0.6	0.5	0.6	1.9	94.1	2.3	2,775
Idaho St U	1.8	1.5	0.8	1.8	92.4	1.8	7,121
Lewis-Clark St C	2.1	0.2	0.4	0.3	96.0	1.1	2,275
North Idaho C	1.2	0.6	0.5	0.9	95.7	1.1	2,565
Northwest Nazarene C	0.4	1.5	0.9	1.4	94.6	1.1	1,138
Ricks C	0.8	0.9	0.2	0.8	93.2	4.1	7,694
U of Idaho	0.8	1.4	0.8	1.2	91.5	4.4	9,450

ILLINOIS

	American Indian	Asian	Black	Hispanic	White	Foreign	Total
Alfred Adler Inst of Chicago ..	0.0	1.4	6.3	3.5	87.3	1.4	142
American Academy of Art	0.4	3.7	5.1	6.8	82.9	1.1	790
American Conservatory of Music	0.0	5.4	10.7	3.6	67.0	13.4	112
American Islamic C	0.0	2.9	32.4	0.0	20.6	44.1	34
Augustana C	0.0	0.5	3.3	0.7	92.5	2.9	2,241
Aurora U	0.4	1.5	11.7	4.3	81.4	0.8	2,066
Barat C	0.0	1.6	0.3	0.3	95.0	2.8	674

	American Indian	Asian	Black	Hispanic	White	Foreign	Total
Belleville Area C	0.7%	1.8%	6.1%	1.1%	90.2%	0.2%	12,511
Bethany Theol Sem	0.0	0.0	2.5	0.8	82.0	14.8	122
Black Hawk C							
East	0.0	0.4	0.9	0.3	97.9	0.5	754
Quad-Cities	0.3	0.8	5.1	3.8	90.0	0.0	5,317
Blackburn C	0.2	0.6	6.7	0.6	89.0	2.9	480
Blessing-Rieman C							
of Nursing	0.0	0.0	0.9	0.0	99.1	0.0	106
Board of Governors of St							
C's and U's							
Chicago St U	0.1	1.0	82.8	2.7	12.2	1.3	6,134
Governors St U	0.1	0.8	17.5	1.8	79.3	0.5	5,089
Eastern Illinois U	0.1	0.5	4.6	0.7	93.4	0.7	11,159
Northeastern Illinois U	0.3	8.2	10.7	11.9	68.0	0.9	9,846
Western Illinois U	0.2	0.9	7.9	1.3	86.0	3.6	12,749
Bradley U	0.0	1.7	6.9	1.1	85.0	5.2	5,171
Brisk Rabbinical C	0.0	0.0	0.0	0.0	100.0	0.0	12
Carl Sandburg C	0.4	0.8	5.0	1.8	91.4	0.6	2,826
Catholic Theol Union	0.0	1.6	1.9	1.0	78.1	17.5	315
Chicago C of Osteopathic							
Medicine	0.5	7.9	1.4	1.9	88.2	0.0	416
Chicago Sch of Professional							
Psychology	0.0	0.0	2.9	0.0	95.6	1.5	136
Chicago Theol Sem	0.0	7.2	21.0	0.6	71.3	0.0	181
City C's of Chicago							
Chicago City-Wide C	0.5	4.7	45.6	21.4	27.8	0.0	12,994
Richard J Daley C	0.4	2.3	20.5	31.3	45.5	0.0	7,406
Harold Washington C	0.7	10.8	59.5	9.0	20.1	0.0	7,915
Kennedy-King C	0.5	2.0	68.8	22.7	6.0	0.0	8,650
Malcolm X C	0.4	16.6	49.3	26.8	6.9	0.0	9,853
Olive-Harvey C	0.8	1.4	76.0	18.3	3.5	0.0	8,080
Harry S Truman C	1.0	18.3	14.4	40.0	26.3	0.0	12,973
Wilbur Wright C	0.4	8.5	13.7	21.6	55.7	0.0	7,043
C of Automation	0.0	0.0	78.3	8.4	10.8	2.4	83
C of Du Page	0.1	6.1	2.2	3.9	87.6	0.1	26,489
C of Lake County	0.2	2.8	5.8	6.4	84.8	0.0	11,587
C of Saint Francis	0.3	0.8	3.3	1.1	94.3	0.1	4,075
Columbia C	0.7	2.5	26.2	6.8	62.9	0.9	6,062
Concordia C	0.1	1.5	4.2	1.0	92.4	0.8	1,121
Danville Area CC	0.8	1.1	8.6	1.8	87.6	0.1	2,925
De Paul U	0.2	5.3	9.8	4.9	78.3	1.5	14,699
DeVry Inst of Tech Chicago ..	0.4	11.3	28.3	15.8	41.8	2.3	3,163
DeVry Inst of Tech Lombard ..	0.2	5.1	7.8	3.7	82.7	0.4	2,370
Dr William Scholl C							
of Podiatric Medicine	0.2	3.3	6.0	2.3	85.2	3.1	487
Elgin CC	0.1	2.5	2.7	3.9	90.6	0.2	5,780
Elmhurst C	0.1	1.4	2.4	1.1	94.2	0.8	3,135
Eureka C	0.0	0.4	6.8	0.6	91.2	1.0	500
Forest Inst of Professional							
Psychology	0.4	2.4	2.8	1.2	93.3	0.0	252
Garrett-Evangelical Theol							
Sem	0.0	5.9	11.5	0.5	72.0	10.1	375
Gem City C	0.0	0.0	2.0	0.0	97.4	0.7	151
Greenville C	0.1	0.8	5.1	4.2	88.9	0.9	745
Harrington Inst of							
Interior Design	0.0	2.9	4.9	1.2	89.1	1.9	411
Hebrew Theol C	0.0	0.0	0.0	0.0	100.0	0.0	235

ILLINOIS, cont.

	American Indian	Asian	Black	Hispanic	White	Foreign	Total
Highland CC	0.1%	0.7%	3.2%	0.0%	95.9%	0.1%	2,878
Illinois Benedictine C	0.2	1.7	2.4	1.2	94.5	0.0	2,550
Illinois Central C	0.1	1.0	3.8	0.8	94.2	0.1	12,022
Illinois C	0.0	0.5	1.4	0.1	97.4	0.6	842
Illinois C of Optometry	0.0	8.4	2.9	3.4	81.8	3.4	583
Illinois Eastern CC	0.1	0.3	0.2	0.3	99.1	0.1	6,571
Illinois Inst of Tech	0.1	10.7	7.6	3.7	66.4	11.4	6,267
III Medical Training Center	0.0	2.1	84.6	6.6	6.8	0.0	487
Illinois Sch of Professional Psychology	0.4	0.4	2.9	1.8	94.0	0.4	448
Illinois St U	0.2	1.2	4.8	0.9	91.6	1.4	22,322
Illinois Tech C	0.0	4.8	67.7	10.2	15.6	1.6	186
Illinois Valley CC	0.2	0.9	2.3	1.1	95.5	0.0	3,850
Illinois Wesleyan U	0.4	1.9	1.8	0.7	92.4	2.8	1,750
ITT Tech Inst	0.0	3.8	5.4	5.9	84.9	0.0	186
John A Logan C	0.2	0.5	4.6	0.4	94.0	0.2	5,183
John Marshall Law Sch	0.0	1.0	5.3	2.7	90.7	0.2	1,273
John Wood CC	0.1	0.7	1.9	0.1	96.8	0.5	2,695
Joliet JC	0.2	1.2	8.3	4.7	85.4	0.2	9,454
Judson C	0.0	0.8	3.3	1.1	94.1	0.8	523
Kankakee CC	0.2	0.8	7.9	0.3	90.7	0.1	3,473
Kaskaskia C	0.4	0.7	5.8	1.1	91.9	0.1	2,806
Keller Graduate Sch of Management	0.0	2.3	5.4	1.3	88.6	2.4	1,120
Kendall C	0.0	0.8	20.6	1.6	74.5	2.6	384
Kishwaukee C	0.4	2.4	4.6	3.2	89.2	0.2	3,113
Knox C	0.2	3.9	4.3	1.3	84.0	6.3	1,024
Lake Forest C	0.0	2.3	5.2	1.2	90.3	0.9	1,149
Lake Forest Graduate Sch of Management	0.0	2.3	2.5	0.8	94.3	0.0	475
Lake Land C	0.5	0.6	3.6	0.6	94.6	0.2	3,952
Lewis and Clark CC	0.3	0.7	4.4	0.4	94.0	0.2	5,012
Lewis U	0.2	1.1	18.7	4.2	75.1	0.6	3,502
Lincoln Christian C and Sem	0.0	0.2	0.6	0.2	98.0	1.0	488
Lincoln Land CC	0.2	0.6	4.2	0.6	94.2	0.2	7,848
Lutheran Sch of Theology	0.0	0.5	4.4	1.5	81.5	12.1	390
MacCormac JC	0.0	0.8	7.3	48.6	41.9	1.4	504
MacMurray C	0.2	0.4	13.9	3.1	82.2	0.2	842
Mallinckrodt C of the North Shore	0.0	3.3	2.6	6.6	69.5	18.0	272
McCormick Theol Sem	0.2	5.9	5.5	8.5	76.3	3.7	544
McHenry County C	0.0	0.5	0.2	1.3	97.9	0.1	3,487
McKendree C	0.2	0.7	14.2	1.4	83.0	0.5	1,012
Meadville / Lombard Theol Sch	0.0	3.1	0.0	0.0	93.8	3.1	32
Mennonite C of Nursing	0.0	0.0	5.9	0.0	94.1	0.0	102
Metropolitan Business C	0.0	1.5	81.6	4.0	12.9	0.0	272
Metropolitan Skill Center	0.0	0.0	97.0	2.0	1.0	0.0	100
Midstate C	0.0	0.2	7.6	1.2	91.0	0.0	420
Midwest C of Engineering	0.0	20.0	0.0	0.0	80.0	0.0	15
Millikin U	0.2	0.7	3.2	0.5	95.3	0.1	1,736
Monmouth C	0.0	5.5	7.4	0.4	86.6	0.0	674
Montay C	0.0	8.2	16.3	16.7	57.1	1.7	233
Moody Bible Inst	0.1	2.0	1.3	0.4	87.0	9.2	1,484
Moraine Valley CC	0.1	0.9	3.9	2.1	92.8	0.2	12,914
Morrison Inst of Tech	0.0	0.0	5.3	3.7	91.1	0.0	246
Morton C	0.2	2.4	0.4	17.6	78.4	0.9	3,625

	American Indian	Asian	Black	Hispanic	White	Foreign	Total
Mundelein C	0.2%	2.0%	17.3%	8.0%	71.7%	0.8%	1,010
National C of Chiropractic	0.4	0.9	1.3	2.4	91.5	3.6	785
National C of Education	0.5	5.6	13.0	6.0	74.9	0.1	4,566
North Central C	0.1	3.0	5.9	1.8	89.0	0.2	2,335
North Park C and Theol Sem	0.7	4.9	5.9	11.2	76.2	1.1	1,218
Northern Baptist Theol Sem	0.0	2.1	15.2	19.4	46.6	16.8	191
Northern Illinois U	0.3	3.0	4.9	2.2	86.8	2.9	24,255
Northwestern U	0.2	7.3	5.8	1.6	78.1	7.0	16,592
Oakton CC	0.2	6.8	2.7	2.2	88.0	0.0	11,596
Olivet Nazarene U	0.2	1.3	4.4	1.0	90.9	2.2	1,823
Parkland C	0.7	2.2	6.6	1.2	88.4	0.9	7,911
Parks C of Saint Louis U	0.1	1.6	4.3	2.9	80.5	10.7	1,105
Prairie St C	0.3	0.9	20.2	4.4	74.2	0.0	4,831
Principia C	0.0	0.3	0.6	0.6	91.9	6.6	654
Quincy C	0.0	0.7	2.6	0.8	95.2	0.7	1,076
Ray C of Design	0.1	6.3	25.8	9.4	55.2	3.1	681
Rend Lake C	0.4	0.3	5.3	0.6	93.4	0.0	3,148
Richland CC	0.1	0.6	9.6	0.3	89.3	0.1	3,743
Robert Morris C	0.3	0.9	42.2	21.1	35.5	0.0	2,313
Rock Valley C	0.2	1.2	3.9	1.7	92.6	0.4	7,703
Rockford C	0.0	1.7	2.1	1.4	94.1	0.8	1,449
Roosevelt U	0.2	2.7	26.5	3.4	60.1	7.0	6,374
Rosary C	0.1	1.3	5.6	4.2	86.8	1.9	1,601
Rush U	0.3	9.8	4.9	2.1	80.3	2.6	1,123
Saint Augustine C	0.0	0.0	0.0	99.7	0.2	0.1	997
Saint Francis Med Ctr C of Nursing	0.0	0.0	3.2	3.2	93.6	0.0	125
Saint Xavier C	0.2	1.2	11.6	3.6	82.9	0.5	2,641
Sangamon St U	0.2	1.0	5.6	0.5	90.2	2.6	3,942
Sauk Valley CC	0.9	0.4	3.2	3.6	91.9	0.0	2,769
Sch of the Art Inst of Chicago	0.1	4.8	5.2	5.4	78.9	5.5	2,147
Seabury-Western Theol Sem	10.0	1.1	3.3	0.0	84.4	1.1	90
Shawnee CC	0.1	0.1	15.2	0.0	84.6	0.0	1,433
Shimer C	0.0	0.0	9.2	3.4	87.4	0.0	87
South Suburban C	1.3	1.0	23.0	3.7	71.0	0.0	8,263
Southeastern Illinois C	0.4	0.4	12.7	1.7	84.7	0.1	2,756
Southern Illinois U							
Carbondale	0.3	1.6	9.4	1.8	80.0	6.9	24,217
Edwardsville	0.2	1.1	11.2	0.8	84.7	2.0	11,352
Spertus C of Judaica	0.0	3.4	31.0	3.4	62.1	0.0	87
Spoon River C	0.1	0.5	1.6	0.2	97.2	0.6	1,723
Springfield C	0.3	0.5	5.5	0.3	92.7	0.8	385
State CC at East Saint Louis	0.1	0.3	97.1	0.0	2.4	0.0	1,184
Telshe Yeshiva Chicago	0.0	0.0	0.0	3.7	92.7	3.7	82
Trinity Christian C	0.0	1.1	9.3	2.0	86.0	1.6	550
Trinity C	0.3	2.2	6.5	1.4	88.6	1.0	630
Trinity Evangelical Divinity Sch	0.0	7.2	3.3	0.8	86.9	1.9	1,132
Triton C	0.3	3.4	14.0	10.6	71.4	0.3	17,691
U of Chicago	0.2	8.3	3.6	2.0	76.3	9.7	10,409
U of Health Sciences Chicago Med Sch	0.1	12.7	4.0	0.9	79.4	2.9	892
U of Illinois							
Chicago	0.2	12.5	9.1	8.5	64.4	5.3	23,986
Urbana-Champaign	0.2	6.8	4.8	2.5	78.7	7.0	38,337
U of Saint Mary of the Lake Mundelein Sem	0.0	2.1	0.7	6.2	89.7	1.4	291

ILLINOIS, cont.

	American Indian	Asian	Black	Hispanic	White	Foreign	Total
VanderCook C of Music	0.0%	0.0%	13.9%	4.9%	79.2%	2.1%	144
Waubonsee CC	0.6	0.7	5.2	14.9	77.1	1.5	5,378
Wheaton C	0.2	3.8	1.0	0.9	91.7	2.4	2,529
William Rainey Harper C	0.1	4.4	1.4	4.3	89.0	0.8	16,121

INDIANA

	American Indian	Asian	Black	Hispanic	White	Foreign	Total
Ancilla Domini C	0.0	0.2	1.1	0.7	97.8	0.2	456
Anderson U	0.9	0.3	3.5	0.2	94.0	1.0	2,050
Ball St U	0.2	0.6	3.4	0.5	94.2	1.1	18,732
Bethel C	0.2	0.2	2.2	0.4	96.5	0.6	539
Butler U	0.2	1.3	4.4	0.5	93.4	0.2	3,912
Calumet C of Saint Joseph ...	0.5	0.5	22.9	13.1	63.0	0.1	1,049
Christian Theological Sem ...	0.4	1.5	8.8	0.8	87.3	1.2	260
Concordia Theological Sem ..	0.0	1.4	1.4	0.7	96.0	0.5	424
Davenport C South Bend	0.0	0.0	26.5	2.1	71.4	0.0	238
Davenport C Merrillville	0.3	0.3	37.7	5.7	56.1	0.0	369
De Pauw U	0.1	1.0	2.4	0.5	94.7	1.3	2,480
Earlham C	0.2	1.4	3.9	0.6	92.3	1.7	1,249
Fort Wayne Bible C	0.0	0.3	4.0	0.3	94.9	0.5	371
Franklin C of Indiana	0.0	1.1	2.3	0.4	95.9	0.2	812
Goshen Biblical Sem	0.0	0.0	0.0	2.4	85.9	11.8	85
Goshen C	0.3	1.1	2.9	2.8	86.8	6.2	1,073
Grace C	0.5	0.9	0.5	0.7	95.6	1.8	769
Grace Theological Sem	0.3	3.1	2.8	0.9	90.6	2.2	319
Hanover C	0.0	0.0	0.8	0.3	98.0	0.8	1,075
Holy Cross JC	0.0	0.0	6.7	1.2	90.1	1.9	416
Huntington C	0.2	0.0	1.9	0.2	90.1	7.7	574
Indiana Inst of Tech	0.0	0.0	28.0	1.1	47.6	23.3	464
Indiana St U	0.2	0.5	6.9	0.7	86.1	5.5	11,677
Indiana U Sys							
Bloomington	0.1	2.0	3.8	1.3	87.6	5.2	33,776
East	0.1	0.5	3.0	0.4	95.9	0.1	1,628
Kokomo	0.4	0.4	2.3	1.1	95.7	0.2	3,115
Northwest	0.1	0.7	22.4	6.6	70.0	0.2	4,812
Purdue U Indianapolis	0.2	2.0	7.3	0.9	88.8	0.8	24,808
Purdue U Fort Wayne	0.1	0.8	3.1	0.8	94.6	0.5	11,073
South Bend	0.1	0.7	4.2	0.9	93.4	0.6	6,447
Southeast	0.2	0.2	1.7	0.1	97.6	0.2	5,192
Ind Vocational Tech C							
Central Indiana	0.7	0.8	19.1	0.5	78.9	0.0	4,407
Columbus	0.3	0.4	1.3	0.2	97.7	0.0	2,255
Eastcentral	0.1	0.2	5.6	0.5	93.7	0.0	1,646
Kokomo	0.6	0.3	3.5	0.6	94.9	0.0	2,197
Lafayette	0.5	0.5	1.7	0.3	97.0	0.0	1,783
North Central	0.6	0.7	6.7	1.3	90.7	0.0	2,445
Northeast	0.1	0.5	3.9	0.8	94.7	0.0	2,895
Northwest	0.3	0.3	30.0	4.7	64.6	0.0	2,816
Southeast	0.1	0.1	0.4	0.0	99.3	0.0	750
Southcentral	0.3	0.1	2.7	0.1	96.8	0.0	1,455
Southwest	0.3	0.6	4.3	0.1	94.5	0.0	2,011
Wabash Valley	0.5	0.7	3.7	0.3	94.8	0.0	1,935
Whitewater	0.8	0.2	5.6	0.2	93.1	0.0	854
Indiana Wesleyan U	0.1	0.3	5.8	1.2	91.8	0.7	2,019
International Business C	0.0	0.4	3.9	1.1	94.7	0.0	567
Interstate Tech Inst	0.0	0.0	15.2	0.0	83.7	1.1	92
ITT Tech Inst Fort Wayne	0.1	0.7	15.7	2.0	81.5	0.0	1,034

	American Indian	Asian	Black	Hispanic	White	Foreign	Total
ITT Tech Inst Indianapolis	0.2%	0.6%	8.7%	1.1%	89.5%	0.0%	1,236
ITT Tech Inst Evansville	0.0	0.2	6.3	0.4	93.1	0.0	448
Lockyear C Indianapolis	0.0	0.4	62.6	0.4	36.6	0.0	257
Lockyear C Evansville	0.9	0.3	13.8	0.0	85.1	0.0	348
Manchester C	0.2	0.6	1.8	1.2	93.9	2.3	1,028
Marian C	0.0	0.0	12.8	0.7	84.0	2.4	1,215
Martin Center C	0.0	0.0	78.7	0.9	20.1	0.3	328
Mennonite Biblical Sem	0.0	0.0	0.0	0.0	71.1	28.9	76
Mid American C of Funeral Service	1.0	0.0	12.1	0.0	86.9	0.0	99
Oakland City C	0.0	1.0	0.6	0.0	98.4	0.0	627
Purdue U							
Main	0.3	2.4	3.1	1.3	87.0	5.8	36,517
Calumet	0.2	1.1	8.4	7.0	83.3	0.1	7,393
North Central	0.2	0.4	2.8	0.9	95.6	0.0	3,065
Rose-Hulman Inst of Tech	0.4	3.1	0.6	0.4	95.5	0.0	1,424
Saint Francis C	0.2	1.0	4.3	1.1	93.0	0.3	960
Saint Joseph's C	0.1	0.3	4.4	1.5	92.8	0.9	1,003
Saint Mary-of-the-Woods C ...	0.3	0.9	2.3	1.2	94.1	1.2	910
Saint Mary's C	0.0	1.1	0.3	1.8	95.5	1.3	1,782
Saint Meinrad C	0.0	2.3	0.8	3.1	87.7	6.2	130
Saint Meinrad Sch of Theol ..	0.0	3.1	3.9	3.1	89.0	0.8	127
Taylor U	0.1	0.6	0.8	0.4	96.9	1.3	1,635
Tri-State U	0.0	1.2	1.8	0.9	82.0	14.2	1,037
U of Evansville	0.1	0.7	2.5	0.2	92.6	3.9	3,379
U of Indianapolis	0.3	0.7	5.5	0.6	91.3	1.5	3,274
U of Notre Dame	0.4	2.0	3.3	3.8	87.2	3.4	9,335
U of Southern Indiana	0.4	0.5	2.4	0.3	95.7	0.7	5,264
Valparaiso U	0.2	0.7	1.7	1.0	95.3	1.1	3,890
Vincennes U							
Main	0.1	0.3	7.3	2.0	88.3	2.0	7,556
Jasper	0.0	0.3	0.4	0.0	99.2	0.1	729
Wabash C	0.0	2.1	3.0	1.1	91.7	2.1	872

IOWA

American Inst of Business	0.1	0.9	0.8	0.3	97.9	0.0	1,120
Briar Cliff C	0.2	0.4	0.7	0.8	97.0	0.9	1,090
Buena Vista C	0.1	0.4	0.3	0.2	98.9	0.0	2,721
Central U of Iowa	0.0	0.9	0.9	0.5	95.4	2.4	1,507
Clarke C	0.0	0.0	1.6	0.2	97.5	0.7	830
Coe C	0.0	0.6	1.6	0.5	86.6	10.8	1,242
Cornell C	0.4	2.0	3.0	1.8	90.6	2.2	1,129
Des Moines Area CC	0.3	2.4	3.4	0.8	92.7	0.4	9,861
Divine Word C	0.0	56.1	0.0	1.5	28.8	13.6	66
Dordt C	0.0	2.2	0.4	0.1	85.0	12.3	987
Drake U	0.1	0.9	2.7	0.7	93.3	2.3	6,618
Emmaus Bible C	0.0	1.0	2.9	6.3	82.0	7.8	205
Faith Baptist Bible C and Sem	0.3	1.6	0.3	0.7	97.1	0.0	307
Graceland C	0.4	0.7	3.1	0.4	92.7	2.8	1,622
Grand View C	0.1	2.1	3.4	1.4	89.8	3.1	1,359
Grinnell C	0.1	3.0	4.3	0.8	85.5	6.3	1,302
Hawkeye Inst of Tech	0.3	0.2	3.4	0.2	95.9	0.1	1,885
Indian Hills CC	0.3	0.5	0.9	0.4	97.9	0.0	2,588
Iowa Central CC	0.1	1.0	2.3	0.2	96.4	0.0	2,036
Iowa Lakes CC	0.2	0.6	0.6	0.2	98.4	0.1	1,787
Iowa St U	0.1	1.3	2.1	0.9	87.7	7.9	26,475

IOWA, cont.

	American Indian	Asian	Black	Hispanic	White	Foreign	Total
Iowa Valley CC Dist							
Ellsworth CC	0.0%	0.3%	8.0%	0.0%	91.7%	0.0%	959
Marshalltown CC	2.6	1.1	0.6	0.1	94.8	0.9	1,229
Iowa Wesleyan C	0.1	0.6	2.1	0.0	94.7	2.5	679
Iowa Western CC	0.2	0.7	1.7	0.7	96.5	0.2	2,604
Kirkwood CC	0.1	0.9	1.3	0.9	96.0	0.7	7,053
Lincoln Tech Inst	0.0	0.7	4.2	2.1	93.0	0.0	143
Loras C	0.0	0.7	1.7	0.0	97.6	0.0	1,933
Luther C	0.0	2.5	1.2	0.2	93.0	3.0	2,160
Maharishi International U	0.6	2.4	1.2	0.9	58.8	36.1	782
Marycrest C	0.1	0.1	2.3	2.9	93.7	0.8	2,002
Morningside C	2.0	0.5	2.0	0.2	95.3	0.0	1,229
Mount Mercy C	0.3	0.4	1.2	0.4	97.0	0.6	1,568
Mount Saint Clare C	0.0	0.3	8.2	0.6	89.3	1.6	317
North Iowa Area CC	0.0	0.4	2.3	1.1	96.1	0.0	2,510
Northeast Iowa Tech Inst	0.1	0.2	0.1	0.2	99.5	0.0	1,153
Northwest Iowa Tech C	0.0	0.9	0.0	0.0	99.1	0.0	528
Northwestern C	0.1	0.3	0.7	0.1	95.4	3.3	965
Palmer C of Chiropractic	0.6	0.7	0.4	0.7	87.5	10.1	1,622
Saint Ambrose U	0.3	0.8	3.2	2.4	92.9	0.4	2,110
Scott CC	0.5	0.6	3.3	1.5	93.6	0.6	5,374
Simpson C	0.1	0.5	1.0	0.2	98.1	0.2	1,710
Southeastern CC	0.1	0.7	2.4	0.8	95.9	0.0	2,341
Southwestern CC	0.0	0.2	1.2	0.1	97.8	0.7	907
U of Dubuque	0.5	0.8	5.1	0.6	86.3	6.8	1,187
U of Iowa	0.4	2.2	2.2	1.3	87.6	6.5	30,001
U of Northern Iowa	0.1	0.5	1.3	0.4	96.4	1.2	12,396
U of Osteopathic Medicine							
and Health Sciences	0.1	5.4	3.7	3.0	85.3	2.5	1,150
Upper Iowa U	0.2	0.7	6.3	1.0	91.5	0.2	1,725
Vennard C	0.0	0.7	0.0	0.7	95.8	2.8	144
Waldorf C	0.0	0.6	2.3	0.2	94.0	3.0	529
Wartburg C	0.1	0.1	1.5	0.2	93.9	4.3	1,358
Wartburg Theological Sem ...	0.0	0.9	0.5	0.9	91.0	6.6	211
Western Iowa Tech CC	4.9	1.5	1.5	1.1	90.8	0.1	1,576
Westmar C	0.0	0.4	4.6	1.0	93.7	0.4	505
William Penn C	0.1	0.6	2.7	0.3	95.4	0.9	675

KANSAS

	American Indian	Asian	Black	Hispanic	White	Foreign	Total
Allen County CC	1.4	0.6	2.7	0.8	94.2	0.3	1,267
Baker U	0.1	0.5	3.1	0.6	93.9	1.8	873
Barton County CC	0.4	0.5	5.0	1.4	92.7	0.1	3,531
Benedictine C	0.4	0.5	3.1	3.3	90.9	1.8	735
Bethany C	0.3	0.3	3.2	1.4	92.4	2.4	715
Bethel C	0.2	1.1	5.6	1.1	87.2	4.8	623
Butler County CC	1.2	2.0	6.2	2.3	87.0	1.4	4,048
Central Baptist							
Theological Sem	2.1	0.7	25.5	1.4	69.5	0.7	141
Central C	0.8	1.5	12.5	5.3	79.6	0.4	265
Cloud County CC	0.4	0.6	1.8	0.9	96.2	0.1	2,128
Coffeyville CC	0.2	0.9	8.0	0.7	87.1	3.0	1,938
Colby CC	0.1	0.2	0.6	1.0	97.8	0.2	1,624
Cowley County CC	2.1	0.5	3.3	2.1	92.0	0.0	2,191
Dodge City CC	0,1	0.7	1.9	4.2	92.9	0.2	2,213
Donnelly C	0.9	4.9	51.7	7.9	16.2	18.4	445
Emporia St U	0.3	0.2	2.3	1.1	93.9	2.1	5,763

	American Indian	Asian	Black	Hispanic	White	Foreign	Total
Fort Hays St U	0.6%	1.2%	1.3%	1.0%	95.9%	0.0%	5,005
Fort Scott CC	0.9	0.4	3.7	0.3	94.7	0.1	1,379
Friends Bible C	1.0	1.0	1.0	3.8	89.4	3.8	104
Friends U	0.3	0.7	4.6	1.3	90.0	3.3	1,185
Garden City CC	0.6	2.8	5.4	9.3	81.6	0.4	1,117
Haskell Indian JC	100.0	0.0	0.0	0.0	0.0	0.0	842
Hesston C	0.4	1.5	2.9	1.7	86.2	7.3	521
Highland CC	1.6	0.2	3.3	0.9	94.0	0.0	1,861
Hutchinson CC	0.7	0.5	3.8	2.1	92.0	0.9	3,456
Independence CC	0.6	0.5	5.4	1.2	92.3	0.1	1,471
Johnson County CC	0.4	1.8	2.6	1.7	93.2	0.3	11,161
Kansas City C and Bible Sch .	0.0	2.2	11.1	4.4	82.2	0.0	90
Kansas City Kansas CC	0.6	1.3	18.3	3.6	76.1	0.0	4,167
Kansas C of Tech	0.1	0.5	1.2	1.1	96.9	0.1	737
Kansas Newman C	1.0	0.9	4.8	5.5	85.7	2.2	691
Kansas St U	0.3	0.9	2.9	1.8	88.0	6.1	19,301
Kansas Wesleyan	0.8	0.2	14.6	3.8	79.3	1.3	474
Labette CC	2.4	0.4	3.9	1.1	91.6	0.7	2,667
Marymount C	0.0	0.8	3.7	1.7	93.3	0.6	653
McPherson C	0.4	1.0	4.6	2.1	88.8	3.1	482
MidAmerica Nazarene C	0.4	1.0	1.6	1.3	91.7	3.9	1,112
National C	1.6	0.0	81.1	1.6	15.6	0.0	122
Neosho County CC	1.0	0.3	2.3	1.9	94.2	0.3	1,180
Ottawa U	1.5	0.8	7.3	2.9	79.1	8.4	521
Pittsburg St U	0.7	0.8	1.2	0.7	93.4	3.2	5,637
Pratt CC	0.1	0.0	3.2	1.5	94.9	0.3	984
Saint Mary C	3.4	1.0	24.9	5.2	63.7	1.9	1,066
Saint Mary of the Plains C ...	0.3	0.0	2.7	4.4	90.4	2.2	930
Seward County CC	0.7	1.2	2.2	3.4	92.5	0.1	1,370
Southwestern C	0.6	0.8	10.9	2.6	84.2	1.1	663
Tabor C	0.6	0.6	3.2	1.1	92.4	2.1	476
U of Kansas							
Main	0.6	1.6	2.6	1.4	86.9	7.0	26,020
Medical Center	0.4	4.7	1.8	2.4	89.6	1.2	2,383
Washburn U of Topeka	0.9	1.1	4.9	3.4	88.9	0.8	6,586
Wichita St U	0.9	3.4	4.7	2.2	84.0	4.7	16,673

KENTUCKY

	American Indian	Asian	Black	Hispanic	White	Foreign	Total
Alice Lloyd C	0.0	0.0	0.0	0.0	100.0	0.0	507
Asbury C	0.2	0.7	0.8	1.2	95.6	1.4	988
Asbury Theological Sem	0.3	0.6	0.6	0.4	92.9	5.3	717
Bellarmine C	0.0	0.1	1.6	0.2	97.6	0.4	3,343
Berea C	0.1	0.7	8.6	0.3	84.7	5.6	1,527
Brescia C	0.0	0.0	2.0	0.2	97.1	0.8	666
Campbellsville C	0.1	0.7	5.3	0.0	92.8	1.1	732
Centre C	0.0	1.4	1.2	0.0	96.9	0.6	860
Clear Creek Baptist Bible C...	0.0	0.0	0.6	1.2	98.2	0.0	168
Cumberland C	0.1	0.1	5.6	0.3	90.4	3.5	1,904
Eastern Kentucky U	0.1	0.3	5.9	0.2	92.4	1.0	13,635
Georgetown C	0.1	0.2	2.7	0.3	96.1	0.5	1,471
Inst of Electronic Tech	0.0	0.0	9.4	0.0	89.7	0.9	224
Kentucky Christian C	0.0	0.2	0.9	0.0	98.7	0.2	548
Kentucky St U	0.1	0.3	41.6	0.3	56.4	1.3	2,218
Kentucky Wesleyan C	0.0	0.4	4.3	0.0	94.4	0.9	765
Lees C	0.0	1.9	7.2	0.0	91.0	0.0	432
Lexington Theol Sem	0.0	0.0	5.5	0.0	92.2	2.3	128

KENTUCKY, cont.

	American Indian	Asian	Black	Hispanic	White	Foreign	Total
Lindsey Wilson C	0.0%	0.0%	4.2%	0.0%	95.3%	0.5%	1,059
Louisville Tech Inst	0.0	0.2	6.9	0.8	92.1	0.0	505
Mid-Continent Baptist Bible C	0.0	0.0	2.0	0.0	95.1	2.9	102
Midway C	0.0	0.0	2.0	0.5	93.7	3.8	396
Morehead St U	0.0	0.1	3.2	0.1	95.7	0.9	7,360
Murray St U	0.3	0.4	5.0	0.3	92.7	1.4	7,593
National Education Center Kentucky C of Tech	0.2	0.2	14.7	0.2	84.4	0.2	475
Northern Kentucky U	0.1	0.2	1.4	0.1	97.5	0.7	9,490
Owensboro JC of Business ..	0.0	0.0	5.0	0.0	95.0	0.0	318
Pikeville C	0.0	0.0	0.9	0.0	99.0	0.1	915
RETS Electronic Inst	1.4	0.1	10.3	0.1	88.0	0.1	740
Saint Catharine C	0.0	0.0	10.2	0.0	86.1	3.8	266
Spalding U	0.1	0.6	8.7	0.1	90.6	0.0	1,196
Sue Bennett C	0.0	0.4	1.5	0.2	97.8	0.2	551
Sullivan JC of Business	0.1	0.1	15.0	0.4	83.6	0.9	1,989
Thomas More C	0.4	0.2	1.8	0.3	97.1	0.3	1,097
Transylvania U	0.0	0.1	0.9	0.3	97.4	1.3	1,041
Union C	0.0	0.5	4.7	0.3	94.3	0.3	1,048
U of Kentucky	0.4	1.1	3.2	0.7	93.1	1.6	22,230
Ashland CC	0.7	0.3	0.8	0.2	98.0	0.0	2,609
Elizabethtown CC..........	0.7	1.1	6.0	1.4	90.7	0.1	2,710
Hazard CC	1.3	1.0	1.1	0.0	96.6	0.0	1,038
Henderson CC	0.0	0.3	4.4	0.2	95.0	0.0	1,239
Hopkinsville CC...........	0.6	1.6	13.7	2.9	81.2	0.0	1,741
Jefferson CC	0.4	0.6	12.7	0.3	85.7	0.3	8,197
Lexington CC	0.9	0.7	6.1	0.6	91.6	0.1	3,401
Madisonville CC	0.9	0.4	3.7	0.1	94.8	0.1	1,819
Maysville CC	0.2	0.1	2.0	0.1	97.6	0.0	870
Paducah CC	0.4	0.2	3.8	0.2	95.3	0.2	2,437
Prestonsburg CC	0.7	0.2	0.5	0.3	98.2	0.1	2,085
Somerset CC	1.3	0.5	0.5	0.1	97.5	0.1	1,583
Southeast CC	0.3	0.4	1.5	0.1	97.6	0.0	1,601
U of Louisville	0.3	1.8	8.4	0.9	87.1	1.6	21,313
Western Kentucky U	0.2	0.3	5.8	0.2	92.5	1.0	14,056

LOUISIANA

	American Indian	Asian	Black	Hispanic	White	Foreign	Total
Bossier Parish CC	0.0	0.6	11.1	1.6	86.7	0.0	2,221
Centenary C of Louisiana	0.3	0.5	6.3	0.5	91.4	1.1	1,110
Delgado CC	1.0	2.6	30.9	5.3	58.4	1.8	7,315
Dillard U	0.0	0.1	98.9	0.0	0.1	0.9	1,400
Grambling St U	0.0	0.1	94.1	0.1	3.8	1.9	6,003
Louisiana C	1.3	1.0	4.6	0.6	91.2	1.3	985
Louisiana St U Sys Louisiana St U and A&M C .	0.3	2.1	7.1	1.5	84.4	4.6	27,348
Alexandria	0.5	0.6	9.7	0.7	88.5	0.0	2,203
Eunice	0.3	0.2	13.6	0.5	85.2	0.2	1,723
Medical Center	0.2	4.2	8.4	2.5	82.2	2.4	2,415
Shreveport	0.6	1.4	8.5	0.7	88.7	0.2	4,499
U of New Orleans	0.2	2.5	15.2	4.7	75.3	2.0	16,076
Louisiana Tech U	0.2	0.8	12.3	0.9	83.1	2.7	10,044
Loyola U	0.4	1.9	11.6	5.7	77.9	2.5	4,961
McNeese St U	0.6	0.5	13.6	0.8	83.1	1.5	7,378
New Orleans Baptist Theological Sem	0.1	0.4	3.4	4.8	90.7	0.4	1,351
Nicholls St U	0.5	0.1	11.4	1.3	86.3	0.4	7,159

	American Indian	Asian	Black	Hispanic	White	Foreign	Total
Northeast Louisiana U	0.6%	1.0%	14.7%	0.2%	80.6%	2.9%	10,498
Northwest St U	1.1	1.3	20.4	2.2	74.4	0.6	6,455
Notre Dame Sem	0.0	24.2	4.2	3.2	68.4	0.0	95
Our Lady of Holy Cross C	0.8	1.5	26.2	2.5	68.8	0.2	848
Phillips JC	0.2	1.7	24.0	7.6	66.2	0.3	1,099
Saint Bernard Parish CC	0.7	1.0	2.1	2.7	93.6	0.0	828
Saint Joseph Sem C	0.0	9.6	2.6	6.1	81.6	0.0	114
Southeastern Louisiana U	0.3	0.5	6.6	0.7	91.0	0.9	8,520
Southern Tech C Lafayette ...	0.0	1.0	35.1	2.8	55.6	5.6	502
Southern Tech C Monroe	0.0	0.0	47.5	0.0	52.1	0.4	259
Southern U and A&M C Sys							
Baton Rouge	0.0	0.2	92.5	0.4	3.5	3.5	8,968
New Orleans	0.1	0.5	89.8	0.4	6.5	2.7	3,434
Shreveport	0.0	0.2	90.2	0.2	9.5	0.0	1,229
Tulane U	0.2	3.3	7.1	3.6	80.3	5.5	10,778
U of Southwestern Louisiana	0.2	1.2	16.4	0.7	74.8	6.7	15,033
Xavier U	0.1	0.4	90.5	0.5	4.9	3.5	2,528

MAINE

	American Indian	Asian	Black	Hispanic	White	Foreign	Total
Andover C	0.0	0.6	1.1	0.4	97.8	0.0	464
Bangor Theological Sem	0.0	0.0	0.0	0.0	99.0	1.0	104
Bates C	0.1	2.4	2.1	1.0	92.0	2.5	1,557
Beal C	0.0	0.4	0.0	0.0	98.6	1.1	279
Bowdoin C	0.1	2.5	2.9	1.7	91.2	1.5	1,426
Casco Bay C	0.0	0.0	0.4	0.0	99.6	0.0	253
Central Maine Medical							
Center Sch of Nursing	0.0	0.0	0.0	0.0	100.0	0.0	74
Central Maine Tech C	0.1	0.3	0.3	0.0	99.2	0.0	906
Colby C	0.1	1.3	1.2	0.8	94.6	2.0	1,736
C of the Atlantic	0.0	0.0	0.5	0.0	97.0	2.5	197
Husson C	0.6	0.8	1.3	0.4	95.6	1.3	1,789
Kennebec Valley Tech C	0.0	0.0	0.0	0.0	100.0	0.0	977
Maine Maritime Academy	0.6	1.2	1.2	0.6	89.2	7.3	507
Northern Maine Tech C	3.1	0.1	0.4	0.0	96.4	0.0	828
Portland Sch of Art	0.0	1.0	0.0	0.7	98.0	0.3	300
Saint Joseph's C	0.2	0.5	0.7	0.3	97.7	0.5	572
Southern Maine Tech C	0.4	0.7	0.1	0.3	98.5	0.0	1,907
Thomas C	0.0	0.0	0.1	0.2	99.2	0.5	1,013
Unity C	0.5	0.3	0.5	0.0	97.7	1.0	395
U of Maine Sys							
U of Maine	0.9	0.6	0.5	0.3	97.5	0.3	10,967
Augusta	0.0	0.1	0.1	0.0	99.7	0.1	3,853
Farmington	0.0	0.1	0.0	0.1	99.9	0.0	1,931
Fort Kent	0.3	0.0	0.8	0.2	98.7	0.0	620
Machias	2.8	0.0	0.5	0.1	94.9	1.6	851
Presque Isle	1.0	0.7	2.0	0.7	93.6	1.9	1,398
U of Southern Maine	0.4	0.1	0.0	0.1	99.4	0.0	10,071
U of New England	0.1	1.2	1.5	0.2	96.6	0.4	1,071
Westbrook C	0.0	0.9	1.0	0.4	97.0	0.6	677

MARYLAND

	American Indian	Asian	Black	Hispanic	White	Foreign	Total
Allegany CC	0.1	0.2	2.0	0.1	97.6	0.0	2,220
Anne Arundel CC	0.4	1.4	7.8	1.2	88.8	0.4	11,664
Baltimore Hebrew U	0.0	0.0	0.0	0.0	100.0	0.0	231

MARYLAND, cont.

	American Indian	Asian	Black	Hispanic	White	Foreign	Total
Baltimore International Culinary C	0.3%	2.7%	18.4%	3.6%	75.0%	0.0%	332
Capitol C	0.1	11.7	15.6	2.3	66.6	3.7	778
Catonsville CC	0.2	2.1	14.0	0.7	82.7	0.3	11,444
Cecil CC	0.7	0.6	3.5	0.3	94.5	0.3	1,447
Charles County CC	0.4	0.9	8.2	0.9	89.5	0.1	4,966
Chesapeake C	0.0	0.4	11.1	0.3	88.2	0.0	2,247
C of Notre Dame of Maryland	0.0	0.9	13.4	1.9	82.5	1.4	2,461
Columbia Union C	0.1	6.3	33.5	4.3	55.8	0.0	1,096
CC of Baltimore	0.6	1.3	71.0	1.0	24.1	2.0	4,487
Dundalk CC	0.4	1.4	10.8	0.7	86.7	0.0	3,206
Eastern Christian C	0.0	0.0	8.1	0.0	89.2	2.7	37
Essex CC	0.4	1.4	6.5	0.7	91.0	0.0	10,218
Frederick CC	0.2	0.8	3.4	0.8	93.9	0.9	3,470
Garrett CC	0.0	0.0	1.6	0.3	98.0	0.0	612
Goucher C	0.2	4.5	4.3	2.7	86.9	1.4	974
Hagerstown Business C	0.0	0.0	1.3	0.0	98.7	0.0	463
Hagerstown JC	0.4	0.5	6.4	0.8	92.0	0.0	2,641
Harford CC	0.6	1.5	6.5	0.8	90.6	0.0	4,454
Hood C	0.1	2.2	5.5	3.2	86.8	2.2	1,859
Howard CC	0.2	3.2	13.1	1.1	81.8	0.5	3,925
Johns Hopkins U	0.2	5.9	4.7	1.4	80.8	7.0	12,647
Loyola C	0.1	2.0	3.1	1.1	92.6	1.1	5,821
Maryland C of Art and Design	1.2	3.7	20.0	5.0	70.0	0.0	80
Maryland Inst C of Art	0.4	3.5	6.5	2.1	85.0	2.5	1,285
Montgomery C							
Germantown	0.4	4.3	5.8	2.3	86.8	0.5	3,124
Rockville	0.4	9.8	9.0	5.8	72.3	2.8	14,113
Takoma Park	0.3	8.2	33.9	5.6	47.9	4.1	4,328
Morgan St U	0.2	0.4	91.7	0.4	3.0	4.4	4,066
Mount Saint Mary's C	0.1	0.4	3.4	0.7	95.4	0.1	1,783
Ner Israel Rabbinical C	0.0	0.0	0.0	0.0	95.2	4.8	352
Peabody Inst of Johns Hopkins U	0.0	4.8	4.5	1.3	73.7	15.8	463
Prince Georges CC	0.4	4.1	44.1	2.0	48.4	1.0	13,443
Saint John's C	0.0	2.1	1.9	1.1	93.4	1.5	467
Saint Mary's C of Maryland	0.3	1.5	5.6	1.8	90.5	0.4	1,585
Saint Mary's Sem and U	0.0	0.0	1.7	0.0	98.0	0.3	297
Sojourner-Douglass C	0.0	0.0	98.3	0.0	1.7	0.0	353
Uniformed Services U of the Health Sciences	0.3	7.7	2.7	1.8	84.8	2.7	943
U S Naval Academy	0.6	4.5	5.5	5.4	83.3	0.7	4,557
U of Maryland Sys							
Baltimore	0.3	6.7	10.6	1.7	78.1	2.7	4,563
Baltimore County	0.2	7.2	12.0	1.2	77.2	2.3	9,868
C Park	0.2	7.4	8.6	2.4	75.1	6.3	36,681
Eastern Shore	0.3	1.2	71.4	0.7	21.4	5.1	1,559
U C	0.6	6.3	18.3	2.9	71.6	0.4	14,263
Bowie St U	0.2	1.9	64.0	0.5	32.2	1.1	3,325
Coppin St C	0.3	2.0	90.0	0.1	4.7	2.9	2,246
Frostburg St U	0.2	0.6	6.5	0.6	92.0	0.1	4,525
Salisbury St U	0.1	0.8	6.8	0.4	91.6	0.4	5,260
Towson St U	0.2	1.7	8.2	0.9	87.5	1.4	15,169
U of Baltimore	0.2	1.6	14.5	0.9	80.9	1.9	5,228
Villa Julie C	0.0	0.8	15.9	0.6	82.7	0.0	1,271
Washington Bible C	0.0	9.6	24.9	1.6	54.9	8.9	437
Washington C	0.0	0.9	1.2	0.9	95.2	1.7	988

	American Indian	Asian	Black	Hispanic	White	Foreign	Total
Washington Theological Union	0.0%	1.4%	1.8%	3.9%	92.9%	0.0%	280
Western Maryland C	0.0	0.8	2.2	0.6	95.2	1.1	2,002
Wor-Wic Tech CC	0.0	0.2	20.8	0.4	78.6	0.0	1,032

MASSACHUSETTS

	American Indian	Asian	Black	Hispanic	White	Foreign	Total
American International C	0.0	1.1	9.3	1.7	84.3	3.7	1,869
Amherst C	0.2	6.8	5.3	4.4	81.0	2.3	1,592
Andover Newton Theological Sch	0.0	0.2	4.8	2.1	88.6	4.3	421
Anna Maria C	0.0	0.4	1.9	0.9	94.1	2.7	1,180
Aquinas JC							
Milton	0.0	0.0	1.4	0.8	97.8	0.0	359
Newton	0.0	0.0	0.4	0.0	99.6	0.0	262
Arthur D Little Management Education Inst	0.0	0.0	0.0	1.9	5.8	92.3	52
Assumption C	0.1	0.1	1.1	2.1	96.0	0.6	2,904
Atlantic Union C	0.1	0.3	18.4	12.6	52.8	15.8	795
Babson C	0.1	0.8	0.8	1.5	91.7	5.0	2,971
Bay Path JC	0.5	1.2	2.8	2.8	92.6	0.2	579
Bay St JC of Business	0.0	0.5	7.0	2.4	89.4	0.8	631
Becker JC							
Leicester	0.0	4.0	1.5	1.5	90.9	2.1	529
Worcester	0.0	0.1	3.2	0.3	95.4	0.9	965
Bentley C	0.2	1.9	1.5	2.2	90.9	3.3	7,151
Berklee C of Music	0.1	1.6	4.7	3.1	68.7	21.8	2,830
Boston Architectural Center	1.8	2.1	1.8	2.3	92.0	0.0	661
Boston C	0.2	4.7	3.2	4.2	84.4	3.3	14,594
Boston Conservatory	0.0	0.7	3.2	2.3	89.0	4.8	435
Boston U	0.2	6.4	3.0	2.7	75.2	12.6	28,555
Bradford C	0.5	0.5	3.5	2.3	86.0	7.2	428
Brandeis U	0.0	4.0	3.0	1.9	82.2	9.0	3,755
Cambridge C	0.4	0.6	20.1	5.7	72.7	0.4	472
Catherine Laboure C	0.0	1.0	14.9	1.0	83.1	0.0	302
Central New England C of Tech	0.2	2.0	0.5	0.5	96.1	0.7	562
Clark U	0.2	2.7	2.1	2.2	83.2	9.6	3,350
C of the Holy Cross	0.0	0.8	3.6	1.9	93.5	0.2	2,647
C of Our Lady of the Elms	0.0	1.3	3.8	3.4	91.0	0.6	1,065
Conway Sch of Landscape Design	0.0	0.0	0.0	0.0	100.0	0.0	17
Curry C	0.1	0.2	3.1	1.3	94.2	1.2	1,270
Dean JC	0.0	0.4	0.4	0.3	98.3	0.7	2,538
Eastern Nazarene C	0.3	1.0	6.0	3.8	86.5	2.3	979
Emerson C	0.2	1.0	3.0	1.6	91.9	2.2	2,668
Emmanuel C	0.1	1.0	7.5	3.9	83.6	3.9	977
Endicott C	0.2	0.4	1.1	1.3	90.3	6.8	843
Episcopal Divinity Sch	0.8	1.7	2.5	2.5	81.7	10.8	120
Fisher C	0.4	1.0	7.5	1.7	88.5	0.9	2,115
Forsyth Sch of Dental Hygienists	0.0	5.1	1.7	0.8	91.5	0.8	118
Franklin Inst of Boston	0.2	7.1	10.7	4.2	77.0	0.9	553
Gordon C	0.2	1.2	2.2	0.7	93.7	2.1	1,184
Gordon-Conwell Theol Sem	0.0	2.6	17.3	9.1	68.1	2.9	717
Hampshire C	0.1	2.1	2.6	1.7	88.2	5.3	1,282
Harvard U	0.4	6.1	4.9	3.7	75.0	9.8	24,194

	American Indian	Asian	Black	Hispanic	White	Foreign	Total
Hebrew C	0.0%	0.0%	0.0%	0.0%	88.5%	11.5%	78
Hellenic C-Holy Cross Greek Orthodox Sch of Theology .	0.0	0.8	0.0	0.0	81.1	18.2	132
Lasell JC	0.0	1.4	1.6	2.3	89.8	5.0	441
Lesley C	0.2	1.0	3.0	1.9	92.1	1.7	4,460
Marian Court JC	0.0	0.6	1.8	3.0	94.5	0.0	165
Mass Bd of Regents Sys Southeastern Mass U	0.2	1.3	1.9	0.8	94.0	1.8	7,589
U of Lowell	0.2	4.7	1.9	1.2	88.4	3.6	14,493
U of Mass Amherst	0.3	2.1	3.1	2.8	85.0	6.7	27,918
U of Mass Boston	0.4	4.4	8.6	2.9	81.0	2.7	13,666
U of Mass Medical Sch Worcester	0.7	5.6	2.9	2.7	88.2	0.0	449
Bridgewater St C	0.2	0.5	1.4	0.6	97.2	0.2	8,962
Fitchburg St C	0.0	1.0	2.5	1.0	95.3	0.1	6,224
Framingham St C	0.3	0.7	1.8	1.0	95.8	0.5	6,677
Massachusetts C of Art	0.3	2.4	2.3	1.5	90.7	2.7	2,371
Mass Maritime Acad	0.2	0.7	2.7	6.6	89.9	0.0	602
North Adams St C	0.0	0.3	2.3	0.6	96.5	0.3	2,743
Salem St C	0.4	0.7	2.5	1.3	94.4	0.7	9,565
Westfield St C	0.3	0.4	2.2	1.1	95.9	0.1	5,106
Worcester St C	0.5	0.7	1.4	1.1	95.1	1.2	6,435
Berkshire CC	0.2	0.5	0.6	0.4	96.5	1.8	3,158
Bristol CC	0.7	1.1	2.7	1.0	93.7	0.8	4,699
Bunker Hill CC	0.4	11.6	13.9	6.8	62.3	4.9	6,456
Cape Cod CC	0.4	0.2	0.8	0.9	97.5	0.1	4,991
Greenfield CC	0.0	0.9	1.0	1.3	95.9	0.9	2,231
Holyoke CC	0.5	0.3	2.3	5.1	91.2	0.5	5,283
Massachusetts Bay CC	0.2	1.8	5.6	2.2	87.8	2.3	4,125
Massasoit CC	0.3	1.1	4.6	1.0	92.8	0.3	6,591
Middlesex CC	0.6	3.8	1.3	3.1	91.0	0.2	6,469
Mount Wachusett CC	0.2	0.2	1.4	1.8	95.8	0.5	3,793
North Shore CC	0.2	2.1	4.9	4.8	87.1	0.9	5,810
Northern Essex CC	0.5	1.4	0.3	11.6	85.6	0.6	6,349
Quinsigamond CC	0.5	1.7	3.2	5.7	88.8	0.2	4,411
Roxbury CC	0.2	7.1	62.8	12.3	17.1	0.5	2,467
Springfield Tech CC	0.2	0.8	9.8	6.3	82.3	0.6	5,941
Mass C of Pharmacy & Allied Health Sciences	0.9	6.9	3.7	5.5	70.4	12.6	1,073
MGH Inst of Health Professions	0.0	3.6	1.0	0.0	94.9	0.5	197
Mass Inst of Tech	0.3	9.7	3.5	3.7	62.0	20.9	9,500
Massachusetts Sch of Professional Psychology ...	0.0	0.0	1.2	0.0	97.6	1.2	169
Merrimack C	0.2	1.7	1.5	1.4	92.3	2.9	3,483
Montserrat C of Art	0.0	0.9	2.3	0.0	96.7	0.0	215
Mount Holyoke C	0.2	4.8	4.2	1.9	81.6	7.2	1,987
Mount Ida C	1.0	1.4	6.4	2.5	79.6	9.0	1,537
New England C of Optometry	0.0	6.4	3.5	4.8	77.6	7.7	375
New England Conservatory of Music	0.4	2.9	2.4	4.0	69.0	21.3	755
New England Inst of Applied Arts and Sciences	0.0	0.0	2.0	0.0	96.9	1.0	98
New England Sch of Law	0.1	0.5	1.4	1.4	96.6	0.0	1,192
Newbury C	0.0	3.4	20.3	18.7	54.9	2.8	3,385
Nichols C	0.0	0.4	0.4	0.4	98.2	0.6	1,489
Northeastern U	0.5	3.7	5.6	1.7	85.1	3.4	32,385

	American Indian	Asian	Black	Hispanic	White	Foreign	Total
Pine Manor C	0.0%	2.6%	2.2%	4.5%	79.1%	11.6%	646
Quincy JC	0.3	1.9	4.9	0.8	88.3	3.8	2,644
Radcliffe C	0.3	12.2	9.6	5.4	66.7	5.8	2,691
Regis C	0.2	0.5	1.0	4.5	89.3	4.6	1,005
Saint Hyacinth C and Sem	0.0	0.0	3.3	0.0	90.0	6.7	30
Saint John's Sem	0.0	6.0	1.3	3.3	84.1	5.3	151
Sch of the Museum of Fine Arts Boston	0.1	3.2	0.9	0.9	91.7	3.2	1,371
Simmons C	0.1	1.6	2.9	1.6	90.2	3.6	2,878
Simon's Rock of Bard C	0.0	6.3	6.3	2.5	81.9	2.9	315
Smith C	0.2	7.0	3.2	2.0	80.7	6.9	3,039
Springfield C	0.0	0.1	2.4	0.7	94.6	2.2	3,204
Stonehill C	0.0	0.2	0.4	0.3	98.6	0.4	3,054
Suffolk U	0.1	1.7	3.6	1.3	89.2	4.1	5,390
Tufts U	0.1	5.9	2.9	2.4	80.3	8.4	8,013
Wellesley C	0.3	14.6	6.1	3.8	71.3	4.0	2,237
Wentworth Inst of Tech	0.2	4.1	6.1	2.0	81.4	6.2	3,861
Western New England C	0.2	0.7	2.7	1.3	93.8	1.3	5,182
Weston Sch of Theology	0.0	0.0	0.0	0.0	90.3	9.7	186
Wheaton C	0.2	1.7	3.1	1.6	87.5	5.9	1,161
Wheelock C	0.4	0.6	7.4	2.6	88.1	0.8	1,648
Williams C	0.0	6.6	6.6	3.5	79.9	3.4	2,076
Worcester Polytechnic Inst	0.0	3.5	0.5	0.6	86.5	8.8	3,767
Worcester JC	0.2	1.5	1.2	1.1	94.9	1.0	1,325

MICHIGAN

	American Indian	Asian	Black	Hispanic	White	Foreign	Total
Adrian C	0.6	1.1	3.5	1.3	91.7	1.9	1,229
Albion C	0.0	1.7	2.4	0.2	94.9	0.8	1,652
Alma C	0.1	0.4	1.2	0.7	97.2	0.4	1,198
Alpena CC	0.1	0.4	2.4	0.5	96.5	0.2	2,281
Andrews U	0.6	5.4	15.1	6.4	57.2	15.4	2,858
Aquinas C	0.3	1.0	4.1	1.1	92.7	0.8	2,532
Baker C Owosso	0.7	0.4	0.4	1.4	97.0	0.0	900
Baker C Flint	0.6	1.3	13.5	0.6	84.1	0.0	2,654
Bay De Noc CC	2.6	0.0	0.0	0.2	97.1	0.0	2,171
Calvin C	0.1	0.9	1.0	0.4	89.1	8.4	4,448
Calvin Theological Sem	1.3	7.1	1.3	3.4	56.7	30.3	238
Center for Creative Studies C of Art and Design	0.2	1.4	6.4	1.1	89.2	1.7	1,114
Center for Humanistic Studies	1.4	0.0	5.6	0.0	93.0	0.0	71
Central Michigan U	0.5	0.4	2.1	0.8	95.1	1.1	19,024
Charles S Mott CC	1.2	0.4	14.3	1.9	82.1	0.1	10,516
Cleary C	0.2	1.9	5.3	2.1	89.9	0.6	1,003
Concordia C	0.2	0.9	6.9	0.0	90.6	1.3	533
Cranbrook Academy of Art	0.0	2.2	1.5	0.0	91.0	5.2	134
Davenport C Grand Rapids	0.3	0.3	3.9	0.7	94.8	0.0	3,232
Davenport C Kalamazoo	0.3	0.6	9.5	0.8	88.8	0.0	1,009
Davenport C Lansing	0.7	2.6	13.4	15.0	68.3	0.0	1,287
Delta C	0.3	0.5	5.7	3.1	90.3	0.1	9,651
Detroit C of Business Dearborn	0.4	0.6	45.8	3.0	50.1	0.2	2,331
Detroit C of Business Madison Heights	0.0	0.3	30.3	0.6	68.7	0.0	630
Detroit C of Business Flint	0.0	0.1	47.5	0.1	52.3	0.0	1,100
Detroit C of Law	0.3	1.4	11.3	0.8	85.2	1.0	711
Eastern Michigan U	0.3	1.1	6.8	1.3	86.5	4.0	23,060

MICHIGAN, cont.

	American Indian	Asian	Black	Hispanic	White	Foreign	Total
Ferris St U	0.4%	0.5%	3.9%	0.7%	93.1%	1.5%	11,762
GMI Engineering and Management Inst	0.3	5.0	5.5	1.3	79.9	8.0	3,068
Glen Oaks CC	0.2	0.4	1.3	0.4	97.5	0.1	1,370
Gogebic CC	1.7	0.3	0.6	0.0	97.5	0.0	1,178
Grace Bible C	1.5	0.0	2.3	3.1	89.3	3.8	131
Grand Rapids Baptist C and Sem	0.1	0.2	1.3	0.2	97.1	1.1	929
Grand Rapids JC	0.9	1.3	6.4	1.6	89.6	0.2	10,634
Grand Valley St U	0.3	0.8	2.9	1.1	94.7	0.3	9,768
Great Lakes Bible C	0.0	0.8	0.0	0.0	99.2	0.0	123
Great Lakes JC of Business	0.3	0.3	12.6	4.8	81.9	0.0	1,756
Henry Ford CC	0.5	1.4	13.3	2.1	82.6	0.1	15,791
Highland Park CC	1.6	0.0	98.2	0.0	0.2	0.0	2,342
Hillsdale C	0.0	0.0	1.1	0.0	97.4	1.5	1,071
Hope C	0.4	0.9	0.9	1.0	94.4	2.5	2,781
Jackson CC	0.6	0.7	11.3	1.5	85.6	0.2	5,782
Jordan C	0.4	0.2	58.3	0.7	40.3	0.0	2,271
Kalamazoo C	0.2	4.7	1.8	0.7	87.8	4.9	1,255
Kalamazoo Valley CC	1.0	0.8	7.4	1.2	88.2	1.5	9,161
Kellogg CC	0.4	0.8	6.7	1.0	90.1	1.0	4,478
Kendall C of Art and Design	0.7	0.7	2.7	2.0	91.8	2.2	744
Kirtland CC	0.6	0.2	5.1	0.4	93.6	0.0	1,146
Lake Michigan C	0.7	0.9	12.7	0.9	84.7	0.2	3,020
Lake Superior St U	4.8	0.3	1.3	0.4	70.9	22.3	3,155
Lansing CC	0.7	1.5	6.2	2.3	88.4	0.9	21,470
Lawrence Tech U	0.6	1.7	7.3	1.3	86.8	2.3	5,443
Lewis C of Business	0.0	0.0	99.0	0.0	1.0	0.0	291
Macomb CC	0.4	1.0	1.5	0.6	96.3	0.3	31,462
Madonna C	0.4	0.6	7.6	1.5	88.1	1.8	3,950
Marygrove C	0.4	0.0	70.7	0.5	26.6	1.8	1,205
Mercy C of Detroit	0.2	1.3	37.5	1.3	59.4	0.4	2,362
Michigan Christian C	0.4	0.8	19.2	1.9	74.1	3.8	266
Michigan St U	0.3	1.8	6.1	1.4	85.3	5.1	44,480
Michigan Tech U	0.5	1.4	0.6	0.5	92.2	4.8	6,502
Mid Michigan CC	0.6	0.2	0.4	0.5	97.4	0.8	1,910
Monroe County CC	0.2	0.4	1.1	0.8	97.2	0.2	3,083
Montcalm CC	0.7	0.6	10.0	2.4	86.3	0.0	1,918
Muskegon C	0.1	0.1	8.0	1.6	90.2	0.0	1,741
Muskegon CC	2.9	0.3	7.4	1.8	87.5	0.1	4,941
Nazareth C	0.0	1.0	5.6	1.2	92.2	0.0	730
Northern Michigan U	1.6	0.4	2.2	0.6	94.7	0.5	8,185
Northwestern Michigan C	1.9	0.4	0.3	0.5	96.9	0.1	4,307
Northwood Inst	0.7	0.2	7.4	0.0	76.6	15.1	1,809
Oakland CC	0.5	1.4	9.5	1.5	86.7	0.3	26,854
Oakland U	0.2	1.9	5.2	1.0	90.9	0.9	12,254
Olivet C	0.0	0.6	9.1	0.8	89.5	0.0	783
Reformed Bible C	1.1	3.7	0.0	2.1	61.7	31.4	188
Sacred Heart Major Sem	0.0	0.0	9.1	4.6	86.3	0.0	197
Saginaw Valley St U	0.5	0.7	5.5	2.7	90.1	0.6	5,850
Saint Clair County CC	0.2	0.1	1.5	1.2	96.3	0.7	4,064
Saint Mary's C	0.4	5.8	3.9	1.5	85.7	2.7	259
Schoolcraft C	0.2	0.9	3.5	0.6	94.2	0.6	8,499
Siena Heights C	0.1	0.5	6.5	4.0	87.6	1.3	1,667
Southwestern Michigan C	0.7	0.5	6.3	1.0	89.3	2.2	2,492
Spring Arbor C	0.2	0.7	14.4	0.8	82.3	1.7	1,319
Thomas M Cooley Law Sch	0.0	1.4	3.7	3.0	91.2	0.6	1,254

	American Indian	Asian	Black	Hispanic	White	Foreign	Total
U of Detroit	0.4%	1.8%	18.3%	1.1%	73.1%	5.3%	6,021
U of Michigan							
Ann Arbor	0.4	5.8	5.8	2.3	78.8	6.9	36,001
Dearborn	0.6	3.3	5.7	1.9	88.1	0.5	7,494
Flint	1.0	1.1	8.3	1.2	88.4	0.0	6,310
Walsh C of Accountancy							
and Business Admin	0.3	1.7	4.3	0.5	92.9	0.3	2,663
Washtenaw CC	0.9	2.8	11.4	1.2	83.4	0.3	9,523
Wayne County CC	0.8	1.2	64.7	2.1	29.6	1.6	12,098
Wayne St U	0.6	3.5	21.9	1.6	67.8	4.6	30,751
West Shore CC	0.7	0.3	1.1	1.1	96.8	0.0	1,186
Western Michigan U..........	0.3	0.6	4.6	0.7	90.1	3.7	24,861
Western Theological Sem	0.0	0.7	1.4	0.7	91.4	5.7	140
William Tyndale C	0.2	1.2	30.4	0.5	67.2	0.5	418
Yeshiva Gedolah							
Rabbinical C	0.0	0.0	0.0	0.0	100.0	0.0	43

MINNESOTA

	American Indian	Asian	Black	Hispanic	White	Foreign	Total
Alexandria Tech Inst	0.7	0.2	0.0	0.3	98.8	0.1	1,674
Augsburg C	1.7	1.9	3.3	0.4	89.9	2.7	2,506
Bethany Lutheran C	0.3	0.3	2.2	0.0	95.5	1.6	312
Bethel C	0.2	0.7	0.8	0.2	98.1	0.0	1,800
Bethel Theological Sem	0.4	2.8	3.0	0.6	90.0	3.2	501
Carleton C	0.4	5.6	3.3	2.5	87.5	0.7	1,897
C of Saint Benedict	0.1	1.1	0.2	0.6	96.8	1.3	1,961
C of Saint Catherine	0.6	1.2	0.9	1.3	93.4	2.5	2,727
C of Saint Catherine							
Saint Mary's campus	1.1	0.6	6.3	0.7	90.9	0.4	536
C of Saint Scholastica	1.9	0.4	0.3	0.2	96.6	0.6	1,849
C of Saint Teresa	0.4	0.8	0.8	2.0	96.0	0.0	249
C of Saint Thomas	0.3	1.2	1.0	0.5	96.3	0.8	8,810
Concordia C Moorhead	0.7	0.8	0.2	0.3	95.2	2.8	2,880
Concordia C Saint Paul	0.3	4.2	3.2	0.0	91.5	0.8	1,133
Dakota County Tech Inst	0.2	1.3	0.4	0.4	97.8	0.0	1,613
Dr Martin Luther C	0.4	0.0	1.3	0.0	98.2	0.0	447
Gustavus Adolphus C	0.1	0.3	1.2	0.1	96.5	1.8	2,451
Hamline U	0.1	1.8	2.1	0.6	94.2	1.3	2,223
Luther Northwestern							
Theological Sem	0.4	1.4	1.2	0.6	94.5	1.9	724
Macalester C	0.9	2.2	3.2	1.5	84.1	8.1	1,847
Mayo Foundation							
Grad Sch of Medicine	0.4	3.7	2.4	1.4	75.2	16.9	1,105
Medical Sch	1.9	7.0	1.3	1.9	87.9	0.0	157
Medical Inst of Minnesota	0.8	5.0	3.7	1.7	88.7	0.0	240
Minneapolis C of Art and							
Design	0.7	2.8	2.1	1.3	92.1	1.0	713
Minnesota Bible C	0.0	2.2	0.0	0.0	94.4	3.3	90
Minnesota CC Sys							
Anoka-Ramsey CC	0.6	0.5	0.3	0.3	98.3	0.1	5,844
Arrowhead CC Region							
Hibbing CC	1.3	0.0	0.4	0.0	98.3	0.0	1,345
Itasca CC	7.8	0.0	0.8	0.1	91.2	0.2	1,245
Mesabi CC	4.5	0.1	1.2	0.1	93.8	0.3	1,481
Rainy River CC	15.2	0.2	0.7	0.2	82.7	1.1	613
Vermilion CC	1.6	0.2	0.3	0.5	97.4	0.0	576
Austin CC	0.1	0.3	0.3	0.2	98.2	0.9	1,196

	American Indian	Asian	Black	Hispanic	White	Foreign	Total
Minnesota CC Sys							
Brainerd CC	2.6%	0.5%	0.5%	0.1%	96.0%	0.3%	1,526
Fergus Falls CC	0.2	0.0	0.4	0.1	99.0	0.4	1,090
Inver Hills CC	0.1	1.1	1.5	0.6	96.6	0.1	4,853
Lakewood CC	0.2	2.3	0.7	0.7	96.0	0.1	5,277
Minneapolis CC	2.7	2.6	13.5	1.2	75.5	4.5	3,266
Normandale CC	0.1	1.4	0.7	0.2	96.9	0.6	8,560
North Hennepin CC	0.3	0.4	1.1	0.4	96.1	1.7	5,498
Northland CC	7.4	0.1	0.9	0.3	91.4	0.0	1,033
Rochester CC	0.4	2.2	0.6	0.4	95.8	0.6	3,839
Willmar CC	0.3	0.3	0.2	0.8	98.4	0.1	1,325
Worthington CC	0.5	1.1	1.1	0.2	96.4	0.8	854
National C at Saint Paul	1.5	12.3	4.5	6.3	68.8	6.6	333
National Education Center							
Brown Inst	1.3	5.2	4.1	1.0	87.7	0.7	1,655
North Central Bible C	0.5	1.0	2.6	1.0	92.6	2.4	1,146
Northwestern C	0.2	0.6	1.6	0.4	96.4	0.7	973
Northwestern C of							
Chiropractic	0.0	0.7	0.2	0.9	93.3	4.9	569
Oak Hills Bible C	0.0	0.0	0.0	0.8	99.2	0.0	129
Pillsbury Baptist Bible C	0.5	0.0	1.3	1.8	94.9	1.5	391
Rasmussen Business C	0.2	0.0	1.4	0.5	97.7	0.2	427
Saint John's U	0.3	1.0	0.8	0.7	95.1	2.2	1,998
Saint Mary's C	0.8	0.8	1.1	0.7	95.2	1.4	1,938
Saint Olaf C	0.2	1.8	0.5	0.4	95.5	1.6	3,118
Saint Paul Bible C	0.2	7.4	0.4	0.2	91.1	0.8	526
Saint Paul Tech Inst	1.4	1.1	1.2	0.7	95.1	0.5	1,678
Sch of the Associated Arts ...	0.7	1.5	1.5	0.0	96.3	0.0	134
St U Sys							
Bemidji St U	3.8	0.0	0.3	0.3	94.6	0.9	4,996
Mankato St U	0.2	1.0	0.7	0.4	95.9	1.9	15,944
Metropolitan St U	0.7	0.9	3.3	0.9	94.2	0.0	5,799
Moorhead St U	0.6	0.6	0.3	0.3	97.1	1.2	8,103
Saint Cloud St U	0.3	0.7	0.7	0.3	97.3	0.7	16,252
Southwest St U	0.1	0.2	1.3	0.0	97.4	1.0	2,475
Winona St U	0.5	0.9	0.6	0.4	95.1	2.5	7,079
U of Minnesota							
Crookston	0.5	0.2	0.2	1.0	97.4	0.7	1,221
Duluth	1.0	0.7	0.7	0.3	96.2	1.2	9,523
Morris	2.0	1.7	2.0	1.0	92.9	0.5	2,178
Twin Cities	0.5	3.0	1.6	1.0	90.0	4.1	61,556
Waseca	0.1	0.2	0.2	0.0	99.1	0.4	1,169
United Theological Sem							
of the Twin Cities	1.0	1.4	1.4	1.0	93.7	1.4	207
William Mitchell C of Law	0.6	1.2	2.2	1.2	94.8	0.0	1,089

MISSISSIPPI

Alcorn St U	0.0	0.4	91.6	0.2	7.8	0.0	2,757
Belhaven C	0.1	0.3	7.1	1.0	88.2	3.3	693
Blue Mountain C	0.0	0.3	7.5	0.3	91.6	0.3	332
Clarke C	0.0	0.0	22.4	0.0	77.6	0.0	116
Coahoma CC	0.0	0.0	98.6	1.4	0.0	0.0	1,407
Copiah-Lincoln CC	0.4	0.4	25.2	0.4	73.6	0.1	1,382
Delta St U	0.1	0.5	19.5	0.1	79.8	0.0	3,672
East Central JC	2.7	0.0	5.7	0.0	91.6	0.0	3,624
East Mississippi CC	0.1	0.1	36.5	0.1	63.2	0.0	896

	American Indian	Asian	Black	Hispanic	White	Foreign	Total
Hinds CC Raymond	0.1%	0.4%	35.3%	0.2%	63.9%	0.2%	8,228
Holmes JC	0.0	0.1	19.9	0.1	79.7	0.2	1,827
Itawamba CC	0.0	0.1	16.1	0.0	83.6	0.2	2,633
Jackson St U	0.1	0.4	93.0	0.1	3.5	2.9	6,777
Jones County JC	0.3	0.1	18.5	0.2	80.9	0.0	3,252
Mary Holmes C	0.0	0.0	99.2	0.0	0.2	0.6	519
Meridian CC	1.5	0.8	25.3	0.6	71.6	0.1	2,844
Millsaps C	0.0	1.8	4.8	0.6	91.9	0.8	1,445
Mississippi C	0.1	0.5	11.8	0.4	86.9	0.3	3,540
Mississippi Delta JC	0.1	0.4	41.9	0.2	57.5	0.0	1,712
Mississippi Gulf Coast JC	0.8	1.0	13.7	0.9	82.7	0.9	8,393
Mississippi St U	0.2	1.2	11.1	0.2	82.8	4.5	12,407
Mississippi U for Women	0.3	0.3	17.8	0.2	81.3	0.0	2,063
Mississippi Valley St U	0.0	0.0	99.3	0.0	0.7	0.0	1,756
Northeast Mississippi JC	0.0	0.1	11.2	0.0	88.7	0.0	2,735
Northwest Mississippi JC	0.0	0.1	24.2	0.1	75.6	0.0	3,619
Pearl River JC	0.2	0.1	16.1	0.1	83.5	0.0	2,336
Phillips JC Gulfport	0.0	0.5	21.6	0.1	77.7	0.0	772
Phillips JC Jackson	0.1	0.0	43.4	0.0	56.4	0.0	677
Prentiss Normal and							
Industrial Inst	0.0	0.0	100.0	0.0	0.0	0.0	47
Reformed Theological Sem ..	0.3	1.1	0.8	0.6	86.0	11.3	363
Rust C	0.0	0.0	96.1	0.0	2.8	1.1	925
Southeastern Baptist C	0.0	0.0	5.1	0.0	94.9	0.0	79
Southwest Mississippi JC	0.0	0.0	20.9	0.0	79.1	0.0	1,353
Tougaloo C	0.0	0.0	99.7	0.0	0.3	0.0	794
U of Mississippi Main	0.1	0.5	6.6	0.2	87.6	5.1	9,927
U of Mississippi Medical Ctr ..	0.1	2.0	10.8	0.5	83.5	3.1	1,404
U of Southern Mississippi	0.3	0.7	13.4	0.4	83.2	2.1	12,581
Wesley Biblical Sem	0.0	0.0	10.7	0.0	83.9	5.4	56
Wesley C	1.8	0.0	5.4	0.0	92.9	0.0	56
William Carey C	0.2	0.2	18.7	0.6	79.1	1.2	1,931
Wood JC	0.0	0.0	10.5	0.0	88.3	1.2	486

MISSOURI

	American Indian	Asian	Black	Hispanic	White	Foreign	Total
Aquinas Inst of Theology	0.0	0.0	0.9	0.9	98.1	0.0	107
Assemblies of God Theol							
Sem	0.3	1.3	1.7	2.7	91.6	2.3	298
Avila C	0.7	1.5	8.5	2.0	87.4	0.0	1,585
Baptist Bible C	0.1	0.4	0.4	0.8	97.3	1.0	781
Calvary Bible C	0.0	1.6	4.7	0.6	90.5	2.5	317
Central Bible C	0.9	2.0	1.1	2.4	92.7	0.8	881
Central Christian C of the							
Bible	0.0	0.0	1.2	0.0	96.4	2.4	83
Central Methodist C	0.0	0.1	7.5	0.4	89.4	2.5	710
Central Missouri St U	0.0	0.4	7.5	0.3	88.8	2.9	10,104
Cleveland Chiropractic C	0.3	1.3	1.0	2.3	90.3	4.9	308
Columbia C	1.5	1.7	13.7	2.3	79.9	0.8	3,566
Conception Sem C	0.0	2.6	0.0	6.4	88.5	2.6	78
Concordia Sem	0.0	0.8	0.6	0.0	95.3	3.2	493
Cottey C	0.3	0.9	0.6	1.7	91.4	5.1	350
Covenant Theological Sem ...	0.0	3.3	3.3	0.0	88.9	4.6	153
Crowder C	1.1	0.3	0.9	0.3	97.2	0.1	1,487
Culver-Stockton C	0.0	0.9	5.0	0.0	94.1	0.0	1,032
DeVry Inst of Tech	0.5	4.2	9.8	1.1	83.9	0.7	1,692
Drury C	0.4	0.3	2.4	0.4	95.8	0.7	3,156

MISSOURI, cont.

	American Indian	Asian	Black	Hispanic	White	Foreign	Total
East Central C	0.2%	0.0%	0.3%	0.1%	99.3%	0.1%	2,509
Eden Theological Sem	0.0	3.0	5.6	0.0	89.4	2.0	198
Evangel C	0.4	0.4	3.4	1.2	94.4	0.3	1,564
Fontbonne C	0.0	1.2	10.6	0.4	82.0	5.8	1,036
Forest Inst of							
Professional Psychology ...	1.3	2.5	2.5	1.3	91.1	1.3	79
Hannibal-La Grange C	0.4	0.3	1.3	0.3	97.4	0.4	763
Harris-Stowe St C	0.2	0.2	78.3	0.4	20.2	0.8	1,725
ITT Tech Inst	0.0	0.2	21.2	0.0	78.6	0.0	617
Jefferson C	0.2	0.4	0.6	0.3	98.4	0.1	3,294
Kemper Military Sch and C ...	1.0	5.8	28.8	2.6	60.2	1.6	191
Kenrick-Glennon Sem	0.0	1.5	1.5	0.0	97.1	0.0	68
Kirksville C of							
Osteopathic Medicine	0.8	4.5	0.2	3.4	90.6	0.6	531
Lincoln U	0.5	0.4	26.8	0.2	69.5	2.7	2,743
Lindenwood C	0.1	1.4	11.0	0.5	86.7	0.3	1,771
Logan C of Chiropractic	0.3	1.1	1.9	0.4	92.3	4.0	699
Maryville C	0.2	0.6	3.2	0.6	92.8	2.6	2,934
Metropolitan CC Sys							
Longview CC	0.2	0.6	5.4	0.8	92.8	0.2	7,684
Maple Woods CC	0.3	0.6	0.8	1.0	97.2	0.1	3,848
Penn Valley CC	0.4	2.4	34.8	3.1	55.9	3.5	5,481
Mineral Area C	0.0	0.2	0.3	0.0	99.5	0.0	2,205
Missouri Baptist C	0.4	1.2	14.0	0.5	79.9	4.1	849
Missouri Southern St C	1.2	0.5	0.9	0.5	96.7	0.1	5,404
Missouri Valley C	1.3	1.6	26.1	2.2	68.4	0.3	1,175
Missouri Western St C	1.8	0.4	3.0	0.6	94.2	0.0	4,083
Moberly Area JC	0.4	0.3	9.5	0.5	88.0	1.3	1,317
National Education Ctr							
Kansas City	2.8	0.6	42.5	4.4	48.6	1.1	181
Nazarene Theological Sem ...	0.7	1.2	2.2	1.5	85.8	8.6	409
North Central Missouri C	0.3	0.3	1.5	0.0	98.0	0.0	737
Northeast Missouri St U	0.0	0.2	3.1	0.2	93.8	2.5	6,419
Northwest Missouri St U	1.0	0.1	2.4	0.3	93.7	2.5	5,306
Ozark Christian C	0.0	0.0	0.6	1.4	96.3	1.8	514
Platt JC	1.5	1.1	4.6	1.5	91.2	0.0	262
Research C of Nursing	0.0	0.9	3.6	0.9	94.6	0.0	112
Rockhurst C	0.1	1.9	7.5	2.0	87.6	1.0	3,125
Saint Louis Christian C	0.0	0.0	2.5	0.0	89.8	7.6	118
Saint Louis C of Pharmacy ...	0.0	2.6	3.2	0.3	92.7	1.2	772
Saint Louis CC	0.1	0.8	15.0	0.8	83.2	0.2	30,291
Saint Louis Conservatory							
of Music	0.0	4.4	2.6	3.5	67.5	21.9	114
Saint Louis U	0.2	3.7	6.0	1.6	85.2	3.3	12,935
Saint Paul Sch of Theology ..	0.0	0.8	5.1	0.4	92.0	1.7	237
Sch of the Ozarks	0.0	0.3	1.7	0.1	95.6	2.4	1,310
Southeast Missouri St U	0.1	0.3	7.6	0.2	88.9	2.9	8,778
Southwest Baptist U	0.3	2.6	3.5	0.4	93.2	0.1	1,834
Southwest Missouri St U	0.2	0.9	1.4	0.5	96.4	0.6	17,006
State Fair CC	0.3	0.2	3.0	0.7	95.7	0.0	1,750
Stephens C	0.2	0.8	3.7	0.7	94.7	0.0	1,256
TAD Tech Inst	0.0	5.1	8.6	1.7	84.6	0.0	175
Tarkio C	0.0	0.4	13.7	7.5	78.0	0.3	2,063
Three Rivers CC	0.0	0.2	2.1	0.1	97.6	0.0	1,776
U of Missouri							
Columbia	0.3	1.3	3.4	0.8	88.5	5.7	23,568
Kansas City	0.6	3.1	6.7	1.8	84.3	3.6	11,628

	American Indian	Asian	Black	Hispanic	White	Foreign	Total
Rolla	0.4%	4.8%	2.4%	0.9%	85.4%	6.2%	5,724
Saint Louis	0.2	2.2	9.5	0.8	86.9	0.4	13,932
Washington U	0.1	5.6	4.5	1.5	82.0	6.4	11,498
Webster U	0.4	1.2	11.7	2.9	82.6	1.3	8,120
Wentworth Military Academy and JC	0.5	0.5	4.4	1.1	92.1	1.4	366
Westminster C	0.4	0.7	1.9	0.1	96.7	0.1	689
William Jewell C	0.2	0.3	1.5	0.1	97.9	0.1	1,984
William Woods C	0.1	0.0	0.4	0.1	99.3	0.0	760

MONTANA

	American Indian	Asian	Black	Hispanic	White	Foreign	Total
Blackfeet CC	91.9	0.0	0.3	0.0	7.7	0.0	297
Carroll C	0.6	0.8	0.3	0.2	96.1	2.0	1,413
C of Great Falls	5.0	0.8	2.4	1.7	88.2	1.9	1,187
Dawson CC	4.0	0.0	0.6	0.4	94.5	0.6	531
Dull Knife Memorial C	84.9	0.0	0.6	0.0	14.5	0.0	179
Flathead Valley CC	2.2	0.6	0.0	1.5	95.4	0.3	1,900
Fort Peck CC	84.6	0.0	0.0	0.4	15.0	0.0	234
Miles CC	3.5	0.0	0.0	0.3	95.3	0.8	593
Montana U Sys							
Eastern Montana C	5.0	0.4	0.3	1.2	92.9	0.2	3,992
Montana C of Mineral Science and Tech	0.4	0.2	0.3	0.8	92.8	5.5	1,818
Montana St U	2.0	0.4	0.3	0.6	94.7	2.1	10,024
Northern Montana C	8.8	0.3	0.4	0.4	89.3	0.8	1,593
U of Montana	2.3	0.3	0.5	0.7	93.2	3.0	8,879
Western Montana C	0.7	0.4	0.2	0.5	98.3	0.0	1,097
Rocky Mountain C	1.4	1.0	0.6	2.4	91.1	3.5	705
Salish Kootenai CC	68.5	0.0	0.0	0.0	31.5	0.0	704

NEBRASKA

	American Indian	Asian	Black	Hispanic	White	Foreign	Total
Bellevue C	1.5	0.5	5.4	2.0	90.0	0.5	1,862
Bishop Clarkson C	0.0	0.4	2.3	0.7	96.6	0.0	565
Central Tech CC Area	0.3	0.3	0.2	0.7	98.5	0.0	9,676
Chadron St C	0.2	0.7	0.3	0.2	98.6	0.0	2,450
C of Saint Mary	0.3	0.4	4.0	1.1	94.1	0.2	1,133
Concordia Teachers C	0.1	0.1	1.3	0.3	96.8	1.4	779
Creighton U	0.3	4.3	2.5	2.6	87.4	3.0	5,958
Dana C	0.6	1.2	5.6	0.6	89.1	2.8	496
Doane C	0.2	0.0	2.4	0.5	93.4	3.5	935
Gateway Electronics Inst	0.0	0.0	1.6	0.5	97.9	0.0	188
Grace C of the Bible	1.9	1.5	2.2	0.4	90.0	4.1	269
Hastings C	0.2	0.5	4.6	1.0	93.4	0.3	935
Kearney St C	0.1	0.2	0.2	0.6	97.9	0.9	9,094
McCook CC	0.1	0.2	0.8	0.9	97.6	0.4	922
Metropolitan CC	2.4	1.8	11.1	2.2	82.5	0.0	6,629
Mid Plains CC	0.2	0.1	0.2	1.5	98.0	0.0	1,983
Midland Lutheran C	0.4	0.7	4.3	1.1	92.7	0.8	910
Nebraska Christian C	0.0	0.0	0.0	0.7	98.6	0.7	148
Neb C of Tech Agriculture ...	0.0	0.0	0.0	0.0	100.0	0.0	208
Nebraska Methodist C of Nursing and Allied Health ..	0.0	0.4	3.8	0.8	94.1	0.8	238
Nebraska Wesleyan U	0.2	0.8	1.0	0.6	96.8	0.7	1,527
Northeast CC	0.3	0.1	0.2	0.2	99.2	0.0	2,687
Peru St C	0.3	0.2	3.6	0.4	95.1	0.3	1,441

NEBRASKA, cont.

	American Indian	Asian	Black	Hispanic	White	Foreign	Total
Southeast CC							
Beatrice	0.0%	0.4%	1.4%	0.0%	98.1%	0.2%	569
Lincoln	0.4	0.9	1.3	0.9	96.3	0.2	4,409
Milford	0.1	0.2	0.1	0.2	98.9	0.5	883
Union C	0.8	0.8	2.1	2.9	84.9	8.5	615
U of Nebraska							
Lincoln	0.2	0.7	1.6	0.9	92.4	4.1	23,985
Medical Center	0.4	2.6	2.3	1.6	90.6	2.5	2,278
Omaha	0.2	1.0	4.1	1.4	92.2	1.1	14,985
Wayne St C	0.3	0.2	1.3	0.2	97.6	0.4	2,874
Western Nebraska CC	1.0	0.0	0.4	4.2	94.2	0.2	2,508
York C	1.8	0.0	3.3	1.1	91.3	2.5	276

NEVADA

	American Indian	Asian	Black	Hispanic	White	Foreign	Total
Sierra Nevada C	0.0	0.0	0.0	0.0	96.9	3.1	161
U of Nevada Sys							
Las Vegas	0.5	3.6	5.5	5.0	84.1	1.2	14,673
Reno	1.1	2.5	1.9	2.5	88.5	3.6	10,506
Clark County CC	1.3	3.9	9.6	6.8	78.4	0.0	10,519
Northern Nevada CC	5.6	1.3	0.4	6.6	86.2	0.0	1,596
Truckee Meadows CC	2.1	3.4	1.4	4.0	87.9	1.3	9,006
Western Nevada CC	2.7	3.0	4.5	6.0	83.4	0.5	2,346

NEW HAMPSHIRE

	American Indian	Asian	Black	Hispanic	White	Foreign	Total
Antioch New England							
Graduate Sch	0.0	0.0	1.1	0.5	96.7	1.7	645
Castle JC	0.0	0.0	0.0	1.4	97.9	0.7	146
Colby-Sawyer C	0.0	0.4	0.7	0.0	98.7	0.2	446
Daniel Webster C	0.1	0.6	1.4	0.6	96.0	1.2	1,088
Dartmouth C	1.7	5.3	5.6	2.3	78.7	6.3	4,777
Franklin Pierce C	0.1	0.6	2.2	1.5	95.1	0.5	3,568
Franklin Pierce Law Center	0.9	0.9	0.6	0.3	97.4	0.0	341
Magdalen C	0.0	0.0	0.0	0.0	98.1	1.9	52
New England C	0.1	0.0	0.3	0.0	97.2	2.5	1,128
New Hampshire C	0.0	1.2	1.0	4.6	89.1	4.1	6,308
NH Tech C Berlin	0.2	0.0	0.0	0.0	99.8	0.0	496
NH Tech C Claremont	0.0	0.0	0.0	0.0	100.0	0.0	460
NH Tech C Laconia	0.9	0.2	0.4	1.1	97.4	0.0	539
NH Tech C Manchester	0.0	0.3	0.0	0.0	99.7	0.0	1,190
NH Tech C Nashua	0.6	1.1	1.2	0.8	96.3	0.0	1,045
NH Tech C Stratham	1.6	0.9	0.6	0.6	96.0	0.2	849
New Hampshire Tech Inst	0.0	0.2	0.5	0.0	99.2	0.0	2,098
Notre Dame C	0.5	0.1	0.0	0.4	98.9	0.1	842
Rivier C	0.2	1.4	0.9	1.5	94.4	1.4	2,427
Saint Anselm C	0.1	0.1	0.1	0.2	99.2	0.5	1,934
U Sys of New Hampshire							
U of New Hampshire	0.2	0.5	0.3	0.5	97.2	1.2	12,984
Plymouth St C	0.3	0.5	0.3	0.3	98.3	0.3	3,936
Sch For Lifelong Learning	0.3	0.4	0.9	1.1	97.0	0.3	1,592
U of NH Manchester	0.6	0.4	0.4	0.5	98.0	0.1	1,564
White Pines C	0.0	0.0	0.0	0.0	87.5	12.5	48

NEW JERSEY

	American Indian	Asian	Black	Hispanic	White	Foreign	Total
Assumption C for Sisters	0.0	40.7	0.0	0.0	59.3	0.0	27

	American Indian	Asian	Black	Hispanic	White	Foreign	Total
Atlantic CC	0.5%	2.5%	10.0%	3.3%	82.1%	1.6%	4,303
Bergen CC	0.1	4.8	4.2	7.5	79.5	3.8	10,923
Berkeley Sch C of Business ..	0.0	0.1	9.4	11.4	79.1	0.0	731
Beth Medrash Govoha	0.0	0.0	0.0	0.9	93.6	5.4	1,161
Bloomfield C	0.1	2.1	36.8	6.9	53.4	0.7	1,484
Brookdale CC	0.1	2.9	6.1	2.4	88.2	0.3	10,633
Burlington County C	0.3	2.0	14.3	2.3	80.3	0.8	6,252
Caldwell C	0.0	1.8	10.1	3.1	83.1	2.0	945
Camden County C	0.1	2.4	11.6	2.2	83.7	0.1	9,358
Centenary C	0.0	1.1	9.5	2.8	83.4	3.3	613
C of Saint Elizabeth	0.1	2.7	7.5	6.9	80.5	2.3	1,039
County C of Morris	0.2	3.2	2.5	3.0	89.2	1.9	8,401
Cumberland County C	1.3	0.1	10.7	7.2	79.1	1.5	2,246
Don Bosco C	0.0	17.1	0.0	7.3	75.6	0.0	41
Drew U	0.2	2.9	5.8	2.2	83.4	5.5	2,346
Essex County C	0.2	1.6	55.2	17.2	20.0	5.7	5,664
Fairleigh Dickinson U							
Main	0.8	4.6	6.7	4.2	77.4	6.3	4,972
Edward Williams C	0.1	3.9	14.9	8.2	70.8	2.1	1,549
Madison	0.2	2.4	6.6	1.2	89.0	0.7	3,709
Rutherford	0.2	2.5	6.7	4.1	80.7	5.9	2,447
Felician C	0.2	4.2	7.3	5.7	80.5	2.3	619
Georgian Court C	0.1	0.6	2.9	2.5	93.6	0.3	2,054
Glassboro St C	0.5	1.2	8.2	2.5	86.0	1.7	9,495
Gloucester County C	0.1	0.6	7.0	1.0	87.5	3.8	3,672
Hudson County CC	0.6	10.0	14.5	46.6	23.9	4.4	2,736
Jersey City St C	0.1	5.2	13.7	14.9	52.8	13.3	7,482
Katharine Gibbs Sch	0.3	1.5	18.3	10.7	69.1	0.0	327
Kean C of New Jersey	0.1	2.6	12.3	9.0	74.3	1.7	12,404
Mercer County CC	0.3	2.2	12.9	4.2	78.5	1.9	8,643
Middlesex County C	0.8	7.5	7.3	7.4	75.7	1.2	11,220
Monmouth C	0.1	2.3	3.8	1.9	87.2	4.7	4,430
Montclair St C	0.7	1.9	7.3	7.9	80.4	1.8	12,657
New Brunswick Theol Sem ...	0.0	7.4	31.9	5.2	53.3	2.2	135
Northeastern Bible C	0.5	2.6	13.8	5.6	74.4	3.1	195
Ocean County C	0.8	0.9	2.2	1.7	94.3	0.0	6,214
Passaic County CC	0.1	5.2	20.9	45.3	23.3	5.1	2,837
Princeton Theological Sem ..	0.1	5.7	7.4	1.2	77.1	8.5	767
Princeton U	0.2	6.4	4.7	3.2	70.5	15.0	6,338
Ramapo C of New Jersey	0.1	1.5	7.6	2.6	85.6	2.7	4,046
Raritan Valley CC	0.5	3.7	3.2	2.0	90.6	0.0	4,841
Rider C	0.7	0.8	4.6	3.2	89.4	1.3	5,415
Rutgers U							
Camden	0.4	2.7	8.7	2.7	85.1	0.4	5,187
New Brunswick	0.1	7.3	7.6	4.9	74.6	5.4	32,901
Newark	0.1	6.9	18.0	9.2	61.5	4.3	9,694
Saint Peter's C	0.1	5.7	7.0	13.0	72.6	1.6	3,346
Salem CC	0.4	1.2	13.6	3.2	81.6	0.0	1,202
Seton Hall U	0.1	2.1	7.3	4.6	84.6	1.3	9,284
Stevens Inst of Tech	0.2	12.1	3.3	5.1	52.6	26.7	2,859
Stockton St C	0.4	1.4	10.7	2.5	84.5	0.6	5,287
Sussex Co CC Commission ...	0.0	0.1	0.2	0.4	99.3	0.0	1,759
Thomas A Edison St C	0.5	0.8	8.3	2.9	83.6	4.0	6,842
Trenton St C	0.2	1.7	8.4	2.8	86.0	0.8	7,416
Union County C	0.0	1.1	15.7	5.7	64.0	13.4	8,741
U of Medicine and Dentistry of New Jersey	0.1	7.8	7.4	4.9	72.6	7.2	2,901

	American Indian	Asian	Black	Hispanic	White	Foreign	Total
Upsala C							
Main	0.0%	2.3%	36.9%	4.8%	54.4%	1.6%	1,093
Wirths	0.0	1.2	0.3	0.6	97.9	0.0	329
Warren Co CC Commission ..	0.1	0.1	1.2	0.5	96.7	1.4	999
Westminster Choir C	0.3	3.7	8.6	2.6	82.7	2.0	347
William Paterson C	0.2	1.2	5.8	4.8	87.3	0.7	9,222

NEW MEXICO

	American Indian	Asian	Black	Hispanic	White	Foreign	Total
Albuquerque Tech-Voc Inst ..	8.5	1.6	3.4	35.1	51.3	0.0	7,778
C of Santa Fe	10.1	0.9	3.9	28.2	56.8	0.2	1,289
C of the Southwest	0.0	1.0	1.9	13.8	79.0	4.3	210
Eastern New Mexico U							
Main	1.3	1.0	4.7	15.4	75.5	2.0	3,765
Roswell	1.1	0.1	1.7	24.8	72.3	0.1	1,595
Clovis	0.9	1.3	6.1	13.0	77.8	0.9	2,806
Inst of American Indian and Alaska Native Culture and Arts Development	94.1	0.0	0.0	0.0	5.9	0.0	119
National C Albuquerque	5.5	2.4	1.6	48.8	41.7	0.0	127
New Mexico Highlands U	3.7	0.3	2.3	70.8	22.0	0.8	2,017
NM Inst of Mining and Tech ..	3.0	1.6	0.3	9.7	74.0	11.4	1,222
New Mexico JC	0.6	0.3	4.4	12.5	81.5	0.7	2,513
New Mexico Military Inst	0.7	5.1	5.6	16.0	69.3	3.3	449
New Mexico St U							
Main	2.1	0.5	1.4	24.0	68.6	3.4	14,279
Alamogordo	2.9	1.5	4.6	15.2	75.8	0.0	1,680
Carlsbad	1.2	0.7	0.6	19.7	77.7	0.0	964
Dona Ana	2.9	0.3	1.9	42.1	51.4	1.5	1,366
Grants	16.9	0.4	0.2	28.0	54.4	0.0	485
Northern New Mexico CC	10.0	0.6	0.4	73.0	16.1	0.0	1,445
Saint John's C	0.2	1.4	0.9	2.1	95.1	0.2	430
San Juan C	27.5	0.2	0.1	10.1	61.6	0.4	2,851
Santa Fe CC	1.7	0.6	0.5	49.0	48.1	0.2	2,351
U of New Mexico							
Main	3.2	2.0	1.6	21.3	69.6	2.4	24,433
Gallup	68.8	0.5	0.6	8.3	21.7	0.1	1,610
Los Alamos	1.5	1.7	0.4	18.2	76.6	1.5	920
Valencia	2.0	0.1	0.7	49.7	47.6	0.0	1,066
Western New Mexico U	1.9	0.5	2.1	38.2	56.0	1.4	1,680

NEW YORK

	American Indian	Asian	Black	Hispanic	White	Foreign	Total
Adelphi U	0.1	2.3	8.6	3.8	85.0	0.3	9,068
Albany Business C	0.3	0.6	26.6	0.3	70.3	2.0	357
Albany C of Pharmacy	0.3	3.8	1.5	1.1	91.6	1.7	653
Albany Law Sch	0.3	2.1	3.8	1.6	91.6	0.7	765
Albany Medical C	0.0	13.6	2.1	2.2	80.3	1.7	631
Alfred U	0.2	1.2	3.5	1.4	92.2	1.6	1,736
American Academy of Dramatic Arts	0.5	0.0	3.5	4.0	76.7	15.3	202
American Acad McAllister Inst of Funeral Service	0.0	0.0	28.6	10.7	60.7	0.0	112
Bank Street C of Education ..	0.3	1.6	8.1	9.4	80.6	0.0	639
Bard C	0.0	1.5	3.2	2.6	90.2	2.5	929

	American Indian	Asian	Black	Hispanic	White	Foreign	Total
Barnard C	0.0%	16.2%	3.4%	3.3%	74.1%	2.8%	2,192
Berkeley Sch of Long Island	0.0	1.5	17.0	7.3	73.3	1.0	206
Berkeley Sch of Westchester	0.0	1.2	10.2	7.2	81.3	0.0	566
Beth Jacob Hebrew Teachers C	0.0	0.0	0.0	0.0	100.0	0.0	539
Bramson ORT Tech Inst	0.0	0.0	1.1	0.8	98.1	0.0	471
Briarcliffe Sch	0.4	0.4	12.8	13.6	68.8	4.0	522
Brooklyn Law Sch	0.0	3.2	3.9	5.2	87.3	0.4	1,335
Bryant & Stratton Business Inst	0.5	0.6	12.7	4.7	81.5	0.1	3,256
Bryant & Stratton Business Inst main	0.6	0.4	16.3	0.6	82.2	0.0	1,795
Canisius C	0.2	0.6	5.3	1.2	92.0	0.7	4,514
Cathedral C of the Immaculate Conception	0.0	5.9	0.0	11.8	82.4	0.0	17
Cazenovia C	0.2	0.7	3.4	0.5	94.6	0.5	914
Central Yeshiva Tomchei Tmimim Lubavitz	0.0	0.0	0.0	0.0	52.9	47.1	448
Christ the King Sem	0.0	0.0	0.0	0.0	100.0	0.0	99
City U of New York							
Bernard Baruch C	0.4	19.0	17.7	13.5	46.1	3.3	16,463
Borough of Manhattan CC	0.1	7.0	54.1	29.5	7.4	1.9	12,651
Bronx CC	0.8	4.2	48.4	42.3	2.7	1.7	5,725
Brooklyn C	0.1	9.5	18.8	12.6	56.7	2.3	15,933
City C	0.4	12.4	32.0	22.7	25.1	7.5	12,778
C of Staten Island	0.7	4.2	8.2	5.7	77.3	3.8	10,678
Graduate Sch and U Center	0.5	5.7	13.2	8.2	68.4	4.1	4,139
Hostos CC	0.1	1.0	12.1	83.4	1.6	1.8	4,024
Hunter C	0.5	8.1	19.0	16.6	52.5	3.3	20,755
John Jay C of Criminal Justice	0.3	2.3	35.3	27.6	33.7	0.8	7,308
Kingsborough CC	0.3	4.6	22.3	10.6	61.5	0.7	12,817
La Guardia CC	0.4	10.8	33.1	42.0	13.6	0.0	8,994
Lehman C	7.4	4.9	24.7	26.4	35.6	1.0	9,494
Medgar Evers C	0.3	0.6	91.0	3.7	0.3	4.2	2,431
New York City Tech C	0.1	7.9	55.7	21.4	12.8	2.1	10,324
Queens C	0.2	9.1	10.6	10.6	65.0	4.5	16,944
Queensborough CC	0.6	10.1	20.8	15.2	53.2	0.0	11,644
Sch of Law Queens C	0.4	5.3	13.7	8.2	68.6	3.8	452
York C	0.3	6.2	60.0	15.7	7.1	10.6	4,832
Clarkson U	0.2	1.0	0.4	0.4	89.1	8.9	3,602
Cochran Sch of Nursing	0.0	3.5	39.5	12.8	44.2	0.0	86
Colgate Rochester-Bexley Hall-Crozer Divinity Sch	1.0	2.5	14.6	1.0	79.9	1.0	199
Colgate U	0.2	5.5	3.7	2.1	85.1	3.4	2,750
C for Human Services	1.4	0.4	71.1	18.3	8.7	0.0	703
C of Aeronautics	0.4	10.9	26.2	30.0	29.4	3.1	1,255
C of Insurance	0.0	7.7	11.8	7.0	69.4	4.1	712
C of Mount Saint Vincent	0.0	4.3	7.0	8.7	78.6	1.4	1,007
C of New Rochelle	0.1	0.8	45.5	8.9	44.4	0.2	4,491
C of Saint Rose	0.1	0.2	1.4	0.2	97.1	0.9	3,231
Columbia U	0.1	8.7	4.2	3.2	78.3	5.4	17,296
Columbia U Teachers C	0.1	3.4	10.8	5.4	69.5	10.8	4,143
Concordia C	0.6	2.3	11.2	2.7	73.2	10.1	526
Cooper Union	0.0	23.9	4.1	3.5	62.0	6.5	1,001
Cornell U Endowed C's	0.3	10.8	3.7	3.7	70.3	11.2	11,525
Cornell U Medical Center	0.0	9.4	6.8	5.2	68.4	10.1	572
Culinary Inst of America	0.1	0.4	1.1	0.8	96.2	1.5	1,835

NEW YORK, cont.

	American Indian	Asian	Black	Hispanic	White	Foreign	Total
Daemen C	0.4%	1.3%	15.3%	3.4%	79.4%	0.1%	1,630
Dominican C of Blauvelt	0.0	1.3	5.1	3.5	90.1	0.0	1,443
Dowling C	0.0	0.9	2.3	1.8	94.8	0.3	3,977
D'Youville C	0.8	0.7	9.9	3.8	79.5	5.4	1,061
Edna McConnell Clark Sch of Nursing	0.0	2.1	64.9	10.3	22.7	0.0	97
Elizabeth Seton C	0.7	2.3	42.8	14.9	39.0	0.2	979
Elmira C	0.2	1.1	1.6	0.6	96.6	0.0	1,880
Five Towns C	0.0	0.0	17.1	6.7	75.3	0.9	461
Fordham U	0.1	1.7	3.5	5.1	87.2	2.4	13,036
Friends World C	0.0	3.1	6.2	2.6	79.9	8.2	194
Hamilton C	0.1	2.7	2.4	2.0	88.7	4.1	1,643
Hartwick C	0.0	0.8	0.7	0.6	96.8	1.2	1,543
Helene Fuld Sch of Nursing	0.0	1.2	82.6	4.1	12.2	0.0	172
Hilbert C	0.6	0.0	4.6	0.9	93.7	0.2	653
Hobart and William Smith C's	0.3	0.6	3.4	1.2	93.0	1.6	1,964
Hofstra U	0.2	2.1	5.5	2.8	88.3	1.0	12,329
Holy Trinity Orthodox Sem	0.0	0.0	0.0	2.9	47.1	50.0	34
Houghton C	0.3	1.4	2.0	0.6	91.3	4.3	1,181
Inst of Design and Construction	0.0	4.1	31.7	9.9	53.1	1.2	243
Iona C	0.2	1.1	5.1	3.7	89.4	0.5	5,987
Ithaca C	0.1	0.5	2.1	1.2	95.1	1.0	6,105
Jamestown Business C	0.3	0.3	1.6	0.6	97.1	0.0	309
Jewish Theological Sem of America	0.0	0.0	0.2	0.0	96.4	3.4	494
Juilliard Sch	0.0	12.0	4.1	3.5	53.7	26.8	1,084
Katharine Gibbs Sch Melville	0.0	0.0	4.9	1.4	93.7	0.0	347
Katharine Gibbs Sch New York City	0.0	1.5	22.1	21.9	52.8	1.7	411
Keuka C	0.5	0.5	7.7	2.3	88.8	0.2	596
King's C	0.0	3.8	6.0	3.4	84.0	2.8	501
Kol Yaakov Torah Center	0.0	0.0	0.0	0.0	100.0	0.0	39
Laboratory Inst of Merchandising	0.0	3.1	7.7	8.7	79.5	1.0	195
Le Moyne C	0.2	0.8	2.4	0.6	95.8	0.2	2,270
Long Island C Hospital Sch of Nursing	0.0	1.4	57.2	6.5	34.8	0.0	138
Long Island U							
Administration	0.5	0.8	4.5	3.0	91.0	0.2	1,003
Brooklyn	0.3	6.2	42.6	12.6	34.7	3.7	5,960
C W Post	0.1	1.5	6.8	3.2	81.4	7.0	8,947
Rockland	0.0	0.6	5.0	2.1	92.1	0.2	483
Southhampton C	0.9	0.8	6.0	2.8	87.9	1.7	1,262
Machzikei Hadath Rabbinical C	0.0	0.0	0.0	0.0	100.0	0.0	119
Manhattan Sch of Music	0.0	6.5	4.0	2.6	62.5	24.4	774
Manhattanville C	0.1	2.3	4.1	4.9	81.6	7.0	1,518
Mannes C of Music	0.2	11.9	5.8	4.7	69.4	8.0	536
Maria C	0.0	0.6	4.6	1.1	93.3	0.3	927
Maria Regina C	0.0	10.0	0.0	0.0	90.0	0.0	10
Marist C	0.2	0.6	8.2	5.4	85.1	0.5	4,545
Maryknoll Sch of Theology	0.0	0.0	0.0	2.5	78.7	18.8	80
Marymount C	0.0	1.6	13.0	9.5	74.2	1.7	1,248
Marymount Manhattan C	0.2	2.7	14.6	9.9	70.0	2.6	1,277
Mater Dei C	15.4	0.6	3.0	1.7	79.0	0.2	525
Medaille C	0.5	0.2	31.1	3.9	64.4	0.0	1,053

	American Indian	Asian	Black	Hispanic	White	Foreign	Total
Mesivta Eastern Parkway							
Rabbinical Sem	0.0%	0.0%	0.0%	0.0%	100.0%	0.0%	55
Mesivta Torah Vodaath							
Rabbinical Sem	0.0	0.0	0.0	0.0	100.0	0.0	435
Mirrer Yeshiva Central Inst ...	0.0	0.0	0.0	0.0	100.0	0.0	235
Molloy C	0.4	0.9	7.9	3.3	87.3	0.3	1,384
Monroe Business Inst main ..	0.7	0.4	44.9	51.0	3.0	0.0	2,101
Mount Saint Mary C	0.1	0.4	8.2	3.2	86.1	2.0	1,226
Mount Sinai Sch of Medicine	0.0	11.4	3.9	6.7	77.8	0.2	492
Nazareth C of Rochester	0.3	0.4	2.8	0.9	95.2	0.4	2,935
New Sch for Social Research	0.4	5.6	7.0	5.3	69.8	11.8	6,381
New York Chiropractic C	0.1	0.9	1.6	4.2	92.6	0.5	758
New York C of Podiatric							
Medicine	0.0	3.1	12.8	4.7	78.8	0.6	486
New York Inst of Tech							
Main	0.1	2.7	5.0	3.1	75.2	14.0	7,566
Central Islip	0.1	0.4	7.4	2.0	79.7	10.4	2,057
Metro	0.1	4.0	13.8	9.7	32.4	40.2	2,952
New York Law Sch	0.1	3.6	4.1	3.9	88.0	0.3	1,246
New York Medical C	0.1	9.9	9.6	3.9	75.7	0.8	1,248
New York Sch of Interior							
Design	0.0	8.9	8.2	19.9	58.9	4.1	637
New York Theological Sem ...	0.0	19.2	40.1	14.5	25.2	0.9	317
New York U	0.2	10.5	5.5	5.6	70.7	7.5	30,750
Niagara U	0.4	0.5	5.5	0.6	80.4	12.7	3,048
Nyack C	0.1	12.7	5.3	4.8	73.8	3.4	861
Ohr Somayach Insts	0.0	0.0	0.0	0.0	100.0	0.0	51
Olean Business Inst	1.3	0.0	1.3	1.3	96.1	0.0	154
Pace U							
New York	0.6	8.9	15.1	10.6	55.2	9.7	9,780
Pleasantville-Briarcliff	0.6	1.5	3.7	4.1	88.0	2.2	4,342
White Plains	0.8	4.3	5.3	3.3	84.6	1.7	4,254
Paul Smith's C of Arts							
and Sciences	0.1	0.0	1.4	0.4	93.4	4.8	813
Phillip Beth Israel Sch							
of Nursing	0.0	6.3	48.3	8.0	35.8	1.7	176
Plaza Business Inst	0.0	12.0	30.4	28.2	29.0	0.4	493
Polytechnic U	0.0	27.4	4.9	4.5	53.2	10.0	4,219
Pratt Inst	0.0	9.2	11.3	7.4	60.0	12.0	3,639
Rabbi Isaac Elchanan							
Theological Sem	0.0	0.0	0.0	0.0	97.2	2.8	319
Rabbinical C Bobover							
Yeshiva B'nei Zion	0.0	0.0	0.0	0.0	100.0	0.0	293
Rabbinical Sem M'kor Chaim	0.0	0.0	0.0	0.0	100.0	0.0	112
Rabbinical Sem of America ..	0.0	0.0	0.0	0.0	100.0	0.0	203
Rensselaer Polytechnic Inst ..	0.2	8.0	2.3	2.8	76.8	9.9	6,706
Roberts Wesleyan C	0.9	0.4	5.7	2.7	82.4	7.9	820
Rochester Business Inst	0.4	0.0	32.8	1.7	65.1	0.0	241
Rochester Inst of Tech	0.3	2.4	3.1	1.4	90.1	2.6	12,346
Rockefeller U	0.0	3.4	0.9	0.9	54.7	40.2	117
Russell Sage C main	0.2	0.8	5.8	1.8	90.7	0.6	4,165
Saint Bernard's Inst	0.0	0.0	1.0	4.0	95.0	0.0	100
Saint Bonaventure U	0.4	0.4	0.9	0.6	97.2	0.5	2,853
Saint Elizabeth Hospital							
Sch of Nursing	0.0	0.0	2.2	0.0	97.8	0.0	136
Saint Francis C	0.4	1.6	22.9	10.4	61.1	3.7	1,929
Saint John Fisher C	0.2	0.7	3.5	1.2	93.8	0.6	2,359

NEW YORK, cont.

	American Indian	Asian	Black	Hispanic	White	Foreign	Total
Saint John's U	0.1%	5.3%	7.2%	6.7%	76.2%	4.5%	19,143
Saint Joseph's C							
Main	0.0	7.9	37.3	7.6	47.2	0.0	794
Suffolk	0.0	0.1	3.7	6.2	90.0	0.0	1,766
Saint Joseph's Sem & C	0.0	0.0	1.2	2.7	94.6	1.5	259
Saint Lawrence U	1.2	0.4	2.7	0.4	92.2	3.3	2,232
Saint Thomas Aquinas C	0.0	0.9	2.7	2.8	93.3	0.2	2,038
Sarah Lawrence C	0.0	3.4	5.2	2.7	88.1	0.7	1,202
Sch of Visual Arts	0.1	4.2	7.0	4.8	81.2	2.8	4,832
Sem of the Immaculate							
Conception	0.5	0.0	0.5	2.2	96.2	0.5	185
Siena C	0.0	1.2	1.3	1.3	96.0	0.2	3,481
Skidmore C	0.0	2.0	5.0	2.4	89.1	1.5	2,595
St U of New York							
Albany	0.1	3.0	6.5	4.0	82.2	4.2	16,561
Binghamton	0.1	5.2	4.6	3.6	82.9	3.6	12,588
Buffalo	0.5	4.3	5.6	2.3	80.5	6.8	28,005
Stony Brook	0.2	10.3	6.9	4.9	69.4	8.3	16,728
Empire St C	0.3	0.8	8.2	5.1	85.1	0.5	6,495
C at Brockport	0.2	0.8	6.2	1.5	90.5	0.8	8,840
C at Buffalo	0.5	0.6	7.6	2.0	88.2	1.1	12,721
C at Cortland	0.2	0.4	1.5	1.1	96.4	0.5	7,261
C at Fredonia	0.3	0.3	2.1	1.2	95.8	0.3	4,994
C at Geneseo	0.2	0.7	1.3	1.0	96.7	0.1	5,321
C at New Paltz	0.3	2.0	7.8	4.9	83.2	1.9	8,093
C at Old Westbury	0.2	4.7	27.2	8.7	56.9	2.2	3,923
C at Oneonta	0.1	0.8	1.8	1.7	94.4	1.1	6,017
C at Oswego	0.2	1.1	2.5	1.4	94.6	0.2	8,672
C at Plattsburgh	0.3	0.7	2.2	1.3	94.4	1.1	6,594
C at Potsdam	0.6	0.6	1.0	0.6	96.4	0.8	4,310
C at Purchase	0.1	1.4	4.1	2.8	90.2	1.3	4,143
Health Science Center							
Brooklyn	0.2	6.5	27.6	2.9	59.0	3.7	1,681
Health Science Center							
Syracuse	0.2	5.1	6.6	2.0	82.7	3.3	979
C of Optometry	0.0	12.5	3.0	4.1	74.9	5.5	271
C of Ag & Tech Cobleskill	0.0	0.2	3.7	1.8	94.0	0.3	2,729
C of Ag & Tech Morrisville	0.3	0.6	4.7	1.3	92.9	0.2	3,362
C of Tech Alfred	0.8	0.7	2.3	0.7	95.2	0.4	3,775
C of Tech Canton	0.6	0.4	2.3	0.5	95.9	0.3	2,326
C of Tech Delhi	0.2	1.0	4.7	2.0	92.0	0.1	2,453
C of Tech Farmingdale	0.1	2.1	9.3	4.7	83.6	0.2	10,802
C of Tech Utica-Rome	0.2	1.0	3.1	0.6	93.6	1.6	2,620
C of Environmental							
Science and Forestry	0.4	0.7	1.1	1.4	87.0	9.4	1,398
Maritime C	0.1	6.3	2.3	3.9	76.4	11.0	828
Fashion Inst of Tech	0.0	10.4	18.0	9.7	59.5	2.4	11,944
C of Ceramics Alfred U	0.6	1.3	1.4	1.3	90.0	5.5	869
C of Ag and Life Sciences							
Cornell U	0.3	5.1	1.9	2.2	79.2	11.3	4,221
C of Human Ecology							
Cornell U	0.3	8.5	4.8	3.3	77.7	5.4	1,471
C of Veterinary							
Medicine Cornell U	1.7	2.1	1.7	4.3	78.9	11.4	421
Sch of Industrial and Labor							
Relations Cornell U	0.8	2.0	12.0	5.2	78.5	1.5	2,043
Adirondack CC	0.2	0.3	0.6	0.5	98.2	0.2	3,096

	American Indian	Asian	Black	Hispanic	White	Foreign	Total
Broome CC	0.1%	0.9%	1.2%	0.4%	95.9%	1.5%	5,815
Cayuga County CC	0.1	0.1	2.0	0.8	96.8	0.1	2,683
Clinton CC	0.2	1.2	8.8	3.6	86.0	0.2	1,812
Columbia-Greene CC	0.6	0.4	4.2	2.0	92.8	0.0	1,613
CC of the Finger Lakes	0.3	0.1	1.1	0.4	98.1	0.0	3,355
Corning CC	0.3	0.3	1.9	0.7	96.8	0.0	3,229
Dutchess CC	0.4	1.9	7.7	2.9	86.8	0.4	6,417
Erie CC City	0.9	0.6	26.0	4.9	67.6	0.1	3,089
Erie CC North	0.3	0.8	4.3	0.4	92.7	1.5	6,062
Erie CC South	0.4	0.3	0.8	0.4	98.1	0.0	3,418
Fulton-Montgomery CC	0.5	0.3	2.2	1.5	94.1	1.4	1,843
Genesee CC	0.2	0.1	1.0	0.1	98.5	0.1	2,955
Herkimer County CC	0.0	0.2	1.5	0.1	98.1	0.1	2,219
Hudson Valley CC	0.2	0.5	2.7	0.5	95.7	0.4	8,596
Jamestown CC	0.9	0.2	1.5	0.6	96.7	0.1	4,038
Jefferson CC	0.3	1.4	6.3	2.2	89.8	0.0	2,194
Monroe CC	0.4	2.0	8.2	2.4	86.6	0.4	12,768
Mohawk Valley CC	0.3	0.8	4.6	1.4	92.1	0.7	6,147
Nassau CC	0.4	1.6	9.2	4.2	83.2	1.5	20,130
Niagara County CC	1.6	0.4	4.0	0.4	93.3	0.3	4,693
North Country CC	0.5	0.2	3.4	1.4	94.0	0.5	1,520
Onondaga CC	1.5	1.0	5.8	1.1	89.8	0.8	7,173
Orange County CC	0.1	0.8	3.5	3.6	91.4	0.5	4,826
Rockland CC	0.5	3.9	10.4	5.2	76.9	3.2	7,644
Schenectady County CC ...	0.2	0.5	2.2	0.8	96.3	0.0	3,026
Suffolk County CC Eastern .	0.2	0.5	3.1	1.5	94.7	0.0	2,031
Suffolk County CC Selden .	0.2	1.1	1.7	2.5	94.6	0.0	11,267
Suffolk County CC Western	0.3	0.7	6.3	6.3	86.4	0.0	4,317
Sullivan County CC	0.1	0.6	14.8	4.8	79.6	0.1	1,889
Tompkins-Cortland CC	0.3	1.1	2.6	0.8	94.8	0.3	2,595
Ulster County CC	0.1	0.9	6.1	3.2	89.6	0.1	2,816
Westchester CC	0.3	3.1	12.7	7.2	75.6	1.1	8,241
Stenotype Academy	0.0	1.0	28.8	16.3	50.9	2.9	583
Syracuse U	0.2	2.2	4.7	1.6	84.4	7.0	22,086
Utica C	0.1	0.6	5.0	1.7	91.1	1.4	2,523
Taylor Business Inst	0.0	3.7	49.3	39.0	8.0	0.0	536
Tech Career Insts	0.0	34.0	27.0	18.1	15.6	5.3	1,910
Tobe-Coburn Sch of Fashion Careers	0.0	2.8	10.5	18.0	68.4	0.3	399
Trocaire C	0.5	0.6	5.4	1.0	92.1	0.4	826
Union C	0.0	3.5	2.1	1.8	90.5	2.0	2,980
U S Merchant Marine Acad ...	0.2	3.8	1.4	2.4	90.2	2.0	851
U S Military Academy	0.7	4.0	7.3	4.2	83.8	0.0	4,310
U of Rochester	0.1	5.0	4.2	1.9	80.0	8.9	9,195
U of the St of NY Regents C Degrees	0.5	5.7	13.2	8.2	68.3	4.1	16,480
Utica Sch of Commerce	0.0	0.0	3.0	0.0	97.0	0.0	502
Vassar C	0.1	5.8	7.5	3.4	80.1	3.1	2,395
Villa Maria C Buffalo	0.0	0.0	7.1	0.4	91.9	0.7	567
Wadhams Hall Sem and C	0.0	0.0	0.0	0.0	100.0	0.0	62
Wagner C	0.1	1.0	8.3	2.5	75.9	12.3	1,767
Wells C	0.2	1.2	3.2	1.0	93.6	0.7	408
Westchester Business Inst ...	0.0	0.0	28.4	24.5	47.0	0.0	897
Wood Sch	0.2	2.0	18.3	46.3	33.2	0.0	404
Yeshiva Gedolah Bais Yisroel	0.0	0.0	0.0	0.0	84.8	15.2	46
Yeshiva Derech Chaim	0.0	0.0	0.0	0.0	100.0	0.0	130
Yeshiva Karlin Stolin	0.0	0.0	0.0	0.0	94.9	5.1	79
Yeshiva U	0.0	1.5	2.8	1.9	89.5	4.1	4,543

NORTH CAROLINA

	American Indian	Asian	Black	Hispanic	White	Foreign	Total
Alamance CC	0.3%	0.3%	16.5%	0.3%	82.6%	0.0%	3,096
Anson CC	0.1	0.1	24.0	0.3	75.5	0.0	797
Asheville Buncombe Tech CC	0.3	0.6	5.2	0.3	93.3	0.3	3,050
Atlantic Christian C	0.1	0.5	9.4	0.5	88.4	1.1	1,382
Barber-Scotia C	0.0	0.0	98.8	0.0	0.2	0.9	422
Beaufort County CC	0.1	0.4	20.9	0.4	78.2	0.0	1,202
Belmont Abbey C	0.6	2.1	3.9	1.5	89.6	2.3	1,052
Bennett C	0.0	0.0	97.6	0.0	0.3	2.1	615
Bladen CC	1.4	0.2	34.7	0.6	63.1	0.0	510
Blue Ridge CC	0.1	0.4	3.4	0.5	95.0	0.5	1,168
Brevard C	0.4	0.1	5.8	0.6	88.0	4.9	668
Brookstone C of Business ...	0.0	0.0	48.7	0.0	51.3	0.0	156
Brunswick CC	0.3	0.3	18.7	0.3	80.4	0.0	621
Caldwell CC and Tech Inst ...	0.0	0.4	3.8	0.2	95.6	0.0	2,553
Campbell U	0.7	14.3	6.9	1.2	75.6	1.3	4,375
Cape Fear CC	0.5	0.2	13.3	0.7	85.2	0.1	2,480
Carteret CC	0.4	0.4	7.6	0.5	91.0	0.0	1,344
Catawba C	0.3	0.1	9.4	0.3	89.4	0.5	1,030
Catawba Valley CC	0.2	0.6	5.8	0.6	92.8	0.0	2,641
Cecils C	0.0	0.0	6.9	0.0	93.1	0.0	189
Central Carolina CC	1.0	0.5	21.0	0.6	76.9	0.1	2,424
Central Piedmont CC	0.3	2.3	15.6	0.6	79.4	1.8	16,442
Chowan C	0.4	0.8	29.7	0.7	64.9	3.5	973
Cleveland CC	0.1	1.1	17.8	0.5	80.6	0.0	1,425
Coastal Carolina CC	0.4	1.8	15.4	4.1	78.1	0.2	3,404
C of the Albemarle	0.1	0.6	17.3	0.6	81.3	0.0	1,603
Craven CC	0.3	0.9	18.7	2.5	77.5	0.1	2,108
Davidson C	0.3	4.5	4.0	0.8	90.4	0.0	1,395
Davidson County CC	0.2	0.5	7.6	0.2	91.4	0.1	2,212
Duke U	0.2	3.4	4.4	2.0	83.9	6.1	10,689
Durham Tech CC	0.3	2.1	35.3	0.7	61.0	0.5	4,430
East Coast Bible C	0.0	0.8	7.1	1.6	90.5	0.0	252
Edgecombe CC	0.5	0.3	47.1	0.0	51.8	0.3	1,341
Elon C	0.2	0.3	4.8	0.3	93.8	0.7	3,314
Fayetteville Tech CC	1.8	2.1	28.9	3.2	63.9	0.1	6,043
Forsyth Tech C	0.2	0.7	19.8	0.4	78.8	0.0	4,422
Gardner-Webb C	0.1	0.4	10.7	0.4	87.7	0.7	2,139
Gaston C	0.1	0.6	9.4	0.3	89.5	0.1	3,300
Greensboro C	0.3	0.4	12.2	0.6	84.8	1.7	967
Guilford C	0.5	0.8	5.6	0.6	89.2	3.3	1,755
Guilford Tech CC	0.7	1.2	17.6	0.6	79.6	0.4	6,232
Halifax CC	1.1	0.4	37.6	0.3	60.5	0.0	983
Haywood CC	0.9	0.1	0.7	0.5	97.8	0.1	1,026
High Point C	0.1	0.4	6.0	0.6	91.1	1.9	1,930
Isothermal CC	0.2	0.3	7.9	0.1	91.6	0.0	1,554
James Sprunt CC	0.6	0.1	24.8	0.4	74.0	0.1	846
John Wesley C	1.8	0.0	8.8	0.0	89.5	0.0	57
Johnson C Smith U	0.0	0.0	99.6	0.0	0.1	0.3	1,197
Johnston CC	0.2	0.1	16.8	0.4	82.2	0.1	2,030
Lees-McRae C	0.0	0.4	10.7	0.1	87.5	1.3	787
Lenoir CC	0.2	0.2	28.8	0.5	70.2	0.1	2,178
Lenoir-Rhyne C	0.1	0.4	4.4	0.4	94.5	0.1	1,596
Livingstone C	0.0	0.0	97.3	0.0	0.4	2.3	558
Louisburg C	0.1	0.1	8.3	0.0	91.0	0.4	904
Mars Hill C	0.4	0.1	5.0	0.1	93.4	1.0	1,345
Martin CC	0.2	0.3	38.3	0.5	60.8	0.0	655
Mayland CC	0.3	0.0	3.2	0.3	96.1	0.1	775

	American Indian	Asian	Black	Hispanic	White	Foreign	Total
McDowell Tech CC	0.2%	0.3%	3.5%	0.3%	95.5%	0.2%	600
Meredith C	0.3	0.6	2.6	0.5	94.7	1.4	2,124
Methodist C	0.9	1.9	13.0	4.1	79.5	0.7	1,501
Mitchell CC	0.1	0.3	10.8	0.2	88.6	0.1	1,392
Montgomery CC	3.1	0.0	24.6	0.2	72.1	0.0	524
Montreat-Anderson C	0.3	0.0	5.7	0.0	87.8	6.2	386
Mount Olive C	0.0	0.8	15.6	1.3	82.2	0.0	997
Nash CC	1.6	0.3	22.3	0.2	75.5	0.0	1,501
North Carolina Wesleyan C ...	0.7	0.1	17.4	0.6	80.2	0.9	1,513
Pamlico CC	0.0	0.0	23.7	0.6	75.6	0.0	160
Peace C	0.4	1.1	0.4	0.4	97.5	0.2	530
Pfeiffer C	0.2	0.5	8.6	0.9	88.6	1.3	875
Piedmont Bible C	0.0	0.4	3.1	0.0	94.7	1.8	227
Piedmont CC	0.4	0.3	41.4	0.6	57.3	0.0	990
Pitt CC	0.4	0.4	22.9	0.2	75.9	0.2	3,247
Queens C	0.3	0.1	6.0	0.4	91.3	1.9	1,373
Randolph CC	0.2	0.3	4.3	0.2	94.7	0.2	1,267
Richmond CC	3.5	0.2	26.7	0.7	68.8	0.0	936
Roanoke Bible C	0.0	0.0	4.6	0.0	94.4	0.9	108
Roanoke-Chowan CC	0.8	0.2	50.8	0.5	47.8	0.0	634
Robeson CC	32.3	0.2	23.8	0.3	43.3	0.0	1,345
Rockingham CC	0.0	0.2	14.8	0.1	84.8	0.1	1,576
Rowan-Cabarrus CC	0.2	0.5	11.9	0.2	87.1	0.1	2,606
Rutledge C Durham	0.0	0.0	92.0	0.0	8.0	0.0	224
Rutledge C Fayetteville	0.3	0.9	74.2	2.9	21.7	0.0	341
Rutledge C Raleigh	0.5	0.5	92.1	0.5	6.5	0.0	214
Rutledge C Winston-Salem ...	0.0	0.0	72.1	0.9	26.6	0.4	233
Saint Andrews Presbyterian C	0.2	1.2	7.6	0.4	86.4	4.1	802
Saint Augustine's C	0.0	0.3	96.5	0.1	0.3	2.7	1,788
Saint Mary's C	0.0	0.3	0.7	0.7	95.0	3.3	303
Salem C	0.0	0.9	3.3	0.6	94.3	1.0	819
Sampson CC	1.8	0.5	24.4	0.5	72.8	0.1	848
Sandhills CC	2.5	0.4	14.1	0.4	82.6	0.1	1,961
Shaw U	0.0	0.0	90.6	0.1	9.3	0.0	1,507
Southeastern Baptist Theol							
Sem	0.1	1.0	2.4	0.0	94.6	1.8	819
Southeastern CC	4.5	0.4	16.1	0.2	78.9	0.0	1,376
Southwestern CC	9.5	0.1	1.8	0.2	88.5	0.0	1,249
Stanly CC	0.2	0.4	11.3	0.3	87.6	0.1	1,338
Surry CC	0.1	0.1	5.3	0.3	94.2	0.0	2,768
Tri-County CC	1.4	0.0	0.8	0.5	97.3	0.0	867
U of North Carolina							
Asheville	0.1	0.6	3.5	0.8	94.2	0.8	3,124
Chapel Hill	0.6	1.9	7.8	0.7	86.3	2.7	23,626
Charlotte	0.3	1.9	9.7	0.7	84.9	2.5	13,181
Greensboro	0.3	0.9	9.7	0.6	87.0	1.4	11,477
Wilmington	0.3	0.8	7.3	0.3	91.1	0.2	6,953
Appalachian St U	0.2	0.4	4.5	0.3	94.2	0.3	11,548
East Carolina U	0.5	0.7	10.4	0.6	87.2	0.6	16,501
Elizabeth City St U	0.1	0.1	81.5	0.2	17.6	0.4	1,641
Fayetteville St U	0.8	0.8	70.0	1.2	27.1	0.1	2,726
North Carolina A&T St U ...	0.2	0.4	83.8	0.2	12.8	2.6	6,297
North Carolina Central U ...	0.4	0.8	82.6	0.5	15.5	0.2	5,182
NC Sch of the Arts	0.2	0.2	11.1	2.9	82.7	2.9	515
North Carolina St U	0.3	2.4	9.3	0.8	83.1	4.1	25,725
Pembroke St U	23.4	1.0	12.1	0.3	63.2	0.1	2,835
Western Carolina U	1.5	0.5	4.7	0.2	91.8	1.4	6,162

	American Indian	Asian	Black	Hispanic	White	Foreign	Total
U of North Carolina							
Winston-Salem St U	0.2%	0.3%	84.6%	0.1%	14.7%	0.0%	2,532
Vance-Granville CC	1.2	0.4	37.2	0.3	60.9	0.1	1,900
Wake Forest U	0.1	1.4	4.3	0.4	92.9	0.9	5,337
Wake Tech CC	0.3	2.1	17.2	0.5	78.8	1.1	5,405
Warren Wilson C	0.2	1.7	2.7	0.8	87.4	7.3	523
Wayne CC	0.1	0.9	21.7	0.6	76.5	0.1	2,166
Western Piedmont CC	0.3	0.5	4.8	0.3	94.1	0.1	2,290
Wilkes CC	0.1	0.1	4.6	0.1	95.0	0.1	1,765
Wilson Tech CC	0.2	0.0	30.6	0.9	68.3	0.0	1,439
Wingate C	0.0	0.2	6.4	0.5	92.0	0.9	1,709

NORTH DAKOTA

	American Indian	Asian	Black	Hispanic	White	Foreign	Total
Fort Bethold CC	83.2	0.0	0.0	0.8	16.0	0.0	125
Jamestown C	2.1	0.5	0.9	0.6	93.3	2.5	796
Little Hoop CC	100.0	0.0	0.0	0.0	0.0	0.0	120
ND St Bd of Higher Ed Sys							
U of North Dakota							
Main	2.3	0.7	0.3	0.5	93.6	2.6	11,824
Lake Region	2.7	0.7	4.3	1.2	90.6	0.5	923
Williston	7.3	0.2	0.0	0.3	92.0	0.2	586
North Dakota St U Main	0.6	0.7	0.3	0.2	94.8	3.5	9,536
Dickinson St U	0.8	0.1	0.3	0.4	97.6	0.9	1,417
Mayville St U	0.8	0.5	1.3	0.1	92.5	4.8	755
Minot St U	2.0	0.3	1.3	0.6	89.5	6.3	3,246
ND St C of Science	1.9	0.7	0.5	0.1	96.1	0.7	2,385
ND St U Bottineau	5.1	0.2	1.4	0.0	87.3	5.9	489
Valley City St U	0.6	0.1	0.8	0.5	96.2	1.8	1,154
Bismarck St C	2.5	0.1	0.1	0.1	96.8	0.4	2,492
Standing Rock CC	93.1	0.0	0.0	0.0	6.9	0.0	262
Trinity Bible C	1.6	0.0	2.5	1.1	92.8	2.0	445
Turtle Mountain CC	93.2	0.0	0.0	0.0	6.8	0.0	309
U of Mary	6.0	1.1	0.1	0.4	91.5	0.9	1,418

OHIO

	American Indian	Asian	Black	Hispanic	White	Foreign	Total
Air Force Inst of Tech	0.1	1.4	4.9	0.7	87.8	5.2	737
Antioch C	0.4	0.4	8.5	1.4	85.7	3.7	566
Antioch Sch for Adult and							
Experiential Learning	1.3	0.7	9.1	2.4	86.1	0.4	453
Art Academy of Cincinnati ...	0.0	0.4	5.8	0.0	93.3	0.4	223
Antonelli Inst of Art and							
Photography	0.0	0.8	19.5	1.6	78.0	0.0	123
Ashland U	0.0	0.2	8.5	0.3	88.5	2.4	4,053
Athenaeum of Ohio	0.0	0.7	1.0	0.0	98.3	0.0	294
Baldwin-Wallace C	0.1	1.2	5.5	0.5	91.8	0.9	4,563
Belmont Tech C	0.0	0.3	1.7	0.1	97.9	0.0	1,901
Bluffton C	0.0	0.5	4.4	0.0	91.8	3.3	608
Borromeo C of Ohio	0.0	0.0	1.8	3.6	94.6	0.0	56
Bowling Green St U							
Main	0.1	0.6	3.5	0.8	93.5	1.5	18,345
Firelands C	0.1	0.1	1.7	0.8	97.3	0.0	1,206
Bradford Sch	0.0	0.5	5.1	0.0	94.5	0.0	217
Capital U	0.0	0.4	8.0	0.3	90.2	1.0	3,016
Career Com C of Business ...	0.0	0.0	59.9	0.0	40.1	0.0	187

	American Indian	Asian	Black	Hispanic	White	Foreign	Total
Case Western Reserve U	0.2%	5.0%	4.7%	1.0%	76.8%	12.4%	8,333
Cedarville C	0.0	0.3	0.7	0.5	97.4	1.0	1,879
Central Ohio Tech C	0.3	0.4	2.0	0.2	96.8	0.2	1,446
Chatfield C	0.0	1.7	0.0	0.0	98.3	0.0	115
Cincinnati C of Mortuary Science	0.0	0.0	4.1	0.0	95.9	0.0	122
Cincinnati Metropolitan C	0.0	0.3	43.9	0.0	55.8	0.0	351
Cincinnati Tech C	0.5	0.7	16.3	0.4	82.1	0.0	4,404
Circleville Bible C	0.0	0.6	5.6	0.0	93.8	0.0	161
Clark St CC	0.3	0.6	8.1	0.1	90.5	0.2	2,154
Cleveland Inst of Art	0.0	2.1	5.5	1.4	89.7	1.4	513
Cleveland Inst of Music	0.0	2.2	2.6	1.7	81.5	12.0	416
Cleveland St U	0.7	0.5	10.0	1.0	84.2	3.6	17,346
C of Mount Saint Joseph	0.0	0.2	4.5	0.2	93.3	1.8	2,209
C of Wooster	0.1	0.7	4.7	0.3	87.6	6.5	1,895
Columbus C of Art and Design	0.3	1.9	5.5	1.9	88.8	1.5	1,557
Columbus St CC	0.4	1.3	15.8	1.1	80.6	0.8	9,520
Cuyahoga CC	0.5	1.4	23.6	1.4	71.9	1.2	22,010
Davis C	0.0	3.0	10.0	1.5	85.0	0.5	400
Defiance C	0.1	0.1	3.3	1.6	93.0	1.9	1,026
Denison U	0.0	0.8	4.3	0.5	93.4	1.0	2,133
DeVry Inst of Tech	0.0	1.9	13.3	0.8	83.1	0.9	3,013
Dyke C	0.0	1.4	46.9	1.3	50.3	0.1	1,334
Edison St CC	0.3	1.0	1.7	0.1	96.7	0.1	2,574
ETI Tech C	0.0	1.7	41.0	3.2	54.0	0.0	692
Franciscan U of Steubenville .	0.0	0.4	1.3	3.1	92.6	2.6	1,369
Franklin U	0.2	1.2	12.5	0.5	84.5	1.1	4,280
Hebrew Union C-Jewish Inst of Religion	2.5	0.0	0.0	0.0	91.6	5.9	119
Heidelberg C	0.3	1.4	3.3	1.2	92.3	1.6	1,178
Hiram C	0.0	0.9	4.0	0.6	94.4	0.1	1,220
Hocking Tech C	0.1	0.3	6.1	0.4	92.0	1.1	4,108
ITT Tech Inst	0.0	0.0	13.3	1.3	85.4	0.0	624
ITT Tech Inst Stanley campus	0.0	0.5	11.0	0.3	87.8	0.3	617
Jefferson Tech C	0.0	0.0	4.2	0.0	95.7	0.1	1,410
John Carroll U	0.1	0.8	2.5	0.6	95.3	0.6	4,081
Kent St U							
Main	0.1	0.8	5.0	0.5	91.3	2.3	22,753
Ashtabula	0.2	0.2	0.8	0.7	97.8	0.2	868
East Liverpool	0.2	0.0	1.8	0.2	97.8	0.0	546
Geauga	0.0	0.0	0.2	0.4	99.4	0.0	471
Salem	0.0	0.0	1.3	0.1	98.6	0.0	791
Stark	0.1	0.2	2.9	0.1	96.6	0.1	1,811
Trumbull	0.2	0.4	4.7	0.5	94.1	0.1	1,681
Tuscarawas	0.0	0.2	1.0	0.0	98.6	0.1	955
Kenyon C	0.0	1.8	1.3	1.2	93.8	1.9	1,588
Kettering C of Medical Arts ..	0.8	1.0	4.5	0.7	93.0	0.0	597
Lake Erie C	0.1	0.6	2.6	1.0	95.6	0.0	685
Lakeland CC	0.2	0.6	2.0	0.3	96.9	0.0	7,840
Lima Tech C	0.2	0.5	6.1	0.6	92.3	0.3	1,945
Lorain County CC	0.2	0.2	4.6	3.7	91.0	0.2	5,963
Lourdes C	0.4	0.1	4.9	0.9	93.5	0.1	773
Malone C	0.1	0.2	4.0	0.1	95.0	0.6	1,318
Marietta C	0.0	0.4	1.3	0.1	96.8	1.5	1,339
Marion Tech C	0.2	0.7	5.7	0.3	92.9	0.1	1,350
Medical C of Ohio	0.0	6.2	5.7	1.6	79.5	7.0	757
Miami-Jacobs JC of Business	0.0	0.4	31.0	0.2	68.4	0.0	548

OHIO, cont.

	American Indian	Asian	Black	Hispanic	White	Foreign	Total
Miami U							
Hamilton	0.1%	0.7%	2.7%	0.1%	96.3%	0.0%	2,154
Middletown	0.1	0.3	2.3	0.3	96.7	0.4	1,904
Oxford	0.1	1.2	2.3	0.4	94.8	1.3	16,027
Mount Union C	0.0	0.6	5.6	0.7	89.6	3.6	1,294
Mount Vernon Nazarene C	0.0	0.2	0.5	0.4	98.4	0.6	1,087
Muskingum Area Tech C	0.5	0.1	2.3	0.2	96.9	0.0	1,944
Muskingum C	0.3	0.9	1.3	0.2	96.1	1.2	1,142
North Central Tech C	0.3	0.3	2.6	0.6	96.2	0.0	1,828
Northeastern Ohio U's C							
of Medicine	0.3	20.5	1.1	1.8	76.3	0.0	380
Northwest Tech C	0.1	0.1	0.3	2.6	96.9	0.0	1,869
Northwestern Business							
C-Tech Center	0.0	0.2	3.1	0.7	96.1	0.0	1,221
Notre Dame C	0.3	0.8	26.0	4.0	67.2	1.7	749
Oberlin C	0.1	7.2	8.8	2.6	78.4	2.8	2,876
Ohio C of Podiatric Medicine	0.2	3.8	15.3	4.2	75.0	1.4	424
Ohio Dominican C	0.0	0.6	10.5	3.2	78.4	7.3	1,331
Ohio Northern U	0.1	1.1	2.6	0.6	93.9	1.7	2,537
Ohio St U							
Main	0.2	2.5	4.7	1.2	85.9	5.5	53,661
Agricultural Tech Inst	0.3	0.1	4.1	0.0	94.8	0.6	677
Lima	0.0	0.2	2.2	0.5	97.1	0.0	1,276
Mansfield	0.4	0.4	2.0	0.5	96.8	0.0	1,276
Marion	0.4	0.4	4.5	0.1	94.6	0.0	1,134
Newark	0.1	0.3	1.7	0.1	97.7	0.0	1,503
Ohio U							
Main	0.3	0.3	4.7	0.6	87.2	6.9	17,836
Belmont	0.3	0.0	0.6	0.3	97.0	1.9	1,090
Chillicothe	0.1	0.0	1.2	0.1	98.0	0.5	1,468
Ironton	0.2	0.0	1.2	0.0	98.5	0.1	1,303
Lancaster	0.4	0.1	1.9	0.2	97.2	0.2	1,809
Zanesville	0.1	0.2	1.7	0.1	97.8	0.2	1,261
Ohio Wesleyan U	0.1	1.0	3.3	0.5	90.1	5.0	1,773
Otterbein C	0.0	0.4	1.9	0.2	95.3	2.2	2,177
Owens Tech C	0.3	0.3	7.0	2.4	89.8	0.2	6,014
Pontifical C Josephinum	0.0	5.0	2.2	7.7	79.6	5.5	181
Saint Mary Sem	0.0	1.4	0.0	0.0	98.6	0.0	72
Shawnee St U	0.6	0.1	5.3	0.3	93.5	0.1	2,967
Sinclair CC	0.4	1.4	12.7	0.8	84.5	0.2	16,632
Southern Ohio C	0.0	0.7	29.8	0.0	69.5	0.0	574
Southern St CC	0.2	0.0	0.3	0.2	99.2	0.2	1,317
Stark Tech C	0.4	0.2	4.7	0.4	94.4	0.0	3,275
Tiffin U	0.0	0.0	9.4	0.8	87.6	2.2	777
U of Akron							
Main	0.4	0.9	7.6	0.4	87.5	3.2	27,818
Wayne C	0.8	0.5	0.9	0.4	97.1	0.2	1,220
U of Cincinnati							
Main	0.3	2.3	9.3	0.7	84.3	3.1	31,432
Clermont C	1.0	0.6	0.8	0.0	97.7	0.0	1,251
Raymond Walters C	0.6	1.4	7.2	0.5	89.6	0.5	3,725
U of Dayton	0.1	1.1	4.1	1.2	91.7	1.8	11,121
U of Findlay	0.5	0.5	15.4	3.3	79.1	1.3	1,686
U of Rio Grande	0.2	0.2	2.1	0.1	95.8	1.8	1,884
U of Toledo	0.5	0.8	6.1	1.4	83.8	7.5	22,806
Urbana U	0.3	1.3	28.9	0.0	69.0	0.5	765
Ursuline C	0.0	0.8	10.2	1.1	86.9	1.0	1,298

	American Indian	Asian	Black	Hispanic	White	Foreign	Total
Virginia Marti C of Fashion and Art	0.0%	0.4%	29.8%	2.1%	67.2%	0.4%	238
Walsh C	0.0	0.0	5.2	2.5	89.5	2.7	1,297
Washington Tech C	0.5	0.1	0.9	0.2	98.3	0.0	1,716
West Side Inst of Tech	0.0	0.5	19.4	1.1	79.0	0.0	372
Wilberforce U	0.0	0.0	99.7	0.0	0.1	0.1	767
Wilmington C	0.0	0.0	18.3	0.1	79.6	1.9	1,473
Wittenberg U	0.0	0.8	3.5	0.7	92.7	2.4	2,273
Wright St U							
Main	0.1	1.7	5.0	0.6	90.6	2.0	16,149
Lake	0.2	0.5	0.0	0.5	98.7	0.1	828
Xavier U	0.2	1.5	6.9	1.7	87.9	1.8	6,412
Youngstown St U	0.1	0.4	7.0	0.7	90.2	1.5	14,710

OKLAHOMA

	American Indian	Asian	Black	Hispanic	White	Foreign	Total
Bacone C	46.9	0.2	12.5	0.2	40.2	0.0	463
Bartlesville Wesleyan C	3.0	0.9	1.2	1.2	85.5	8.2	427
Cameron U	3.6	2.3	14.6	4.0	75.1	0.4	5,777
Carl Albert JC	12.6	0.2	2.4	1.5	83.3	0.0	1,479
Central St U	1.8	1.5	7.5	1.2	82.7	5.2	14,269
Connors St C	7.1	0.2	8.7	0.5	83.5	0.0	1,740
Dickinson Business Sch	2.0	0.3	30.7	1.1	65.9	0.0	745
East Central U	7.6	0.4	3.0	0.8	88.0	0.2	4,244
Eastern Oklahoma St C	10.9	0.2	6.2	0.5	82.1	0.2	1,772
El Reno JC	2.6	1.1	5.5	1.4	88.0	1.4	1,328
Flaming Rainbow U	50.8	0.0	2.5	0.8	45.9	0.0	122
Hillsdale Free Will Baptist C ..	4.3	0.9	7.8	0.0	87.0	0.0	115
Langston U	1.5	1.2	54.2	1.0	39.6	2.5	2,308
Mid-America Bible C	2.6	0.0	9.8	0.4	86.0	1.3	235
Murray St C	7.0	0.3	3.6	0.9	88.2	0.0	1,401
National Education Ctr- Spartan Sch of Aeronautics	4.1	2.7	5.9	3.5	80.0	3.8	2,293
Northeastern Okla A&M C	14.0	0.2	7.1	0.2	77.0	1.5	2,469
Northeastern St U	16.1	0.2	4.3	0.7	77.9	0.9	8,742
Northern Oklahoma C	6.3	0.5	1.8	1.1	89.8	0.5	1,897
Northwestern Oklahoma St U	1.8	0.1	2.5	1.0	94.2	0.5	1,751
Oklahoma Baptist U	3.2	1.0	6.5	0.5	87.5	1.2	1,847
Oklahoma Christian C	0.9	2.0	4.6	0.9	91.1	0.4	1,617
Oklahoma City CC	2.6	2.9	5.0	1.6	87.0	1.0	8,511
Oklahoma City U	3.0	3.0	5.0	1.9	69.1	18.0	2,957
Oklahoma JC	0.2	1.3	37.7	1.4	59.2	0.2	559
Oklahoma JC of Business and Tech	4.8	1.0	20.9	1.6	71.4	0.3	2,103
Oklahoma Mission Baptist C .	1.2	2.4	10.8	0.0	85.6	0.0	167
Oklahoma St U							
Main	2.7	1.2	2.7	0.9	85.4	7.1	21,258
Okmulgee	2.4	3.6	6.4	1.5	85.5	0.7	3,290
C of Osteopathic Medicine .	4.5	1.9	4.1	2.6	86.2	0.7	269
Oral Roberts U	0.7	2.2	13.4	4.0	74.5	5.2	4,148
Oklahoma Panhandle St U ...	0.4	0.4	3.9	5.9	89.4	0.1	1,140
Phillips U	0.7	0.2	4.1	1.0	83.2	10.7	942
Rogers St C	9.9	0.8	1.6	0.7	82.7	4.4	3,055
Rose St C	2.9	2.6	14.0	2.4	77.3	0.8	9,460
Saint Gregory's C	2.7	2.0	6.0	5.3	79.4	4.7	301
Seminole JC	10.2	0.3	4.7	0.7	82.9	1.1	1,486
Southeastern Oklahoma St U	25.3	2.9	3.6	0.9	66.3	1.0	3,563

OKLAHOMA, cont.

	American Indian	Asian	Black	Hispanic	White	Foreign	Total
Southern Nazarene U	0.8%	0.4%	4.5%	0.9%	87.2%	6.2%	1,393
Southwestern C of							
Christian Ministries	0.8	6.7	2.5	0.8	89.2	0.0	120
Southwestern Oklahoma St U	2.8	1.3	2.7	1.3	91.4	0.6	5,309
Tulsa JC	2.2	1.1	5.1	0.9	90.6	0.0	16,778
U of Oklahoma							
Health Sciences Center	4.2	4.2	4.7	1.4	83.0	2.5	2,459
Norman	2.4	2.3	4.4	1.4	84.0	5.5	22,224
U of Science and Arts of							
Oklahoma	7.2	0.9	4.5	1.0	84.4	2.0	1,374
U of Tulsa	2.2	1.8	3.1	1.1	83.1	8.8	4,344
Western Oklahoma St C	1.8	1.3	7.8	5.0	84.1	0.0	2,056

OREGON

	American Indian	Asian	Black	Hispanic	White	Foreign	Total
Bassist C	0.5	3.4	1.4	1.0	88.9	4.8	208
Blue Mountain CC	2.0	0.8	0.5	2.4	94.3	0.0	1,617
Central Oregon CC	1.6	0.4	0.1	0.7	96.0	1.2	2,314
Chemeketa CC	1.4	2.2	0.7	2.1	93.5	0.1	8,726
Clackamas CC	0.5	3.0	0.8	3.9	90.8	0.8	5,456
Clatsop CC	2.4	2.7	0.1	1.6	93.2	0.0	821
Columbia Christian C	0.0	2.9	3.2	0.7	91.1	2.1	280
Concordia C	0.4	4.9	4.2	0.9	74.0	15.6	450
Eugene Bible C	0.0	0.0	0.8	4.1	91.0	4.1	122
George Fox C	0.1	1.7	0.7	1.8	94.0	1.7	828
ITT Tech Inst	0.8	2.3	1.7	1.5	93.6	0.2	660
Lane CC	2.0	2.2	1.0	1.4	90.9	2.5	7,254
Lewis and Clark C	0.8	4.5	1.2	1.3	85.9	6.3	3,225
Linfield C	0.7	4.6	0.8	0.7	87.7	5.5	2,035
Linn-Benton CC	0.6	0.9	0.4	0.6	96.6	0.9	5,492
Marylhurst C for							
Lifelong Learning	1.0	1.0	1.4	0.8	95.6	0.2	1,005
Mount Angel Sem	0.0	6.7	0.0	4.8	79.0	9.5	105
Mount Hood CC	0.8	2.8	1.6	1.3	93.3	0.2	7,885
Multnomah Sch of the Bible .	0.7	2.8	1.4	1.1	90.8	3.1	710
Northwest Christian C	0.5	1.8	0.5	1.4	90.8	5.0	218
Oregon Graduate Center	0.0	11.4	0.0	0.0	61.2	27.3	245
Oregon Polytechnic Inst	0.3	2.7	2.1	1.8	92.5	0.6	332
Oregon St Sys of Higher Ed							
Eastern Oregon St C	1.4	2.8	0.8	1.5	89.3	4.2	2,224
Oregon Health Science U ..	0.6	7.5	0.8	1.2	87.3	2.6	1,288
Oregon Inst of Tech	1.9	3.2	1.8	1.4	89.9	1.8	2,987
Oregon St U	1.4	5.2	1.0	1.3	81.2	9.8	16,042
Portland St U	0.9	5.8	1.8	1.5	85.5	4.6	17,316
Southern Oregon St C	1.3	1.3	0.5	1.5	93.9	1.5	5,164
U of Oregon	0.8	4.4	1.2	1.5	84.5	7.6	18,840
Western Oregon St C	0.7	0.9	0.5	5.5	89.6	2.8	4,571
Pacific Northwest C of Art ...	1.5	3.4	0.5	1.5	89.7	3.4	203
Pacific U	1.4	12.8	1.5	2.0	79.3	3.1	1,364
Portland CC	0.6	5.9	2.6	1.7	88.0	1.2	20,904
Reed C	0.2	6.1	1.4	1.9	89.0	1.5	1,286
Rogue CC	1.2	0.7	0.1	0.0	97.4	0.5	2,460
Southwestern Oregon CC	1.6	1.0	0.7	1.1	95.1	0.5	2,570
Treasure Valley CC	0.6	2.2	0.9	3.5	89.4	3.4	1,268
Umpqua CC	1.1	0.6	0.9	0.9	96.4	0.1	1,408
U of Portland	0.5	5.3	1.1	1.4	79.1	12.5	2,367
Warner Pacific C	0.6	2.5	2.5	0.6	90.1	3.7	354

	American Indian	Asian	Black	Hispanic	White	Foreign	Total
Western Baptist C	0.6%	1.5%	1.8%	0.9%	95.1%	0.0%	328
Western Conservative							
Baptist Sem	0.0	0.5	0.0	0.0	93.1	6.4	423
Western Evangelical Sem	0.0	0.8	2.5	0.0	80.2	16.5	121
Western Sts Chiropractic C ..	0.5	1.8	0.3	2.3	87.2	8.0	399
Willamette U	0.6	4.2	0.9	1.7	89.9	2.7	2,089

PENNSYLVANIA

	American Indian	Asian	Black	Hispanic	White	Foreign	Total
Academy of the New Church .	0.0	0.0	0.0	0.6	74.7	24.7	158
Albright C	0.1	1.9	1.7	0.7	93.9	1.7	1,892
Allegheny C	0.1	1.4	3.3	1.1	91.3	2.8	1,997
Allentown C of Saint							
Francis De Sales	0.1	0.1	0.3	0.6	98.8	0.1	1,679
Alvernia C	0.2	0.4	1.3	1.6	96.1	0.4	1,060
American C	0.0	0.0	0.0	0.0	100.0	0.0	437
Annenberg Research Inst	0.0	8.3	0.0	0.0	91.7	0.0	12
Antioch C Philadelphia	0.3	0.0	76.1	3.8	19.8	0.0	343
Baptist Bible C of Pa	0.2	0.5	1.3	0.7	96.9	0.5	613
Beaver C	0.0	1.7	7.4	1.0	89.0	0.7	2,197
Berean Inst	0.0	1.6	95.8	1.6	0.0	1.0	192
Biblical Theological Sem	0.0	6.6	1.1	0.0	87.9	4.4	182
Bryn Mawr C	0.2	8.2	3.7	2.2	79.3	6.4	1,847
Bucknell U	0.1	1.2	2.0	0.9	93.3	2.5	3,412
Bucks County CC	0.1	1.1	1.3	0.7	96.8	0.0	10,028
Butler County CC	0.0	0.2	0.8	0.3	98.8	0.0	2,488
Cabrini C	0.0	0.6	2.2	0.4	96.8	0.0	1,262
Carlow C	0.8	0.6	14.4	0.4	82.5	1.1	962
Carnegie Mellon U	0.1	2.2	2.2	0.2	83.5	11.8	6,993
Cedar Crest C	0.2	0.4	0.5	1.2	97.4	0.4	1,039
Center for Degree Studies ...	0.2	0.6	18.9	1.8	78.1	0.4	17,738
Central Pennsylvania							
Business Sch	0.1	0.7	1.6	0.9	96.6	0.1	696
Chatham C	0.0	1.2	8.3	0.7	87.9	1.9	686
Chestnut Hill C	0.0	2.1	6.7	2.4	88.4	0.3	1,191
C Misericordia	0.0	0.0	0.6	0.0	98.9	0.5	1,232
CC of Allegheny County	0.3	0.8	10.8	0.3	87.5	0.3	18,211
CC of Beaver County	0.0	0.0	4.9	0.0	95.1	0.0	2,603
CC of Philadelphia	0.4	5.3	38.8	4.1	51.4	0.0	14,215
Curtis Inst of Music	0.0	6.1	2.5	3.1	57.1	31.3	163
Dean Inst of Tech	0.0	0.0	13.9	0.8	85.2	0.0	122
Delaware County CC	0.1	1.0	4.0	0.4	94.4	0.0	8,273
Delaware Valley C	0.0	0.0	2.6	0.0	97.4	0.0	1,654
Dickinson C	0.0	2.3	0.7	0.9	94.8	1.3	2,041
Dickinson Sch of Law	0.0	1.2	1.3	0.7	95.0	1.8	596
Drexel U	0.2	5.5	4.4	1.0	83.6	5.3	12,263
Du Bois Business C	0.0	0.7	0.0	0.0	99.3	0.0	278
Duquesne U	1.0	1.4	3.3	1.0	92.9	0.4	6,366
Eastern Baptist Theol Sem ...	0.0	2.8	27.4	2.0	64.7	3.1	351
Eastern C	0.1	1.2	6.8	1.5	84.1	6.3	1,155
Elizabethtown C	0.0	0.8	0.7	0.2	97.9	0.4	1,788
Erie Business Center	0.0	0.0	4.8	0.0	95.2	0.0	248
Evangelical Sch of Theology .	0.0	4.8	0.0	0.0	95.2	0.0	62
Faith Theological Sem	0.0	43.4	0.0	1.9	5.7	49.1	53
Franklin and Marshall C	0.0	3.0	2.8	1.2	90.7	2.2	2,410
Gannon U	0.2	1.0	1.8	0.3	94.9	1.7	3,687
Geneva C	0.2	1.1	4.7	0.2	93.1	0.7	1,234

PA., cont.

	American Indian	Asian	Black	Hispanic	White	Foreign	Total
Gettysburg C	0.0%	0.9%	1.7%	0.6%	95.2%	1.5%	2,022
Gratz C	0.0	0.0	11.5	0.0	86.1	2.4	582
Grove City C	0.0	2.2	0.2	0.8	96.7	0.0	2,152
Gwynedd-Mercy C	0.2	1.4	3.0	0.4	92.9	2.2	1,795
Hahnemann U	0.3	6.0	12.8	1.9	77.5	1.6	2,042
Harcum JC	0.0	1.7	7.3	1.4	85.0	4.5	762
Harrisburg Area CC	0.1	2.0	5.1	1.0	91.5	0.3	6,686
Haverford C	0.0	6.9	4.8	3.7	84.6	0.0	1,105
Holy Family C	0.1	0.7	1.3	1.0	95.3	1.6	1,657
Hussian Sch of Art	0.0	0.0	7.3	2.2	90.4	0.0	178
Immaculata C	0.0	0.8	3.1	3.2	91.3	1.6	2,095
Johnson Tech Inst	0.0	0.2	0.0	0.0	99.5	0.2	440
Juniata C	0.0	0.8	0.7	0.0	96.0	2.5	1,137
Keystone JC	0.1	0.2	2.7	0.3	95.7	1.0	1,245
King's C	0.0	0.2	0.2	0.5	98.8	0.3	2,304
La Roche C	0.0	0.6	1.6	0.6	97.0	0.1	1,852
La Salle U	0.0	0.4	5.3	0.6	93.7	0.0	6,364
Lackawanna JC	0.2	0.3	1.6	0.3	97.7	0.0	1,192
Lafayette C	0.0	2.0	3.0	0.9	90.9	3.1	2,352
Lancaster Bible C	0.0	0.8	1.8	1.1	94.2	2.1	380
Lancaster Theological Sem ..	0.0	0.5	8.9	0.5	87.9	2.3	214
Lebanon Valley C	0.2	1.0	0.5	0.5	97.6	0.2	1,274
Lehigh County CC	0.0	1.6	1.1	1.8	95.2	0.3	3,487
Lehigh U	0.0	3.1	1.5	1.4	86.1	7.8	6,569
Lincoln Tech Inst	0.0	0.9	1.3	1.2	95.8	0.9	687
Lincoln U	0.0	0.5	90.5	1.4	7.1	0.6	1,251
Lutheran Theological Sem at Gettysburg	0.0	0.4	2.2	0.7	95.9	0.7	270
Lutheran Theological Sem at Philadelphia	0.0	1.8	22.3	1.8	73.3	0.7	273
Luzerne County CC	0.1	1.1	1.2	0.4	97.2	0.1	5,688
Lycoming C	0.0	1.2	0.7	0.5	97.5	0.1	1,150
Manor JC	0.3	1.1	9.2	2.2	86.7	0.5	368
Mary Immaculate Sem	0.0	0.0	0.0	2.7	97.3	0.0	37
Marywood C	0.1	0.2	0.3	0.7	97.9	0.9	3,006
McCarrie Schs of Health Sciences & Tech	0.0	0.0	61.1	13.0	25.9	0.0	54
Medical C of Pennsylvania ...	0.2	9.7	5.4	1.1	81.4	2.2	554
Median Sch of Allied Health Careers	0.0	0.0	16.3	0.0	83.7	0.0	252
Mercyhurst C	0.2	0.4	4.1	0.2	95.1	0.0	2,018
Messiah C	0.1	1.4	2.0	1.0	93.8	1.8	2,184
Montgomery County CC	0.5	2.8	4.5	0.9	91.3	0.0	7,170
Moore C of Art and Design ...	0.1	2.9	6.7	1.3	86.1	2.8	685
Moravian C	0.1	0.7	0.7	0.3	98.2	0.0	1,804
Mount Aloysius JC	0.0	0.2	1.2	0.2	98.0	0.4	943
Muhlenberg C	0.0	1.9	0.6	0.8	96.0	0.7	2,084
Neumann C	0.1	1.1	6.1	0.7	91.7	0.4	1,139
Northampton County Area CC	0.2	1.0	1.7	2.5	94.1	0.4	4,712
Northeastern Christian JC	0.6	0.0	22.9	1.7	65.4	9.5	179
Peirce JC	0.3	1.4	40.7	2.5	54.3	0.8	1,197
Pennsylvania C of Optometry	0.2	4.1	5.4	2.1	87.5	0.8	634
Pennsylvania C of Podiatric Medicine	0.2 ·	4.6	6.2	2.1	84.4	2.5	437
Pennsylvania C of Tech	0.1	0.3	1.2	0.2	98.2	0.0	3,700
Pennsylvania Inst of Tech	0.0	1.7	19.7	0.3	78.1	0.3	360

	American Indian	Asian	Black	Hispanic	White	Foreign	Total
Pennsylvania St U							
Main	0.2%	2.1%	3.9%	1.4%	87.8%	4.7%	37,269
Allentown	0.0	3.2	0.6	1.4	94.5	0.3	781
Altoona	0.2	1.2	3.7	0.7	94.0	0.2	2,604
Beaver	0.1	0.9	4.7	0.8	93.4	0.1	1,104
Berks	0.0	1.6	0.3	1.0	97.1	0.0	1,440
Delaware	0.1	2.5	6.4	1.0	90.1	0.0	1,861
Du Bois	0.5	0.4	0.3	0.2	98.3	0.2	957
Erie-Behrend C	0.1	1.3	3.7	0.7	94.0	0.1	2,830
Fayette	0.0	0.3	2.7	0.4	96.4	0.1	894
Great Valley	0.9	6.8	4.2	0.8	87.2	0.1	886
Harrisburg-Capital C	0.1	2.2	3.7	0.8	92.4	0.8	3,144
Hazleton	0.2	1.9	2.0	2.4	93.4	0.1	1,276
Hershey Medical C	0.3	3.4	4.0	0.9	87.7	3.7	698
McKeesport	0.1	1.4	9.0	0.1	89.3	0.1	1,463
Mont Alto	0.3	2.6	4.5	0.9	91.4	0.2	970
New Kensington	0.1	0.6	1.8	0.1	97.4	0.1	1,428
Ogontz	0.1	3.1	5.9	1.1	89.8	0.1	3,502
Schuylkill	0.0	1.8	1.1	0.7	96.4	0.0	1,122
Shenango Valley	0.1	0.4	2.9	0.1	96.6	0.0	1,078
Wilkes-Barre	0.1	0.9	1.0	0.4	97.4	0.1	980
Worthington-Scranton	0.2	0.6	0.2	0.7	98.3	0.0	1,321
York	0.2	2.8	2.3	0.9	93.8	0.0	1,662
Philadelphia C of Bible	0.7	1.4	5.7	2.7	86.1	3.4	584
Philadelphia C of							
Osteopathic Medicine	0.0	2.0	2.8	1.2	93.8	0.1	808
Philadelphia C of							
Pharmacy and Science	0.0	8.9	2.1	0.6	86.0	2.6	1,603
Philadelphia C of Textiles							
and Science	0.0	2.1	8.3	0.5	84.5	4.6	3,417
Pinebrook JC	0.0	2.7	14.2	0.0	73.6	9.5	148
Pittsburgh Inst of Aeronautics	0.1	0.1	2.1	0.1	97.6	0.0	878
Pittsburgh Theological Sem	0.0	1.3	5.8	0.3	92.5	0.0	308
Point Park C	0.0	1.1	8.0	0.7	86.1	4.1	2,820
Reading Area CC	0.4	1.3	6.9	5.3	85.7	0.4	1,640
Reformed Presbyterian							
Theol Sem	0.0	0.0	38.7	0.0	58.7	2.5	80
RETS Electronic Sch	0.3	0.9	14.4	1.1	83.0	0.3	348
Robert Morris C	0.2	0.3	4.4	0.2	94.2	0.6	5,500
Rosemont C	0.0	1.1	2.9	1.4	94.3	0.3	648
Saint Charles Borromeo Sem	0.0	1.7	3.1	2.6	92.6	0.0	351
Saint Francis C	0.0	0.3	1.6	0.2	98.0	0.0	1,791
Saint Joseph's U	0.0	1.3	5.9	1.9	87.7	3.2	5,787
Saint Vincent C	0.1	0.3	1.2	1.0	96.6	0.7	1,205
Saint Vincent Sem	0.0	0.0	0.0	0.0	100.0	0.0	55
Seton Hill C	0.1	0.6	3.3	4.8	90.0	1.1	870
Spring Garden C	0.1	2.8	10.9	1.3	83.6	1.2	1,545
St Sys of Higher Education							
Bloomsburg U of Pa	0.1	0.5	2.3	0.6	95.8	0.7	6,804
California U of Pa	0.2	0.7	3.9	0.4	94.1	0.7	6,313
Cheyney U of Pa	0.1	0.1	92.5	0.4	3.9	3.1	1,361
Clarion U of Pa	0.1	0.2	2.2	0.1	94.9	2.4	6,601
East Stroudsburg U of Pa	0.1	0.7	2.6	1.1	94.0	1.6	4,910
Edinboro U of Pa	0.2	0.4	3.5	0.3	94.3	1.3	7,001
Indiana U of Pa	0.1	0.5	4.0	0.4	92.6	2.4	13,650
Kutztown U of Pa	0.1	0.6	3.0	0.9	94.5	0.9	7,167
Lock Haven U of Pa	0.2	0.3	3.0	0.3	94.3	1.9	3,012

PA., cont.

	American Indian	Asian	Black	Hispanic	White	Foreign	Total
St Sys of Higher Education							
Mansfield U of Pa	0.1%	0.1%	2.9%	0.3%	95.8%	0.9%	2,980
Millersville U of Pa	0.2	1.5	4.7	1.3	92.0	0.4	7,389
Shippensburg U of Pa	0.1	0.7	3.1	0.4	94.7	1.0	6,352
Slippery Rock U of Pa	0.3	0.3	3.1	0.4	94.2	1.8	7,360
West Chester U of Pa	0.1	1.1	6.0	0.7	90.8	1.3	11,475
Susquehanna U	0.1	0.5	0.4	0.5	97.8	0.8	1,697
Swarthmore C	0.3	4.6	6.7	1.7	81.6	5.1	1,356
Temple U	0.3	3.9	14.2	2.1	76.0	3.5	32,139
Thiel C	0.0	0.2	5.6	0.0	93.0	1.2	917
Thomas Jefferson U	0.5	6.1	7.1	1.7	83.1	1.5	2,112
Trinity Episcopal Sch for							
Ministry	0.0	0.0	2.6	0.9	92.2	4.3	116
United Wesleyan C	0.0	0.0	6.6	1.3	76.3	15.8	152
U of the Arts	0.6	2.7	7.8	1.7	82.7	4.5	1,396
U of Pennsylvania	0.2	5.6	5.2	2.2	74.7	12.1	22,169
U of Pittsburgh							
Main	0.1	1.9	8.2	0.8	84.1	4.9	28,524
Bradford	0.2	0.9	2.9	0.5	95.4	0.0	954
Greensburg	0.0	0.6	0.6	0.1	98.7	0.0	1,452
Johnstown	0.0	0.4	1.4	0.2	98.0	0.1	3,270
Titusville	0.0	0.8	0.5	0.3	98.5	0.0	394
U of Scranton	0.1	0.6	0.2	0.4	98.0	0.6	4,929
Ursinus C	0.2	1.0	1.1	0.5	96.7	0.4	2,286
Valley Forge Christian C	0.2	3.8	3.6	1.8	89.7	1.0	506
Valley Forge Military JC	0.0	1.0	4.1	2.6	87.8	4.6	196
Villa Maria C	0.0	1.0	2.3	0.0	96.8	0.0	708
Villanova U	0.1	1.6	2.2	0.7	95.0	0.4	12,054
Washington and Jefferson C	0.1	1.3	1.7	0.6	96.0	0.4	1,390
Watterson Career Center	0.0	0.0	89.0	9.9	1.1	0.0	91
Watterson Sch of							
Business and Tech	0.0	0.0	72.1	26.2	1.6	0.0	305
Waynesburg C	0.0	0.4	5.1	0.0	92.6	1.9	990
Westminster C	0.0	0.1	0.5	0.0	99.2	0.1	1,475
Westminster Theol Sem	0.2	18.1	3.9	1.0	66.0	10.7	485
Westmoreland County CC	0.1	0.3	1.4	0.0	98.2	0.0	4,570
Widener U	0.2	1.1	7.5	0.6	90.3	0.3	6,173
Wilkes C	0.0	0.9	0.3	0.2	98.0	0.6	3,626
Wilson C	0.0	0.0	0.9	0.4	97.4	1.3	702
York C of Pennsylvania	0.0	0.9	1.7	0.5	96.8	0.1	4,873

RHODE ISLAND

	American Indian	Asian	Black	Hispanic	White	Foreign	Total
Brown U	0.1	7.6	6.0	2.7	76.8	6.8	7,612
Bryant C	0.0	0.5	0.7	1.0	96.9	0.9	5,658
CC of Rhode Island	0.7	1.7	4.2	2.7	90.4	0.3	14,715
Johnson & Wales U	0.3	1.0	6.0	1.6	88.3	2.9	7,210
New England Inst of Tech	0.1	0.6	1.5	0.3	97.3	0.3	1,770
Providence C	0.0	0.4	1.0	0.6	97.4	0.6	5,750
Rhode Island C	0.2	1.0	1.9	1.4	95.0	0.6	8,431
Rhode Island Sch of Design	0.1	2.9	2.5	1.1	83.5	9.8	1,943
Roger Williams C	0.3	0.7	0.5	0.7	95.8	2.1	3,655
Salve Regina the Newport C	0.2	0.3	0.5	0.4	97.2	1.4	2,252
U of Rhode Island	0.3	1.6	2.0	1.4	91.5	3.1	15,843

SOUTH CAROLINA

	American Indian	Asian	Black	Hispanic	White	Foreign	Total
Aiken Tech C	0.7%	0.9%	28.4%	0.7%	69.1%	0.2%	1,485
Anderson C	0.0	0.2	9.8	0.3	87.8	2.0	1,045
Baptist C at Charleston	0.2	0.8	20.6	0.8	77.7	0.0	1,926
Benedict C	0.0	0.0	98.5	0.0	0.0	1.5	1,448
Bob Jones U	0.0	0.5	29.6	0.4	68.6	0.9	4,384
Career Com C of Business	0.0	0.0	88.0	0.0	12.0	0.0	92
Central Wesleyan C	0.0	0.6	8.8	0.0	89.5	1.0	679
Chesterfield-Marlboro Tech C	1.2	0.3	24.2	0.1	74.1	0.0	731
Citadel Military C of SC	0.2	0.5	7.8	0.3	90.5	0.7	3,628
Claflin C	0.0	0.0	99.1	0.0	0.5	0.4	742
Clemson U	0.1	0.6	5.3	0.5	89.5	3.9	14,794
Clinton JC	0.0	0.0	100.0	0.0	0.0	0.0	88
Coker C	0.4	0.4	25.8	1.1	71.1	1.2	814
C of Charleston	0.2	1.5	6.5	0.5	89.7	1.7	6,205
Columbia Bible C and Sem . .	0.0	2.0	2.6	1.8	85.8	7.8	929
Columbia C	0.2	1.1	20.5	0.6	77.4	0.2	1,213
Columbia JC of Business	0.0	0.0	86.9	0.2	12.6	0.2	427
Converse C	0.1	0.4	3.2	0.5	95.4	0.4	1,251
Denmark Tech C	0.0	0.0	98.6	0.0	1.4	0.0	699
Erskine C and Sem	0.1	0.3	7.0	0.6	90.4	1.6	674
Florence Darlington Tech C . .	0.1	0.2	25.5	0.3	73.9	0.1	1,875
Francis Marion C	0.2	0.6	14.2	0.2	84.5	0.3	3,929
Furman U	0.0	0.8	3.8	0.3	95.0	0.0	3,205
Greenville Tech C	0.1	0.9	12.5	0.6	85.7	0.2	6,135
Horry-Georgetown Tech C	0.2	1.0	16.0	0.5	82.2	0.1	1,661
Johnson & Wales U							
Charleston	1.0	1.0	14.3	0.8	82.8	0.0	495
Lander C	0.1	0.4	16.1	0.3	81.8	1.4	2,461
Limestone C	0.0	0.1	17.7	0.5	81.1	0.5	921
Lutheran Theol							
Southern Sem	0.0	0.0	6.9	0.0	93.1	0.0	160
Medical U of South Carolina . .	0.2	2.8	7.0	0.6	88.4	1.0	2,118
Midlands Tech C	0.3	0.7	28.5	1.2	69.2	0.0	6,082
Morris C	0.0	0.0	100.0	0.0	0.0	0.0	774
Newberry C	0.4	0.4	16.8	0.3	81.8	0.3	686
Nielsen Electronics Inst	0.0	2.6	60.7	0.0	36.7	0.0	229
North Greenville C	0.4	0.6	33.3	0.4	65.0	0.4	532
Orangeburg-Calhoun Tech C .	0.2	0.4	42.3	0.3	56.5	0.3	1,149
Piedmont Tech C	0.0	0.2	28.3	0.2	71.3	0.0	1,745
Presbyterian C	0.0	0.2	4.1	0.2	95.0	0.5	1,108
Rutledge C Charleston	0.0	2.2	49.3	2.5	45.9	0.0	357
Rutledge C Spartanburg	0.0	0.0	44.4	0.0	55.6	0.0	135
Sherman C of Straight							
Chiropractic	0.0	1.6	4.1	0.0	81.1	13.1	122
South Carolina St C	0.1	0.4	91.8	0.0	7.5	0.2	4,399
Spartanburg Methodist C	0.0	0.5	20.5	0.3	78.5	0.2	976
Spartanburg Tech C	0.2	1.4	13.3	0.2	84.8	0.1	1,725
Sumter Area Tech C	0.1	0.8	37.4	1.2	60.4	0.1	1,564
Tech C of the Lowcountry	2.0	0.6	34.7	1.1	60.8	0.7	950
Tri-County Tech C	0.1	0.3	9.0	0.8	89.1	0.7	2,327
Trident Tech C	0.3	2.6	18.2	1.0	77.6	0.4	5,594
U of South Carolina							
Columbia	0.1	1.3	12.4	0.8	82.2	3.3	26,435
Aiken	0.0	0.5	14.6	0.8	83.8	0.3	2,532
Beaufort	0.5	1.3	13.6	2.5	81.6	0.6	1,010

S.C., cont.

	American Indian	Asian	Black	Hispanic	White	Foreign	Total
U of South Carolina							
Coastal Carolina	0.2%	0.7%	7.9%	0.5%	89.6%	1.1%	4,135
Lancaster	0.1	0.4	13.6	0.0	85.7	0.2	1,004
Salkehatchie	0.3	0.6	26.6	0.0	72.1	0.3	628
Spartanburg	0.0	1.0	8.7	0.4	89.0	0.8	3,265
Sumter	0.1	1.2	15.8	1.1	81.7	0.2	1,440
Union	0.3	0.0	16.9	0.3	82.5	0.0	343
Williamsburg Tech C	0.0	0.0	35.8	0.2	63.9	0.0	402
Winthrop C	0.1	0.4	14.8	0.7	81.6	2.4	5,351
Wofford C	0.1	1.0	6.4	0.5	91.6	0.4	1,118

SOUTH DAKOTA

	American Indian	Asian	Black	Hispanic	White	Foreign	Total
Augustana C	0.3	0.4	0.7	0.1	94.9	3.5	2,048
Dakota Wesleyan U	8.8	0.3	0.7	0.0	89.4	0.7	667
Huron U	14.9	0.0	10.1	0.8	71.4	2.7	483
Kilian CC	1.3	0.0	0.8	0.0	97.9	0.0	237
Mount Marty C	1.5	0.5	0.5	0.1	97.3	0.1	850
National C	5.1	0.5	4.7	2.7	86.2	0.8	918
National C Sioux Falls	2.8	0.8	1.7	1.4	93.2	0.0	355
North American Baptist Sem .	0.0	1.6	0.0	0.0	94.3	4.1	123
Oglala Lakota C	90.5	0.0	0.0	0.0	9.5	0.0	897
Presentation C	14.1	0.6	0.0	0.3	84.5	0.6	354
Sinte Gleska C	74.5	0.0	0.0	0.0	25.5	0.0	502
Sioux Falls C	0.8	0.8	0.6	0.1	97.4	0.3	880
SD St Bd of Regents Sys							
U of South Dakota	1.7	0.5	0.7	0.1	96.5	0.6	6,759
South Dakota St U	0.7	0.3	0.2	0.1	95.8	2.9	7,735
Black Hills St U	1.6	0.2	0.7	0.4	97.1	0.1	2,282
Dakota St C	0.4	0.6	1.2	0.2	97.3	0.4	1,111
Northern St U	2.5	0.2	0.1	0.0	97.1	0.1	3,066
Sisseton-Wahpeton CC	85.5	0.0	0.0	0.0	14.5	0.0	145
SD Sch of Mines and Tech .	1.4	0.7	0.5	0.2	85.2	12.1	2,048

TENNESSEE

	American Indian	Asian	Black	Hispanic	White	Foreign	Total
American Baptist C	0.0	0.0	86.5	0.5	0.0	13.0	185
Aquinas JC	0.5	1.4	5.2	1.6	89.3	2.0	440
Belmont C	0.1	0.5	3.0	0.3	92.8	3.3	2,580
Bethel C	0.0	0.0	6.5	0.0	92.1	1.3	596
Bristol U	0.0	0.0	13.0	1.0	85.5	0.5	193
Career Com C of Business ...	0.4	0.0	21.9	0.7	76.3	0.7	274
Carson-Newman C	0.3	0.2	3.6	0.4	94.9	0.7	1,999
Christian Brothers C	0.3	1.6	19.5	0.8	75.4	2.4	1,798
Church of God Sch of Theol .	0.5	1.0	3.4	3.4	72.4	19.2	203
Cooper Inst	0.0	0.0	30.4	0.0	69.6	0.0	79
Crichton C	0.0	0.3	35.0	0.3	63.4	1.0	314
Cumberland U	0.0	1.1	7.4	0.3	90.6	0.6	651
David Lipscomb U	0.1	0.3	2.6	0.2	96.2	0.6	2,320
Draughons JC Bristol	0.0	0.0	4.1	0.0	95.9	0.0	197
Draughons JC Johnson City ..	0.0	0.3	3.0	0.0	96.7	0.0	300
Draughons JC Kingsport	0.0	0.6	3.7	0.0	95.1	0.6	164
Draughons JC Knoxville	0.2	0.0	19.0	0.4	79.6	0.9	568
Draughons JC Memphis	0.0	0.0	78.6	0.0	21.4	0.0	388
Draughons JC Nashville	0.0	0.6	30.1	10.0	59.4	0.0	512
Emmanuel Sch of Religion ...	0.0	0.6	1.3	0.6	92.3	5.1	156

	American Indian	Asian	Black	Hispanic	White	Foreign	Total
Fisk U	0.0%	0.0%	98.1%	0.0%	0.1%	1.8%	774
Free Will Baptist Bible C	0.7	0.0	0.3	0.7	96.5	1.7	286
Freed-Hardeman C	0.1	0.5	5.7	0.1	90.7	2.9	1,144
Harding U Grad Sch of Religion	0.0	0.0	3.7	0.0	90.7	5.6	162
Hiwassee C	0.0	0.0	6.8	0.0	89.2	3.9	584
Johnson Bible C	0.0	0.2	0.7	0.9	95.6	2.6	430
King C	0.0	1.9	0.9	4.3	91.2	1.9	588
Knoxville Business C	0.0	2.0	20.0	0.0	78.0	0.0	250
Knoxville C	0.2	0.0	98.9	0.0	0.3	0.7	1,310
Lambuth C	0.0	0.3	13.5	0.1	82.3	3.7	747
Lane C	0.0	0.0	99.6	0.0	0.0	0.4	541
Lee C	0.5	0.7	2.0	3.1	89.8	4.0	1,535
Lemoyne-Owen C	0.0	0.0	98.1	0.0	0.3	1.6	1,130
Lincoln Memorial U	0.0	0.1	1.5	0.1	86.5	11.8	1,582
Martin Methodist C	0.3	0.0	9.7	1.2	80.6	8.2	330
Maryville C	0.1	0.4	3.8	0.9	90.6	4.2	787
McKenzie C	0.0	0.0	29.1	1.3	69.6	0.0	237
Memphis C of Art	0.0	1.2	14.6	1.2	82.3	0.8	254
Memphis Theological Sem	0.0	0.7	24.5	0.0	74.8	0.0	143
Mid-America Baptist Theol Sem	0.0	0.2	1.4	0.0	95.7	2.7	414
Milligan C	0.0	0.8	1.8	1.4	95.4	0.6	658
Rhodes C	0.0	1.6	4.5	0.5	92.6	0.8	1,346
Rutledge C Memphis	0.0	0.0	92.9	0.0	6.5	0.6	170
Southern C of Optometry	0.8	2.1	3.9	1.8	91.4	0.0	382
Southern C of Seventh-Day Adventists	0.4	2.3	7.5	4.9	82.9	2.1	1,443
St U and CC Sys of Tenn							
Austin Peay St U	0.3	1.3	15.4	2.5	80.0	0.5	5,177
East Tennessee St U	0.3	0.5	2.6	0.4	95.3	0.9	10,983
Memphis St U	0.2	0.5	16.8	0.3	78.7	3.4	20,267
Middle Tennessee St U	0.2	0.3	8.1	0.4	88.8	2.2	13,174
Tennessee St U	0.2	3.3	62.8	0.4	33.4	0.0	7,352
Tennessee Tech U	0.1	0.8	3.2	0.5	92.9	2.6	7,901
Chattanooga St Tech CC	0.3	0.7	10.7	0.4	87.9	0.1	7,365
Cleveland St CC	0.3	0.3	5.0	0.8	93.4	0.2	2,977
Columbia St CC	0.3	0.2	8.1	0.2	89.5	1.8	2,665
Dyersburg St CC	0.3	0.2	12.0	0.2	87.3	0.0	1,742
Jackson St CC	0.0	0.1	12.8	0.1	86.9	0.0	2,774
Motlow St CC	0.1	0.4	5.4	0.4	93.7	0.0	2,396
Nashville St Tech Inst	0.1	1.4	12.1	0.7	85.6	0.1	5,358
Pellissippi St Tech CC	0.3	1.0	3.9	0.3	93.8	0.8	2,981
Roane St CC	0.2	0.5	2.9	0.2	96.1	0.1	3,868
Shelby St CC	0.2	0.5	56.8	0.3	42.3	0.0	3,822
St Tech Inst Memphis	0.2	0.9	30.7	0.5	67.5	0.1	7,398
Tri-Cities St Tech Inst	0.1	0.3	1.1	0.0	98.4	0.0	1,667
Volunteer St CC	0.3	0.4	4.9	0.5	93.9	0.1	3,473
Walters St CC	0.8	0.2	2.6	0.2	96.1	0.2	3,332
Tennessee Temple U	0.1	0.6	3.3	1.6	93.3	1.0	1,406
Tennessee Wesleyan C	0.3	0.5	6.5	0.2	87.7	4.8	600
Tomlinson C	0.0	0.3	6.6	3.7	81.7	7.6	301
Trevecca Nazarene C	0.1	0.3	20.5	0.2	78.4	0.5	1,977
Tusculum C	0.0	0.0	9.3	0.2	89.4	1.0	953
Union U	0.0	0.0	7.1	0.0	92.1	0.7	2,031
U of Tennessee Chattanooga	0.3	1.2	10.1	0.9	85.5	2.1	7,526

TENNESSEE, cont.

	American Indian	Asian	Black	Hispanic	White	Foreign	Total
U of Tennessee							
Knoxville	0.2%	1.0%	4.5%	0.4%	90.8%	3.1%	24,985
Martin	0.1	0.5	13.0	0.2	82.5	3.7	4,653
Memphis	0.2	3.7	6.3	0.6	86.5	2.7	1,773
U of the South	0.1	0.3	1.0	0.4	96.2	2.0	1,171
Vanderbilt U	0.1	2.0	3.9	0.7	87.3	5.9	8,960
William Jennings Bryan C	0.0	0.2	5.6	0.4	89.6	4.3	517

TEXAS

	American Indian	Asian	Black	Hispanic	White	Foreign	Total
Abilene Christian U	0.1	1.6	4.0	2.0	91.6	0.8	4,181
Alamo CC Dist							
Palo Alto C	0.7	0.7	5.9	55.1	37.2	0.5	3,386
St Philip's C	0.4	1.6	24.5	37.2	35.6	0.6	5,867
San Antonio C	0.4	1.5	5.7	42.9	48.9	0.6	21,593
Amarillo C	0.6	2.4	2.9	9.6	84.0	0.5	5,395
Amber U	0.7	0.9	19.5	4.0	71.9	2.9	1,233
American Tech U	0.8	1.2	20.4	8.3	67.6	1.7	593
Angelina C	0.7	0.3	12.6	2.1	84.2	0.0	2,962
Angelo St U	0.3	0.8	4.5	11.8	80.8	1.8	6,334
Art Inst of Houston	0.3	2.2	13.6	18.8	65.0	0.0	987
Austin C	0.5	3.3	2.9	3.7	88.7	0.9	1,269
Austin CC	0.4	3.3	6.6	14.9	74.1	0.7	21,418
Austin Presbyterian							
Theol Sem	0.4	1.2	2.5	3.3	90.5	2.1	241
Baptist Missionary							
Association Theol Sem	0.0	0.9	16.7	0.0	81.5	0.9	108
Bauder Fashion C	0.0	0.7	1.4	6.3	90.2	1.4	441
Baylor C of Dentistry	0.0	10.0	3.2	5.8	78.4	2.6	468
Baylor C of Medicine	0.1	11.0	1.1	5.2	73.0	9.6	937
Baylor U	0.3	2.4	2.1	2.5	91.0	1.6	11,789
Bee County C	0.4	0.7	2.6	52.7	43.6	0.0	2,550
Blinn C	0.3	0.7	7.0	6.8	82.8	2.4	5,889
Brazosport C	0.3	0.9	7.0	10.8	80.8	0.3	3,550
Central Texas C	0.5	2.9	20.8	9.0	65.8	1.0	6,079
Cisco JC	0.2	0.7	6.6	6.3	86.2	0.0	1,972
Clarendon C	0.3	0.0	5.0	4.1	90.5	0.0	916
C of the Mainland	0.6	1.2	14.8	9.0	73.3	1.2	3,458
Collin County CC	0.3	1.8	2.1	3.2	92.4	0.2	7,153
Concordia Lutheran C	0.4	0.6	5.1	7.9	86.0	0.0	507
Cooke County C	0.6	0.7	3.2	2.8	90.8	1.9	2,968
Criswell C	0.3	2.9	7.3	6.0	78.9	4.7	383
Dallas Baptist U	0.3	2.9	22.0	4.1	66.8	3.8	2,018
Dallas Christian C	1.0	1.0	6.0	4.0	86.0	2.0	100
Dallas County CC Dist							
Brookhaven C	0.4	5.8	7.5	7.0	78.2	1.1	7,929
Cedar Valley C	0.5	0.8	39.2	5.2	54.1	0.1	3,083
Eastfield C	0.8	4.4	8.6	7.8	77.9	0.5	9,396
El Centro C	0.5	2.4	44.8	9.3	41.4	1.6	5,761
Mountain View C	0.7	3.7	20.5	14.0	60.7	0.4	5,967
North Lake C	0.5	4.9	7.6	7.5	78.9	0.7	6,126
Richland C	0.4	6.0	7.5	5.4	79.8	0.9	13,101
Dallas Theological Sem	0.2	5.5	5.5	1.0	79.3	8.7	1,244
Del Mar C	0.4	0.9	3.1	47.5	48.0	0.2	9,972
DeVry Inst of Tech	0.6	5.6	21.2	14.9	55.8	1.9	2,354
East Texas Baptist U	0.5	0.9	7.3	1.1	88.8	1.5	809
East Texas St U	0.6	0.7	9.3	2.6	82.8	4.0	7,315

	American Indian	Asian	Black	Hispanic	White	Foreign	Total
East Texas St U Texarkana ...	0.5%	0.2%	9.6%	0.7%	88.5%	0.5%	1,286
El Paso County CC	0.5	0.8	4.5	71.5	21.9	0.8	14,820
Episcopal Theological Sem							
of the Southwest	0.0	0.0	1.4	4.3	88.6	5.7	70
Frank Phillips C	0.9	0.1	3.2	5.5	89.8	0.4	965
Galveston C	0.1	2.6	19.6	16.0	60.9	0.7	2,215
Grayson County C	0.9	0.7	5.2	1.6	91.6	0.0	4,003
Hardin-Simmons U	0.3	0.5	2.6	5.9	89.7	1.0	1,928
Hill C	0.1	0.2	7.1	6.1	86.3	0.3	1,534
Houston Baptist U	0.2	9.8	9.0	8.3	69.4	3.3	2,429
Houston CC	0.2	7.5	20.2	13.0	58.2	0.8	30,236
Houston Graduate Sch							
of Theology	0.0	11.1	21.5	5.6	59.0	2.8	144
Howard County JC Dist	0.2	0.9	6.2	18.5	73.8	0.3	1,645
Howard Payne U	0.2	0.2	6.5	6.7	86.1	0.2	1,247
Huston-Tillotson C	0.0	1.2	70.6	2.2	3.2	22.9	506
Incarnate Word C	0.4	1.1	7.3	39.4	49.0	2.9	2,240
Inst for Christian Studies	0.0	1.4	5.5	5.5	84.9	2.7	73
ITT Tech Inst	0.0	6.5	16.3	27.1	50.2	0.0	658
Jacksonville C	0.0	0.4	8.3	0.8	71.8	18.8	266
Jarvis Christian C	0.0	0.0	99.4	0.0	0.6	0.0	538
Kilgore C	0.2	0.3	11.7	1.1	86.5	0.1	4,289
Lamar U							
Main	0.3	1.8	17.0	2.5	75.4	3.0	11,809
Orange	0.6	0.5	9.6	2.2	87.0	0.0	1,110
Port Arthur	0.3	2.5	27.5	4.8	64.6	0.3	1,707
Laredo JC	0.0	0.4	0.2	89.6	6.2	3.7	4,891
Le Tourneau C	0.3	0.5	0.9	0.9	91.6	5.7	749
Lee C	0.4	0.5	16.1	11.3	71.3	0.3	5,163
Lon Morris C	0.0	0.0	13.2	4.4	74.2	8.2	341
Lubbock Christian U	0.2	0.8	3.6	3.8	86.9	4.7	1,073
McLennan CC	0.1	0.8	13.4	6.5	79.0	0.2	5,411
McMurry C	0.7	0.7	8.3	7.4	81.2	1.8	1,683
Midland C	0.2	1.3	4.8	13.5	79.5	0.8	3,680
Midwestern St U	0.5	2.4	4.5	4.3	86.5	1.8	5,149
Miss Wade's Fashion							
Merchandising C	0.5	2.7	27.3	12.3	56.2	1.0	406
Navarro C	0.0	3.3	17.4	4.3	74.8	0.2	2,310
North Harris County C Dist ...	0.6	3.1	5.4	7.9	82.5	0.4	13,302
Northeast Texas CC	0.4	0.4	7.5	1.0	90.7	0.0	1,673
Northwood Inst	0.0	0.0	10.1	10.6	78.3	0.9	217
Odessa C	0.5	1.2	5.5	19.2	73.4	0.1	4,625
Our Lady of the Lake U	0.4	0.6	7.7	45.0	45.1	1.2	2,245
Panola C	0.0	0.1	14.6	1.0	84.3	0.1	1,454
Paris JC	1.0	0.4	10.2	0.9	84.9	2.6	2,221
Parker C of Chiropractic	0.5	2.0	2.0	3.3	92.1	0.0	393
Paul Quinn C	0.0	0.0	95.7	0.4	3.1	0.8	517
Ranger JC	0.5	0.2	32.1	9.1	57.8	0.0	635
Rice U	0.1	4.8	3.2	3.6	78.3	10.0	4,202
Saint Edward's U	0.2	1.3	5.5	20.5	65.1	7.4	2,823
Saint Mary's U	0.3	2.1	5.0	38.5	53.1	1.1	3,654
Sam Houston St U	0.3	0.5	8.8	4.7	84.2	1.5	11,561
San Jacinto C Sys							
Central	0.3	2.1	4.3	10.4	76.9	6.0	9,180
North	0.4	2.6	12.3	13.2	69.7	1.8	3,442
South	0.2	5.2	6.0	10.5	76.1	2.1	4,681
Schreiner C	0.2	1.0	3.3	11.3	82.4	1.8	602

TEXAS, cont.

	American Indian	Asian	Black	Hispanic	White	Foreign	Total
South Plains C	0.4%	0.8%	6.5%	17.8%	73.8%	0.7%	4,394
Southern Methodist U	0.2	3.5	3.1	3.6	85.8	3.9	8,944
Southwest Texas JC	0.3	0.6	1.2	59.1	38.2	0.7	2,450
Southwest Texas St U	0.3	0.8	4.6	12.7	80.7	1.0	20,505
Southwestern Adventist C	1.0	1.8	6.5	12.6	71.1	7.0	771
Southwestern Assemblies of God C	0.8	0.5	1.9	8.3	87.7	0.7	731
Southwestern Christian C	0.0	0.0	87.3	0.0	1.5	11.3	275
Southwestern U	0.1	2.7	2.6	6.3	86.6	1.6	1,171
Stephen F Austin St U	0.2	0.7	4.7	2.4	91.7	0.3	12,574
Sul Ross St U	0.1	0.1	4.1	36.7	57.5	1.5	2,236
Tarrant County JC Dist	0.4	2.4	8.4	6.7	81.9	0.2	25,946
Temple JC	0.2	0.9	9.5	9.1	79.6	0.6	2,383
Texarkana C	0.1	0.3	9.7	0.5	89.3	0.1	3,755
Texas A&M U Sys							
Corpus Christi St U	0.4	0.8	1.9	30.1	66.4	0.4	4,045
Laredo St U	0.1	0.4	1.1	80.8	12.0	5.7	1,076
Prairie View A&M U	0.1	0.8	83.1	1.2	8.8	6.0	5,640
Tarleton St U	0.2	0.2	2.2	2.5	94.5	0.4	5,667
Texas A&I U	0.2	1.5	3.5	55.5	36.1	3.2	5,614
Texas A&M U Main	0.2	2.3	2.7	6.8	83.2	4.7	39,163
Texas A&M U Galveston	0.3	1.5	0.9	4.9	91.0	1.5	742
Texas Chiropractic C	0.0	2.6	1.3	5.1	90.0	1.0	390
Texas Christian U	0.2	1.1	3.7	2.7	89.4	2.9	6,993
Texas C	0.0	1.0	87.1	0.0	0.2	11.7	410
Texas C of Osteopathic Med	0.5	7.7	1.3	6.1	84.4	0.0	391
Texas Lutheran C	0.2	1.5	4.9	10.2	82.0	1.1	1,319
Texas Southern U	0.2	1.1	77.5	3.9	3.5	13.9	8,666
Texas Southmost JC	0.2	0.2	0.1	85.6	12.1	1.8	5,526
Texas St Tech Inst Sys							
Amarillo	0.7	2.7	5.0	11.4	80.2	0.0	858
Harlingen	0.1	0.2	0.6	82.2	16.4	0.5	2,623
Waco	0.3	0.7	10.7	9.0	78.3	0.9	4,022
Sweetwater	0.1	1.6	4.9	17.9	75.4	0.0	748
Texas Tech U							
Main	0.2	0.7	2.4	6.8	85.9	3.9	24,605
Health Science Center	0.4	4.6	1.9	8.2	82.2	2.7	826
Texas Woman's U	0.4	1.1	13.7	6.1	74.2	4.4	8,898
Trinity U	0.5	4.0	1.3	8.1	83.9	2.2	2,412
Trinity Valley CC	0.4	0.4	14.9	4.9	78.6	0.7	4,276
Tyler JC	0.4	0.2	13.6	1.3	83.4	1.1	7,820
U of Dallas	0.6	3.9	3.1	4.4	77.3	10.6	2,649
U of Houston							
Clear Lake	0.2	4.0	4.5	6.1	83.6	1.6	7,196
Downtown	0.2	11.3	24.4	18.7	41.8	3.7	7,409
U Park	0.4	8.3	7.2	7.8	70.1	6.2	30,372
Victoria	0.6	0.7	2.5	9.5	86.8	0.0	1,059
U of Saint Thomas	0.2	5.8	4.7	12.9	68.2	8.2	1,646
U of Texas Sys							
Arlington	0.4	6.9	6.8	4.8	76.2	4.8	23,383
Austin	0.2	5.3	3.6	9.9	74.3	6.8	50,106
Dallas	0.3	5.9	4.4	3.1	82.1	4.3	7,667
El Paso	0.3	1.1	3.1	55.3	35.5	4.8	10,491
Tyler	0.6	0.4	6.7	0.9	90.2	1.2	3,859

	American Indian	Asian	Black	Hispanic	White	Foreign	Total
Health Science Center							
Houston................	0.3%	10.1%	7.5%	9.3%	68.4%	4.3%	2,837
Health Science Center							
San Antonio	0.2	6.9	3.2	16.0	71.9	1.8	2,219
Medical Branch Galveston .	0.6	9.1	6.7	9.6	71.3	2.7	1,705
Permian Basin	0.1	0.5	1.9	8.0	89.0	0.5	2,132
Pan American U	0.2	0.5	0.9	81.6	16.5	0.4	11,204
Pan American U							
Brownsville	0.2	0.0	1.3	74.2	24.1	0.3	1,516
San Antonio	0.2	2.6	3.4	26.7	66.3	0.8	13,134
SW Medical Ctr Dallas	0.1	6.4	3.2	6.8	79.7	3.8	1,458
U of North Texas	0.3	1.3	6.4	3.6	83.2	5.1	24,498
Vernon Regional JC	0.7	2.0	8.2	6.7	82.5	0.1	1,729
Victoria C	0.4	0.5	3.1	18.6	77.2	0.2	3,229
Wayland Baptist U	0.1	0.4	3.5	5.4	89.1	1.4	1,755
Weatherford C	2.1	0.1	3.2	0.5	91.5	2.5	2,040
West Texas St U	0.4	0.9	2.9	6.6	86.8	2.6	5,756
Western Texas C	0.1	0.1	4.2	9.2	86.0	0.3	966
Wharton County JC	0.1	0.6	10.6	15.9	72.3	0.4	2,553
Wiley C	0.0	0.0	97.0	0.3	0.3	2.4	369

UTAH

	American Indian	Asian	Black	Hispanic	White	Foreign	Total
Stevens Henager C	1.4	0.5	4.2	3.8	90.1	0.0	212
Utah Higher Education Sys							
U of Utah	0.5	2.6	0.6	2.4	87.1	6.8	23,756
Utah St U	0.8	1.3	0.5	0.7	89.0	7.8	13,777
Southern Utah St C	3.0	0.6	0.6	0.7	94.6	0.5	2,952
Weber St C	0.5	2.0	1.1	2.0	92.9	1.3	12,146
C of Eastern Utah	10.5	0.0	0.8	4.6	84.1	0.0	2,210
Dixie C	1.6	1.0	1.0	1.0	94.8	0.6	2,166
Salt Lake CC	1.2	3.3	0.5	4.0	90.9	0.1	9,048
Snow C	1.2	1.7	0.9	0.8	87.6	7.8	1,544
Utah Valley CC	1.6	1.3	0.1	1.8	92.9	2.3	6,833
Westminster C of Salt Lake City	0.3	1.6	1.4	3.9	90.8	2.0	1,854

VERMONT

	American Indian	Asian	Black	Hispanic	White	Foreign	Total
Bennington C	0.2	2.1	2.1	1.5	87.6	6.5	613
Burlington C	0.0	0.5	3.0	0.0	95.9	0.5	197
Champlain C	0.3	0.5	0.7	0.0	97.9	0.5	2,029
C of Saint Joseph	1.2	0.7	1.2	0.7	95.9	0.5	434
Goddard C	1.4	0.8	1.6	0.9	92.8	2.5	1,005
Green Mountain C	0.0	0.2	0.9	0.2	96.0	2.6	529
Landmark C	0.0	0.0	0.0	0.0	95.7	4.3	23
Marlboro C	0.0	0.4	0.8	0.8	94.6	3.3	240
Norwich U	0.6	1.5	2.2	1.9	91.8	2.0	2,488
Saint Michael's C	0.0	0.1	0.7	0.2	96.3	2.6	2,231
Sch for International Training	0.4	1.7	0.8	1.5	86.9	8.6	521
Southern Vermont C	0.2	0.8	1.3	0.8	95.9	1.1	635
Sterling C	0.0	0.0	1.5	0.0	96.9	1.5	65
Trinity C	0.2	0.5	0.3	0.4	98.7	0.0	1,043
U of Vermont	0.2	2.3	0.6	0.9	94.8	1.2	11,287
Vermont St C's Sys							
Castleton St C	0.1	0.3	0.4	0.3	98.7	0.2	1,803

VERMONT, cont.

	American Indian	Asian	Black	Hispanic	White	Foreign	Total
Vermont St C's Sys							
CC of Vermont	0.5%	0.3%	0.1%	0.2%	97.1%	1.7%	3,465
Johnson St C	0.2	0.2	0.1	0.3	98.3	1.0	1,547
Lyndon St C	0.0	0.1	0.3	0.2	99.1	0.4	1,125
Vermont Tech C	0.0	0.7	0.4	0.4	98.2	0.3	740

VIRGINIA

	American Indian	Asian	Black	Hispanic	White	Foreign	Total
Averett C	0.1	1.8	11.9	0.9	81.3	4.0	982
Bluefield C	0.0	1.6	4.4	0.0	92.1	1.9	366
Bridgewater C	0.1	1.1	2.4	0.5	94.7	1.2	973
Christendom C	0.0	0.0	0.0	1.3	93.7	5.0	159
Christopher Newport C	0.4	1.4	10.7	0.9	86.3	0.3	4,647
C of William and Mary	0.1	2.4	5.9	0.9	87.7	3.1	7,372
Richard Bland C	0.6	2.0	18.3	1.7	76.8	0.6	1,015
Community Hospital of Roanoke Valley C of Health Sciences	0.0	0.0	11.6	0.0	88.4	0.0	181
Commonwealth C	0.0	0.5	66.3	0.0	32.2	1.0	202
Commonwealth C Hampton ..	0.0	1.9	64.3	0.0	33.9	0.0	322
Commonwealth C Virginia Beach	0.0	0.8	14.3	4.4	80.5	0.0	502
Eastern Mennonite C	0.0	0.6	2.0	0.8	91.5	5.1	1,049
Eastern Va Medical Sch of the Medical C of Hampton Roads	0.0	9.6	6.7	1.3	82.4	0.0	448
Emory and Henry C	0.0	0.4	2.5	0.0	97.1	0.0	788
Ferrum C	0.4	0.6	6.8	1.2	90.1	0.9	1,206
George Mason U	0.4	6.5	4.8	2.6	82.4	3.4	18,965
Hampden-Sydney C	0.1	0.5	1.6	0.5	97.2	0.0	937
Hampton U	0.1	0.2	91.3	0.1	6.0	2.3	5,305
Hollins C	0.0	0.2	2.0	0.4	96.6	0.8	1,063
Inst of Textile Tech	0.0	0.0	2.9	2.9	94.3	0.0	35
James Madison U	0.1	1.5	7.8	1.2	89.1	0.3	10,906
Liberty U	0.1	0.2	4.4	0.5	93.6	1.2	10,902
Longwood C	0.2	1.5	8.7	0.4	88.8	0.4	3,042
Lynchburg C	0.1	0.5	4.9	0.3	91.9	2.2	2,447
Mary Baldwin C	0.2	0.8	3.4	0.8	92.9	1.9	1,186
Mary Washington C	0.1	1.3	3.4	1.0	93.3	0.9	3,427
Marymount U	0.2	4.3	7.2	3.3	78.1	7.0	2,977
Norfolk St U	0.2	0.4	84.6	0.3	12.7	1.8	8,123
Old Dominion U	0.5	3.0	9.8	1.2	82.9	2.7	16,364
Presbyterian Sch of Christian Education	0.0	3.8	3.8	0.0	74.5	17.9	106
Protestant Episcopal Theol Sem in Va	0.0	0.0	3.2	0.5	93.1	3.2	218
Radford U	0.3	1.2	3.1	0.9	92.9	1.7	8,764
Randolph-Macon C	0.0	1.2	1.9	0.4	95.3	1.3	1,117
Randolph-Macon Woman's C	0.1	0.8	2.5	1.1	92.2	3.2	746
Roanoke C	0.2	0.8	1.5	0.2	97.1	0.3	1,594
Saint Paul's C	0.0	0.0	97.3	0.0	1.6	1.1	555
Shenandoah C and Conservatory of Music	0.1	2.7	7.5	0.5	89.2	0.0	1,007
Southern Sem C	0.3	0.3	1.0	0.7	94.7	3.0	302
Sweet Briar C	0.0	0.2	4.5	0.7	90.2	4.3	553
Union Theological Sem in Va	0.0	2.7	2.2	0.5	88.7	5.9	186
U of Richmond	0.2	0.9	3.3	0.6	94.5	0.4	4,948

	American Indian	Asian	Black	Hispanic	White	Foreign	Total
U of Virginia							
Main	0.0%	3.7%	7.6%	0.6%	85.3%	2.8%	20,802
Clinch Valley	0.1	0.3	1.2	0.4	97.8	0.2	1,688
Virginia Commonwealth U	0.4	2.7	13.1	1.0	81.6	1.2	20,645
Virginia CC Sys							
Blue Ridge CC	0.2	0.5	2.9	0.3	96.1	0.0	2,483
Central Virginia CC	0.1	0.3	13.1	0.1	86.3	0.0	3,721
Dabney S Lancaster CC	0.1	0.1	5.4	0.2	94.3	0.0	1,277
Danville CC	0.2	0.1	19.7	0.2	79.8	0.0	2,680
Eastern Shore CC	0.2	0.4	19.5	0.4	79.4	0.0	456
Germanna CC	0.3	0.4	7.6	0.8	90.7	0.2	2,250
J Sargeant Reynolds CC	0.5	1.6	23.4	0.5	73.7	0.3	9,747
John Tyler CC	0.1	1.1	19.1	0.9	78.1	0.7	4,243
Lord Fairfax CC	0.2	0.4	2.7	0.2	96.5	0.0	2,473
Mountain Empire CC	0.0	0.1	1.4	0.0	98.4	0.0	2,350
New River CC	0.1	0.4	4.0	0.2	95.1	0.2	3,044
Northern Virginia CC	0.4	7.7	8.0	3.9	78.0	2.0	31,896
Patrick Henry CC	0.3	0.3	13.1	0.1	86.2	0.0	1,726
Paul D Camp CC	0.1	0.5	29.8	0.3	68.9	0.3	966
Piedmont Virginia CC	0.1	1.0	8.6	0.5	89.4	0.3	4,053
Rappahannock CC	0.6	0.1	17.4	0.3	81.6	0.1	1,559
Southside Virginia CC	0.2	0.3	34.1	0.4	64.9	0.1	2,416
Southwest Virginia CC	0.0	0.1	1.1	0.0	98.7	0.0	4,082
Thomas Nelson CC	0.4	2.1	22.2	1.2	73.9	0.2	6,640
Tidewater CC	0.3	4.9	12.3	1.3	80.1	1.1	16,557
Virginia Highlands CC	0.1	0.1	2.6	0.1	97.2	0.0	1,975
Virginia Western CC	0.1	0.8	7.5	0.2	91.3	0.1	6,755
Wytheville CC	0.2	0.1	3.2	0.0	96.5	0.1	1,843
Virginia Intermont C	0.0	1.1	3.1	0.9	90.9	4.0	450
Virginia Military Inst	0.1	3.0	6.6	1.6	87.0	1.8	1,285
Virginia Polytechnic Inst and St U	0.1	4.2	3.6	0.9	85.5	5.7	24,280
Virginia St U	0.1	0.4	88.4	0.2	10.3	0.6	3,855
Virginia Union U	0.2	0.0	98.5	0.2	0.8	0.4	1,248
Virginia Wesleyan C	0.4	1.4	5.0	0.9	91.2	1.1	1,261
Washington and Lee U	0.1	1.1	3.1	0.5	94.8	0.4	1,971

WASHINGTON

	American Indian	Asian	Black	Hispanic	White	Foreign	Total
Antioch C Seattle	1.3	0.3	1.9	0.3	93.6	2.7	376
Art Inst of Seattle	0.3	3.2	3.1	3.0	89.4	0.9	1,269
Bellevue CC	0.3	4.4	1.0	0.8	93.3	0.2	9,138
Big Bend CC	0.8	1.7	0.4	6.3	83.1	7.7	1,843
Central Washington U	1.2	2.8	1.6	2.7	90.3	1.3	7,109
Centralia C	1.7	0.8	3.9	1.5	92.0	0.1	3,372
Clark C	1.3	2.9	1.0	1.2	93.5	0.1	7,460
Cogswell C North	0.0	8.1	1.0	1.4	89.5	0.0	210
Columbia Basin C	0.6	2.2	0.4	2.2	94.6	0.0	5,186
Cornish C of the Arts	1.0	2.3	2.5	2.7	89.1	2.5	521
Edmonds CC	1.4	3.3	2.9	1.9	90.4	0.1	7,059
Everett CC	1.9	3.2	0.8	1.2	92.8	0.2	6,636
Evergreen St C	1.6	3.3	3.6	1.9	88.5	1.2	3,165
Gonzaga U	1.0	3.6	0.6	2.1	88.8	3.7	3,592
Grays Harbor C	3.5	0.8	0.4	0.7	94.4	0.3	2,132
Green River CC	1.2	2.3	1.1	1.3	94.1	0.0	5,421
Griffin C	0.1	4.7	8.3	2.5	79.6	4.8	1,756
Heritage C	23.0	4.0	2.1	17.2	52.2	1.6	379

WASHINGTON, cont.

	American Indian	Asian	Black	Hispanic	White	Foreign	Total
Highline CC	1.3%	6.7%	2.9%	2.1%	86.0%	0.9%	7,368
Lower Columbia C	0.7	1.0	0.2	0.8	97.2	0.0	3,163
Lutheran Bible Inst of Seattle	0.0	2.9	2.2	0.0	91.2	3.7	136
Olympic C	1.6	4.8	2.9	2.0	88.7	0.1	5,601
Pacific Lutheran U	0.6	2.9	1.4	1.1	87.6	6.3	3,970
Peninsula C	3.6	1.5	1.2	1.8	90.7	1.2	2,669
Pierce C	1.5	5.4	9.1	3.3	80.3	0.5	7,715
Puget Sound Christian C	0.0	2.3	2.3	1.1	93.2	1.1	88
Saint Martin's C	0.6	5.2	5.7	2.6	82.8	3.2	1,200
Seattle CC Dist							
North Seattle CC	0.9	10.7	2.6	2.0	83.7	0.1	6,485
Seattle Central CC	2.0	16.7	12.4	2.3	66.5	0.1	5,886
South Seattle CC	2.1	13.3	5.7	2.0	76.6	0.2	5,335
Seattle Pacific U	0.8	2.9	0.9	0.8	89.0	5.6	3,356
Shoreline CC	0.9	7.8	0.9	1.3	88.7	0.4	6,485
Skagit Valley C	1.6	2.4	0.7	2.4	92.8	0.1	5,092
South Puget Sound CC	1.7	4.2	1.0	1.9	91.3	0.0	3,655
Tacoma CC	1.5	6.1	7.3	2.0	83.0	0.0	4,503
U of Puget Sound	0.6	4.5	1.3	1.2	91.8	0.7	4,234
U of Washington	1.0	12.6	3.1	2.1	76.5	4.8	33,460
Walla Walla C	0.5	2.8	1.8	3.4	85.4	6.2	1,428
Walla Walla CC	1.5	1.1	7.5	3.7	85.8	0.3	4,093
Washington St CC Dist							
Spokane CC	1.9	2.2	0.7	1.2	93.9	0.1	6,242
Spokane Falls CC	2.2	2.4	1.5	2.2	91.4	0.3	10,345
Washington St U	0.8	3.8	1.8	1.2	86.2	6.1	16,405
Wenatchee Valley C	6.2	1.1	1.0	1.8	89.8	0.1	2,147
Western Washington U	0.9	2.6	1.0	1.2	93.1	1.2	9,837
Whatcom CC	2.1	1.7	0.6	1.2	94.2	0.2	2,252
Whitman C	0.1	5.8	0.7	1.4	89.7	2.3	1,284
Whitworth C	0.4	2.6	0.9	0.8	92.6	2.8	1,840
Yakima Valley CC	4.0	1.5	1.5	7.3	85.6	0.1	3,750

WEST VIRGINIA

	American Indian	Asian	Black	Hispanic	White	Foreign	Total
Alderson Broaddus C	0.0	1.0	3.7	0.5	91.6	3.2	728
Appalachian Bible C	0.0	2.7	2.2	1.1	93.4	0.5	182
Beckley C	0.0	0.5	5.7	0.3	93.5	0.0	1,605
Davis & Elkins C	1.6	2.4	2.3	1.4	90.2	2.0	789
Huntington JC of Business	0.0	0.2	6.0	0.2	93.5	0.0	448
Ohio Valley C	0.0	0.0	4.5	0.0	93.2	2.3	221
Parkersburg CC	0.1	0.2	0.3	0.1	98.7	0.5	3,219
Salem-Teikyo U							
Main	0.2	0.9	12.2	3.9	79.3	3.5	564
Clarksburg	0.0	0.0	6.6	0.0	93.4	0.0	166
U of Charleston	0.4	0.5	3.3	0.7	92.9	2.2	1,528
U of West Virginia Sys							
Marshall U	0.2	0.6	3.0	0.4	94.9	0.9	12,350
C of Graduate Studies	0.1	0.7	3.4	0.4	94.9	0.6	2,596
West Virginia U	0.1	1.5	2.6	0.5	91.2	4.2	18,746
Potomac St C	0.1	0.3	5.1	0.1	94.4	0.1	1,081
West Virginia Sch of Osteopathic Medicine	0.4	3.0	2.2	1.7	91.8	0.9	232
West Virginia St C Sys							
Bluefield St C	0.1	0.1	8.5	0.1	90.5	0.7	2,487
Concord C	0.2	0.9	4.2	0.1	94.6	0.0	2,450

	American Indian	Asian	Black	Hispanic	White	Foreign	Total
West Virginia St C Sys							
Fairmont St C	0.2%	0.2%	2.0%	0.4%	97.2%	0.0%	5,758
Glenville St C	0.0	0.2	1.7	0.0	96.7	1.3	2,205
Shepherd C	0.3	0.1	2.4	0.4	96.7	0.0	4,010
West Liberty St C	0.1	0.2	2.0	0.3	96.9	0.5	2,435
West Virginia Inst of Tech ..	0.2	0.5	6.3	1.2	87.1	4.7	2,955
West Virginia St C	0.1	0.5	11.8	0.4	87.0	0.2	4,509
Southern West Virginia CC .	0.1	0.1	1.9	0.1	97.8	0.0	2,688
West Virginia Northern CC .	0.0	0.2	2.9	0.3	96.1	0.5	2,660
West Virginia Wesleyan C	0.3	0.9	3.7	0.6	92.3	2.2	1,484
Wheeling Jesuit C	0.2	1.1	0.9	0.2	95.0	2.6	1,206

WISCONSIN

Alverno C	0.5	0.8	11.5	3.2	83.9	0.2	2,191
Bellin C of Nursing	3.5	0.0	0.0	0.0	96.5	0.0	143
Beloit C	0.1	2.9	2.2	1.1	88.9	4.7	1,203
Blackhawk Tech C	0.2	0.6	2.2	0.6	96.4	0.0	1,738
Cardinal Stritch C	0.2	1.1	5.9	0.8	92.0	0.0	3,044
Carroll C	0.4	0.7	2.2	1.3	94.9	0.5	2,202
Carthage C	0.1	0.5	4.7	1.4	93.1	0.3	1,842
Chippewa Valley Tech C	0.6	0.6	0.0	0.1	98.6	0.0	3,407
Concordia U	2.9	0.9	5.3	0.3	89.0	1.6	1,175
Edgewood C	0.1	0.8	0.6	0.4	95.0	3.2	1,076
Fox Valley Tech C	0.8	1.3	0.3	0.8	96.7	0.0	3,906
Gateway Tech C	0.7	1.0	5.3	1.6	90.9	0.6	8,153
Inst of Paper Science							
and Tech	0.0	0.0	0.0	0.0	91.2	8.8	68
Lakeland C	0.2	0.7	5.1	1.1	92.2	0.7	1,535
Lakeshore Tech C	0.3	1.3	0.0	0.2	98.2	0.0	2,352
Lawrence U	0.2	1.5	1.9	0.2	93.4	2.8	1,231
Madison Area Tech C	0.4	0.8	1.9	1.0	95.5	0.4	10,611
Madison Business C	0.0	0.0	0.0	0.0	99.5	0.5	374
Maranatha Baptist Bible C ...	0.2	2.2	1.7	2.0	93.4	0.4	458
Marian C of Fond Du Lac	0.3	0.7	2.5	0.7	95.6	0.1	869
Marquette U	0.3	3.5	2.9	2.9	86.1	4.2	12,142
Medical C of Wisconsin	0.2	12.6	1.5	3.2	80.8	1.6	849
Mid-State Tech C	0.4	0.5	0.1	0.4	98.5	0.1	2,219
Milwaukee Area Tech C	0.7	1.8	17.7	2.8	76.9	0.1	19,693
Milwaukee Inst of Art and							
Design	0.6	1.5	2.1	1.1	94.2	0.4	466
Milwaukee Sch of							
Engineering	0.2	2.3	2.0	1.2	93.2	1.0	2,808
Moraine Park Tech C	0.4	0.9	0.2	0.4	98.1	0.0	4,921
Mount Mary C	0.4	0.7	3.4	1.2	92.8	1.5	1,367
Mount Senario C	14.4	1.9	2.8	1.1	78.7	1.1	1,701
Nashotah House	0.0	0.0	5.4	3.6	83.9	7.1	56
Nicolet Area Tech C	3.1	0.5	0.6	0.3	95.5	0.0	1,311
North Central Voc-Tech							
Adult Ed Dist	0.9	0.9	0.1	0.2	97.3	0.5	3,489
Northeast Wisconsin Tech C .	1.7	1.1	0.1	0.3	96.8	0.0	5,558
Northland C	9.1	1.2	1.4	2.2	84.4	1.7	647
Northwestern C	0.0	0.0	0.0	0.0	100.0	0.0	202
Ripon C	0.2	1.3	0.7	0.9	93.8	3.0	857
Sacred Heart Sch of Theology	0.8	0.8	0.0	4.6	86.2	7.7	130
Saint Norbert C	0.8	0.3	0.4	0.5	97.7	0.3	1,827
Silver Lake C	0.1	0.6	0.0	0.4	98.6	0.3	796

	American Indian	Asian	Black	Hispanic	White	Foreign	Total
WISCONSIN, cont.							
Stratton C	1.5%	0.5%	27.6%	5.3%	65.1%	0.0%	601
U of Wisconsin							
Madison	0.4	2.6	1.7	1.5	87.4	6.4	43,364
Eau Claire	0.3	0.6	0.4	0.3	96.8	1.6	11,038
Green Bay	1.7	0.5	0.7	0.4	95.4	1.2	5,221
La Crosse	0.3	0.7	0.7	0.4	97.1	0.8	9,242
Oshkosh	0.5	1.1	1.2	0.6	95.7	0.9	11,209
Milwaukee	0.7	1.7	5.9	2.2	86.5	2.9	25,212
Parkside	0.2	1.2	3.2	2.5	92.3	0.5	5,172
Platteville	0.3	0.7	0.6	0.4	97.0	1.0	5,334
River Falls	0.3	0.6	1.0	0.4	96.8	0.9	5,544
Stevens Point	0.9	0.7	0.6	0.4	95.4	2.1	9,318
Stout	0.4	1.4	0.9	0.6	95.1	1.5	7,597
Superior	1.6	0.9	1.4	0.4	94.2	1.6	2,437
Whitewater	0.2	0.7	2.4	1.0	94.8	1.0	10,458
Centers	0.4	0.7	1.1	0.8	96.3	0.6	11,184
Viterbo C	0.5	0.8	1.2	0.4	97.2	0.0	1,060
Waukesha County Tech C	0.2	0.3	0.2	1.1	98.0	0.1	4,424
Western Wisconsin Tech C	0.3	1.1	0.1	0.2	98.3	0.0	3,452
Wisconsin Indianhead Tech C	3.0	0.3	0.3	0.3	96.2	0.0	3,157
Wisconsin Lutheran C	0.0	0.0	1.8	0.4	96.4	1.3	224
WYOMING							
Casper C	0.5	0.2	0.8	1.2	97.1	0.2	3,471
Central Wyoming C	10.8	0.2	0.6	1.7	86.3	0.4	1,406
Eastern Wyoming C	0.8	0.1	1.0	2.1	96.0	0.0	1,362
Laramie County CC	0.8	0.6	2.7	4.3	91.6	0.0	3,676
Northwest C	0.3	0.0	0.3	1.7	96.5	1.2	1,739
Sheridan C	0.7	0.2	0.5	0.7	97.4	0.6	1,980
U of Wyoming	1.3	0.2	0.8	2.2	91.2	4.2	10,773
Western Wyoming CC	0.6	0.9	0.9	5.0	92.6	0.1	1,504
Wyoming Tech Inst	0.3	0.6	0.5	5.4	93.2	0.0	629

Higher Education in the 80's: Some Highlights

1980

- The College Board and several other testing organizations agree to develop procedures to allow students to verify their scores on standardized tests. (*The Chronicle of Higher Education*, 1/7/80)

- In a move that the Association for Intercollegiate Athletics for Women decries as a "power grab," the National Collegiate Athletic Association votes to establish women's championship events in five sports for small and medium-sized colleges. (*The Chronicle*, 1/14/80)

- In "Three Thousand Futures: The Next 20 Years for Higher Education," the Carnegie Council on Policy Studies in Higher Education says that predicted enrollment declines will create a "new academic revolution." (*The Chronicle*, 1/28/80)

- President Jimmy Carter says that he will ask Congress to begin draft registration. (*The Chronicle*, 1/28/80)

- The Supreme Court rules that faculty members at Yeshiva University have managerial roles and are thus not entitled to bargain collectively under the National Labor Relations Act. (*The Chronicle*, 2/25/80)

- The council of the National Academy of Sciences votes to suspend for six months all bilateral symposia, seminars, and workshops with its counterpart in the Soviet Union to protest the arrest and exile of the dissident physicist Andrei D. Sakharov. (*The Chronicle*, 3/3/80)

- In two decisions, the Supreme Court limits the use of the Freedom of Information Act by researchers, journalists, and the general public. (*The Chronicle*, 3/10/80)

- A U.S. District Court judge rules that the federal government cannot cut off aid to students at Grove City College because the institution refuses to file a form certifying that it is complying with an anti-sex-bias law. (*The Chronicle*, 3/17/80)

- White House officials say that Iranian students in good standing at American colleges will be allowed to complete their studies despite President Carter's severing of diplomatic relations with Iran and the barring of any future travel of Iranians to the United States. (*The Chronicle*, 4/14/80)

- The American Council on Education predicts that despite the sharp drop in the number of 18-year-olds, enrollments could rise by as much as 3.5 per cent by the end of the decade if colleges recruit more low-income, minority, and adult students. (*The Chronicle*, 4/21/80)

■ The U. S. Department of Education begins operation, with Shirley M. Hufstedler at the helm. (*The Chronicle*, 5/12/80)

■ At least 20 colleges and universities in Washington, Idaho, and Montana are forced to close for several days because of the fallout of volcanic ash from the eruption of Mount St. Helens. (*The Chronicle*, 5/27/80)

■ The Supreme Court rules that bacteria created by genetic engineering may be patented. The decision is expected to spur commercial development of organisms and biological substances produced in genetic laboratories. (*The Chronicle*, 6/23/80)

■ Faculty salaries rose 7.1 per cent in 1979-80 to an average of $21,620 for all ranks combined, but failed to keep up with the inflation rate of 13.5 per cent. (*The Chronicle*, 6/30/80)

■ James A. Dinnan, a professor of adult education and reading at the University of Georgia, is jailed for refusing to tell a federal judge how he voted on a tenure decision. (*The Chronicle*, 9/2/80)

■ Predicting a physician surplus by 1990, a federal commission calls for a 17-per-cent cut in medical-school enrollments and for limits on the number of graduates of foreign medical schools allowed to practice in the United States. (*The Chronicle*, 10/6/80)

■ The highest educational priority for the 1980's should be the "dramatic" improvement of the quality of elementary and secondary schools, a Rockefeller Foundation commission reports. (*The Chronicle*, 10/14/80)

■ In a protest against the jailing and oppression of dissident Russian scholars, 7,900 scientists and engineers from 44 countries suspend professional relations with their counterparts in the Soviet Union. (*The Chronicle*, 10/27/80)

■ President-Elect Ronald Reagan says he will not move immediately to abolish the Department of Education, a step he advocated during his campaign. (*The Chronicle*, 11/17/80)

■ After weeks of intense debate, Harvard University abandons a plan to participate in forming a genetic-engineering company on the grounds that it would create "a number of potential conflicts" with academic values. (*The Chronicle*, 11/24/80)

1981

■ A rash of cross burnings and racial and ethnic slurs on college campuses leads educators to believe the problem of racism is worsening. (*The Chronicle*, 1/12/81)

■ Barbara W. Newell, named to the post of chancellor of the nine-campus State University System of Florida, becomes the first woman to head a statewide university system. (*The Chronicle*, 1/12/81)

■ President-Elect Ronald Reagan selects Utah's commissioner of higher education, Terrel H. Bell, to be his Education Secretary. (*The Chronicle,* 1/12/81)

■ In response to scandals involving the doctoring of academic records, the National Collegiate Athletic Association votes for the first time to require athletes to complete a specific number of credit-hours each term to remain eligible for varsity sports. (*The Chronicle,* 1/19/81)

■ Amid charges that it had run a "power play" against the Association for Intercollegiate Athletics for Women, the traditionally all-male N.C.A.A. extends its umbrella over women's sports by establishing new women's championships and developing plans to create policies to govern both men's and women's sports. (*The Chronicle,* 1/19/81)

■ For the first time, the cost of attending college will run into five figures. Harvard and Stanford Universities and Bennington College announce that costs for tuition, board, and room for 1981-82 will top $10,000. (*The Chronicle,* 2/9/81)

■ The federal government would drastically curtail its commitment to aid middle-income college students, educational research, and the arts and humanities in a package of budget cuts proposed by President Reagan. [Many of the proposals were later rejected.] (*The Chronicle,* 2/23/81)

■ As many as 750,000 students could be forced to drop out of college if the Reagan Administration's sweeping austerity plan is adopted, higher-education representatives warn. (*The Chronicle,* 3/2/81)

■ The Corporation for Public Broadcasting receives a $150-million gift from Walter H. Annenberg, the publisher of *TV Guide,* to produce courses to be offered for credit by colleges and universities. (*The Chronicle,* 3/9/81)

■ The latest version of the Reagan Administration budget for fiscal 1982 includes cuts for the National Science Foundation and in federal grants for college libraries, international education, and the renovation of campus buildings, as well as increases in direct grants to low-income students and in aid to black colleges. (*The Chronicle,* 3/16/81)

■ New postal-rate increases are expected to raise the average college's mailing costs by about 14 per cent. (*The Chronicle,* 3/16/81)

■ Because of a decline in the number of students majoring in teacher-education programs, a "critical" shortage of schoolteachers is likely by 1985, education deans warn. (*The Chronicle,* 3/23/81)

■ In the first such action of its kind, the Educational Testing Service raises the scores of 240,000 students who took the Preliminary Scholastic Aptitude Test after a Florida high-school student proved the service wrong on a geometry question. (*The Chronicle,* 3/23/81)

■ The College Board says students may ask for and receive copies of their own responses and the correct answers to questions on the Scholastic Aptitude Test, extending nationwide an option that New York State residents have under a 1980 "truth in testing" law. (*The Chronicle,* 4/6/81)

■ General education remains a "disaster area" at most colleges and universities, but the times are propitious for a "contemporary revival," according to Ernest L. Boyer and Arthur Levine of the Carnegie Foundation for the Advancement of Teaching. (*The Chronicle,* 4/13/81)

■ In one of the most sweeping actions ever taken at a single institution, Michigan State University trustees declare a financial crisis and cut the 1981-82 budget by 9 per cent, an action that could leave jobless 108 faculty members who have tenure or who are eligible for it. (*The Chronicle,* 4/13/81)

■ The presidents of five leading universities protest government attempts to restrict the flow of research data in the name of national security, even when the information is not classified as secret. (*The Chronicle,* 4/27/81)

■ The U.S. Commission on Civil Rights says the government's efforts to eliminate traces of segregation in state higher-education systems have been weak and largely ineffective. (*The Chronicle,* 5/18/81)

■ Colleges plan to fight an effort by the Internal Revenue Service to tax one of higher education's most cherished perquisites, free tuition for employees' dependents. (*The Chronicle,* 6/8/81)

■ Scholar Gerda Lerner becomes the first woman in 50 years to be elected president of the 8,500-member Organization of American Historians, an action that many see as symbolic of a growing acceptance of both women historians and women's history. (*The Chronicle,* 6/8/81)

■ Engineering schools at American colleges are on the "eve of disaster" because a faculty shortage is causing institutions to limit enrollments at a time when the demand for engineers is growing, according to engineering educators. (*The Chronicle,* 6/29/81)

■ In a look at campus life after the sexual revolution of the late 1960's, a *Chronicle* survey of student-personnel administrators at 150 four-year colleges shows that cohabitation is firmly entrenched as "living alternative" for many students, that interracial dating is accepted on many campuses, and that homosexual students are "coming out of the closet" in growing numbers. (*The Chronicle,* 6/29/81)

■ In actions that critics charge will significantly weaken affirmative action, the Reagan Administration moves on several fronts to modify civil-rights and affirmative-action requirements affecting women, members of minority groups, and the handicapped. (*The Chronicle,* 9/2/81)

■ President Reagan signs into law tougher eligibility requirements for Guaranteed Student Loans and the requirement that borrowers pay banks a 5-per-cent origination fee on their loans. (*The Chronicle,* 9/2/81)

■ The much-publicized 18-year decline in scores on the Scholastic Aptitude Test is halted, with average verbal and mathematical scores unchanged from 1980. (*The Chronicle,* 10/7/81)

- In 34 states, support for higher education from state appropriations failed to keep up with inflation during the past two years. (*The Chronicle*, 10/21/81)

- Education Secretary Terrel H. Bell announces plans to lay off between 200 and 250 of the department's 6,500 employees by January, and says the department has already eliminated some 1,000 jobs through attrition and by shifting loan-collection jobs to private contractors. (*The Chronicle*, 10/28/81)

- Duke University's academic council approves a plan to locate Richard M. Nixon's Presidential Library—but not an accompanying museum—at Duke. [The foundation responsible for raising funds for the project later decides to build the library and museum in Yorba Linda, Cal.] (*The Chronicle*, 11/11/81)

- Colleges must develop programs "to combat growing illiteracy about public issues," says a report by Ernest L. Boyer, president of the Carnegie Foundation for the Advancement of Teaching, and Fred M. Hechinger, president of the New York Times Foundation. (*The Chronicle*, 11/25/81)

- Academic freedom does not entitle professors to refuse to testify about their role in tenure decisions, a federal appeals court rules in a case involving James A. Dinnan, a University of Georgia professor who was jailed for refusing to say in court how he voted on a tenure case. However, in a case at La Guardia Community College, a federal district judge rules that the secrecy of tenure votes is essential to preserving academic freedom. (*The Chronicle*, 11/25/81)

- President Reagan nominates William J. Bennett, director of the National Humanities Center in North Carolina and a self-described "disaffected Democrat who voted for Reagan," to head the National Endowment for the Humanities. (*The Chronicle*, 11/25/81)

- Because of substantial gains in enrollments at two-year colleges, overall enrollment rises 1.9 per cent to a record 12,322,469, according to the Education Department. (*The Chronicle*, 12/9/81)

- Faced with an overload of underprepared students and financial problems that could force them to limit enrollment, many public colleges and universities begin to raise their entrance requirements. (*The Chronicle*, 12/9/81)

- The Supreme Court upholds the right of students to hold religious services on public university campuses, rejecting a claim by the University of Missouri that allowing regular services would violate federal and state constitutional prohibitions against governments' establishment or advancement of religion. (*The Chronicle*, 12/16/81)

- With the imposition of martial law, riot police shut down Poland's universities, driving students from the campuses. Many students and faculty members fear academic life in Poland will never be the same. (*The Chronicle*, 1/6/82)

1982

- Officials of the Association for Intercollegiate Athletics for Women hold what they fear will be their last conference. Many say they will go out of business unless they win a lawsuit against the National Collegiate Athletic Association to prevent it from sponsoring women's championships. (*The Chronicle*, 1/6/82)

■ The American Association for the Advancement of Science warns that "creationist groups are imposing beliefs disguised as science upon teachers and students to the detriment and distortion of public education in the United States." (*The Chronicle*, 1/13/82)

■ Scientists warn that a 10-year decline in mathematics test scores of entering freshmen presages a critical shortage of competent scientists and technologists in the future. (*The Chronicle*, 1/13/82)

■ The Education Department rejects Alabama's proposal for desegregating the state's higher-education system and asks the Justice Department to take action. (*The Chronicle*, 1/13/82)

■ The Ford Foundation's Commission on the Higher Education of Minorities calls on colleges and universities to adopt a "value added" system in which students would be admitted and evaluated "on the basis of their potential for learning and growth rather than their relative standing on tests and grades." (*The Chronicle*, 2/3/82)

■ Texas A&M University's new football coach, Jackie Sherrill, signs a six-year, $1,722,000 contract—the largest in the history of college sports. College athletics officials fear a "ripple effect" on salaries. (*The Chronicle*, 2/3/82)

■ President Reagan announces a "new federalism" that will shift financial responsibility for billions of dollars in social programs—including $3.3-billion in education—to the states. (*The Chronicle*, 2/3/82)

■ *The New York Times Selective Guide to Colleges* hits the stands, delighting some and provoking others of the 250 "best and most interesting" four-year institutions rated in the book. (*The Chronicle*, 2/10/82)

■ President Reagan's budget for fiscal 1983 proposes demoting the Education Department, cutting 23 education programs, and renaming the revamped federal agency the Foundation for Education Assistance. [Many of the proposals were later rejected.] (*The Chronicle*, 2/17/82)

■ Thousands of students rally on Capitol Hill chanting "Books, not bombs" and hawking T-shirts to protest against the Reagan Administration's proposed cuts in federal student aid. (*The Chronicle*, 3/10/82)

■ President Reagan signs a new executive order to beef up protection for national-security information. Scientists say it will limit their access to government documents and make it easier for officials to keep information secret indefinitely. (*The Chronicle*, 4/14/82)

■ The Supreme Court rules that Title IX of the Education Amendments of 1972 bars sex discrimination against employees of educational institutions as well as against students. (*The Chronicle*, 5/26/82)

■ The Association for Intercollegiate Athletics for Women suspends all activities, pending the outcome of an antitrust suit filed against the National Collegiate Athletic Association. (*The Chronicle*, 6/16/82)

■ The Supreme Court refuses to review the contempt-of-court conviction of James A. Dinnan, a University of Georgia professor who went to jail rather than reveal how he voted in a tenure decision. The lower court had ruled that the right to academic freedom must be limited by other goals of society and that confidentiality "cannot be used to give an institution of higher learning *carte blanche* to practice discrimination." (*The Chronicle*, 6/16/82)

■ David S. Dodge, acting president of the American University of Beirut, is kidnaped as the institution is caught up in the ideological and religious battles that have plagued Lebanon. (*The Chronicle*, 7/28/82)

■ The Presidential Commission for the Study of Ethical Problems in Medicine and Biomedical and Behavioral Research finds that gene-splicing work has not yet presented "a fundamental danger to human values, social norms, or ethical principles." The panel urges greater federal scrutiny of human genetic engineering. (*The Chronicle*, 11/24/82)

1983

■ The members of the National Colle-

giate Athletic Association's Division I vote to toughen academic standards for freshman athletes, requiring them to meet minimum standardized-test score requirements and earn at least a 2.0 grade-point average in a high-school core curriculum. The rule, commonly known as Proposition 48, passes despite bitter opposition from black-college presidents who say the inclusion of test-score requirements makes the standards discriminatory. (*The Chronicle*, 1/19/83)

■ The United States Football League signs Herschel Walker, the country's top collegiate player, before his eligibility ends at the University of Georgia. (*The Chronicle*, 3/2/83)

■ Several states begin raising their minimum drinking ages, worrying college officials who say they are losing their ability to monitor and control the use of alcohol by students in the mixed-age college population. (*The Chronicle*, 3/9/83)

■ Barney B. Clark dies 112 days after doctors at the University of Utah implanted an artificial heart. (*The Chronicle*, 3/30/83)

■ Nine book publishers withdraw a lawsuit charging New York University and several of its professors with copyright infringement. In return, the university agrees to step up efforts to prevent unauthorized photocopying of copyrighted works. (*The Chronicle*, 4/20/83)

■ The National Commission on Excellence in Education warns in a report to President Reagan and the American people that "our nation is at risk." The report says: "The educational foundations of our society are presently being eroded by a rising tide of mediocrity that threatens our very future as a nation and a people." (*The Chronicle*, 5/4/83)

■ Rejecting a plea from Bob Jones University, the Supreme Court rules that tax exemptions cannot be granted to schools and colleges that violate "fundamental public policy" by practicing racial discrimination. The university had cited religious grounds for its restrictive policies. (*The Chronicle*, 6/1/83)

■ Riot police in Paris clash with right-wing students during widespread protests over President François Mitterrand's proposed overhaul of France's higher education system. (*The Chronicle*, 6/1/83)

■ The U. S. Supreme Court allows the Education Department to bar young men from receiving federal student aid if they have not registered for the draft. The order lifts a lower-court injunction until the Supreme Court rules on the constitutionality of the requirement. (*The Chronicle*, 7/6/83)

■ The Supreme Court upholds a state law allowing parents to deduct from their state income taxes the tuition and other educational expenses paid for their children's elementary- and secondary-school educations. (*The Chronicle*, 7/6/83)

■ The Supreme Court rules that paying women lower retirement benefits than men constitutes sex discrimination. (*The Chronicle*, 7/13/83)

■ A federal panel recommends that the Energy Department abandon a half-finished atom smasher at the Brookhaven National Laboratory in New York State in favor of a more powerful, $2-billion accelerator—the Superconducting Supercollider. (*The Chronicle*, 7/20/83)

■ The Chinese government awards doctoral degrees to Chinese students taught by Chinese professors for the first time since the Communists came to power. (*The Chronicle*, 7/20/83)

■ Kidnapers release David S. Dodge of the American University of Beirut, a year after abducting him. (*The Chronicle*, 7/27/83)

■ The Soviet Union's shooting down of a South Korean airliner halts the United States decision to set up new cultural, scientific, and scholarly exchanges with the Russians. (*The Chronicle*, 9/14/83)

■ "Our children could be stragglers in a world of technology" warns the National Science Board's Commission on Precollege Education in Mathematics, Science, and Technology. "We must not let this happen; America must not become an industrial dinosaur." (*The Chronicle*, 9/21/83)

■ The Carnegie Foundation for the Advancement of Teaching says colleges and universities should establish links with high schools to create "comprehensive partnerships." (*The Chronicle*, 9/21/83)

■ A Court of Appeals judge for the District of Columbia upholds Georgetown University's refusal to recognize two organizations for homosexual students, saying that the First Amendment guarantee of religious freedom outweighs the District of Columbia's law protecting homosexuals from discrimination. (*The Chronicle*, 10/26/83)

■ Several hundred American medical students are evacuated from St. George's University School of Medicine during the United States invasion of Grenada. (*The Chronicle*, 11/2/83)

■ More than 1,500 American physicists and some 11,500 others in 42 countries sign a plea for an immediate freeze in the testing, production, and deployment of nuclear weapons. (*The Chronicle*, 11/23/83)

■ Catholic educators express concern over a revision in the Roman Catholic Church's canon law that says "those who teach theological subjects in any institute of higher studies must have a mandate from the competent ecclesiastical authority." (*The Chronicle*, 12/7/83)

■ The United States serves notice that it will withdraw from the United Nations Educational, Scientific, and Cultural Organization by the end of 1984 unless Unesco makes dramatic changes in its management and corrects its "anti-West bias." (*The Chronicle*, 1/4/84)

1984

■ State spending on need-based aid to undergraduates tops $1-billion for the first time. (*The Chronicle*, 1/4/84)

■ The National Collegiate Athletic Association establishes a commission of college presidents to solve prob-

lems plaguing college sports, but refuses to give it as much authority as some say it needs. (*The Chronicle*, 1/18/84)

■ Malcolm H. Kerr, president of the American University of Beirut, is assassinated outside his office. (*The Chronicle*, 1/25/84)

■ To refurbish or replace their deteriorating facilities, colleges will need to spend at least $40-billion, says Harvey H. Kaiser in *Crumbling Academe*. (*The Chronicle*, 1/25/84)

■ Apple Computer Inc. introduces the Macintosh, an easy-to-use, graphic computer, and establishes the Apple University Consortium, which becomes the standard for arrangements between microcomputer manufacturers and higher education. For significant discounts on the machine, the colleges would write software for it. (*The Chronicle*, 2/1/84)

■ Tuition of up to $100 a year, the first such charge in the 73-year history of the California Community Colleges system, will go into effect next fall to avert a fiscal crisis. (*The Chronicle*, 2/1/84)

■ The Reagan Administration's budget for fiscal 1985 calls for more spending for basic scientific research on college campuses and requires students and their parents to pay more of the cost of a college education. (*The Chronicle*, 2/8/84)

■ A National Institutes of Health advisory committee refuses to require researchers to file environmental-impact statements before conducting field tests of genetically engineered organisms. (*The Chronicle*, 2/15/84)

1984
Continued

■ William J. Bennett, chairman of the National Endowment for the Humanities, says too many graduate programs in the humanities are "insignificant, lifeless, and pointless." (*The Chronicle*, 2/29/84)

■ Faculty members at public colleges and universities have no constitutional right to a voice in policy decisions made by their institutions, the Supreme Court says in a case involving the Minnesota Board for Community Colleges. (*The Chronicle*, 2/29/84)

■ In a case involving Grove City College, the Supreme Court rules that a law barring sex bias in education covers not an entire college, but only its programs that get direct U.S. aid. (*The Chronicle*, 3/7/84)

■ In an investigation called "Dipscam," the Federal Bureau of Investigation cracks down on the sale of fake college diplomas. (*The Chronicle*, 3/28/84)

■ Many public community colleges are establishing non-profit foundations to raise money from private sources for activities that are not adequately supported by government funds. (*The Chronicle*, 4/18/84)

■ American and French scientists report finding the virus that causes AIDS. (*The Chronicle*, 5/2/84)

■ In its first action against a woman's program, the N.C.A.A. censures the women's basketball program at Alcorn State University for rules violations. (*The Chronicle*, 5/9/84)

■ A federal judge issues an order stopping researchers at the University of California from conducting the first deliberate release of genetically engineered organisms into the environment. (*The Chronicle*, 5/23/84)

■ In a surprise move, Edward A. Knapp, director of the National Science Foundation for one and a half years, resigns; his replacement will be Erich Bloch, a vice-president of the International Business Machines Corporation, who will be the first director to come from industry. (*The Chronicle*, 6/13/84)

■ The Supreme Court strikes down the N.C.A.A.'s control of televised intercollegiate football games, agreeing with a lower court that the association violates antitrust laws by acting as a "classic cartel." (*The Chronicle*, 7/5/84)

■ The Supreme Court upholds the ban on financial aid to students who refuse to register for the draft. (*The Chronicle*, 7/11/84)

■ The growing popularity of dormitory living—and, in some cases, unanticipated enrollment increases—has created severe housing shortages on many campuses this fall. (*The Chronicle*, 9/5/84)

■ Violations of rules on recruiting and financial aid to athletes are so rampant in big-time college sports that the N.C.A.A. is having a difficult time tracking down the cheaters, says Walter Byers, the association's executive director. (*The Chronicle*, 9/5/84)

■ Women's colleges, to the surprise of many who were sounding their death knell as recently as a decade ago, are thriving: Enrollments, applications, and gifts from alumnae are up. (*The Chronicle*, 9/12/84)

■ Researchers planning field tests involving the release of some types of genetically engineered microbes into the environment must first obtain approval from the Environmental Protection Agency. (*The Chronicle*, 9/19/84)

■ Scores on both parts of the Scholastic Aptitude Test rose last year by a total of four points, adding to evidence that the long and worrisome decline in scores has been reversed. (*The Chronicle*, 9/26/84)

■ American colleges are suffering from a pervasive lack of strong presidential leadership, concludes the Commission on Strengthening Presidential Leadership, headed by Clark Kerr. At many institutions the president's job has become too difficult, too stressful, too constrained by outside influences, and too unrewarding to attract or long retain the kind of person who is probably best qualified to serve, the group says. (*The Chronicle*, 9/26/84)

■ Some 1,800 non-academic workers at Yale University strike after protracted contract negotiations fail. (*The Chronicle*, 10/3/84)

■ The Supreme Court rules that both men and women who retired after May 1, 1980, must get the same pension benefits from the Teachers Insurance and Annuity Association and the College Retirement Equities Fund. (*The Chronicle*, 10/17/84)

■ In an effort to signal applicants that the Scholastic Aptitude Test "is not the be-all and end-all of college admissions," Bates College drops the test as an admissions requirement and requires instead that applicants submit scores on three achievement tests. (*The Chronicle*, 10/17/84)

■ Education Secretary Terrel H. Bell says one of his goals in a second Reagan Administration would be to protect the federal education budget from cuts by David A. Stockman, director of the Office of Management and Budget. (*The Chronicle*, 10/17/84)

■ Colleges should revitalize liberal education and set higher standards for graduation because the curriculum has become "excessively vocational," warns a National Institute of Education panel in "Involvement in Learning: Realizing the Potential of American Higher Education." (*The Chronicle*, 10/24/84)

■ Colleges must hire 500,000 professors in the next 25 years, thereby replacing virtually the entire professoriate, according to a study by Howard R. Bowen and Jack H. Schuster, both faculty members at the Claremont Graduate Schools. (*The Chronicle*, 11/7/84)

■ For personal reasons, Education Secretary Terrel H. Bell announces he will resign to become a professor of school administration at the University of Utah; he is the first Cabinet member to leave since the re-election of President Reagan. (*The Chronicle*, 11/14/84)

■ Citing "arid teaching" and a "self-service curriculum," William J. Bennett, the chairman of the National Endowment for the Humanities, assails the state of the humanities on college campuses in his report "To Reclaim a Legacy." (*The Chronicle*, 11/28/84)

■ Robert H. Atwell, vice-president of the American Council on Education, is named president of the group. He replaces Jack W. Peltason, president since 1977, who resigned to become chancellor of the University of California at Irvine. (*The Chronicle*, 12/5/84)

■ Frank Newman, a fellow at the Carnegie Foundation for the Advancement of Teaching and former president of the University of Rhode Island, is named executive director of the Education Commission of the States. (*The Chronicle*, 12/12/84)

1985

■ Making good on a threat issued 12 months earlier, the United States withdraws from the United Nations Educational, Scientific, and Cultural Organization, saying Unesco has failed to make progress on a series of reforms intended, among other things, to make it more impartial. (*The Chronicle*, 1/9/85)

■ President Reagan nominates William J. Bennett, controversial head of the National Endowment for the Humanities, to be Secretary of Education. (*The Chronicle*, 1/16/85)

■ The United States and the Soviet Union reach tentative agreement to resume scientific exchanges, which have been suspended since 1980 when members of the governing council of the U.S. National Academy of Sciences voted to break off contact with their Soviet counterparts as a way of protesting the arrest and banishment of Andrei D. Sakharov, the dissident Soviet physicist. (*The Chronicle*, 2/6/85)

■ To help speed the confirmation of William Bennett as Education Secretary, President Reagan assures Congress that he has "no intention of recommending abolition" of the Department of Education "at this time." (*The Chronicle*, 2/6/85)

■ The Association of American Colleges issues a report that places much of the blame for what it calls the "decline and devaluation" of undergraduate education on faculty members and calls on them to take the lead in restoring "coherence" to the curriculum. (*The Chronicle*, 2/13/85)

■ In his first news conference as Secretary of Education, William J. Bennett endorses President Reagan's plans to cut federal spending on student-aid programs and suggests that some students now receiving aid may have to consider "divestitures of certain sorts—like a stereo divestiture, an automobile divestiture, or a three-weeks-at-the-beach divestiture." His comments draw fire from students, higher-education groups, and the chairman of the Senate Education Committee, Robert T. Stafford, Republican of Vermont. (*The Chronicle*, 2/20/85)

■ The National Commission for Excellence in Teacher Education issues

"A Call for Change in Teacher Education," which urges colleges to stiffen admission and graduation requirements for prospective teachers and recommends better working conditions for schoolteachers. (*The Chronicle*, 3/6/85)

■ In response to government pressure, U. S. scientific and engineering associations begin to limit attendance at their meetings to American citizens. The government is concerned about the possible "export" of military technology to the Soviet Union and certain other nations. (*The Chronicle*, 3/6/85)

■ Surgeons at the University of Arizona implant an untested, unapproved artificial heart in a human patient in what they call a desperate attempt to keep the patient alive between human heart transplants. The patient dies, and specialists in medical ethics condemn the surgeons' actions. (*The Chronicle*, 3/20/85)

■ Clark Kerr declares that the federal era in higher education has "clearly ended." (*The Chronicle*, 4/3/85)

■ Tulane University's president, Eamon M. Kelly, says the university will abolish its men's basketball program, which is beset by recruiting violations and allegations of gambling. (*The Chronicle*, 4/10/85)

■ In a report called "Equality and Excellence: The Educational Status of Black Americans," the College Board says the gains made by black students in the 60's and early 70's have eroded during the preceding 10 years and are endangered by policies that "threaten to reverse the movement toward equality." (*The Chronicle*, 4/17/85)

■ A wave of 60's-style protests hits the campuses. They are aimed at South Africa and divestment, recruiting by the Central Intelligence Agency, and minority issues. (*The Chronicle*, 4/24/85)

■ 370 students are arrested in South Korean protests to mark the 25th anniversary of a student uprising that led to the downfall of an earlier government. (*The Chronicle*, 5/1/85)

■ The Carnegie Foundation for the Advancement of Teaching issues "Sustaining the Vision," a report that says the "historic partnership" between higher education and the federal government is being challenged by a shortsighted emphasis on budget cutting and abuses of federal programs. (*The Chronicle*, 6/5/85)

■ Thomas Sutherland, dean of agriculture at the American University of Beirut, is taken hostage. Some experts say the continuing strife in Lebanon is threatening the very existence of the university. (*The Chronicle*, 6/12/85 and 6/19/85)

■ The Howard Hughes Medical Institute becomes the world's richest private research organization with the sale of its sole asset, the Hughes Aircraft Company, to the General Motors Corporation for an estimated $5-billion. (*The Chronicle*, 6/12/85)

■ Thousands of U.S. and Canadian scientists urge their governments to oppose President Reagan's Strategic Defense Initiative. (*The Chronicle*, 6/12/85)

■ Texas A&M University, after twice failing in attempts to get the U. S. Supreme Court to hear its appeal of a ruling that it must grant recognition to a homosexual student group, gives the group, Gay Students Services, official recognition and the right to hold meetings on the campus. (*The Chronicle*, 6/19/85)

■ China announces a plan to end its Soviet-style education system and adopt a Western model. (*The Chronicle*, 6/26/85)

■ At a special meeting called by its presidents' commission, the National Collegiate Athletic Association adopts changes in 12 rules aimed at reforming intercollegiate athletics, including the "death penalty" for colleges caught cheating. (*The Chronicle*, 7/3/85)

■ A three-judge panel in the District of Columbia Court of Appeals reverses a trial-court ruling and tells Georgetown University to grant official recognition to two gay-student organizations. (*The Chronicle*, 8/7/85)

■ South Africa calls a "state of emergency." Black students are among those who bear the brunt of police action. (*The Chronicle*, 8/7/85)

■ The Carnegie Foundation for the Advancement of Teaching, in a report by Frank Newman, calls for a "fundamental re-examination" of national policies toward higher education. (*The Chronicle*, 9/18/85)

■ A call for increased community service by students is made by a newly formed coalition of 75 college presidents. (*The Chronicle*, 10/23/85)

■ South Africa widens its state of emergency; students and faculty members are detained. (*The Chronicle*, 11/6/85)

■ Three athletes, two coaches, and a trainer from Iowa State University women's cross-country team are killed when their plane crashes in bad weather. (*The Chronicle*, 12/4/85)

1986

■ Despite impassioned pleas from the presidents of predominantly black institutions, members of the National Collegiate Athletic Association reject an attempt to abolish the standardized-test score requirement from Proposition 48, the association's academic standards for freshman athletes. The academic rule, first adopted in 1983, takes effect immediately. (*The Chronicle*, 1/22/86)

■ Deteriorating research facilities, outdated scientific equipment, and shortages of science and engineering faculty must be corrected with "significant increases" in federal support to universities if the United States is to maintain its economic and military strength in the decades ahead, a White House panel concludes. (*The Chronicle*, 1/29/86)

■ Fifteen Dartmouth College students, armed with sledgehammers and sponsored by the conservative Dartmouth *Review*, demolish three shanties erected on the college green by anti-apartheid protesters. After 200 students and faculty members occupy the administration building, the college agrees to suspend classes for one day and convene a campus forum on "racism, violence, and disrespect for diversity of opinion." (*The Chronicle,* 1/29/86)

■ The Supreme Court unanimously rules that providing government aid to students who are preparing for careers in the ministry does not necessarily violate the constitutional separation of church and state. (*The Chronicle,* 2/5/86)

■ A jury in a federal court in Atlanta awards more than $2.5-million to Jan Kemp, a former remedial-English instructor at the University of Georgia who charged that two university officials had fired her because she had complained publicly about the practice of giving preferential treatment to athletes. [The award was eventually reduced to $1.08-million.] (*The Chronicle,* 2/19/86)

■ A wave of terrorism in Europe and the Mediterranean causes the cancellation of some study-abroad programs and the rearrangement or postponement of others. (*The Chronicle,* 2/19/86)

■ The Vatican orders the Rev. Charles E. Curran, a professor of moral theology at the Catholic University of America, to retract his positions on abortion, birth control, and other issues or face the loss of his authorization to teach Roman Catholic doctrine. (*The Chronicle,* 3/19/86)

■ Urging America's research universities to "respond to the crisis in public education," education deans from several dozen such institutions outline an ambitious program for reforming teacher education and the school-

teaching profession. The deans, known collectively as the "Holmes Group," call their report "Tomorrow's Teachers." (*The Chronicle,* 4/9/86)

■ The National Academy of Sciences and the Soviet Union's Academy of Sciences announce they will resume a program of exchanges and cooperation that was suspended in February 1980. (*The Chronicle,* 4/16/86)

■ In academic 1984-85, for the first time ever, corporate gifts to colleges and universities topped contributions from alumni and alumnae. A total of $6.3-billion in voluntary financial support included $1.6-billion in company contributions. (*The Chronicle,* 5/7/86)

■ The Supreme Court, ruling in a case involving Franklin and Marshall College, lets stand a lower-court decision that allows the Equal Employment Opportunity Commission to inspect confidential documents in college faculty tenure cases. (*The Chronicle,* 6/11/86)

■ Len Bias, a star basketball player at the University of Maryland at College Park, dies of a heart attack after ingesting cocaine, one day after being picked second in the National Basketball Association draft. (*The Chronicle,* 7/2/86)

■ The Danforth Foundation gives Washington University $100-million, believed to be the largest grant ever made to a college by a philanthropy. (*The Chronicle,* 7/9/86)

■ A survey by the American Council on Education shows that national reports calling for reform of undergraduate education have led to changes in

1986

Continued

academic programs at one in three colleges. (*The Chronicle*, 7/30/86)

■ The House of Representatives votes to bar any college, university, or school from receiving money from the Education Department unless it can prove it has a program to prevent student drug abuse. (*The Chronicle*, 8/6/86)

■ Negotiators from the United States and the Soviet Union sign agreements for 13 specific exchange projects and predict substantial expansion of educational and cultural contacts between the two countries. (*The Chronicle*, 8/13/86)

■ Harvard University—and American higher education—marks its 350th anniversary. (*The Chronicle*, 9/3/86)

■ The National Governors' Association calls on all colleges and universities, public and private, to start comprehensive programs to measure what undergraduates learn. (*The Chronicle*, 9/3/86)

■ Walter Byers, the only executive director the National Collegiate Athletic Association has ever had, announces plans to retire. (*The Chronicle*, 9/3/86)

■ About 400 freshmen at colleges with big-time sports programs are deemed ineligible to play football or basketball because they did not meet the new academic requirements under the N.C.A.A.'s Proposition 48. An overwhelming majority of the athletes are black. (*The Chronicle*, 9/10/86)

■ The House of Representatives passes compromise tax-reform legislation that is later approved by the Senate and signed by the President. The sweeping bill causes concern among higher-education and philanthropic groups that fear a drastic drop in charitable giving. (*The Chronicle*, 10/1/86)

■ The National Labor Relations Board rules that faculty members at Boston University are managerial employees and are not entitled to bargain collectively. (*The Chronicle*, 10/8/86)

■ Washington University announces it has set a record in American higher education for funds raised in a capital campaign—$503.5-million in a drive it began in May 1982. (*The Chronicle*, 10/15/86)

■ Clifton R. Wharton, Jr., says he will resign as chancellor of the State University of New York—America's largest university system—to head the nation's largest private pension companies, the Teachers Insurance and Annuity Association and College Retirement Equities Fund. (*The Chronicle*, 10/22/86)

■ Congress sends President Reagan legislation that would bar colleges from forcing tenured faculty members to retire at age 70, effective in 1994. (*The Chronicle*, 10/29/86)

■ In a new book, *College: The Undergraduate Experience in America*, Ernest L. Boyer, president of the Carnegie Foundation for the Advancement of Teaching, warns that undergraduate colleges in the United States are confused over their purposes and racked by tensions that prevent them from providing coherent educational experiences for their students. (*The Chronicle*, 11/5/86)

■ A committee of the National Academy of Sciences and the Institute of Medicine recommends more involvement by universities and industry in efforts to stop the spread of AIDS and find a cure for it. (*The Chronicle*, 11/5/86)

■ A panel of educators, business leaders, and government officials calls for a state-by-state overhaul of education "comparable to the Marshall Plan," in a report published by the American Association of State Colleges and Universities. The panel was headed by former U.S. Secretary of Education Terrel H. Bell. (*The Chronicle*, 11/12/86)

■ Challenging colleges to curb their costs, Secretary of Education William J. Bennett announces he is considering a federal policy to reduce financial aid to students whose institutions increase tuition charges much beyond the rate of inflation. (*The Chronicle*, 11/26/86)

■ A massive protest movement against government education policies sweeps across France. Critics say proposed reforms threaten to produce inequality of opportunity and excessive selectivity among universities. (*The Chronicle*, 12/3/86 and 12/10/86)

■ Michigan's Legislature approves a plan to let parents start paying for college tuition before their children are out of diapers. It is the first such statewide plan in the nation. (*The Chronicle*, 12/17/86)

■ A Congressional report shows borrowing by students to pay for college has quintupled in the last 10 years, raising the specter of a "debtor generation" of young Americans. (*The Chronicle*, 1/7/87)

1987

■ The presidents' commission of the National Collegiate Athletic Association calls a special convention to consider measures to reform college sports. (*The Chronicle*, 1/14/87)

■ President Reagan's education budget calls for student aid to be slashed 45 per cent, from $8.2-billion this year to $4.5-billion in fiscal 1988. [Congress later rejected the cuts.] (*The Chronicle*, 1/14/87)

■ The Chinese government's early tolerance of student protests in 12 Chinese cities gives way to a crackdown as Deng Xiaoping, the nation's top leader, calls the unrest a mistake. The dissident astrophysicist Fang Lizhi is fired from his university post for defaming Communist Party leaders. (*The Chronicle*, 1/21/87)

■ Catholic University temporarily suspends the Rev. Charles E. Curran from all teaching duties. The liberal theologian, whom the Vatican declared unfit to teach Catholic theology because of his dissent from church teachings, threatens to sue the university. (*The Chronicle*, 1/21/87)

■ A study by the University of California at Berkeley declares unfounded the charges that the university imposed discriminatory admissions policies or practices to hold down the enrollment of Asian Americans. (*The Chronicle*, 2/4/87)

■ H. Ross Perot, the Texas billionaire, joins Carnegie Mellon and Stanford Universities in providing the capital that Steven P. Jobs says will enable him to produce and deliver a powerful new microcomputer and software for higher education within 12 months. (*The Chronicle*, 2/11/87)

■ President Reagan decides to back the construction of a $4.4-billion particle accelerator known as the Superconducting Supercollider, bringing scientists one step closer to realizing a long-held scientific dream. (*The Chronicle*, 2/11/87)

■ Stanford University announces plans for a five-year campaign to raise $1.1-billion, the largest fund-raising drive in the history of American higher education. (*The Chronicle*, 2/11/87)

■ A study by the American Council on Education finds that college tuition fees have risen markedly faster than consumer prices since 1980. But from 1970 to 1986, they rose at an average annual rate of only 1 percentage point above inflation. The study comes during an increasingly sharp debate about skyrocketing college costs. (*The Chronicle*, 3/4/87)

■ The N.C.A.A.'s infractions committee imposes for the first time its "death penalty" for repeat violators, barring Southern Methodist University from playing football for a year and restricting its schedule for an additional year. The penalties are the harshest ever issued for rules violations in college football. (*The Chronicle*, 3/4/87)

■ The University of Michigan closes a campus radio station after it broadcasts remarks that insulted blacks. The university president appoints a panel to investigate the incident and adds $1-million to the affirmative-action budget. (*The Chronicle*, 3/4/87)

■ The Rev. Charles E. Curran sues Catholic University, seeking to overturn its decision to suspend him from teaching Catholic theology. (*The Chronicle*, 3/4/87)

■ Paul C.W. Chu of the University of Houston and colleagues at the University of Alabama at Huntsville report the discovery of the first material that retains its superconductive properties above liquid-nitrogen temperatures. The announcement produces a frantic race among scientists to find materials with no electrical resistance that retain their superconductive properties at even higher temperatures. (*The Chronicle*, 3/18/87)

■ In its most sweeping endorsement of affirmative action, the Supreme Court upholds voluntary plans that help qualified women and members of minority groups gain jobs traditionally dominated by white men. (*The Chronicle*, 4/1/87)

■ E.D. Hirsch, a professor of English at the University of Virginia, decries cultural ignorance in America in a new book, *Cultural Literacy: What Every American Needs to Know*. (*The Chronicle*, 4/22/87)

■ A $2.5-million fire started by arsonists and linked to animal-rights activists heavily damages a veterinary diagnostic laboratory under construction at the University of California at Davis. (*The Chronicle*, 4/29/87)

■ South Korean students stage a new wave of violent protests against their government. Demonstrations are held at about 40 universities. (*The Chronicle*, 4/29/87)

■ Allan Bloom, author of *The Closing of the American Mind*, draws widespread attention with his argument that students are dispirited and universities are in disarray. (*The Chronicle*, 5/6/87)

■ After 35 years as president of the University of Notre Dame, the Rev. Theodore M. Hesburgh retires. (*The Chronicle*, 5/13/87)

■ The Carnegie Forum on Education and the Economy creates a national board to certify schoolteachers. The National Board for Professional Teaching Standards, a voluntary body, hopes to begin issuing certificates within five years. (*The Chronicle*, 5/20/87)

■ A federal grand jury will subpoena about 60 college athletes to testify in an investigation into alleged extortion, fraud, and racketeering by at least two sports agents. (*The Chronicle*, 6/3/87)

■ Education Secretary William J. Bennett presses the Reagan Administration to abandon its seven-year effort to reduce drastically the federal government's spending on education. (*The Chronicle*, 6/10/87)

■ Richard D. Schultz, director of athletics at the University of Virginia, is selected to succeed Walter Byers as executive director of the National Collegiate Athletic Association. (*The Chronicle*, 6/17/87)

■ Delegates to a special convention of the N.C.A.A. reject virtually all of the proposals to cut costs in college sports put forth by the presidents' commission. The commission, handcuffed by a lack of consensus among its members, begins an 18-month "national dialogue" consisting of studies and forums to try to shape an accord. (*The Chronicle*, 7/8/87)

■ The Education Department finds that students at proprietary schools are getting a growing share of federal aid. College officials fear the trend means that students seeking bachelor's degrees are receiving less. (*The Chronicle*, 7/22/87)

■ Increases in college tuition will exceed the nation's inflation rate for the seventh straight year, according to a study by the College Board. (*The Chronicle*, 8/12/87)

■ A *Chronicle* survey finds most Americans are worried about spiraling tuition, but many either think higher education is more expensive than it actually is or have no idea of its cost. (*The Chronicle*, 9/2/87)

■ Education Secretary William J. Bennett urges candidates for the Presidency to encourage colleges and universities to improve their quality and hold down tuition costs. (*The Chronicle*, 9/16/87)

■ Trustees of higher education's leading pension companies recommend several new and flexible investment funds for their policy holders. The report follows years of acrimonious de-

1988

bate between the pension companies and various education associations. (*The Chronicle*, 10/7/87)

■ The stock market plunges 500 points, threatening the value of pension funds and endowments at colleges and universities and raising fears that fund raising will be more difficult. (*The Chronicle*, 10/21/87)

■ South Africa issues stringent regulations requiring its universities to prevent campus unrest as a condition for receiving state subsidies. Academic leaders regard the action as the most serious infringement of university autonomy in the country's history. (*The Chronicle*, 10/28/87)

■ The Education Department moves to crack down on student-loan defaulters. Colleges with default rates of more than 20 per cent will have three years to reduce them or risk losing all of their federal student aid. (*The Chronicle*, 11/11/87)

■ The District of Columbia Court of Appeals rules that Georgetown University must offer equal treatment to homosexual student groups, but need not recognize them officially. (*The Chronicle*, 12/2/87)

■ A federal judge dismisses landmark litigation—known as the *Adams* case—that for nearly 15 years forced states in the South to submit college-desegregation plans. (*The Chronicle*, 1/6/88)

■ The number of doctorates earned by black Americans has declined 26.5 per cent from 1976 to 1986. The National Research Council blames it on a sharp drop in Ph.D.'s earned by black males. (*The Chronicle*, 2/3/88)

■ Newly released documents show the Federal Bureau of Investigation spied on campus groups at eight universities while investigating organizations opposed to the Reagan Administration's policies in Central America. (*The Chronicle*, 2/3/88 and 2/10/88)

■ Education Secretary William J. Bennett releases a scathing report on for-profit trade schools, accusing them of defrauding students and wasting federal student-aid money. (*The Chronicle*, 2/17/88)

■ Civil-rights groups are angered when the Education Department declares that four states—which have been under court order to desegregate their public colleges—are now in compliance with federal civil-rights laws. Six other states under similar court orders are still in violation of the 1964 Civil Rights Act and face a cutoff of federal funds, the department says. (*The Chronicle*, 2/17/88)

■ In a shift in his education policy, President Reagan sends a budget proposal to Congress that would increase spending on student aid by 9 per cent in fiscal 1989. He also recommends a 6-per-cent rise in federal spending for basic research. (*The Chronicle*, 2/24/88)

■ Rutgers University closes a fraternity and suspends all fraternity and sorority activities on its New Brunswick campus following the alcohol-related death of a freshman who took part in an initiation rite. (*The Chronicle*, 2/24/88)

■ The South African government imposes a sweeping ban on opposition organizations. University officials and students denounce the move. (*The Chronicle*, 3/2/88)

■ Fearful that the United States may lose the race to commercialize superconductivity, President Reagan asks Congress to prevent federal laboratories from releasing some scientific information to foreign competitors. (*The Chronicle*, 3/2/88)

■ Congress approves a bill that expands the scope of anti-bias rules that apply to colleges and other recipients of federal aid. The bill is designed to counteract the 1984 Supreme Court decision involving Grove City College. (*The Chronicle*, 3/9/88)

■ The appointment of a hearing person as president of Gallaudet University, the nation's only university for the deaf, triggers bitter student protests that close the campus and force the newly elected president to submit her resignation. Trustees select Irving King Jordan as the university's first hearing-impaired president. (*The Chronicle*, 3/16/88 and 3/23/88)

■ Educators criticize a recent spate of incidents involving excessive drinking, hazing, and abuse of women in fraternities and sororities on campuses. Meanwhile, membership in Greek organizations soars. (*The Chronicle*, 3/16/88)

■ Gov. James J. Blanchard of Michigan announces that the Internal Revenue Service plans to allow parents to participate in his state's prepaid-tuition program without paying additional federal income tax. (*The Chronicle*, 3/23/88)

■ Kenneth H. Keller, the architect of a long-term plan aimed at making the University of Minnesota one of the nation's top public institutions, resigns as president amid controversy over a $1.7-million renovation of his campus office and his official residence. (*The Chronicle*, 3/23/88)

■ The University of Michigan sets penalties—up to expulsion—for students found guilty of committing discriminatory acts, including verbal harassment. (*The Chronicle*, 3/30/88)

■ More than 20 universities across the country are expected to participate in a blood-testing program that would give health researchers their first reliable figures on the number of college students with H.I.V., the virus that causes AIDS. (*The Chronicle*, 4/6/88)

■ Stanford University's faculty votes to replace the Western-culture requirement with a new year-long requirement that will give "substantial attention" to the issues of race, sex, and class. The controversy sparks a national debate about what Western culture means and who defines it. (*The Chronicle*, 4/13/88)

■ Allegations of scientific misconduct against a Nobel Laureate and his collaborators bring into question the efficiency of federal and university systems for investigating such charges. The dispute involves David Baltimore, a Nobel Prize–winning biologist at the Massachusetts Institute of Technology. (*The Chronicle,* 4/20/88)

■ The Patent and Trademark Office grants the first patent ever issued on animals to Harvard University for genetically altered mammals that can be used to detect cancer-causing substances. (*The Chronicle,* 4/20/88)

■ The trustees of TIAA-CREF approve a plan to allow policy holders to transfer their accumulations to other funds under certain conditions—a concession that critics have sought for years. (*The Chronicle,* 5/4/88)

■ Colleges and universities report modest increases in the number of black students who plan to enroll in next fall's freshman classes, suggesting that the drought of blacks in institutions of higher learning may be easing. (*The Chronicle,* 5/18/88)

■ Education Secretary William J. Bennett announces he will resign. (*The Chronicle,* 5/18/88)

■ The American Council on Education releases a report, "One Third of a Nation," that declares the future prosperity of the country is at stake unless the United States renews its commitment to the advancement of members of minority groups. The Education Commission of the States cosponsors the report. (*The Chronicle,* 5/25/88)

■ A new plan to encourage students to participate in community or military service in exchange for federal financial aid attracts wide attention and re-

vives debate about the establishment of a national service corps. (*The Chronicle,* 5/25/88)

■ American and Soviet leaders agree to renew, extend, and broaden cooperation in education, atomic energy, and peaceful uses of outer space. The pacts will lead to increased scholarly ties. But officials fail to reach agreement on a proposal to broaden Soviet-American cooperation in the basic sciences. (*The Chronicle,* 6/8/88)

■ Temple University agrees to give more than 40 per cent of its athletic scholarships to women, settling an eight-year-old, sex-discrimination lawsuit. (*The Chronicle,* 6/22/88)

■ The British Parliament votes to end tenure for new faculty members at universities, but for the first time codifies the principles of academic freedom in British law. (*The Chronicle,* 8/3/88)

■ College tuition fees rise 7 per cent, outpacing inflation for the eighth consecutive year. (*The Chronicle,* 8/10/88)

■ President Reagan nominates Lauro F. Cavazos, a Hispanic who heads Texas Tech University, to be Secretary of Education. (*The Chronicle,* 9/1/88)

■ In a controversial report called *Humanities in America,* Lynne V. Cheney, chairman of the National Endowment for the Humanities, charges that the teaching of the humanities on many campuses is overly specialized and intensely politicized. (*The Chronicle,* 9/21/88)

■ Education Secretary Bennett announces new rules that will cut off federal student aid to colleges and trade schools where more than 20 per cent of the former students fail to repay their loans. (*The Chronicle*, 9/21/88)

■ Congressional leaders and President Reagan reach agreement on sweeping reforms under which tens of thousands of welfare recipients may enroll in job-training programs at community colleges and for-profit trade schools. (*The Chronicle*, 10/5/88)

■ University and science groups develop guidelines to help research institutions cope with incidents of scientific fraud. In the meantime, the federal government proposes new regulations to govern university behavior in misconduct investigations. (*The Chronicle*, 10/5/88)

■ Steven P. Jobs unveils his new NEXT computer, ending three years of secrecy and anticipation. He plans to sell it only to colleges and universities. (*The Chronicle*, 10/19/88)

■ After years of plummeting enrollments in the early 1980's, enrollment rises at many black colleges. The increases are attributed to better recruiting and to racist incidents at predominantly white colleges. (*The Chronicle*, 10/26/88)

■ Congress approves a bill to allow judges to strip federal student grants and loans from people who are convicted of using or selling illegal drugs. (*The Chronicle*, 11/2/88)

■ Early data from a nationwide study of AIDS infection on college campuses clearly establish that the virus has reached significant numbers of students. (*The Chronicle*, 11/9/88)

■ George Bush is elected President. He decides to keep Lauro F. Cavazos on as Education Secretary. (*The Chronicle*, 11/16/88 and 11/30/88)

■ The competition for the most-sought-after federal science project in history ends when Energy Secretary John S. Herrington selects Texas as the site for the $4.4-billion Superconducting Supercollider. (*The Chronicle*, 11/16/88)

■ A computer "virus" brings national research and communications networks to a halt. A first-year graduate student at Cornell University is believed to have created the virus. (*The Chronicle*, 11/16/88)

■ Urging blacks to support black higher education, the comedian Bill Cosby gives $20-million to Spelman College. (*The Chronicle*, 11/16/88)

■ The Education Department announces it will examine admissions policies at Harvard University and the University of California at Los Angeles out of concern that they may illegally limit the enrollment of Asian American students. (*The Chronicle*, 11/30/88)

■ The Teachers Insurance Annuity Association and College Retirement Equities Fund reach a final settlement with critics who were pressing the pension companies to become more flexible. (*The Chronicle*, 1/4/89)

■ Louis W. Sullivan, president of the Morehouse School of Medicine, is nominated Secretary of Health and Human Services in the Bush Administration. (*The Chronicle*, 1/4/89)

■ The Supreme Court rules the Na-

1988

Continued

tional Collegiate Athletic Association is not a governmental entity, thus exempting it from the Constitution's due-process requirement. (*The Chronicle*, 1/4/89)

1989

■ In "Speaking for the Humanities," the American Council of Learned Societies defends the humanities against charges that they are overspecialized and in decline. (*The Chronicle*, 1/11/89)

■ Controversy erupts over Proposition 42, a new rule adopted by the National Collegiate Athletic Association that bars Division I institutions from giving financial aid to freshman athletes who fail to meet minimum academic standards. (*The Chronicle*, 1/25/89)

■ The National Research Council reports that American students are not receiving the high-quality education in mathematics that is crucial for science, technology, and the economy of the nation. (*The Chronicle*, 2/1/89)

■ A National Institutes of Health panel concludes that David Baltimore, a Nobel Prize–winning biomedical scientist, and some of his colleagues are innocent of fraud but guilty of including significant errors in a scientific paper. (*The Chronicle*, 2/8/89)

■ In his first budget proposal, President Bush seeks increases in spending for education and science beyond those proposed by the Reagan Administration. (*The Chronicle*, 2/15/89)

■ A District of Columbia judge upholds the right of Catholic University of America to bar a tenured professor from teaching theology, rejecting the claims made in a lawsuit brought by the Rev. Charles E. Curran. (*The Chronicle*, 3/8/89)

■ The Education Department declares that the public higher-education systems of Georgia, Missouri, and Oklahoma are in compliance with federal civil-rights laws, ending nearly 20 years of court battles and federal supervision. (*The Chronicle*, 3/29/89)

■ Two chemists claim to have sustained a nuclear-fusion reaction in a flask of water during a freshman-level laboratory experiment—a claim that causes a furor among scientists. (*The Chronicle*, 4/5/89)

■ Almost 30 years after the civil-rights movement made improved race relations a top priority for higher education, ugly and embarrassing incidents between white and black students continue to plague colleges nationwide. (*The Chronicle*, 4/26/89)

■ Massive student demonstrations marking the sudden death of Hu Yaobang, a popular former chief of the Chinese Communist Party, take Beijing by storm. (*The Chronicle*, 4/26/89)

■ Concerned about tax-law changes and shaken by the stock-market crash, alumni cut back on giving to their alma maters in 1987-88, causing the first decline in private contributions in more than a decade. (*The Chronicle*, 5/3/89)

■ Student protests in China explode into a mass uprising, turning a momentous state visit by the Soviet leader Mikhail S. Gorbachev into a humiliating sideshow. (*The Chronicle*, 5/24/89)

■ A growing share of the corporate philanthropic dollar is going to public colleges and universities, a fact that has many private institutions worried about what they see as erosion of their support. (*The Chronicle*, 5/31/89)

■ The first federally approved experiment to transfer non-human genes into human patients begins at the National Institutes of Health, shortly after the settlement of a lawsuit seeking to halt the procedure. (*The Chronicle*, 5/31/89)

■ The Chinese government launches a bloody crackdown on pro-democracy students and demands that leaders of the student movement turn themselves in. (*The Chronicle*, 6/14/89)

■ Universities in parts of Eastern Europe are in the midst of far-reaching and sometimes startling liberal reforms. (*The Chronicle*, 6/21/89)

■ Colleges, universities, and trade schools race to comply with federal regulations that are intended to deter drug abuse and fraud, or face a cutoff of funds for some federal student-aid programs. (*The Chronicle*, 6/28/89)

■ The Supreme Court gives colleges and universities significantly more leeway to regulate commercial activity on their campuses in a case involving the State University of New York System. (*The Chronicle*, 7/5/89)

■ The Supreme Court upholds a Missouri law restricting abortion, clearing the way for states to enact legislation to bar the faculty members and hospitals of public universities from performing most such operations. (*The Chronicle*, 7/12/89)

■ In a victory for civil-rights groups, a federal appeals court revives a lawsuit—known as the *Adams* case—that forced the Education Department to monitor the desegregation of public colleges in 18 Southern and border states. (*The Chronicle*, 7/19/89)

■ The Department of Justice begins an investigation into whether private colleges and universities violated federal antitrust laws in the way they set tuition rates and award financial aid. (*The Chronicle*, 8/16/89)

■ Two national fraternities eliminate pledging in an effort to stop alcohol abuse and violence by their members. (*The Chronicle*, 9/6/89)

■ The settlement plan reached between TIAA-CREF and its critics is approved by the Securities and Exchange Commission, clearing the way for more pension flexibility for TIAA-CREF policy holders. (*The Chronicle*, 9/6/89)

■ "Greekfest," a Labor Day gathering of black college students and other black youths in Virginia Beach, ends in looting and clashes with the police. (*The Chronicle*, 9/13/89)

■ The National Aeronautics and Space Administration selects 81 universities, colleges, and research institutes to participate in a new network of "space-grant" colleges. (*The Chronicle*, 9/13/89)

- Arts-and-sciences faculties face severe shortages in the future, especially in the humanities and social sciences, a new study finds. (*The Chronicle,* 9/20/89)

- Two federal agencies propose conflict-of-interest guidelines to govern almost all federally supported biomedical and behavioral research. The rules would require scientists to file financial-disclosure forms. (*The Chronicle,* 9/20/89)

- A national commission is formed to build a consensus on the reforms needed in big-time college athletics. The Rev. Theodore M. Hesburgh, president emeritus of the University of Notre Dame, and William C. Friday, president emeritus of the University of North Carolina system, will lead the panel. (*The Chronicle,* 10/4/89)

- More and more colleges move to adopt tough penalties for students who use slurs and epithets to harass others, raising fears the institutions are infringing on free-speech rights. (*The Chronicle,* 10/4/89)

- Higher education takes a back seat to elementary and secondary education at President Bush's "Education Summit," while some governors criticize the "greediness" of colleges and universities. (*The Chronicle,* 10/4/89)

- Congress reaches a compromise on legislation that would prohibit the use of federal funds to support "obscene" art, but removes some other restrictions. (*The Chronicle,* 10/11/89)

- A model curriculum for colleges is proposed by Lynne V. Cheney, chairman of the National Endowment for the Humanities. The plan emphasizes traditional Western texts but also suggests students take courses on other cultures. (*The Chronicle,* 10/11/89)

- Room-temperature nuclear fusion is resurrected when a group of scientists organized by the National Science Foundation and the Electric Power Research Institute concludes that unusual effects in some of the experiments cannot be explained and need further tests. (*The Chronicle,* 10/25/89)

- A panel of leading scientists formed by the U.S. Energy Department declares it can find no convincing evidence that the phenomenon of room-temperature fusion exists. (*The Chronicle,* 11/8/89)

- Professors are increasingly optimistic about their profession, but deeply troubled by the attitudes and academic credentials of their students and the quality of academic administration, a national survey commissioned by the Carnegie Foundation for the Advancement of Teaching shows. (*The Chronicle,* 11/8/89)

- CBS agrees to pay the National Collegiate Athletic Association $1-billion over seven years for the exclusive right to broadcast the Division I men's basketball tournament. (*The Chronicle,* 11/29/89)

- Eastern European academics play key roles in reform movements sweeping the Warsaw Pact countries. (*The Chronicle,* 12/6/89)